A~Z
of
Bahamas
Heritage

Macmillan Caribbean A–Z Series

A~Z *of* Bahamas Heritage

Michael Craton

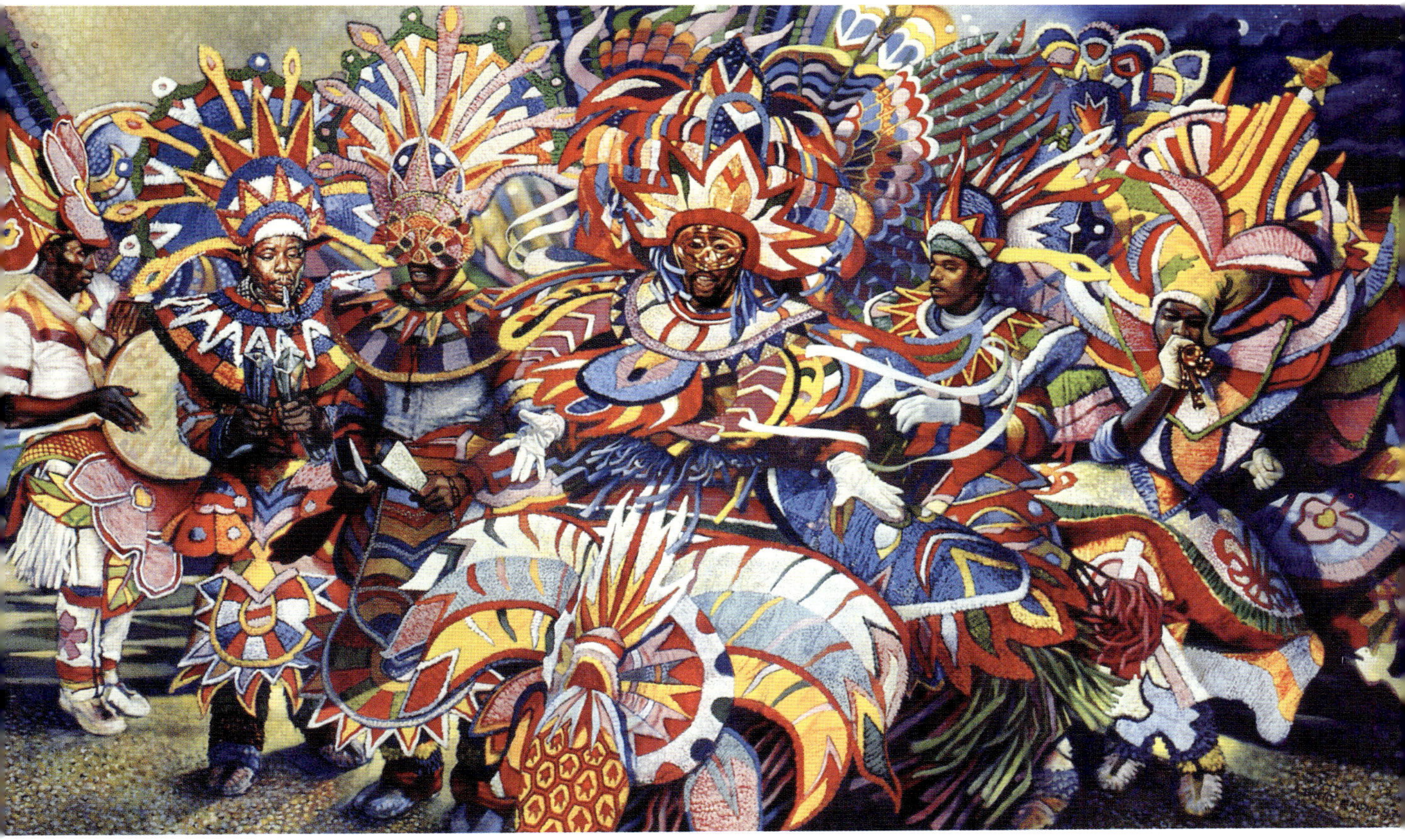

MACMILLAN
CARIBBEAN

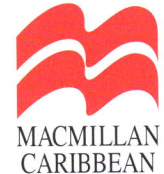

Macmillan Education
Between Towns Road, Oxford OX4 3PP
A division of Macmillan Publishers Limited
Companies and representatives throughout the world

ISBN 978-1-4050-0242-4

Text © Michael Craton 2007
Design and illustration © Macmillan Publishers Limited 2007

First published 2007

All rights reserved; no part of this publication may be
reproduced, stored in a retrieval system, transmitted in
any form, or by any means, electronic, mechanical, photocopying,
recording, or otherwise, without the prior written permission
of the publishers.

Designed by Mike Brain
Typeset by Carol Hulme
Cover design by Gary Fielder
Cover photographs by Michael Craton, except image of Debbie Ferguson, by Empics.

Printed and bound in Thailand

2011 2010 2009 2008 2007
10 9 8 7 6 5 4 3 2 1

Contents

Author's Acknowledgements	vi
Preface	vii
Map of The Bahamas	viii
Abaco–Aviation	1
Bacardi–Butlin	29
Cable Beach–Customs Duties	72
Dance–Dupuch	115
Education–Exumas	127
Family–Funerals	139
Gambier Village–Guy Fawkes Day	162
Haiti–Hurricanes	184
Iguana–Isaacs	197
Jerome–Junkanoo	206
Key West – Kweyole	214
Lake Cunningham–Lyford Cay	216
McKay–Museums	239
Names–Norman's Cay	265
Oakes–Owens-Illinois Company	274
Paradise Island–Proverbs	284
Queen's College–Queen Victoria	313
Raccoon–Russell	317
Sailing–Symonette	332
Taylor–Typhoid	365
United Bahamian Party–University of the West Indies	383
Vanguard Party–Vodun	386
Walker's Cay–Wylly	389
Yellow Fever – Young	404
Zemis	405
Index	406
Text Credits	415
Picture Credits	416

Author's Acknowledgements

In a book of this scope and kind the debts owed by the author are legion. Wherever possible, suggestions for further reading are given after each entry, which in many cases indicate sources which have proved invaluable to the compiler. Special gratitude however must be expressed to those, such as David Campbell, Robert Douglas, Patricia Glinton-Meicholas, Mizpah Tertullien, Dr Alison Shilling and the late Clement Bethel, whose works have been quoted because they have described aspects of Bahamian heritage far better and more definitively than the author can. One can only hope that the publicity hereby given their admirable work is sufficient recompense for the borrowing.

Beyond the ever-expanding store of writings on The Bahamas, innumerable Bahamians and Bahamianists have contributed verbally to the author's array of useful and interesting Bahamian material, not just over the four or five years that this book has been in the making, but over the period ten times as long that he has been accumulating information and deepening his affection and respect for The Bahamas and its people. In a real sense this multitude of friends and willing informants have been contributors to the work in progress – deserving the credit for its possible merits while not being responsible for its idiosyncrasies and flaws. At the risk of being overly selective, or slighting equally valuable informants, the author/compiler would like to mention the following individuals, listed alphabetically: Anthony Aarons, Hon. Paul Adderley, Dr Roseanne Adderley, Paul Aranha, Peter Barratt, Dr Keva Bethel, Dr Nicolette Bethel, Howland Bottomley, Dr Anthony Dahl, Sir Clifford Darling, Dr Steve Dodge, Eileen Dupuch Carron, the late Dr Cleveland Eneas, Hon. Sir Arthur Foulkes, Drs Don and Kathy Gerace, Lady Patricia Isaacs, Dr Bill Keegan, Ronald Lightbourn, the late Brent Malone, Hon. Sir Clement Maynard, Hon. Sean McWeeney, Eric Minns, Dr Eugene Newry, Keith and Sara Parker, the late Sir Lynden Pindling, Sir Sidney Poitier, Antonius Roberts, the late Oris Russell, Dr Gail and Winston Saunders, Dr Neil Sealey, Paul Thompson, Dr John Winter.

As suggested, to name all helpers is impossible and to try to pick out the most helpful might risk being invidious. But special thanks beyond the call of duty are nevertheless due to the perennial help so willingly and efficiently provided by the former Chief Archivist Dr Gail Saunders and her staff at the Bahamas Archives, to the fledgling Antiquities, Monuments & Museums Corporation and Clifton Heritage Authority, and the staffs of the various other libraries, museums, government departments and institutions consulted. Thanks are perhaps (with apologies) imperfectly accorded to those who provided permissions for quotations and illustrations – in most cases requiring no more than mere acknowledgment – most notably the Bahamas National Archives and the former Bahamas News Bureau.

More directly, the winnowing and shaping of this work – triangulated between England, Canada and the Bahamas – posed the difficulties which were only to be expected. But the author must gratefully acknowledge above all others the tactful, professional and prompt marshalling and co-ordination of text, illustrations and maps of the publisher's freelance editor Belinda Baker. As ever, fulsome credit is also due to my family for their patience, forbearance and practical help during the many months of the book's preparation – notably the electronic expertise of my son Darius in the collation and editing of illustrations during the summer of 2004, and the thorough proof-reading of the text by my wife Pat closer to the publication deadlines in 2006.

Preface

This book is aimed at a wide audience. Its target is all those who have an interest in the heritage and culture of the Commonwealth of The Bahamas. This includes all Bahamians, adults or still at school, first or frequent tourist visitors, or that multitude of non-Bahamians who for one reason or another have been intrigued and fascinated by the unique characteristics and quirks of the Bahamian archipelago and its people, and wish to know more.

What then is the Bahamian heritage which this book sets out to itemize and explain? A nation's and its people's heritage is taken to mean everything which renders them distinctively different from any other country and people in the world. Heritage is a concept even more all-encompassing in the case of a young and evolving nation with such a multifaceted history and culture, consisting of hundreds of subtropical islands and islets, located between the Atlantic Ocean and the Caribbean Sea, historically between the imperial worlds of Britain, Spain, France and the United States, and culturally between African, British, North American and Caribbean Creole influences.

Accordingly, the reader can expect a book that if not quite definitive is very diverse. It shares the features of a gazetteer or guidebook — giving accounts of almost 50 different islands and settlements — and a Who's Who and Who Was Who, with a select cast of at least 140 significant persons, living or dead. Besides, it provides a survey of the country's unique geology, flora and fauna, natural resources, industries, arts, crafts and architecture, cuisine, sports and diversions, social, political, economic and religious institutions, and the complex mix and melding of ethnicities, races and classes. Though history is not quite synonymous with heritage, the book can serve, last but not least, as an introductory, but up-to-date, History of The Bahamas. Overall it is the widest-ranging of all books yet written on The Bahamas — completely original in its form and array of information.

Stylistically, this Bahamian A–Z is designed to be a lively and well-illustrated mini-encyclopedia — equally useful and rewarding as a work of reference and for more casual dipping. Some entries — on Land Tenure, Citizenship and Education for example — are short technical essays. But at the other end of the scale are more light-hearted titbits — such as the quoted examples of proverbs, riddles, poems, goombay calypsos and picturesque slang. Whereas great efforts have been made to be accurate, inevitably in a work of such scope by a single author there will be items that readers will look for in vain, statements with which they disagree or know to be erroneous and, perhaps even more obviously, examples of authorial subjectivity.

In these respects, the author is only partially apologetic or repentant. Of course he will be happy to be informed of errors and will endeavour to have them corrected in subsequent reprintings. He is always ready to discuss and if necessary argue for interpretations with which readers may disagree. But, while acknowledging that this work is indeed to a degree subjective, he would argue that this could be as much a positive as a negative feature. In one respect he is actually dogmatic. 'Heritage' is too often regarded as a purely positive and celebratory concept. Rather, as this Preface began by stating, it includes *all* things that have contributed to a nation's and a people's shaping — the less creditable or pretty as well as the wholly admirable and worthy of celebration. Anything less would be a distortion and a disservice to the Bahamian nation and people to which and whom the author — though not a born ('true-true') Bahamian — has dedicated more than a half-century of scholarship, and affirms an indissoluble affection and respect.

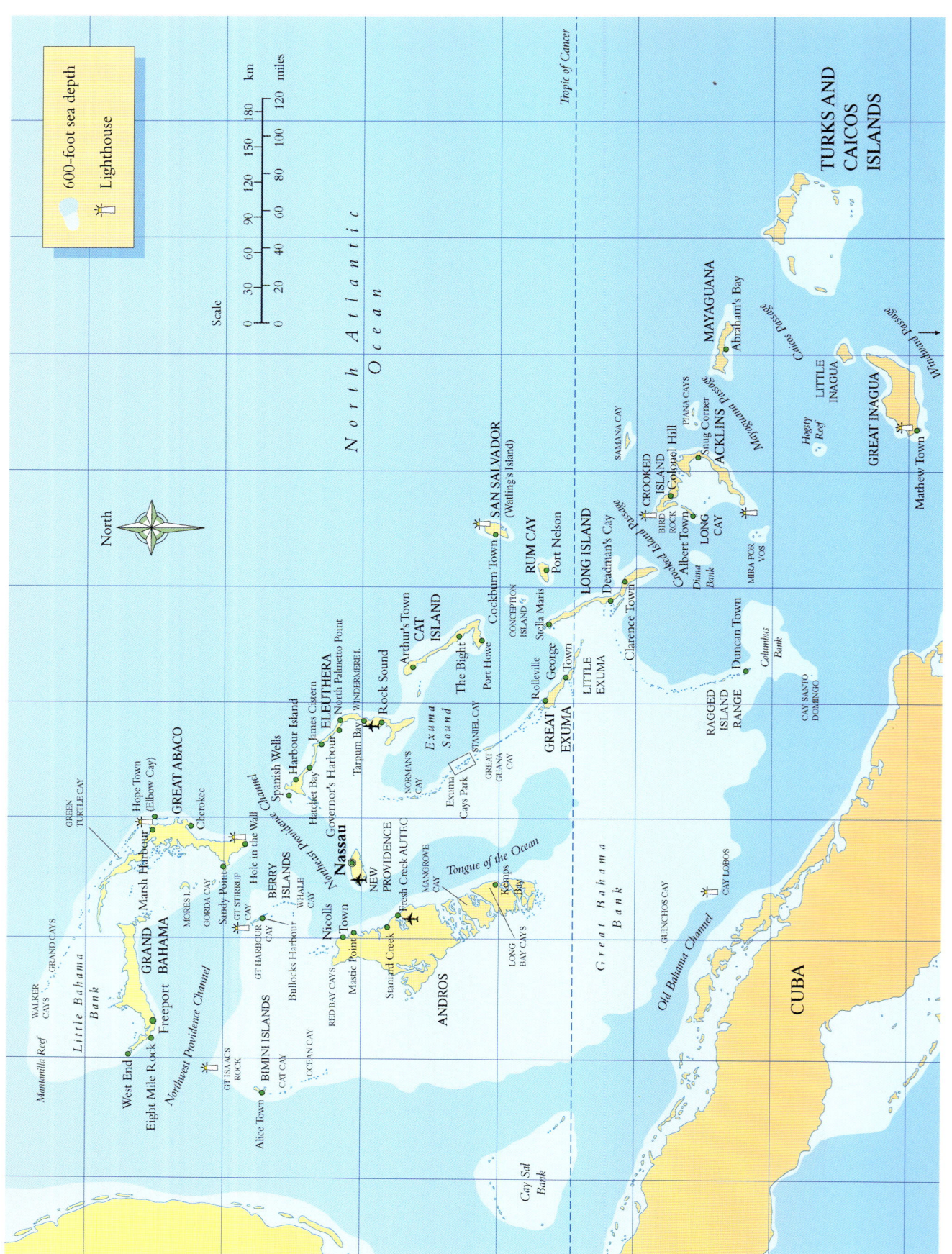

The Bahama Islands

**ABACO** The extreme north-eastern district of the Bahamian archipelago, occupying the eastern half of the Little Bahama Bank and fronting the Atlantic Ocean in the directions of Bermuda and the United States. With its angled mainland – consisting of Great Abaco and the causeway-joined Little Abaco – along with numerous small offshore cays, it constitutes the second largest section of The Bahamas (649 square miles, 1681 square kilometres). On the mainland, the grand-sounding Great Abaco Highway – still not entirely paved – extends 125 miles (200 km) from Crown Haven in the north-west to Hole-in-the-Wall and Sandy Point on the North-West Providence Channel in the south. The northern half of the mainland is protected by one of the longest barrier reefs in the northern hemisphere, extending more than 100 miles (160 km) from Walker's Cay south-east to Elbow Cay, and south to Little Harbour. This encloses the comparatively shallow but safe Abaco Sound (also known as the Sea of Abaco), the finest yacht-cruising ground adjacent to the United States.

Formerly it was believed that Abaco's northerly location dissuaded the aboriginal AMERINDIANS from settling there, but numerous archaeological discoveries since the 1980s have proved this incorrect. Depopulated (like the rest of The Bahamas) before the first English colonists arrived, Abaco was resettled in 1783–5 by American LOYALISTS, mainly from New York though indirectly also from the American South. At first the emigrés consisted of penurious whites, and non-whites ostensibly freed after fleeing to the British lines during the American Independence War. The initial settlement, called Carleton, was on the sandy bay now named Treasure Cay. But the poverty of the soil and the arrival of southern planters and their slaves led to other settlements, notably at Marsh Harbour, Spencer's Bight and Eight Mile Bay, to the south.

With the failure of attempted COTTON plantations and the decline of slavery, many Loyalists left Abaco for more promising islands. Of the hardy souls who remained, most of the non-whites remained on the mainland, while the whites (initially almost as poor) migrated to form exclusive settlements on the offshore cays; at HOPE TOWN on Elbow Cay, MAN-O'-WAR CAY, GREAT GUANA CAY, GREEN TURTLE CAY and CHEROKEE. Then and later they were augmented by migrants from the relatively overcrowded pre-Loyalist settlements of Harbour Island and Spanish Wells, off northern Eleuthera. According to Bahamian historian Paul ALBURY, most of these were young men attracted by the Abaco girls' reputation for beauty, which accounts for the recurrence of Eleutheran surnames among the whites of the Abaco cays: Albury, Bethel, Pinder, Roberts, Russell, Sands and Sawyer.

All Abaconians practised subsistence farming and fished for turtle, conch, crawfish and sponges. But the whites enjoyed relatively greater success through their boatbuilding skills, using the plentiful resources of timber on Great Abaco and gleanings from wrecks. Though Abaconian whites became intrepid sailors and roamed widely (being prominent among the early settlers of Key West), they remained deeply conservative, racially exclusive and educationally backward until the mid-twentieth century. However, as Abaco was opened up for the exploitation of timber and agricultural resources by American companies, and a rising tide of American tourists discovered its cruising grounds and beaches, wealth multiplied, facilities improved and horizons widened, even for the relatively disadvantaged non-whites of the Abaco mainland. Abaconians continued to feel distanced from Nassau and complained of neglect, and some even threatened to secede from The Bahamas at the time of Independence in 1973. Such sentiments though were undoubtedly mitigated when a black son of Cooper's Town, Abaco, Hubert Ingraham, became the second Prime Minister of The Bahamas in August 1992.

As an index of rising prosperity, the population of Abaco, which was static around 3,400 from 1901 to 1953, rose to 6,500 in 1970 and 10,000 in 1990; Abaco is one of only three Bahamian islands with an inflow rather than outflow of population. Though more open to outside influences

Hope Town, on Elbow Cay, the eastern extension of Abaco

ABACO INDEPENDENCE MOVEMENT (AIM)

and rather better integrated than formerly, Abaconians still retain pride in their special place in Bahamian history and a strong regional identity. These feelings are manifested by the Wyannie MALONE Museum at Hope Town and the Albert Lowe Museum and Loyalist Memorial Sculpture Garden at New Plymouth on Green Turtle Cay.

Further reading: S. Dodge, *Abaco: The History of an Out Island and its Cays*, 2nd ed., White Sound Press, 1995.

ABACO INDEPENDENCE MOVEMENT (AIM)

When the black PROGRESSIVE LIBERAL PARTY government came to power in 1967–8, white Abaconians felt more than ever isolated from Nassau. Subsequently, even non-white Abaconians complained of neglect by the central government. Such feelings increased as the PLP moved The Bahamas towards INDEPENDENCE. The most conservative Abaconians professed their complete loyalty to the British Crown and said that they would rather remain a British colony and even secede from The Bahamas than have Abaco become, in effect, an exploited colony of the regime in Nassau. The chief of their spokesmen were the white former UNITED BAHAMIAN PARTY Minister and RAF veteran Leonard Thompson, and the black former policeman Errington Watkins.

Receiving some encouragement from the anti-Independence forces in the FREE NATIONAL MOVEMENT Opposition in Parliament, Abaconians formed a lobby group called the Greater Abaco Council (GAC) in 1971. Yet when the PLP won the 1972 general election on the Independence issue, loyal petitions from Abaco to London fell on deaf ears, and the FNM declared that Independence was the will of the Bahamian people and Abaco's secession unthinkable, more radical and even violent counsels prevailed among the minority of Abaconian extremists. These were disowned by Leonard Thompson and Errington Watkins, with the active leadership falling to the fire-eating white Chuck Hall.

As The Bahamas became independent, the extremists set up a Council for a Free Abaco (CFA) in place of the GAC, and easily found a shady crew of allies in the United States. These included a 'libertarian' from Nevada, Michael Oliver, and an arms-dealer from Georgia, Mitchell Wer-Bell, who was said to be ready to train Abaconian 'freedom fighters' and to provide 300 armed mercenaries, helicopter gun-ships and motor torpedo boats. As a respectable cover, the Abaco Independence Movement (AIM) was formed in August 1973, with a well-written newspaper, *The Abaco Independent*, providing propaganda.

AIM always professed its intention to seek secession only through constitutional means, but became discredited as more violent plans were gradually uncovered. An armed coup was planned for January 1975, but it fizzled out through a combination of prompt government action and cold feet on the part of the conspirators, including Chuck Hall. AIM was disbanded and replaced by the Abaco Home Rule Movement (AHRM). This kept the secessionist cause going for a further two years. But the overwhelming victory of the PLP in the 1977 general election, a canny conciliatory policy towards Abaco by Prime Minister PINDLING, and generally improving economic and social conditions in Abaco led to its extinction. Symbolically, *The Abaco Independent* ceased publication in August 1977.

Further reading: S. Dodge, *Abaco: The History of an Out Island and its Cays*, 2nd. ed., White Sound Press, 1995, ch. 6, 109–37.

ACKLINS ISLAND

This 50-mile (80 km) long, tadpole-shaped island encloses the eastern half of the huge inverted triangle which with CROOKED ISLAND and LONG CAY constitutes the Crooked Island District. Within the triangle are the 400 square miles (1,036 squ.

Bagging cascarilla, Acklins Island

km) of the shallow Bight of Acklins, while to west and east are the deep and dangerous Crooked Island and Mayaguana Passages from the Atlantic to the Caribbean.

Densely populated by the Lucayans, who found the eastern bluffs protection against marauders and the leeward shallows very suitable to their lifestyle, Acklins Island has always been attractive to its inhabitants but resistant to development. The names of coves on the island's western side – Lovely Bay, Delectable Bay, Snug Corner – display the islanders' affections, but disguise the fact that while small boats were almost the sole means of communication between settlements, the shallow Bight and rough eastern edge meant that there were almost no landing places for deep-draught vessels.

Acklins Island was always remote but its people were famously hard-working and ingenious in making a living. They built their own boats, engaged in fishing and sponging, grew produce and raised stock to supply the steamships using the Crooked Island Passage, and exported to Europe bundles of the aromatic bark stripped from the CASCARILLA shrub for use in medicines and Campari liqueur. The decline of this lifestyle in the 1930s and the relative attractions of the Bahamian capital led to a steady migration, so that the entire population of the Crooked Island District in 2000 was less than half that of Acklins Island alone a century earlier. The descendants of the islanders living abroad, though, retain strong feelings for their island and family roots, and hold an annual homecoming. Among the most distinguished sons of Acklins Island have been Sir Lynden PINDLING (through his Bain mother), his almost lifelong friend and colleague Arthur HANNA, and Sir Clifford DARLING, Speaker and fourth Governor-General of The Bahamas.

The 400 or so permanent residents of Acklins are now better served than ever before in terms of amenities, with a road almost the length of the island, electricity, telephones, and two clinics. But they have more or less deserted the outlying settlements, to congregate around Spring Point at the island's centre, close to the airport with its thrice weekly BAHAMASAIR flights and the dock where the mailboat from Nassau calls once a week on its way to Inagua. There is virtually no tourism, much less farming than formerly, and the chief remnant of the traditional way of life is the collection of cascarilla bark.

ADDERLEY FAMILY (BLACK) A distinguished black dynasty, founded by a LIBERATED AFRICAN Yoruba probably named Oloudah (Anglicised as Alliday), who assumed the Bahamian surname Adderley around 1840. By the 1860s, Alliday Adderley's 'industrious habits' had made him the first black Bahamian of substance. Two of his sons were elected to the House of Assembly, and a grandson, predictively christened William Parliament (1868–1944), was long an MHA for Andros. Graduating from the family business of farming, selling produce and small-scale contracting, he became the owner of the modest but grandly named Big Store opposite Nassau's Christ Church Cathedral. Though not approaching the affluence, let alone the power, of the wealthiest white Bay Street merchants, W. P. Adderley was able to send his son Alfred to an English 'public' boarding school (Denstone), from where he went on to St Catharine's College, Cambridge, and finally the Inns of Court in London.

Alfred Francis Adderley (1883–1953) became the most able and busiest black Bahamian lawyer of his time, and a politician of considerable influence. A social icon and spokesman for the black majority, he long represented Nassau's Western District in the Assembly. He appeared as a prosecutor for the Crown in the trial of Count Alfred de Marigny for the murder of Sir Harry OAKES (1943) – said to have been the only murder case he ever lost, acting on either side. A staunch Anglican, he was Chancellor of the Anglican Diocese of Nassau, and one of the founders of the Anglican ST JOHN'S COLLEGE.

A. F. Adderley and his formidable wife Ethel lived in considerable style in the mansion called Poinciana Hill, in the non-white district close to Government House known as DELANCEY TOWN. Though respected by the BAY STREET whites for his abilities and moderate views, he did not mix with them socially, or desire to do so – one of the secrets of his success with blacks and whites alike. Raised to the Legislative Council by

PLP Foreign Minister Paul Adderley negotiates territorial fishing rights with the US, 1975

ADDERLEY FAMILY (WHITE)

Governor DUNDAS in 1938, A. F. Adderley and his wife were official guests from The Bahamas at the coronation of QUEEN ELIZABETH II in 1953. He died of a heart attack on the BOAC plane returning from London following the ceremony.

Paul Lawrence Adderley (b. 1928), in his early days nicknamed 'the Prince of Poinciana Hill' was thought by some to be a likely candidate to fulfil his father's ambitions and become the first black Premier or Prime Minister of The Bahamas. Lacking quite the personal charisma of Lynden PINDLING, he fell short of this goal. Yet his great abilities led him to perform distinguished service for The Bahamas and Bahamian people as a PROGRESSIVE LIBERAL PARTY Minister.

Educated at GOVERNMENT HIGH SCHOOL and, like his father, at Cambridge and the Inns of Court, Paul Adderley returned to Nassau and a career in law and politics in 1953. Courted by Etienne DUPUCH'S middle-of-the-road Bahamas Democratic League, along with Orville TURNQUEST, he threw in his lot with the now unequivocally black and populist PLP in 1960. Elected for the Western District with a large majority in 1962, he was disaffected by the radical events of 'BLACK TUESDAY' (1965) and left the PLP with Turnquest and others, to form the NATIONAL DEMOCRATIC PARTY (NDP).

Any hope of leading that party to victory was demolished by the PLP's first victory in 1967. The NDP did not contest the subsequent election, and after the PLP landslide Adderley was not among those who formed the new Opposition FREE NATIONAL MOVEMENT (FNM). Instead, he was persuaded by the offer of a ministerial post from Premier Pindling to rejoin the PLP in 1972. Thereafter, he gave loyal (though not always uncritical) service in a variety of important Cabinet posts, until the PLP's demise in 1992, most notably as Minister of External Affairs.

Not all of the descendants of Alliday Adderley prospered or remained in The Bahamas. Among the family members who took flight to a more comfortable life in the northern United States in the early twentieth century were the parents of the famous jazz musicians Nat and Julian 'Cannonball' Adderley.

ADDERLEY FAMILY (WHITE)

One of the most interesting, if sometimes confusing, features of Bahamian genealogy is that most families have branches, even immediate family members, spanning the entire spectrum between 'recognised white' and 'unequivocally black'. This admixture is the inevitable consequence of gradual miscegenation over the generations, whether or not acknowledged or still traceable. Less common are entire families which share the same surname, but seem to have had no genetic crossovers, and can accurately distinguish themselves as a unit as either whites or blacks. This situation is usually ascribed to slaves and ex-slaves having taken the names of their masters when the possession of a surname became socially important or beneficial to them.

Perhaps the outstanding Bahamian example of two families sharing a surname but nothing else is that of the 'white' and 'black' Adderleys. As described in the previous entry, the latter were descendants of a LIBERATED AFRICAN (not a slave) who chose the Bahamian surname closest to his native African name. The other Adderleys, however, claimed equal distinctiveness – and even greater distinction – through descent from the earliest of the white settlers of Virginia, Bermuda, Jamaica and The Bahamas. So certain were they of their identity that as late as the year 2000 a family member was able to write a well-researched article for the *Journal of the Bahamas Historical Society* entitled 'The Adderley Family in the New World' without a single mention of the black Adderleys.

The Adderley Building, Central Bay Street, 1870s. The white Adderleys were probably the last of the 'Conchy Joe' merchant oligarchs to live above their shop in downtown Nassau

According to the family historian, the patriarch of the white Adderleys was one William Adderlie, who settled in Bermuda from Virginia around 1612 and was one of the original shareholders by the charter of 1615. His eldest son, Abraham, was one of the ELEUTHERIAN ADVENTURERS who settled The Bahamas in 1648, and three or four further generations of Abraham Adderleys carried on commercial and privateering activity between Bermuda, Jamaica and The Bahamas, before finally settling in New Providence around the middle of the eighteenth century. Though an 'Old Inhabitant' not a LOYALIST migrant, Abraham Adderley IV (or V) benefited richly from the share-out of land after the end of the American War of Independence, with an estate in northern Long Island that, under his acquisitive son Nehemiah, eventually extended to 2,000 acres (a section of it is now part of the STELLA MARIS Resort).

Almost needless to say, the Adderleys were slave-owners and staunch opponents of Amelioration and EMANCIPATION, to which they erroneously attributed the decline of their Long Island plantation. Nehemiah's son, Henry, however, recouped the family fortune by becoming a prominent Nassau merchant. Wealthy from the proceeds of WRECKING and running the blockade during the AMERICAN CIVIL WAR, he was said to have been the first Bay Street millionaire. Long a landmark, his place of business, the Adderley Building at the corner of Bay Street and Rawson Square, was finally pulled down only in the 1960s.

In typical Victorian style, the Adderley family was prolific, and its members naturally were at the centre of the conservative local oligarchy and social elite. Several of the men were Assemblymen and Members of the Executive Council, while the women almost invariably married into the close-knit circle of prominent local white families. Henry and his son Augustus, however, chafed at Nassau's narrow bounds. Henry retired to London in the 1860s and left his business in the capable hands of his nephew George Butler Adderley, who engaged profitably in the notoriously exploitative SPONGE industry. Augustus spent much of his later life in London, promoting The Bahamas and acting as a spokesman for its ruling class. He was knighted for services to the Empire, which included the management of the West Indies Pavilion at the Colonial and Indian Exhibition of 1836. His most typical remark about The Bahamas, in a speech to the Royal Colonial Society, was that 'he was in favour of the continuance of local self-government as at present obtained. The Bahamians were good honest traders, and would be a credit to any community.'

In the twentieth century the line of male white Adderleys died out or migrated. The last of the family in Nassau were women. These included Kathleen, daughter of George Butler Adderley, who married the arch-conservative Speaker of the Assembly and local historian, Harcourt Gladstone Malcolm (1875–1936). They had no children. Probably the last of all was George Butler Adderley's granddaughter Enid Boyce, a pillar of both the IMPERIAL ORDER OF DAUGHTERS OF THE EMPIRE and of the BAHAMAS HISTORICAL SOCIETY, who died, also childless, in 1995.

Further reading: J. Gorman, 'The Adderley Family in the New World', *Journal of the Bahamas Historical Society*, 22, 2000, 31–41.

ADELAIDE VILLAGE A settlement 16 miles (25 km) from Nassau on New Providence's South West Bay. It was founded in 1831 under Governor Carmichael SMYTH to locate 157 LIBERATED AFRICANS from the seized Portuguese slave ship *Rosa*. The original settlers were provided with one-third acre plots, tools and other provisions, a rudimentary school and a church, but were expected to build their own houses and establish subsistence farms. As late as the 1960s, Adelaide remained isolated and poor and retained much of its original character, with houses made of lime 'tabby' and palmetto thatch and its families, proud that they had never been slaves, eking a livelihood out of the meagre soil. African methods, customs and folklore lingered, and the settlement was considered picturesque and quaint by outsiders. Better roads, cars and other aspects of modernisation have changed almost all of that; but ghosts remain.

Further reading: *Settlements in New Providence*. Department of Archives booklet, 1982.

AFRICAN HERITAGE Though probably no more than 10 per cent of the Bahamian population is of purely African descent, nine out of ten Bahamians have varying degrees of African ancestry. The African cultural heritage is accordingly very important, though in ways subtle and complex as well as evident and simple, and to a degree that has only come to be generally acknowledged with pride in the last half century. Among the baleful legacies of SLAVERY, and the fact that only blacks were slaves, was a denigration of things African – shared by Afro-Bahamians themselves (see BLACK CRAB MENTALITY). This long survived the formal emancipation of the slaves and a phase of white condescension, into the era of black majority rule.

Black slaves accompanied the first English settlers from Bermuda, and the numbers and proportions of blacks

AGOUTI (alias Hutia)

greatly increased with the coming of the American LOYALISTS in the 1780s. These were blacks who were quickly or already 'creolised' and Christianised by their sojourn in the Americas, and there was never a large infusion of slaves directly from Africa. Because many of the blacks who came with the white Loyalists were already free, as a result of miscegenation, and because the growing number of slaves outran the labour needs of decaying plantations, there was already a sizeable proportion of FREE COLOUREDS before slavery ended. These, and their descendants in the upper ranks of non-white society after EMANCIPATION, were especially concerned to put slavery behind them and to emulate the dominant whites in cleaving to 'civilised' European norms and condemning Africa as the home of barbarity and superstition.

Yet as many as a fifth of Bahamian blacks in 1860 were LIBERATED AFRICANS, who had come directly from Africa and had never been slaves in The Bahamas. Though for the most part Christianised, these proudly kept their African beliefs, customs, folklore and even, for at least a generation, their languages. Liberated Africans and their children in fact formed and sustained FRIENDLY SOCIETIES identified by their separate ethnic origins. These included the Yoruba, Ibo and Congo Societies – for persons originating on either side of the Niger Delta and from the Congo Basin respectively – which survived well into the twentieth century. As late as 1970, the Congo Society still had more than 60 adult members. The African legacy has also been kept alive in recent years through contacts with HAITIANS – who have never been as creolised as the majority of black Bahamians.

The belief and practice of OBEAH has suffered especially from the misunderstanding of African culture. Though widely believed in and at least partially therapeutic in nature, it has been officially condemned and legislated against as 'black magic', rather than recognised as authentic African sorcery medicine – for good more often than evil purposes. Other survivals, notably in DANCE, DRUMMING, MUSIC, FOLKLORE and PROVERBS, have had a happier fate, achieving respectability and being sought out and preserved (if somewhat condescendingly) by ethnologists, mostly American, since the early twentieth century. The ASUE (or Su-su) system, BUSH MEDICINE, and aspects of African CUISINE have also lasted because of their obvious usefulness. The most successful of all customs of African derivation, however, is the twice-yearly celebration of JUNKANOO – which has become the quintessential and distinctive Bahamian national festival.

AGOUTI (alias Hutia) A large indigenous rodent (*Geocapromys ingrahami*) long thought to be extinct, but rediscovered in large numbers on uninhabited East PLANA CAY in the mid-1960s. Hutia are thought to have been domesticated, perhaps even introduced, by the aboriginal Lucayans for food (CATESBY in 1725 called their flesh 'very good … more of the taste of a Pig than a Rabbit'). They were probably the creature which COLUMBUS described as a 'small, barkless dog'. Once widely distributed through the islands, they were almost exterminated by the dogs and cats of the English settlers – if not by hungry settlers themselves. Non-aggressive and trusting, agouti communicate with whistles and squeals. The pathetic noises they make when taken by humans, draw others to the scene.

The hutia of East Plana Cay, which may number 10,000 on an island no more than 3,000 acres in extent, have adapted remarkably to an inhospitable environment. Mainly nocturnal, they shelter from the sun during the day, and obtain all their moisture from the vegetation which constitutes their diet. Their vulnerability, however, is increased by the fact that the females only produce a single offspring in each annual litter – itself, ironically, a response to the present high population density on the cay.

In 1973 conservationists relocated pairs of East Plana hutia on Little Wax Cay in the EXUMA CAYS LAND AND SEA PARK. A survey in 1985 estimated that about 1,200 hutia were then present, and a further study in 1989 demonstrated their considerable impact on the vegetation.

Further reading: G. C. Clough, 'A Most Peaceable Rodent', *Natural History*, 82 (6), 1973, 66–79.

Agouti (hutia)

AGRICULTURE

AGRICULTURE With its thin and rocky soils, limited fresh water and often broiling sun, The Bahamas has never been ideal for agriculture. Farming, along with fishing, was a toilsome necessity for the islanders' subsistence during pre-Columbian and colonial times, and brave attempts to produce crops for export – COTTON, SISAL, PINEAPPLES, citrus and tomatoes – soon petered out. Likewise, in post-colonial times, efforts to lessen the dependence of The Bahamas on imports of agricultural produce – through more expert advice, more modern machinery and methods, economies of scale, better distribution and marketing, and even a degree of economic protection and subsidy – have so far had disappointingly limited effects.

In the past, of necessity, island peasant farmers showed great fortitude and ingenuity. Armed simply with the cutlass, hoe and woven straw baskets, they wrested a subsistence in food for their families, plus the small surplus for export to Nassau in the form of corn, peas and other vegetables, pigs, sheep, goats or even a few cattle, needed to buy those few essentials which they could not produce or improvise for themselves. Often ranging miles from their homesteads and using the labour of all able-bodied family members, they practised a rotational slash-and-burn and 'pothole' farming method, on land for which they rarely had more than customary title. 'Banana holes' (recesses in the honeycomb rock with exceptionally rich pockets of soil) were prized and jealously guarded, as were the sources of fresh water and bat and bird guano in caves.

The white landowners – who had pre-empted and obtained legal title for the best lands – tried to make money through plantation produce, first with slave labour and then in an unequal partnership with black sharecroppers, but without lasting success. The LOYALIST cotton plantations had all failed by the 1820s, and attempts to grow sisal and pineapples from the 1840s eventually foundered because of competition from more efficiently productive areas and US protectionism. Similarly, the trade in tomatoes grown in ELEUTHERA and CAT ISLAND and carried to market in Florida in the 1920s and 1930s did not resume after World War Two because of the development of large-scale Florida farms and tighter US import regulations.

During the BAY STREET era, the ruling regime had little incentive to improve native Bahamian agriculture. Its general interest was to keep Family Island farmers backward and dependent, while those who controlled the Nassau retail food market wished to protect the greater profits that could be made from importing produce from the United States. Moreover, from the 1940s to the 1960s, Family Island farmers much preferred to sign up as relatively well-paid itinerant agricultural labourers in the United States.

Under the Bay Street regime, however, much was done to encourage foreign investors to initiate major agricultural projects in the Family Islands, especially if they were geared for export. Such operators were the first to use heavy ground clearing and rock pulverising machinery, and large quantities of imported fertilisers. Substantial leases were granted on 'sweetheart' terms to US companies in southern Eleuthera, central Abaco and northern Andros. Some of these had spectacular success on the short term, particularly in the production and export of cucumbers, strawberries and papayas, but none lasted more than a decade.

The most outstanding of the offshore agricultural projects was the short-lived attempt by a subsidiary of the OWENS-ILLINOIS COMPANY called the Bahamas Agricultural Industries Limited (BAIL) to make The Bahamas a major sugar producer. Forty square miles (104 squ. km) of former pine forest in Abaco were planted in cane, which was processed through a shipped-in state-of-the-art sugar mill. Beginning in 1966, production reached a peak of 15,000 tons of sugar and a million gallons of molasses in 1969. However, cane productivity was low and not cost-efficient, and when the surge in the world sugar price was not sustained, BAIL was suddenly shut down in 1971.

When black majority rule came in 1967, determined efforts were made by the PROGRESSIVE LIBERAL PARTY government to revive, modernise and expand native Bahamian agriculture. The Ministry of Agriculture was reorganised and expanded, and its budget allocation tripled. Students were sent to be trained in such schools as the black Tuskeegee Institute in Alabama. Agricultural science was introduced as a subject in Bahamian schools for the first time. Packing stations were established on all

Traditional slash-and-burn agriculture

AIDS

Hoe and cutlass peasant farmers, Rock Sound, Eleuthera, 1950s

the agricultural islands, trained local advisers appointed, transportation facilities improved, and a new produce exchange set up on POTTER'S CAY. In 1970 a central agricultural station was established on Gladstone Road in New Providence, in 1974 an act was passed to set up farmers' co-operatives, and in the later 1970s tariffs were introduced to give a degree of protection for local produce, especially in the most productive seasons, and for the importation of feedstuffs, fertilisers and farm machinery duty free.

The most notable PLP initiative (and sadly one of its salient failures) was The Bahamas Agricultural Research, Training and Development programme (BARTAD) set up in northern Andros immediately following INDEPENDENCE in 1973. Funded by an initial $10 million grant from the US, the project did undertake some useful research and training but was dogged by mismanagement, misfortunes with the weather, and the decline in enthusiasm with the lack of continuing subsidies. An equally lamentable disaster was the failure of the government's 1975 initiative in taking over the formerly highly successful Hatchet Bay Farms Eleuthera established by Austin Levy in the 1930s – which had reverted to bush by 1980.

The PLP administration looked for what help it could get and from 1989 welcomed the agricultural aid and advice notably proffered by the government of Taiwan. The solution to the problems of mismanagement and underfunding proved elusive, however, and the government wavered between a commitment to helping out Bahamian farmers and encouraging foreign investment.

The only section of the agricultural industry which could point to great success was the production of broiler chickens and eggs. By 1996, Bahamian poultry farms were satisfying almost 100 per cent of local demand. This was the result almost entirely of large-scale private enterprise operations (helped by protective tariffs against chicken imports), rather than government-aided small producers. In the 1970s and 1980s an increasing proportion of locally produced vegetables were being grown on moderate to large-scale farms, and production of meat by small farmers rapidly declined.

Bahamian agriculture has suffered from a lack of native Bahamians willing to be farmers or, even more, content to be mere farm labourers. Despite the government's attempts to facilitate the acquisition of land for farming, the number of persons classified as farmers decreased from 4,246 in 1978 to 1,780 in 1994.

Further reading: W. J. G. Eneas, *Agriculture in the Bahamas: Historical Development, 1492–1992*, Media Publishing, 1998.

AIDS An incurable and usually fatal disease that first manifested itself in 1980 and within a decade had become a dangerous epidemic. At first, AIDS and its preliminary HIV infection, were attributed solely to Haitians, homosexuals, and drug addicts using dirty needles. Soon, however, the plague had spread throughout the population, and was more common among non-drug-using heterosexual couples, women and even children, than among those originally thought most vulnerable and to blame.

By the end of 1998, a total of 3,185 AIDS cases had been reported in the Bahamas, with a further 4,235 persons infected with HIV. In the previous 13 years, 2,413 persons with AIDS had died. On a per capita basis (with roughly one person in 39 affected) this seemed to indicate the Bahamas the worst afflicted country in the region – Haiti not excepted. The only solace offered was that the high figures were due in part to comparatively efficient reporting procedures.

In 1988, a non-government caring service called the Samaritan Ministry was established, mainly by Catholic nuns, to give counsel and sympathy to individuals and families stricken with AIDS. The Ministry was extended to Freeport in 1999. Spurred by public concern, the Ministry of Health set up an AIDS Secretariat in 1989, to organise the training of carers and counsellors, to educate the public in safe sexual practices, and to devise long-term prevention strategies. The AIDS Secretariat was reinforced by the creation of the AIDS Foundation of The Bahamas, a non-profit, non-governmental organisation, founded on World AIDS Day (1 December) 1992.

Bahamians have benefited from health and public education facilities well above average in the region (and immeasurably better than in sub-Saharan Africa). Since 1995, annual totals of HIV cases reported have slowly declined. But AIDS continues to be the most severe health, social and even psychological menace which the Bahamas faces.

For more information, contact The AIDS Secretariat, Ministry of Health, PO Box N-3729, Nassau.

AIRPORTS As airline and private planes have augmented and improved the international and inter-island transportation provided by steamers and MAIL BOATS, the islands of The Bahamas have been provided with an impressive array of government and private airports.

Nassau Harbour was used by numerous seaplanes from the 1920s to the present day. Landplanes soon followed. The earliest 'airfield' was Westward Villas Flying Field, described as 'difficult' and the scene of many accidents, but active in the 1930s. Later in the same decade the Nassau airfield was constructed by and later named after Sir Harry OAKES. By 2000 there were no fewer than 55 airfields in The Bahamas.

Bahamian airports range from Nassau International on western New Providence (first built as Windsor Field in World War Two), with its three runways, to the unpaved strip on Little Fowl Cay in the Exumas. The government owns and runs 27 airports, of which 14 have runways 5,000 feet (1,524 m) or more in length, more than sufficient for jets. Those at Governor's Harbour, Eleuthera, San Salvador and Mayaguana were inherited from the United States, which constructed them as part of their space shuttle programme when The Bahamas was still a British colony. The largest private airport is Freeport International, the 11,000 foot runway of which (like Nassau's) was occasionally used by the supersonic *Concordes* of British Airways. The highest concentrations of private airports are in the Exumas (seven) and Berry Islands (six), some of which, like isolated airstrips elsewhere, were reportedly used for drug-running in the 1980s.

ALBURY, Dr Paul (1934–1997) Born in HARBOUR ISLAND to a family dating back to the first English settlers in the seventeenth century, Paul Albury was schooled at QUEEN'S COLLEGE in Nassau and trained as a dentist in the United States. Though dentistry was his livelihood, Bahamian history was his passion . A famous raconteur, much in demand as a public speaker, he was a member of the BAHAMAS HISTORICAL SOCIETY from its foundation and its president during the years of transition from white minority to black majority rule. In 1975, he published with Macmillan his own long-awaited version of Bahamian history, *The Story of The Bahamas*. Not surprisingly, it was a lively narrative that ruffled no feathers, at the same time disappointing both those who wished for the traditional celebration of the white regime and who wanted a radical re-evaluation. Much more original and useful, though equally cautious was Dr Albury's *Paradise Island Story*, published in 1984, also by Macmillan.

Unfortunately, illness and his untimely death did not allow Dr Albury to bring his general history past the year of Bahamian INDEPENDENCE, or to recount the huge changes involving Paradise Island since 1984. However, *The Story of the Bahamas* remained in print and in 2004 a second edition of *Paradise Island Story* was published, revised and updated by Paul Albury's daughter, Ann Lawlor.

AMBERGRIS A solid gummy substance with almost magical attributes which is formed in the intestines of the sperm whale, disgorged and usually found washed up on tropical shores, especially in The Bahamas. Originally black and soft with a disagreeable odour, ambergris hardens and fades in the sun and develops a pleasant scent. Most remarkably, it was found to have the almost priceless ability to fix perfumes indefinitely. This made it so valuable that even in the seventeenth century it commanded £4 an ounce. Though usually small, lumps weighing many pounds were sometimes discovered – the record one of an almost incredible 922 pounds – which held out the promise to searchers of riches for life.

It was chiefly ambergris that lured sailors from Bermuda to The Bahamas in the early seventeenth century. Some fortunes were made, but the supply was much more finite than the searchers wished or realised, and was all but exhausted by 1700. By that time venturers had turned to other pursuits, including timber and dye-wood cutting, PRIVATEERING, WRECKING, and even planting.

AMERICAN CIVIL WAR The Bahamas, like Bermuda, played an important subsidiary role in the American Civil War (1861–5), serving as a neutral base for running the Union blockade, to export cotton and import arms and other supplies.

President Lincoln declared a blockade of Confederate ports in the first week of the war, but the Union grip did not tighten until 1863, with as many as 700 blockade-busting vessels eventually deployed. To counter them, special sleek paddle-wheelers were built in British shipyards, capable of steaming up to 17 ½ knots. In all, some 1,650 vessels were involved, making about 8,000 voyages to and from the Southern ports.

As the neutral port closest to the chief Southern ports of Charleston and Wilmington, NASSAU enjoyed a tremendous boom. Losses in vessels captured or sunk were immense, but were much more than offset by the profits.

AMERICAN INVASION, 1776

Blockade running bonanza during the American Civil War, 1860s

Of the Nassau blockade-running steamships, 42 were captured and 22 sunk. But supplies purchased in England or Nassau were sold for at least five times as much in the Confederacy, while cotton bought in Charleston for 10 cents a pound could fetch a dollar a pound in Nassau three days later. Bahamian imports and exports worth no more than £390,000 in 1860, soared to £10 million in 1864. Merchants and captains made fortunes, and even ordinary sailors and stevedores reaped undreamed-of wages.

Some of the earliest Bahamian photographs show Nassau harbour – visited by only a handful of steamships a year before the war – crammed with up to 20 tall smoke-stacked paddle-wheelers, with the dock piled high with cotton bales. The ROYAL VICTORIA HOTEL was built and became the rowdy resort of blockade-runners celebrating their gains.

Union cruisers roamed as close as the Providence Channel approaches to Nassau, but by denying entry to hostile but not trading vessels, Governor Charles Bayley, with the backing of the British government, preserved the Bahamian capital as a safe haven. Protests by the Union government were offset by British anger when the USS *Trent* seized two Confederate officials from a British vessel on the high seas, bringing cotton-hungry Great Britain close to war on the Confederate side.

In all, almost a thousand voyages were made through the blockade to and from Nassau within five years. But the cutting of Confederate communications on the landward side and the capture of Wilmington and Charleston in 1865 first slowed then suddenly stopped the traffic. Almost sharing the fate of the Confederacy, The Bahamas slipped into a slump so deep that some regretted the brief boom that preceded it, and had raised false hopes.

Further reading: M. Craton, *A History of the Bahamas*, 3rd ed., San Salvador Press, 1986, 212–25.

AMERICAN INVASION, 1776 Bahamians did not join cause with the mainland colonists in the American War of Independence. However, they were not universally loyal to the British Crown at that time and did not offer serious resistance on the several occasions during the War when the islands were 'invaded' by the Americans or their Spanish allies. Apart from the SPANISH INVASION (1783), the most important of these incursions was the first, in March 1776, largely because it was the first enterprise of the infant United States Navy, under the command of Commodore Ezekial Hopkins.

Hopkins was given a ragtag flotilla of eight small warships, mustering 100 guns in total, and left from the Chesapeake to seize much needed gunpowder and armament from The Bahamas in February 1776. Sailing by way of Abaco, he arrived off Nassau on 3 March. Panic ensued in the town, but a volley of cannon fire from the fort dissuaded Hopkins from crossing the harbour bar. Instead, he passed Hog Island and landed 250 marines 2 miles (3 km) east of Fort Montagu, to march on Nassau.

The defence was more comic than bellicose. The ill-armed local militia advanced gingerly and then retreated without firing a shot, leaving Fort Montagu undefended. Governor Montfort Browne, despairing of the preparedness of Fort Nassau and the willingness of the inhabitants to resist, ordered the guns spiked and the gunpowder shipped away – only the second part of his orders being obeyed.

Entering Nassau without bloodshed on either side, the Americans stayed two weeks, dismantling the forts and openly entertained by many townsfolk. When they sailed away on 17 March, they carried with them not only the 24 remaining barrels of gunpowder, but 103 cannon and mortars and 16,500 shells and cannon balls. Governor Browne and another senior colonial official were taken as hostages – though soon exchanged. The success of

American marines coming ashore east of Fort Montagu, 3 March 1776

the American venture was only marred by the serious sickness of 200 of Hopkins's men (said to have been incurred through excessive carousing in Nassau) and a bloody encounter with the formidable HMS *Glasgow* on the way home.

Further reading: G. W. Allen, *A Naval History of the American Revolution*, New York, 1962, i. 120; M. Craton, *A History of the Bahamas*, 136–47.

AMERINDIANS Three successive waves of Amerindians are likely to have settled the Bahamian archipelago before Christoper COLUMBUS arrived in the islands in 1492. Each influx came in the direction of winds and sea currents from the larger islands to the south and east, the second two migrant peoples displacing their less accomplished and less politically organised forerunners. The first-comers may have been Palaeo-Indians some thousand years before the Christian era, who arrived on rafts, lived in caves, made no pottery, did not farm, and left no discernible traces. Rather better known are the Meso-Indian cave-dwelling fisher-folk whom the first Spaniards found still living in the far south-west of Hispaniola and western Cuba; they were called *Siboney*. These people, whom ethnologists have preferred to call by the name they gave themselves, *Guanahatabey*, did some farming and pottery, but were not able to defend their settlements and were easily displaced and even enslaved by their Neo-Indian successors. They have left little evidence of their existence in The Bahamas – mainly in the form of rough pottery sherds and shaped shell implements.

The Bahamians who encountered Columbus in 1492 were the Arawak-speaking maritime sub-branch of the Taino people of the Greater Antilles who called themselves *Lukku-cairi* ('off-shore islanders'), transliterated as *Lucayans* by the Europeans. The custom of labelling all Taino and sub-Taino peoples *Arawaks* is outdated, just as the notion that they were a peaceable people driven onwards from the Lesser Antilles by the fiercer *Caribs* is now seen as a simplistic explanation, if not actually false. More likely, the *Lucayans* were adventurous and adaptive canoe-based colonists, forced out of Hispaniola and Cuba and onwards through The Bahamas by population pressure – itself the result of the ecological, economic and social sophistication and success of Tainan culture.

Arriving in the TURKS AND CAICOS ISLANDS and the south-eastern Bahamas from Hispaniola and Cuba some time in the first Christian millennium, the Lucayans had colonised virtually every habitable island in the archipelago by 1492, and may have numbered 40,000 people at their peak. More than 500 Lucayan sites have been located by modern archaeologists, consisting of sizeable townships around a central oblong plaza, satellite

Projected Lucayan migration routes and settlements

ANDROS

villages, temporary fishing camps, and caves used for refuge, burial and sacred ceremonies. Lucayan rubbish middens are a treasure ground for archaeological explorers. Lucayans were accomplished potters, wood-workers, basket-weavers and stone-carvers. They worked cotton into ropes and strands but did not weave it. Their caves were adorned with elaborate petroglyphs and contained sacred charms called ZEMIS and carved ceremonial stools called *duhos*. Animistic and fatalist, by all accounts Lucayans had a coherent set of beliefs, a vivid cosmology and pantheon of gods.

The Lucayans made delicate stone and shell beads, bangles and bracelets, elaborate head-dresses and skirts of cotton, feathers and shells. They knew gold and the magical amalgam of gold and copper called *guanin*, but no metals suitable for tools or weapons. Expert canoe-builders, sailors, swimmers, fishers and farmers, they built sturdy if impermanent houses of tree trunks and boughs, wattles and thatch, and slept in hammocks. The Lucayan diet was healthily balanced and plentiful, except in times of drought or storm. Unusually for Amerindians, Lucayans cultivated both cassava and corn, rather than one or the other. These staple starch foods were augmented with peas, beans and native fruits, including guavas and pineapples. Their protein was derived from a healthy mixture of fish, shellfish, turtles and seals, supplemented by agouti, iguana and the migrant and native fowls. Lucayan shamans, like later Bahamians, were adept in BUSH MEDICINE.

Organised effectively in small island units, the Lucayans lived a relatively peaceful, healthy and fertile life, in harmony with their environment. They were no match for the armed and armoured Spaniards, who killed those few who resisted, inadvertently infected the majority with European diseases against which they had no resistance, and rounded up the survivors to work the mines of Hispaniola. Within 20 years, The Bahamas was completely depopulated, remaining without permanent inhabitants for almost a century and a half, and with fewer people than in pre-Columbian times until about 1870.

The Lucayans (with other Arawakan speakers) have left a small legacy in several words adopted by the English language, such as *canoe, hammock* and *tobacco*. The Lucayan names for many Bahamian islands have survived in the early records, but only *Mayaguana, Samana* (probably Long Island, not the cay now bearing that name), *Exuma, Abaco,* and perhaps *Inagua* and *Bimini,* have avoided renaming to be found on modern maps. Others, recorded by Spanish chroniclers, were *Guanahani* (San Salvador), *Someto* (Crooked Island), *Guanima* (Cat Island) and *Segatoo* (Eleuthera).

The Lucayans formed a unitary culture, effectively bounded in the north by the swift-flowing Florida Channel. Speculations that there may have been cultural contact with the Amerindians of Florida in the pre-Columbian period are unproven. At the time of the expansion of the United States into Florida in the early nineteenth century, however, small groups of SEMINOLE Indian refugees crossed the Gulf Stream to settle Red Bay Cays in north-western ANDROS, where some of their descendants remain to this day. Most, however, have fully integrated into the Bahamian population – to a tiny extent reversing the Columbian genocide and displacement that had earlier deprived The Bahamas of an Amerindian component in its ethnic mix. The Bowleg family in particular derives its surname from Billy Bowlegs, the redoubtable resistance leader in the Seminole Wars.

Further reading: W. Keegan, *The People Who Discovered Columbus,* Florida, 1992; W. Keegan, *Bahamian Archeology*, Media Publishing, 1977; Craton and Saunders, *Islanders,* i. 3–59.

ANDROS Colloquially known as 'the Big Yard', Andros is by far the largest, and among the last and least developed of Bahamian islands. It is situated between the huge flats of the Great Bahama Bank in the west (known as 'the Mud' when it was one of the world's chief SPONGING grounds) and the mile-deep TONGUE OF THE OCEAN

Captive Lucayans visualised by artist Brent Malone

in the east. Mostly completely flat, with a single low ridge down its eastern side, Andros is really an archipelago of three large islands and innumerable islets, split by three wide, shallow bights and a network of tidal creeks. There are also more than two hundred BLUE HOLES, on land or just off shore, in which the water rises and falls with the tide, in some cases with spectacular energy.

The exact land area of this perforated jigsaw depends in effect on the state of the tide and whether or not 'land' includes only areas permanently dry. But in any case, Andros stretches over an area more than 100 miles (160 km) north to south and as much as 45 miles (72 km) east to west, containing almost as much land as the rest of The Bahamas put together – some 2,300 square miles (5,957 squ. km). The fringing reef that stretches almost the entire length of the eastern shore is said to be the third most extensive in the world, behind only Australia's Great Barrier Reef, and that off the coast of Belize. Andros is the only Bahamian island large enough to generate its own clouds and substantial convectional rainfall. It is therefore well watered and has vast natural reservoirs of fresh water underground, especially in the north and central parts. Before it was clear-cut for pulpwood in the 1950s and 1960s, Andros was largely covered with pine forest, interspersed with groves of palmetto and stands of hardwoods such as mahogany. In the areas of tidal 'swash', MANGROVES still carry out their primeval task of recovering land from the sea.

Andros was not named, as is sometimes said, either by nineteenth-century Greek sponge fishermen after the Aegean island of Andros, or for the seventeenth-century Governor of New England, Sir Edmund Andros. The earliest Spanish explorers called it *Espirito Santo* but later Spaniards *San Andreas*, which was turned into English as *St Andrew's*, and modified in common usage to *Andros*.

With no good harbours and not deemed suitable for slave plantations, Andros was ignored by the early English colonists and Loyalists – in fact it was so little known that in the nineteenth century there were legends that its interior was peopled with descendants of the aboriginal Lucayans. The truth behind the rumours may have been occasional visits by SEMINOLES from Florida, or, more likely, the existence of the small band of refugees from the Seminole Wars who formed what is still the only settlement on the west coast of Andros, Red Bay, in the 1830s.

The other earliest settlers were ex-slaves crowded out by population growth and limited land from the central islands, notably EXUMA. These were a proud and hardy people, exclusively of African descent, subsistence farmer-fishermen who built their own boats and were ignored and almost totally neglected by Nassau. But at the same time they retained and developed their own culture, based on African roots overlaid with a fervent homespun Christianity. Living only on the far eastern edge of the island, they looked to the sea rather than the forested and swampy interior, which remained in their folklore an area of darkness and mystery. It was said to be the home of the mischievous *chickcharnie* – 'red-eyed, three-fingered, owl-like elves with beards and feathered scalps who hang by their tails from cottonwood trees'. And in the depths of the interconnecting blue holes was said to lurk the sinister submarine monster called the *Lusca*.

Conditions changed for Andros with the development of the sponge industry in the late nineteenth century, but

Fresh Creek, Andros

ANDROSIA

not for the better. The population expanded, but fewer of the inhabitants had the land, skill or time to be subsistence farmers. Androsian sponge fishermen were the most exploited and desperate of the Bahamian poor and their plight grew even worse during the Great Depression and with the sponge blight of the late 1930s. Andros became a byword for backwardness until after the middle of the century. However, at the same time it was recognised by folklorists as the strongest remaining bastion of the authentic Afro-Bahamian culture – even referred to by one folk musicologist as 'The Real Bahamas'.

In 1965 the British government agreed to the establishment of the AUTEC base from which to test submarines and weapons in the Tongue of the Ocean. After Independence, the Americans were taxed more heavily for their use of the AUTEC facility, and while Prime Minister Lynden PINDLING was one of its parliamentary representatives (1967–97) Andros received considerable development in the form of roads, bridges, airports (it has four), schools and clinics. The government offices at Nicholl's Town in north Andros are housed in what is described in one guidebook as the loveliest neo-Georgian building in The Bahamas. But government schemes to modernise farming have failed through mismanagement, and for Nassauvians Andros is regarded as important only as the place from which six million gallons of fresh water are barged each day to top up their supply.

At the beginning of a new century Andros is still regarded as a 'sleeping giant' or 'land of the future'. With much to attract tourists (especially scuba divers, blue hole explorers, bonefishers and eco-tourists), some potential for farming, and enough fresh water to support a million people, it is still home to barely 8,000 Bahamians.

ANDROSIA An imaginative and successful *batik* textile-dyeing and small garment-manufacturing operation established at Fresh Creek, ANDROS since 1973. Androsia has adapted an ancient Indonesian technique to the Bahamian context, employing the traditional craft and needlework skills of local islanders. It provides discriminating tourists with a memento of their stay that combines beauty and elegance, as well as being authentically Bahamian.

Androsia was established by the Canadian-born, Andros-resident Birch family (owners of the famous diving and fishing resort called Small Hope Bay) in the year of Bahamian INDEPENDENCE (1973). It had the encouragement of the government (especially of the two Andros representatives, Prime Minister Lynden PINDLING and Minister Darrell Rolle) but resolutely

Typical Androsia batik fabric

maintained its own autonomy and resisted the temptation to grow too large too quickly at the expense of quality and authenticity. It now employs some 45 local waxers, dyers, cutters and sewers – many of them women with skills in making straw baskets and handbags with cotton linings. Androsia uses only the highest quality cotton cloth and colour-fast cold dyes and specialises in colours and designs that are characteristically Bahamian. It favours such lively sea and flower colours as emerald, turquoise and deep-sea blue, poinciana red, poui pink or bougainvillea orange, and such distinctive motifs as conch shells, birds and flowers.

Often cited as a model for rationally sized Family Island industries, Androsia's achievement was fittingly recognised by the award of the prestigious Silver Jubilee Award during the celebrations of the twenty-fifth anniversary of Bahamian Independence in 1998.

ANGLICANISM Although the colony of The Bahamas was founded by Puritan dissidents from Bermuda, the Church of England was its official 'established' church from the royal takeover in 1718 until 1869. Even after its disestablishment, the Anglican Church retained much prestige, and despite competition from BAPTISTS, METHODISTS, ROMAN CATHOLICS and numerous other denominations, and periodic internal crises, it still claimed a quarter of the Bahamian population as its adherents at the start of the twenty-first century.

Under the Old Colonial System, the Anglican Church was expected to work hand in glove with the colonial government. As in England, apart from their purely ecclesiastical functions, clergymen kept local records. Parishes, with their 'vestries' of laymen, were intended to be responsible for most aspects of local government, including education, the relief of the poor, and the maintenance of roads and bridges – the expenses of which were paid for by local taxation. Even the local militia was usually organised on a parochial basis. This system worked satisfactorily enough in the West Indian plantation colonies, but it was less practicable in The Bahamas, with its widely scattered islands and small and poor (not to say ungodly) population.

The early royal Governors (in their official role as 'ordinaries' of the Anglican Church) did their best to furnish a church building and obtain ordained ministers who could also teach. They raised what money they could through a poor and reluctant Assembly to augment the meagre subventions of the overstretched Society for the Propagation of the Gospel (SPG). The nominal authority of the Bishop of London over all the American colonies was tenuous to the point of non-existence in The Bahamas. The entire Bahamas was a single parish (with CHRIST CHURCH in Nassau its only church) down to 1768, when HARBOUR ISLAND and ELEUTHERA were made the separate parish of St John's, with its own minister, church and school. The records of the SPG, however, reveal a Bahamian ministry struggling against the poverty, ignorance and indifference of the whites and free coloureds, and not ministering to the black slaves at all. In 1780 there were only three ministers in the entire colony.

The coming of the American LOYALISTS in the 1780s and 1790s initiated the first major changes. Though not all the immigrant whites were Anglicans (and those Scots PRESBYTERIANS among them managed to obtain establishment privileges for their own kirk in Nassau), they nearly all regarded the setting up of parishes, churches and schools as necessary functions. In 1795, funds were voted by the Assembly for the establishment of six new parishes in the newly settled areas: a second parish for New Providence (ST MATTHEW'S), the separation of Eleuthera from Harbour Island (as St Patrick's), Exuma (St Andrew), Long Island (St Paul), Cat Island (San Salvador), Long Cay, Crooked Island and Acklins (St David) and Turks' Island (St George). By 1815 there were as many as a dozen Anglican ministers in The Bahamas, and their ministry had begun to extend towards the non-white majority.

The next significant advances were made under the influence of the evangelical and abolitionist reformers within the Anglican Church in England. In 1824, The Bahamas was placed under the authority of the newly created diocese of Jamaica and the first bishop, Lipscomb, visited the islands four times between 1826 and 1839, recommending and implementing reforms. Equally important were the allocations for 'negro education' made by the imperial government from 1824, which were to be administered through the established church.

Christ Church Anglican Cathedral

Conflicts, however, arose between the Anglicans and the Nonconformists over the question of the former's establishment status, and within the Anglican Church itself. The number of Anglican clergy reached a peak of 16 in 1845, but had fallen to 13 by 1880. The government continued to give aid to the church to the extent that the church provided primary schooling, and Christ Church continued to be the colony's most prestigious place of worship. But the influence of the church would have waned disastrously were it not for two interrelated factors: the heroic evangelical and missionary activities of Bishop Addington VENABLES (1864–76) and his successors and Anglo-Catholic priests such as Fr. W. L. Woodcock in Nassau and Fr. F. B. Matthews in Cat Island and Andros; and the undoubted attraction that the Anglo-Catholic type of ritual and congregational participation held for many black Bahamians. The Anglican Church also gained much credit and recruited followers through the foundation of a mission for seamen on the Nassau harbour-front by Rev. Weigell in 1891.

Under its succession of staunchly Anglo-Catholic bishops (sometimes at variance with 'Low Church' Deans and parsons in Nassau's Christ Church and St Matthew's) the Anglican Church survived strongly into the twentieth century. Its chief new problems were to withstand the

ARAWAK CAY

onslaught of financially better supported ROMAN CATHOLIC missionaries from the United States, to regain a stronger presence in the colony's educational system, and to overcome the situation (increasingly uncomfortable for Bahamian nationalists) that it was a church consisting of predominantly black congregations ministered to by white expatriate priests. This clergy, moreover, never numbered more than a score before the mid-twentieth century.

The Anglicans undoubtedly lost ground first to the Roman Catholics, both in respect of numbers of adherents and in the educational field, and later to revivalist and pentecostal churches. Under its American Bishop Spence Burton (1942–61) it strengthened its parochial schools and founded two non-segregated and co-educational high schools; ST JOHN'S (1947) in Nassau and ST ANN'S (1955) in eastern New Providence – to which Freeport High School was added a few years later. More drastic reforms, however, awaited the first Bahamian (and black) bishop, Michael ELDON (1972–96). Personally an Anglo-Catholic, but diplomatic and exercising the best Anglican traditions for doctrinal and ritual flexibility, Eldon healed the ecclesiastical rift in the church and became one of the strongest proponents of ecumenical cooperation with other churches. Taking advantage of the winds of change that accompanied Bahamian INDEPENDENCE, the church attracted a growing number of local ordinands, so that, with the previous generation of expatriates gradually declining through death or retirement, it fielded more than 50 clergy by the year 2000, almost exclusively black Bahamians.

Largely through the initiatives of Bishop Eldon and prominent members of the Anglican Synod, Anglican schools became much more generously state-aided, many new churches were built (especially in newly settled but previously neglected areas of New Providence and Grand Bahama) and dozens of churches repaired and renovated throughout the Family Islands. These advances were continued, and the prestige of the Anglican Church enhanced, by the appointment of Rt Rev. Drexel Gomez to succeed Bishop Eldon in 1996. Already having served as Bishop of Barbados, Gomez was further elevated to combine his role of Bishop of The Bahamas and Turks Islands with that of Anglican Archbishop of the West Indies.

Most remarkable, perhaps, is the way that the Anglican Church has countered its rivals, on both right and left wings. Though equally conservative on some issues (such as the ordination of women priests) the Anglicans have outdone the Catholics and challenged the revivalists in such areas as lay participation, modernised liturgies, indigenous music and charismatic worship.

Further reading: C. F. Pascoe, *Two Hundred Years of the S.P.G., 1701–1900*, London, 1901; Rt Rev. Roscow Shedden, *Ups and Downs in a West Indian Diocese*, London, 1927.

ARAWAK CAY A 250-acre artificial island controversially created in the mid-1960s at the western end of NASSAU Harbour from material dredged during the deepening of the harbour to accommodate more and larger cruise-ships. Joined to the mainland by a short bridge and causeway, leaving only a narrow channel between itself and Silver Cay. Arawak Cay has affected not just the nearby road traffic but the water-flow channels and beach patterns further west.

The intention of the BAY STREET legislators who planned Arawak Cay was to provide an area for profitable new residential and business buildings. But public opposition and the unwillingness of the government to allow private developers to acquire what was declared to be Crown Land, has meant that nearly forty years later the cay has developed as an extension of the harbour area. It now functions as a major cargo and container port, and is the fresh-water tanker terminal for water from Andros. More picturesquely, it is noted for its HAITIAN schooners – up to a dozen of which, either awaiting checking or impounded, are normally to be seen anchored on its eastern side. The cay is marked by two failed projects: the rusting wreck of an abandoned customs warehouse, and the closed tower of the Coral World Aquarium, to which it provided access via a small bridge.

On the landward side of Arawak Cay, also a landfill site, an area usually called Arawak Cay Village, one of the busiest

Arawak Cay

areas of informal commercial enterprise and interaction between tourists, native Nassauvians and Haitians, has developed, initially of its own accord but with increasing government sanction. It consists of a thriving collection of more than thirty gaily painted wooden houses and stalls, selling fresh and cooked seafood, cold beers and other drinks, vegetable produce and fruits, and all manner of tourist mementos.

ARCHAEOLOGY With ever-increasing sophistication, three branches of the science of archaeology – prehistoric, historic and marine – help to fill gaps in our knowledge of the Bahamian past. Once the realm of inadequately monitored amateur diggers and treasure hunters, archaeological activities first came under the supervision of an enthusiastic but over-worked Department of ARCHIVES in the 1970s and 1980s. It was not until the passage of the Antiquities, Monuments and Museums Act in 1998, setting up a comprehensive infrastructure with a specialised staff under a full-time board, that the archaeological side of the exploration and preservation of Bahamian heritage was placed in more professional hands.

Archaeology is of paramount importance in finding out about the aboriginal AMERINDIANS of The Bahamas, who left no written records and had totally disappeared from the islands more than a century before the first English settlers landed. Evidence about the Lucayans (beyond what the Spanish explorers wrote) dates from the late nineteenth century, with the findings of the pioneer archaeologists Otis Mason (1877), William Brooks (1888) and Charles Maynard (1890) being followed up by the early professionals Jesse Fewkes (1907), Theodore DeBooy (1912), Herbert Krieger (1937) and John Goggin (1937–52). At the same time, scientific understanding was not advanced by the casual explorations and appropriations of 'Arawak' materials by amateurs, including at least two Catholic missionary priests, and an American resident who chipped out priceless petroglyphs from a cave on RUM CAY.

Largely inspired by the pan-Caribbean work of Irving Rouse from the late 1940s, there was a steady increase in professional explorations and writings on the Lucayans and their predecessors. Among those doing important work were Julian Granberry (1956–87), Charles Hoffman (1967–87), William Sears and Shaun Sullivan (1974–81) and John Winter (1978–90); particularly significant was the summary of his own wide-ranging discoveries and hypotheses by William Keegan of the University of Florida in *The People Who Discovered Columbus* (1992).

At least equally important was the increasing involvement in archaeological enterprises and their co-ordination by the Department of Archives during the tenure of the Jamaican consultant Tony Aarons (1988–93). Besides leading prehistoric digs in western New Providence and Long Island and cataloguing important finds in Grand Bahama and Andros, Aarons made invaluable compilations of the almost 400 prehistoric sites so far discovered in The Bahamas and of the 40 or so ceremonial *duhos* discovered (and mainly dispersed) over the years. In doing so, he and his willing helpers not only greatly increased the knowledge of the Lucayan way of life and revised the known patterns and extent of Lucayan settlement, but alerted the Bahamian public to the need for retaining their prehistoric heritage. In an act symbolising this new awareness the Archives purchased the three *duhos* uniquely discovered in a cave at Mortimer's, Long Island in 1988 from their finders and kept them as part of the Bahamian national patrimony – to be a possible centrepiece for the long-planned national museum.

Also important, though perhaps less glamorous, have been scientific efforts to explore sites from the early colonial period, thereby augmenting what is known from documentary sources of the lives and lifestyles of slaves and their planter masters. Here the salient problems are twofold. While the steady depopulation of many of the

'Dig' at Long Bay, San Salvador led by Professor Charles Hoffman, July 1983, which discovered certain evidence that this was the American landfall of Christopher Columbus

ARCHITECTURE

Family Islands leaves the ruins of many old 'great houses', slaves' quarters and other plantation buildings neglected, the encroachment of bush makes archaeological work difficult and costly. Conversely, some of the most interesting sites in more developed locations – such as the original house of William Lyford at LYFORD CAY and the great house and slave quarters on William WYLLY's nearby CLIFTON Estate – have been threatened by uncaring developers. The heated controversy over the latter, however, has successfully brought the need for preservation to public attention.

Probably most problematic, though, is the control of treasure hunting. From the earliest years of English settlement The Bahamas has been recognised as one of the world's most promising locations for treasure-bearing wrecks. Among the most famous finds were two as early as 1657: a Spanish treasure ship found on a reef off north Eleuthera and the much richer wreck of the galleon *Maravilla* on Memory Rock, the north-east tip of the Little Bahama Bank. Though not quite matching the famous Phipps treasure found off Hispaniola in 1687 or the wreck of the *Atocha* off Florida discovered almost two hundred years later, two chance finds off Gorda Cay in 1950 and Freeport in 1965 generated almost equal excitement.

The Freeport treasure of 1965 motivated the UNITED BAHAMIAN PARTY government to pass a more rigorous act to control marine treasure-hunting. But this was inspired more by a wish to share in the monetary proceeds than to retain heritage items within The Bahamas (companies had to be licensed for a specific search and also had to have Bahamian partners). Following the fabulous returns made from the use of modern search and recovery equipment on the *Atocha* site and the rediscovered wreck of the *Maravilla*, applications for exploration licences have multiplied in recent years. Most significant from a historical viewpoint have been the searches that led to the discovery of two Spanish wrecks dating from the lifetime of COLUMBUS himself, located on the Molasses Reef off West Caicos and near Highborn Cay in the Exumas. Both were at first thought to have been the remains of Columbus's own lost *Pinta*. But subsequent studies suggested the equally interesting possibility that they were the wrecks of vessels scouring The Bahamas for Lucayan slaves, sent by Columbus's immediate successors.

Further reading: W. F. Keegan, *The People Who Discovered Columbus: The Prehistory of The Bahamas*, University Press of Florida, 1992; I. Rouse, *The Taino: Rise and Fall of the People who Greeted Columbus*, Yale University Press, 1993.

ARCHITECTURE

Thanks largely to the drawings of the artist Robert Douglas, Bahamian architecture – FORTS, public buildings, great houses and vernacular dwellings – has been recognised as possessing distinctive and elegant traditional styles, shaped through adaptation to local materials and climatic conditions. At the same time, through the voluntary work of such conservationists as the Historic Committee of the BAHAMAS NATIONAL TRUST, this heritage has to a great extent been able to resist the onset of an incongruous modernism. Since 2003, a licence has been required to alter or demolish any public building over 50 years old.

Forts (considered separately), public buildings and the houses of the planter and mercantile ruling class employed the native limestone, which had the properties of being easily cut but subject to weathering. Most limestone buildings were plastered for this reason. Where there were no facilities for cutting limestone blocks (as in the Family Islands), substantial buildings were constructed from cemented free-stone rocks, though in modern times cement blocks became the universal medium (easier to work with than free stones, and far cheaper than cut limestone). The more modest houses of the great majority of the people were constructed from wattle-and-daub, cemented free-stone or, like the native boats, from the wide variety of local hard and soft woods. They were roofed with native palm thatch or imported cedar shingles. Even the great houses of the upper classes, to moderate the sweltering heat of the summer, had their cut limestone cores clad in a wooden carapace of galleries, jalousies, dormers and projecting roofs, requiring carpentry skills equal to those developed in boat building. Unlike the West Indies proper, corrugated iron was not used for roofing until comparatively late, and even then not generally.

Probably no Bahamian public buildings (including the oldest churches) antedate the coming of the LOYALISTS. Consequently, they derive their style from the North American variant of the classical style developed in the mid-eighteenth century, rather than directly from British models. For example, Joseph EVE's Nassau Public Library (built in 1800 as the town jail) and ST MATTHEW's Church (1802) are very reminiscent of buildings in Williamsburg, Virginia, while the central government buildings facing Parliament Square (1805–13) were said to be consciously modelled on the Governor's Palace at New Bern, North Carolina. Subsequent public buildings, such as the Supreme Court in Bank Lane (1921) and many banks and office buildings built even later, closely echo such original models. Thought by some to be the finest building in Nassau, the Villa Doyle on West Hill Street, built in the 1860s as a private mansion and from 2000 renovated to house the National Gallery, is designed much on the

ARCHITECTURE

same lines, being reminiscent of some of the grandest ante-bellum mansions in the United States' South.

The pride of NASSAU are the 20 or 30 elegant residences dating from the eighteenth century carefully preserved by their private or corporate owners. Among the finest and most typical are Jacaranda on East Hill Street, Cascadilla on East Street, Georgeside on George Street, and The Deanery on Cumberland Street. Several of the Loyalist era houses on Queen Street give that quiet, dead-end street an ambience likened by some to colonial Charleston, South Carolina. There are undoubtedly stylistic derivations from the port cities of the colonial South – quite natural given their close connections with Nassau in earlier times. However, Nassau's old town houses are subtly distinct in most respects, particularly in their use of faux quoins on the inner core, and the all-round galleries designed to catch the breeze from any direction.

(a) Georgeside, George Street, Nassau

So well have the houses followed traditional styles in both building and restoration that it is often difficult to date them precisely or to tell which is the oldest and therefore the likely original model. Robert Douglas suggests that The Deanery originally dates from about 1710, though it was probably almost entirely rebuilt by the vestry of CHRIST CHURCH as a parsonage house in 1802. What may well be the oldest house still in its original form, BALCONY HOUSE on Market Street, a comparatively modest edifice mostly built of wood, was probably in fact constructed no earlier than 1790. At the other end of the timescale, the building at the corner of West and Marlborough Streets with some of the features of Balcony House which Douglas includes as a fine example of traditional style, was actually custom-built as an office building in the 1970s (albeit on a rather older original core).

(b) Harbour Island

Not one of the great houses once found in the Family Islands settled by LOYALIST planters has survived intact or been preserved, though the cut or free-stone cores of many are still to be found in the bush, in various late stages of decay. The most imposing example is the original core of the mansion of Andrew Deveaux Sr. at Port Howe, CAT ISLAND, which Robert Douglas, making an urgent plea for its restoration in 1992, claimed was probably the finest house in The Bahamas in its day. Much more modest were the wooden houses of those Loyalist mariners who settled in the small islands off northern ELEUTHERA and ABACO, which have survived along with their tenacious communities. These houses, like many others constructed over the years on traditional models, display strong influences from the American mainland – but the north-eastern maritime towns rather than the southern ports – allowing many travel writers to suggest, with their customary hyperbole, that Dunmore Town, HARBOUR ISLAND and HOPE TOWN, Abaco appear as if transplanted from Cape Cod.

(c) Old Bight, Cat Island

As Robert Douglas powerfully argues, though, the houses of the most prosperous Conchy Joes of Eleuthera and

ARCHITECTURE

Abaco are but the most elaborate of a whole range of vernacular houses with features that, while subtly distinct from island to island, are distinctive to The Bahamas as a whole. Douglas selects examples from five islands to illustrate his contention. His typical shingled and weather-boarded Hope Town house has a distinctive 'cranked' roof extending forward over the front porch to give extra bedroom space for the traditionally large families. The example chosen as typical of the many handsome houses in Harbour Island is rather larger, with a simply pitched roof but with double dormers front and back and two gable windows at each end. The full-length front gallery has elegant timber pillars and ship-style brackets supporting the front of the roof, and wooden guttering. All windows have sashes but also shutters. The top-hinged shutters on the side windows provide shade as well as rain protection, whereas the front, back and dormer windows are side-hinged.

The typical houses in Spanish Wells, as befits a traditionally puritan community, have an almost severe simplicity, which, says Douglas, would appeal to twentieth-century Cubist painters. Little more than wood-framed and weather-board boxes with a hipped porch at the front, they are traditionally painted white, with the shutters alone painted a different colour by way of contrast. As Douglas says of Spanish Wells as a whole, 'In spite of its spartan appearance, or perhaps because of it, this settlement is extremely beautiful.'

Douglas also has favourable things to say about the even simpler traditional houses of the poorer non-white islands, though he concentrates on the stone-walled houses rather than the far more impermanent wattle-and-daub framed and thatched-roof structures of the poorest islands and settlements. Of his 'typical' example from Old Bight, CAT ISLAND, he says: 'This simple structure has great elegance. A pyramidical shingle roof covers the stone walled house and timber framed gallery. Rear wall corners have battered stone buttresses. Similar houses are shown in early photographs of Grant's Town, Nassau – they were, however, thatched and of heavy board construction.'

The house chosen by Douglas from Simms settlement in LONG ISLAND is the simplest of the five: a four-sided, stone-walled block, with a shingled hipped roof that may originally have been thatched. Without a front porch, it is probably divided into four small rooms inside, each with a single sash-less window, protected by side-opening shutters. A similarly constructed but much smaller kitchen building was separate but adjacent, and an earth latrine somewhat further away at the back. Traditional features found in Long Island were the stone walling continued up into the roof to give 'a firmer holding capacity during hurricane', and an elaborately carved ridge pole to provide otherwise almost identical buildings with a distinctive identity.

Church buildings in The Bahamas seem to follow styles even more varied than the different modes of religion practised inside. It would be difficult, if not impossible, to make architectural generalisations between different faiths and sects. The one exception to the general eclecticism is the stylistic consistency of the many churches and religious buildings designed and constructed by the remarkable architect-monk Father JEROME (1876–1956). Though they show traces of influence from other parts of the world and do not noticeably derive from native models, Father Jerome's buildings lay claim to a consistent style unique to The Bahamas.

By the year 2000, architects practising in The Bahamas were almost as numerous as doctors. The *Bahamas Handbook* lists almost fifty architectural firms in Nassau and another dozen in Freeport. With few exceptions, however, this multiplicity has not led to stylistic incongruities. This is no accident. Not only do all practising architects have to be licensed by a Professional Architects Board in accordance with the Professional Architects Act of 1994, but all building plans are required to have official approval. It no doubt also helps that a majority of practising architects are now native Bahamians, with an inherent sensitivity to the Bahamian architectural heritage.

Usually the government of The Bahamas has followed tradition in the design of its own official buildings, as well as being laudably willing to pass building and other regulations aimed at preventing The Bahamas becoming quite like South Florida. Besides a ban on the use of large or lurid advertising signs, there is supposed to be a height restriction on new buildings. Notably, new government offices in the Family Islands have been tastefully designed, sometimes providing an elegant focus for settlements that are otherwise somewhat down-at-heel. The *Lonely Planet* guidebook even describes the 'Georgian style' government building at Nicholls Town, ANDROS, as being both modern and beautiful.

In controlling buildings put up by major foreign investors, though, the government's record has been less consistent. Freeport, as a consequence of its virtual autonomy in the early years, has been marred by several buildings more appropriate to Miami or Las Vegas than The Bahamas. These include the Moorish-style Princess Casino and the architectural mishmash of the International Bazaar. Nassau's hotels and resorts are similarly exotic in style. Mercifully, downtown Nassau has not been allowed to become a miniature Manhattan, despite its importance as a major financial centre. The sensitive remodelling of what is now the British Colonial Hilton Hotel, originally built in 1899 and rebuilt in 1923, has done much to make up for the demolition of the historic Royal Victoria Hotel.

Further reading: S. Russell, *Nassau's Historic Buildings*, Nassau, 1979; R. Douglas, *Island Heritage: Architecture of The Bahamas*, Nassau, Darkstream Publications, 1992; G. Saunders and L. Huber, *Nassau's Historic Landmarks*. Oxford, Macmillan Caribbean, 2001.

ARCHIVES Before 1967 the public records of The Bahamas were in a sorry state. Each government department was responsible for its own records, and these were kept haphazardly and inefficiently, if at all. The pioneer survey of all British West Indian materials carried out by Bell and Parker under the auspices of the Carnegie Institute in 1926 disclosed a wealth of local records, but revealed that few of them were catalogued and many suffering from tropical damp, the ravages of insects and neglect. Partial exceptions were the Assembly and Council records, preserved in print (as abstracts, not verbatim) and the records in the Lands and Surveys Department and Registry regarded as vital in establishing titles to land, property transactions, and genealogical ties. Almost too late, a programme of microfilming the Registry records began in 1956.

Following recommendations made by a United Nations expert in 1968, a public records office was set up subordinate to the Ministry of Education and located in the old Post Office on Mackey Street in Nassau. This was officially opened on 15 September 1971. The first major operation of the new department was a survey of all Bahamian records, including those located outside The Bahamas. This was made by another UN expert, Mr E. A. Carson, in collaboration with Mrs Gail SAUNDERS, a seconded high school teacher just returned from an archives course in London. This invaluable work was published as a fat booklet towards the end of 1973, by which time Mrs Saunders had been appointed Chief Archivist, and several of her staff had been sent for specialist archival training to Jamaica, Barbados, the Virgin Islands and Washington DC.

Though many of the most important records (notably those of the Legislature, Judiciary, Registry and Lands and Surveys Department) remained where they were, the Archives Department faced a monumental task in gathering in and preserving what other old records lay scattered around Nassau, while at the same time trying to accommodate and catalogue the growing collection of new documents emanating from ministries and other institutions. A repair and bindery section was set up in January 1973 (located at first in the Ministry of Education building), followed shortly afterwards by a microfilming facility. Periodically, the Mackey Street facilities were extended and upgraded – most notably in 1990 when the existing building was constructed.

Despite funding difficulties, the Archives Department admirably strove to fulfil all the functions to be expected of a proper modern public records office. From the beginning it was an indispensable resource for researchers, with a reading room much frequented by scholars, school students and interested ordinary members of the public. As well as steadily expanding its holdings of documentary records and newspapers, the Archives gradually became the unofficial national library of Bahamiana – with an ever-increasing collection of books and articles by scholars who had used its facilities. As far as they could given the pressure of other work, the staff became involved in oral history projects, and built up an invaluable array of taped and transcribed interviews.

From 1974 the Archives held an annual series of exhibitions – either at Mackey Street or in downtown Nassau – each on a different aspect of Bahamian history and culture. Each was accompanied by an informative illustrated booklet. Given virtual control over Bahamian archaeology (including treasure hunting), the Archives over the years also built up a priceless collection of Bahamian artefacts – most famous of which were the three Lucayan *duhos* discovered in a cave on LONG ISLAND in 1988. Replicas of these are displayed inside the main entrance of the main Mackey Street building. With many other artefacts on show, along with documents, photographs, prints and paintings, this foyer constitutes an excellent if small museum of Bahamian history, culture and life.

Further reading: G. Saunders and E. A. Carson, *Guide to the Records of The Bahamas*, Nassau, Government Printing Department, 1973.

ARDASTRA GARDENS Five-acre tropical gardens and zoo in Nassau's suburban CHIPPINGHAM, famous for their parading FLAMINGOS.

Named for the motto of the ROYAL AIR FORCE (*Per ardua ad astra,* 'Through difficulties to the stars') the Ardastra Gardens were established as a tourist attraction in the early 1950s by the Jamaican-born resident Hedley Edwards. Besides the unique – not to say bizarre – daytime spectacle of captive flamingos marching to barked commands like Alice in Wonderland guardsmen, it was for many years also the location of one of Nassau's most popular nightclubs.

With the shift of the nightclub scene to the hotels and the retirement of Hedley Edwards, the Ardastra Gardens almost faded away. But they were rescued in the late 1980s by a consortium headed by the BAY STREET entrepreneur Norman Solomon. The nightclub was

ART

Ardastra Gardens

not revived and the emphasis was now placed on the display and preservation of Bahamian and West Indian flora and fauna. The thrice-daily parade of the flamingos was retained (at 11 am, 2 pm and 4 pm, except for a Sunday rest day) but tourists were equally encouraged to enjoy an impressive array of native and exotic trees, plants and flowers, to view and even, under supervision, to pet, Bahamian AGOUTIS (hutias), IGUANAS, boa constrictors and PARROTS, as well as more cautiously to admire alligators, monkeys, jaguars and ocelots from points further south. With its concern for conservation, the management is particularly proud of its breeding programme for the endangered Bahama parrot, and of the fact that, after half a century of recruiting only from the wild, it was responsible for the first successful breeding of a Bahamian flamingo in captivity in the year 2000.

ART Artwork has not been a traditional feature of Bahamian culture; but during the last half century it has become one of the most remarkable and vital forms of Bahamian creativity. The most obvious reasons are not the only ones, or even the most salient. Bahamian art has undoubtedly been unlocked by new opportunities and stimuli: teaching in schools, professional training, increased leisure, the easier availability of materials, patronage and, above all, the synergistic growth of a profitable market. Yet it is clear that there was a natural reservoir of talent and subject matter – environmental, social and cultural – waiting to be melded into a recognisably distinctive national school.

Historians of Bahamian art – and some of the artists themselves – are able to point to significant events and influences. The most distinguished and successful of Bahamian painters, Brent MALONE (1941–2004) cited the joint inspiration of three exceptionally gifted English art teachers at QUEEN'S COLLEGE, along with the dedicated black Bahamian Don Russell (trained at the Art Students League in New York), who ran an Academy of Fine Art on Nassau's Elizabeth Avenue in the mid-1950s. Another pioneer black Bahamian teacher was Horace Wright (1915–76), who after some training in England was from 1951 an itinerant art teacher in government schools, and from 1961 to 1975 Supervisor of Art in all schools under the Board and later Ministry of Education. Brent Malone and other apprentice artists (including Maxwell TAYLOR, Kendall Hanna and Eddie MINNIS) also praised the influence of the Englishman David Rawnsley, whose Chelsea Pottery ran a branch in Nassau for a decade in the 1950s and 1960s under the patronage of Sir Harold CHRISTIE.

Several important artists, such as Malone, Taylor, the Abaconian Alton LOWE and, rather later, John Beadle and Antonius Roberts, were able to further their studies in Europe and the United States. But this mainly gave them technical skills and versatility; their chief inspiration and subject matter remained or became essentially Bahamian. Lack of foreign training did not hinder a much greater range of purely home-bred practitioners, be they intuitive talents like Amos FERGUSON, 'Joe Monks' (Joseph Weaver) and Tony 'Exuma' MCKAY, or brilliant realists such as Chan Pratt, Rolfe Harris, Malcolm Rae, and Eddie MINNIS's even more accomplished daughters, Nicole and Roshanne.

In *Islanders in the Stream* (1998), Michael Craton and Gail Saunders considered the source of inspiration for Bahamian artists:

> *Despite their creative individualism, the work of Ferguson, Taylor, Lowe, Malone and Roberts – and that of other important Bahamian artists – is linked by a celebration of Bahamian light and colour; the invocation of the surrounding element of the sea and the people's responses to it; the common identity of the people themselves; their shared legacies, from Europe and elsewhere as well as Africa; and above all, the symbolic importance to them all of the syncretic, if predominantly African, Junkanoo festival, with its bloodbeat rhythm of the goombay drums.* (ii. 486).

ASUE (SU-SU)

Long-planned Art Gallery in renovated Villa Doyle on West Hill Street, opened 2003

Bahamian art has achieved prominence in such landmark integrating events as the exhibition 'Bahamian Art Today' held at Malone's Matinee Gallery in 1977; the 'Ten Artists' show held to celebrate the tenth anniversary of Bahamian Independence in July 1983; the formation of the artists' cooperative B-CAUSE (Bahamian Creative Artists Unified for Serious Expression) in 1991, and the widely applauded installation of the work of Amos Ferguson in a permanent exhibition in NASSAU's Pompey Museum in 1993 (moved to the National Art Gallery in 2003). Just as important was the encouragement of generous local patrons and collectors, including FINCO and the Central Bank.

It is a nice irony that the poor but picturesque islands which in colonial times had been subjects for visiting artists (the greatest of whom was the American Winslow HOMER) had become by the time of Bahamian INDEPENDENCE the home of a veritable school of proud and prosperous island-born artists. The fact that single works of at least a dozen Bahamian artists could command prices in five figures was only a commercial indicator. A more significant indication that Bahamian artwork had come of age was the opening in 2003 of the long-planned National Art Gallery in the elegant and expensively restored Villa Doyle, atop Nassau's ridge on West Street. Fittingly, its first exhibition, held in February 2004 and entitled 'One Man's Vision', was a selection of more than forty works from the D'Aguilar Collection, splendidly showcasing both the range and the combining essence of contemporary Bahamian painting.

Further reading: P. Glinton, C. Huggins and B. Smith, *Bahamian Art, 1492–1992*, Counsellors Limited for Finance Corporation of The Bahamas, 1992; *One Man's Vision: The D'Aguilar Collection*, Collectors Series 1, National Art Gallery of The Bahamas, 2003; E. M. Dahlyzen, *Randolph Wandell Johnston: Feel Intensely, Imagine Vividly, Control Precisely*, Washington DC, 1993.

ASUE (SU-SU) A folk savings system originating in West Africa and found throughout the West Indies under different names (*Su-su*, 'partner', 'meet and turn'). It still flourishes in The Bahamas despite the country's well-earned reputation as a centre of more sophisticated forms of banking.

An *asue* is formed by a group of people who agree to put a fixed amount regularly (weekly or, more usually, monthly) into a common pool, which is held by a trusted *asue*-keeper. The total amount paid in each time is paid out to each participant in rotation, with the keeper rewarded by being given a rotational share without having to put in a regular contribution. Participants are often prepared to contribute a very large proportion of their weekly wage or monthly salary, for the enticing prospect of a relatively large lump sum when their '*asue* draw'.

Ordinary Bahamians seem to like the *asue* system because it gives the sense of belonging to a club or cooperative rather than dealing with an impersonal bank. It involves a great deal of trust; both that the participants will all pay in regularly and that the *asue*-holder will not abscond with the money. Besides this, each participant is under a communal form of compulsion that is by experience more effective than putting money into a personal savings account in a formal bank. Perhaps too, the habit of scrimping to the point of poverty for the prospect of a future bonanza is

ATHLETICS

subtly attuned to that aspect of the Bahamian national experience by which years of hardship are followed by brief bursts of heady prosperity.

ATHLETICS Bahamians, irrespective of gender, have in the last half century demonstrated a remarkable aptitude for field and track athletics. This attribute is innate, but it only became manifest and reached a peak once conditions proved right in key respects. These included more leisure and encouragement for training in the local schools, opportunities to compete both locally and internationally, better facilities and coaching, and perhaps most important of all, the increased availability of athletics scholarships to universities in the United States.

The first Bahamian world-class athlete made his impact in the United States almost unnoticed by his countrymen at the time. Charles William Major (1904–84) was born in Nassau but brought up in New York, where his parents had taken him just after World War One. Enrolled at St Bonaventure University, he excelled in the high jump, winning gold medals at the Boston Amateur Athletics Championships in 1926, the Millrose Games in 1927, and the inaugural USAAU Championships in Madison Square Gardens in 1929. Though high jumping technique was then limited to the 'hitch-kick' or 'straddle' method, 'Charley' Major is reputed to have equalled the existing world record (then 6 feet, 8 inches) in 1929, his last year in competitive athletics. He returned to Nassau in 1938, and though briefly appointed national track and field coach for the 1962 Commonwealth Games he was chiefly noted as a boxing and wrestling trainer and promoter, first based at a gym in the 'Pond' area of eastern Nassau and then, from 1953, at the Nassau Stadium on Fowler Street off East Bay Street.

By that time, the star in the Bahamian athletics firmament was the sprinter Thomas Augustus Robinson, after whom the national track at the Queen Elizabeth Sports Centre was to be named in 1981. Born in Nassau in 1938, 'Tommy' Robinson was one of the first students to graduate from ST JOHN'S COLLEGE, going on to attend the University of Michigan on a four-year athletics scholarship. While at Michigan, he won nine 'Big Ten' conference titles and set ten Michigan records, being inducted into the University of Michigan Hall of Fame in 1985.

Tommy Robinson's greatest achievements, however, were made while wearing the vest of The Bahamas. In 1956 he was the sole track athlete in the first Bahamian Olympic team at Melbourne, Australia. In the following year he teamed up with Tom Grant, Oscar Francis and Enoch Beckford to win the first ever track medal for The Bahamas, a bronze in the sprint relay of the West Indies Federation Games in Jamaica. Far outshining this, and getting much attention in the British press, Tommy Robinson, as the sole Bahamian representative and flag carrier at the Commonwealth Games in Cardiff, Wales, in 1958 won silver behind Keith Gardner of Jamaica in the 100 yards and defeated Gardner to take the gold in the 220. Not even setting a world record in the not-often-run 300 metres in Canada in 1965 quite lived up to these heady events. In all, though, Tommy Robinson competed for his country in four Commonwealth Games (winning one gold and three silver medals), and in four Olympics between 1956 and 1970 – the highlights being to lead the 1964 Tokyo 100 metres final at the two-thirds stage before pulling a hamstring, and to be placed second to the current world record holder, Harry Jerome, after a photo-finish that took 90 minutes to resolve, in the 1966 Commonwealth Games in Kingston, Jamaica.

The exploits of Tommy Robinson aroused interest in Bahamian sprinters among American track coaches, but it was largely through the coaching of a former British decathlete turned Bahamian, Keith Parker, that Bahamians began to develop their natural talents in all track and field endeavours (except long distance running). Combining

Debbie Ferguson triumphantly crosses the line for the gold medal in the 4 x 100 m women's relay at the Sydney Olympics, 5 a.m. (Bahamian time), Saturday 30 September 2000

sprinting and jumping skills with a difficult technique, triple-jumping became something of a craze among young high-schoolers, producing several medal-winners, including Timothy Barrett and the future Prime Minister, Perry CHRISTIE. However, the most remarkable achievement of the early local coaching era occurred at the Commonwealth Games in 1982, when Keith Parker led a team of just seven athletes that came away with six medals. Shonel Ferguson (long jump) and Bradley Cooper (discus) broke Commonwealth records in winning golds, while Stephen Wray equalled the record in coming second (on a count-back) in the high jump (with a leap of 7 feet 4 ½ inches).

By this time, American university coaches were competing with each other to attract Bahamian athletes, female as well as male. By 1992 they had brought on a world-class 400 metres hurdler, Danny Smith, and the first Bahamian Olympic athletics medallist, Frank Rutherford, who came third in the long jump at Barcelona. But this was only the beginning of an astounding flowering. On the same day in August 1995, Pauline Davis won the silver medal in the 400 metres and Troy Kemp the gold in the high jump (with 7 feet 9 ¾ inches) at the World Championships in Gothenburg, Sweden. Equally meritorious was the triumph of Avard Moncur, US universities champion for two years, in winning the 400 metres at the 2001 World Championships in Edmonton, Canada, in a time of 44.64 seconds – the first athlete apart from the great American Michael Johnson to win the event over the previous 12 years.

These performances, however, were eclipsed by those of the five great female Bahamian sprinters collectively known as the 'Golden Girls': Eldece Clarke, Pauline Davis, Debbie Ferguson, Sevatheda Fynes and Chandra Sturrup. Trained at five different universities in the US (Hampton, Alabama, Georgia, Michigan State and Norfolk State) they won numerous medals individually. But it was as a 4 x 100 metre relay team that they proved themselves supreme – and probably the most outstanding sports team ever produced from such a small country. They first burst on the international scene by coming a narrow second to the US quartet at the Atlanta Olympics in 1996. This they topped by winning the gold medal at the 1999 World Championships in Seville, Spain – a feat they were to repeat in Edmonton in 2001. But their most glorious moment came just after 4 am (Bahamian time) on Saturday 30 September 2000, the last day of the Sydney Olympics.

Eldece Clarke, a veteran at 35, had run valiantly to help the team through the preliminary heats (while the others were competing in individual events) but stood down for the final. In that climactic event Sevatheda Fynes (aged 25 and individual bronze medal winner at the Atlanta Olympics) led off with a blistering run that carried her 5 metres ahead of the pack. Chandra Sturrup (29, and reigning Pan American Games gold medallist) sustained the lead down the back straight, handing over to the curve-running specialist Pauline Davis. At 34, Davis was the oldest member of the quartet and fatigued from her splendid performance in the individual 200 metres, in which she had taken the silver medal. But digging deep, she still managed to hand the baton to her youngest team-mate, 24-year-old Debbie Ferguson, with a short lead. It proved enough. While the TV-watching Bahamas held its collective breath, Debbie ran the race of her life in the anchor leg, triumphantly throwing up her arms as she crossed the line 2 metres ahead of the world record holder Marion Jones of the USA – closely followed by the almost equally famed Merlene Ottey of Jamaica and Christine Aron of France.

Unprecedented celebrations greeted the return of the Golden Girls to The Bahamas on a BAHAMASAIR plane three days later, and on their subsequent trips to the Family Islands (including Sevatheda Fynes' ABACO birthplace). A grateful nation awarded each of the five a specially minted gold medallion, $40,000, and a plot of land overlooking the sea on western NEW PROVIDENCE. For their part, the quintet (two of whom were on the point of retirement) set up a Golden Girls Scholarship fund, to help sustain the athletic achievements which they had brought to such a thrilling climax.

ATLANTIS RESORT First there were guest-houses, then there were hotels. Many hotels. Then there were casino hotels and all-inclusive resorts. And finally there was Atlantis.

Atlantis outruns superlatives. More than an all-inclusive resort and casino-hotel, the Atlantis complex re-creates the beauties and treasures of The Bahamas within its own perimeter, in an even more spectacular and idealised form. Atlantis was the brainchild of the South African Sol Kerzner, owner of the mega-resort of Sun City, which flourished as an oasis of hedonism in the 'African homeland' enclave of Bophutswana. Simple commercial expansionism occasioned the purchase of Resorts International's Atlantic City and PARADISE ISLAND interests by Kerzner's Sun International company in 1990. Demolition and rebuilding began in the early 1990s, involving the replacement of 550 hotel rooms and the creation of the largest and most dazzling casino in The Bahamas.

AUTEC

Royal Towers, Atlantis resort

Even greater changes were effected in the second stage of development between 1996 and 1998 when Sun International transformed Paradise Island almost before the public knew what was happening. At a cost of $850 million, an immense interlocking range of accommodation, restaurants and other indoor facilities was constructed on each side of the giant casino. This was set in a dazzling maze of tropical gardens, lagoons, aquaria, swimming pools, 'river' rides and slides, enclosed beaches, sporting facilities and other outdoor amusements. Connected by a network of new roads are a splendid new marina, smart rental villas and condominiums, the ultra-exclusive Ocean Club, and the excellent 18-hole golf course at the eastern end of Paradise Island. Altogether, the Atlantis complex can accommodate 5,000 guests at a time, in more than 2,300 rooms.

In 2002 the renamed Kerzner and One & Only Enterprises announced the building of Atlantis Stage III, with 1,200 additional rooms, for completion in 2005. In September 2003 Kerzner announced the purchase for $40 million of the adjacent CLUB MEDITERRANÉE property (stretching across Paradise Island and including the original Paradise Beach) for the development of Stage IV, bringing the mega-resort's capacity up to 5,000 rooms by 2006.

For guests and visitors the most stunning features of Atlantis are the sea-water aquaria – the most extensive and most lavishly endowed in the world. In outdoor pools swim immense sharks, sawfish and rays, which draw crowds at their feeding times. Even more fascinating is the range of fish and sea creatures – from tiny luminescent gobies and elegant multicoloured jellyfish to huge grumpy looking groupers, scuttling conchs and crawfish, and darting schools of jacks – that can be viewed by means of a 100-foot submarine plexiglass walkway. In all there are said to be 20,000 fish of more than a hundred species in three million gallons of sea water, which is recycled four times a day.

From outside the well-guarded boundaries of Atlantis, the most dramatic sight is the central range of buildings themselves. These are dominated by the 500-foot (150-metre) twin Royal Towers and their scarcely smaller flanking wings. Twice as tall as any other buildings in The Bahamas, they are visible from almost any point in New Providence and 30 miles (50 km) out to sea. In 2002, the smallest room in the cheapest season at Atlantis cost $205 a night, without food, taxes, surcharges or any other extras. At the top of the advertised rates, a luxury suite in the peak season could cost $1,600 a night. However, the pinnacle of extravagance was the Bridge Suite, suspended between the twin pink skyscrapers, the nightly rate for which was reported to be $28,000.

AUTEC The Atlantic Undersea Testing and Evaluation Centre, covering the 3,000 square miles (7,770 squ. km) of the TONGUE OF THE OCEAN from a base near Fresh Creek, ANDROS, represents the most important and secretive continuing operation by the United States on Bahamian territory and in Bahamian territorial waters.

Bases had been granted in The Bahamas to the United States by the British imperial government without reference to Bahamians as long ago as 1940. These were greatly extended by the addition of missile tracking stations by a treaty in 1950, as the Cold War began. AUTEC was founded in 1965.

In great secrecy and with tight security, a major base, commanded from Palm Beach, Florida and Newport, Rhode Island, was set up just south of Fresh Creek, Andros. Submarines, missiles, mines and sonar devices were tested on several nearby ranges. A network of small satellite stations was also set up at several points further south in both north and south Andros.

Soon after INDEPENDENCE, in 1973, the Bahamian government negotiated lease payments for installations hitherto granted free and a $10 million loan for the BARTAD agricultural project in Andros. By the 1980s, further negotiations had focused on AUTEC as the most indispensable of the remaining bases, and in July 1983 it was announced that agreement had been reached over the continuing leases on AUTEC and the remaining bases in GRAND BAHAMA, ELEUTHERA and SAN SALVADOR. All these bases except for AUTEC have since been closed and their facilities handed over to The Bahamas.

AUTEC's activities continue to expand. In 2002, its website announced the initiation of an Electronic Support Measures (ESM) Threat Simulator, and a Buoyed Acoustic Range Tracking System (BARTS) – and the expansion of activities in the comparatively shallow northern section of its ranges, between north Andros and the Berry Islands. AUTEC has not been without its critics, however, and in 2002 (and subsequently) the beaching and death of a large number of whales was attributed to the use of mid-range frequency sonar by US Navy ships traversing the North West Providence channel.

Further reading: www.npl.nuwc.navy.mil/autec/mbs.hlm; K. Balcombe *et al.*, 'A Mass Stranding of Cetaceans Caused by Naval Sonar in The Bahamas', *Bahamas Journal of Science*, 8 (2), 2001.

AVIATION Beginning in the 1920s and with a huge surge after WORLD WAR TWO, airplanes proved of vital importance in developing The Bahamas, bringing the islands closer together as well as closer to the outside world. Bahamian aviation, though, has never been problem-free. Even more difficult than providing and maintaining infrastructural and servicing facilities has been the problem of maintaining a viable national airline in the face of cut-throat international competition.

It is claimed that the first scheduled passenger air service in the world was initiated by A. B. CHALK between Miami and BIMINI in July 1919. An efficient and regular service between Miami and NASSAU was firmly established by Juan Trippe's Pan American Airways in 1929 PAA's twin-engined Sikorsky seaplanes alighted like giant ducks in Nassau harbour and docked at a terminal near the Eastern Parade, later the headquarters of The Bahamas Air–Sea Rescue Association (BASRA). For lack of landing grounds, air services were restricted to seaplanes for a further decade, and while five times as fast as tourist ships, the aircraft were cramped, noisy and expensive, carrying no more than 25 passengers on a flight that took up to three hours each way.

The first landplane to land in The Bahamas, on 9 November 1934, was a single-engined 90 h.p. Lambert Monocoupe christened 'The Spirit of Booker T. Washington'. It was piloted by the Bahamian-born Dr Albert E. Forsyth (1897–1986) who, in company with C. Alfred 'Chief' Anderson, was following up the achievement of the first round-trip flight across the United States by black pilots by making a 'good will flight' to the Caribbean, Central and South America. Watched by a large and enthusiastic crowd, Forsyth flawlessly brought his plane down after dark on a cleared section of road at Westward Villas, and a few days later successfully performing the even more difficult task of taking off again.

Modern aviation in The Bahamas began in the last two years before the outbreak of WORLD WAR TWO, with the building of Oakes Field on the southern outskirts of Nassau and the creation of Bahamas Airways (BAL). This was thanks to the vision and enterprise of Sir Harry OAKES and his associates in the Development Board section of the BAY STREET oligarchy, notably Harold CHRISTIE and Stafford SANDS. The obvious benefits for Bahamian tourism were postponed by the six years of war, but were immensely boosted thereafter by the building and subsequent bequest of ultra modern airfields (far more costly than The Bahamas could afford) by the Americans – in NEW PROVIDENCE during the war itself, and in ELEUTHERA, SAN SALVADOR, MAYAGUANA and ANDROS during the Cold War which followed. Airfields multiplied with the expansion of tourist traffic, private flying and optimistic efforts to modernise Out Island communications during the rapidly escalating boom years of the 1950s and 1960s – until nearly every inhabited island had its own airport or airstrip, and airplanes hugely outnumbered MAIL BOATS and cruise ships alike.

Yet though proven indispensable, aviation posed perennial problems for the emergent Bahamian nation. Providing and maintaining the essential infrastructure and technology for larger, faster and more sophisticated aircraft was a serious enough problem at the central hub of tourist traffic, New Providence (and later, Freeport). But to sustain the same level of services over the whole archipelago repeatedly

AVIATION

stretched Bahamian resources and capabilities close to the breaking point.

The story is best told by briefly tracing the tortuous history of the attempts to create and run a successful national airline. Almost from its beginning, BAL (like many new airlines in other colonies) came under the protective umbrella as major shareholder of BOAC (formerly called Imperial Airways). Though an invaluable partnership while the British Empire still existed – making The Bahamas part of an almost worldwide network and able to tap a reservoir of expertise – BAL never made a profit for its imperial masters. In 1968 85 per cent of BAL's shares were sold to the Hong Kong-based Swire Corporation, which in October 1970 quite suddenly placed BAL in 'voluntary liquidation,' flew its seven leased aircraft back to their owners, and put its 750 employees out of work (they were compensated later).

The competing small companies licensed by the government (Out Island Airways and Flamingo Airways) struggled in vain to fulfil the country's needs. The following two and a half years were a time of severe crisis, made all the worse by the world-wide rise in oil prices and the withdrawal of services to The Bahamas of both BOAC and Pan Am. Accepting the inevitable, the government took over. In cooperation with OIA (but not Flamingo) it floated a $3 million loan for an 87.5 per cent shareholding, and formed the first truly national air carrier, Bahamasair, in May 1973, just two months before The Bahamas achieved its political independence.

Bahamasair began operations with a single small jet (with three more on order) and several already aged DC3s. It failed in its efforts to find a 'big brother' partner (such as Air Jamaica then had in its relationship with Air Canada) or to break the stranglehold which the major air carriers had over the most profitable international routes. Yet, while never achieving the elusive goal of making a profit, it had much to be proud of during its first two decades – not least in sustaining the record of BAL never to have had a fatal accident. By 1979 Bahamasair's gross revenues had risen from $9 million to $24 million and as well as regularly serving all the major Family Islands, it was carrying 10 per cent of all passengers arriving in The Bahamas and 42 per cent of those coming in from Florida. At its peak in the later 1980s, Bahamasair jets and turbo-props were flying between Nassau and seven US cities, as well as having a shuttle service between Nassau and Freeport and frequent flights between Freeport and Miami.

In the 1990s, despite the cutting of several routes, the sale of all jet aircraft and some trimming of staff, Bahamasair continued to lose money. The government actively considered privatising the national airline, but found no interested buyers.

Despite its problems Bahamasair continues to serve the Family Islands and has increased its international destinations in an attempt to find profitability. The beginning of the twenty-first century also saw the rise of several alternative local airlines notably Western Air and Southern Air, which took over several of Bahamasair's Family Island routes, notably to Andros.

Further reading: L. M. Thompson, *I Wanted Wings: The Autobiography of Leonard M. Thompson, OBE*, White Sound Press.

BACARDI With one brief exception, The Bahamas has never been a substantial SUGAR producer; nor, despite its prominence in the rum-running business during the PROHIBITION era, had it ever developed its own distilling industry. Yet fortuitous events and other factors – Castro's Cuban revolution and the structures of the world's liquor markets and fiscal arrangements – have determined that NEW PROVIDENCE is currently a major operational hub of one of the world's largest producers of rum and other liquors. This development is obviously of mutual benefit to both The Bahamas and the Bacardi Company, and will continue as long as it remains so.

The first Bacardi distillery was set up in Santiago de Cuba in 1862 by Don Facundo Bacardi, a wine merchant who had emigrated from Spain to Cuba in 1830. The company having been granted the right to include the Spanish royal coat of arms on its label as 'Purveyors to the Royal Court' in the 1880s (a right renewed as recently as 1988 by King Juan Carlos), it called its product 'The King of Rums and the Rum of Kings'. The famous company trademark of a bat was chosen for the creatures which lived in the original wooden buildings – the bat being regarded as a symbol of luck in Spain and Cuba. However, it has been acumen, hard work and family solidarity more than good luck that has allowed the Bacardi Company to survive all vicissitudes and expand to its present size, while remaining entirely a family firm (the largest family liquor business in the world, with the numerous members of the Bacardi clan worth an estimated total of $2.5 billion).

Having successfully survived the Cuban civil wars, the US invasion, and the official closure of the American market in the 1920s, what seemed the worst setback of all turned out to be simply a turning point on the way to the greatest success. In October 1960, Fidel Castro's government confiscated all the company's Cuban assets (worth $75 million) and the entire family fled into exile – in The Bahamas as well as the US and Puerto Rico. Having already made contingency plans, the family leaders astutely restructured the business over the following decades. Taking advantage of Puerto Rico's virtual integration with the US, the company's major distillery was built in San Juan in order to supply the American market. Similarly, the Bahamian distillery (still huge but its capacity only a sixth of that in Puerto Rico) was set up between 1962 and 1965 to target European and Commonwealth markets through Britain, of which The Bahamas was still a dependency. After The Bahamas became independent in 1973, the company guaranteed its continuing association with Britain by setting up its head office in Bermuda (which remained a British dependency), and actually expanded its European exports through the preferential concessions made when the independent Bahamas signed the Lomé Convention in 1989. As part of its continuing expansion, during this period Bacardi also acquired Martini & Rossi, Dewar's Scotch and Sapphire Bombay Gin.

Bacardi's New Providence distillery, situated on a landscaped 60-acre tract of formerly remote bush near

The Bacardi distillery

BAHAMAS (name)

the swampy southern shore, is the island's largest and most impressive industrial complex. At its centre is a huge five-storey distilling tower, the five units of which are capable of producing 27 million litres of over-proof rum a year. Surrounding it are the facilities for the preliminary fermentation process, the 44,000 barrel warehouses in which the product is aged, the buildings where rums are blended, diluted and bottled for the local market, and a visitors' centre, where tourists are offered samples (including the local liqueur, called Nassau Royale) before, or after, being taken on a guided tour.

Though the company proudly claims that the local demand is the highest per capita of anywhere in the world (ignoring the fact that most of it is bought and carried away by tourists), the bottled rum sold locally amounts to less than 10 per cent of the total produced in The Bahamas. The remainder, left in over-proof form, is carried to Clifton Pier in tanker trucks, and stored in ten stainless steel tanks with a capacity of over ten million litres, before being piped to the Company's 350-foot tanker ship, which visits up to eight times a year, and takes away the equivalent of a million cases of liquor every trip. These volatile cargoes are carried to England, Germany or Canada, for local dilution, bottling and distribution. On the return voyage the tanker ship brings in the molasses, rum's raw material, originating mainly from the Dominican Republic, which is piped and transported by truck back to the distillery.

Most obvious of the advantages to the host country from Bacardi's operations in The Bahamas is the duty paid on the product sold locally and (at a much lesser rate) on that which is exported. The imported molasses does not attract duty under the Spirits and Beer Manufacture Act. The company provides employment for Bahamians, giving them technical training and paying them well – though with the high level of automation achieved in the plant in recent years, the total number employed has fallen to 155, a decreasing number of them being skilled technicians. As by-products of its fermentation and distillation processes the company makes available valuable quantities of carbon dioxide gas (used, for example, in the soft drinks industry) and provides two million gallons of water a day, a quarter of New Providence's needs.

Added to this are the many contributions made by the Bacardi Company, and members of the Bacardi family to Bahamian charities and other worthy local causes. Most notably, Bacardi sponsors several sailing regattas and an annual basketball jamboree on a court provided by the company near its plant, and has been involved in several restoration projects, including the refurbishment of the old VENDUE HOUSE on Bay Street as the POMPEY MUSEUM. Even more directly beneficial have been the scholarships and other contributions made by the Bacardi Family Foundation and by the senior family member and former CEO of Bacardi, Manuel Cutillas (long time resident of LYFORD CAY and now a Bahamian citizen) through his work as chairman of the board of the Lyford Cay Foundation.

Further reading: Dawn Lomer, 'Bacardi in The Bahamas: A resilient family of rum-makers travelled the bumpy road to success', *Bahamas Handbook and Businessman's Annual, 2003*, Dupuch Publications, 2003, 250–66.

BAHAMAS (name)

It has plausibly been suggested that the word Bahama derives from the Spanish for 'shallow sea', *baja mar*. Much more likely is that it was a Lucayan name for the island now called GRAND BAHAMA that was easily adopted by the Spaniards because it seemed to make sense in Spanish. It was the English settlers who first applied the plural, 'The Bahamas' or 'The Bahama Islands', to the entire archipelago. Until the twentieth century the Spanish and French called the islands *Las Islas Lucayas* (or *Les Iles Lucayes*) after the people whom the first Europeans found there – who called themselves simply *luku-kairi*, 'island people', to distinguish them from other Tainos living in the Greater Antilles.

BAHAMAS CHAMBER OF COMMERCE

Founded during the period of commercial expansion that followed the LOYALIST migration of the 1780s, and for long an organisation representing the shared interests of the white BAY STREET merchants who then dominated Bahamian politics as well as commerce, The Bahamas Chamber of Commerce in Nassau has since the 1960s resolutely moved with the times, now being open to 'any reputable person, firm, partnership, estate, association or corporation conducting business in The Bahamas' wishing to promote their particular commercial interests.

The original BCC was founded in 1797 and 'established' by 1799. It was described in 1801 by the Loyalist Joseph EVE (inventor, editor and architect of ST MATTHEW'S CHURCH) as having the objects 'to unite the strength of the mercantile interest for any purposes that are thought to promise advantages to the commerce of the colony, to give members an opportunity to gain information by occasional discussions on mercantile subjects, and to procure relief from litigation by means of a perpetual court of arbitration.'

With the exception of the last, the Chamber has persisted in these objects through many changes over the last two hundred years. In 2003, it listed the following benefits which it still sought to provide: 'Opportunity for direct impact on legislation and public policy; linkage with foreign companies, organisations and individuals seeking trade and services locally; networking opportunities with business colleagues at meetings, seminars, conventions, etc.; opportunity to receive information on or participate in publications, business-to-business exchanges, training workshops, etc.' Among the services offered to members were a well-stocked reference centre and commercial library, an information and complaints service, website advertisement and promotion, monthly business luncheons, regular promotional forums, a 'mentoring programme' and an annual business plan review and business directory.

Though it claims to be a non-political as well as a non-profit organisation, since it is concerned with all phases of the Bahamian economy, the BCC maintains active standing committees which parallel the areas of responsibility of most government ministries. These committees meet usually on a monthly basis, routinely offering recommendations to government and receiving requests from government officials for advice and cooperation from the private sector on such important matters as the involvement of The Bahamas in the projected Free Trade Area of the Americas (FTAA). In such respects, the political influence of the modern equivalent of 'Bay Street' is far from dead.

In friendly association with the BCC and with similar aims and features, since the 1960s there has also been a Grand Bahama Chamber of Commerce, based in Freeport.

Further information: www.bahamaschamber@coralwave.com; www.thegrandbahamachamberofcommerce.com

BAHAMAS CHRISTIAN COUNCIL

The BCC was an optimistic child of the new Bahamian nation emerging in the 1960s. Its stated motivations were the wish of Christian ministers to heal the traditional divisions between the numerous denominations, to engender mutual tolerance and respect, to improve communications and, equally important, to provide a permanent forum for the discussion and promotion of sound Christian social and moral principles.

Though ministers from almost all Christian denominations now routinely participate together at national functions, and religious services are sometimes shared, full concord is far from attainment. Better communications may have stemmed from (and facilitated) greater tolerance and increased respect, but a clearer understanding of each other's beliefs has tended to emphasise fundamental differences as often as to promote ecumenicism. Not surprisingly, religious leaders are united on nearly all major moral issues – the centrality of the family, and the evils of violence, promiscuity, crime, drugs and alcohol abuse. But they are seriously divided on two issues: GAMBLING and homosexuality.

Gambling has always been a hot potato, for Bahamian religious leaders and politicians alike. Nonconformist ministers traditionally opposed all forms of gambling, and won at least partial victories in the past in having 'numbers' remain technically illegal and Bahamians banned from casino gambling. Other churchmen took a softer stance, especially over such matters as charity raffles. The BCC, however, remained adamant, coming out strongly against government plans to grant further casino licences and any moves to establish a national lottery – despite the undoubted benefits such lotteries have demonstrated in most other countries, including Britain. Most divisive of all was the BCC's militant stance in the 1990s on homosexuality. The issue of homosexual tourism not only sharply divided the Bahamian Christian community but stirred up a political storm, with Prime Minister Hubert INGRAHAM (himself a practising Baptist) actually condemning the BCC.

BAHAMAS ELECTRICITY CORPORATION (BEC)

As a consequence of the islands' wide dispersion, scattered population and general poverty, the provision of electricity to The Bahamas before the 1950s was patchy and slow, with government supply limited to Nassau and dependence on private suppliers elsewhere. Almost universal electrification was achieved within 40 years of the formation of the Bahamas Electricity Corporation in 1956 – a virtual revolution. Yet in the 1990s, manifold operational problems and ideological arguments kept alive the question of whether it would not be more efficient to return the whole system to private enterprise.

BEC repair hurricane damage

BAHAMAS HISTORICAL SOCIETY

Electricity was first generated in The Bahamas as early as 1900, to illuminate a private club in Nassau. But it was not until an Electric Light Act was passed in 1907 that any effort was made by government to provide a general supply. A small gasoline generator in the VENDUE HOUSE on BAY STREET power first distributed power to a few public buildings and a few dozen street lamps in June 1909. Increases in the power supply enabled the production of ice by refrigeration and the projection of the first movies, but there were only 443 private subscribers and 276 street lights in Nassau by 1916. Ironically, the outpost of Wilson City, Abaco, home of the American-owned Bahamas Timber Company, was well ahead of the colonial capital in the sophistication of its power supply.

The first significant advance occurred during the relatively prosperous 1920s, when much more powerful diesel generators extended power lines and street lights over most of Nassau and brought electricity into shops and the homes of the well-to-do. Further expansion was slowed by the Great Depression, and while Nassau was generally electrified by the end of World War Two, supply to the Family Islands was entirely dependent on private companies and individually owned generators.

The creation of the Bahamas Electricity Corporation by the Electricity Act of October 1956 was a major step forward. But change really accelerated when a separate Ministry of Electricity was set up under the 1964 Constitution, with a mandate to extend supply throughout the islands and exercise supervision over private suppliers. Especially in the first phase, BEC had to work hard simply to satisfy the rapidly expanding demand in New Providence. A large and still experimental combined generator and water distillation plant was constructed at Clifton Pier by 1960, which, while failing in its secondary function, almost quadrupled electricity output. From 35 million kWh in 1955, BEC's two stations were generating 155 million kWh a decade later. However, it was not until a third generating plant was established at BLUE HILLS in the centre of the island in the 1970s, and doubled in size in the 1980s, that the supply of electricity caught up and even marginally exceeded demand in New Providence.

A serious setback for BEC and consumers alike was the quadrupling of oil prices during the 1970s. Nevertheless, the years following Bahamian INDEPENDENCE saw BEC take advantage of the availability of international loans to extend its operations from New Providence to almost every inhabited Bahamian island. With a final spurt in the 1990s and with the help of loans from the Inter-American Development Bank and the European Investment Bank, the Family Islands Electrification Programme was said to have been completed in 1997.

By that year, besides New Providence, there were five BEC generating plants in Abaco, three each in Eleuthera and Andros, two each in the Exumas and Crooked Island, and one each in Bimini, the Berry Islands, Cat Island, San Salvador, Rum Cay, Long Island and Ragged Island. Altogether, these power sources generated over a million kWh in 1997. Besides this, three major power plants remained in private hands: the ultra-efficient 150,000 kWh Freeport plant of the Grand Bahama Power Company, the community-owned power station in Spanish Wells, and that owned and run by the Morton Salt Company in Matthew Town, Inagua.

Unfortunately, not all has been plain sailing for BEC during recent decades. In the 1980s it got into serious financial difficulties and came under attack from the political Opposition for mismanagement, featherbedding and fiscal inefficiency. In 1992 the Corporation was threatened with privatisation if it did not mend its ways. This caused low morale and provoked industrial unrest among its workers, and occasioned protests among a public generally satisfied with the level of service and afraid that privatisation would lead to much higher charges for power (as already existed in Grand Bahama). Radical debt restructuring, internal reforms and staff trimming, however, seem to have staved off the threat of a BEC sell-off to private interests, at least for the time being.

BAHAMAS HISTORICAL SOCIETY It is probably not unfair to attribute the foundation of the Bahamas Historical Society in 1959 to the will of the Bahamian elite to preserve their own version of Bahamian history, and not inaccurate to ascribe the Society's early failings very largely to the fact that they were attempting to flog a moribund horse. The Society was initiated by the wife of Governor Sir Raynor Arthur, and the initial committee consisted entirely of pillars of the local establishment. Lady Arthur was Patron, Sir George Roberts (Chairman of Ex.Co,) was President, and Miss Mary MOSELEY was Honorary President. Mrs Harcourt Malcolm, wife of the long-time Speaker of the House of Assembly, was Vice President, and the two Secretaries were the wives of Harold G. Christie (who became the second President on Sir George's death in 1964) and Harry P. Sands.

The first meetings of the BHS were held (thanks to Lady Arthur) in the ballroom of Government House. The first important talk was given by the distinguished British historian Sir Steven Runciman, on the topic 'What Columbus expected to find in The Bahamas'. Other early talks were on such subjects as Loyalist genealogy, the great sponge blight of 1938, and the notion that Atlantis had been found off Bimini. The first permanent home for the BHS and its eclectic collection of Bahamiana was the hall of the IMPERIAL ORDER OF DAUGHTERS OF THE EMPIRE, bequeathed by that society on the verge of its demise in 1976.

The enthusiastic local historian and peerless raconteur, Dr Paul ALBURY, the third President, did much to sustain the BHS during the tumultuous late 1960s and 1970s. However, the revival of the fortunes and increase in the credibility of the BHS occurred under two influences; those of the new Department of ARCHIVES under the leadership of Dr Gail SAUNDERS (President of the BHS 1989–99), and of the COLLEGE OF THE BAHAMAS and its professional historians. Highlights of this transitional phase were the initiation of the *Journal of the Bahamas Historical Society* in October 1979, and the official opening of the former IODE hall as the BHS Museum by Governor General Sir Gerald CASH in January 1987.

Though run entirely by volunteers and not able to remain permanently open, the Museum was visited by up to 6,000 tourists a year in the 1990s. It will have served an invaluable interim purpose until the projected new National Museum and Art Gallery is fully in operation. The first 20 issues of BHS *Journal* (edited continuously by Dr Saunders since 1980), though uneven in quality, have made almost a hundred contributions to Bahamian historiography, of which 28 have emanated from the staff of the Department of Archives, and eight from faculty members at the College of The Bahamas. In addition, the more than 130 lectures and talks hosted by the BHS over the years have ranged ever more widely and deeply into all aspects of Bahamian history.

Further reading: P. Albury, 'A Short History of the Bahamas Historical Society', *Journal of the Bahamas Historical Society*, 6, 1984; Geoffrey Johnstone CMG, 'The History of the Bahamas Historical Society', *Journal of the Bahamas Historical Society*, 22, 2000, 44–50.

BAHAMAS HUMANE SOCIETY Founded by a Colonial Secretary's wife in 1924 as 'Our Dumb Friends League', the Bahamas Humane Society is, next to the BAHAMAS RED CROSS, the oldest and most active of Bahamian charities. Sustained almost entirely by donations and largely through the work of volunteers, the BHS has been living proof for more than three-quarters of a century that The Bahamas is a truly caring – indeed, civilised – nation.

BHS maintains a full-time staff of 14, including three trained veterinarians. These are augmented by many part-time volunteers. It has an animal hospital and shelter and provides a 24-hour emergency ambulance service. Animal cruelty investigations are carried out by trained inspectors. As recently as 1998 modern grooming and routine care facilities were added. BHS also conducts an education programme for schools and youth groups and provides tours of the animal shelter at its CHIPPINGHAM headquarters.

The BHS is not responsible either for the collection of dead animals or the rounding up of strays (which are the responsibility of the Departments of Environmental Health and Agriculture respectively). The Society, however, is very concerned by the problem of stray cats and dogs, caring for those brought in sick or wounded and doing its best to relocate them in responsible and caring homes. As part of its humane ethos the Society is opposed to reducing the number of unwanted strays by a callous culling, advocating instead a general programme of spaying and neutering. For example, besides ensuring that all dogs and cats taken up for adoption have a full set of inoculations, it insists that they are spayed or neutered – either before adoption or, if puppies or kittens, before they reach reproductive maturity.

Bahamas Humane Society

BAHAMAS NATIONAL TRUST Established by an Act of Parliament in 1959, the Bahamas National Trust is dependent on collaboration between those in the private sector, the world of science and the government who are dedicated to the conservation of the natural and historic resources of the islands for the enjoyment of the people of The Bahamas and visitors to its shores.

The BNT traces its origins to the formation of the Society for the Protection of the Flamingo in 1952 and the creation by the government of the 176-square mile (456-squ. km) Exuma Cays Land and Sea Park in 1958. With

BAHAMAS NATIONAL TRUST

barely 100 members in its first year, it has steadily expanded its activities and powers and now has more than 4,000 members, many of whom are benefactors and voluntary helpers. Approximately two-thirds of members are non-Bahamians. Under the 1959 Act, the BNT is governed by a 21-person council, consisting of nine persons elected annually from the general membership, and 12 appointed by five designated Bahamian government departments and seven international scientific organisations – including the American Museum of Natural History, the Smithsonian Institute and the Audubon Society. But its immediate direction is under the supervision of an elected president and smaller executive committee.

The BNT headquarters are at the Retreat in Village Road, Nassau, an 11-acre site that includes an area of native Bahamian woodland and one of the finest collections of rare palms in the Americas. There is a branch office of the BNT at the 100-acre Rand Nature Centre in Freeport, and facilities in each of the main national parks. The Trust employs a professional executive director at the Retreat, several full-time educational officers, park wardens and administrative and technical staff, but still depends largely on voluntary assistance.

The Trust divides its activities into six main areas. Much the most extensive and expensive is the management of the expanding number of national parks – which by 2002 covered some 650,000 acres, or about a fifth of the entire land area of The Bahamas. This responsibility stems from the dedicated and successful management of the original parks in INAGUA and the EXUMA Cays. To these by the 1990s were added 20,000 acres on the mainland and three off-shore cays in ABACO, the Rand Nature Centre, Peterson Cay and the Lucayan National Park in GRAND BAHAMA (site of the world's longest underwater cave system), and the whole of uninhabited CONCEPTION ISLAND in the central Bahamas. In April 2002 Prime Minister Hubert INGRAHAM announced to the 43rd annual meeting of the BNT the creation of ten new national park areas, more than doubling the area protected and managed by the Trust. Besides two large tracts in central ANDROS, the whole of Little Inagua, three more cays in the Exumas and the WALKER'S CAY marine environment off Abaco, these included three pond, wetland and primeval forest areas in seriously population-threatened NEW PROVIDENCE.

Closely related to the management of national parks has been the BNT's work in helping to save, protect and expand threatened wildlife and flora and their habitats. The most spectacular success has been the establishment of colonies of flamingos, roseate spoonbills, reddish egrets and Bahama parrots in Inagua. But successes have also been achieved with the white crowned pigeon and green parrot in Abaco, the iguana and the agouti (hutia) in the Exumas, and the green turtle on Conception Island and elsewhere.

A third important role assumed by the BNT is the protection of the national heritage and identity through the preservation of buildings, historic sites and places of interest. A national register of historic buildings has been compiled and laws promoted to facilitate their preservation. The BNT has produced a five-part education video of historic buildings, and has supervised the restoration by volunteers of such historic ruins as the eighteenth-century gun battery on POTTER'S CAY in Nassau's harbour.

BNT regards the raising of public awareness and especially the teaching of children about environmental and conservation issues as one of its important duties. It has been responsible for the introduction of such matters into the national school curriculum and teacher training, for many publications, workshops and special events, and for the Discovery Club, a young members' programme for children between six and eleven. For itself, the BNT acts as a major resource centre and clearing house for scholars, organisations and government agencies conducting research relating to all aspects of conservation in The Bahamas. Last but not least, through its association with international scientific bodies, the BNT also takes on the tasks of advising government and suggesting strategies on fishery management, sustainable development and eco-tourism. One of its important recent functions has been to act as a liaison between the government's Bahamas Environment, Science and Technology Commission

Bahamas parrot

(BEST) and the United Nations Biodiversity Convention, and to make a major contribution to the production of a National Biodiversity Strategy and Action Plan for The Bahamas.

The BNT now spends more than a million dollars a year. In the year 2000 its operations were financed through proceeds from a Heritage Endowment Fund (50 per cent), membership fees (19 per cent), annual donations (14 per cent), sales and other fees (9 per cent), and a comparatively modest government grant (8 per cent).

BAHAMAS RED CROSS The Bahamas branch of the Red Cross is often said to have been founded at the beginning of WORLD WAR TWO under the inspiration of the Duchess of Windsor. In fact, a branch was formed by a much earlier Governor's wife, Lady Allardyce, during WORLD WAR ONE. The writer Amelia DEFRIES explained that the motive was to mobilise those philanthropic middle-class, non-white ladies excluded by their colour from the IMPERIAL ORDER OF DAUGHTERS OF THE EMPIRE. Thereafter, Red Cross and IODE ladies competed in raising funds and providing comforts for Bahamian servicemen away at the war.

The Duke and Duchess of Windsor visit the reconstituted Bahamas Red Cross during World War Two

The local Red Cross seems to have faded between the wars. But it was instantly revived in 1939, being enthusiastically adopted as her main social service activity by the Duchess of Windsor after her arrival in NASSAU a year later. Considerable social cachet was attached to helping the Duchess, and volunteers (of all shades and most classes) flocked to provide nursing assistance and help raise funds – especially through the grand Annual Red Cross Fair in the grounds of GOVERNMENT HOUSE, which was initiated by the Duke and Duchess of Windsor in 1941.

During World War Two, under the supervision of the British Red Cross, the main priority was the nursing and after-care of injured and sick servicemen based in New Providence. But far from fading away with the coming of peace in 1945, the local Red Cross expanded its services and went from strength to strength. Besides providing nursing training until that was taken over by the government in 1953, it gave courses in first aid, resuscitation, disaster relief and preparedness, and it provided first aid services at public functions, and transport, welfare and rehabilitation for the sick and disabled. An increasing number of men were recruited as well as women.

The local organisation continued to be directed by field officers from the British Red Cross until 1968, but it appointed its own Director from 1970. A new constitution was drafted for it in 1972, and in June 1975 an Act of Parliament incorporated it as a National Society. After vetting by official delegates from Geneva, The Bahamas Red Cross Society was officially recognised as the one hundred and twenty-third member of the International Red Cross in December 1976. Over the next quarter century, the following services were augmented or added: meals on wheels for the elderly; home visits for 'shut-ins'; milk for needy schoolchildren; welfare packages for the destitute; rental of medical equipment; testing for the deaf; after-school programmes and other activities for children through a special Youth Department; occupational therapy for the disabled; prison visits; and assistance for refugees, especially HAITIANS and Cubans. In all, The Bahamas Red Cross had become not only an indispensable general welfare agency but a perfect modern example of the age-old willingness of the Bahamian community to rally round voluntarily to help those in need.

Although now receiving some financial aid from government and working in conjunction with government agencies, The Bahamas Red Cross is still very dependent on voluntary help and public donations. It has ten permanent employees at its headquarters on John F. Kennedy Drive in Nassau and its regional office in Freeport, and an annual budget approaching half a

BAHAMAS TELECOMMUNICATIONS CORPORATION (Batelco)

million dollars. The chief fund-raising efforts include a glitzy annual ball and monster raffle as well as the annual fair. But voluntary assistance by professionals and non-professionals, young and old, continues to be vital.

BAHAMAS TELECOMMUNICATIONS CORPORATION (Batelco) Although, as in most aspects of modernisation, The Bahamas was relatively slow to develop telecommunications, it rapidly caught up after the formation of Batelco as a government-supported monopoly in 1966. However, the further spurt in technologies during the 1980s and 1990s outpaced local capabilities, and Batelco became targeted first for selective and eventually for complete privatisation.

Batelco's first seed was the Telegraph Department set up to operate the cable laid between Jupiter, Florida and Goodman's Bay, Nassau in 1892. When the first few telephones were installed in downtown Nassau in 1906, the department (located in VENDUE HOUSE on downtown BAY STREET) was renamed the Telegraph and Telephone Department. The troublesome undersea cable was replaced by wireless telegraphy in 1913, and over the next few years morse-transmitting wireless stations were established between Nassau and most of the key Family Islands. In Nassau, the telephone service extended steadily if slowly, but a radio-telephone voice connection between Nassau, Florida and the rest of the world was not established (through ATT) until 1932. As described elsewhere, local RADIO broadcasting through Station ZNS began only in 1937.

In New Providence, direct dial telephoning was installed in 1938. But technology lagged behind the US even in the Bahamian capital, and the service in the Family Islands was limited to a few single-line connections between some of the more populous settlements until the early 1960s. In 1952, the progressive Director Kenneth R. Ingraham recommended to government that the Telecommunications Department be made into a Crown Corporation, but this was not effected until the Batelco Act of 9 June 1966.

Granted virtually a monopoly jurisdiction over telecommunications throughout The Bahamas (initially with the exception of Grand Bahama), Batelco strove to extend services throughout The Bahamas and to bring them into line with the latest technology. For the first four years the corporation was managed by a US-based company, Page Communications, and foreign technicians were brought in to set up equipment and train local staff. A technical centre was set up on Nassau's Poinciana Drive early in 1972, and by the time of Independence in the following year both the management and technical staff were almost all Bahamians, as were the entire support staff and corps of manual workers.

A giant step forward was the installation of a direct distance dialling service, first between Nassau and Grand Bahama and onwards to the United States and the rest of the world in 1978, and its steady expansion thereafter to almost all other islands. In the early 1980s digital exchanges were installed throughout the country, and in 1986 Batelco completed its monopoly over telephone services by buying out the Grand Bahama Telephone Company from the American Continental Telephone Company. These moves, however, were overshadowed by the subsequent flurry of developments, as Batelco sought to keep pace with worldwide revolutions in technology.

A standard 'A' earth station was inaugurated in June 1987 to provide direct international telephone, telex, data, fax and television services, and in the following year Batelco initiated its cellular mobile radio system – which within a few years covered the islands as far south as Exuma. In the mid-1990s fibre optic cables were introduced, along with such innovations as internet facilities, video conferencing, mobile trunking, pagers and phonecards. By 1997, The Bahamas was given its own '242' area code number.

However, in similar ways but to an even greater extent than the other important government corporation, the BAHAMAS ELECTRICITY CORPORATION, all was not well with Batelco. Though the local telephone service (free to subscribers) was generally satisfactory, the international telephone and other services were regarded as both inefficient and over-priced when compared with other countries outside the region. Worst of all was that Batelco could never be a profitable business because – contrary to the argument that advances in technology lead to reductions in manpower – it had become hugely over-staffed.

In the early 1990s the government advocated the selective privatisation of Batelco's peripheral services as the first phase of a necessary move towards complete privatisation. As a result the government did indeed open up internet services to three, and paging services to five private companies, as well as authorising five independent RADIO stations and giving cable television to a private company. Nevertheless, when the government made it clear that massive downsizing (reducing the workforce from 2,100 to 1,000) would be necessary before any private investors might be interested in buying Batelco, a storm of opposition arose from the two unions representing Batelco's staff. In a forceful speech to the public on 31 March 1999, Prime Minister Hubert INGRAHAM condemned the demonstrations as misguided and foolish and affirmed his government's intention to press ahead.

Despite assurances that the privatisation process would be phased and that the government and private Bahamian investors would hold a majority of the shares in the new company, and the announcement of generous early retirement and retraining packages, the opposition led by the unions was not quelled. Downsizing proceeded with a generous payoff of surplus staff, but Batelco's finances continued in a parlous state, and despite receiving five proposals from prospective consortia, the government failed to conclude a deal with any of them; Batelco remained a state corporation into the twenty-first century.

BAHAMIANISATION Tighter restrictions on immigration, work permits and CITIZENSHIP, and on the ownership of land and businesses by non-Bahamians, were natural concomitants of the achievement of majority rule in 1967 and of national INDEPENDENCE in 1973.

During colonial days, Bahamians had to be content with the status of British subjects, and ordinary Bahamians had absolutely no say as to who might settle, do business or acquire land in the islands. From the 1920s, the local white oligarchy did chafe at such imperial dictation, and revising the rules was one of the chief motives for such magnates as Roland SYMONETTE and Stafford SANDS to work for the degree of self-government achieved in 1964. However, though they were proud Bahamians under their own terms, the BAY STREET group which Symonette and Sands led made rules that ensured that 'suitcase' companies established in The Bahamas had to have at least one Bahamian officer on their boards – almost invariably the lawyer who set up the company. Foreign investors were welcomed and rewarded with extravagant concessions, and non-Bahamians with useful skills were sought and allowed to settle permanently, as long as they were white and could be expected to vote for their Bay Street benefactors.

This (with the possible exception of the 'suitcase' companies) was the situation which the populist PROGRESSIVE LIBERAL PARTY was committed to change from the time of its first manifesto in October 1953. Initially, though, they were impeded by the undoubted economic boom that accompanied (if it was not directly caused by) Bay Street's policies, by the genuine lack of qualified Bahamians, and by the long-implanted BLACK CRAB mentality that inclined the Bahamian majority to believe that white economic and political domination were permanently ordained.

This changed, if gradually and with a wise lack of impetuosity, once the victories of the PLP in 1967 and 1968 entrenched the rule of the black majority. The basic and general policy was to educate the people; to give them self-belief along with relevant skills. More directly, the PLP soon abolished the 'Bahamian Belonger' status which their predecessors had used to bolster the white minority, and moved to challenge the excessive privileges (in the matters of land grants, business concessions and work permits) accorded to the non-Bahamian concessionaires at Freeport, Grand Bahama, by the Hawksbill Creek Agreements of 1955–65. In this campaign, the famous 'Bend or Break' speech by Prime Minister Lynden PINDLING on 26 July 1969 threw down the gauntlet. It provoked a local storm and more widespread panic – and the first migration of banks and other companies from The Bahamas to what they regarded as safer locations. But it was calmed by the government's caution and the Wooding Report of March 1971.

The second phase of Bahamianisation, following the achievement of Independence in 1973, was a much more vigorous and accordingly heated phase. Buoyed by their decisive electoral victories in 1972 and 1977, by the nationalistic energy and fervour generated by Independence, and disappointed by the slow pace of change up to that point, the PLP pushed ahead with Bahamianisation on all fronts. This policy became identified with the fiery and sometimes abrasive Deputy Prime Minister A. D. HANNA even more than with Prime Minister Pindling. It was a situation further complicated because the government had become just as concerned to restrict and control the immigration of 'blue collar' HAITIAN and West Indian blacks, as that of 'white collar' workers of whatever ethnicity.

By the Independence Constitution the rules for obtaining Bahamian citizenship were tightened (automatic in fewer cases and in others completely dependent on a board's approval), at the same time that immigration, permanent residence and work permits were progressively made more difficult and expensive to obtain. Over citizenship, the key case was that of D'Arcy Ryan (1975–80), which was a victory for the government only after appeals all the way to the Privy Council and the threatened imprisonment of the then Immigration Minister, Clement MAYNARD. For the regulations that allowed companies to employ foreigners only if there were no qualified Bahamians available, and to set up training programmes until there were, there was virtually no appeal. The granting of work permits became a notoriously protracted business as well as costing applicants or their sponsors annual fees that eventually ranged between $350 and $10,000, depending on the level of employment. From the mid-1970s such immigration and work permit regulations were applicable to Freeport as well as the rest of The Bahamas.

Even more severe were the rules proposed and first implemented in the later 1970s governing permanent residency and the ownership of houses, land and businesses by non-Bahamians. In October 1976, Home Affairs Minister Darrell Rolle announced that only 500 residency permits would be issued per year, and those only to 'worthy' or 'distinguished' persons with a high disposable income, prepared to spend at least $50 thousand on a permanent home and invest a further $100 thousand in The Bahamas. Moreover, it was stated that such residents should be prepared to live among Bahamians rather than in such virtually foreign enclaves as E. P. Taylor's LYFORD CAY.

Land was to be much more difficult to acquire by foreigners even if Bahamians were willing to sell to them. Not only were all real estate agents to be Bahamians, but, as laid down in the Immovable Property (Acquisition by Foreign Persons) Act of 1980, all foreigners wishing to buy land in The Bahamas had to provide suitable character, police and financial references, and state what they intended to do with the land. If it was to build a home, they had to say whether they expected to live there part or full time, and if the latter, whether they were retired or had sufficient independent means not to have to work. In any case, permanent residents had to provide full details of the family members living with them and provide guarantees that they were not seeking employment in The Bahamas.

Most draconian were the PLP's plans for the eventual Bahamianisation of all businesses operating in The Bahamas. As outlined in Prime Minister Pindling's 1975 PLP Convention speech, there were four main levels of the policy. First, all essential services – including water, sewerage, electricity, telephones, radio and television – were to be retained as public corporations overseen by the government for the benefit of the Bahamian people. Second, a huge range of businesses – including all but the largest import and export, wholesale and retail outlets and construction companies, all small farms and small hotels, all restaurants except gourmet and ethnic establishments, and all internal transportation, cinemas, nightclubs, newspapers, advertising and real estate agencies, security operations, handicraft factories and repair shops – were to be reserved exclusively for Bahamian citizens. Third, another echelon of larger businesses – including external transportation, medium-sized hotels, and all local industries producing for the local market – were earmarked for majority Bahamian ownership 'as soon as was practicable'. Fourth, though the largest industrial, agricultural and commercial operations – especially if producing goods for export – might remain under majority or even sole ownership by foreigners, they were all to be vetted in respect of their benefit to The Bahamas, licensed and controlled. Finally, though no existing businesses were to be closed down or appropriated without compensation, a timetable was laid down that anticipated complete implementation within a decade – that is, by 1985.

All these requirements were clearly irrelevant to the Haitians and poor West Indians who were simply in The Bahamas to work. They were almost completely subject to the work permit system, which regarded them as either temporary migrants or illegal immigrants. Because of the intentionally exclusive wording of the relevant acts, it was extremely difficult if not impossible for such persons to reside permanently in The Bahamas, let alone become Bahamian citizens.

During the 25-year regime of the PLP much progress was made, especially in the raising of the general level of education and the upward socio-economic movement of black Bahamians. Perhaps the most remarkable development was the Bahamian takeover of the management and manning of the Nassau casinos. But during the 1980s it was increasingly thought that the PLP's Bahamianisation policy had attempted to go too far and too fast – and, if not unworkable, was mired in bureaucracy and open to manifold abuses. The full implementation of the plan of 1975 was far from complete by 1985. Yet the Bahamianisation policy was blamed for the second wave of investor panic and capital migration which, coupled with a general down-turn in the economy, was regarded as a major reason for the downfall of the PLP in the general election of 1992.

During the subsequent ten-year tenure of the free market-oriented FREE NATIONAL MOVEMENT the government marked time or even backtracked on Bahamianisation – for example, allowing the temporary importation of hundreds of foreign construction workers and craftsmen for the building of the second PARADISE ISLAND bridge and the gigantic ATLANTIS complex (although the previous administration had made the same concessions for the building of the Crystal Palace resort and new international airport terminal). In addition this administration undertook a massive legalising of migrant Haitians by awarding citizenship to virtually all who had worked in The Bahamas for a lengthy period and demonstrated their commitment to The Bahamas. To counterbalance this it also established an illegal migrant holding facility and the quick repatriation of all illegal migrants.

Further reading: F. R. Wilson, 'Bahamianisation and Economic Development' in D. Collinwood and S. Dodge (eds.), *Modern Bahamian Society*, Caribbean Books, 1989.

BAILEY, Robert Melville (1875–1960) Master tailor and tireless speaker for progressive causes. Born in Barbados, the third child of a carpenter and a seamstress, his outstanding abilities gained him a place to study Latin, Greek and music at Codrington College in Barbados. Denied opportunities for advancement by his colour and the depressed economy, he went to Nassau at the time of the building of the original Colonial Hotel (1899) and never returned to Barbados. As adept with his needle and shears as in the cut and thrust of debate, he became the most accomplished and sought-after Bahamian tailor. Eager for a political role and ever critical of the educational backwardness and passivity of Bahamian blacks, he did not fulfil his ambition to sit in the Assembly. But his home and workshop on Dorchester Street in downtown Nassau became a perennial meeting place and forum for non-white Members of the House of Assembly and other would-be activists. First and last an Anglican, he was for some years an important member and choirmaster of Bethel Baptist Church on Meeting Street, where he often spoke publicly on political and educational issues. His most notable achievement was to influence the creation in 1925 of GOVERNMENT HIGH SCHOOL, where three of his nine children were among the very first pupils and distinguished alumni.

BAIN, Hon. Clarence A. (1904–71) Influential black politician and most distinguished son of ANDROS. Born at Love Hill and meagrely educated at Calabash Bay primary school in northern Andros during the poverty and oppression of the SPONGING era, Clarence Bain migrated for a better life in New York at the close of the First World War. During his 36 years in the United States, he educated himself, honed his natural oratorical skills, and became heavily involved in the Elks brotherhood and the nascent civil rights movement. When he opted to return to The Bahamas in 1954, shortly after the formation of the PROGRESSIVE LIBERAL PARTY, he was not only a successful businessman but Grand Regional Director of the Elks in Florida, Georgia and the Carolinas. His commitment, organisational experience and incomparable ability to win over black audiences with homely analogies and wit as well as his unanswerable political arguments, were indispensable to the fledgling PLP, especially in his home island of Andros.

Clarence Bain, 1960s

None was more impressed and influenced than the young Lynden PINDLING, whom Clarence Bain introduced to the leaders of the US civil rights movement and the canny black voters of Andros alike. One of Pindling's most famous sayings: 'If you can't fish, cut bait; if you can't cut bait, get out of the boat', was actually borrowed from the man he always called 'CB'.

One of the 'Magnificent Six' PLP candidates successful in the 1956 Election, CB was almost inevitably a key member of Pindling's shadow Cabinet once self-government was achieved in 1964. He was instrumental in Pindling's decision to transfer his candidacy from Nassau to Andros to confront the disaffected Cyril Stevenson in the 1967 election, the success of which was a key factor in the PLP coming to power. Though not entrusted with a specific ministry, CB was appointed Minister without portfolio in Pindling's first Cabinet, becoming, with Milo BUTLER, one of the two father figures in that youthful body.

His health, however, declined and he died, much lamented, in July 1971, having been appointed CBE in the Queen's Birthday Honours list just one month earlier.

BAIN TOWN Distinctive district of Over-the-Hilll Nassau, first settled by LIBERATED AFRICANS, especially Yoruba, as a westerly overspill from GRANT'S TOWN.

BALCONY HOUSE, Nassau

As slavery ended and Liberated Africans as well as emancipated slaves competed for living space, Over-the-Hill, the area laid out under Governor Lewis Grant in the 1820s became overcrowded. In 1840 an enterprising free black named Charles H. Bain purchased a 140-acre tract of bush immediately to the west of Grant's Town, extending from Blue Hill Road as far as the present Nassau Street to the west, and from just north of what was soon called Meadow Street as far as what was later named Poinciana Drive to the south.

In the area named after him, Charles Bain offered house lots and garden plots even cheaper than those in Grant's Town, and in a far more haphazard way. The lack of regimentation, as well as the price, attracted a rapid influx of Liberated Africans who rejected the desperate conditions in the distant parts of New Providence originally chosen for them, while wishing to retain their community spirit. Many of them hailed from the southwestern part of what is now Nigeria and still spoke the Yoruban language. Yet if the new settlement retained a strong African feel, it also allowed for its own small social gradations. Most Bain Towners were very poor, living in flimsy 'tabby' and thatch houses and working as manual labourers for pitiful wages. But at the same time some of their fellows boasted wood and shingle houses with small verandahs and sizeable garden plots. In general, though, it was a poor area which waited even longer than the rest of Over-the-Hill for modern improvements: piped water, electricity and paved roads.

As early as 1847, the ANGLICAN rector of St Agnes in Grant's Town, Rev. W. L. Woodcock, expressed concern about the spiritual and educational needs of neighbouring Bain Town, setting up a small school in the area as a missionary enterprise. The school was a notable success, but the people of Bain Town as a whole never took to the religious regime of the established Anglican Church. They much preferred Christian sects more attuned to African lifestyles and systems of belief, if not – as many other more proper Nassauvians claimed – still retaining an adherence to 'African superstitions'.

Yet if Bain Town was looked down on as a relatively poor and 'primitive' district, on the positive side it had a strong sense of its separate identity and its proud African – especially Yoruban – heritage. According to its historian, Dr Cleveland ENEAS, its people always had a strong work ethic and a great respect for education, were notably enterprising and ingenious, and never had a sense of inferiority. They even looked down on the inhabitants living in the area called Conta Butta to the south (around Dumping Ground Corner and Big Pond) as being socially and morally as well as economic inferiors – above all, because they lacked all sense of ethnic pride and cohesion.

Further reading: Cleveland W. Eneas, *Bain Town*, Nassau, 1976; *Let the Church Roll On*, Nassau, 1992.

BALCONY HOUSE, Nassau A charming pink and white wooden town house on Market Street, built around 1790 or earlier – the oldest surviving such building in downtown Nassau.

A two-story clapboard and shingle building with a cellar cut into the bedrock and a detached stone-built kitchen in its small back yard, it may have been the home of a moderately prosperous sea captain. Almost certainly it was crafted by someone familiar with ship carpentry. Mainly constructed of imported American cedar (used for ships' planking and decking), its distinctive balcony, jutting into the street, is supported on curved brackets of native hardwood, like the inner structure of a typical Bahamian sloop. The mahogany inside staircase is also said to have come from a ship – perhaps a product of the flourishing Bahamian WRECKING industry.

Threatened with decay while concrete and glass offices went up around it, Balcony House was bought by the Central Bank (which it faces) in 1985, restored with the help of the Ministry of Works, Department of Archives, and a firm called Antique Warehouse, and opened as the Balcony House Museum in 1993. It is open most days during daylight hours. Admission is free but donations for upkeep are gratefully accepted.

Balcony House, Nassau

BALTIMORE GEOGRAPHICAL SOCIETY REPORT, 1905 In 1902–3, members of the Geographical Society of Baltimore made an extensive survey of The Bahamas, published in a fat book edited by George B. Shattuck, in 1905. Most of the scientific findings were useful and unexceptionable. But a study of the people of the all-white settlements of HOPE TOWN, ABACO and SPANISH WELLS was tainted by misconceptions and misinformation and stirred up lasting controversy and local anger.

The researchers regarded these isolated and almost endogamous communities as ideal subjects for a study of the effects of a restricted gene pool. At Hope Town they painstakingly drew up a genealogy of the thousand white inhabitants reaching back more than a century. They were cheerfully helped by the oral testimonies of people positively proud of a lineage going back to a single matriarch, the LOYALIST widow Wyannie MALONE, and inevitably involving (and to their mind reinforced by) frequent close cousin marriages. Unfortunately, though, the Baltimore researchers seem to have been predisposed to regard such 'in-breeding' as inevitably regressive, leading to what they loftily referred to as 'degeneracy'.

Ignoring the reality that poverty, the preoccupation with making a subsistence living, and the lack of educational resources were bound to result in a low level of scholastic learning, the chief commentator (Clement Penrose, MD) remarked that 'the mental acumen of many of the inhabitants was rather low.' There was indeed some scattered evidence of the effects of regressive genes – including polydactylism, dwarfism, deafness and dumbness, and even idiocy – but these traits were grossly exaggerated. Worse, through sheer ignorance the researchers sought to buttress their case by adding symptoms solely due to infectious disease – such as locomotor ataxia (syphilis) and leprosy.

'Early in the history of the Malone family these symptoms of degeneracy were absent,' wrote the egregious Penrose, 'but they began in the fourth generation and rapidly increased afterwards until they culminated by the presence of five idiots in one family. The original stock was apparently excellent but the present state of the descendants is deplorable …'. He concluded 'At once the idea of bringing in new blood suggests itself … On the other hand there is no reason to believe that the people, if left to themselves, will do in the future otherwise than they have done in the past. Future generations will sink to even a lower state of degeneracy than at present.'

Needless to say, such eugenicist predictions were hopelessly awry – and not just because the twentieth century was to see tremendous improvements in social and material conditions and the injection of what Penrose called 'new blood'. But the damage had been done. As the political power of white Bahamians increased and racial tensions heightened in the 1950s and 1960s, some non-whites seized on the Baltimore 'findings' with malicious glee. For their part, irate CONCHY JOES defaced the offending pages of the copy of the Report in the Nassau Public Library and refused to allow the sale in Abaco of a history of The Bahamas that quoted it (in their opinion) too uncritically.

The following half century has seen such controversies and animosities cool. This has been helped by the judicious re-evaluation of the 1905 Report and its context in such works as Steve Dodge's excellent *Abaco: The History of an Out Island and its Cays* (2nd ed., White Sound Press, 1995); and Craton and Saunders's *Islanders*.

BANKING From extremely modest and shaky beginnings in the early nineteenth century, local banking in The Bahamas expanded gradually in tune with the growing needs of the colonial mercantile community, with a rapid acceleration as the economy took off after World War Two and The Bahamas made its transition from colony to independent nation. The Commercial banks alone in 2000 claimed total domestic assets of $4 ½ billion, and a total of loans and advances of almost $4 billion. The total assets and the annual flow of transactions through the remaining 'public licensees' were incalculable.

The embryo of Bahamian banks was the Savings Bank created in 1835. This became the Public Bank of The Bahamas in 1837 once it had developed full banking functions – including deposit and current accounts, loans, discounting and the issue of currency notes. The trifling scale of the local economy and the weakness of the bank, however, were shown by the facts that the total currency in circulation in 1844 was £21,000, and that when it eventually failed in 1885 the bank had a cash balance of only £466, despite accounts crediting £86,000 to its depositors. The colonial government settled the affairs of the Public Bank by raising a £35,000 loan at what was then a high rate of interest, set up a Post Office Savings Bank as a stop-gap or alternative, and in 1888 authorised and backed the incorporation of a Bank of Nassau, floated by a consortium of ten BAY STREET merchants, with an initial capitalisation of a thousand pounds apiece.

The Bank of Nassau operated for 27 years, but hampered by the shortage of money and hemmed in by tight government regulations (particularly the Banking Act of 1909) it never flourished. It was unable to compete with the far richer and more aggressive Royal Bank of Canada,

Bank House

which had opened a branch in Nassau in 1908. Affected by wartime conditions, the Bank of Nassau suddenly failed in December 1916, to be almost immediately swallowed up by the Royal Bank – which paid off all depositors in full, yet within a year had as much money on deposit in Nassau as both banks combined before the collapse.

The Royal Bank of Canada did not enjoy its monopoly for long, soon having to compete with two other Canadian banks. A branch of the British Barclay's Bank DCO was added in 1947. Over a half century these efficient competing institutions, with the support and cooperation of an increasingly sophisticated local mercantile community, first helped The Bahamas through the tricky shallows of the Great Depression, then led the colony into the new era of prosperity that followed World War Two.

The first popular efforts to counter 'Bay Street' and the Bay Street banks were heroic but of limited immediate effect. In 1952, along with a few middle-class non-whites, an enterprising black from LONG CAY who had gained financial experience in the United States, A. Leon McKinney (1906-92), opened the People's Penny Savings Bank in GRANT'S TOWN. 'We are not seeking what is profitable for a few, we are thinking in terms of the many,' explained McKinney. 'This institution, at present, does not boast of being a bank but rather a school of thrift where any man, woman or child may take the first step towards self-sufficiency.'

Though white 'CONCHY JOES' with minimal education readily found jobs behind the counters in the banks, the only non-whites employed were cleaners and doormen. The first black teller (a young woman from GOVERNMENT HIGH SCHOOL who turned down the alternative opportunity of going to university) was not appointed – by Barclay's Bank – until 1965.

Equal opportunities for all was a vital plank of the policy of the black majority's PROGRESSIVE LIBERAL PARTY, and once the party achieved power in 1967 it moved as rapidly as was practicable to change the status quo. While every effort was made to enlarge the reservoir of qualified non-whites through education, all foreign as well as local businesses were required to hire the most qualified applicants irrespective of race, class or gender, and also to institute internal training programmes that would enable junior employees to move progressively into management positions.

By the time that INDEPENDENCE was achieved in 1973 the process was well on its way to completion. In the field of national finance, the symbol (rather, the engine) of the new democratic maturity was the Central Bank, set up in 1974 as the successor to the Monetary Authority created in 1968. It exercised control over the currency, exchange regulations and all the operations of banks and trust companies. Its management from top to bottom, along with those of the Ministry of Finance and other government agencies responsible for financial matters, was in the hands of Bahamians irrespective of colour, class or gender – which, in the natural order of things, meant that the great majority were now non-whites, and steadily increasing proportions were from humble backgrounds and were women. See also OFFSHORE BANKING.

Further reading: A. Thompson, *An Economic History of The Bahamas*, Nassau, Commonwealth Publications, 1979; Neil Hartnell, 'Long Arm of the OECD', *Bahamas Handbook and Businessman's Annual 2002*, Nassau, Dupuch Publications, 2002, 209–46, 340–7; www.centralbankbahamas.com

BAPTISTS Though not a unitary church and with an almost exclusively black following, Baptists constitute the largest Christian denomination in The Bahamas, justifiably proud of their Afro-American origins within the islands, their independence, and their perseverance against opposition.

Baptist ideas and practice spread with wildfire enthusiasm among the black slaves on the American mainland, and were then transferred to The Bahamas and Jamaica by the slaves and recently freed blacks accompanying the white LOYALIST emigrés, following the end of the American War of Independence. Two things in particular attracted these early black converts: the opportunities for personal involvement, even leadership, in church affairs, both secular and spiritual, and for making direct communication with the Almighty through unstructured and extempore worship, with emphasis on preaching, bearing witness and hymn-singing. More generally, involvement in a Baptist church and its services provided joyful, uplifting and fulfilling intermissions in a life that was generally harsh, oppressive and demeaning.

BAPTISTS

Nineteenth-century predecessor of Churches of God, the Shouter Chapel (Baptist)

The nature of Baptist enthusiasm and the reaction of the established church and white regime is admirably conveyed by an oft-quoted report by the SPG missionary Rev. D.W. Rose from LONG ISLAND in 1799. He claimed that the slaves 'had been misled by strange doctrines. They called themselves Baptists, the followers of St John ... Their preachers, black men, were artful and designing, making a merchandise of Religion. One of them was so impious as to proclaim that he had had a familiar conversation with the Almighty, and to point out the place where he had seen Him. At certain times of the year the black preachers used to drive numbers of negroes into the sea and dip them by way of baptism, for which they extorted a dollar, or stolen goods.' According to Rose, some Baptist slaves were so attached to their practices that when their masters attempted to 'check their proceedings', they ran away into the bush.

One Long Island preacher who is sometimes credited with being the founding Black Baptist in The Bahamas is a somewhat shadowy figure called Frank Spence. According to the best evidence, Spence was a slave brought to Long Island from South Carolina by his master in the early 1780s, who saved enough money to buy his own freedom (and that of his wife), moved to Nassau and built a chapel on McCullough Corner just south of Fort Fincastle some time before 1806. Much better documented among the Black Baptist pioneers were the 'Loyalist' ex-slaves Samuel Scriven (c.1730–1822), Prince Williams (c.1760–1840) and Sharper Morris (c.1780–1850). The earliest notice of the first two occurred in a slave runaway advertisement in the *Bahama Gazette* in August 1785, in which their purported owner, Isaac Baillou, offered a reward of two dollars apiece for their apprehension. 'Sambo' was described as 'an old fellow about 55 years of age' who had absconded some time before in St Augustine, Florida claiming to be free, and was now 'often seen in Nassau ... well known by the Negroes as a Baptist Preacher'. He was accompanied by a younger associate called Prince, an undoubted slave thought to be an African ('his Country marks down his face') who had run away recently to join him.

The Baptists in The Bahamas gained most of their modern impetus from two sources: the economic expansion that began in the 1950s, and the involvement of Baptists at large and Baptist pastors in particular in the shift to black majority rule in The Bahamas between 1953 and 1967. This has led to a church that would have surprised – and, in the main, gratified – Frank Spence, Samuel Scriven and Prince Williams: not just still the largest Christian community in The Bahamas, but financially flourishing, politically powerful, and a bastion of traditional values.

It is somewhat ironic that a faith that holds as one of its main principles the separation of church and state has been in the socio-political vanguard in modern times. Bahamian Baptists shared the same motivation that

BARS

inspired the Civil Rights movement in the United States in the mid-twentieth century and reached its apotheosis in the work and words of Martin Luther King. Though the black Bahamian minister who made the initial clarion call for political and social change in a sermon at Governor's Harbour, Eleuthera in January 1946, Rev. H. H. Brown, was a Methodist, Baptists were to the forefront in the PROGRESSIVE LIBERAL PARTY from its foundation in 1953. Most notable was Rev. Harcourt Brown, Pastor of Bethel and President of the Bethel Baptist Association, who was one of the eight PLP delegates to the United Nations in August 1965. Though not himself a Baptist, Prime Minister Lynden PINDLING particularly admired and emulated Martin Luther King, was extremely attentive to the Baptists among the ground-roots followers of the PLP, and appointed several Baptists to his Cabinets, even if he did not always share their ideas and retain their confidence. Among such outspoken eventual defectors were Carlton Francis (who spoke out adamantly against CASINOS) and Hubert INGRAHAM, who was to become the first Baptist Prime Minister when, as leader of the FREE NATIONAL MOVEMENT, he succeeded Pindling in 1992.

Gaining power along with the achievement of black majority rule and political INDEPENDENCE, and increasingly united, the Bahamian Baptists in fact tended to become increasingly conservative. The BBMEC, led by Rev. Michael Symonette and other US-educated pastors, under a new constitution which united six separate Associations in 1971, greatly extended the churches' social work, working towards ecumenical cooperation, and becoming almost the dominant force in the BAHAMAS CHRISTIAN COUNCIL. It was through this body – as well as through sermons from a hundred pulpits – that Baptists carried on a virtual crusade not only against casino gambling but against homosexuality and promiscuity in general.

Despite its inevitable shift towards respectability and the more conservative side of the ideological spectrum, and the inroads made by other denominations (not to mention its own inherent tendency towards fragmentation), the Bahamian Baptist churches still boasted 55,000 active members in 1998, well ahead of the ANGLICANS, ROMAN CATHOLICS and METHODISTS. Constituting 18.6 per cent of the Bahamian population this was by far the highest proportion of adherents for any country in the world – compared with the 12 per cent of Baptists in the population of the United States, in second place, and the mere 2 per cent of Baptist adherents in Jamaica, the country in which the black Baptists were once even more influential than in The Bahamas.

The Compleat Angler bar, Bimini

Further reading: M. C. Symonete and A. Canzonari, *Baptists in the Bahamas: An Historical Review*, Nassau, 1977; H. C. Saunders, *The Other Bahamas*, Bodab Publishers, 1991, *passim*.

BARS In many respects, the traditional Bahamian waterfront and corner bar is the equivalent of the ubiquitous rum shop of the West Indies. Beginning in early post-slavery days, proliferating during the 'rum-running' era of American PROHIBITION, and reaching a peak in the third quarter of the twentieth century, premises licensed to sell spiritous liquors as well as beer and groceries, though often deplored by churchmen and secular moralists, became an essential feature of the lives of ordinary black Bahamians, with a culture all their own.

Though their staff included females and some bars were owned by relatively prosperous non-whites, the traditional bar clientele was exclusively male and drawn from the poorer classes. The crudest bars were those found on the Nassau waterfront, where stevedores, returning sponge fishermen and produce sellers from the Family Islands were persuaded to part with their hard-earned money by bar-owners who were often also boat-owners, sponge-dealers, merchants or liquor wholesalers. Elements of the same process of socio-economic reinforcement also applied to the increasing number of bars in Over-the-Hill and in every Family Island settlement of any size. But these establishments, though not respectable, served other purposes: they were convivial all-male clubs for bonding and sharing political and social opinions and news, for relaxation in games play, or as male refuges from overcrowded family homes dominated by their womenfolk. Only in the worst times and in the most unfortunate circumstances were they places where the most desperate and addicted sought a passport to oblivion.

Though many bars were owned by BAY STREET liquor merchants (who had readier access to the necessary capital and licences) they were invaluable centres for political and social discussion among the black underclass, and also provided opportunities for ambitious blacks to begin the slow upward progress towards wealth and political power. Besides often having an adjacent grocery, several Over-the-Hilll bars became small hotels, with meeting rooms for social functions as well as bedrooms. Over-the-Hill nightclubs, almost all owned by non-whites, made much of their profits from their bars. Notably, some of the first generation of black politicians, including J. W. YOUNG, Milo BUTLER, Spurgeon Bethel, Oscar Johnson and the brothers Edgar and CLARENCE BAIN, were owners of such premises, which served them for political meetings and campaign headquarters as well as business purposes.

In modern times, traditional bars have almost disappeared from the Nassau waterfront as a consequence of the development of tourism and changes in the pattern of employment. Thanks to the general improvement in the standard of living and living styles, they have become rarer elsewhere, or gone several degrees up-market. A good number, however, survive and have not yet descended to the dubious level of being classed as picturesque historic phenomena. To such establishments, the following description of the typical Barbadian rum-shop from *The A–Z of Barbados Heritage* applies: the traditional Bahamian bar is 'a point of social gathering among imbibers, and at almost any time of day, but particularly in the afternoon and at night, groups of men of varying ages can be found "firing one" (having a drink). There is always a discussion of some sort going on, with a wide variety of topics, though the most frequent are those issues currently occupying public attention, including local politics, scandals and sporting events. Conversations are loud, and frequently punctuated with expletives. Very often a game of Dominoes is going on in a corner, characterised by loud slamming and equally loud talking.'

Simple food, such as hamburgers, fries or conch in sundry forms are usually available, but if there is an attached shop the drinking section is clearly demarcated. There are few women found in these areas, and any unaccompanied woman who frequents such a bar is frowned upon – though 'that said, some of the shrewdest shopkeepers are women.' No doubt the character of the traditional Bahamian corner bar, like that of the Barbadian rum-shop, 'will continue to evolve, but it remains a great place to "lime" [hang out] and to eat and drink at an affordable price' (S. Carrington, H. Fraser, J. Gilmore and A. Forde, *A–Z of Barbados Heritage*, Macmillan, Oxford, 2003).

BASEBALL As early as 1900, the travel writer G. J. H. Northcroft reported that 'an occasional game [of baseball] is played on the Eastern Parade under the leadership of certain eager spirits who acquired the art in America.' There were also some casual baseball games between local players and US servicemen during World War Two. But the national American summer game did not begin to challenge the primacy of cricket in The Bahamas until the postwar era, when the gradual integration of the American major leagues begun with Jackie Robinson's 1947 breakthrough hugely increased Bahamian public interest in the game, inspiring local black athletes with the possibility of becoming well-paid professional baseball players in the United States.

Formally organised from 1954, for about 25 years amateur baseball flourished in Nassau and spread to Grand Bahama and other islands. The highlight of this general development was probably the accolade as 'the most disciplined squad' won by a representative Bahamian team when coming seventh out of 32 teams competing in the US National Amateur Baseball Congress tournament held in Wichita, Kansas in 1969. Encouraged by visiting scouts – impressed by the hitting, throwing and general athleticism of those playing cricket, SOFTBALL and BASKETBALL, as well as baseball – almost 50 young Bahamians were persuaded to try their luck in the intensely competitive pyramid structure of American professional baseball between 1954 and 1985.

Of these, only five ever made it into the stratospheric elite of the major leagues, including the pitcher Wenty Ford, who played just four games for Atlanta in 1973, and Wil Culmer, who batted in seven games for Cleveland ten years later. Much more successful were Tony Curry, who played in 129 games over three years for Philadelphia and Cleveland between 1960 and 1966, averaging .246 with the bat, and Ed Armbrister, who played 224 games over five consecutive seasons for Cincinnati (1973–7) and averaged .246. Easily the most talented of all (who Bahamians maintain might, with better luck, have become a Hall of Famer) was Kenneth Andre Ian Rodgers, a former local

Baseball

BASKETBALL

star cricketer, born in 1934. Andre (or Andy) Rodgers played 854 games over 11 seasons in the major leagues, mainly as short stop, averaging .249 with the bat overall. Making his debut for the New York Giants in April 1957, he moved with them to San Francisco in the following year, reached his peak after transfer to the Chicago Cubs between 1961 and 1964, and, plagued with injuries and other problems, finished up with three years of limited playing time with the Pittsburgh Pirates (1965–7).

During the 1970s and 1980s baseball was the most played summer game in The Bahamas, in inter-school and little league as well as adult play. But it never became a fervent national avocation – and was no longer seen as a possible route to fame and riches for impoverished youngsters – as in Cuba and other Latin American countries. Like other sports, baseball also suffered from declining spectator support, from a populace now hooked on TV and turned off by organisational slackness and dissension, and by on-field indiscipline – which many saw as part of a general national malaise. By the 1990s The Bahamas Baseball Association, bitterly divided, was almost moribund.

A fresh beginning was attempted with the establishment of the New Providence Amateur Baseball League in April 1994. A five-team league was organised, and there was much talk about an increase in inter-island and international competition. That the old problems remained unresolved was, however, made clear by the fiasco of November 2003, when disagreement over the selection process and the failure to raise the necessary funds led to the last-minute non-appearance of a representative Bahamas team for the trials for the 2004 Olympic Games.

BASKETBALL The natural aptitude of Bahamians for basketball was first recognised and developed by American Catholic schoolteachers in Nassau in the 1950s. The game caught fire and very soon excellent youth teams were eagerly competing on the Priory grounds, with the St Augustine's and St Anselm's teams being the most notable rivals among the boys. In the early days at least the game was almost as popular among girls, with the 'Dizzy Dames' team led by Betty Cole (later a long-time and much respected coach) to the fore.

The Bahamas Amateur Basketball Association was formed in 1962 and under the leadership of Winston 'Tappy' Davis, Bahamians teams first participated in regional competitions. Such a hold had basketball taken that in the West Indies it was almost taken for granted that to be a Bahamian was to be a basketball player, much as to be a British West Indian was to be presumed to be adept at CRICKET. For example, for several years the representative men's basketball team of the UNIVERSITY OF THE WEST INDIES in Jamaica consisted entirely of Bahamians. For a halcyon period in the early 1970s The Bahamas seemed to be destined to become a power in the basketball world, with the national men's team defeating all West Indian and most Latin American nations, and even on one heady occasion coming within a few points of a win over the giants from the United States.

However, even in the rich soil of such success, the seeds of decline in the amateur and local game had already been sown. Such a consuming force had professional basketball become in the US that it sucked up talent from all promising sources, including The Bahamas. Moreover, unlike athletics, in which recruiting began at the college level and signally benefited the sport in the athletes' home nation, basketball recruitment began much earlier, at the high school level, holding out the prospects of financial rewards that almost precluded a return to amateur and local play. This is borne out by the history of the many Bahamian young men who strove to break into the golden world of the American NBA, and the comparatively few who succeeded.

About the time of Bahamian Independence, four of the most brilliant young Bahamian prospects were scouted and recruited by the Florida high school power-house, Jackson High School in Miami. Bahamians Cecil Rose, Osborne Lockhart, Charles Thompson and Michael Thompson were four of the 'Jackson Five' who made their school's basketball team the most successful in Florida's history. Charles Thompson and Rose went on scholarships to star at the University of Houston, while Lockhart and Michael (soon to rename himself Mychal) Thompson had even more stellar careers at the University of Minnesota. The Houston pair never made the crucial transition to professional basketball. But Osborne 'Goose' Lockhart had a long and lucrative career with the Harlem Globetrotters (filling the shoes of the more famous 'Goose' Tatum), while Mychal 'Sweet Bells' Thompson outshone all four, becoming All-American and acknowledged as the finest college player in the US. Perhaps the tallest of all Bahamians at 6 foot 10 inches (2.08 m), but with the soft touch round the basket that gave him his nickname, Thompson was drafted first overall in the first round of the NBA entry draft in 1978, at the age of 23. Playing for seven stellar seasons for the Portland Trailblazers, he went for a year to San Antonio (1986–7), but had probably the four finest of his 12 NBA years with the Los Angeles Lakers, sharing in two of the five NBA championship years the team enjoyed under the leadership of 'Magic' Johnson. Overall, Mychal Thompson played as a centre in

935 NBA games between 1978 and 1991, on the court an average of 29.7 minutes and scoring 13.7 points per game – a huge 12,810 points in total.

At least equally brilliant and long lasting (if not quite so consistent) has been the career of the only other Bahamian so far to have achieved stardom in the NBA, Ulrick Alexander (Rick) Fox. Born in Toronto in 1969 to a Bahamian father who took his family back home two years later, Rick was hooked on basketball as a preteen and went to a high school in Warsaw, Illinois, to polish his natural skills. From there he became a star at the University of North Carolina, being drafted by the Boston Celtics as a forward in 1991, at the age of 22. After six years with the Celtics he went to join Mychal Thompson's old team, the Lakers (six years after Mychal's retirement), teaming with Shaquille O'Neal and Kobe Bryant in three of their four consecutive NBA titles. Three inches shorter than Thompson at 6 foot 7 inches (2 m), Rick Fox by February 2004 had played in 895 NBA games over 13 seasons, scoring 8,771 points at an average of 9.8 per game, spending an average of 25.6 minutes per game on court.

Off the court, Rick Fox has been much more of a celebrity than his great Bahamian predecessor with the Lakers. Having majored in radio, TV and film at UNC, Fox has had a cameo part in the basketball film *He Got Game* and a recurring role in the gritty HBO TV drama *Oz*, confidently expecting to expand his acting career once he retires from basketball. A dedicated investor, he has already multiplied the millions he has made by playing the game and acting, and lives in a mansion in Malibu, California. Even more famously, he is married to the beautiful actress-singer Vanessa Williams.

This a far cry indeed from the basketball first played by barefoot boys and girls in Nassau backyards a mere half-century ago. It is almost as far removed from the current game in The Bahamas, with its perennial shortage of funds, often undisciplined play, and fierce disputes. Rick Fox and Osborne Lockhart have signalled their wish to contribute to the development (or recovery) of Bahamian basketball; it remains to be seen whether they, or anyone else, can successfully reignite the spark in their homeland.

BASRA An organisation maintained and run by volunteers and financed by membership fees and donations from the public, The Bahamas Air Sea Rescue Association is a modern extension of the Bahamian tradition of rallying round to aid those (whether natives or foreigners) who encounter difficulties while sailing in Bahamian waters.

In 1958, the yachting Speaker R. H. 'Bobby' Symonette had Parliament create an Air Sea Rescue Board, under the command of another Olympic yachtsman, Durward KNOWLES. But the necessary conjunction between government encouragement and private enterprise did not occur until 1963, when the Outboard Marine Company gave a hugely successful safe boating course in Nassau, headed by the American resident sailor and airman Ben Astarita. The foundation of BASRA was an immediate outcome of the course, with half of the 200 persons attending becoming foundation members. Ben Astarita himself was Commodore of the Association from 1968 to 1972, and Honorary Life Commodore thereafter.

From the beginning, the air component of BASRA was vital, thanks to the enthusiastic participation of the rapidly expanding Nassau Flying Club. Over the following 40 years BASRA has been a model of efficient and unstinting voluntary organisation, despite steadily increasing calls upon its services, and escalating costs. Going into the new century, it has only one paid employee but a permanent roster of volunteers, a 24-hour radio monitoring service from its headquarters on East Bay Street, and two small boats specially adapted for rescue work. It also maintains branch facilities on the Queen's Highway in Freeport, Grand Bahama and at four sites in Abaco. Government provides

Mychal 'Sweet Bells' Thompson, Los Angeles Lakers, 1970s

BATS

some financial and material aid and the cooperation of police and defence forces, and the US Coast Guard, DEA and AUTEC base willingly help whenever called upon. But BASRA continues to depend on the unpaid services, annual fees, donations and fund-raising efforts of its 700 local and 400 offshore members, and is always eager to augment their number.

BATS As David Campbell has written, 'Most people journey through life unaware that they are surrounded by bats, a state of ignorance which both humans and bats generally prefer.' Yet bats, and not least those of The Bahamas, are far more interesting, and more beneficial, than is generally realised.

Being nocturnal and roosting by day in secluded places, bats largely escape notice. Yet next to rodents they are the second most abundant mammals on earth, both in numbers of species and sheer numbers. In The Bahamas, despite being endangered by modern development, they can be found in huge clusters in caves by day and in squeaking clouds of foragers at night. One of the earliest and hardiest colonisers of the archipelago, bats serve the islands' ecology and their human population well, by dispersing seeds, pollinating the flora, providing bat guano ('cave dirt'), invaluable as a fertiliser, and by devouring insects that are a nuisance if not dangerous to humans.

There are 13 native mammal species in The Bahamas, of which only the AGOUTI (hutia) is not a bat. Bats colonised The Bahamas from the Antilles soon after the islands emerged from the receding ocean, some 70,000 years ago. Bats were able to survive through their habitual avoidance of the sun, not needing much water, their mobility, and ability to find a plentiful diet of insects and fruits by night. They also showed great powers of adaptability, diversifying and specialising over the succeeding millennia. All Bahamian bats are comparatively small – with a wingspan between 5 and 8 inches (12.7 and 20.3 cm) – and like all bats are aerodynamically distinct from birds, and even more agile. Rather than planing like birds' wings, bats' wings scoop the air, obtaining great manoeuvrability from the aerofoil action of a membrane between the bats' legs. In some species, this flap is used to scoop up insects, which the bat then consumes while still in flight. One indigenous Bahamian species, the free-tail bat (*Tadarida bahamensis*) is especially versatile, being able not only to outfly any insect but, having hook-like fingers on the edge of its short wings, also uniquely to pick up crawling insects from the ground. Most bats feed on insects, some on insects and fruits, and a few on fruits alone.

Bats in a cave in Andros

The most amazing skill of bats is their ability to forage in complete darkness. Though with tiny brains and with very poor eyesight, they all have the facility to 'see' objects, however minute and fast moving, by a form of sonar. This is probably most highly developed in the three Bahamian species of leaf-nosed bats (especially *Europhylla plantifrons*). Their curiously shaped proboscides act as a kind of radar dome, directing and focusing the high-frequency squeaks that the bats emit. These are bounced back, to be gathered by the bats' external ears, instantly analysed and translated into flight commands. By this means, bats are able both to avoid obstacles and to catch their flying prey without needing sight at all.

Bats in The Bahamas offer no danger to humans (they do not attack, bite, suck blood or convey disease) and their aura of evil in folk mythology tells more about the humans' psychological distaste for mysterious things that flap and squeak in the night than about the creatures' fascinating and beneficial attributes. The *Lonely Planet* guide does well to make Bahamian bat caves an important focus of interest and study for eco-minded tourists. Notable examples cited are the Hatchet Bay cave on ELEUTHERA, the Griffin Bat Cave near Orange Creek, CAT ISLAND, Cartwright and Hamilton Caves on LONG ISLAND, and the Gordon's Bluff cave near Landrail Point, CROOKED ISLAND.

Further reading: D. G. Campbell, *The Ephemeral Islands: A Natural History of the Bahamas*, Macmillan, 1978, 67–9; Karl F. Koopman, 'Notes on the Mammals of The Bahamas, with Special Reference to the Bats,' *Journal of Mammalogy*, 38 (2), 1975, 164–75; D. W. Buden, 'Bahamian Land Mammals with a Guide to the Identification of Bats', *Bahamas Journal of Science*, 3 (2), 1995.

BAY STREET Literally, the main street of NASSAU, fronting the harbour and still containing all the principal downtown shops. Figuratively, the name Bay Street was given to the white commercial oligarchy that owned those shops and dominated the political life of The Bahamas in colonial days – and in the last phase (1953–67) was synonymous with the UNITED BAHAMIAN PARTY.

A road along the bay (or harbour) was probably made at the time of Governor William SHIRLEY (1758–68). The earliest plan of Nassau, dated 1739, shows no street along the shore, with the first thoroughfare back of the harbour-front houses called King Street. A map of the time of the Loyalists (1788) shows a Bay Street that stretched from the Parade in front of Fort Nassau, past the new public buildings and East Street as far as what was then called Culmer Street and was renamed Victoria Avenue in 1905.

Central Bay Street now extends just 500 yards (460 m) from the British Colonial Hilton (former site of Fort Nassau) to East Street at Rawson Square. This was the former location of the markets for produce, fish and slaves, later of the first banks, and is now where the tourist-oriented emporia are found. It is also the area taken over on Boxing Day and New Year's morning by the people's JUNKANOO, and more occasionally by celebratory parades, state funeral processions, and political demonstrations.

East of East Street, Bay Street becomes East Bay Street, extending some 2 miles (3 km) to Fort Montagu, where (though usually still called the same) it is officially named the Eastern Road, which runs a further 5 miles (8 km) to NEW PROVIDENCE's East End Point. Towards the west, Bay Street continues on the other side of the British Colonial Hilton as West Bay Street, along the entire north shore of New Providence, 12 miles (20 km), past CABLE BEACH and GAMBIER VILLAGE, to North West Point by OLD FORT Bay.

BERMUDA TRIANGLE Alleged black hole of mysterious disappearances; staple of check-out counter magazine sensationalism, with only the flimsiest basis in fact.

The Bermuda Triangle (sometimes called 'the Devil's Triangle') has its apexes north on Bermuda, south-west on Miami and south-east on San Juan, Puerto Rico, thus including the entire archipelago of The Bahamas. It was christened and first publicised in a February 1964 article in *Argosy* magazine by an American journalist called Vincent Gaddis, who in a subsequent book cited nine unexplained incidents, notably the disappearance without trace of an entire squadron of Grumman Avenger planes from Fort Lauderdale in 1944. Catching the public fascination for such maritime mysteries, Gaddis's speculations soon moved into the realm of accepted fact, with dozens of further alleged occurrences being added to the roll, along with many outlandish explanations.

Countering public disquiet, the US Navy and Coast Guard have come closest to exploding the myths. While they admit that the area is 'noted for a high incidence of unexplained losses of ships, small boats and aircraft', they point out that this is no more true than for certain other areas in the world, and that most if not all of the occurrences can be attributed either to special geographical features of the region, or to plain human error.

Study of ocean currents and low and high altitude winds shows that the Bermuda Triangle is very subject to sea and air disturbances and fluctuations. The GULF STREAM has a particularly strong influence on navigation and weather, adding to the area's reputation for sudden thunderstorms

West central Bay Street in the 1920s, with the Market and Ice House on the north side and Hotel Colonial in the background

BERRY ISLANDS

and water-spouts. Likewise (as anyone who has flown between Nassau and Bermuda can testify), the conflict of jet-streams over that area of the Atlantic leads to an almost invariably bumpy, even scary, ride. Added to this are the well-known dangers of sailing through an area where shoals and reefs alternate with submarine chasms, leading to wrecks that sink into the depths without trace.

Vastly improved meteorology and navigational equipment has almost removed the danger of unexpected and unexplained mishaps such as the fate of the Grumman Avengers in 1944. However, in its last word, the US Coast Guard is not quite so sanguine about the chances of small boats avoiding the dangers of the Bermuda Triangle: 'Not to be underestimated is the human error factor. A large number of pleasure boats travel the waters between Florida's Gold Coast and The Bahamas. All too often, crossings are attempted with too small a boat, insufficient knowledge of the area's hazards, and a lack of good seamanship. The Coast Guard is not impressed with supernatural explanations of disasters at sea. It has been their experience that the combined forces of nature and unpredictability of mankind outdo even the most far fetched science fiction.'

Further reading: V, Gaddis, *Invisible Horizons: True Mysteries of the Sea*, Philadelphia, Chilton Books, 1964; H. Rosenberg, 'Exorcising the Devil's Triangle', *Sealife Magazine*, 24 (6), 1974, 11–15; US Navy, 'The Bermuda Triangle: A Selective Bibliography', www.history.navy.mil/faqs/faq 8-1. html

BERRY ISLANDS A necklace of some 20 cays around the eastern edge of a shallow bank almost surrounded by the oceanic chasms of the Northwest and Northeast Providence Channels. Ideally located on the sailing route between Florida and Nassau and with splendid beaches, excellent dive sites and superlative fishing of all types, the Berry Islands are a favourite resort for well-heeled yachtsmen, and in recent years have become a stopping place for Florida-based cruise ships.

The Stirrup Cays, the northernmost of the Berry Islands, were the location of a failed attempt by the colonial government to settle Africans liberated from illegal slavers in the 1830s. The 650 native Bahamians who now inhabit the Berry Islands (three-quarters of whom live in the village of Bullock's Harbour on Great Harbour Cay) are descended from ex-slaves who squatted on land then thought worthless, poor fishermen and spongers, or later migrants who came to serve rich foreign settlers or the tourist traffic.

From the 1920s until the 1950s, the Berry Islands (like the Abacos and the Exumas) became the target of those who could afford to indulge the dream of owning a private tropical island – or, as prices escalated, at least a slice of one. Two of the most notable owners were Marion 'Joe' CARSTAIRS, the English 'Queen of Whale Cay', and Wallace Groves, the American founder of Freeport, who made Little Whale Cay into an elegant private domain, complete with gardens, aviary and zoo. After World War Two, several lavish developments sprang up, with marinas, airstrips, golf courses, and house-lots. Of these, the Great Harbour Cay Club, on the largest island, and the Chub Cay Club and Marina, on the southernmost cay, were the smartest and most exclusive. Between them they boasted

Whale Cay, Berry Islands

such diverse jet-set owners and visitors as Cary Grant, Bridget Bardot, Bill Cosby, several Rockefellers, and the mobster Meyer Lansky.

The phases of private and corporate developments faded somewhat in the 1970s and 1980s, around the time that the four airstrips in the Berry Islands were rumoured to be links in the international drug-running chain. But a new era opened up in the 1990s when Norwegian Cruise Line and Royal Caribbean Cruise Line bought up the northernmost islands of Great Stirrup Cay and Little Stirrup Cay, renamed them more glamorously, and transformed them into one-day paradises for their middle to lower income passengers.

BETHEL, Cecil Valentine (1904–1999) Inspiring teacher and education pioneer. Orphaned early and largely self-taught, he was apprenticed as a tailor, but at the age of 20 won a place at Codrington College, Barbados, to study for the Anglican ministry. Deciding against joining the priesthood, he returned to tailoring, finding his true vocation in the tutoring he did on the side. With a single colleague, he founded the private St Cyprian's school, which 'crammed' many later non-white leaders to a level and in subjects not then available in government schools. He taught practically any subject for which there was a call. Legend has it that 'CVB', who became justly famed as a teacher of Spanish, learned the subject entirely on his own in order to convey the winning numbers in the Cuban national lottery from the radio to the local masters of the 'numbers game'.

In 1941 CVB gave up tailoring and tutoring on obtaining a coveted position as assistant teacher at GOVERNMENT HIGH SCHOOL. Though a brilliant natural teacher, respected and loved by his pupils, like other non-white teachers he suffered discrimination at the hands of colonialist headmasters, who preferred expatriates. With the first wafts of the winds of change, however, he became the first Bahamian headmaster of GHS in 1964. Three years later, at the age of 63, he retired from GHS, but continued an active and increasingly honoured life as private tutor and public servant for many years, culminating in the chairmanship of the Public Service Commission. He died in August 1999, a few days after Anna Louise (née Russell), his devoted wife of almost 70 years.

BETHEL, Clement (1938–1987) Classical pianist, composer, choreographer, choirmaster and folklore scholar, whose untimely death deprived The Bahamas of one of its foremost cultural leaders.

Showing precocious talent while studying piano under Meta Davis in Nassau, Clement Bethel was sent to the Royal Academy of Music in London, earning a sheaf of diplomas and awards. Opting for a career in teaching and the public service rather than that of a concert pianist, he taught music in several government schools and became deeply immersed in many cultural activities, as well as giving an annual piano recital. In 1976 he was awarded a Fulbright Scholarship for graduate study at the University of California, which led to his ground-breaking MA thesis on the ethnomusicology of The Bahamas, entitled 'Music in The Bahamas: Its Roots, Development and Personality'.

On his return to Nassau from California, Clement Bethel was appointed the first Director of Culture at the Ministry of Education. In this role he tirelessly promoted the teaching of music in schools and served as producer, artistic and music director, composer and arranger for numerous cultural productions, at home and abroad. Before and after his appointment as Director of Culture, he was involved in the music and choreography for the Mexico Olympic Games (1968) and was an active committee member for Carifesta in Guyana (1972), Cuba (1979) and Barbados (1981). He was also largely responsible for the impressive music and folklore show which was part of The Bahamas INDEPENDENCE celebrations in July 1973. In his private time he was the founder and director of the distinguished chorale called the Renaissance Singers, the first president of The Bahamas Music Society, and several times chairman of The Bahamas Festival of Culture and Drama. Perhaps his finest and most original achievement, however, was the production of the pioneer Bahamian folk opera, *The Story of Sammy Swain,* in 1975.

Clement Bethel was married to Dr Keva Bethel (née Eldon), President of the COLLEGE OF THE BAHAMAS, and was the father of two talented children. In August 1987, at the age of 49, he succumbed to hereditary nephritic cystitis. His important manuscript entitled 'Junkanoo: Festival of The Bahamas' was posthumously edited and expanded by his daughter Nicolette, beautifully illustrated by Brent MALONE, and published by Macmillan in 1991.

Further reading: C. Bethel, 'Music in the Bahamas: Its Roots, Development and Personality', MA thesis, University of California, 1978; 'Music in The Bahamas', *Bahamas Handbook and Businessman's Guide*, Nassau, Dupuch Publications, 1983; E. C. Bethel, *Junkanoo: Festival of The Bahamas*, ed. N. Bethel, London, Macmillan Caribbean, 1991.

BIMINIS Two almost contiguous small islands and four tiny cays, famed far beyond their size, situated on the eastern edge of the Florida Channel, within sight of the night-glow of Miami.

BIRDS

North Bimini

Though the total area of the Biminis is less than 10 square miles (26 squ. km), almost their entire population of 1,700 lives on the southern half of the 3 ½ mile long and less than 200 yard wide (5.5 km by 182 m) ribbon of land in North Bimini that comprises the twin towns of Alice Town and Bailey Town. To the east are the uninhabited mangrove flats of North Bimini, and the whole is separated by a 150-yard (136 m) channel from the scarcely populated expanse of South Bimini, where the airport lies. With houses, hotels, shops and bars packed as tight as cutlery in a box, the strip of settlement running from Alice Town through Bailey Town to Porgy Bay is rarely somnolent, and at JUNKANOO time, and during the annual regatta, main fishing tourneys and American college breaks, is almost riotously active.

Throughout its history, Bimini has attracted legends as much as it has drawn explorers, big game fishermen, rum-runners, drug smugglers, marine biologists, writers and frolicking students. It was named for the 'two islands' which the Lucayans told the gullible Spaniards were the site of a fountain of eternal youth. This the early governor of Puerto Rico Juan Ponce de LEON went looking for, dismissing the islands now called Bimini or missing them altogether, and going on to find Florida instead (1513). Modern Biminites try to convince visitors that the famed fountain was either a small stone-walled well on South Bimini (more often than not dry), or a sulphurous muddy spring deep in the mangroves of North Bimini – which they have christened the Healing Hole.

Even less credible, though a draw for scuba-divers, is the claim that the natural formation of limestone blocks off North Bimini called the Bimini Road is a remnant of the fabulous drowned island of Atlantis. Divers are also lured with tales of sunken Spanish galleons, or to swim with dolphins and explore the wreck of the freighter which served as an entrepôt for liquor during the rum-running days of American PROHIBITION (1919–33). During that era Bimini was said to be the busiest port in The Bahamas, as well as a favourite destination for Americans looking for a legal drinking spot in picturesque surroundings. Bimini's reputation as a partying hideaway was later sustained by such characters as the rapscallion Rev. Adam Clayton Powell Jr. in the 1960s and the would-be US presidential contender Gary Hart, detected cavorting there by the media in the 1980s. Locals also claim, with limited evidence, that Martin Luther King wrote the draft of his 'I Have a Dream' speech while staying in Bimini.

The chief of Bimini's legendary expatriates, though, was Ernest Hemingway, who often visited and stayed there during the 1930s. Credited with popularising if not starting the game-fishing industry, the hard-drinking and sometimes bellicose 'Papa' Hemingway is said to have written much of his immortal *To Have and Have Not* in Bimini. The Biminis are the location of the semi-autobiographical, posthumously published novel which gives the Biminis their best nickname, *Islands in the Stream*. The lounge of Hemingway's favourite watering-hole, the *Compleat Angler Hotel* (founded by Helen Duncombe in 1935), is now a museum to his larger-than-life memory.

Further reading: A. B. Saunders, *History of Bimini*, 1998.

BIRDS Though without the range of birds found in either the North or South American subcontinents, or even in the larger and more fertile islands of the Greater Antilles, The Bahamas is still a happy hunting ground for 'twitchers' (bird-watchers), with a fascinating variety of woodland, wetland and marine resident species, seasonal migrants and occasional visitors. Thanks largely to the Ornithology Group, a subcomittee of the BAHAMAS NATIONAL TRUST, bird-watching is already said to

Bananaquit

draw as many visitors as those who come to The Bahamas for golf.

There are some 230 species of birds to be seen in The Bahamas, of which three are found nowhere else in the world. About 40 species are permanent residents, 70 winter visitors from the north, 10 summer visitors from the south, 70 passage migrants and the remainder occasional vagrants. The three endemic species are the rare Bahama Yellowthroat, the tiny but colourful Bahama Woodstar hummingbird, found wherever there are nectar-bearing flowers, and the Bahama Swallow, which can be seen even in downtown Nassau. An indigenous subspecies, once common and hunted as a pest or as a pet but now threatened and rigorously protected, is the Bahama Parrot. This raucous and gregarious bird, a relative of the Cuban and Caymanian Green Parrots, is mainly green in colour but with a white head, tufts of pink and violet-tinged wing feathers. It is now found only in the less inhabited parts of ABACO and INAGUA. Though of the same sub-species these two colonies exhibit different nesting habits; the Abaconian parrots make their nests in rocky nooks close to the ground and the Inaguans nest in trees.

Each Bahamian habitat – whether north, central or south, remote blackland coppice, coastal whiteland or mangrove swamp, or cultivated gardens in NASSAU, HARBOUR ISLAND or Freeport – has its own ornithological character and delights, by night as well as day. To the most casual spectator, the table-hopping antics of the yellow Bananaquit (perhaps the most common of all Bahamian birds), the fishing techniques of the cormorants and pelicans, or the sight of a hummingbird hovering over a hibiscus flower (its wings oscillating at up to 200 times a second) are endlessly intriguing. Equally arresting are the sudden sighting of a statuesque Green Heron, known locally as 'Poor Joe' on account of its plaintive cry, by a pond in the evening twilight, the silent passage of a Barn Owl through the dusk, or the infinitely varied and often beautiful song of the Northern Mockingbird (*Mimus polyglottos*) in the night. For many, though, the most thrilling sight of all is the effortless soaring flight of the aptly named Magnificent Frigate Bird (with a 7-foot (2.1 m) wingspan), which aeroplane pilots have reported at 9,000 feet (2,740 m) above the islands.

Perhaps the favourite Bahamian destination for avid bird-watchers is the far southern island of INAGUA, where besides the once-again flourishing population of FLAMINGOS (numbering as many as 60,000) may be spied large numbers of the rare Roseate Spoonbill and a high proportion of the world population of Reddish Egrets. Another prized sighting is the rare and protected night-feeding West Indian Whistling Tree Duck. More easily accessible to less dedicated bird-watchers than remote Inagua are the 'bird walks' organised through the 100-acre Rand Nature Centre on GRAND BAHAMA and from the Retreat, the headquarters of The Bahamas National Trust, off Village Road in Nassau.

Further reading: P. G. C. Brudenell-Bruce, *The Birds of New Providence and the Bahama Islands*, Collins, 1975; D. G. Campbell, *The Ephemeral Islands: A Natural History of The Bahamas*, Macmillan, 1978.

'BLACKBEARD' (Edward Teach)

'BLACKBEARD' (Edward Teach) The most infamous of Bahamian PIRATES, whose larger-than-life legend has dominated the extensive literature on the piracy era (*c*.1690–1718). As the author of *A History of the Bahamas* wrote in 1962:

> The Edward Teach of whom we read was a villain of more than vile aspect. The hair of his beard he wore in plaits. Ranting into battle, he wore six brace of pistols in a special belt and fuming slow matches in his hatband. In a cruel age, his cruelties were legendary. A physical giant, he was said to have had fourteen 'wives' and when eventually cornered in 1718 to have gone on fighting after five musket wounds and three sabre-thrusts. His drinking powers were unmatched. One favourite story tells how, at the climax of a drunken spree, he forced his companions to enter the hold of a ship where he had set trays of burning sulphur. Closing the hatches, he shouted, 'We have made our own hell. Let us see who is closest kin to the devil by staying longest in it!' One by one his spluttering cronies pushed up the hatches and gasped in the fresh air. Needless to say, the triumphant Blackbeard was the last on deck, hardly the worse for his experience.

The reality was much less picturesque or spectacular. Edward Teach was an ordinary seaman from Bristol who served as a privateer in 'Queen Anne's War' (1702–13). Unemployed at the peace, like many other privateers he joined up with the pirates then beginning to terrorise shipping throughout the Caribbean and off the mainland American colonies. Serving under Benjamin Hornigold, Teach did not gain a command of his own until 1716. This was a captured merchantman which he renamed the *Queen Anne's Revenge*. In 1717 Teach was listed as one of the five pirate captains (along with Hornigold, Jennings, Burgess and White) using The Bahamas as their base. His active career was bloody but short, and he gained more fame by his death than by his depredations – being brought to account off the coast of North Carolina in November 1718.

Nevertheless, Blackbeard came almost to epitomise Bahamian piracy, in both its more sordid and its most

BLACK CRAB MENTALITY

Edward Teach, alias 'Blackbeard, the Notorious Pirate'

romanticised versions. In 1784, a refugee LOYALIST planter wishing to disparage the established inhabitants of The Bahamas characterised them as 'the Offspring and Successors of the famous Blackbeard the Pirate'. Like Captain Henry Avery, Blackbeard became the subject of a stage play in London. He was a favourite figure in pantomimes (including one put on in Nassau by a company from Cuba in 1813) and the hero of a verse epic by the self-styled 'Poet Laureate of The Bahamas', Henry Christopher Christie (1925). As Bahamian TOURISM developed, visitors were invited to view a 'Blackbeard's Tree' in the Public Square (since cut down) and a 'Blackbeard's Well' (since filled in), to visit a 'Blackbeard's Tower' on the Eastern Road (which can have had nothing to do with the pirate), and to carouse and ogle the show in allegedly pirate fashion in the bar-nightclub called Blackbeard's Tavern (which closed down in the 1980s).

BLACK CRAB MENTALITY A term used, if not coined, by Prime Minister Lynden PINDLING to describe and condemn the Bahamian variant of that state of false consciousness by which, through the years of enslavement and socioeconomic and political subordination, Afro-Americans were brainwashed into an inferiority complex. It effects were not just a belief that blacks were incapable of competing with whites and a denigration of all things African, but a jealous bringing down of those who sought to advance – dragging them back into the common mass, like the behaviour of crabs in a barrel.

It was Lynden Pindling's greatest achievement, through words and personal example, to consign such sentiments to the rubbish bin where they belonged. His intention was to restore pride, self-confidence and a sense of unity, to all Bahamians, while at the same time resolutely avoiding the kind of aggressive negritude which is the Black Crab Mentality's antithesis.

Further reading: P. J. Wilson, *Crab Antics: The Social Anthropology of English-Speaking Negro Societies in the Caribbean*, New Haven, Yale University Press, 1973.

'BLACK TUESDAY', 27 April 1965 The day that saw the dramatic events which threatened fatally to divide the opposition to the UNITED BAHAMIAN PARTY but in fact laid the groundwork for the achievement of majority rule by the PROGRESSIVE LIBERAL PARTY in January 1967.

Beset by a loaded electoral system and by UBP propaganda that they were led by Black Power extremists, the PLP had failed to make much progress in the 1962 general election (though they polled most votes, they won only a quarter of the seats). This accorded the UBP the kudos of bringing internal self-government to The Bahamas in January 1964 and allowed the party to make the claim that it alone was capable of leading the colony to greater prosperity.

When it became clear that the promised electoral reforms would continue to block majority rule, the activist core of the PLP decided that more forthright tactics were necessary. Its model was the type of mass protest and symbolic actions short of actual violence which were beginning to prove effective in the Civil Rights movement in the United States. Stormy debates inside Parliament (which saw the physical ejection of Milo BUTLER and Arthur HANNA) were accompanied by well-organised demonstrations in the streets outside. These rose to a dramatic and apparently spontaneous, but in fact completely premeditated and orchestrated climax on Tuesday 27 April 1965.

Contingents of PLP supporters under party marshals filled the area around the House of Assembly, chanting and singing, while inside, party leader Lynden PINDLING made a blistering attack on the regime's denial of democracy. At the climax of his speech, with words to the effect that democracy belonged to the people, Pindling suddenly seized the sacred mace – symbol of the Assembly's authority – and threw it out of an open window into the square below. Not to be outdone, Milo Butler followed by tossing out the Speaker's hourglass, which symbolised for him the UBP's curtailment of the people's freedom of speech.

Before the stunned Speaker could stop them, the PLP Members left the chamber and joined their cheering supporters. Well disciplined, the crowd sat down on the road and Pindling spoke to them from the top of a van. Privately nervous that the protest might suddenly explode into a riot as in 1942 and prove counter-productive, he spoke out against the regime but counselled peaceable behaviour. As armed police appeared to clear the streets and a magistrate prepared to read the Riot Act, Pindling announced an adjournment to the Southern Recreation Ground, Over-the-Hill, and the marshals efficiently led the entire crowd away from Bay Street within a few minutes.

The PLP officially boycotted Parliament for almost a year, but were bitterly divided internally. Three of the eight PLP Members (Paul ADDERLEY, Orville TURNQUEST and Spurgeon Bethel) who had not been made privy to the plan because it was certain they would have disapproved it, returned to the House within two weeks, were expelled from the party and went on to form the rival NATIONAL DEMOCRATIC PARTY, taking with them many of the more conservative middle-class non-whites. In addition, Cyril Stevenson, who knew but disapproved of the plan and absented himself, left the party, while the maverick labour leader Randol FAWKES veered further away from an alliance with the PLP.

For some time it seemed that the PLP radicals had overplayed their hand – and played into the hands of the UBP, which confidently expected to extend its mandate for a further five years in 1967. However, Lynden Pindling's firm but judicious leadership, the publicity generated from the PLP delegation to the United Nations in August 1965 and, even more, the revelations of UBP corruption which followed the bombshell article in the *Wall Street Journal* in October 1966, led to the cliff-hanging PLP victory of 10 January 1967 and the legislation that guaranteed majority rule thereafter.

Further reading: D. L. Johnson, *The Quiet Revolution in The Bahamas*, Nassau, Family Islands Press, 1972, 51-84; C. A. Hughes, *Race and Politics in the Bahamas*, St Lucia, Queensland University Press, 1981, 95-123; M. Craton, *Pindling: The Life and Times of Sir Lynden Pindling, First Prime Minister of The Bahamas, 1930-2000*, Oxford, Macmillan Caribbean, 2002.

'BLIND BLAKE' (ALPHONSO HIGGS)

'BLIND BLAKE' (ALPHONSO HIGGS) (1915–1985) Legendary maestro and composer of GOOMBAY music. Born in INAGUA in 1915, Alphonso Higgs had lost his sight at the age of 16 and turned his natural musicality to a means of livelihood, borrowing his more familiar nickname from a formerly famous blind American blues guitarist. A self-taught pianist and adept on all stringed instruments, 'Blind Blake' usually played a banjo or ukelele, in a trio with a drummer and guitarist. Earning merely a local reputation and little money in the depressed 1930s, he became a popular nightclub entertainer once TOURISM developed, and quite often travelled abroad to publicise The Bahamas. One of his specialties was to perform goombays with his trio while being driven down Bay Street in a horse-drawn surrey.

Blind Blake's secret was not just his command of the distinctively Bahamian goombay rhythms but his inventiveness in writing songs with catchy tunes and relevant lyrics, which he delivered in his distinctive gravelly voice. In these respects his only peers were the pianist George SYMONETTE and 'the Bahamas Songbird', Eloise LEWIS. Among Blind Blake's notable goombay songs were 'Run Come See Jerusalem' (recalling the effects of the 1929 hurricane), 'Jones Oh Jones' and 'My Name is Morgan (But I ain't J. P.)'. Most famous of all was 'Love, Love Alone'—a kindly comment on the love affair between the Duke of WINDSOR and Wallis Simpson, which Blind Blake was at first forbidden to sing in the couple's hearing, but was later commanded to do so by the Duke and Duchess themselves, receiving a standing ovation.

If they had a fault, Blind Blake's songs were too bland, lacking the satirical edge and salacious innuendoes of Trinidadian calypso or the driving beat of Jamaican reggae. Though affectionately regarded and locally honoured, he spent the last dozen years of his life not living the life of an international superstar like the Mighty Sparrow or Bob Marley (if that were truly enviable), but genially greeting arrivals at Nassau International Airport as an employee of the Tourist Board.

Blind Blake

BLUE BOOKS Easily accessible in the ARCHIVES, these are not, as the name may suggest, pornography, but invaluable and under-used historical sources – the Bahamian version of the annual sets of answers to printed questionnaires about each colony which Governors (or their Colonial Secretaries) were required to send to their masters in London, between 1834 and 1940.

The Blue Books were eventually discontinued once superseded by the printed annual reports for which colonial Governors were also made responsible between the early decades of the twentieth century and each colony's achievement of independence. Already the compilers, even in a comparatively minor colony like The Bahamas, had almost become inundated by a flood of information. But with the multiplication of ministries and burgeoning bureaucracy that invariably accompanied the process of self-government, the distillation of information within a single volume became virtually impossible. Sadly, the historical researcher, instead of tapping annual summary compilations of between 170 and 385 pages, now has to round up and digest a veritable paper mountain from a plethora of elusive, widely differing and often expensive sources.

BLUE HILLS A 90-foot (27-m) transverse ridge in the centre of NEW PROVIDENCE, 3 miles (4.8 km) south of NASSAU's waterfront. Once marking the southern boundary of the well-known parts of the island's interior, since the 1950s it has been overleapt by Nassau's suburban sprawl.

Sometimes said to have been named after a LOYALIST landowner, Isaac Baillou, the ridge had in fact been called the Blue Hills at least 50 years before Baillou arrived. In the 1740s, Governor John Tinker famously wrote that the thriftlessness of his troublesome subjects 'would make a stranger at first sight imagine we had golden mines no further than the Blue Hills'.

During slavery days the Blue Hills were trackless bush and a notorious hideout for runaways. A cleared area at the end of a path due south from Nassau that was a base for searches for fugitives was appropriately called Lookout Farm. Later the path became Blue Hill Road, taking a turn to the west just south of the ridge to serve the LIBERATED AFRICAN settlements of Carmichael and ADELAIDE, and by 1890 also carrying on straight to New Providence's southern shore. Within another century both sides of this extension were completely developed into housing subdivisions, with such grandly attractive names as Golden Gates, Sunshine Park, Fair View, Seven Hills, and South Beach Estates.

BLUE HOLES Found either on land or in offshore shallows, Bahamian 'blue holes' are submerged and inundated ancient sinkholes. Usually circular, sometimes tidal, and varying in size and depth, there are at least 175 on the mainland and 50 off the shores of ANDROS alone – a magnet for scuba divers interested in scientific research or simply pursuing adventure.

Since the sinkholes from which the blue holes originate could only have been created through the action of rainwater at a time when the Bahamian limestone base was above sea-level, their depth is a scientific indicator of the lowest points reached in sea-level (and hence the largest extent of Bahamian land masses) during ancient ice ages. The fact that many blue holes and their offshoot branches contain stalactites and stalagmites (built up through aeons from dripping water containing calcium carbonate) both confirms that they were formed during 'high island' glacial periods, and helps scientists to measure more precisely when and for how long such ice ages occurred.

The linked caverns and branching passages from most blue holes (extending sometimes for miles and interconnecting with other blue holes and the sea) are also, of course, the sub-marine relics of water-formed karst formations to be seen on dry land. These, which are largest and most

Divers exploring blue hole, Andros

extensive in the least flat Bahamian islands, not inundated for millions of years – such as ELEUTHERA, CAT ISLAND and LONG ISLAND – offer similar and related opportunities for exploration and scientific study, without adding the risk of drowning!

From the enthusiastic divers' accounts, however, nothing is more exciting and rewarding than blue hole diving. Each hole seems to have its own character and surprising features, and only a minority have yet been fully explored. The cloudiness and salinity of the water usually varies with the depth of the hole. In many onshore blue holes there are upper levels infused with tannin from leaves and hydrogen sulphide from decayed organisms. But these are succeeded by crystal clear freshwater, standing atop brackish and saltwater levels. Some, holes with high concentrations of hydrogen sulphide and low levels of oxygen, are comparatively lifeless, while others, filled with sea water, teem with fish. None has yet been found to harbour the monsters, such as the 'half-giant squid, half-shark' *lusca* assigned to blue holes in Androsian folklore. Undreadful but just as fascinating, however, has been the discovery of the completely new group of crustacean called *remipede*, first in GRAND BAHAMA in 1980 and later in Andros.

Almost certainly the largest Bahamian blue hole (maybe the largest in the world) is the so-called 'Black Hole' between Fresh Creek and South Bight in southern Andros. Almost perfectly circular, it measures more than 330 yards (300 m) across. It is thought to be very deep but has not yet been fully plumbed. The deepest blue hole so far measured, near Twin Lakes in central north Andros, went down 363 feet (110 m), which suggests a huge main Bahamian island with hills almost 500 feet (150 m) high. Some of the Andros blue-hole cave systems are very extensive, but none are quite as far reaching and multi-passaged as those in the Lucayan National Park in Grand Bahama, which the *Guinness Book of Records* has described as the most extended underwater cave system in the world.

For the historian and archaeologist the blue holes in Grand Bahama and Andros have proved even more wonderful. In both islands (once thought to have been uninhabited before the Europeans came) large numbers of aboriginal skeletons have been found. The blue hole called 'Stargate' on Andros has also produced the first Lucayan canoe ever recovered. What these discoveries most probably disclose is that the Lucayans used blue holes as underwater burial places – perhaps burying men with the canoes they had built and used. But an even more intriguing possibility exists. If the Grand Bahama and Andros aboriginals buried their dead in caves above sea-level, as Lucyans did elsewhere in The Bahamas, these underwater skeletons may be far more ancient than previously thought – antedating the earliest known human habitation in the islands by several thousand years.

A far less thrilling feature of Bahamian blue holes is the way that they have been plundered by unscientific curio-hunters and used as refuse dumps by careless locals. The Lucayan Cavern system on Grand Bahama was closed in 1999 because of plundering and pollution. Some blue holes near settlements in Andros are in a worse state. Divers encounter skeletons of dead animals and discarded rubbish, including wrecked cars, and some holes are virtual sumps for sewer seepage. After one Andros dive in 1987 all three divers immediately came down with septicaemia that but for antibiotics might have been fatal. It is against these by-products of 'development' that such organisations as the Blue Holes Foundation and the BAHAMAS NATIONAL TRUST strive as best they can.

Further reading: N. E. Sealey, *Bahamian Landscapes: An Introduction to the Geography of The Bahamas*, London, Collins Caribbean, 1985, 47-56; G. J. Benjamin, 'Diving into the Blue Holes of Andros', *National Geographic Magazine*, 1970, II, no. 360, 347-63; R. Palmer, *Deep Into Blue Holes: The Story of the Andros Project*, Nassau, Media Publications, 1997; S. Schwabe, 'Blue Holes of The Bahamas: A Silent Death', *Immersed*, 2001, 6 (2); www.blueholes.org.

BOATBUILDING Proudest, most sophisticated and most essential of all traditional Bahamian crafts, the making and shaping of boats with native materials gave the colony of The Bahamas an independent viability, responding successfully to changing economic conditions throughout the colonial period. In the modern era, traditional boatbuilding is narrowly saved from becoming a mere folk museum curiosity by the nostalgia of wealthy wooden boat enthusiasts and by the popularity of competitive sailing in 'work boat' REGATTAS.

The ELEUTHERIAN ADVENTURERS brought skills and boat types from Bermuda and the LOYALISTS imported methods and design influences from New England and the Chesapeake. But it was the Bahamian settlers, of necessity committed to a largely maritime existence, who learned how to employ the plentiful local resources of hardwood and pine to produce boats effectively, even elegantly, adapted to local conditions and needs.

Since the Bahamian archipelago consists of huge shallow banks with dangerous coral heads and reefs, split by comparatively narrow stretches of deep water, small, manoeuvrable vessels with a moderate draught suitable for the shallows but sufficient for the deeps were required. In the first phase of settlement, shallow-draught Dutch-style 'shallops' were used, as well as Bermudian sloops designed more for ocean-roaming. Very few of the PRIVATEERING vessels which scoured the nearby seas from a base in NASSAU during the frequent wars down to 1815 (and probably none of the PIRATE ships of the earlier period) were actually constructed in The Bahamas. Hoping that their settlements might become bases for an export trade to North America and even Europe, the ABACO LOYALISTS first constructed ocean-going vessels of up to 150 tons. But these had little local use, and most were sold abroad.

Instead, over the following century native boat-builders in all the settled islands (but particularly Abaco, Eleuthera, Exuma, Andros and New Providence) developed three distinctive types of Bahamian sailboat for different local purposes. Smallest and most numerous was the so-called Abaco dinghy, an open boat from 9 to 20 feet (2.7 to 6 m) in length, with a single mast and 'leg-of-mutton' sail, a straight keel and outboard rudder. There was a notch in the transom that enabled it to be sculled effectively when the wind failed. Similar in build but up to twice the length was the Bahamian fishing smack or sloop. These were relatively broad in beam (one third of the length) but of shallow draught, with a single mast and with a jib-sail bent to a bowsprit as well as a comparatively huge 'loose-footed' mainsail, on a boom as long as the boat itself. The boat was decked over, with no cockpit and only a small trunk cabin aft. A hatchway forward led to a cargo hold and below there was a 'live well' in which to keep the fish fresh for market. The crew of seven to ten men cooked, ate and normally slept on deck, rather than below. A dismasted Bahamian fishing sloop is the centrepiece of Winslow HOMER'S dramatic 1899 oil-painting *The Gulf Stream*.

A variant of the Bahamian fishing sloop, showing the continuing influence of the Bermudian sloop (having a curved prow and a rather deeper draught) was found in the 'salt islands' of the south-eastern Bahamas. This, the so-called Turks Island sloop, was used for carrying SALT as far as North America, but also other cargoes to and from Cuba, HAITI and other parts of the Caribbean.

Schooners, with at least two but up to four masts, were the largest and most complex of Bahamian-built boats. The basic type was the two-masted SPONGE schooner, some 35 to 38 feet (10.5 to 11.5 m) on the keel and 50 to 55 feet (15.2 to 16.7 m) overall, 16 feet (4.8 m) wide and drawing 5 feet (1.5 m). Besides its main masts and mainsails and one or two jibs to a long bowsprit, it carried topmasts and topsails and a foretopmast stay-sail bent to a jib boom. Serving as the mother ship for expeditions to 'the Mud' off Andros, sponge schooners carried on deck, or towed, eight to ten dinghies. They carried crews of up to 20, who used the dinghies to search for and hook sponges but returned to the anchored schooner to eat and sleep. Bahamian schooners were built in all the Abaco island settlements, Harbour Island and Andros. At the peak of the sponge industry there were at least 200 in operation, many of those from Abaco and Harbour Island being made and wholly owned by the men who sailed them.

Schooners were also used in the nineteenth century for carrying PINEAPPLE, during PROHIBITION (1919–33) for transporting liquor; and in the early twentieth century for lumber.

To a remarkable degree, but of necessity, the materials used for building the different styles of Bahamian boat were obtained in the islands, the tools were of the simplest, and the painstaking methods, time and effort employed had no relevance to such foreign concepts as labour cost. The chief raw materials were the rich variety of native woods. The most vital and difficult to harvest were the naturally curved hardwoods that made the structural skeleton of each boat: madeira (mahogany), horseflesh, LIGNUM

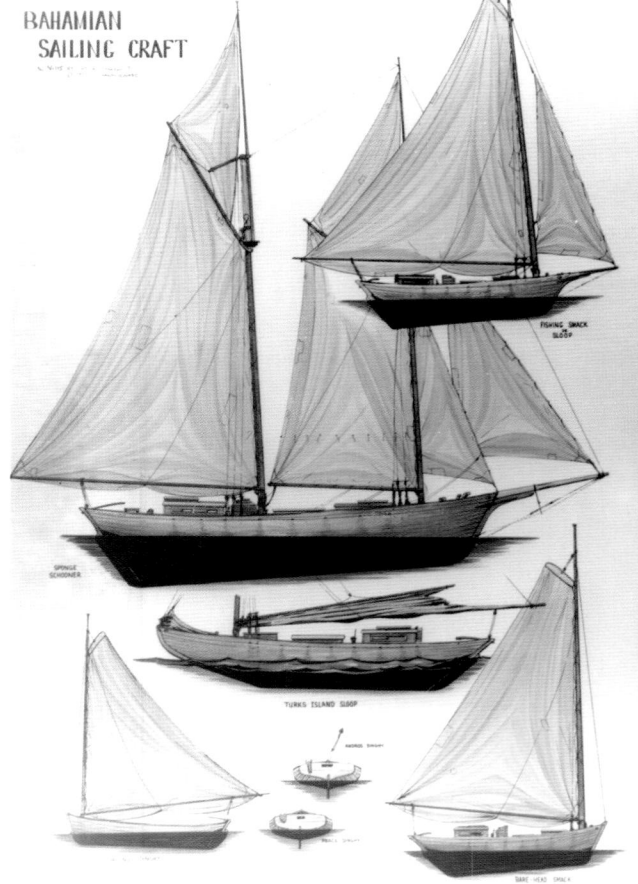

Types of traditional Bahamian working sailboats, from William Johson Jr., *Bahamian Sailing Craft* (1973).

VITAE, dogwood, corkwood, bullwood or tamarind. Gangs roamed deep in the bush in search of suitable timbers, which were laboriously chopped out, dragged down to the shore and shipped back to the settlement. The pines that provided the masts, side and deck planking, false keels and other relatively softer woodwork were easier to locate and transport, though once the export lumber industry developed, the best specimens became ever more scarce and distant from the settlements (eventually to be replaced by pine wood from other islands or the southern United States).

The boats themselves were constructed in the open air on the shore under the shade of large trees. There was no secrecy about methods but very great skill involved, with the work under the direction of acknowledged master craftsmen. The basic tools were axe, adze, saw, plane and spokeshave, which were preferred even after power tools became available and could be afforded. The builders relied on their eye and experience and there were no formal plans – though in the later years some of the Abaco and Harbour Island craftsmen worked from half-models, which were themselves works of art. The greatest skill of all went into the shaping of the ribs to provide the required beam and planing contours, shaping the lines from prow to transom, and the 'spiling' of the sideplanks (that is, chamfering them longitudinally to fit the ribs, strongly and as near as possible watertight). Also important was the placing and seating of the mast, or masts.

For the rest, it was mostly just skilled carpentry and providing the sails, rigging and fitments. Planks were caulked with local cotton fibre or kapok from the silk cotton tree, with a home-made tool fashioned from a holed penny on a stick and a tamping mallet. Rope was made from local SISAL at least in Abaco, but a much more common source was rigging salvaged from wrecks. WRECKING, indeed, was an essential concomitant for Bahamian boatbuilding in the years when cash was almost non-existent. Sailcloth and metals were not natural products of the Bahamas, so the all-too-frequent wrecks during the sailing era were relied on as a vital source – of ships' timber as well as rigging, canvas and metal fittings. This was not mere cannibalisation, though, for Bahamians in the maritime settlements were famously adept at reshaping sailcloth to their special needs, and using forges to fashion nails, bolts, cleats, hinges, swivels and hooks.

Finishing and launching a dinghy was such a frequent occurrence that it occasioned no great ceremony. But the launch of a sloop, even more of a schooner, was a settlement occasion. Men, women and children lent a hand at helping the boat into the water. There was a formal christening and blessing, followed by a picnic meal and much jollity. In the semi-puritanical white settlements, though, there was noticeably less alcohol and dancing involved than in other places.

During the century from the end of SLAVERY to the great sponge blight of 1938 perhaps 1,500 sloops and schooners were built in The Bahamas, along with innumerable dinghies. In boom periods, like the 1860s and first two decades of the twentieth century, as many as 30 sizeable vessels were launched every year, and scarcely ever less than ten in the most depressed years. In 1912, the Commissioner at Hope Town, Abaco, reported that in his district alone three schooners, six sloops and no less than 140 dinghies had been built and launched in the past year. The 32 Abaconian schooners in the sponging business had procured sponge worth £20,000, with the most successful making almost £1,000.

A typical sponge schooner displaced no more than 65 tons, but the 'lumber draggers' were of 150 tons and upwards. The three-masted *Abaco Bahamas*, built by Jenkins Roberts of Hope Town in 1922, was 150 feet (45 m) long with 110-foot (33-m) masts and displaced 484 tons – the largest ever built in Abaco. But this was exceeded by the four-masted *Marie J. Thompson* built at Harbour Island by Edward Roberts and launched in the same year, which at 696 tons was the largest Bahamian-built schooner ever. The building of such leviathans, however, was a doomed enterprise that probably did more harm than good to the native industry. From the beginning, the much greater costs of construction tended to take ownership out of the hands of the local builders. But this process was accelerated when wholesale lumber prices and freight charges tumbled with the onset of the Great Depression, making carriage by even the largest sailing ships impractical. With the total collapse of the sponge-fishing industry in 1938, the great days of not just the Bahamian schooner but the entire native shipbuilding industry were suddenly over.

Schooners, though, continued to be used for inter-island travel and supply until long after motor vessels were available. The first regular Family Island MAIL BOAT was said to have been a small two-masted schooner called the *Dart* which started sailing between Nassau and Harbour Island in 1870. The last sailing mailboat was Captain Sherwin Archer's former sponge schooner *Arena*, which served Abaco until the 1950s. At that time, however, most of the mail boats – such as the famous *Stede Bonnet, Richard Campbell, Noel Roberts* and *Ena K* – were still either dismasted and motorised former schooners, or custom-built motor boats with wooden hulls constructed largely with local materials in traditional ways.

BODYBUILDING

By the mid-twentieth century most of the boatbuilding activity had shifted to Nassau, and Abaco was virtually the last refuge of traditional methods – and even there most of the great boatbuilders had died, retired, or been forced to take up other occupations, such as house construction or merely servicing foreign yachts. As Winer Malone, the last builder of traditional Abaco dinghies in Hope Town, complained in 1995, what had once been the poor man's work-boat, which of necessity he built himself, was now a rich man's plaything. In the 1930s a 10-foot (3-m) Abaco dinghy could command no more than $25 (or its equivalent in supplies) in Nassau. Malone sold his first boat to an American in 1950 for $65. By 1982 the price was $1,000, and in 1995 $350 a foot for the bare boat and $600 for the mast, boom and rudder – and that was without the cost of the sail and sailing hardware. The sole saving factor was that those who no longer needed a boat to make a living and had other far more lucrative livelihoods were being attracted to competing in the 'traditional work-boat' regattas that started in Exuma in 1954, and had spread back to New Providence and ten other islands by the 1980s.

The cost of a truly competitive vessel had risen almost to the point where the saying of J. P. Morgan about his personal yacht almost applied: 'If you have to ask how much it costs, you cannot afford it.' Yet those who flock to Bahamian regattas today can still echo the nostalgic enthusiasm of American yachtsman-photographer Art Paine in 1994 about the Family Island sailors and their boats: 'They had three attributes which were and are pertinent. Firstly they were incredibly good seamen. Secondly, living a peaceful but challenging life in harmony with their world and untouched by outside contact, they were interesting and gregarious by nature. Finally, and significantly, the vast majority had an extremely artistic bent. … What was unique to the Bahamian craftsmen was a seemingly inborn sense of form.'

Further reading: *The Boat-Building Industry of The Bahamas*, Nassau, Department of Archives, 1981; A. Paine, 'Boats of the Shallow Sea', *The Boatman*, April 1994, 15-25; S. Dodge, 'Boat Building in Abaco', in *Abaco: The History of an Out Island and Its Cays*, 2nd ed., Decatur, Ill., White Sound Press, 1995, app., 208-36;

BODYBUILDING

It is significant that, even more than with other organised sports, bodybuilding grew in popularity, sophistication and success along with the emergence (even, one might say, the muscle-flexing) of The Bahamas as an independent nation. With the related activities of weightlifting, powerlifting and general fitness training, bodybuilding also appears to be avoiding the decline being suffered by many sports in a nation now more dedicated to watching sport on cable TV than actually participating.

Veteran Bahamian bodybuilders attribute the original impetus to their sport to its promotion by the Americans Charles Atlas and Ben Wieder from the 1930s to the 1950s. Almost uniquely among sports, bodybuilding's appeal crossed most, if not all, lines of class and ethnicity. Amateur enthusiasts, including Calvin Pinder, Hubert Wong and Cyril Smith, instituted a Mr Bahamas Contest long before they had a formal organisation, Smith becoming the first title-holder as early as 1950. So quickly and strongly did the sport develop, that when Wong, Richard Demeritte and Edison Deleveaux founded The Bahamas Body Building Association (BBBA) in 1962 it was immediately granted membership by the chief international organisation (IFBB), and within a further three years the black Bahamian Kingsley Poitier had won the IFBB's Mr World Contest and the equally statuesque white Bahamian Glen Wells was placed third in the tall class of the IFBB's even more prestigious Mr Universe competition.

Bahamian bodybuilding gained a boost when the Progressive Liberal Party came to power in 1967 under the leadership of a former weightlifter, Lynden Pindling, and especially when one of bodybuilding's chief local aficionados, Dr Norman Gay, became Minister of Health. However, almost all Bahamian bodybuilders, not necessarily through choice, remained self-supporting amateurs. Sponsorship was intermittent and unreliable and, though reaching championship form demanded almost

Bodybuilding: former Mr Universe (1975) and stage and screen star, Tony Carroll, with Eartha Kitt

full-time work in the gym, there was little prospect of making a career in bodybuilding, especially from a base in The Bahamas. The one notable exception almost proved the rule. Originating (like 'Sweet Richard' DEAN) from Long Island, Anthony (Tony) Carroll showed tremendous potential but decided that he had to migrate to the United States to make bodybuilding a career, along with acting. In bodybuilding his rise was meteoric: successively he won the Mr New York, Mr America, Mr World titles and, climatically in 1975, that of Mr Universe. At the same time, Carroll deliberately courted publicity and took every opportunity to find a place on the acting stage.

On the posing podium, Tony Carroll's virtual nemesis was the phenomenal Arnold Schwarzenegger, who burst on the scene in the late 1970s. Yet, though overshadowed as a competitor, Carroll was able successfully to ride in Arnold's wake once the Austrian followed the brilliant success of the film *Pumping Iron* (1977) to become the megastar of a whole new genre of action movies. For his part, Carroll, zealously honing his natural (and typically Bahamian) acting talent and related skills, was in demand for almost every film, TV show or theatre performance that needed a character who combined a spectacular physique and convincing skills in 'stunt fighting, fencing, broadsword fighting, wrestling, taekwondo, horseback riding, tossing the caber and dancing' with more than average acting ability. Although the statement of one admirer that 'Carroll with the exception of Academy Award-winning actor Sidney POITIER, is perhaps the most world famous Bahamian of all time', is overblown, Carroll's list of cinema, TV and theatre credits is hugely impressive, and an infinitely greater achievement than had he remained simply a bodybuilder based in The Bahamas.

Back in The Bahamas, however, the sport continued to grow in popularity, while making adjustments to fresh interests and demands. In the 1970s women began to take up bodybuilding, and Donna Dorsett became the first female champion of The Bahamas in 1977. In 1980, the BBBA expanded its scope and became The Bahamas Bodybuilding, Weightlifting and Powerlifting Federation (BBWPF). Focusing more on regional than on the increasingly confusing world competition scene, Bahamian lifters won several medals in the Central American and Caribbean Championships, including a women's gold medal by Della Thomas. For the first time a Bahamian bodybuilder, Charles Kemp, won the overall men's competition in the CAC Championships in El Salvador in 1998, receiving an IFBB professional card – also a first for a Bahamas-based competitor This success was almost repeated when Joel Stubbs won the CAC gold medal in the heavyweight division in 2003 – going on to be voted Bahamian Sportsman of the Year.

In 2000 the BBWPF split into two 'separate but cooperative' federations, The Bahamas Bodybuilding and Fitness Federation (BBFF) and The Bahamas Powerlifting Federation (BPF).

BOND, James Two James Bonds, the one fictitious, the other real, have bonds both with each other and The Bahamas. In 1952, when writing his first potboiler spy novel *Casino Royale* in Jamaica, the English author Ian Fleming cast around for a name to give his hero. What he sought was a plain, even dull, two-syllable name that was not already well known. His eye lit on a book on his coffee-table, *Birds of the West Indies* by James Bond, and the character who was to become the world's best-known fictional spy was christened.

The real James Bond, of whom Fleming had never previously heard (and guessed was long dead) was in fact an American ornithologist well known in his field, though not outside it. Born in 1900, he had published his book in 1936, and already spent a quarter-century researching the birds of the Caribbean and The Bahamas as a curator at the Academy of Natural Sciences in Philadelphia. Dr James Bond met with Fleming only once, at the author's Jamaican villa Goldeneye (fittingly, the name of a bird), in 1963. The handsome but decidedly un-spy-like birdman introduced himself in the words made immortal by Sean Connery: 'My name's Bond. James Bond.' Fleming was amused to hear that the success of his own bestsellers had given a spin-off boost to the sales of Bond's solitary and very different book, and asked as recompense that if ever the ornithologist discovered a new species of bird he might name it after him (which did not happen).

Thunderball Grotto

BOSTWICK, Hon. Janet G

Over the course of 40 years, several of the 20 James Bond films were filmed largely in The Bahamas, beginning with the third film, *Thunderball* in 1965. Cashing in on the perennial success and glamour of the Fleming novels, a number of tour companies promote their Bahamian offerings with such slogans as 'Share the James Bond experience.' More directly, some operations promise dives in the very 'Thunderball Grotto' used in filming. Stretching credibility, though, these are located in two widely separated places: at Staniel Cay in the Exumas (probably the authentic site), and off Rose Island – conveniently much closer to Nassau.

Though he sold the film rights to all of his James Bond novels, Ian Fleming was not to see any of them filmed on location in The Bahamas. He died of a heart attack the year before the filming of *Thunderball.* Ironically, the real James Bond outlived Fleming by 25 years, often visiting The Bahamas and dining out on his vicarious connection with Agent 007. His book, still in print, remained the only work even partially covering The Bahamas until the publication of P. G. C. Brudenell-Bruce's *Birds of New Providence and the Bahama Islands* (1975) – which can now be supplemented by Peter Evans's *Birds of the Eastern Caribbean* (London, Macmillan Caribbean, 2004).

BOSTWICK, Hon. Janet G. A tireless and fiery champion of women's and children's rights and family values, Janet Bostwick was the first woman elected to the House of Assembly and the second female Cabinet Minister, holding many important posts in the FREE NATIONAL MOVEMENT government after 1992. These included appointments as the first female Attorney General and Minister of Foreign Affairs.

Born Janet Musgrove in 1939, she was educated at GOVERNMENT HIGH SCHOOL, where she was head girl at the same time that her future husband, Henry Bostwick (in due course President of the Senate), was head boy. Called to The Bahamas Bar in 1971, Janet Bostwick had a distinguished career as prosecutor, defence attorney and expert in family law, and served as President of The Bahamas Bar Association from 1980 to 1982.

Earlier an adherent of the PROGRESSIVE LIBERAL PARTY, Ms Bostwick made a strong but unsuccessful showing for The Bahamas Democratic Party in the 1977 election, being nominated instead for one of the four Opposition seats in the Senate. With the fading away of the BDP, she joined the FNM, winning the Yamacraw constituency for the party in the 1982 and in four subsequent elections, by increasingly wider margins. Serving as President of the FNM's Women's Association and of Caribbean Women for Democracy, Janet Bostwick was immediately drafted into Prime Minister Hubert INGRAHAM'S Cabinet once the FNM triumphed in August 1992.

Despite her array of other concerns in her successive roles as Minister of Social Services, National Insurance, Housing, Justice and Immigration, Attorney General and Minister of Foreign Affairs, Janet Bostwick is the driving force in the move to remove all sexual bias in the laws. She was a fervent advocate for Bahamian participation in the United Nations' Decade for Women, and Convention on the Rights of the Child. She and her husband Henry are the parents of four children.

BOXING Sometimes referred to by its supporters as 'the noble art of self-defence', boxing does indeed demand athletic skills that verge on the balletic, and produces popular heroes. Yet, at least in its prize-fighting form, it can also be regarded as a human blood sport, satisfying the demand of spectators for a form of legitimised violence and of promoters and gamblers to make money, with its combatants drawn mainly from the roughest and most financially desperate members of society. These contradictory factors help to explain both the emergence of boxing as a professional sport in The Bahamas in the mid-twentieth century, and its virtual collapse by the end of the century.

The origins of competitive boxing in The Bahamas can be traced to four more or less distinct sources. The earliest was the English tradition that pugilism was a way of promoting 'manly qualities': fitness, agility and physical toughness – as well as settling scores in a refereed context. Consequently, it was encouraged first among the soldiers of the army garrison (with rank more or less irrelevant within the ring) and was carried over into the British-influenced POLICE force by the beginning of the twentieth century. Probably the finest product of this tradition was Sergeant Roy Armbrister (a Bahamian in a force then largely West Indian), boxer and trainer as well as all-round sportsman and gentleman.

A second, more commercial influence emanated from the professional game in the northern United States, brought to Nassau by Bahamian returnees during the years of the Great Depression, most notably the former college athlete turned trainer and promoter, Charlie Major Sr. Probably the outstanding Bahamian pugilist of this period was the prizefighter George Edward McKinney, 'Rough House George', the peak of whose achievement was to defeat the self-styled Champion of Florida in 1938. During the same decade, rich American tourists and part-time

BOXING

residents of Bimini, especially Ernest Hemingway, were promoting local boxing as a tourist diversion, making that tiny island a boxing centre to rival Nassau. A fourth strand, and the least Bahamianised, was a spin-off from the huge expansion of tourism after mid-century, when professional boxing contests were occasionally staged by the largest, American-owned, casino-hotels, especially on PARADISE ISLAND, as an attraction for customers.

The confluence of these traditions explains the emergence of a remarkable galaxy of Bahamian boxers between the 1950s and 1980s. Even during World War Two, when Bahamian boxers performed against American, British and Canadian servicemen in amateur contests, interest was shown by American promoters in the potential of local talent. In the immediate post-war years local championship matches were held, in which such boxers as Roy Armbrister, Bert Perry, 'Boston Blackie' Miller, Stony Godet and Battling Douglas featured, and Florida and New York-based trainer/manager/promoters, such as the Dundee brothers, began to make overtures to professionalise and widen the sport. In this phase, it was the Bimini boxers Yama Bahama, Gomeo Brennen and Bobo Reckley who made the most impact, of whom the first-named was the most able, popular and toughest, and the most quintessentially typical, of that era.

Born William Hohalis Butler in 1933, Yama Bahama was the youngest child of a poor Bimini mariner with a large family. From the age of six he was a notable schoolyard scrapper and at 12 began training in the local gym with two of his boxing brothers. Showing exceptional promise, he was invited to train in Miami Beach by manager George Lyon and (unlike his brothers) turned professional, fighting under his colourful new *nom de guerre*. Yama Bahama, a welterweight, later middleweight, fought his first pro contest in Miami Beach in November 1953, winning with an explosive technical knockout in the first round. Undefeated in his first 14 fights, Yama Bahama moved his base of operations to Detroit, Michigan, where he quickly became a favourite with fans for his aggressive style and pleasing personality. First appearing on US-wide TV in December 1955 as a fill-in, he gave such good value that he appeared many times thereafter. Yama Bahama reached his peak with victories over such stars as former world champion Kid Gavilan in 1958, and narrow points losses against former champion Juan Rodriguez and (in a non-title bout) the great Emile Griffith in 1960 and 1961; he progressed as high as seventh in the world middleweight rankings.

Despite suffering severe cuts (one from an accidental head-butt) in a savage replay loss to Rodriguez in May, 1962, Yama Bahama still ended his professional career with three victories, the last being against Harry Monroe in March 1963, appropriately in his home island of Bimini. In a career spanning just over ten years, Yama Bahama fought an almost incredible 102 professional bouts – an average of one every five weeks. Of these, he won no less than 82. Of his 20 defeats some were highly dubious points decisions, and he was cleanly knocked out only once in his entire career. He does not seem to have suffered too severely from all the battering taken, but his financial rewards never matched the efforts expended. He has spent his long retirement in his beloved Bimini, running a modest bar.

Of the Nassau-based Bahamian boxers, the two most outstanding were 'Baby Boy' Rolle and Oswald Ferguson, alias Elisha Obed. Rolle reached the peak of his brief career in a narrow points defeat over 15 rounds in challenging the brilliant John Conteh for the Commonwealth light heavyweight title at Nottingham, England in October 1973. All other achievements by Bahamian boxers, however, were surpassed by Elisha Obed when he became WBC world super welterweight champion by knocking out the Brazilian Miguel de Oliveira in the eleventh round of a 15-round title fight in November 1975. Obed

Boxing: cover of Bert Perry's autobiography

BRAYNEN, Sir Alvin O.

sucessfully defended his title twice, by knocking out the American Tony Gardiner in the second round in February 1976 and defeating the Ivorian Sea Robinson on points over 15 rounds less than three months later – before the German Eckehard Dagge ended his seven month reign with a tenth-round knockout in June 1976. Obed's career was effectively ended when he failed in a challenge to regain the world championship with a defeat by the Italian Romeo Matteoli in March 1978.

Although not quickly acknowledged, Bahamian boxing had already passed its zenith. Ironically the event which effectively sounded its death knell was one that is still misguidedly (and without conscious irony) lauded as a great Bahamian boxing occasion. This was the staging in Nassau on 11 December 1981 of the long overdue final professional fight of the greatest boxer of all time, Muhammed Ali. Grandiosely billed as 'the Drama in Bahama', with a high-class undercard, it turned out to be a sad anticlimax (and financial disaster) as the already brain-damaged Ali lumbered to a pathetic points loss over ten rounds against the Jamaican journeyman Trevor Berbick.

Further reading: B. Perry, *The Fight Goes On*, Nassau, 1995.

BRAYNEN, Sir Alvin O. (1904–1992) White political maverick, Speaker of the House of Assembly, and first Bahamian High Commissioner in London. Born (like Sir Roland SYMONETTE) in the predominantly white settlement of the Current, Eleuthera, Alvin Braynen was educated at local schools and first elected to the House of Assembly in 1939. Always seen as a politician of independent mind, he was chosen as Deputy Speaker under the old BAY STREET regime, first from 1949 to 1953, then (after five years as a Member of Executive Council) from 1963 to 1966, as The Bahamas became a self-governing colony.

A. R. Braynen in his role as Speaker, with historic Bahamian mace

Often chosen to be a member of government boards, but increasingly disenchanted by the directions taken by the Bay Street regime, Alvin Braynen became a key figure in settling the deadlock between the UNITED BAHAMIAN PARTY and the PROGRESSIVE LIBERAL PARTY in the 1967 election. Narrowly winning the second HARBOUR ISLAND seat as an Independent, he accepted the PLP's nomination to the neutral office of Speaker. This, with Labour candidate Randol FAWKES's acceptance of a Cabinet post, gave the PLP a majority of two and brought the government of Lynden PINDLING to power – representing the transition from white minority to black majority rule. Embittered by personal attacks, as Speaker between 1967 and 1972, Braynen noticeably inclined towards supporting the PLP government rather than the UBP Opposition.

The Bay Street diehards never forgave Alvin Braynen, but after his defeat by the UBP's Noel Roberts in north Eleuthera in the 1972 election the PLP government rewarded him with the new post of High Commissioner in London on the achievement of INDEPENDENCE in 1973. In this role, Braynen's hospitality and help to Bahamian students studying in Britain were legendary, though his perennial spirit of independence meant that he ran his office entirely in his own way, with minimal communication with his alleged superiors back in The Bahamas. Retiring in 1978, he lived the remaining 14 years of his life quietly in Nassau, being voted in 2000 one of 20 whites among the hundred most outstanding Bahamians of the twentieth century.

BRAZILETTO A tree (*Caesalpina vesicaria*) up to 20 feet (6 m) tall, with many branches, a spiny bark, leathery leaves, pods, and yellow flowers. Once common throughout the central and southern Bahamas, it was formerly much prized for producing a strong red dye and as a cabinet wood. Apart from AMBERGRIS, braziletto wood was the most valuable product of The Bahamas at the time of first settlement, commanding up to £12 a ton in 1650. A thanksgiving gift by the ELEUTHERIAN ADVENTURERS of 10 tons of braziletto wood was one of the earliest donations to Harvard College. So avidly was it sought out by the first settlers that despite an ordinance by the LORD PROPRIETORS in 1673 restricting its cutting, by 1725 Mark Catesby reported that it was already scarce. Becoming a negligible item of export, it lost commercial value entirely after the discovery of chemical dyes and the decline of cabinet craftsmanship. Today it has recovered somewhat and can be found in coppices and rocky areas in Inagua, Long Island, San Salvador, Cat Island, Exuma and Andros.

BRITISH COLONIAL HOTEL The oldest Bahamian hotel still in operation and the only large hotel in downtown NASSAU itself; it occupies (in its fourth mutation) the site of old Fort Nassau and the barracks of the British West India Regiment garrison.

The ten-acre site was sold by the government to H. M. Flagler's Florida East Coast Hotel Company shortly after the garrison left Nassau, and the original 200-room Colonial Hotel was ready for the winter season of 1899–1900. Built largely of wood, it was completely destroyed in Nassau's most spectacular FIRE in March 1922. Aware of the need to accommodate American tourists during the post-war boom, the government immediately repurchased the site and advanced a £270,000 loan to a subsidiary of the Munson Steamship Line of New York for a complete rebuilding. Allowed to import all materials duty free and to bring in as many foreign craftsmen and labourers as they needed, the contractors, almost incredibly, completed their work within six months. The restored and expanded hotel reopened in February 1923.

The New Colonial Hotel was described in glowing terms in Mary MOSELEY's 1926 *Bahamas Handbook*. A towering structure made of fireproof terracotta blocks in what was said to be Spanish colonial style, it was painted flamingo pink with trimmings of light green and indigo. Its interior decorations, cuisine, ornamental grounds, beach, tennis courts and nearby golf course made it the proud flagship of Bahamian tourism throughout the 1920s, and even during the years of the Great Depression until the onset of World War Two. In 1939 it was purchased by the newly resident Canadian-American tycoon, Sir Harry OAKES. The story that a roughly dressed Oakes bought the hotel in a fit of pique on being refused service is almost certainly apocryphal. More likely, in his usual canny and acquisitive way Oakes was snapping up at a bargain price an asset which was bound to appreciate once tourism revived after the war.

Now named the British Colonial, the hotel certainly did lead the revival of tourism after 1945, though Oakes was no longer alive to see his investment pay off. The most negative aspect of the hotel's operation was that it continued to practise racial discrimination (at its notorious worst during the Munson regime) until pressured to change by the anti-discrimination resolution in the Assembly in 1956. The Oakes family eventually sold out and the 'BC' was operated for many years by the Sheraton Group. In the 1970s and 1980s it began to show signs of its age, and under the pressure of competition from more glitzy hotels on CABLE BEACH and PARADISE ISLAND, gradually faded. Its downtown location, however, was a priceless asset. Instead of being demolished and replaced by offices, shops and parking lots, it was bought by a Canadian group in the mid-1990s and after drastic renovations costing more than $50 million reopened as 'a world-class luxury hotel complex and financial centre', under the Hilton banner.

BRUCE, Peter Henry A fiery Prussian-born military engineer stationed in NASSAU from 1741 to 1745 who was the builder of Fort Montagu and provided an invaluable account of The Bahamas during the tumultuous period of the War of the Austrian Succession.

War had broken out with the Spanish over the question of Captain Jenkins' Ear two years before Bruce arrived in Nassau. The town had become a vital PRIVATEERING base but was poorly defended from assaults, especially on its eastern side. Bruce was given the task by Governor John Tinker of making Nassau 'the Gibraltar of the West' on a budget of £4,000 and almost no resources of men or materials.

Showing great ingenuity in cutting, transporting and using the native limestone (which he described as 'cutting like cheese but hardening like flint') Bruce transformed Fort Nassau into a formidable bastion, barracks and magazine and built Fort Montagu more or less from scratch. This squat miniature fortress still stands, complete with some of its original cannons, though the last remnants of the far larger Fort Nassau were swallowed up in the building of the British Colonial Hotel in 1899.

Though he was the first to describe The Bahamas as a health resort, Peter Henry Bruce found the heat and insects tiresome and had endless trouble with the inhabitants, especially the Governor and his cronies. Though slanted

The British Colonial Hilton, 2000

to his own advantage and somewhat sanitised, Bruce's account gives an impression of Nassau as a seething boom town, little different from piracy days. Its streets and taverns were crowded with privateers spending and quarrelling over the proceeds of the more than a hundred prize vessels brought in for adjudication in the local Vice Admiralty Court during the war. Bruce himself was involved in the share-outs, the accompanying disputes, and doubtless in the drunken carousing too. Virtually accusing the Governor, the Collector of Customs and other leading citizens of corruption and extortion, he was involved in brawls, challenged to a duel, and even went around for a time in fear of assassination.

Bruce was happy to leave Nassau as soon as his fortress work was completed at the beginning of 1745. Accompanying him was a profitable share of a prize cargo of quicksilver, dyewoods and cotton, half of which, to his chagrin, was captured by the French on his voyage back to England.

Further reading: P. H. Bruce, *Memoirs*, London, 1782, reissued as *Bahamian Interlude*, London, Culmer, 1949; Craton and Saunders, *Islanders*, i. 142-8

'BURMA ROAD' RIOTS, 1942
An unprecedented outbreak of labour violence with racial undertones that, while it led to only modest and palliative short-term changes, was seen retrospectively as the first manifestation of concerted action by a repressed black Bahamian underclass.

Interpreted by some commentators as a partially successful 'revolution of rising expectations', the riots stemmed from dissatisfaction with the terms of what workers hoped would be a wartime surge of employment, ending the long purgatory of the Great Depression. After the United States had joined in World War Two and NEW PROVIDENCE was designated a major Allied air base, an American construction company was employed to upgrade OAKES Field near town and build a larger airfield in the western part of the island (later named after Governor WINDSOR), using 2,500 local black labourers.

Hoping to receive something like the normal black labourers' wages in the southern US (then $3 or 12 shillings a day), the Bahamian workers were dismayed to find that the government had agreed to peg wages at the 1936 minimum wage rate of 4 shillings a day (for semi-skilled as well as unskilled workers, and with nothing at all if rain stopped work). White Bahamian overseers were also appointed on the misguided notion that they would best know how to handle their black compatriots. In the last week of May 1942 a hastily and inexpertly formed Federation of Labour held a public meeting and drafted a petition for a minimum wage of 8 shillings a day. When the Labour Officer, John Hughes, and Acting Governor Leslie Heape stalled for time (Governor Windsor being away in Washington), a nucleus of workers went on strike on 31 May – led by a fiery orator from Andros (though born in the Turks Islands) called Leonard Storr (alias Green).

The ostensible labour spokesmen, Charles Rhodriguez and A. F. ADDERLEY, and three non-white Assembly-men (Bert Cambridge, Dr C. R. Walker and Walton Young) counselled patience and thought they had persuaded a majority to continue work. But the situation rapidly deteriorated after the 'CONCHY JOE' police officer Edward Sears attempted to disperse a crowd of vocal strikers by force, including firing his revolver in the air. In the melée, the two supervisors were chased away and the car of one of them was overturned. Though without obvious leaders, a crowd rapidly swelling to 2,000 marched through Over-the-Hill Nassau to Rawson Square on the morning of Monday 1 June, carrying sticks and machetes and clamouring for immediate redress.

The Acting Governor took refuge in GOVERNMENT HOUSE, delegating the expatriate Attorney General Eric Hallinan to mollify the crowd. Hallinan's speech (as far as it was heard or understood) was a disaster, and the angry but peaceable assembly quickly turned into a riot and looting spree. This allegedly began when hotheads pelted bottles from a parked Coca Cola truck through Bay Street shop windows. But the targets, both then and later, were not entirely indiscriminate, being concentrated on the property of such white BAY STREET merchants as Asa PRITCHARD, Stafford SANDS, the Coles, and the Bethell brothers. It was probably at this time that the splendidly named Napoleon McPhee burned the Union Jack and made his famous statement: 'I willing to fight under the flag. I willing to die under the flag. But I ain't gwine starve under the flag.'

Bay Street was cleared by armed police and a detachment of the Cameron Highlanders in the garrison, but this was only the beginning of three days of disorder, centred on GRANT'S TOWN. A curfew was declared and armed soldiers and policemen patrolled the streets. But this did not prevent the looting of white owned bars – the stock of which further inflamed the more aggressive elements in the crowd. Violent confrontations included an attack on the Southern Police Station and other government buildings and the burning of several government vehicles. In all, five rioters and curfew breakers were killed and some 45 persons injured on both sides, including four policemen.

The Duke of Windsor returned hastily from Washington (preceded by 75 US marines disguised as military policemen) and the same night appealed on the radio for calm, promising concessions and an official inquiry as soon as the rioting ended and the workers returned to their jobs. True to his word, the Duke negotiated a 25 per cent pay increase for unskilled workers (to 5 shillings a day) and higher pay for the skilled. The workers were also conceded pay for rain-spoiled days, better transportation and medical facilities, and free midday meals. By 4 June more than half the workers were back at their jobs, and by 8 June when the curfew was lifted, work was almost back to normal.

The general election on 19–21 June, which the authorities feared might be explosive, proved almost an anticlimax, with the composition of the Assembly virtually unchanged. The riots and political events in general were almost overshadowed by the great Bay Street fire at the end of the month. Though 80 persons were brought to trial and 67 convicted for the rioting, sentences were judiciously moderate, except for the eight years of hard labour inflicted on Leonard Storr and another rioter who, like Storr, already had a lengthy criminal record.

As promised by the Duke of Windsor, an official inquiry was held over the following months, under the chairmanship of Sir Alison Russell, former Chief Justice of Tanganyika. The Russell Report candidly described the dire social and economic conditions that were the background, if not the cause, of the riots, and suggested a wide range of solutions, almost none of them immediately practical. For its part, an unrepentant legislature set up its own inquiry (chaired by Stafford Sands), which was almost completely self-excusing. At the same time, the legislature recompensed all those who had suffered damage and losses in the riots.

Neither the Russell nor Sands Report commented on the racial tensions that everyone privately acknowledged were an integral component of socio-economic discord. However, both reports did propose the implementation of the minimal labour legislation which had already been recommended in a report made by Major George Orde-Brown four years earlier. This was accomplished in March 1943. Largely because of the distractions of the war and the substantial improvement in employment conditions both before and immediately after 1945, further advances for Bahamian workers and for black Bahamians in general had to wait for other favourable trends and triggering events in the 1950s and 1960s.

The 1942 outbreak got its popular name after the nickname given to the new road joining the two New Providence airfields (itself derived from the wartime lifeline constructed between Burma and China). Its significance as an example of black proletarian tactics, and an indication of the essentially Bahamian way of seeking change without violence, was encapsulated in the goombay calypso said to have been sung by the rioters: 'Burma Road declare war on the Conchy Joe. Do' Nigger, don't lick nobody, don't lick nobody.'

Further reading: G. Saunders, 'The Social History of the Bahamas, 1890–1953', unpublished PhD thesis, University of Waterloo, 1985, 420–46.

BUSH MEDICINE Often treated in guidebooks as if it were a kind of folk magic akin to OBEAH, Bahamian bush medicine derives in fact from times before modern pharmaceuticals were available or could be afforded. The Bahamas has always been especially rich in its range of bush medicines, and their usage persists to the present day. Not only do many Bahamians still attest to their proven efficacy, but at least two influences sustain their use. 'New Age' trends include, perhaps paradoxically, the search for alternative traditional remedies, while the traditionally religious find biblical endorsement: 'The Most High hath created medicines out of the earth and a wise man will not abhor them' (*Ecclesiaticus* 38: 4).

The ethnobotanist Laurel Richey (of Miami University, Ohio) has discovered no less than 163 plants that are, or have in the past, been used medicinally in CAT ISLAND alone, and 140 in LONG ISLAND – with 120 used in both islands. Though the bush medicines are often said to be a legacy from Africa, it is clearly only the generic custom and the search for local remedies that can have been brought by the African slaves, since the overwhelming majority of Bahamian medicinal plants are natives of the American, not African tropics. Equally clearly, trial and error – by AMERINDIANS as well as later newcomers – must have played an important part in sorting out the poisonous plants (for example, oleander, datura, euphorba and croton) from the obviously and the possibly efficacious, with the specialists, not unlike today's GPs, occupying a role and status somewhere between the shaman and the pharmacist – with an alleged or proven cure for almost every affliction.

Considering the honest claims made for many Bahamian bush medicines, it is perhaps surprising that so few have so far been scientifically tested. Only a handful stand out as having certain efficacy, or properties obviously worthy of scientific study. LIGNUM VITAE (the Bahamian national tree) has long-proven effectiveness against syphilis, while the aloe vera (actually a native of Africa) has proved invaluable for the treatment of burns, as well as having medicinal value. Much more recently, the Bahamian periwinkle (*Vinca rosea* or *alba*) has been found valuable

BUSH MEDICINE

in the treatment of leukaemia, and the Gale of Wind or Hurricane Weed (*Phyllanthus amarus*) has been shown to possess anti-viral qualities that may well be useful to combat both hepatitis and HIV.

Professional scepticism is one reason for the paucity of scientific research. Another is the fact that many Bahamian plants are claimed to have an almost implausible range of effective properties and are deployed in many different ways: as a tea or linctus, powder, poultice or salve, smoked as dried leaves, or even as a leaf worn in a shoe. For example, the bark of the lignum vitae is also used as a cathartic, the fruit as a vegetable and the flower as a laxative. The white juice from the bark is used against what is termed 'scaled head' and an infusion from bark, leaves or flowers employed as a tea or as a bath for 'body pains'. A list of some of the other most commonly used and versatile Bahamian bush remedies follows:

Bay Geranium (*Ambrosia hispida*) can be made into a soap and used to relieve itching skin. Recommended for indigestion and 'cleaning the lungs' and as a strong tea with lime and salt against colds.

Blue Flowers (*Valerianoides jamaicencis*) soothes and eases colic, gas and constipation in babies, and 'cools the blood' and soothes skin irritations in children.

Breadfruit (*Artocarpus altilis*) has leaves used for 'high blood' and, slightly crushed, bound on the forehead as a cure for headache.

Catnip, alias White Sage (*Salvia serotina*) is used for a tea for pregnant women; is given to children for worms; and is also regarded as beneficial in colds and influenza, as a nasal douche for sinus congestion, and to relieve itching skin.

Cerasee, or Serasee (*Mormodica charantia*) is so much a sovereign remedy that it is almost a generic term for all bush medicine. Besides being a skin soother, it is used to counter fever, influenza, congestion and cramps.

Gum Elemi, alias Gumbolimbo, Gamalamee, Kalalamee (*Bursera simarouba*) is perhaps the most versatile plant of all. The natural resin exuded from the tree can be used to staunch wounds. The sap can be used as an antidote for poison wood. The bark is a common topical remedy for skin sores, measles, sunburn, insect bites and rashes. Strips of bark are boiled in water and used as either a bath or tea to treat backaches, urinary tract infections, colds, influenza and fevers. Not least, it provides the chief ingredient of the aphrodisiac bush tea cocktail called colloquially '21-gun Salute' on Cat Island.

Jumbey (*Leucaena glauca*) is used as a cure for 'wind on the stomach', to 'quiet the nerves' and for treating heart conditions.

Life Leaf, alias Live-For-Ever or Ploppers (*Kalanchoe pinnata*) is mainly used for asthma or 'shortness of breath'. A tea made from the crushed leaves soaked in water overnight is drunk to treat heartburn or applied as an antibacterial to skin bruises or sores. Mashed and ground fresh leaves are used as a poultice for headaches, and their juice mixed with salt is regarded as a treatment both for bronchitis and ulcers.

Love Vine (*Cuscuta*), made into a tea, is the most commonly used Bahamian aphrodisiac – euphemistically referred to as 'strong back'. It is also used, perhaps contradictorily, as a soothing bath for itching and prickly heat.

Match-Me-If-You-Can (*Acalypha wilkesina*) has large leaves which are slightly crushed, applied to parts affected by rheumatic pain and bound firmly in place. It is also worn in the sole of a shoe to cure a cold.

Pigeon Plum, alias Stoppers (*Cocoloba*) is used to stop 'free bowels'.

Pound-Cake Bush (*Parthenium hysterophorus*) is used to combat 'weakness' and is also used for coughs and as a wash for skin sores. The flowers are sometimes parched and sprinkled on skin sores. It is also made into a tea for diabetics.

Shepherd's Needle (*Bidens pilosa*) leaves and flowers are steeped and used against prickly heat, for 'cooling the blood', to relieve 'sick stomach', and given daily for nine days to combat worms in children.

Breadfruit

Spotted Basil, alias Basily is used locally to treat asthma, bronchitis, chest colds and skin rashes; in recent years it has become a main ingredient in several commercial preparations for the treatment of intestinal worms and parasites. In 1998, researchers validated the herb's efficacy as an anti-inflammatory, and another research group attested its effectiveness against ulcers and in the treatment of diarrhoea.

White Bells, alias Angel's Trumpet (datura) is poisonous, but its dried leaves and flowers have customarily been smoked in a clay pipe to protect against asthma and influenza.

White Elder *(Sambucus intermedia)* is one of the most popular medicinal plants, applied as a bath during sieges of chicken pox and used as a tea to reduce any kind of fever.

Further reading: L. Higgs, *Bush Medicine in the Bahamas*, Nassau, 1959; J. O. Scott, 'The Role of Herbalists in Health Maintenance on the Biminis, Bahamas', unpublished MA thesis, Florida Atlantic University, 1980; S. A. McLure, 'Bush Medicine of Andros Island, Bahamas', unpublished MA thesis, Miami University, Oxford, Ohio, 1981; L. R. Randolph, 'An Ethnobiological Investigation of Andros Island, Bahamas', unpublished PhD thesis, Miami University, Oxford, Ohio, 1994; L. R. Richey, unpublished PhD thesis on ethnobotanical research on bush medicine in Cat Island and Long Island, Bahamas, Miami University, Oxford, Ohio, 2002.

BUTLER, Hon. Sir Milo Boughton (1906–1979)
Fearless champion of the black Bahamian majority and first Bahamian Governor-General.

Descended from an African slave named Glasgow who took the surname of his planter-owner George Butler, Milo Butler himself was named after his great grandfather, a peasant farmer of Bannerman Town, Eleuthera in the years immediately after slavery ended. Born in Nassau, the third of ten children, young Milo spent some of his earliest years living with his grandfather on impoverished and isolated RUM CAY, returning to the capital as a teenager and attending the Boys Central School up to the age of fifteen.

Milo Butler always claimed that he learned habits of industry and enterprise from his father, George Raleigh Butler (1885–1921), but his political commitment from his even more remarkable mother, Frances Manester Butler (née Thompson, 1889–1955). On the early death of her husband (with the last child yet unborn), the intrepid mother took her family to south Florida, where she toiled as a domestic while imbibing progressive ideas as a member of the women's auxiliary branch of the GARVEYITE movement. 'Cousin Fanny' as she was then widely known, ensured that Milo and the other children were well educated, but also insisted that they work hard after school to help support each other. For his part, Milo worked at menial jobs in hotels and restaurants and selling goods from door to door.

As US immigration restrictions tightened, the family returned to Nassau in 1927, and Milo, the sole surviving son, became their chief support. In 1928 he married Caroline Wilson, who, besides bearing him ten children (including seven sons), helped her husband in his fight to counter the effects of the Great Depression and the economic grip which the merchants of BAY STREET held on the black majority. The couple started with a small grocery store, for which Caroline baked bread and other cooked foods and served behind the counter, while Milo sold fish, fruit and vegetables on the street, saving enough money to buy a car, which he drove as a taxi.

As if the struggle for a livelihood were not enough, both Milo and his mother became increasingly involved in politics and social welfare. 'Mother Butler' as she affectionately became called, was the chief founder and sustainer of the Mothers' Club on East Street, Nassau, which provided food, clothing and basic furniture for the most desperately needy, and in due course help for black Bahamians to further their education abroad. Milo moved gradually into politics, first as a lieutenant for A. F. ADDERLEY, MHA for Nassau's Western District, and then, when his chief was elevated to the Legislative Council in 1937, as a contestant for the vacated seat against Bay Street's nominee, Sir Harry OAKES.

This move proved premature. Thanks to the financial clout of Oakes and his backers, Milo Butler was heavily

Sir Milo Butler

defeated. However, when Oakes himself was appointed to the Legislative Council in 1939 Butler won the by-election, and went on to represent the Western District for a decade. During this time, while gradually building up his grocery business against the odds, he gained a reputation as a fiery and fearless champion of the ordinary people – particularly at the time of the 'BURMA ROAD' RIOTS (1942). Bay Street's tactics, which included cutting off Butler's credit at the bank, led to his electoral defeat in 1949, as well as redoubling his populist zeal.

Milo Butler was an early recruit to the PROGRESSIVE LIBERAL PARTY after its formation in 1953, representing the 'black power' wing which came to dominate the party in the 1960s. A physically massive figure with a stentorian voice and preacherly style, Butler was one of the 'Magnificent Six' PLP victors in 1956, and the most prominent and outspoken participant in countless demonstrations – most notably the events of 'BLACK TUESDAY' (27 April 1965). When the PLP came to power in January 1967, Milo Butler was inevitably one of Premier PINDLING's Ministers, successively holding the portfolios of Health and Welfare, Labour, and Agriculture and Fisheries.

Though remaining an idol of the black masses, Milo Butler proved less of a force in office than in Opposition. Moreover, as he aged and began to suffer from heart trouble, he grew physically slimmer and politically more mellow. Resigning his parliamentary seat in 1972 on the eve of INDEPENDENCE, he was the first unequivocally black Bahamian to receive a knighthood, and an immensely popular selection to become effectively the first Governor-General on the achievement of Bahamian Independence – a role which he fulfilled with impeccable dignity until his death on 22 January 1979.

As Hon. Paul Adderley said in his eulogy at the inauguration of the Butler Heritage Foundation (celebrating 'Mother Butler' as well as Sir Milo) in 1996: 'Sir Milo's legacy is to be found in his commitment to the black people of The Bahamas. … His cause was total, complete, unequivocal certain and sure equal treatment for black people, in politics, in business and the social order . . .the inequalities of the legacies of slavery. … He swam against the moderate tide of the partially comfortable black middle class and became the "prophet of black rage". Yet he confronted white supremacy at the institutional level, never the personal, and sought to put a human face on a people who had been devalued and dehumanised for generations.' One of his most significant statements, which could stand as his epitaph, was: 'I do not hate the white man. I hate his ways.'

BUTLIN, Sir 'Billy' (1899–1980) Self-made British millionaire and pioneer of seaside holiday camps in the 1930s, whose attempt to extend his operations to The Bahamas just after World War Two was a good idea years ahead of its time, failing because of factors beyond his control.

Born in South Africa the son of a factory worker, the young Billy Butlin had only a sketchy education and no steady job, working mainly as a circus roustabout. As plausible as he was inventive and with a genius for advertising, he scraped together the finances to open his first holiday camp at Skegness in 1936. His idea of a large, self-contained village of wooden chalets, offering all-inclusive family holidays at a budget price (with decent food and a non-stop round of organised sports and entertainment and an almost Teutonic degree of regimentation), immediately caught on and actually reached its peak of success in the austerity years following World War Two.

By that time the ever-restless Butlin had persuaded backers to join him in applying the same formula to tap the post-war American tourist market in the British colonial base of The Bahamas. In 1948 he obtained a lease on 20,000 acres at the western end of GRAND BAHAMA and set about building a Vacation Village with 500 rooms to accommodate 1,000 holiday-makers, at an all-inclusive cost of $99 per week.

Unexpected snags occurred from the start. A fervent patriot, Butlin was determined to employ a British construction firm and British materials. But a long dock strike in Britain delayed the shipment of materials, and the chosen construction firm found itself incapable of adjusting to the climate and finding sufficiently skilled and hard-working local labourers. The savage devaluation of the pound in 1949 was another unanticipated setback. Even more critical was the fact that the BAY STREET oligarchs showed little support for the brash Britisher when they saw how little there was in the project for themselves.

Butlin's Vacation Village opened for business in December 1950, but with only half the buildings constructed and with the vital airstrip barely half completed. Cost over-runs made Butlin's creditors first nervous then clamorous. Despite the village having attracted 15,000 vacationers in its initial season, an exasperated Butlin decided to cut his losses and closed down the operation within a year. For the rest of his life, as he grew ever richer and more acclaimed in Britain, Sir Billy Butlin (he was knighted in 1965) remained bitter about his Bahamian venture.

What added to Butlin's rancour was the way that his pioneer planting bore profitable fruit for subsequent entrepreneurs. The concept of combining hotel operations with the sale of crown-leased land achieved its apotheosis in the development of FREEPORT under Wallace Groves in the central parts of the same island. Others made at least a transient success of Butlin's own West End enterprise – most notably the Texas-based Jack Tar hotel chain, which added what was said to be the largest swimming pool in the world, an 18-hole golf-course and a boat marina, and persuaded The Bahamas government to provide a fully equipped airport, opened by Governor Stapledon in 1963. The Jack Tar complex was closed down and demolished in the 1990s, but in 2002 was said to have risen once more 'like a phoenix' as the even smarter Old Bahama Bay Resort and Marina, only to be destroyed again in 2004 by hurricanes Frances and Jeanne.

Such upscaling (to the point when a week's all-inclusive holiday can easily cost $2,000 per person) is a feature of the development of Bahamian tourism over the last half-century. In more general terms, however, Billy Butlin can be credited with pioneering both the gaudily advertised and packaged all-inclusive holiday in an exotic destination, and the type of mass holiday camp experience, with excellent food and non-stop activities and entertainment epitomised, in The Bahamas as elsewhere throughout the world, by CLUB MEDITERRANÉE.

Further reading: B. Butlin, *The Billy Butlin Story*, London, Chrysalis Press, 1982.

The Jack Tar complex

CABLE BEACH The 2-mile strip starting 2 miles (3 km) west of downtown NASSAU; fringing the most beautiful beach on NEW PROVIDENCE it contains most of the island's finest hotels and many of its premium condominiums.

Named for being the place where the new telegraph cable from Florida came ashore in 1892, the area was not thought to be anything special before the era of tourism – merely a stretch of West Bay Street that had marginal value as swampy and rocky farmland for growing pineapples and sisal. Its potential was first visualised in the 1930s by the real estate tycoon Harold CHRISTIE and his chief client Sir Harry OAKES, who purchased most of the land from the sea side, past the parallel Prospect Ridge as far as the picturesque Lake Cunningham. Oakes built mansions at each end of his domain – in one of which, Westbourne, he was famously found dead in July 1943. With BAY STREET associates, Oakes also created the Nassau Country Club, the island's first 18-hole golf course, and its first (and so far only) race track, called Hobby Horse Hall.

The coming of wealthy part-time residents and mass tourism after World War Two transformed Cable Beach within two decades. Beach-front land that had cost a few hundred dollars an acre in the 1920s soon sold for as much per foot of frontage. The original buildings, including Westbourne and the Country Club, gave way to high-rise condos and large ultra-modern hotels – many of the first rich homeowners rebuilding even more grandly on Prospect Ridge. A second wave of even larger and more luxurious hotels followed in the 1970s and 1980s, culminating in the neon-lighted, 850-room Carnival's Crystal Palace Resort and Casino in 1990. By 2000 the nine almost contiguous hotels on Cable Beach, with their combined total of 2,847 rooms, splendid recreation facilities, restaurants, de luxe shopping arcades, and straw-market, formed an almost self-contained resort complex, vying with PARADISE ISLAND and Freeport, GRAND BAHAMA, to be the busiest and most popular tourist destination in The Bahamas. It has also become one of the favourite places for Bahamians themselves to hold weddings and other functions.

CARMAN, BLISS (1861–1929) A Canadian minor poet whose enthusiasm for The Bahamas made him in effect an early promoter of Bahamian tourism. One of the first 'snowbird' refugees from the northern winter, Bliss Carman visited The Bahamas for the first time in January 1899 at the age of 38. The impact of the warmth, light and colours of the islands was similar to that upon the great American artist Winslow HOMER, who, coincidentally, was making the second of his two visits at the very same

Cable Beach hotels

time. While Homer was painting his brilliant watercolours, Carman was inspired to rhapsodise in verse, publishing a half dozen 'Bahaman' pieces on his return to North America, in a slim volume called *A Winter Holiday*.

Carman's poems vividly contrast cold, grey New York, from which he sailed, and the stormy grey Atlantic, with the brilliant waters first seen off ABACO:

> *Cobalt, gobelin, and azure,*
> *   turquoise, sapphire, indigo,*
>
> *Changing from the spectral bluish*
> *   of a shadow upon snow*
>
> *To the deep of canton china,*
> *   one unfathomable glow.*

Nassau, reached after five days from New York (now it takes two hours) was even more magical:

> *Not, my friend, since we were children,*
> *   and all wonder-tales were true,*
> *Jason, Hengest, Hiawatha,*
> *   fairy prince or pirate crew,*
> *Was there ever such a landing*
> *   in a country strange and new.*
>
> *Up the harbour where there gathered,*
> *   fought and revelled many a year,*
> *Swarthy Spaniard, lost Lucayan,*
> *   Loyalist, and Buccaneer,*
> *'Once upon a time' was now,*
> *   and 'far across the sea' was here.*

Though Carman's description of The Bahamas is superficial, somewhat sentimental, and now more than a century old, it does convey something of the magic still felt by first visitors from the north, as well as conjuring up nostalgia for an ideal past with which Bahamians can empathise:

> *This is Bay Street, broad and low-built,*
> *   basking in its quiet trade;*
> *Here the sponging fleet is anchored;*
> *   here shell trinkets are displayed;*
> *Here the cable news is posted daily;*
> *   here the market's made,*
>
> *With its oranges from Andros,*
> *   heaps of yam and tamarind,*
> *Red-juiced shadducks from the Current,*
> *   ripened in the long trade-wind,*
> *Gaudy fish from their sea-gardens,*
> *   yellow-tailed and azure finned.*

> *Here a group of diving boys*
> *   in bronze and ivory, bright and slim,*
> *Sparkling copper in the high noon,*
> *   dripping loin-cloth, polished limb,*
> *Poised a moment and then plunged*
> *   in that deep daylight green and dim.*
>
>   ('Bahaman')

CARMICHAEL VILLAGE First and chief of the settlements for LIBERATED AFRICANS in the interior of New Providence, founded in 1825 and developed during the tenure of Governor Sir James Carmichael SMYTH – after whom it was named.

By the 1820s, so many Africans liberated from illegal foreign slave-ships had been landed in Nassau that they were becoming an embarrassment to Bahamian slave-holders and the government alike. A plan was put forward to locate them away from town, and 400 acres of trackless bush 6 miles (9.5 km) south-west of Nassau were set aside for this purpose. Placed under a Superintendent and at first called Headquarters, the area was treated almost like a military cantonment. The land was geometrically divided into 40 10-acre strips, each of which was allocated to a family head, who was expected to pay ten dollars when he could afford it. Seeds and tools were allotted to each family, who had to clear and plant their land and construct their own houses.

From his first visit in 1830 Governor Smyth wrote optimistically about the settlement. The Africans were generally industrious, and entirely on their own had cut a 3-mile (5-km) road to connect with that running south from Nassau. All they needed to become fully integrated into civilised society, thought Smyth, was Christianity and education. Accordingly, he had a church and schoolhouse built, ordering compulsory attendance at both.

Within a very short time the village, renamed Carmichael, was the home of almost 800 people. But this apparent success was in fact one of the causes of serious friction. The allocated land was insufficient to sustain the numbers living on it, forcing the settlers to farm over a wider area. This brought them into conflict with white landowners. Also, as a home for black freedmen, Carmichael became a refuge for runaway slaves, which led to confrontations when the white owners came into the settlement armed to recover them. Governor Smyth took the side of the Liberated Africans against such incursions by the whites, but the independent spirit of the settlers made them ever more resistant to dictation by the authorities about the way they lived, worked and worshipped.

CARSTAIRS, Marion 'Joe'

The Carmichael settlement almost inevitably faded once slavery ended. Quite apart from the difficulties of farming the rocky soil, the Liberated Africans now had to compete with the newly freed slaves in marketing their produce and finding alternative employment. Nassau was close enough to tantalise but too far for easy daily access. Consequently, within a decade more than three-quarters of the population of Carmichael had drifted away into Nassau's satellite black villages of GRANT'S TOWN, BAIN TOWN and FOX HILL. As these settlements flourished (the last two in particular retaining their Liberated African character), Carmichael never attained the characteristics of a true village – even when compared with more distant ADELAIDE and GAMBIER.

Further reading: *Settlements in New Providence*, Nassau, Department of Archives, 1982; Craton and Saunders, *Islanders*, ii. 5–12.

CARSTAIRS, Marion 'Joe' (1900–1993) One of the most fascinating and eccentric of all expatriates living in The Bahamas, 'Joe' Carstairs was a male-oriented lesbian known as 'the Queen of Whale Cay'. An American heiress to a Standard Oil fortune, she almost invariably dressed in slacks and beret and was never happier than when tinkering with racing cars and boats. A friend of Gar Wood and Malcolm Campbell, she set the women's world record for speedboats in 1928.

Joe Carstairs bought Whale Cay in the BERRY ISLANDS at the height of the Great Depression and constructed a mansion and almost feudal demesne with the help of up to 300 out-of-work Bahamians. Her regime was that of a benign despot. Living in state with a succession of beautiful lovers, she entertained a cavalcade of the rich and famous for forty years. She was a strict but generous employer, hosting an annual camp for black Bahamian children. However, her closest friend from the 1920s onwards was a 2-foot manikin, which she called Lord Tod Wadley.

Concerned by the increasing use of the Berry Islands for drug-running, Joe Carstairs sold Whale Cay in 1975 and moved to Miami. Over her last two decades she made more than 60 wills, restlessly shifting her wealth and possessions between her current favourites and her most faithful employees. As she aged, though, she treated Tod Wadley more and more as a real person, and her only real friend. When she died just short of her ninety-fourth birthday, Joe Carstairs and her marionette were cremated and buried together.

Further reading: K. Summerscale, *The Queen of Whale Cay: The Life of a Great American Eccentric*, London, Penguin Books, 1997.

CASCARILLA A shrub or small tree (*Croton eluteria*) up to 15 feet (4.5 m) tall, the bark of which has long been prized for its aromatic and medicinal qualities. Though alternatively named Eleuthera Bark, it is found most profusely in CROOKED ISLAND, ACKLINS and SAMANA CAY, from which it continues to be exported in significant quantities. As early as 1742, Peter Henry BRUCE reported that between 50 and 70 tons a year were exported to Europe, for use in the making of incense, tonics and laxatives, and for scenting tobacco. Later it became the eseential bitter flavouring component of the Italian liqueur Campari. The growing popularity of this aperitif, in the United States as well as Europe, ensures a high price for cascarilla bark and sustains what is one of the few legitimate money-making activities available to the subsistence farmers of the Crooked Island District. In 2001 The Bahamas exported 73,726 pounds (about 37 tons) of cascarilla bark, valued at $997,000.

CASH, His Excellency Sir Gerald (1917–2003) Non-white lawyer, independent politician, and second Governor-General of the independent Bahamas (1979–88).

Born to relatively prosperous parents, Gerald Cash was educated at GOVERNMENT HIGH SCHOOL, articled to the distinguished black lawyer A. F. Adderley from 1936 and called to The Bahamas bar in 1940. In 1943 he was junior counsel to Adderley in the unsuccessful prosecution of Alfred de Marigny for the murder of Sir Harry OAKES. Between 1945 and 1948 he studied at the Middle Temple in England, passed with honours, and was called to the English bar. Returning to Nassau with conventionally progressive ideas, he soon learned the hard lesson that in the prevailing political climate a prosperous law practice was not compatible with a radical stance, and he became convinced that in pursuing a political career the achievement of personal popularity was more effective than assuming an ardent populist ideology. On such principles he became one of the two Members of the House of Assembly for Nassau's Western District in 1949, and as an Independent retained his seat in 1956. Because of his obvious talents, charm, and value as a middleman, he was chosen as a Member of the Executive Council between 1958 and 1962.

Though he was a member of the moderately progressive Citizen's Committee in the 1950s, Gerald Cash did not follow the example of A. F. Adderley's lawyer son Paul and join the PROGRESSIVE LIBERAL PARTY in advance of the 1962 election, preferring to continue as an Independent. Though consistent with his reputation for sitting on the fence, this was probably a political miscalculation. Conceding his constituency to the PLP (won by Adderley and Milo BUTLER with a huge majority), he stood instead for Nassau City, but was swamped by the UNITED BAHAMIAN PARTY'S Stafford SANDS and R. W. Sawyer. Cash was out of active politics for seven years, becoming extremely successful in the practice of law. But his political skills and ambition could not be gainsaid, and he made an impressive comeback as an Independent Senator from 1969 – two years after the PLP came to power. Appointed Vice-President of the Senate in 1970, he was President from 1972 until the coming of INDEPENDENCE in 1973.

This was merely the prelude to the most distinguished stage of Gerald Cash's career. With Independence, Sir Milo Butler was made the first Bahamian Governor-General. But though much loved and respected, the PLP veteran had neither the suavity nor good health to sustain the post, and Cash seemed the ideal replacement. Standing in as Deputy on numerous occasions from 1973, he was made Acting Governor-General in 1976, knighted in 1977, and fully succeeded to the post on the death of Butler in 1979.

Sir Gerald Cash's nine-year tenure of the Governor-Generalship, though it ended with an alleged indiscretion, was distinguished by a congenial conviviality, scrupulous attention to protocol, and many good works. He was a notable sportsman, especially tennis player, and an ardent supporter of all Bahamian sporting endeavours. Probably the highlight of his tenure was his reception of QUEEN ELIZABETH II at the time of the Nassau Commonwealth Heads of Government meeting in October 1985. He received numerous further honours. He was retired in June 1988 and Sir H. M. TAYLOR made first Acting then full Governor-General in his place. When he died in January 2003, at the age of 85, Sir Gerald Cash, GCMG, GCVO, OBE, JP was duly accorded the honour of a full state funeral.

CASINOS Despite fairy-tales of lucky gamblers 'breaking the bank', the profits from casinos inevitably accrue to the casino operators – even without the returns from slot machines, which can be, and are, mechanically adjusted to guarantee a certain overall profit ratio. Even knowing this has never deterred inveterate gamblers from dreaming of defeating the odds against them, and this quirk of human nature explains why resorts with casinos always outdraw those without them.

Faced with the proven attractions of casino resorts, the Bahamian authorities dedicated to developing a profitable tourist industry were caught in a complex dilemma. Quite apart from the 'inducements' (that is, bribes) offered by foreign would-be operators, successive governments were attracted by the overall boost that casinos would give to Bahamian tourism and the taxes that might benefit the Treasury, while at the same time concerned to reassure local sceptics and churchmen about the potentially impoverishing and demoralising effects that casinos might have upon a people already very fond of other forms of gambling. Their solution was first to ensure that Bahamians themselves would not be allowed to patronise the casinos, then once they had become firmly installed, steadily to increase local participation in their manning, auditing and running, until ownership and profits were, as nearly as possible, completely Bahamianised.

The casino problem long antedated mass tourism. Private clubs, such as the Porcupine Club on what was then Hog Island, saw high-stakes casino-type gambling by well-heeled visitors during the 1920s, and as early as 1939, BAY STREET politicians, including the young lawyer Stafford SANDS, had negotiated exemption certificates for American businessmen to run small-scale casino operations in Nassau and on Cat Cay. As TOURISM began to pick up after World War Two, first the Oakes family and then Huntingdon Hartford attempted, without success, to pick up the existing Nassau exemption certificates and extend them to PARADISE ISLAND.

Sir Gerald Cash

CASSAVA

The sudden cessation of the Cuban tourist industry and expulsion of the casino operatives following the victory of the Castroite revolution in 1959 hugely changed the dimensions of the issue. An unholy trio of Mafia, Freeport and Bay Street interests (popularly represented as, if not actually by, Meyer Lansky, Wallace Groves and Stafford Sands) are reputed to have met secretly in Miami in 1962. 'Consultancy fees' were strategically distributed among the granting authorities, and the exemption certificates duly granted from 1963. Originally for Freeport alone, the licenses were soon extended to Paradise Island (first through a front-company called Mary Carter Paints, and then under the banner of Resorts International), and shortly thereafter to a casino on Cable Beach.

These murky dealings were revealed in a *Wall Street Journal* exposé in October 1966, and contributed largely to the victory of the PROGRESSIVE LIBERAL PARTY in 1967 and 1968. Yet by now the Freeport, Paradise Island and Cable Beach casinos were already firmly installed. Despite the resignation of the Finance Minister Carlton Francis over the further extension of government involvement in 1973, the PLP carefully nurtured the casinos – pointing out that it was the government's revenue from casino taxes alone that had cushioned the recession in tourism in the early 1970s, and satisfying most opponents by its policy of progressively Bahamianising casino operations. The government also prided itself on the wisdom of continuing to forbid Bahamians to patronise the gaming tables and slot machines themselves – ensuring that for the people as the whole the casinos were nothing but a net financial gain.

In 1973, the year of Bahamian INDEPENDENCE, a Casino Management Board was set up and a new schedule of operating fees laid down, along with requirements to train Bahamian managers, croupiers and other staff. A statement was made that the casinos would be completely Bahamianised by 1977. This timetable proved somewhat optimistic. But by the mid-1980s Bahamians essentially manned the casinos – suffering the same scrutiny formerly accorded to the foreign operators, while taking the blame for any shortfall in the anticipated revenues. In a final irony, the proponents of a national lottery – which many on all political sides saw as a potential boon to the national treasury and to worthy public projects, as it had proved in other countries, including the United Kingdom – found opponents among those in government committed to the casinos, as well as among the churchmen inveterately against all forms of gambling.

CASSAVA the product of the tuber of the manioc plant (*Manihot esculenta*), indigenous to the American tropics – though later spread to all tropical areas. Historically it has been of critical importance as a dietary staple and it remains the predominant starch food in many tropical countries. A hardy plant, which grows well even in poor soil and is comparatively resistant to drought, manioc is reckoned to produce 50 per cent more calorific food value per acre than yams, and up to 12 times as much as MAIZE and other grain crops. The chief drawback is that the commonest types of manioc tubers contain dangerous amounts of cyanide, which complicates their preparation for eating. Presumably through trial and error, the AMERINDIANS sliced and grated the tuber and then squeezed out the juice in an ingenious hanging implement made of woven palmetto straw. Then as now, the product was most commonly baked as flour into flat cakes, but also boiled in strips. In modern times at least, the squeezed-out juice is also boiled (to remove the poison) and becomes a piquant sauce or condiment (called *cassareep*) used to spice up the stew called pepperpot throughout the British Caribbean. Today, cassava strips are sometimes deep-fried and eaten like french fries. There is also an almost entirely non-toxic variety called sweet manioc used for making sweet biscuits and desserts.

Almost completely displaced as an essential starch food in the modern Bahamas by imported wheat flour, rice and 'Irish' potatoes, cassava was of vital importance to the pre-Columbian Lucayans – as to most of the people of tropical America. The line between climates respectively more suitable for growing manioc and maize (the latter essentially a subtropical and temperate cultigen) was clearly an important cultural divide, though with considerable overlap. The fact that The Bahamas straddled the climatic

The Princess casino, Freeport

boundary between tropical and temperate zones meant that the Lucayans were able to flourish despite poor soils by combining the cultivation of manioc with maize – evidence for the cultivation, preparation and consumption of both being clear from the archaeological record.

Previously it was thought that the apparent failure of the Lucayans to colonise the northern Bahamas was a consequence of the climate being too cool or seasonally varied there for the successful growing of manioc. This hypothesis, however, has been exploded by discoveries on two fronts in recent years. Archaeological explorations have proved that the Lucayans did in fact settle the entire archipelago, including the far north islands of Abaco and Grand Bahama. At the same time, plant researchers have shown that cassava could have been effectively cultivated in the northernmost Bahamian islands.

Further reading: D. Watts, *The West Indies: Patterns of Development, Culture and Environmental Change since 1492*, Cambridge University Press, 1987 53–66.

CASUARINA A quickly growing and hardy but not handsome or useful tree (*Casuarina equestifolia*) which is a feature of coastal areas throughout The Bahamas. Imported from Australia in the nineteenth century, it was planted as a windbreak around plantations on many Caribbean islands. Subsequently it spread throughout the region and colonised shorelines in particular, where it grew up to 60 feet (18 m) within ten years and self-propagated like a weed. With several main branches springing vertically from the main trunk and then drooping almost like a weeping willow (by which name it is sometimes called), it has a rough, shaggy and furrowed bark. The needle-thin twigs give the tree a feathery appearance and cause a distinctive sighing sound in the breeze, but provide disappointingly meagre shade to beach picnickers.

Botanically, the most interesting feature of the casuarina is that its leaves are too spindly to generate sufficient photosynthesis, which comes instead from the green twigs. Though casuarina bark has been used with limited success to produce a blue dye and tannin, the tree has no practical use as lumber, poles, charcoal or fuel wood. Worse, it has been recognised as an aggressive competitor to native flora, and is increasingly being treated as an arboreal pest by progressive landscapers, and as a major contributor to beach erosion.

CAT CAY One of the six-island BIMINI chain, North Cat Cay was purchased by American millionaire Louis Wasey during the PROHIBITION era and, with the help of one of the first casino licences obtained through BAY STREET lawyer Stafford SANDS, turned into an ultra-exclusive resort. With a luxurious if outlandish Elizabethan-style clubhouse/casino, some 70 private villas, a custom-built harbour and its own nine-hole golf course, it was shuttle-served by A. B. CHALK's flying boats based in Miami, less than 60 miles (95 km) distant. Surviving the loss of the casino licence, the temporary closing of the club in the 1960s, and a severe mauling from Hurricane Andrew in 1992, Cat Cay retains much of its character as an offshore extension of Key Biscayne. Though an official port of entry for The Bahamas, with docking and facilities for up to 80 passing yachts, its renovated club house is still only for members and their guests, and the island itself remains a privileged enclave for the American ultra-rich.

There is also a Cat Cay in Elizabeth Harbour, Exuma, which coincidentally is now being developed with a luxury hotel, villas and a yacht marina.

CATESBY, Mark (1682–1749) An English naturalist, painter and engraver active in the American mainland colonies and The Bahamas over a 14-year period (1712–26). His *Natural History of Carolina, Florida and the Bahama Islands*, eventually published in two volumes in 1747, is the pioneer classic in the field, possessing great visual charm as well as scientific value.

Catesby spent nine months in The Bahamas in 1725 as the guest of Governor George Phenney, visiting Abaco, Eleuthera and Andros as well as New Providence. A painstaking artist, he initially failed to find sponsors to finance his projected book. But he gradually gained recognition and respect as his beautiful illustrations were brought out in instalments as they were completed. Elected a Fellow of the Royal Society, Catesby had the satisfaction of seeing them collected and published just two years before he died. Original copies of the completed work now sell at auction for six-figure sums.

Casuarinas

CAT ISLAND

Catesby's magnum opus contains 220 colour plates. These are said to depict '109 birds, 33 amphibians and reptiles, 7 crabs, 46 fish, 31 insects, 9 quadrupeds and 171 plants'. Of these about a third were derived from The Bahamas, including almost all the fish and crabs, 65 plants, the flamingo, iguana, four types of turtle and the now extinct alligator.

Besides the pictures there is a vivid text, which provides invaluable insights into what The Bahamas was like in the first half-century of its settlement. In purely scientific respects, Catesby's work is said to be significant in at least two ways. Not only was he among the first artists to draw animals against accurate botanical backgrounds from the same habitats, but he was probably the first to establish the systematic seasonal migration patterns of American birds from his observations of rice birds passing over Andros on their way from Cuba to the Carolinas.

CAT ISLAND A fascinating but neglected island, once a populous centre of traditional peasant farming and Afro-Bahamian culture, now with only a third as many inhabitants as a century ago.

Cat Island: the approach to Fr. Jerome's hermitage on Mount Alvernia, at 204 feet (62 m) the highest point in the Bahamas

Like most other Atlantic-facing islands, Cat Island is long and thin, stretching like a skinny boot some 50 miles (80 km) along the edge of the Great Bahama Bank, but averaging only 2 miles (3 km) wide except for a 14-mile (23-km) wide 'foot'. Facing Exuma Sound to the west, it is some three sailing days to and from Nassau. It possesses a well-vegetated spinal ridge of rolling hills, the highest in The Bahamas. Said in the past to top 400 feet, the highest point, called Como Hill or Mount Alvernia, was more precisely measured at 204 feet (62 m) – still almost a mountain by Bahamian standards.

Cat Island was first settled by LOYALIST planters and their slaves in the 1780s. Large COTTON plantations and cattle ranches were started and substantial 'great houses' built, of which the impressive shell of the Andrew DEVEAUX mansion can still be seen at Port Howe in the far south-east of the island. After the failure of cotton and with EMANCIPATION impending, the planter families deserted, leaving their lands to be worked by the slaves and their descendants. As the memoir of the most famous son of Cat Island, Sidney POITIER, describes, it was a hard but healthy peasant life. The rocky soil was worked by family units, to provide food for subsistence and a sufficient surplus in the way of tomatoes, onions and PINEAPPLES to send to Nassau (along with plaited palmetto straw) in exchange for the few necessities that the people could not make for themselves. As Poitier also explains, this way of life could not survive the hardships of the Great Depression and the new values and expectations of the mid-twentieth century – leading to wholesale emigration, either to the United States or up to Nassau.

Though it has miles of splendid pink sand beaches on its ocean side and its sport fishing is said to be as good as anywhere in The Bahamas, Cat Island has only two notable resorts, both small. Fernandez Bay Village, near the only one of the island's four airstrips with scheduled flights, is owned and run by returned descendants of original white planters, the Armbristers. Hawk's Nest Resort and Marina, near Cat Island's 'toe' can only be reached directly by boat or chartered plane – its isolation leading to rumours in the 1980s that it was a drug trans-shipment point.

Because so little was known or written about Cat Island, rumours and legends have abounded throughout its history. Out of local patriotism, and the desire to attract tourists and investors, one of the island's parliamentary candidates in the 1980s, Eris Moncur, confidently declared that Cat Island not Watling's was the first landfall of Christopher Columbus in the New World. This claim was based almost solely on the fact that (out of ignorance) this was once believed to be so, and that the island was officially called

San Salvador until 1926. Others have asserted that ruins to be found in the bush prove that the Spaniards actually settled Cat Island in the early sixteenth century, long before the first English came. Ruins do indeed exist, but none antedate the Loyalist influx in the late eighteenth century.

Much the most interesting extant buildings in Cat Island do seem more ancient than they are, but simply testify to the vision and enterprise in the 1940s of the remarkable 'Hermit of Cat Island', Father JEROME. Of these, the most famous is the hermitage he built and lived his last years in, atop Mount Alvernia. Approached by a rock stairway punctuated with the Stations of the Cross, this rewards toilers up the slope with what is probably the most splendid panorama anywhere in The Bahamas.

CAY SAL BANK A somewhat remote Bahamian atoll, strategically located at the junction of the Old Bahama Channel and the GULF STREAM. Extending over 2,500 square miles (6475 squ. km), the Cay Sal Bank is the largest atoll outside the Pacific – four times the size of Bermuda's, but without its island core. Formerly held by imperial Britain against first Spanish then Cuban claims, its continued possession by the independent Bahamas adds a large swath of ocean to the country's territorial waters, but brings its problems too.

With only a few barren islets around its edges, including Cay Sal itself and the Anguilla Cays, and no oil deposits or other valuable minerals, the Cay Sal Bank itself is not suitable for development. Its chief value lies in the exclusive fishing rights that come with territorial waters, and Bahamian patrol vessels have often had confrontations both with fisherman from nearby Cuba and with Cuban-American lobstermen based on Miami. In the latter case, the diplomatic consequences in the 1960s and 1970s were sometimes referred to as 'the Lobster Wars'.

The Cay Sal Bank is diplomatically troublesome on other grounds. For the Cuban government it is regarded, not without cause, as a dangerous base and launch-pad for anti-Castro guerrillas – as are the Guinchos Cays, Cay Lobos and Cay Santo Domingo further to the southeast, along the Bahamian side of the OLD BAHAMA CHANNEL. For its part, the United States regards the Cay Sal Bank almost as an outlier of their coastal defences, and is also concerned by the role it plays as a natural stop-over point for both Cuban and HAITIAN refugees.

On at least one occasion, events on Cay Sal have also had internal political ramifications in The Bahamas. In February 1963 (shortly after the Cuban Missile Crisis) a group of Cuban exiles was said to have taken possession of the island. This naturally alarmed both Cuba and the United States. Two members of the Opposition PROGRESSIVE LIBERAL PARTY, Cyril Stevenson and Henry TAYLOR, took it on themselves to visit Cay Sal, insist on the raising of the Union Jack, and issue a bellicose statement of policy towards Cuba in Miami – all without authorisation from the PLP Council.

Further reading: K. Boodhoo and J. Hardshaw, 'The U.S.–Bahamian Lobster Dispute: International Legal Perspectives', *Caribbean Studies*, March 1980.

A wreck at Cay Sal, graveyard of unwary vessels

CHALK'S AIRLINE Still proudly flying between Miami and The Bahamas after more than 80 years, Chalk's Ocean Airways lays claim to being the world's oldest scheduled airline as well as the largest remaining operator of passenger flying boats.

The company was founded and run for 56 years by the remarkable Arthur B. Chalk (1889–1977). A car mechanic from Paducah, Kentucky, he obtained flying lessons in return for repair work on the seaplane of the aviation pioneer Tony Janus, in 1911. After barnstorming in the southern US and service during World War One, Chalk settled in Miami and started his airline with a single seaplane. The company's first scheduled passenger flight between Miami and Bimini was in July 1919, a month before the company which grew into Imperial Airways, BOAC and British Airways initiated its regular flights between London and Paris.

From 1926 Chalk's Airline occupied a site on a new landfill area in Biscayne Bay named Watson Island, which remains

Chalk's seaplane, Paradise Island, 1990s

its headquarters to this day. During PROHIBITION Chalk was kept busy flying rum-runners to and fro, though he always denied carrying liquor and often flew US excise inspectors as well. After HURRICANES (such as those of 1926 and 1929) his planes were used in rescue and supply work, and during WORLD WAR TWO, they were used by the US Civil Air Patrol and carried out hundreds of anti-submarine missions in the Florida Straits. The bulk of the airline's work, though, was carrying well-heeled tourists between Miami and Bimini, Cat Cay, Walker's Cay and, less frequently, Nassau. Among the airline's regular passengers were big-game fishermen like Ernest Hemingway (who used Bimini as a favourite base), film stars seeking a quiet and quaint get-away, and Floridian gamblers visiting the exclusive casino on tiny Cat Cay.

Until the 1960s most of the air traffic between Florida and the Bahamian capital was dominated by airlines flying larger planes, first by the seaplanes of PAN AMERICAN AIRWAYS (founded in 1927) and then by the landplanes of many other companies once airports were constructed to service the expanding tourist trade. With the establishment of large casinos in the 1960s, however, Chalk's amphibious aircraft offered a more select and direct access, particularly to PARADISE ISLAND, off Nassau's north shore. The sight and sound of Chalk's ageless and noisy 17-seat Grumman *Mallards* regularly taking off and landing throughout the day became a notable feature of the Nassau Harbour scene.

After 'Pappy' Chalk died in 1977 (he claimed to be the oldest fully certified pilot in the US and had expected to fly till he was a hundred) the airline was bought out by Resorts International, the Paradise Island casino operators. Big efforts were made to update the fleet, adding 30-seater planes (this model was somewhat unfortunately called the *Albatross*). But when first an STOL airstrip was constructed on the eastern end of Paradise Island, and then Resorts International sold off their Bahamian interests, Chalk's Airline fell on hard times.

Of a complex sequence of financial deals, the most interesting was an ill-starred attempt in 1996 to make Chalk's Airline part of a revived Pan American Airways, under the name of Pan Am Air Bridge. The larger enterprise failed within two years, but the Miami–Bahamas seaplane component survived and was rescued by new investors with the full backing of Sol Kerzner's ATLANTIS hotel-casino complex. Firmly re-established on the Miami–Nassau shuttle route, and with renewed scheduled and charter business to other Bahamian destinations, it was also given back its founder's name, as Chalk's Ocean Airways.

CHEROKEE SOUND The most southerly and until recently the most isolated of the 'all-white' settlements of ABACO. Apparently founded by Loyalists around 1800, the origin of its name is obscure. Nor is the reason for choosing such an unpromising location obvious. Though not on a cay like all the Loyalist settlements except MARSH HARBOUR, Cherokee was separated from the Abaco mainland by marshy shallows until a dirt road was constructed in 1990 and it was even later before mains electricity was connected. It had neither much land suitable for cultivation nor a decent harbour – the weekly MAIL BOAT from Nassau still has to stand off and shift goods and passengers by rowing boat.

The extreme isolation of Cherokee Sound is testimony to its settlers' determination to separate from non-whites and make a living entirely on their own, whatever the cost. And by sheer grit, the inhabitants did more than simply subsist, making a living in the only ways possible, boatbuilding and fishing. Cherokee's most famous boatbuilder, Benny Sawyer, built 22 boats in a 50-year career that only ended in 1978. As late as 1957 there were still 56 Cherokee mariners working seven smack boats, catching fish (mainly off the BERRY ISLANDS and northern ANDROS) which they carried to market in Nassau. Their catch was valued at £20,000 a year – more than twice the value of the fish caught by the 185 mariners of the entire Hope Town District. For almost a hundred years, Cherokee Sound was the seat of the Commissioner for Southern Abaco, and its school was famous for producing some of the most literate of Abaconian 'CONCHY JOES' – especially while Walter Sands was the head teacher. Most notable of Sands's pupils was Patrick Bethel, who became Principal of The Bahamas Teachers' College (1965–72), forerunner of the COLLEGE OF THE BAHAMAS.

However, the last resident Commissioner was retired in the 1950s, the last boat built in 1980, and the last working fishing smack sold in 1982. Cherokee Sound is still a community of about 170 permanent residents, proud of its traditional ways – its trim and bright painted houses and Methodist and Pentecostal churches looking like a picture postcard from another century. But it is still too remote and difficult of access to draw many tourists or yachtsmen, and with too little to persuade more than a few to stay. Already most of Cherokee's menfolk commute daily to work in Marsh Harbour or live for much of the year further afield. Inevitably, the young people look to wider horizons, and travel has been made easier by a modern highway. Early in the twenty-first century modern resort development arrived in the form of a golf course and villas for members only, located immediately north of the town along the sand dunes facing Cherokee Sound.

Further reading: P. J. Bethel, *Growing up in Cherokee 1935–1950*, privately published, n.d., c.1995.

CHINESE BAHAMIANS

CHINESE BAHAMIANS A small but distinctive ethnic minority that established itself in the boom years of the 1920s, survived intermittent opposition and prejudice, and continues to make a significant if unobtrusive contribution in the commercial sphere.

The first Chinese (jocularly called 'Celestials' from China's title, 'the Celestial Empire') arrived in Nassau as early as 1879 – a tiny fragment of the worldwide diaspora that followed the opening up of China, the development of steamships, and the demand for cheap 'coolie' labour in places like Cuba. Their pioneer was an ex-coolie from Cuba called Pan Yuong, who set a precedent by opening a small restaurant in which he employed even poorer fellow migrants and family members. 'It is astonishing how the Chinese settlers are thriving in our midst,' wrote the *Nassau Guardian*. 'We now have about a dozen Celestials, who are patterns of industry, ingenuity and perseverence.'

It seems that these original Chinese carried their ingenuity elsewhere, for the first permanent migrants arrived in the mid-1920s – as a result of the end of the 'dance of the millions' boom in the Cuban sugar industry and the relative attractions of the rum-running era in The Bahamas. Two families predominated; the Wongs and the Cheas, who opened three restaurants and a lunch counter and two laundries on or near Bay Street between 1923 and 1925. Since these filled a need and catered mainly to non-Bahamians they were more or less tolerated. But when the Wongs, Cheas and other migrants began to diversify into the dry goods, grocery and bakery fields, the established Bay Street merchants campaigned against them in the legislature – using arguments that appealed to ordinary Bahamians as well as serving their own self-interest.

By the end of the 1920s, the entry of further Chinese was heavily restricted and even well-established families were denied naturalisation as British subjects. Tenacious and frugal, the Chinese families somehow sustained themselves through the Great Depression, shared in the rising prosperity following World War Two, and gained a few further recruits among refugees from Mao's Communist takeover in 1949. Undoubtedly they have benefited since from the general familiarity with and tolerance for people

Cherokee Sound

CHIPPINGHAM

and things Chinese (not least, Chinese cuisine) that have followed from the second great Chinese diaspora. Yet the legacy of opposition and their own clannishness has tended to make even modern Bahamian Chinese rather more reclusive and introverted than other minority groups.

Third, fourth and fifth generation Bahamian Chinese are now respected members of the Bahamian community – as likely as any other Bahamians to resent later migrants who act without sufficient sensitivity. A critical issue, however, looms: the effect on the Bahamian Chinese of recent political changes in China itself – including the Chinese reacquisition of Hong Kong in 1997. All the immigrants from the 1920s until the Communist takeover of Cuba in 1959 were firm supporters of Sun Yat Sen, Chiang Kai-Shek, and the Nationalist China that was established in Taiwan after 1949. In the 1990s, however, the People's Republic of mainland China began to make strong diplomatic overtures towards The Bahamas, being (with the United States, United Kingdom and Haiti) one of only four countries with a formal legation, with resident officials, in Nassau.

Further reading: E. Johnson, *The Bahamas: From Slavery to Servitude, 1783-1933*, University of Florida Press, 1995.

CHIPPINGHAM A distinct and almost self-contained western suburb of Nassau, developed by the middle-class non-white E.A. Chipman in the later 1920s and 1930s. Set in an approximately 40-acre tract of former bush, it consists of a tight grid of four north–south and eight east–west streets that were unmade until the 1950s. Bounded, almost hemmed-in, on the north by Fort Charlotte and the government's experimental farm, on the east by three cemeteries, and on the west by Nassau's original well-field (Perpall's Tract), the community of modest but neat houses with small gardens had its own small shops and bars – though without its own school or churches before the 1960s. Settled mainly by migrants, either from Jamaica and Barbados, or from the southern Bahamas (especially Long Island and Inagua), the community was appropriately first called Rainbow Village. The English-sounding Chippingham – derived from the name of its first developer and the several members of his family who lived there – became its name later by common usage. Perhaps Chippingham's best known inhabitant today is the brilliant drummer, and RAKE N' SCRAPE and JUNKANOO band leader, John 'Chippie' Chipman.

CHOLERA Originating in South East Asia, cholera spread in periodic waves to most of the world's ports and their hinterlands along with improvements in steamship navigation during the nineteenth century. Reaching the Americas as early as 1817, it peaked during the 1850s and 1860s. It first struck Nassau from New York in September 1852, spreading rapidly through the slum areas both to east and west as well as Over-the-Hill. Approximately a tenth of the population was infected, of whom a quarter died. At the height of the epidemic, 70 persons a week were dying, with some of the dead lying a long time in their coffins above ground for want of grave-diggers.

From Nassau, cholera spread with terrible speed to those settlements best served by boats from the capital. So great were the fears of contagion that in November 1852 the people of Governor's Harbour, Eleuthera refused to let the stipendiary magistrate and his retinue land, holding them at bay with sticks and stones. When they returned later under the protection of a detachment of soldiers and the epidemic subsequently took hold, the government was blamed. Before Governor John Gregory was able to announce in February 1853 that the five-month epidemic was over (declaring a public holiday and day of prayer and thanksgiving), cholera had claimed well over a thousand victims, including 696 in Nassau, 178 in Harbour Island, 200 in the rest of Eleuthera, 108 in Abaco and even 40 in tiny and distant Ragged Island.

The Bahamas was further ravaged by cholera during the blockade-running period of the AMERICAN CIVIL WAR, though never seriously again thereafter. All the same, deaths from cholera were one of the main reasons why the general population did not greatly increase during the third quarter of the nineteenth century, and why migration from the comparatively healthy Family Islands to unhealthy Nassau was slowed until even later. The Bahamas has not had a fatality, far less an epidemic outbreak, for over a century.

CHRIST CHURCH CATHEDRAL The oldest extant church in The Bahamas. Situated since 1723 at the junction of George and King Streets in downtown NASSAU, it became a cathedral (and Nassau a city) with the establishment of the ANGLICAN bishopric of The Bahamas in 1861.

Christ Church's forerunner, remnants of which can be seen as part of the fabric of the house called GRAYCLIFF on West Hill Street, was built before Charles Town was renamed Nassau. As a Protestant place of worship it was dutifully sacked by the invading Catholic Spaniards in 1684, and again in 1703. When the first royal Governor, Woodes ROGERS, arrived (1718) there was no proper church building, no church organisation, and no ordained minister.

CHRIST CHURCH CATHEDRAL

Christ Church Cathedral

These deficiencies were remedied by the second Governor, GEORGE PHENNEY, with the help of the inhabitants and the Society for the Propagation of the Gospel. The garrison chaplain was sent to England to be properly ordained, and in 1723 a prefabricated wooden frame for a church was brought from England at a cost of 450 pieces of eight (£75 sterling at that time). This was erected on the present site and the finished building called Christ Church. As shown in a contemporary sketch in the Public Record Office in London, it was a modest and quaint building which could hold 300 persons, with a five-windowed nave, three-windowed chancel apse and a porch, shingled roof, cupola and spire, topped with a gilded weather vane. In traditional style, the church was aligned west (the main entrance and font) to east (the pulpit, lectern, choir-stalls and altar).

Also in 1723, following the parochial pattern of the established Church in England (with Christ Church as the parish church of the entire Bahamas as well as Nassau), the parishioners were instructed to elect 12 vestrymen and two churchwardens, whose duties, besides looking after the church and ordaining dues to pay for a minister and church upkeep, included responsibility for the care of orphans, the poor, aged, and sick, and even the maintenance of roads and other public works within the parish. The minister, paid the relatively generous stipend of £400 a year, also kept a school, which in 1770 was reported to have 54 pupils, all baptised, including, surprisingly, six black children.

The original Christ Church building, though suffering from periodic hurricanes and steady deterioration from termites and tropical decay, survived for 114 years. An American visitor around Christmas-time in 1823 was impressed, not so much by the church ceremonies (or even by the report that the organist was paid $500 a year) as by the social display. The Governor and his retinue attended, with a 'mace guard of black troops ... The people dress as much to go to church as if they were in a populous city or as if all the world were looking at them ... There was quite a parade of all the gigs & curricles in town before the church door, with starved diminutive horses arrayed in burnished harness & accompanied with plenty of black equerries, all of which ostentation appears ludicrous when contrasted with the meanness of the cavalry.'

The symbolic importance of Christ Church, especially as SLAVERY came to an end, was stressed by the dismantling of the old edifice and the erection of the far larger present building between 1837 and 1840 – with a grant of £10,000 from the government, obtained through a public loan. Though somewhat elongated by the addition of a chancel, and having had an impressive stained glass east window installed in the 1860s, Christ Church today looks almost exactly as it did when it was consecrated by Bishop Spencer of Jamaica in 1845. It is built of the white local stone in the neo-gothic style, with lancet windows and arched doorways, and a simple but elegant square clock-tower. Inside there are a main and two side aisles, with a war memorial chapel taking the place of the former vestry at the eastern end of the north aisle, and a fine pipe organ in the corresponding place in the southern aisle. Over the doorway and vestibule at the west end is a gallery.

Altogether there is seating in Christ Church for 1,200 people. Until the 1940s, 800 seats were in family rented pews. In the front and centre pews sat the most prominent whites, with the less affluent, including a few coloureds occupying the rest. Blacks sat in the free seats in the side aisles and in the gallery. As late as the 1950s the churchwarden, himself a black, would usher white tourists to the traditionally privileged places, while directing any blacks, even well-known Nassauvians, into the side aisles, or upstairs.

The prestige that Christ Church gained when it became a cathedral in 1861 was somewhat eroded when the Anglican Church in The Bahamas was disestablished (that is, lost its financial support from the government) in 1869. It also lost popularity among black Anglicans because of its stuffiness, and its retention of 'low church, prayer book' ritual. Most blacks preferred the more participatory and lively 'Anglo-Catholic' type of worship practised in almost all of the other Anglican churches. All the same, though Christ Church (like the Church of England in England) can no longer be said to represent 'the Establishment at prayer' it still has the kudos of being the head church of the Anglican diocese,

CHRISTIE, Sir Harold George

the scene of many state religious occasions, and the place in which many, if not most, Bahamian Anglicans would choose to hold their christening, marriage and funeral ceremonies if they could.

CHRISTIE, Sir Harold George (1896–1973) Millionaire realtor, pioneer promoter of foreign investment and tourism, and one of the chief pillars of the BAY STREET regime. A descendant of one of the founding white settler families, 'HG' was the eldest of the eight children of the usually impoverished dreamer Henry Christopher Christie, author of the epic poem *Blackbeard or The Pirate of the Isles* (1925) and sometimes exaggeratedly called 'the poet laureate of The Bahamas'. Educated in Nassau and the United States, young Harold joined the Canadian Air Force as a trainee pilot towards the end of World War One, before spending a few unsuccessful years as a junior reporter in New York. He returned to Nassau almost penniless in the early 1920s and drifted into rum-running. Pretty soon, however, he became the first serious entrant into the real estate business – accurately assessing the long-term potential of land in NEW PROVIDENCE and the Out Islands that could then be bought or optioned for next to nothing.

From modest beginnings, H. G. Christie Ltd. rode the boom of the PROHIBITION era and stayed ahead of the competition through the 1930s and 1940s by its efficiency in buying cheap and selling dear, by imaginative advertising, and by Harold Christie's almost magic ability to charm rich investors seeking the sun, a haven from taxation during the Depression, and an escape from the effects of World War Two. Among the tycoons attracted were Harry OAKES, Axel Wenner-Gren, Arthur Vining Davis and Edward Plunkett Taylor. 'HG' was the brains behind the development of such expatriate enclaves as LYFORD CAY, Great Harbour Cay in the Berry Islands, Windermere Island, Eleuthera, and Hawksnest Creek, Cat Island.

Harold Christie was also a visionary pioneer for Bahamian tourism, a founder of Bahamas Airways (1935) and one of the most enterprising members of The Bahamas Development Board. Like his youngest brother and business partner Frank, but unlike the other brother, Percy (a shoe merchant and political populist), 'HG' was among the most inventive in exploiting the profitable connection between politics and business. An MHA for Abaco and Cat Island from 1927 to 1966 and a Member of Executive Council from 1939 to 1949, he was knighted in 1964, the year that the UNITED BAHAMIAN PARTY led The Bahamas into self-government.

With Sir Roland SYMONETTE and Sir Stafford SANDS, Sir Harold Christie was one of the trio who spearheaded and epitomised the so-called 'Bay Street Boys'. Undoubtedly ruthless, though also a promoter of the arts and personally charming, he never fully dispelled the cloud of rumour and innuendo that arose from the circumstances surrounding the murder of Sir Harry Oakes in 1943.

CHRISTIE, Rt. Hon. Perry Gladstone Populist lawyer who overcame many difficulties to become the third Prime Minister of The Bahamas on leading the PROGRESSIVE LIBERAL PARTY to its landslide victory in the general election of 2 May 2002. Only in retrospect does it seem predictive that his second given name was that of the great British Liberal Prime Minister of the late nineteenth century.

Perry Gladstone Christie was born on 21 August 1943 to Gladstone L. Christie, an activist member of the Taxi-Cab Union and early supporter of the PLP, and his wife Naomi, a nurse. The family lived in the lower middle-class Nassau suburb just east of COLLINS' WALL called Centreville, alias 'the Valley'. As a boy, Perry was regarded as talented but harum-scarum, more noted for athletics than schoolwork (he won a bronze medal for the triple-jump in the 1962 Central American and Caribbean Games). His future career might have been blighted when he was asked to leave the GOVERNMENT

Hon. Perry G. Christie

HIGH SCHOOL without graduation, but this setback jolted him into a determination to succeed on his own. Studying assiduously at the University Tutorial College in London, he went on to receive an LLB with honours from Birmingham University, distinguishing himself as the leading light of the University's debating society. He was called to the Bar at the Middle Temple and admitted to The Bahamas Bar in 1970 at the age of 27.

Christie began his law career with the old-established and conservative firm of McKinney, Bancroft and Hughes, but soon set up his own practice in partnership with Hubert INGRAHAM, a locally trained lawyer from Abaco. Both Christie and Ingraham were very active in the idealistic (and far from uncritical) youth wing of the PLP called Unicomm, which had been born out of discussions between Christie, Bernard Nottage and others while studying in the United Kingdom. Christie and Ingraham were particularly encouraged by Prime Minister Lynden PINDLING, who saw them as valuable allies among the younger generation, if not quite yet as potential future leaders of the PLP.

In 1973, following his work in helping to unseat the FREE NATIONAL MOVEMENT's Orville TURNQUEST in Centreville in the 1972 general election, Christie was appointed to the Board of Directors of the Broadcasting Corporation, and in 1974 Pindling selected him as the youngest ever Member of Senate – aged 30. In 1977 he was appointed Chairman of the Gaming Board. In the same year's general election he successfully stood as candidate for Centreville himself, being immediately appointed to Pindling's Cabinet as Minister of Health and National Insurance. In 1982, Christie easily retained his Centreville seat and was shifted to the more important post of Minister of Tourism in the new Cabinet.

For a time Christie's star still seemed in the ascendant, but in 1984 it was suddenly threatened with extinction. At the time that Pindling was under heavy fire on account of the drug-running scandals, and there were suggestions even within the party that he should step down. Christie was suspected of involvement with his law partner Ingraham in a plot to take over. Both were summarily sacked from the Cabinet and almost immediately resigned from the PLP. Christie stood as an Independent in the 1987 general election and demonstrated his personal popularity by retaining his Centreville seat. But unlike Ingraham, who went on to join and then lead the FNM, Christie ate humble pie and returned to the PLP in 1990. Pledging no intention to overthrow Pindling (then or earlier) he was straightaway brought back into the inner circle as Minister of Agriculture, Trade and Industry. Almost needless to say, the professional partnership of Christie and Ingraham was sundered.

Though keeping his Centreville seat once more, Christie shared in the ignominy of the FNM's victory under Ingraham in 1992. But he so convinced Pindling of his fidelity and value that he was made Co-Deputy Leader with his old schoolfriend and associate Bernard Nottage in 1993. Recognising in him his own qualities of popular charisma and political pragmatism, Pindling increasingly came to favour Christie over his more cerebral and forthright rival. Once Pindling decided to retire after a second PLP defeat at the hands of the FNM in 1997 (when Christie was one of only six party members to retain their seat) he was duly chosen to be the Chief's successor, over Bernard Nottage and Philip Galanis.

Facing an apparently hopeless task, Perry Christie tirelessly restructured the PLP, rethought and revised its ideology, and re-enthused its demoralised supporters. With the help of a Cabinet of new and younger faces (including as Deputy Leader the redoubtable Rev. Cynthia 'Mother' Pratt), the party won a stunning victory (by 29 seats to nine) in May 2002; Perry Gladstone Christie became Prime Minister at the age of 58. Not least of those who came out to celebrate were the oft-time winning JUNKANOO group from Centreville called 'the Valley Boys', of whom Christie was a founding member and ardent annual participant.

CHRISTMAS CUSTOMS 'Momma bake a johnny cake. Christmas coming …' As in all Christian countries, for The Bahamas the week between Christmas and New Year is, and always has been, the premier holiday season of the year; a favourite time for food and drink, general jollification and present-giving, as well as the formal rituals commemorating the birth of Christ, and the end of one year and the start of another. Yet it is as difficult to unravel the interwoven secular and religious, European, American and even African origins of the seasonal celebrations, as it is to distinguish those that are uniquely and traditionally Bahamian.

As in the true plantation colonies of the West Indies, Christmas was ardently celebrated in The Bahamas in slavery days – by the slaves even more than by their masters – with little or no religious connotation. The one surviving diary of life on a Bahamian slave plantation gives a vivid description of the seasonal rituals on the Farquharson estate on San Salvador in December 1832, without any reference to any religious observance. There was no work done from 24 to 27 December, and precious little before 2 January. On the 24th the master had a fat hog and heifer slaughtered and each slave was issued several pounds of fresh meat, along with a few ounces of sugar, a bottle of rum for each adult, handkerchiefs for the women and older children, and 'a good westcot' for each of the men. On Christmas Day, while the master and his family had several neighbours over for a relatively lavish dinner in the big house, the slaves enjoyed their own unaccustomed plenty in their separate family quarters. On 26 December, Farquharson recorded succinctly: 'Some of our people gon abroad to see some of their friends and some at home amusing themselves threw the day, but all of them at home in the evening and had a grand dance and keep it up until near daylight.' And the following day he wrote: 'Everything very still today the people mostly sleeping being much fatigued in dancing last night.'

In Nassau, the colonial capital, the celebrations were more formal and elaborate among the whites, and more nearly riotous on the part of the slaves – and these traditions continued almost unchanged after slavery ended. Besides noisy carousing Over-the-Hill, many of the blacks, as in Jamaica and other West Indian islands, dressed up in tattered costumes, forming groups that played RAKE N' SCRAPE and GOOMBAY drum music outside the houses of the whites, soliciting money, rum and cake. Costumes and music were clearly derived from Africa, though to some they were also reminiscent of the traditional Christmas mummers in England. This annual custom gradually developed into the full-blown JUNKANOO masquerade, in which first hundreds then thousands of masked and costumed revellers woke the echoes on downtown BAY STREET on Christmas morning.

The secular mayhem on Christmas Day scandalised the churches and alarmed the forces of law and order, and Junkanoo was periodically banned altogether, and in due course postponed to the morning of 26 December – called Boxing Day since it was the day that employees, in The Bahamas as well as England, expected 'boxes' or bonuses from their employers. From the 1920s, the Boxing Day Junkanoo grew in size and well-controlled exuberance as the most distinctive Bahamian Christmastide custom – with a second parade added on New Year's morning in the late 1940s.

Once the religious significance of Christmas had been firmly established, Bahamian year-end customs, with the exception of the Junkanoos, became increasingly mere local variants of those derived from and developed in Europe and North America – including, in the late twentieth century, their ever more pervasive commercialisation. For almost all Bahamians, the season is incomplete without attendance at church services – most commonly the watch-night services on Christmas Eve and New Year's Eve. The rest of the holiday time is largely given over (much as in San Salvador in 1832) to food, drink and socialising, visiting friends and exchanging gifts. Until the invasion of American turkeys and English Christmas puddings, the food would have a Bahamian flavour (and always more elaborate and special than simply johnny cake) and feature rum more largely than other spirits and wines elsewhere. The custom of dressing a tree and surrounding it with presents (imported from Germany by way of the UK in Victorian times) was Bahamianised by employing a small Caribbean pine cut by permit on the payment of a small fee on a special expedition to the pine barrens – at least until supplanted by shapelier conifers imported from the US or Canada, or by storable plastic versions. Likewise, in simpler and less affluent times, the wrapped presents would consist largely of hand-crafted local items.

Further reading: O. J. McDonald and D. A. Peggs (eds.), *A Relic of Slavery: Farquharson's Journal for 1831–32*, Nassau, Deans Peggs Research Fund, 1957; L. Glover, *Ilun Peepul: A Jaunt through Bahamian Culture and Folklore*. Nassau, National Archives, uncirculated publication, n.d., c. 2000.

CHURCHES OF GOD The various branches of the Church of God in The Bahamas trace their foundation directly to the overflow of the pentecostalism that erupted in the southern United States and California at the beginning of the twentieth century. Yet there is clear evidence that similar beliefs and practices had already long existed among Afro-Bahamians. Similarly, the splits that later characterised the Bahamian Churches of God were as much the consequence of a will on the part of many adherents to indigenise their church as they were a reflection of divisions among the American evangelists.

Perhaps merging Wesleyan ideas about the baptism of the Holy Spirit with worship practices derived from Africa, there were 'Jumper' or 'Shouter' churches in Nassau at least by the 1880s, when, shamefully, they were objects of wonder and derision to such white visitors as Dickinson and Dowd, Drysdale and POWLES. A fresh impetus, invoking the spirit of the biblical Pentecost, faith healing, and speaking in tongues, however, did emanate from the confluence of two distinct, and distinctly American sources: the 'camp meetings' and 'Holiness' churches of whites in the hills of Tennessee and Georgia, and the mixed-race (but black-led) pentecostalist revivalism that exploded in Los Angeles, California, in 1906. Drawing from several different sects, the movement spawned several new churches, of which among the most evangelical was the Church of God, founded by A. J. Tomlinson (a former Quaker and Holiness preacher) and other whites, in the small town of Cleveland, Tennessee, in 1907.

Church of God: pastors, officials and choir members

Church of God missionaries carried the word to Florida (where many black Bahamians were living) and onwards to The Bahamas – their first foreign mission – by 1910. There, their most ardent converts were the Yoruba Bain Town mason (former Baptist), Wilmore Venable Eneas (1883–1961), and his wife Arabella. Meeting first in a wattle-and-daub hut on a site nicknamed 'the Camp Ground' on south Hospital Lane, the new pentecostals encountered actual persecution and ridicule, before beginning to earn respect for their dedication and rigidly puritan lifestyle. By 1920, W.V. Eneas had been consecrated Bishop by the authorities in Tennessee and the church had moved to the 'new road' (East Street), where they built a more substantial wooden church on what became popularly known as 'Eneas Jumper Corner'.

The early 1920s, however, saw a serious schism in the mother church, which spilled over into The Bahamas. In Cleveland, the followers of A. J. Tomlinson formed a faction which regarded itself as the one true Church of God. They consecrated a new bishop, Stanley Ferguson, and sent him to Nassau as Colonial Overseer of The Bahamas, to take over from Bishop Eneas. Not only the members of Eneas's congregation saw this as a foreign intrusion, and Ferguson and his followers were physically ejected from the 'Eneas Jumper' church and forced to set up their own place of worship further up East Street, at the junction of Taylor Street. The split was not healed, and though both branches continued to have their headquarters in Tennessee, the Tomlinson sect (including its Bahamian followers) were compelled by a court decision to redesignate themselves as the Church of God of Prophecy – with its rivals triumphantly retaining the original name.

From 1923, the Church of God and the Church of God of Prophecy in The Bahamas, though professing virtually identical beliefs and practices, continued in not always brotherly and sisterly competition – each claiming to be the more authentically Bahamian. In 1952, in the last decade of Bishop Eneas's ministry, the Church of God consecrated its first stone structure, at the junction of East Street and Lily of the Valley Corner, christening it the Church of God Cathedral. Some years later it built a far more spacious cathedral, church headquarters and school on Joe Farrington Road in the Yamacraw area of south-eastern New Providence. By the 1990s, the Bahamian Church of God had 15 churches in New Providence alone (three of them styled cathedrals) and 36 in ten of the Family Islands. This growth was almost exactly matched by the Bahamian Church of God of Prophecy, which in 1992 claimed a dozen churches in New Providence, and 52 congregations in all, distributed through 15 Bahamian islands. Its membership, though, might have been somewhat smaller than that of the Church of God – calculated as approximately 3,300 full members and 10,000 'followers'.

Unfortunately, the tendency of the Churches to God to split (often around the leadership of favourite pastors)

CITIZENSHIP

was a continuing feature, in The Bahamas much as in the United States. In Tennessee, when the founder Tomlinson died his church divided under the leadership of his two sons, and none of the Tomlinson foundations were quite able to keep pace with the rival Church of God in Christ, the all-black church also founded in 1907. In The Bahamas in the 1960s, many members of the Church of God specifically felt the call of Bahamian nationalism (if not necessarily Black Power) and resented the direct ties to the United States and the continuing influence of white southern evangelists. The result were heated debates held at the East Street CG Cathedral and the CG church on Dixie Highway, which (after a decision in the courts) led to the creation of the breakaway Church of God in The Bahamas Incorporated in 1965. By 1992, the CGBI, with its headquarters at a cathedral on Cooper's Terrace in eastern Nassau, boasted at least four bishops and seven churches (besides the cathedral) in New Providence and about a dozen in various Family Islands. Nor was this the sum of breakaway splits within the Bahamian Churches of God. At least two single breakaway churches still carry variations of the Church of God name, and many others with different names (including Bahamas Faith Ministries and the Latter Rain Ministries) have similar pentecostalist roots.

The questions as to which of the Churches of God is the most authentically Bahamian, and which follows most strictly the original pentecostalist beliefs and practices, are still matters of debate. Perhaps the Church of God most recognisably follows the teachings and style of Bishop Eneas – though all of the Churches of God have had much of their pentecostalist thunder stolen by the phenomenal spread of charismatic styles of worship to almost all Bahamian churches, including the Anglican and Catholic, over the last half century. All three main Churches of God are now exclusively led by fully trained Bahamian ministers. The Church of God in The Bahamas Incorporated has a strong claim to have been a direct product of the era of black majority rule and political INDEPENDENCE – and continues to make subtle currency of the fact that its two main rivals still acknowledge some allegiance to Cleveland, Tennessee, with both of their two presiding Bishops still bearing the limiting title of National Overseer (their own presiding bishop is termed General Superintendant).

However, in two respects the Church of God of Prophecy may claim to have moved most with the times and to have an edge over its two main rivals. Its rituals are much less tuned to the practices of the old 'jumper' and 'shouter' zealots and its congregations, at least in Nassau, now include rather more members of the respectable new Bahamian black middle class. The CGP also possesses, in its East Street Tabernacle (completed in 1946) what is probably still the largest single church building in The Bahamas. This, as well as its convenient central location, rather than a greater sense of respectability and ecumenism, probably explains what might otherwise have been regarded as a *coup de prestige* – its choice as the location for the state funeral of Sir Lynden PINDLING on 4 September 2000.

Further reading: C.W. Eneas, *Let The Church Roll On*, Nassau, 1985; C.W. Conn, *Like a Mighty Army: A History of the Church of God*, Cleveland, Tennessee, Pathway Press, 1996; V. Synan, *The Origins of the Pentecostal Movement*, www.oru.edu/university/library/holyspirit/pentorgl.html

CITIZENSHIP The rules governing citizenship (much like those relating to work permits and the right to permanent residency) have been determined by the principles of international law as far as they are in accord with the special conditions and needs of The Bahamas.

In colonial times, those born and living in The Bahamas who were not citizens of a foreign country were simply regarded as British colonial subjects. Once passports became necessary and customary in the twentieth century, Bahamians travelling abroad were issued with British passports prominently indicating the holders' status and place of birth.

On the eve of the achievement of internal self-government, the Immigration Act of 1963 introduced the unique status of Bahamian Belonger. Those who automatically 'belonged' were all British subjects over 21 who were either born in The Bahamas or, if born elsewhere, had a Bahamian-born father or mother – along with their wives and children. However, those persons not fulfilling these requirements might apply for and be granted Belonger status. These conditions were having lived in The Bahamas for at least five years, having the intention of staying permanently, and – here was the crux – satisfying the Immigration Board as to his or her good character and that their 'continued residence and association with the Colony may afford some advantage to The Bahamas'. For those not automatically Belongers, the Belonger's certificate might be revoked if they resided elsewhere continuously for seven years, were convicted of a serious crime, including treason, or became in any way *persona non grata*.

The status of Belonger was disliked by the Bahamian majority both because of its complexity, and the suspicion that it was a subterfuge by the ruling BAY STREET oligarchy to facilitate the immigration and voting rights of those whom they favoured, and to restrict all others. Accordingly it was replaced by the narrower and less flexible concept of 'Bahamian Status' soon after the

PROGRESSIVE LIBERAL PARTY came to power in 1967.

The whole question of citizenship necessarily came under review once The Bahamas became a fully independent country in 1973. The situation was particularly delicate because the policy of BAHAMIANISATION aimed to strengthen the rights of unequivocal Bahamians and to control both the influx of white 'white-collar' immigrants and of poor 'blue-collar' non-whites from HAITI and other parts of the West Indies. Such motives helped to shape the Bahamian Nationality Act of 1973, which became a part of the Independence Constitution and remained in force with only minor modifications (though with considerable flexibility in practice) into the twenty-first century.

The 1973 Act had to begin by differentiating between those born before and after INDEPENDENCE. Any person born in The Bahamas before 10 July 1973, or if born elsewhere, having a father qualified for Bahamian citizenship, and who was at that date a citizen of the UK and colonies, was automatically a Bahamian citizen. This also applied to anyone not born in The Bahamas or without a Bahamian father who had been registered as a British citizen in The Bahamas under the British Nationality Act of 1948, as long as they were still resident in The Bahamas and had not obtained the nationality of any other country.

For those persons born in The Bahamas after 9 July 1973, those who had either a father or mother who was a Bahamian citizen were to enjoy like status. Those born in The Bahamas neither of whose parents were Bahamian citizens had the right to apply for Bahamian citizenship once they reached 18, 'subject to exceptions or qualifications prescribed in the interests of national security or public policy'. Before being granted a certificate of citizenship they would be required to renounce any foreign citizenship, to take an oath of allegiance to The Bahamas, and make a declaration of intent regarding residence within the country.

These rules were relatively straightforward; it was different and exceptional circumstances which were most problematic – the most controversial being those rules which seemed to discriminate in favour of Bahamian men or which involved children born illegitimately. A person born after 9 July 1973 whose father was a Bahamian by birth and whose parents were married was a Bahamian citizen regardless of the nationality of the mother. If the child was illegitimate and the mother non-Bahamian, or if legitimate and the father born outside The Bahamas (if with Bahamian parents) he or she was not a Bahamian citizen. However, even if born legitimately of a Bahamian mother outside The Bahamas (of a non-Bahamian father), a person had to make a formal application for citizenship between the ages of 18 and 21, and would only be granted it subject to the conditions and exceptions applied to other young applicants.

Any woman who after 9 July 1973 was married to a Bahamian citizen was entitled to Bahamian citizenship, but only provided she was still married and satisfied the studiously vague 'national security and public policy considerations'. Somewhat curiously (and probably as a consequence of United Nations concerns about children's rights) it was decreed that if a child were born illegitimately abroad of a Bahamian mother, he or she was automatically Bahamian by birth.

The principles of international law were also behind the seemingly liberal provision of the Bahamian Nationality Act that allowed even aliens not entitled to be registered or naturalised on the strength of an existing status to make an application for Bahamian citizenship. The qualifications, though, were stringent and successful applications so rare as to be negligible. At the minimum, the applicant had to have been legally resident at least seven years, to intend to reside permanently, to renounce any foreign citizenship and take an oath of Bahamian allegiance, to have (unspecified but substantial) assets to contribute to The Bahamas, to have an unblemished character and record, and, final hurdle, to be demonstrably literate in English.

A particularly grey area was the status of persons whose claim to citizenship was based on the provisions special to the former 'Belonger' and 'Bahamian Status' categories. Here, the test case was that of the Canadian-born but long-time resident Belonger D'Arcy Ryan, who was denied citizenship in 1975. This went through the entire gamut of the British appeals system and appeals to international law and the United Nations, and saw the Bahamian Minister responsible for citizenship come close to imprisonment for non-compliance; the Bahamian government belatedly charged Ryan with misdemeanours and even threatened to change the law retrospectively (see BAHAMIANISATION).

Further reading: *Bahamas Handbook and Businessman's Annual 2003*, Nassau, Dupuch Publications, 2003, 357–8, 425–31.

CLIFFORD, Governor Hon. Sir Bede (1890–1969)

A genial aristocrat, whose superficial efforts to lead The Bahamas through the worst of the Great Depression were made to seem even slighter by the somewhat flippant memoirs he published in 1964.

CLIFTON CAY CONTROVERSY

Sir Bede Clifford

A younger son of the tenth Baron Clifford of Chudleigh who delighted in his descent from the buccaneering Earl of Cumberland, Bede Clifford was successively private secretary and aide-de-camp to the Governor Generals of Australia, South Africa and Canada in the 1920s. An ardent sportsman and socialite, he married an American heiress in 1926 and fathered three famously beautiful daughters, arriving in The Bahamas as Governor in 1932 like an exotic butterfly alighting in a shabby back yard.

Clifford's first responses to conditions in the colony were typically insouciant. Insensitive to the fact that the rum-running boom was already over, he joked that the legislators ought to raise a statue to the prohibitionist Senator Volstead to accompany those of Christopher COLUMBUS and QUEEN VICTORIA. More seriously but even less adroitly, he proposed to the horrified Assembly that an income tax might both equalise wealth and ease the economic condition of the colony.

Another famous one-liner was both more thoughtful and better received. On getting advance notice from his friend President Roosevelt that the Volstead Act was about to be repealed, Clifford quipped: 'If we can't take the liquor to the Americans we must bring the Americans to the liquor.' With the enthusiastic support of the BAY STREET-run Development Board, this in effect is what he did – concentrating on the richer American tourists and potential winter residents. Hotels and cruise lines were strongly encouraged, docking, seaplane landing and international telephone facilities improved, and Nassau itself made more attractive for the well-heeled visitor. To a golf course and tennis courts were added a race-track (HOBBY HORSE HALL), and, of all things, a polo field was levelled in front of Fort Charlotte. This, though now used for important national occasions as well as soccer games, is still called Clifford Park. Besides, Clifford involved government with private estate agents in the development of Prospect Ridge and CABLE BEACH as the sites of luxurious expatriates' mansions, while wealthy Americans were also encouraged to buy their own private Bahamian cays.

During Clifford's tenure the number of tourists more than doubled (to 25,000 a year), and one magazine was able to gush in 1935 that Nassau had become 'the social centre of the South' where 'the society set of Palm Beach and other Florida resorts mingled with the fashionable colony in a gay whirl of parties prompted by the visit of Their Royal Highnesses the Duke and Duchess of Kent.'

The real effects of underemployment in seething Over-the-Hill, and the even worse consequences of the regime's almost total neglect of the Out Islands, were left to be faced by Clifford's Colonial Secretary and successor as Governor, Sir Charles DUNDAS.

From The Bahamas, Sir Bede Clifford was moved laterally to Mauritius in 1937 and marginally upwards to be Governor of Trinidad and Tobago between 1942 and 1946. In neither colony does he seem to have made even as much impact as he did on Nassau. Though the autobiography Clifford wrote in retirement is compulsively readable, his use of such terms as 'coons' or 'darkies' for non-white colonials, and his caricaturing account of Bahamian 'Holy Rollers' diminish the author as much as they demean his subjects.

Further reading: B. Clifford, *Proconsul: Being Incidents in the Life and Career of the Honourable Sir Bede Clifford, GCMG, CB, MVO*, Evans Bros., 1964; V. Moseley Moss, *Reminiscing: Memories of Old Nassau*, Ronald Lightbourn, 1999, 143–52.

CLIFTON CAY CONTROVERSY

A bitter dispute over an area in western NEW PROVIDENCE that exemplifies and highlights the conflict between developers and the forces of conservation at the turn of the twenty-first century.

Adjacent to the gated millionaires' enclave of LYFORD CAY, Clifton is one of the last attractive uninhabited parts of New Providence. Including areas of woodland, wetlands, cliffs and beaches, it was at one time chief of the several extensive estates of the Loyalist planter William WYLLY. After slavery ended, cultivation declined and eventually ceased. The estate went through different ownerships and by the 1930s was a neglected part of the huge acreage acquired by the OAKES family – over which the public roamed unhindered. From the 1970s, archaeological explorations under the supervision of the Department of ARCHIVES uncovered first the old plantation house and slaves' quarters and then several unique Lucayan sites.

Long on the market, in 1998 Clifton's central 600 acres became the focus of a development plan put forward by Americans James Anthony and James Chaffin. The plan visualised a gated community like Lyford Cay, called Clifton Cay, with 600 luxury homes surrounding an 18-hole golf course, served by a yacht marina, and with private-access beaches. Despite the planners' assurance that the old plantation ruins would be preserved as 'an interesting historical feature', that the wetland areas would be 'cleaned and upgraded', and that a separate beach would be provided for the public, there was an immediate outcry. This stemmed from four more or less distinct constituencies: ecologists, historic preservationists, those who believed that NEW PROVIDENCE was already overdeveloped, and those who vehemently opposed another exclusive enclave like Lyford Cay. Together they formed the Clifton Cay Coalition, whose vociferous leader was Rev. C. B. Moss.

The fate of Clifton Cay became the hottest political issue of the year 2000, with the ruling free-market FNM government of Hubert Ingraham citing the potential economic benefits of the development plan and declaring its intention to give permission for a go-ahead as soon as the thorny question of who actually owned the land was resolved. Meanwhile, the PLP Opposition led by Perry Christie just asw adamantly supported the CCC position and threatened to cancel any permissions given once it came to power.

A Supreme Court decision and parliamentary vote gave the government the right to go ahead and sell, but this seemed to come too late since by then Anthony and Chaffin had given up their project in despair. The defeat of the FNM by the PLP in 2002 at first seemed an unequivocal win for the CCC, cemented by the passing of an act in 2004 creating a Clifton Heritage Authority. In November 2006, however, Prime Minister Perry Christie, in an apparent change of heart, announced his government's endorsement of what was essentially the Clifton Cay development plan under a different name – the Albany Golf and Beach Resort – the brainchild of the English billionaire resident of Lyford Cay Joe Lewis,

Aerial view of Clifton Cay

with the active support of the golfing superstars Ernie Els and Tiger Woods. Time alone would tell whether this was a victory for developers or conservationists, or even an acceptable and wise compromise solution.

Further reading: *Bahamas Index and Yearbook, 1999*; P. L. Adderley, 'The History of the Clifton Plantation, 1788–2000', *Journal of the Bahamas Historical Society*, 2000, 4–11.

CLIMATE Except for the very occasional visitations by HURRICANES, the climate of The Bahamas is regarded as one of the most benign in the world, without extremes of heat or cold, drought or rain – giving the islands the only slightly exaggerated label of 'the Isles of Perpetual June'.

In rather more precise terms, The Bahamas, situated between the subtropical and tropical belts of the northern hemisphere, enjoys a maritime environment dominated by the prevailing north-east trade winds, the influence of which are only temporarily and mildly disrupted by cold fronts from North America in winter and warm masses of tropical air from the south in summer. Unlike North America (and many other parts of the world) there is neither a perceptible spring nor autumn season in The Bahamas. For an archipelago covering such a large area there is also a remarkably small variation in climate from north to south – owing to the large proportion of The Bahamas which consists of warm ocean water, and to the insulation provided by the massive northwards flow of the GULF STREAM which forms its north-western geographical boundary.

Though Florida can experience freezing temperatures and even snow, only once in history have a few snow flakes been recorded in The Bahamas, at West End, Grand Bahama on 17 January 1977 – and even then the air temperature at ground level was no lower than 5.5 °C (42 °F). The average temperature in January at West End is 18 °C (64.5 °F) (compared with 23.6 °C, 74.5 °F at Matthew Town, Inagua, at the other end of the chain) and even at West End, the January mean of daily maximum temperatures is 25.3 °C (77.7 °F), and the highest January temperature recorded a broiling 30.5 °C (86.9 °F). Surface water temperatures, moreover, never fall below 23 °C (74 °F). Such statistics explain why The Bahamas is such a favoured destination for 'snowbird' tourists during the northern winter – despite the fact that native Bahamians often swathe themselves in woollens in January and February, and rarely disport on the beaches or in the sea between November and March.

At the height of the summer, high humidity can make the temperatures somewhat oppressive to northerners. But the highest temperature ever recorded anywhere in The Bahamas is less than 37.7 °C (100 °F) and the monthly means are remarkably moderate, and uniform from north to south. For West End (and for Nassau) the July mean is 27.7 °C (82 °F), and for Matthew Town only one degree warmer. The average hours of daily sunshine, though somewhat greater in the southern than in the central and northern Bahamas (especially in islands like ANDROS that are large enough to generate their own cloud systems) are still impressive by North American or European standards – averaging 8.2 hours in Nassau and more than nine hours in Matthew Town throughout the year.

There is, however, a greater range of rainfall between the northern and southern Bahamas and between summer and winter throughout the islands. The average annual rainfall for West End is 1354 mm (53.3 in.) (and for Nassau, 1341 mm, 52.8 in.), but for Matthew Town only 696 mm (27.4 in.). The monthly totals for Nassau vary from 39 mm (1.55 in.) in January to 236 mm (9.28 in.) in August, and all islands show similar proportional variations. Thus, historically it has been the amount and seasonality of rainfall as much as the temperatures, amount of sunshine and fertility of the soil that has determined the patterns of Bahamian natural vegetation and agriculture. This factor has also been critical in determining the boundary between those islands in the south-eastern Bahamas which could profitably manufacture SALT, and those which could not.

The reasons for these differences are largely related to the prevailing winds and seasonal incursions of air masses from north and south already referred to. In summer the north-east trade-wind belt shifts somewhat to the north, leaving The Bahamas at its southern margin. This area is heavy with moisture, which means that quite minor disturbances bring more rain in the summer than during the winter, when the trade-wind belt is further to the south. Added to this, the central and northern Bahamas receive more rain than the south both in the summer, when they are most in the path of masses of moist tropical air, and even during the winter, when the frequent cold fronts from frigid North America collide with the warmer trade winds, as soon as they reach and cross the Gulf Stream.

Further reading: N. E. Sealey, *The Bahamas Today: An Introduction to the Human and Economic Geography of The Bahamas*, Macmillan Caribbean, 1990, 1–10; Michael Halkitis et. al. *The Climate of The Bahamas*. Bahamas Geographical Association, 1980.

CLUB MEDITERANÉE

A French holiday colossus that began as an ostensibly non-profit concern providing camping holidays in Majorca in 1950 and by 2000 boasted 120 elegant all inclusive (and decidedly profit-conscious) holiday resorts in 30 countries, including The Bahamas. The key to their charm (and success) has been their location on splendid sunny beaches that at least gave the impression of being far from the madding crowd, and combining the ultimate in gourmet food and leisure activities with casual living and lack of hassle. One of Club Med's most potent selling points is that (while very expensive 'up front') it virtually frees its clients from worrying about money while in residence. All food, drinks and activities are paid for with bead tokens, and tipping is actually forbidden. Though some Club Meds cater imaginatively for children as well as adults, most target hedonistic adult couples, and are closed to persons below the age of 12.

There are (or have been) three Club Mediterranée operations in The Bahamas (not counting Club Med

CLUB MEDITERANÉE

Turkoise on Providenciales in the Caicos Islands). These, for different reasons, have had somewhat mixed fortunes. The first was set up in December 1977 on three tracts totalling 35 acres formerly owned by two American millionaires and the exclusive Porcupine Club on PARADISE ISLAND. For a quarter century this 300-room facility was able to disguise its actual propinquity to bustling Nassau and the increasing number of nearby hotels, and its non-exclusive access to the ocean-side beaches. But in September 2003 it was announced that it had sold out to the imperialistic ATLANTIS resort complex, for $40 million. Though the Paradise Island Club Med would not cease operations until the end of 2004 and its employees were promised transfers to Atlantis, its facilities were to suffer the indignity of becoming the temporary living quarters of the army of workmen engaged in the third and fourth phases of development destined to double the capacity of Atlantis to 5,000 rooms by 2006.

The second Bahamian Club Med was created in a more promising location in 1985, taking over the magnificent beach-side site long occupied by the famous but fading French Leave resort, a mile across pencil-thin ELEUTHERA from the settlement of Governor's Harbour (and within a few miles of its jet-capable airport). One of relatively few Club Meds catering for families, it became a favourite with its regular clientele and kept a profitably high occupancy rate for more than a decade. Like much of Eleuthera, however, it suffered catastrophic damage from Hurricane Floyd in September 1999 and was forced to close down. This closure was at first said to be temporary, while repairs were being completed, but it soon became clear that Club Med was not interested in further investment in Eleuthera. Fortunately, in 2003 a buyer was found and the site is to be redeveloped with a luxury hotel, villas and marina, a project regrettably delayed following two hurricanes in 2004.

Similar problems and criticisms were not unknown but have not yet become insistent concerning the third Bahamian Club Med operation: Club Med Columbus Isle on the remote island of SAN SALVADOR. So far at least, it has provided an unequivocal economic boost for one of the many decaying outer Family Islands, and has even reversed the demoralising tide of emigration. Founded in 1992, it owed its impetus not only to the island's white beaches, crystal waters and incomparable dive sites, but also to the attention drawn to San Salvador by the COLUMBUS Quincentennial. Located on 80 acres fronting the beautiful 3-mile (5 km) Bonefish Bay, it was somewhat slow to succeed, largely because of the government's delay in its promised upgrading of the adjacent airport. But by the end of the decade it was regarded as one of Club Med's flagship operations – and also rated 'Best Dive Resort in the World' by *Scuba Diving* magazine.

Specifically served by four charter flights a week from Miami and New York (as well as the daily BAHAMASAIR flights from Nassau), the *Columbus Isle* resort has almost 300 luxury rooms and three gourmet restaurants, as well its superb dive facilities, 12 tennis courts, and other aids to fitness. The public rooms are said to boast 'exotic antique art valued at more than $2.5 million: carved Nepalese doorways, Pakistani urns covered with a rich-coloured

Club Méditerranée, Columbus Isle, San Salvador

patina, Indonesian temple gods, Brazilian headdresses, Turkish rugs and African statues and masks'. Each unit is custom-furnished and air-conditioned, with refrigerator, satellite TV, telephones and internet access. Though somewhat delayed by the fall-out from New York's 9/11, plans were afoot to construct an 18-hole golf course and install a full-scale CASINO. All these things (as well as the minimum daily rates of $350 per couple) were a world removed from the austerity and camp-ground ambience of the original Club Med of 1950 – or even the Club Meds of the 1980s which ostracised TVs and telephones. They also indicated an investment more irreversibly rooted in its chosen location than any previously, a view substantiated by the resort's prompt reopening after San Salvador suffered massive damage from Hurricane Frances in September 2004, and lesser damage a few weeks later from Hurricane Jeanne.

COLLEGE OF THE BAHAMAS (COB)

Founded in 1974 to combine the meagre facilities for tertiary education then available in The Bahamas, the College of The Bahamas has proceeded steadily and responsibly towards becoming a fully fledged university. Already by 2000 it offered a wide range of courses towards a Bachelor degree and was making plans to offer Master's courses and other graduate studies in the near future.

Shortly following Bahamian INDEPENDENCE, an Act of Parliament created the COB by amalgamating the operations of the two teacher training colleges, the Technical College, and the sixth-form programme of the GOVERNMENT HIGH SCHOOL. Commencing classes in the existing buildings in September 1975, the fledging college took over the Oakes Field premises of GHS in September 1976. All facilities were concentrated on that campus by the summer of 1984 – with building steadily expanding to a point where it became necessary to locate satellite accommodation and branch components elsewhere.

At one stage it seemed likely that COB would proceed to full university status only as a campus of the UNIVERSITY OF THE WEST INDIES. Preparation for UWI entry was a marked feature of early teaching, a UWI resident tutor was maintained in Nassau, and a direct connection was established when the COB became the location for the UWI school of hotel management and training. Similar close cooperation in degree studies was also established pragmatically with several reputable universities in the United States.

However, as COB gradually expanded and matured, and as the government's commitment to it steadily grew, the institution increasingly stood on its own feet. In 1991, the nursing and other health related programmes run by the Ministry of Health were transferred to the College as a School of Nursing, housed in Grosvenor Close in downtown Nassau. A separate research unit was set up in 1992 in response to the government's intention that the College should be the national research centre, planning for future development and 'nurturing the local intellectual climate'.

A revised College of The Bahamas Act was passed in 1995, strengthening the organisational structure, giving the College greater financial autonomy (particularly in seeking private funding) and, most importantly, giving it formal permission to grant degrees. In 1997, a centre for entrepreneurship was established by the College Council, in close association with the University of Maryland, and in 2000 The Bahamas Tourism Training Centre was formally amalgamated to the COB. By that time, local demand and opportunities in the Family Islands had led to the creation of a northern campus in Freeport and a smaller local facility in Exuma. The Bahamian Field Station in San Salvador formerly run by a consortium of universities in upper New York State was taken over, and a Bahamas Environmental Research Centre (BERC) set up in northern Andros, in collaboration with George Mason University in Virginia.

Besides the remaining direct links and the general high regard earned with foreign universities, close connections are fostered by the College with many local businesses and government departments – for the purposes of training employees, generating scholarships, and providing internships for COB students. Part-time studies are strongly

College of the Bahamas: COB main building, Poinciana Drive, Nassau, 2004

encouraged, and there is an extremely active Centre for Continuing Education and Extension Services. In fact it was through the Continuing Education Department that the first graduate course was offered in The Bahamas: a Master's in Health Administration, taught in collaboration with Western Connecticut State University.

Entry to the various schools and divisions of COB is carefully tied to the general Bahamian education system. The basic requirement is normally five satisfactory Bahamas General Certificate of Secondary Education passes, including in English and Mathematics. In some fields, a two-year Associate Degree (adequate for entry to any foreign university) is still the highest qualification obtainable. But in those fields in which a Bachelor's degree is offered an Associate Degree is the minimum entrance requirement.

By 2000, the total enrolment at COB was approximately 3,100, of whom just over half were full-time students. Fairly accurately reflecting career aspirations, some 35 per cent were enrolled in the School of Business and Administration, 19 per cent in Teacher Training, 13 per cent in Humanities and Social Sciences, 10 per cent in Tourist and Hospitality Services, 9 per cent alike in Natural Sciences and Nursing, and 6 per cent in Technology. Full-time and part-time teaching staff totalled about 225, of whom 13 per cent held doctoral, 75 per cent Master's, and virtually all Bachelor degrees or their equivalent.

A parallel institution to COB, emphasising the technical rather than purely academic aspects of tertiary education and deriving essentially from the original Technical College founded in the later 1960s, is The Bahamas Technical and Vocational Institute (BTVI). With its main campus in Nassau and a smaller facility in Freeport, BTVI had approximately 1,800 students enrolled in 2000. Much smaller, and maintaining close connections with UWI as well as COB (with which it shares accommodation) is the Eugene DUPUCH Law School, set up in 1995 to formalise the hallowed tradition that Bahamian lawyers do not necessarily have to go away to study in order to practise at the local bar.

As part of the general expansion into higher education, several other institutions besides COB, BTVI and EDLS have received at least qualified government approval to offer tertiary education in The Bahamas in recent years. These include Success Training College, the first private college in The Bahamas (1982), Grosvenor Academy (a language school), and an offshore campus of Sojournor-Douglass College of Baltimore, Maryland. The University of the West Indies retains a practical connection with The Bahamas by offering reciprocal training between its own Hotel Management and Training School and COB's School of Tourism and Hospitality Services, and between the Eugene Dupuch Law School in Nassau and the UWI Law School in Barbados.

Further information: website: www.cob.edu.bs; e-mail: advc04ai@cob.edu.bs

COLLINS' WALL An unbroken barrier, 10 feet (3 m) high and 1.5 miles (2.4 km) long, between GRANT'S TOWN and Centreville, erected in 1930; the most obvious, and increasingly odious, evidence of the system of practical *apartheid* in Nassau. The campaign that led to its breaching in three places in 1961 symbolised the first phase of the dismantling of racial and social divisions and discrimination in The Bahamas.

Ralph G. Collins was an American-born millionaire rum-runner, whom the white BAY STREET oligarchy co-opted into its ranks during the 1920s. To provide a demesne for the mansion that he built on the south side of Shirley Street opposite Deveaux Street (later the premises of ST ANDREW'S SCHOOL, and later still of the Ministry of Education), he purchased the 600-acre tract running from Shirley Street as far as Plaxtol Street, just north of Wulff Road, now bisected by what is still called Collins Avenue. Collins's announced intention was to create a citrus farm, but this soon changed into a plan to develop a somewhat upmarket garden suburb, mainly for whites.

Ostensibly to keep out poachers and squatters, but mainly to keep up the market value of his residential lots, Collins surrounded his land with iron railings to the north and a continuous wall to west, south and east – of which by far the most substantial and significant was that hemming in the teeming population of Grant's Town to the west. Ironically, the wall-builders were drawn from the very people whom Collins aimed to exclude, the hundreds of black labourers out of work because of the Great Depression, who were willing to toil for a shilling a day plus a free midday meal.

For twenty years, Collins' Wall was an uncomfortable fact of life for black Bahamians. Though unguarded and unpatrolled, it was a barrier to traffic, and forced individuals, including black domestics working in Centreville homes, to scramble ignominiously up and down makeshift ladders. It became a scandal with the rising race- and class-consciousness of the 1950s, particularly when, after the death of Ralph Collins, Bay Street's paramount leader, Roland SYMONETTE, became the most active developer of Centreville. The opening up of Collins' Wall was one of the demands (along with the desegregation of restaurants and the ending of film censorship) of the moderate Citizens' Committee, formed in 1950, and it

COLUMBUS, Christopher

was the subject of a petition by Etienne DUPUCH's Bahamas Democratic League in 1955 at the same time that demands were being made for the end of racial discrimination in general – nominally achieved in 1956. But it was not until the burgeoning PROGRESSIVE LIBERAL PARTY took up the issue as a major plank of their platform, and Bay Street's UNITED BAHAMIAN PARTY were prepared to make a tactical concession in the run-up to the 1962 general election, that the breakthrough was (literally) accomplished.

Late in 1961 the UBP voted $18,000 for the making of gaps in Collins' Wall, creating four new east–west routes (joining Grant's Town's MacCullough, Gibbs and Toote Shop Corners and Sunlight Village to Centreville's Fifth, Sixth, Seventh and Eighth Terraces, respectively). This concession was one of the factors that helped the UBP win the 1962 election. Remnants of the wall, however, survive to this day, and its effects are still clear on the map of Over-the-Hill Nassau. No less than ten 'corners' branching eastwards off East Street still have dead-ends. These are of more than antiquarian or archaeological interest – they are a reminder of social and racial divisions no more than a half century ago that in today's Bahamas seem almost incredible.

Further reading: P. Deveaux, 'The Story of Centreville and Collins Wall', *Nassau Guardian*, 17 October 1983; *Street Map of Nassau and New Providence Island. Book One*, Nassau, Lands and Surveys Department, 1973.

COLUMBUS, Christopher

(1451–1506) Most famous of all European maritime explorers, whose 'discovery' of America began with his landfall on the Bahamian island which the Lucayan natives called Guanahani and which he christened SAN SALVADOR, on Friday 12 October 1492.

Columbus was born in the Italian maritime republic of Genoa. He gained wide sailing experience in the Mediterranean and nearer stretches of the Atlantic before proposing his great western enterprise. Knowing (as did most mariners) that the world was round not flat, he realised that the Far East could therefore be reached by sailing west as well as east – a conclusion only flawed by his underestimate of the size of the globe and his ignorance (which he never fully acknowledged) of an intervening continent.

After vain efforts to interest the kings of Portugal, France and England, Columbus eventually found patrons in the husband and wife monarchs of recently united Spain. King Ferdinand and Queen Isabella helped fund a flotilla of three small caravels in 1492, promising Columbus the titles of Admiral of the Ocean Sea and Viceroy of any lands he might discover and effectively claim for Spain.

Symbolic engraving of landing at San Salvador, 12 October 1492, by Theodore de Bry (1594)

The *Santa Maria*, *Pinta* and *Nina* left Palos, Spain on 3 August 1492 and set out into unknown waters from Gomera in the Canary Islands on 8 September. Taking advantage of what were later called the north-east trade winds, Columbus and his 125 crewmen traversed the dreaded Sargasso Sea without incident and after 33 days of plain sailing sighted the white cliffs of a small island by moonlight at 2 a.m. on 12 October. After landing, claiming and exploring the island and attempting to communicate with its people, Columbus pushed on southwards to nearby islands, which he christened Santa Maria de la Concepcion, Fernandina and Isabela, then on 27 October left the shoals, rocks and flat islands of the Lucayans for the far larger and more promising island of Cuba, which he took to be part of the domain of Marco Polo's Kublai Khan.

Curiously, there is still avid debate as to quite where Columbus first landed in the New World, and about his precise route through The Bahamas. Some dozen locations have been claimed as the landfall site with varying degrees of plausibility – many of the claims (like those for the TURKS AND CAICOS ISLANDS, CAT ISLAND and ELEUTHERA) based mainly on local patriotism and wishful thinking. Despite hugely funded efforts by the National Geographic Society to promote SAMANA CAY in time for the 1992 quincentennial, the actual first landing site was almost certainly at Fernandez or Long Bay on the western side of the island formerly called Watling's but officially since 1926 San Salvador.

COMPASS POINT

As most strongly argued by Samuel Eliot Morison in 1941, Watling's/San Salvador more than any other island fulfils the description given by Columbus in the third-hand account written by Bartolemé de las Casas. The clinching evidence, however, would seem to be that discovered by a team of archaeologists under Charles Hoffman in July 1983. This was a so far unique small collection of the type of Spanish trade goods described by Columbus, in conjunction with the artefacts of a Lucayan village, in exactly the landing spot deduced by Morison and others from Columbus's account – where an authoritative monument has stood since 1992.

Christopher Columbus did not revisit The Bahamas on the further three voyages he made before his death in 1506. Gradually losing his reputation as a leader, he was deprived of his title and rights as Viceroy of the Indies by Ferdinand and Isabella. Nonetheless, because of his obsession with mines and plantations and his remarks of the Lucayans that they would make 'good servants' (quite casually abducting half a dozen himself on his first voyage) he surely deserves some of the blame for the Spaniards' subsequent deportation of the entire Lucayan population to be slaves in Hispaniola, if not for Spanish imperialist crimes in general. The near veneration of Columbus as the founder of American civilisation which reached a peak at the time of the quatercentenary in 1892, was almost erased by a backlash of condemnation led by American native peoples and their Afro-American, slave-descended allies during the quincentennial of 1992. As a consequence, there was a movement in The Bahamas in the year 2000 to redesignate Columbus Day (12 October) as National Heroes Day; but by 2004 this had largely been discredited as counterproductive for tourism. The romanticised statue of Columbus commissioned by Washington Irving and erected by Governor Carmichael SMYTH in 1831 still proudly stands looking down on George Street, Nassau, from the steps of GOVERNMENT HOUSE.

Further reading: S. E. Morison, *Admiral of the Ocean Sea*, New York, Little, Brown, 1941; J. Judge, 'Where Columbus Found the New World', *National Geographic*, 170 (5), 1986, 563–99; F. Fernandez-Armesto, *Columbus*, Oxford Unversity Press and New York, Morrow, 1991; Craton and Saunders, *Islanders*, i. 48–59, 404–6.

COMPASS POINT A chic and imaginative combined resort and recording studio which reflects the style of its owner and creator, Chris Blackwell, English-born but Jamaican-bred founder of Island Records and discoverer, friend and admirer of the late Bob Marley.

Having already branched into film production (beginning with the brilliant reggae-inspired *The Harder They Come* in 1971), Blackwell spent much of the 1980s producing a sequence of films that achieved commercial success without

Compass Point, western New Providence

compromising his artistic standards. But by 1989 he lost interest in Hollywood, sold Island Records to Polygram for $200 million, and turned his restless energy to creating a chain of small hotels that would combine luxury with an authentic local ambience. In Jamaica he saved Noel Coward's hill-top house for the nation and turned Ian Fleming's nearby Goldeneye into a luxurious guest house, and in Miami's South Beach saved four historic art deco hotels. Next, through his Islands Outpost Company, he rescued and transformed HARBOUR ISLAND'S Pink Sands after its near destruction by Hurricane Andrew in 1992, and turned his main attention to creating Compass Point.

The Compass Point complex was opened by Prime Minister Hubert INGRAHAM in March 1995. Situated a dozen miles west of Nassau on a rocky promontory close to Love Beach, the resort combines luxury with a tasteful evocation of native Caribbean and Bahamian features. While the two recording studios and accommodations boast the latest technology and facilities, the buildings simulate a West Indian village of clapboard tin-roofed cottages, painted in vivid JUNKANOO colours, and the restaurant offers gourmet versions of West Indian dishes with fresh local ingredients. Top recording artists and millionaires arrive in chartered jets, relishing the opportunity to work in seclusion and to dress and relax pretending to be care-less beach-bums. In this respect, Compass Point – if not also Pink Sands or Goldeneye – are the polar opposites of such palaces as ATLANTIS or the Nassau Marriott, matching them only, perhaps, in the prices charged.

CONCEPTION ISLAND

Chris Blackwell's Bahamian ventures have once more demonstrated his golden touch. Yet, equally characteristically, he has shared his financial success with the country of his adoption. In 1993 he set up the Bahamian Chris Blackwell Foundation, which annually provides $50,000 in prizes for Junkanoo, as well as five scholarships a year for young Bahamians to study abroad.

Further reading: 'Chris Blackwell's Island Life', *Bahamas Handbook and Businessman's Annual, 2000*, Nassau, Dupuch Publications, 2000, 183–96; www.compasspoint.islandoutpost.com

CONCEPTION ISLAND A competitor with Little San Salvador and Little Inagua for the title of most interesting and explorable uninhabited Bahamian island. Conception Island, which Christopher COLUMBUS almost certainly saw on his way onwards from SAN SALVADOR, and may or not be that island which he christened Santa Maria de la Concepcion, is 3 miles long, 2 miles wide (4.8 by 3.2 km), with hills up to 90 feet (27 m) in height. It is one of the few places in The Bahamas where the endangered green TURTLE comes ashore to nest, and where it is unlikely to be molested – thanks to the fact that the island and its surrounding waters have recently been declared a land and sea park in the care of the BAHAMAS NATIONAL TRUST. Conception Island is also an excellent place to study migratory birds, especially boobies – who give their name to tiny nearby Booby Cay.

CONCH The emblematic Bahamian queen conch (*Strombus gigas*) is a large marine snail with a spectacular pink shell. It has a fascinating life cycle, most stages of which are perilous. The female of the species lays up to 300,000 eggs, the survivors developing into larva-like pinhead-sized creatures called veligers, living on minute plankton, if not being eaten themselves. After a month, those surviving, now about a millimetre long, drop to the sea floor, change their diet to algae and begin to develop a shell for protection. The process of maturing takes four years, during which the shell grows to accommodate the creature inside, until it has developed the distinctive wide pink lip and upward pointing spires. Conchs do not slide slowly like terrestrial snails, but rather move in a sedate dragging motion on a protruding foot. A trunk-like proboscis with an eye on each side scours around for food. Adult conchs, now from 8 to 12 inches (20 to 30 mm) long and weighing up to half a pound (250 g), copulate in the summer months – an especially delicate operation since the male conch penis is said to be regarded as a delicacy by marauding eels.

Conch drying

The most voracious of the conch's predators, though, is man. Long the favourite protein source for Bahamians (of whom the whites even got to be nicknamed 'Conchs' or 'CONCHY JOES'), the conch was sufficiently prolific to survive the islanders' taste for it raw (as conch salad or 'scorched' conch), marinated ('conch souse'), stewed in a chowder, or cooked in batter and deep fried ('cracked conch' and 'conch fritters') when the Bahamian population was still numbered in tens of thousands. Now the population has passed a quarter of a million, and tourists – encouraged to eat conch by fables about its aphrodisiac qualities – are numbered in the millions, conch are almost fished out within a hundred miles of Nassau. As long ago as 1992 the Bahamian *Strombus gigas* was said to be on the brink of being listed as an endangered species.

Despite this melancholy assessment, Bahamians and tourists continue to consume hundreds of tons of conch each year, with the piles of shells in the harbour growing ever higher. The one relieving factor is that the price has risen so high that conch is now being farmed in the Caicos Islands for the Bahamian market. In the hope that this development will staunch or even reverse the depletion (or, if not, to give visitors a chance to find what the Bahamians' enthusiasm for *Strombus gigas* is all about, before it is too late) here is a recipe for the most economical way of using the conch for food, the chowder:

Ingredients: ¼ cup salt pork or bacon, diced; six conchs; two onions, finely chopped; two green peppers, diced;

two celery sticks, finely sliced; three potatoes, diced; five medium-sized ripe tomatoes; ¼ cup tomato paste.

Method: Beat the conchs until tender, then dice them finely. Fry the pork or bacon until golden brown. Remove or leave, as desired, adding onions, peppers and celery to the pan. Cook until the liquid is almost evaporated, then pour in tomatoes and tomato paste. Add the diced conch, bring to the boil, and season according to taste. Add sufficient water to cover and allow to simmer for 25 minutes, adding water if it becomes too dry. Serve conch chowder in bowls or mugs with a dash of pepper sherry – which is made by steeping six or more whole hot peppers in a bottle of good sherry for at least a month.

Further reading: D. Carstaphen, *The Conch Book*, Pen and Ink Press. 2000.

'CONCHY JOES' Familiar and not necessarily derogatory term used for native white Bahamians. Originally it was somewhat dismissively used by others for the poor and disadvantaged whites living in the northern Out Islands. Later, in an unfriendly way, it was linked to a stereotypical characterisation of such people as having an unjustified sense of ethnic superiority, on account of which they claimed special civic and economic privileges. In the modern, more prosperous and egalitarian Bahamas, however, the term is used as a badge of distinction by the whites themselves, and as a merely humorous, even affectionate, label by the non-white Bahamian majority.

This is amusingly detailed by Patricia Glinton-Meicholas in her best-selling *How to be a True-True Bahamian: A Hilarious Look at Life in the Bahamas* (Nassau, Guanima Press, 1994). According to this author, you are likely to qualify as a Conchy Joe if you have the surname Albury, Curry, Higgs, Lowe, Malone, Pinder, Roberts, Russell, Sands, Sawyer or Saunders, and are married to someone born with the same surname as yourself; if you have a familiar forename such as 'Maudie', 'Charlie', 'Donnie', 'Debbie', 'Willie', 'Jimmy', or just plain 'Junior'; if you follow a maritime version of the culture of whites from the American South; and if you speak a dialect quite distinct from that of black Bahamians and more akin to that of seventeenth-century rural England than modern English. This last includes saying *horbour* for *harbour*, *cor* for *car*, and *Cholly* for *Charlie*, and switching aitches and vowels, as in '*hanimals 'ate to heat hon ons*.' Tongue in cheek, Ms Glinton-Meicholas claims that the modern Conchy-Joes 'believe that going to heaven is "sailing" for all eternity through the Exuma Cays on a boat equipped with two nine hundred h.p. Evinrudes, a cooler that stays full of beer, a hairdresser and a telephone to gossip with "Charlie", "Maudie", etc.'

CONTRACT, The (1943–63) Name popularly given to the system of contract labour employing Bahamians in the United States during and after WORLD WAR TWO, which had profound economic and social effects on The Bahamas, especially the Family Islands.

The Contract was not the first phase of Bahamian MIGRATION to the United States and was similar in some respects to the 'Miami Craze' before WORLD WAR ONE and the employment of migrant labourers during that wartime period. It differed, though, in its scale, duration and effects. If the earlier migrations opened the door to a land of seeming opportunity, this door was cruelly shut during the Great Depression. The two decades of the Contract, on the other hand, gave thousands of Bahamians access to a country enjoying a wartime and postwar economic boom but on the threshold of social change, and in the process gave them the knowledge, means and will to help their own country in its own relatively even greater changes. As one veteran of the Contract put it in 1992, 'We didn't actually enjoy it. But the way t'ings was home, it beat home. Any way you was livin' better than you was home. … An' then it gave you chance to grab at somethin' bigger.'

When World War Two began in Europe, ordinary Bahamians were in the throes of a depression made all the more grievous by the recent collapse of the SPONGE industry. Cash was so short that men were prepared to work for a shilling a day and a hot meal. Thus the entry of the United States into the war in December 1941 and the subsequent demand for labour to build two airfields on New Providence and other smaller bases was seen as a windfall. Though the pay was still a measly four shillings a day, what was generically called 'the Project' drew thousands of desperate applicants, including Out Island farmers and office-workers.

The workers on the Project proved themselves a volatile proletariat with the 'BURMA ROAD' RIOTS of June 1942 (which were followed by marginally improved pay and conditions), so that the regime greatly feared the consequences once the work came to an end. The American wife of the Governor, the Duke of WINDSOR, went so far as to write privately to her aunt, 'The negroes are busy complaining now that the base is nearing completion and some of them are being laid off. I should not be surprised to see more trouble – but this time one is somewhat prepared and there is enough fire-power on the island to deal with the situation.' It was largely to allay the perceived threat that the Duke negotiated an agreement in Washington in March 1943 for the employment under contract of up to 5,000 Bahamians on agricultural labour in the United States – probably the most significant achievement of his generally undistinguished tenure as Governor. Because of its continuity with the war-work on the bases, this arrangement was sometimes also referred to as 'the Project', as well as 'the Contract'.

Recruiting began through a specially created Labour Bureau in Nassau in April 1943. The first 2,500 workers were dispatched within a month, and by August 1943 the full quota had been reached. At its peak in July 1944, almost 5,800 Bahamians were under contract – roughly a twelfth of the entire population, a sixth of all adult Bahamian males, and perhaps a third of all able-bodied male Out Islanders. The first migrant workers were employed on fruit farms in Florida, but soon gangs were employed much farther afield. Limited by their contract to agricultural work, they harvested 'tobacco in Tennessee, apples in New York, peanuts in North Carolina, citrus or sugar cane or beans in Florida'. A few tended livestock, cooked for other workers, or operated farm machinery. The great majority were black males; fewer than 10 per cent were black females. Of these, a few were the wives of male contractees – the remainder being left behind to look after their families and farms as best they could. Less than a hundred Bahamian poor white males were recruited (as dairy farm workers) but nearly all, disliking the climate rather than the work, returned within a year.

Selection for the Contract was rigorous, the work was hard, and the experience an eye-opening novelty for those engaged. Contract workers had to be at least 18 years of age and pass a strict medical test. Their contracts were for six or nine months but easily renewable. Their transportation to the United States was paid for by The Bahamas government, their onward journey by the US authorities. For many of those engaged it was their first departure from their home island, and for nearly all their first venture abroad, as well as their first experience of travel by plane or train. Their pay ($3 to $5 a day, or more at piecework rates) was low by US standards but up to five times what they might receive in The Bahamas. Accommodation, transportation and a midday meal were free. Living conditions were normally more spartan than in American army camps, but, with amenities such as flush toilets, hot showers, electric light and radios, were comfortable by Bahamian standards.

Bahamians found it difficult to adjust to the harsher climate and to a work regime set by the farm owners rather than by themselves. They commonly laboured twelve hours a day and sometimes seven days a week, especially when engaged on piecework. Naturally what galled them most was having to accept the restrictions and racism of the Jim Crow system of segregation, particularly in the Southern States. These they ignored as best they could – by keeping to themselves, restraint, and remaining outwardly cheerful under stress – taking comfort in the fact that, unlike American blacks, they did not have to endure the worst indignities all their lives. All in all, Bahamian workers on the Contract gained a reputation for being harder working and more reliable than other black workers, American or West Indian. Many of them had positive and lasting relationships with their white employers, who encouraged them to renew their contracts time and again. This largely accounted for the continuation of the Contract for almost two decades after World War Two ended; the system eventually came to an end because improving conditions at home made it no longer necessary or a preferred option for Bahamians, rather than because the American employers wished to end it.

It was the money that could be saved by normal frugality that made the toil and conditions worth while. A quarter of workers' earnings was automatically deducted and remitted to Nassau on their behalf, providing their families with a guaranteed $10 a month for their subsistence. Many workers, however, remitted much more, and the most hard-working and frugal were able to build up nest-eggs of hundreds of pounds in their Nassau Post Office savings accounts. By the end of World War Two, Bahamians on the Contract were earning more than half a million pounds a year and transferring at least a third of that back to The Bahamas – and these amounts greatly increased after the war ended, despite a gradual decrease in the numbers engaged. In what was probably a peak year for earnings, the 4,000 Contract workers in 1951 were said to have made five million dollars in wages.

All in all, Bahamians on the Contract saw both the worst and the best aspects of life in the United States. They became aware of the material benefits available in that booming country for the hard-working and ambitious, and the growing potential even for blacks to improve themselves and get organised politically. Generally speaking, however, they did not get on well with American blacks, who tended to regard them as aliens, and whom they in turn criticised for being too passive, if not lazy. Unlike many earlier migrants, few of those on the Contract chose to make a permanent home in the United States. Beyond a normal homesickness, they saw The Bahamas, where they constituted the great majority of the population, as a more comfortable place, as well as the natural arena for their own aspirations for a better life, economically, socially and politically.

CORALS AND CORAL REEFS

The two decades of the Contract certainly had a lasting effect on the Bahamian homeland and its people. Though some of those on the Contract used their earnings to buy land and build houses in their home islands, the migration of workers both accelerated the shift of population from the Out Islands and sounded the death knell for traditional subsistence farming. Few of the returnees were happy to go back to the back-breaking and unrewarding toil on the land, and probably a majority instead sought a better life in the Bahamian metropole – as non-agricultural wage-earners if not owners of small businesses or as entrepreneurs. Both the Contract and the shift to Nassau had even more significant effects on Bahamian society. The absence of men abroad had damaged traditional family life, by removing the male head of the family as well as leading to marital break-ups and infidelities. The increased authority of women consequent to running the family and farm on their own was only a small and inadequate compensation. On the more positive side, it was the immigrants to Nassau, especially those with experience in the United States, who were to fuel and spark the political revolution of the 1960s, as well as to provide the backbone for the economic changes which followed the victory of the black majority in 1967.

Further reading: D. Greenberg, 'The Contract, the Project, and Work Experiences', in Joel Savashinsky (ed.), *Strangers No More: Anthropological Studies of Cat Island, the Bahamas*, Ithaca, Ithaca College, 1978; T. Thompson and O. Culmer Jenkins, *Bahamian Memories: Island Voices of the Twentieth Century*, Gainesville, University Press of Florida, 2000, 207–14; T. L. Thompson, 'Remembering the Contract: Insights Towards a Thesis', ACH conference paper, Mona, Jamaica, 1993.

CORALS AND CORAL REEFS

Beautiful and fascinating, corals are primitive salt-water animals which are the principal agents in the creation of the fringing and barrier reefs and atolls for which The Bahamas is famous. Both corals and reefs are priceless but fragile resources, in constant need of protection and conservation.

Corals originated 2 billion years ago, and even the 9,000 species which exist today date back to the beginning of the tertiary era, some 65 million years. The existing reefs which they helped create, however, were formed virtually yesterday in geological terms – in the 10,000 years of rising and warming sea waters since the last Ice Age.

Some kinds of coral are found in all the world's seas, submerged as deep as 19,700 feet (6,000 m). But the great majority flourish only in warm, clear waters which sunlight can penetrate – no deeper than 150 feet (45 m). The ideal water temperature range is between 20 °C and 28 °C (68 to 82.5 °F), which limits the growth of most species to tropical and subtropical seas, only as far as 30 ° latitude north and south of the Equator. Other optimal conditions include minimal tides so as not to alternate between exposing the corals and plunging them too deep, moderate but not excessive wave action to wash food and nutrients towards the corals without causing damage, and a firm geologic base to which the corals can adhere. In all respects, the Bahamian archipelago is naturally ideal – not least in its crystal clear waters, which display the wealth of corals as well as facilitating their growth.

Corals occur in a wonderful array of shapes and colours: in mounds, globes, leaves, flowers, stars, fans and bush-like sprays; coloured brilliant white, red, orange, yellow, green, blue and purple as often as more nondescript browns and greys. All corals consist of individual polyps (some tiny but all usually in conjoined clusters or colonies), each one a tubular sac with a mouth and digestive tract, a 'nerve net' that can detect useful prey and nutrients, tentacles to stun and attract the plankton, small fish and algae on which it feeds, and an apparatus of reproduction, which may be male or female, hermaphroditic, or even asexual.

No one seems to know how long the individual polyps live, but colonies exist for decades or even hundreds of years, given freedom from natural disasters or predators. Corals, however, live in symbiosis with the algae which they consume, as part of the ongoing process of reef formation. Algae help to create the corals' skeletal frameworks of calcium carbonate, which in time become part of the reef, and also act as the cement binding the detritus of dead coral into a solid mass.

Following Charles Darwin's original classification, coral reefs are divided into three types according to their configuration and construction – all of which are to be found in The Bahamas. Most common is the *fringing reef*, formed off the shores of almost all cays where the flat land and shallows give way to deeper water. Where a reef system extends a long distance along the margin between

Corals

a substantial land mass and a deep-water channel, even including islets of its own, it is known as a *barrier reef*. The most notable, if not the only, Bahamian example is the 140-mile (225 km) long reef along the eastern side of ANDROS on the edge of the TONGUE OF THE OCEAN, often said to be the third largest in the world. More questionable examples are the entire chains of cays and reefs north and east of mainland ABACO, between NEW PROVIDENCE and northern ELEUTHERA, and the entire stretch of the EXUMA Cays and RAGGED ISLAND Range – all of them between 70 and 150 miles (110 and 225 km) in length.

The third category of coral reef is the *atoll*. This is a reef system entirely encircling an isolated land mass or subterranean bank. These are far more common in the tropical Pacific than in the Caribbean and Atlantic (though Bermuda is referred to as 'the most northerly coral atoll in the world') and the HOGSTY REEF, between INAGUA and ACKLIN'S ISLAND is sometimes said to be the only Bahamian example. However, far larger Bahamian candidates for the description of atoll are the reef-enclosed CAY SAL Bank and the Great Isaac Bank north of BIMINI, or even the entire reef-surrounded Little Bahama Bank, including the islands of GRAND BAHAMA and Abaco. If the last example were admitted, it would easily oust the Pacific island of Kwajalein from the title of the world's largest atoll.

Though they are an essential feature and the basic building material for coral reefs, live corals are only one ingredient of the ecology of coral reefs – among the richest and most diverse natural habitats in the world. Text books list at least ten types of creature that inhabit, roam and feed on or around coral reefs, drawing scientists, skin-divers and fishermen. Still of huge commercial value are many types of fishes, crustacea and molluscs. Sponges and sea turtles used to be valuable too. Then there are such denizens and visitors (mostly harmless to man but some with formidable defences) as sea anemones, sea urchins, sea cucumbers, sea-worms, sea-snakes, jellyfish, octopuses, eels and sharks and rays. Not least in importance and interest are the tiny but vital micro-organisms, such as plankton and bryozoans (algae) and fungi.

The *Guinness Book of Records* has called Australia's Great Barrier Reef 'the world's largest living organism'. This hyperbole implies that all the living creatures within this gigantic geographical feature are interrelated, interdependent, or symbiotically related to each other. This has been their sustaining strength over aeons. But by the same token, one or more broken links in the symbiotic chain can threaten the whole ecosystem. Some of these are short- or long-term natural disasters or trends, such as cataclysmic storms or climate changes. Sometimes natural predators can inexplicably get out of hand, such as the coral-eating crown of thorns star-fish (*acanthaster planci*) responsible for massive recessions in parts of the Pacific.

Yet by far the most dangerous of the coral reef predators is man and his works. Apart from obvious pollutants or damaging activities such as oil spills, sewage and garbage disposal, run-offs of fertilisers from farming, the illegal use of bleach or dynamite in fishing, dragging anchors, careless dredging and the indiscriminate collection of specimens by divers, there are the less obvious effects of development ashore. These include the clouding of waters through dredging and the run-off of soil from areas deforested and bulldozed, and the general effects of overfishing because of tourist demand. Such effects have already become seriously apparent around New Providence and Freeport, though the government – with much encouragement from the BAHAMAS NATIONAL TRUST, made a major move towards protecting and conserving the marine environment by the establishment of The Bahamas Environment, Science and Technology Commission (BEST) in the year 2000.

Further reading: N. E. Sealey, *Bahamian Landscapes: An Introduction to the Geography of The Bahamas*, Collins Caribbean, 1985, 18–26; I. Greenberg, *Guide to Corals & Fishes of Florida, the Bahamas and the Caribbean*, Miami, Seahawk Press, 1986; *Bahamas Environmental Handbook*, Nassau, Bahamas Environment, Science and Technology Commission, 2002; www.uvi.edu/coral.reefer; www.seaworld.org./coral

COST OF LIVING

In former times, when The Bahamas was poor and of necessity self-sufficient, the cost of living (as far as such a concept was relevant in a cash-scarce economy) was extremely low. Land could be bought for a few pounds an acre, houses built for little more than the cost of the land, and even the comparatively rare wage-earner could exist on a weekly pay that would not buy a single meal today. The situation today is fundamentally different. Greatly enhanced material expectations are coupled with an almost complete dependence on imports, while the absence of an income tax is more than offset by the government's dependence on CUSTOMS DUTIES and other taxes and fees for its revenue. The standard duty rate is 33 per cent, plus a 7 per cent stamp tax. The costs of land, building and all services have escalated hugely. Water, electricity and telephone charges are particularly high. Consequently, the cost of living is one of the highest in the region.

The high cost of living affects the visitor and foreign resident, but at least they have the options of going or living elsewhere, or not staying longer than their purse allows. It is far more damaging for the indigenous

Bahamian population, especially the three-quarters of the people who (because of the distortion of statistical averages caused by the minority of the very prosperous) actually live below the national average income level. For those in regular employment there is mitigation in the relatively high level of wages. For the general population there is limited relief through government controls on the prices of some basic foodstuffs and from the existence of a measure of competition in the local retail trade. In general, Bahamians have the advantage over non-Bahamians of being able to buy land and build with less regulation and more cheaply, and at least some of them have the opportunity to grow and catch their own garden produce and fish. Yet the more they aspire to the standard and mode of living of their North American neighbours, the more they are subject to the cost factors affecting the non-Bahamian.

At a rough general estimate, Bahamian consumer prices are between a third and 40 per cent higher than in the adjacent United States. As in many other respects, tourism and catering to foreign residents is a two-edged sword. The Bahamian economy as a whole could not exist without the money generated by these activities, and the livelihood of at least a third of all Bahamians is dependent upon them.

COTTMAN, Evans W. (1901–1980) An American 'snowbird' whose 1963 account of his adventures as an 'unqualified medical practitioner' is not only a classic of escapist literature but provides a valuable picture of life and conditions in the remoter Family Islands before modernisation.

Born in Indiana and shackled to a career as a teacher, Evans Cottman always hated the winters of the landlocked Midwest and hankered for a carefree life of sailing in the sun. Discovering the Bahamas, he found that the outer islands suited his budget and his spirit and revisited as often as he could. In 1939, he bought ten acres with 500 feet (150 m) of ocean frontage at Gun Bluff, CROOKED ISLAND, for $40, and with local materials and labour built a simple house for little more. A couple of holidays later he visited Abaco to buy a dinghy, meeting his 'CONCHY JOE' wife-to-be, Viola Sawyer, whom he married in 1945.

The problem now was to find an occupation that would allow the Cottmans to stay permanently in The Bahamas. A missionary doctor in Abaco suggested the unexpected solution. The islands were desperately short of doctors and the government was prepared to license willing candidates without professional qualifications and with the sketchiest of scientific training. Cottman applied and was accepted. Provided with a framed certificate and little else, he took his wife to Crooked Island on the mail sailboat and set up practice.

'Doctah' Cottman was amazed by the demand for his services (everything except major surgery) but privately embarrassed by his patients' trust and the well-kept secret of his own incompetence. He put himself through a crash course of reading all the available text books, and also took a voluntary internship in Nassau with a highly skilled and dedicated professional, Dr Charles Maxwell-Joyner (to whom he was to dedicate his book). Though he never did acquire formal qualifications, Evans Cottman found that he had fallen into a thoroughly worthwhile and enjoyable vocation.

Cottman's fees, though numerous, were tiny, and sometimes more difficult to extract than teeth. But in due course he was able to buy a small ketch-rigged Abaco schooner, which he called the *Green Cross*. In this boat he roamed

The cover of Evans Cottman's classic memoir

COTTON

throughout the islands, combining his love for sailing with extending his practice. His voyages were interspersed with longer stints in the lumber camps of Abaco and Grand Bahama. It is the vivid and amusing description of his sailing and medical adventures in the remotest parts of The Bahamas which make his book such a compelling read.

However, it was not Crooked Island but his wife's beloved Abaco that was to become the base and centre of Cottman's practice. Over seven years in the 1950s, as his fees gradually accumulated, he built a small turreted and pillared mansion on the highest bluff in MARSH HARBOUR. Painted a brilliant lime green, it was just a few yards from the dock where the *Green Cross* was moored. 'Seaview House' (locally known as 'the Castle') was a far cry from the original Cottman home at Gun Bluff, Crooked Island. But by the 1960s Cottman was no longer the barefoot and almost penniless adventurer who had first come to The Bahamas; he was now the most famous citizen of what was fast becoming the 'capital' of one of the most rapidly modernising districts in The Bahamas.

Further reading: E.W. Cottman (with Wyatt Blassingame), *Out-Island Doctor*, London, Hodder and Stoughton, 1963; 'Doctor in the Far Flung Islands', *Bahamas Handbook and Businessman's Annual, 1965–6*, Nassau, Dupuch Publications, 1965, 24–35.

COTTON As the Lucayans first discovered, the climate of the central Bahamas (warm and neither too wet nor too dry) is ideal for cultivating the long staple sea island cotton which is still regarded as the best variety found anywhere in the world. COLUMBUS in 1492 was immediately excited by the potential for producing and exporting on a large scale the cotton which the Lucayans already traded and offered the Spaniards in exchange for European goods. Events decreed, however, that plantation production of cotton in The Bahamas was not attempted for almost 300 years, and even then, after an optimistic beginning, unforeseen setbacks doomed the enterprise within 40 years (1785–1825).

The early English colonists had neither the necessary numbers of slaves nor the will to set up large plantations. To the LOYALISTS who flocked to The Bahamas with their slaves after the end of the American War of Independence and the cession of Florida to Spain, however, the cultivation of cotton on the undeveloped central islands seemed to promise compensation for the loss of their plantations on the mainland. The demand for raw cotton from the rapidly expanding British textile industry was open ended; prices were sky-high and promised to remain that way with the continued embargo on imports from the United States.

Within five years, so much Crown land had been allocated and cleared and cotton produced for export that one enthusiast foresaw EXUMA (with its superb natural harbour) superseding NEW PROVIDENCE as the site of the colonial capital. As early as 1787, 4,500 acres had been planted in cotton, with 219 tons exported, worth some £27,000 – five times the total value of all exports before the war. Yet, rather than doubling every year as expected, total cotton production never exceeded 600 tons a year, in 1810, declining to nothing within a further two decades.

The reasons for failure were cumulative. In 1788 began the depredations of an insect called the chenille bug, against which the planters had little protection. More seriously, the planters found that even the best black loam soils were pitifully thin and soon leached out, demanding more and more acreage for similar yields. Productivity was increased by the introduction of a wind-driven variant of Eli Whitney's cotton gin invented by the Loyalist Joseph EVE, but the available slave labour force was stretched painfully thin (not to mention never sharing their masters' incentives). The crucial blow, however, was a steady decline in the price obtainable for raw cotton, as the embargo on American trade ended under pressure from Lancashire cotton spinners, and the cotton plantations of the US South (where slavery lasted until 1865) expanded to meet the accelerating demand.

As early as 1802 Daniel MCKINNEN reported the desertion of plantations in the less productive islands, such as ACKLINS. But long before slavery was ended in The Bahamas (1834–8) the few plantations left had ceased cotton production altogether – with the disconsolate planters and their families having nearly all forsaken their holdings, to live in Nassau, migrate to England, or even return to the United States.

Ironically, cotton was to play a further short-lived role in Bahamian history during the AMERICAN CIVIL WAR. Between 1861 and 1865 Nassau profited spectacularly from being the most convenient neutral base for running arms and supplies into Confederate ports in return for exports of cotton. In January and February 1864 alone, 20 ships evaded the blockade to enter Nassau, carrying more than 14,000 bales of cotton, worth $2,750,000. That almost incredible boom period is recorded in some of the earliest Bahamian photographs. The only mementos of the earlier heyday of Bahamian cotton, though, are the ruins of a few of the cotton planters' mansions – such as the so-called Cotton House in Little Exuma – and the scattered remnants of fluffy wild cotton plants in the surrounding bush, descendants of those planted and harvested by slaves two hundred years ago.

CRABS The Bahamas is rich in crab species, but two stand out in interest and importance: the soft-bodied hermit crab, and the armoured but succulent land crab, a favourite constituent of Bahamian cuisine – its shredded, cooked and seasoned flesh either eaten from the shell, or mixed with PEAS N' RICE.

The different subspecies of hermit crab are distinguished by using the shells of defunct sea or land snails as homes and armour, scuttling laboriously on their projecting front legs and employing their single oversized claw to seize their prey or gather food, or to act as a trap-door when attacked. Clearly, as they mature hermit crabs outgrow their borrowed homes and switch to larger shells. But these transitions are so covert and unpredictable that they have scarcely ever been observed.

Though not palatable, hermit crabs are regarded as quaint and often kept as pets in the United States. Yet the Bahamian land crabs are at least as fascinating, as well as a favourite traditional food source. The largest of the two main species, the giant white (*Cardisoma guanhumi*) may span 2 feet (60 cm), with a carapace that might puncture a car tyre and claws that can almost amputate a human finger. The black land crab (*Gercarcinus lateralis*) is rather smaller, but its flesh is tastier. Both these crabs are hunted at night when they forage, but fall far easier prey when they make their curious mass migrations from land to sea three days before each full moon between May and November.

The geography of The Bahamas, like that of coastal Florida, is ideally suited to the lifestyle and life cycle of the land crab. Air-breathing and adapted to living off terrestrial vegetation and insects, land crabs still need salt water to keep their gills moist and the sea to incubate and mature their offspring. In The Bahamas their favoured land habitats are areas of whiteland coppice, where they construct burrows in the limey soil or sand, down 4 or 5 feet (1.5 m) as far as the water-table. In parts of ANDROS these water-seeking burrows may number thousands to the acre. Intermittent feeders, land crabs are able to survive long periods of drought and food shortage, alternating these with binges, when they consume up to half their weight in leaves, plants, berries and insects.

The annual march to the sea – as curious in its way as the migration of lemmings in Norway, tropical sea TURTLES, or Bahamian crawfish – is an essential part of the land crabs' reproductive process. In early summer the female lays a huge cluster of tiny eggs, which adhere in a glutinous mass to her abdomen to be fertilised by the male. When the embryos, which may number in the hundreds of thousands, reach the stage of self-sufficiency, and the time of the month is right, the land crabs make a concerted rush to the sea. Speed is of the essence in order that the egg mass does not disintegrate and the embryos perish.

The crab embryos – microscopic creatures called *zoea* – are released in the sea, where they join the rest of the myriad creatures collectively called plankton, completely subject to the waves and currents. The tiny fraction of the land-crab zoea who do not become food for plankton-eating species, or succumb later, pass through a series of moults (or *ecdyses*) to become first recognisably crab-like *megalopae* – with ten legs, vestigial claws and carapace – and then fully fledged, if immature, land crabs ready to crawl up and off the beach to construct a burrow like that in which they were conceived. By this time they are sufficiently hardy and armed to be proof against all but their ultimate predator, humankind.

As conservationists point out, it is especially unfortunate that land crabs are most easily captured while they are in the middle of the act of procreation. In densely populated NEW PROVIDENCE they have already been hunted to the point of extinction – a process that was signified when Nola, the famous 'Crab Lady' of Carmichael Village, was forced to close up her cooked crab stall in the 1980s because the crabs were already too scarce.

In Andros, the land crab is such a feature of the local scene, and its life cycle so intertwined with that of the inhabitants, that in recent years a local 'Crab-Fest' has been instituted each June at the height of the crabs' annual march from the land to the sea. For once, it is to be hoped that this celebration of traditional local life does not achieve more than local success – and thus does not serve to hasten the demise of the creature it aims to celebrate.

Crabs a-cooking

CREOLE INCIDENT, 1841

CREOLE INCIDENT, 1841 One of the most dramatic and significant – though almost forgotten – episodes in Bahamian history was the 1841 revolt and takeover by slaves of the American brig *Creole* in Bahamian waters, and the involvement of non-white Bahamians in the subsequent releasing of the slaves.

Full freedom had come for Bahamian slaves as recently as 1838, and a great deal of sympathy was felt for their still enslaved brethren in the United States, not just by the Bahamian ex-slaves and the non-whites long freed, but also by the LIBERATED AFRICANS, freed from foreign slavers and settled in The Bahamas over the previous three decades.

The *Creole*, a two-masted vessel of some 300 tons, set sail from Hampton Roads, Virginia, bound for New Orleans, on 27 October 1841. Besides the Captain, Robert Ensor, his wife, child and a niece, the *Creole* carried a crew of 11, three slave overseers, a cargo of tobacco, and no fewer than 135 slaves – destined to be sold to labour in the rapidly expanding cotton fields of Louisiana. In a manner reminiscent of the more famous revolt on board the *Amistad* two years earlier (though with a different outcome), the slaves first lulled the crew into a false sense of security, then rose up on the night of 7 November, while off the coast of Abaco.

Two crewmen were killed in the fight and two mortally wounded, along with one of the slaves. The slightly wounded captain, his family and the slave overseers were locked up in their cabins, while the mate and the surviving crewmen were ordered to steer the *Creole* for Liberia. Persuaded that the provisions and water aboard were quite insufficient for such a transatlantic voyage, the rebels told them to sail into Nassau instead.

The *Creole* arrived in Nassau harbour on the morning of 9 November, almost immediately to be surrounded by boats full of sympathetic and possibly belligerent blacks. Confident that the British authorities would let them go free (as had happened to the slaves on the American ship *Hermosa*, wrecked at Abaco a year earlier), the rebels allowed the mate to go ashore to report the situation to Governor Cockburn and the American Consul, John Bacon. The Consul angrily demanded that the slaves be compelled to continue to their destination, where the innocent would be sold and the ringleaders indicted for murder.

After consultation with his Council, Governor Cockburn announced that the ringleaders might be extradited but the other slaves would be allowed to go free. To control the situation, he sent a detachment of 24 black soldiers of the West India Regiment garrison under a white officer aboard the *Creole*. These soldiers dissuaded attempts by the local non-whites to liberate all the slaves, but also thwarted a move by armed Americans from other vessels then in the harbour to recapture them and carry them away.

On 12 November, the soldiers escorted the 19 identified ringleaders ashore and into detention, while some 2,000 non-whites rowed all the remaining slaves ashore and jubilantly paraded them through the streets of Nassau. Though three slave women with two children opted to go on to New Orleans, almost all of those released were carried off to more certain safety in Jamaica within a week – though quite what happened to them once there remains obscure. The *Creole* itself left Nassau for New Orleans on 19 November, arriving on 2 December, to provoke outraged cries from American slave-holders and protests from the US government.

However, the demands for the extradition of the rebel ringleaders failed. Despite the delicate British–American negotiations then afoot, British Foreign Secretary Lord Aberdeen ordered all the slaves released in February 1842, a decision that was greeted as a great triumph by all non-white Bahamians and by abolitionists everywhere. What happened to all the ringleaders is not entirely clear. Some are thought to have joined the others in Jamaica, or even to have gone to Liberia. But at least one, Elisha Morris, stayed in The Bahamas, becoming a much respected smallholder in the village of GAMBIER in western New Providence.

Not that this was the end of the *Creole* affair. Demands for reparation for the value of the slaves – some $87,000 – were successful, though not until 1853. In the same year, the great black abolitionist Frederick Douglass, himself a former runaway slave, wrote a semi-fictional account of the *Creole* uprising. In this, the person identified as the slaves' chief leader, the appropriately named Madison Washington, is elevated to the level of a super-hero in the fight against the evil of slavery.

Further reading: H. Jones, 'The Peculiar Institution and National Honor: The Case of the *Creole* Slave Revolt', *Civil War History*, 21, 1975, 30–47; E. Eden, 'The Revolt on the Slave Ship *Creole*: Popular resistance to slavery in post-emancipation Nassau', *Journal of the Bahamas Historical Society*, 22, 2000, 13–20; F. Douglass, 'The Heroic Slave', in W. Andrews (ed.), *The Oxford Frederick Douglass Reader*, New York, Oxford, 1996; M. Montesinos Sale, *The Slumbering Volcano*. Durham, NC, Duke University Press, 1997.

CRICKET The quintessentially English summer game, cricket followed the Union Jack to every corner of the Empire, including The Bahamas. Unlike countries as diverse as Australia, India or Barbados – where the game was so ardently adopted and adapted by the local cultures as to challenge and even outclass its originators – cricket has had a less profound and lasting effect on The Bahamas. Though in its heyday the premier summer team game in

Nassau, cricket has since wilted through competition from many other activities, and is kept alive only by a handful of enthusiasts, most of them not Bahamian-born.

The first reference to cricket in The Bahamas was somewhat negative. Regarded as potentially disruptive if not formally organised, the casual 'playing of Cricket or other like Game or Games on the Parade or public streets' was forbidden by an ordinance in 1853 – the last year of formal slavery. The first mention of a specific game (though probably not the very first played) was a report of a match between the Garrison and a team of civilians in January 1855. The Garrison was also involved in a match with the visiting warship HMS *Galatea* in February 1863, of which the *Nassau Guardian* wrote: 'A number of the fair and beautiful were on the ground, who appeared to take a lively interest in the match if we might judge from their many laughs and sparkling eyes; and the fine band of the 2nd. W.I. regiment added a charm to every thing.'

Though the Garrison teams almost certainly included black players, most of the early games were between white players and watched mainly by white spectators. That ordinary black Bahamians were not enthusiasts at first – or at least felt excluded – was suggested by a riot that occurred in January 1860 at HARBOUR ISLAND. A group of white 'Brilanders' had leased a few acres of flat land in order to play cricket, but their first (and seemingly only) match was disrupted by local blacks who regarded the area in question as common land traditionally earmarked for market gardening. By the 1870s, however, the colonial authorities and Nassau elite had clearly become convinced of cricket's value – long demonstrated in England – in promoting social cohesion without upsetting the social order. In 1873 a Nassau Cricket Club, planned to attract non-white players as well as supporters, was founded, with a custom-built ground and facilities. At the official opening on 25 January 1873, the white Bahamian legislator J. H. Webb exhorted his mixed audience in properly Victorian terms: 'Use your ground well … and learn scientific cricket as a manly outdoor amusement, for the development of pluck and muscle.'

Webb's encouragement seems to have fallen on ready ears. By 1899, the American travel writer G. J. F. Northcroft remarked: 'Cricket, not Baseball, is *the* game of the Bahamian young men. There is a host of Cricket Clubs in Nassau … cricketing interests – as is natural in a British Colony – form a social cement of some adhesiveness; and a cricket match of any importance is generally well patronised by spectators.' Cricket apparently went from strength to strength, gaining such popularity that by the 1920s and 1930s it was almost exclusively played by non-whites, and in the heat of the summer as well as the cooler months of the traditional tourist season. The Bahamas Cricket Association was formed in 1933, initially with five participating clubs: St Agnes, St Alban's, St George's, Melbourne and Wanderers.

A new cricket ground was laid out at Haynes' Oval below Fort Charlotte in the 1930s as part of Governor CLIFFORD'S moves to improve sporting facilities to attract the tourists, and during World War Two the standard of play was raised (and the ethnic range of players temporarily widened) by teams drawn from the forces in Nassau for the duration – particularly the ROYAL AIR FORCE. But it was not until there was an influx of policemen and prison warders from the West Indies, especially Barbados, from the late 1940s that local cricket really took off. Helped by a police policy to encourage sports, a police team of West Indians let by the redoubtable Sergeant Roy Armbrister (perhaps the finest Bahamian all-round player ever) was almost perennial winner of the Bahamas Cricket Association League through the 1950s. The posting of a detachment of the Royal Worcestershire Regiment to Nassau at the time of the GENERAL STRIKE in 1958 gave another boost to the local game, particularly in the person of Treffor Davies, who was to marry and settle in The Bahamas after playing first-class cricket in England and Australia – becoming the captain and star player of a new team, Cosmopolitans.

Inspired by the heightened competition and emulating skills of the newcomers, the number of strong teams and adept players reached a pieak in the early 1960s. Many of the West Indian policemen and prison warders continued to live in The Bahamas after their contracts expired and spread themselves around the league, while more and more Bahamians – already fine fielders through also playing softball and basevall – began to match them in batting and bowling skills. All three of the grounds used – Haynes' Oval, St Bernard's Park off Nassau Street, and Windsor Park at the junction of East Street and Wulff Road – had pitches consisting of matting laid on tarmac. This hard surface meant that the ball soon lost its shine and ability to swing, but had a lively bounce even at medium pace and could be cut quite sharply off the seam. Helped by umpires who ignored the rules against bowling directed at the body, this put a premium on quick rather than spin bowling, and on aggressive rather than defensive batting – both, as it happened, more akin to baseball than classic cricket styles.

CROCODILE

Relatively, the Police team faded as most of its stars finished their term of service and left the force. But there was fierce rivalry to be their successor. Partisanship reached an even higher pitch in the crowd than on the field, a fact not unrelated to the amount of clandestine betting that went on. Probably the two chief contenders were the 'parish' teams of St Bernard's (Catholic) and St Agnes (Anglican), but all the other teams had their good days, especially the three oldest teams still playing, St George's, St Alban's and Westerns, and the newcomer Cosmopolitans. At the height of cricket's popularity in the 1960s, key league matches drew crowds of thousands and the standard of play was of a remarkably high order. The level of umpiring never quite matched this, in knowledge of the laws and judgement, as well, it was widely believed, in impartiality.

However, the glory days of Bahamian cricket faded after the 1960s as the number of active participants declined and other sports, including baseball, softball, TENNIS and GOLF, competed in popularity. By the 1990s Haynes' Oval had become the only location where cricket continued to be played in Nassau. Yet, thanks to the tireless work of the former West Indians and other veterans, the Oval had become the hub and focus of all cricket activity and had more the appearance of an authentic West Indian cricketing arena than ever before – complete with a two-tier pavilion showing international cricket on satellite TV and serving drinks and food, spectator seating, a proper scoreboard and a boundary ringed with advertising boards.

Bahamian cricket had never quite reached either the popularity or the standard achieved by Bermuda, let alone Barbados, Jamaica or Guyana. Yet a handful of Bahamian players have reached or come close to first-class proficiency and, given Bahamians' natural sporting ability and determination, many more would have achieved as much given the right circumstances. Proud cricket fans in The Bahamas have often claimed that at least two Bahamians have had the potential to represent the West Indies in cricket: Roy Armbrister and the St Alban's player who went on to a 12-year career in major baseball, Andre Rodgers. Curiously, the only Bahamian actually to play first-class cricket never played in The Bahamas. This was Ivan Johnson, who learned his cricket at school in England and played a couple of years for Worcestershire, before becoming a journalist and returning to Nassau to found and edit the newspaper *Punch*.

Better days may yet be ahead for Bahamian cricket. The game has caught on in Freeport (mainly among expatriates, largely through sponsorhip and encouragement by Sir Jack HAYWARD. And since the 1990s the BCA has entertained many visiting teams and several international cricketing stars have been welcomed to give clinics to young aspirants. The BCA has also raised funds and found sponsors to send its own representative teams abroad. Encouraged by a successful tour of the United Kingdom in 1999 (albeit only against club opposition), the BCA even sent a Bahamas team all the way to Buenos Aires, Argentina for the inaugural contest for the Americas' Cup in March 2002.

CROCODILE Two species of crocodile, the American and the Cuban, were once numerous throughout The Bahamas, but are now extinct there. Their bones are commonly found in sinkholes, especially in areas of saltwater marsh. They would have been formidable opponents for the aboriginal AMERINDIANS and for the first post-Columbian visitors and settlers. In 1993 a skull and partial skeleton of a fossil crocodile was collected from the bottom of a BLUE HOLE in Abaco. The fossil was dated as nearly 3,000 years old and was considered similar to the modern Cuban crocodile.

Early writers made no distinction between alligators and crocodiles, though the former, which live only in fresh water, probably never lived in the islands. Mark CATESBY, the first naturalist to write on The Bahamas, described ferocious 20–foot (6 m) 'alligators' in the ANDROS swamps in 1725. 'In no place have I ever seen such remarkable scenes of devastation as among the mangroves in Andros,' he wrote, 'where the fragments of half-devoured carcasses [presumably animals, not humans] were usually floating on the water.'

Bahamian 'alligators' were also described by Peter Henry BRUCE in the 1740s, and as late as 1804 Daniel MCKINNEN recorded being served 'alligator' for dinner while visiting ACKLINS Island. They 'were sometimes brought in for the table,' he reported, 'but it required considerable address and some courage to destroy them.' Their meat, said McKinnen, was 'hard, white, and very much resembled the sturgeon's.' His less than enthusiastic report suggests that crocodiles were hunted into oblivion not for food but because of the danger they represented to the settlers and their domestic animals.

Further reading: R. F et al, 'Fossil Skeleton of a Crocodile from Abaco', *Bahamas Journal of Science*, 3 (1), 1995.

CROOKED ISLAND The 84-square mile (218 squ.-km) formerly important island which gives its name to the district that also includes LONG CAY, ACKLINS, SAMANA CAY and the Plana Cays. Well populated by the Lucayans, its first and most famous European visitor was Christopher COLUMBUS. The natives called the island Samoet, but the explorer renamed it Isabella after his Spanish royal patroness. He described it in glowing terms, enthusing about the scented aroma that came off the land (probably the smell of CASCARILLA bark) and exaggerating the suitability of his anchorage as a port (the *Yachtsman's Guide* firmly disagrees). Columbus stayed a few days awaiting an anticipated delegation from a gold-rich king, but moved on towards Cuba when neither king nor gold materialised.

In colonial times, the location of Crooked Island at the Atlantic entrance to the most convenient passage from Europe and North America into the Caribbean gave it considerable strategic and commercial importance. At the end of the eighteenth century, Pitt's Town at the island's north-western tip (named after Britain's famous Prime Minister) was laid out as the site of the General Post Office for The Bahamas, where packet boats would drop off incoming mail for distribution throughout the islands and pick up items destined for abroad. So important was this communication point considered, especially during wartime, that it was guarded by two powerful gun batteries, and a small garrison.

Pitt's Town was the colony's main link with the outside world until NASSAU became a stopping place on the steam mail boat service instituted by James McQueen and Samuel Cunard in the 1840s, and it was a stopping place for ships steaming directly to and from the Caribbean until the end of the century. The surviving name of the overgrown former plantation called Marine Farm indicates that it was the place where fresh produce was available for passing vessels. Little trace of either settlement or post office remain, though eighteenth-century cannons, with their Royal Navy insignia, can still be seen in the bush at Marine Farm and Gun Bluff.

During the era of peace and international trade that followed the Napoleonic Wars, Crooked Island became more important as a landmark than as a stopping place. In 1876 a powerful lighthouse was erected on the rocky islet (described by Columbus) called Bird Rock, a mile or so off Pitt's Town Point. This marked the northern entrance to the wide but tricky Crooked Island Passage, just as a similar lighthouse completed in the same year on Castle Island just south of Acklins, marked its southern end and guided vessels clear of the treacherous reef graphically called *Mira Por Vos* ('Look Out for Yourselves').

At the height of the LOYALIST era Crooked Island boasted 40 COTTON plantations, many of them also with productive SALT-pans. Once cotton production faded and SLAVERY ended, the ex-slaves and their descendants turned to subsistence farming and fishing, WRECKING and SPONGING. The lighthouses virtually ended the wrecking trade, just as the sponge blight ended sponging

Crooked Island post office

CUBA

some sixty years later. Those Crooked Islanders who could not or would not survive on subsistence farming and fishing gradually migrated, mostly to Nassau.

Once home to 2,000 people, Crooked Island now has barely 400 inhabitants. An eighth of these live in the hamlet of Landrail Point, 2 miles (3 km) south of Pitt's Town Point, where the weekly mailboat calls. Some work at Crooked Island's only resort of any size, the 12-room Pittstown Point Landing, which has its own 2,240-foot (683 m) airstrip. Most of the island's population now congregates at Colonel Hill in the hilly centre of the island, where the district's Commissioner resides and the island's airport was built in 1964. This has two scheduled flights a week, along with the occasional charter flight.

A reasonably good road connects Landrail Point to Colonel Hill, but as it passes on eastward through the decayed settlements of Major's Cay, True Blue and Brown's it deteriorates to a track. This terminates at Cove Point, from which a government ferry twice a day crosses the 3-mile (5 km) shallow passage quaintly called the Going Through, which separates quiet Crooked Island from even quieter Acklins. The location is just as beautiful, and hardly more altered by development, than it was when Daniel MCKINNEN visited it in 1802 – and was astounded to be met at the shore by a horse-drawn carriage sent by the Loyalist planter Colonel Douglas.

CUBA The immense island of Cuba is the nearest geographical neighbour to The Bahamas. But the two countries have been politically separated through much of their history; first through the colonial rivalry between Britain and Spain, and since 1959 because of the victory of Castro's Communism and the embargo by the other more powerful neighbour and political ally of The Bahamas, the United States. Yet the Bahamas–Cuba relationship has always actually been closer and more significant than portrayed in the history books, and even today poses ambiguities.

Spain, having claimed the Bahama islands by right of discovery, saw them as more or less worthless but troublesome outliers of their more valuable colonies in the Antilles and on the Spanish Main. Spanish vessels roamed The Bahamas at will, and even during times of official peace Spanish flotillas from Havana or Santiago periodically harried the islands and NASSAU as the haunts of pirates. It needed the capture of Havana by a British expeditionary force sailing through Bahamian waters in 1762, and negotiations for Cuba's return in the subsequent treaty, for the Spanish, somewhat half-heartedly, to acknowledge Britain's possession of The Bahamas. This was reversed by the capture and occupation of Nassau by a Spanish–American expedition from Havana in 1782 – and unequivocal recognition of The Bahamas as a British colony was not accorded until Nassau's 'recapture' by Andrew DEVEAUX and the exchange of Florida for The Bahamas in the Treaty of Versailles (1783).

During the 'free trade' era of the nineteenth century, there was some interchange between the British Bahamas and Spanish Cuba. But relations were never really close or cordial. While slavery still existed in The Bahamas, runaways sometimes fled to Cuba. But this was a chancy enterprise, since re-enslavement grew ever more likely as Cuban sugar plantations developed. A few LOYALIST planters from the American mainland remigrated to grow sugar in Cuba once their cotton plantations had failed in The Bahamas. But this came to an end when the British government forbade them to carry their slaves with them in 1826. When British slavery ended in 1838, many Bahamian ex-slaves were desperate for paid work wherever it could be found. But Cuba was not a favoured option because slavery continued there, and in many respects became more intensive, for fifty years after British EMANCIPATION. Tension between Britain and Spanish Cuba (already high because of British abolitionist tactics) also occurred when remote Bahamian islands were used as bases by Cuban rebels during the Cuban wars of independence, and Spanish *guarda costas* infringed Bahamian territorial waters in hunting them down.

However, during periods of peace, and especially once Cuba had become a virtual US protectorate after the Spanish American War and the Platt Amendment (1898–1902), there was an increasing amount of interchange between The Bahamas and Cuba. From the 1840s, steamer routes connected Nassau with the northern and eastern Cuban ports. Southern Bahamians were recruited as stevedores in ships traversing the Windward Passage and serving Santiago de Cuba as well as other Caribbean ports. A sprinkling of skilled or semi-skilled Cubans migrated to Nassau – including artisans working on the building and rebuilding of the BRITISH COLONIAL HOTEL in 1899 and 1922 who decided to stay on – as well as the few CHINESE who tried their luck in the Bahamian capital after a sojourn of years in Cuba. The Spanish language was heard spoken in Chinese restaurants and grocery stores and among the congregation of Nassau's first Catholic church.

Castro's revolution changed the relationship of The Bahamas with its neighbour. But an ambivalence remained. As an ally and ideological follower (if not quite a client) of the United States, The Bahamas has officially tended to keep its distance from the Cuban Communist regime. This stance was patriotically reinforced by the sinking of the HMBS *FLAMINGO* by Cuban warplanes in 1980. Yet that has not meant that Bahamians have necessarily been sympathetic or welcoming to anti-Castroite Cuban refugees.

It is quite clear that if the 'Miami Cubans' return to their homeland and have their way, the result will be a Cuba much on the freewheeling pre-Castro lines – dominated by a glitzy tourism, combining the undoubted attractions of the Cuban beaches, cuisine, music and countryside, with more sinful pleasures. Some think Cuba will become serious, if not fatal, competition for the more staid (and far from cheap) tourist attractions of The Bahamas. Already at the century's turn, while Castro still ruled, the signs were ominous. A million non-Americans a year were drawn by the Veradero beach hotels (mostly run by non-Cubans, such as the Italian Melia company), by the antique and modern delights of Havana and Santiago, and by a rapidly expanding and increasingly sophisticated eco-tourism. Perhaps the most significant pointer of all, Cubana charter flights were also carrying regular planeloads of young and youngish Bahamians (mainly males) on weekend joy-rides from Nassau to Havana, while others took advantage of cheap medical services and educational programmes.

CUISINE The cuisine of The Bahamas shares much in common with its Caribbean neighbours, through borrowings and from common culinary traditions and ingredients. This includes a few dishes still occasionally found that originally derived from Africa or tropical

Guarded friendliness: Prime Minister Christie enjoys a diplomatic joke with Fidel Castro, 2002

CURRENCY

America. It has also been conditioned by having long been dependent on imported staples, including rice, beans, peas, corn and wheat flour, macaroni and other pastas, and most meats. Like most people in the tropics, however, Bahamians are noted for their preference for hot and spicy foods over the blander dishes found in more temperate climes

The Bahamas has developed an array of distinctive dishes and culinary customs, mainly derived from its special indigenous resources and traditional way of life. Affection for these marks out the native Bahamian, not just at home but abroad. Whenever Bahamians meet together in some alien place, food is not only central to the occasion, but has to include items regarded as Bahamian trademarks, and therefore peerless. Bahamians concede nothing to any other country, claiming, for instance, that their native goat pepper is the hottest in the world.

The core of Bahamian cuisine, naturally, is seafood. Most distinctive of all is the almost ubiquitous CONCH. Bahamians' taste for the emblematic mollusc – which has given them (along with the semi-Bahamians of Key West) their nickname – has sometimes mystified outsiders. 'What *is* the big deal?' almost sacrilegiously asks the *Lonely Planet Guide* – before further jeopardising its credibility by suggesting that conch's popularity is solely due to its mythical qualities as a male aphrodisiac. Bahamians on the contrary, while not dismissing the power of the conch to 'gi'e man strong back', cannot understand why others should not find it intrinsically delicious.

The demand for conch has already overharvested the waters nearest to Nassau, and pessimists have even predicted that it may go the way of another former culinary favourite, the green TURTLE – now protected as an endangered species. Prized as a food since the time of the Lucayans and exported in colonial times as a useful foodstuff for long sailing voyages and to provide the famous soup served at mayoral banquets in London, the turtle was the only Bahamian food for which the short-term resident L. D. POWLES had unstinted praise in the 1880s. He decried the local chickens and other meats and made no comment on the conch as food. But he waxed lyrical on the turtle – especially the local tour de force: turtle baked and served in its own shell, with a pastry crust. This delicacy – said by Powles to have been unique to Nassau – was still the centrepiece for special banquets in the 1930s. Until the 1960s, live turtles were sold from a seawater tank in the fish market on the Nassau waterfront. But turtle steak and soup had already become an extreme luxury before its slaughter for food was finally forbidden.

Besides the conch, Bahamians eat other molluscs, such as 'whelks' and 'curbs', land CRABS, and as much of the great spiny LOBSTER (or crawfish) as is not snapped up by the voracious foreign market. Quantitatively, however, it is the many species of delicious local fish that provide the largest amount of protein food. Bahamians will often buy fresh fried small fish from waterside stalls and eat it there and then, crunching up bones and all. The most popular breakfast or brunch dish is boiled fish-and-grits, held to be the most flavourful way to enjoy the taste of a fresh catch. Stew fish (most notably grouper), prepared with onions, tomatoes, celery and various spices, is another local speciality.

Most main dishes are accompanied by the distinctively Bahamian version of the Caribbean PEAS N' RICE, along with local spices (particularly pepper and thyme), tomatoes and onions. Pigeon peas (once sufficiently produced in the islands but now mainly imported) also figure prominently in an array of tasty Bahamian soups – such as pea soup with dumplings and salt beef or split pea and ham soup. A more substantial stew special to the islands is the Bahamian souse (pronounced 'sowse'). The only ingredients are water, onions, lime juice, celery, peppers and meat – no thickeners are added. The meat is opportunistic and adventurous: chicken, sheep's tongue, oxtail or pig's feet – giving what is described as 'a delicious, rich flavour, new to many visitors'. While these traditional foods, along with goat curry, fried chicken and pork chops, provide a healthy diet, they are today supplemented by all the most popular fast food franchised from the US, and obesity has become a recognised health problem.

Bahamian food can be criticised for being heavy in starches, and Bahamians themselves for being over-dedicated to the pleasures of the table. The excuses are valid enough. Apart from the tastiness of traditional dishes, the custom of providing and eating large amounts whenever possible is said to be a response to previous hard times, when all food had to be garnered by the sweat of the brow and was all too often scarce.

Further reading: C. Williams, *Bahamian Cooking*, Boynton Beach, Florida, Star Publishing, 1976; D. Carstaphen, *The Conch Book: All You Wanted to Know About the Queen Conch, From Gestation to Gastronomy*, Wicomico, Va., Pen and Ink Press, 1982; M. Mendelson and M. Sawyer, *Gourmet Bahamian Cooking*, Iowa City, Best Way Publishing, 1995; 'Galley Guide' section in *Yachtsman's Guide to the Bahamas*, Miami, Tropic Isle Publishers (annually updated).

CURRENCY

Before 1966 there was only ever one coin specific to The Bahamas: a handsome copper half-penny produced by the Royal Mint in London in 1806, with the head of King George III on one side and the old Bahamian coat of arms and motto on the other. It did not gain popular acceptance, and so limited and short-lived was its circulation that specimens change hands today for as much as $650 apiece.

CURRENCY

Before and long after 1806, a whole range of foreign as well as British coins were acceptable currency in The Bahamas. What determined their value was simply the weight of gold or silver in them. British gold sovereigns and guineas and silver coins had a good reputation for standard weight and quality. But they were in shorter supply than foreign coins, especially Spanish. Among the most common silver coins in the eighteenth century were the 'ryal' (from the Spanish *real*), the 'piece of eight' (that is, 8 *reales*, worth about 3 ½ shillings Sterling), and the 'Maria Theresa dollar' (from the German *thaler*—reckoned to be worth 4 shillings and 8 pence). Gold coins, though understandably rare in The Bahamas, were even more varied. Besides British guineas (later, sovereigns and half-sovereigns) these included the *pistole* (worth about 18 shillings), *moidore* (about 27 shillings), *Johannes* (36 shillings) and *doubloon* (66 shillings).

As late as 1880, the BLUE BOOK made the following list of coins current in The Bahamas: British gold sovereigns and half-sovereigns, silver half-crowns, florins, shillings, 6, 4, 3 and 2 penny pieces, and copper pence and half-pence; United States gold ($10) double eagles, single, half and quarter eagles, and silver dollars, half-dollars and quarter-dollars, along with similar coins of various states of South America; old Spanish gold dollars and smaller silver coins, and finally, French silver 5 franc pieces. Confusingly, well into the twentieth century, the tradition of discounting local (or 'Currency') pounds, shillings and pence against Sterling amounts survived in the market custom of regarding (as it suited the transactor) 'tree pence Sterling' actually to mean 5 pence local currency (or 10 cents American, rather than 6).

Though with the expansion of TOURISM the American dollar became almost as current and acceptable, the British denominations of pounds, shillings and pence remained the official Bahamian currency from the 1890s until the achievement of self-government in the 1960s, with all coins and notes being identical with those circulating in the United Kingdom. Apart from the psychological and actual cost to The Bahamas of being dependent on coins and notes produced by the British Royal Mint, there were the long-standing problems of learning in school the mantra '12 pence, 1 shilling, 20 shillings, 1 pound', of understanding the typically British anomalies of the florin (2 shillings) and guinea (21 shillings), and of converting the awkward British currency amounts into those of the United States dollar and other decimal currencies.

The great changeover of 1964–6 was almost entirely the work of the UNITED BAHAMIAN PARTY tycoon Sir Stafford SANDS, the first Minister of Finance. Early in 1964 he officially announced that The Bahamas was converting to a decimal currency of its own. It was decreed that the terms dollars and cents would be used, despite a questionnaire organised by the BAHAMAS CHAMBER OF COMMERCE showing that three-quarters of respondents preferred loyal names such as Crown, Sovereign or Royal, names historically resonant, including Columbus, Santa Maria or Doubloon, or distinctively Bahamian names such as Bahama, Lucaya, Conch, Flamingo or Elder. However, the set of dollar and cent coins and notes introduced in May 1966 were certainly distinctive and distinctively Bahamian. The coins, designed by the British Royal Academician Arnold Machin, with instructions to make them attractive to tourists and collectors (who, it was hoped, would take a proportion out of circulation) included a series of 5, 2 and 1-dollar coins and 50-cent coins in silver, a 25-cent piece

Currency, 2000

CUSTOMS DUTIES

in pure nickel, a square 15-cent, wavy-edged 10-cent and 5-cent piece in cupro-nickel, and a copper 1-cent piece. The equally impressive banknotes, designed and printed in full colour by the British De la Rue Company, were initially in 50-cent, $1, $3, $5, $10, $20, $50 and $100 denominations.

In 1973, the year of Bahamian INDEPENDENCE and a year after Britain had allowed the weak pound to float, the Bahamian dollar was judiciously pegged permanently precisely at par with that of the United States. As a consequence, Bahamian and United States currencies have continued to this day to be virtually interchangeable within The Bahamas – though certainly not outside its shores.

Bahamian coins, which have remained the same since 1966, all have the image of QUEEN ELIZABETH II on one side and a Bahamian motif on the other. The banknotes, which naturally have a much shorter life-span than coins, have been through more changes. Through inflation, the 50-cent note has virtually faded out, and a $500 note has been added to the series. The $3 banknote – an ill-judged attempt to make a collector's item based on the vulgar American saying 'as queer as a three dollar bill' – has been allowed to lapse. A much more important symbolic change is that in the second phase of Bahamian independence it was decided that the Queen's head on all banknotes would be replaced by images of Bahamian heroes and heroines.

CUSTOMS DUTIES

The government's dependence on customs duties (which made up 60 per cent of the total national revenue, and 76 per cent of the revenue from all taxes, in the year 2000) helps to make the COST OF LIVING in The Bahamas one of the highest in the region. This offsets the advantage of the non-existence of an income tax, particularly for those on modest to low incomes. Indeed, it has been argued that the preference for indirect taxation over an income tax and other taxes (a legacy from the days when BAY STREET was supreme) disproportionately benefits the rich at the expense of the poor.

The standard rate of customs duty for imported goods is 35 per cent of their value (including the cost of freight and insurance), plus a further seven per cent for what is termed 'stamp tax'. Yet in reality there is a wide and complex range of customs duties, representing a juggling act aimed at serving different economic and political interests and fiscal and social concerns – some making for lower and others for much higher rates. The resulting complexity of Bahamian tariffs and regulations, and the accompanying paperwork, makes it almost imperative for importers to seek the services of an expert customs broker, which constitutes a hidden further cost.

There are notable reductions on some items intended to benefit the ordinary Bahamian consumer. Items of outer clothing are charged 25 per cent duty and underwear 15 per cent. Certain staple foods not produced in The Bahamas have a low duty tariff, rice, sugar, cheese and pasta being charged 10 per cent, and potatoes no duty at all – though all food products do pay a 2 per cent stamp duty. By arrangement with the Ministry of Agriculture there is also a sliding scale of duties – up to a prohibitive level in some cases – aimed at protecting certain items of Bahamian produce in season (see AGRICULTURE). No levies are made on Bahamian exports, apart from a $10 flat stamp duty on each shipment (with a somewhat higher charge on the export of lobster).

No duty is charged on imported books, computers and outboard engines, among several commodities deemed beneficial to the community, and there are generous duty concessions made on the import of goods for sale to tourists. There is no duty charged at all on the items most popular with tourists, including china and crystal, fine jewellery, cashmere sweaters, perfume, watches and cameras, though again these are subject to a variable amount of stamp duty, up to 20 per cent. Similarly, a variable stamp duty (from $10 a gallon for imported spirits up to 50 per cent of the value of most wines) is a disguised charge on allegedly 'duty-free' liquor.

On the other side of the tariff see-saw there are customs duties in excess of the standard rate for some items in popular demand which are considered to be not necessarily of benefit to The Bahamas or Bahamians. Clearly aimed at the public craving for more and more cars despite the overcrowded roads, there is a swingeing duty on imported vehicles, varying, according to age, size and use, from 45 to 75 per cent of value. Even car parts and accessories are charged 50 per cent, exclusive of stamp duty. Though the curious tax of 100 per cent on the value of pool tables may indicate a somewhat puritanical official attempt to discourage the spread of pool-halls, the most obvious application of a 'sin tax' along the lines of the UK, US and other countries, is the duty of 160 per cent *ad valorem* charged on loose tobacco, and 210 per cent on cigarettes.

Further information: *Bahamas Handbook and Businessman's Annual*, Nassau, Dupuch Publications; Bahamas Tariff Act 1996, copies available from Government Publications, Old Lighthouse Building, Bay Street, PO Box N-7147, Nassau.

DANCE The Bahamas has had an active and interesting tradition of popular dance, derived mainly from Africa. Bahamians have traditionally been keen and adept dancers, and in fairly recent times there have been sundry efforts to establish dance academies. Yet for a variety of reasons the country has not yet produced a truly national school of dance.

As the Bahamian ethno-musicologist Clement Bethel wrote in 1978, the most popular traditional form of entertainment among non-whites was singing and dancing, and he added that secular music, with its emphasis on drumming and dancing (as opposed to religious music that came by way of America) emanated directly from Africa, with only minimal European influences, such as an Africanised version of the quadrille. Despite attempts by Christian ministers to suppress such dances, wherever there was a dominant African element in the population, ring dances to the accompaniment of Goombay drums and perhaps a concertina and two pieces of iron long remained the most popular forms of folk dancing.

Clement Bethel distinguished three distinct types of Afro-Bahamian ring dance: the fire dance, the jumping dance, and the ring play. The basic requirement was a circle of participants and a rhythmic accompaniment, consisting of singing, chanting, clapping, drum rhythms, or a combination of these. The essence of each dance was rotational involvement, singly or in pairs, with an element of exhibition and competition, and a rising climax. Such features also spilled over into the major annual folk celebration of JUNKANOO. Both in ring-dance jamborees and in Junkanoo, the competitive excitement sometimes rose to a point of frenzy and exhaustion not very different from the almost hysterical climaxes of services at the 'shouter' or 'jumper' churches – which, regrettably, became tourist spectacles in the late nineteenth century.

Indeed (with the exception of Junkanoo), such 'native' dancing, especially the fire dance, became gradually relegated to the level of night-club entertainments (with the addition of the limbo dance, quite spuriously claimed to be a relic of slavery times, when slaves would 'get down low' to earn their freedom). Night club and other dance-hall customers, black as well as white, now tended to confine their dancing to more 'proper' (if still somewhat erotically charged) ballroom dancing modes, or, more recently, 'dance hall' styles imported from Jamaica, Trinidad and the United States.

Anyone observing Bahamians at clubs or parties, or watching the annual Junkanoo parades, can have no doubt that Bahamians are enthusiastic natural dancers. But Bahamian dance in general has suffered from confusion between high and low culture, lagging behind the other performing art forms in the Bahamas largely because the country has produced few enduring local visionaries. For example, a local ballet school, the Nassau Civic Ballet, pioneered in the 1960s by classical Bahamian dancer Hubert Farrington, never developed into a national company. It fell uncomfortably between classical European and African-American ballet styles, and the mixture and tension between the two never appealed to a majority of Bahamians.

All other major influences in the realm of formal dance have been introduced by expatriates. During the years that led up to Independence, Alex and Violette Zybine, dancers from Mexico, founded the New Breed Dancers, a company out of which many of the contemporary professional dance teachers and choreographers emerged. From their work came the National Dance School, established in 1976, which was led for several years by Madame Lavinia Williams from Haiti. At the more popular end of the spectrum, the late Shirley Hall-Bass, an American, established the Bahamas Dance Theatre, which also produced a number of professional local and international dancers.

These initiatives, however, were never brought together in a single national vision, with the result that now that Farrington has retired, Williams and the Zybines have left the Bahamas, and Hall-Bass is dead, their influence is a thing of the past. The gap left in the Bahamian dance scene is only imperfectly filled by the National Dance Company or by the chronically underfunded National Dance School, which struggles on without even a proper space to call its own. The work of today's choreographers is mostly visible in Junkanoo, where interpretation is limited by the necessity of fitting into the presentation of the whole, and which now draws heavily on moves borrowed from American musical videos and Brazilian and Trinidadian Carnival.

In 2003, Nicolette Bethel (Clement Bethel's daughter) expressed optimism that Junkanoo, with its ever-expanding popularity, might yet find room for more traditional Afro-Bahamian elements. She also found encouragement in that the attitude of many churchmen that dancing was intrinsically sinful had been moderated in part by the introduction of a decorous form of liturgical dance in some churches. However, she concluded that like the current choreographed moves in Junkanoo, such liturgical

DARLING, Governor-General Sir Clifford

dance forms as yet incorporated very little truly indigenous material, and tended towards the superficial. Dance in the Bahamas, concluded Nicolette Bethel, had far to go before it could emulate the exuberant professionalism, prestige and popular appeal of the Alvin Ailey Dance Company, the Dance Theatre of Harlem, the Ballet Foklorico of Cuba, or the National Dance Companies of Jamaica and Barbados.

Further reading: E. C. Bethel, 'Bahamian Music: From Quadrilles to Junkanoo', *Bahamas Handbook and Businessman's Annual, 1983*, Dupuch Publications, 1983; *Junkanoo: Festival of The Bahamas* (edited and expanded by N. Bethel), Macmillan Caribbean, 1991; Craton and G. Saunders, *Islanders*, ii. 124–8, 220–1, 478–9; W. K. Jones, *Bahamas: Independence and Beyond*, Jones Publications, 2003, 92–104.

DARLING, Governor-General Sir Clifford

Sir Clifford Darling's life story not only demonstrates his remarkable personal qualities but epitomises the modernisation and the democratisation of The Bahamas in the twentieth century.

He was born at the tiny settlement of Chester's on ACKLINS ISLAND, in February 1922, the seventh child of poor but hard-working and godly Baptist parents. Acklins was one of the remotest and least developed 'Out Islands', without electricity or proper roads, and separated from Nassau by a sailboat round-trip that might take a month. The family lived by subsistence farming and fishing, with seasonal visits to nearby SAMANA CAY to harvest CASCARILLA bark and SISAL, which was exchanged for provisions and supplies they could not produce for themselves. The islanders lived almost outside the cash economy. At times of crisis, such as the devastating 1926 HURRICANE or the sudden death of Clifford's father in 1933, the immediate family was only saved from destitution by the rallying round of uncles, aunts and cousins.

Intelligent and industrious, young Clifford did relatively well at the one-room Chester's school and became a 'monitor' (pupil-teacher) – his pay of 6 shillings a month being a vital contribution to the family's finances. In 1938, at the age of 16, he left for Nassau on his own – his worldly goods contained in a single small suitcase. The Great Depression was at its height, but again with help from extended family members, he somehow eked out a living, as assistant in a small grocery store and apprentice barber.

When World War Two came, Clifford Darling, like many of his class, took work on the so-called 'Project' to build an air-base, witnessed without actively taking part the 'BURMA ROAD' riots of 1942, and then eagerly answered the call for migrant agricultural workers in the USA (popularly called 'THE CONTRACT'). By his own account, it was his three-year sojourn in the land of 'Jim Crow' (1943–6) that not only gave him a modest financial start but a determination to strive to better the lot of his fellow black Bahamians.

Life continued a struggle but inexorably upwards. Clifford Darling obtained a taxi licence and his own cab, became an active member of the Taxi-Cab Union, was involved in the infant PROGRESSIVE LIBERAL PARTY, and as recently elected President of the TCU was the key figure in the momentous GENERAL STRIKE of 1958. Entering parliamentary politics, he was chosen as Opposition Senator under the new constitution in 1964, and in 1967, standing for his home constituency of Englerston, was one of the successful candidates who brought the PLP to power. Successfully re-elected on five consecutive occasions, he first entered Prime Minister Lynden PINDLING'S Cabinet in 1969, and between 1971 and 1977 was Minister of Labour and National Insurance.

Clifford Darling's proudest achievement as Minister was the introduction of the NATIONAL INSURANCE scheme in October 1974. But as Labour Minister his breadth of vision and moderation (in contrast to his earlier pro-activism) sometimes brought him into conflict with a new generation of more radical trade unionists. After the 1977 general election he was appointed Speaker, being knighted by the Queen in the same year. He served

Sir Clifford Darling

honourably and judiciously as Speaker (despite the inevitable taunts from the Opposition that he tended to favour the PLP) through three successive parliamentary terms. His career was crowned by his appointment as the fourth Bahamian Governor-General in January 1990. His three-year tenure (before retirement at the age of 70) was uneventful, being chiefly notable for the fact that he was the first Governor-General to serve under both the PLP and the FREE NATIONAL MOVEMENT government.

In retirement, Sir Clifford continued to live in a modest house in Nassau's southern black suburbs, still an active member of Zion Baptist Church, the Prince Hall Masonic Lodge and the Improved Benevolent Protective Order of Elks. The first of two volumes of his biographical memoirs were published in November 2002.

Further reading: C. Darling (as told to Patricia Beardsley Roker), *Sir Clifford Darling: A Bahamian Life Story*, i. *The Years of Struggle, 1922–1958*, privately published, 2002.

DEAN, 'Sweet Richard' (1932–64) Immensely popular nightclub and street entertainer, of limited talents but beauteous physique and notably sweet nature – hence his familiar nickname, 'Sweet Richard'. Dean was a poor and almost illiterate 'Long Island white' who migrated to Nassau to make his fortune in the late 1940s. Too easy-going and trusting, he was a failure as a small shopkeeper Over-the-Hill and soon drifted into the more congenial nightclub world.

Sweet Richard's early partner was his even more comely sister, 'Peaches'. Neither could sing or play an instrument, but both were inventively sexy dancers. When Peaches went solo – being the girlfriend of the leading bandleader and briefly married to the comedian Flip Wilson – Sweet Richard took on an American groupie, rechristened 'Princess Kitty', whose awkward style made her a figure of fun to locals but a hit with American tourists – and who also served to make her partner seem, in contrast, a veritable Rudolf Nureyev.

A tireless exhibitionist, Sweet Richard was a familiar sight on Bay Street, dressed in a brilliant costume midway between that of a pantomime pirate and the clothing worn by Christopher Columbus in the famous statue on Government Hill. Greeting tourists with his favourite catchword, 'Cool it, Daddy!' he would hand out nightclub leaflets and pose for snapshots. No nightclub show was seemingly complete without Sweet Richard, who would make a nightly dash from one to another to satisfy his avid fans with his limbo, sword and fire dance routines.

Many were drawn not so much by the routines themselves as by the chance that Sweet Richard might demonstrate his well-earned reputation for being accident-prone when over-stimulated by applause. However, he was nothing if not a trouper. Once he sliced open his thigh with his cutlass during the sword-dance preliminary to his limbo performance, and another time his fire-dance grew so extravagant that he ignited the fabric hangings of the Spider Web nightclub. On the first occasion he was egged on by his rum-fuelled audience to complete his limbo, with the thigh wound gaping and spurting blood. On the other occasion he continued his fire-dance routine until the building looked like going up in flames, and then tried in vain to calm the panicked crowd with his almost inevitable exhortations to 'Cool it, Daddy!'

Sweet Richard, of course, was in his element during any JUNKANOO celebrations. His end was tragic. In 1964, at the age of 32, he died at the Club Pigalle in Miami while on a promotional Junkanoo junket organised by The Bahamas Tourist Board, when he choked on a chicken bone.

'Sweet Richard' Dean struts his stuff on Bay Street during Junkanoo, 1960s

DEFRIES, Amelia Dorothy (*c.*1880–1935) An intrepid English lady traveller and writer who, while exhibiting some of the prejudices of her nationality and class, still provides valuable insights into Bahamian social life and culture in the second and third decades of the twentieth century.

DELANCEY TOWN

Amelia Defries produced two books about The Bahamas following her visits during and after World War One. *In a Forgotten Colony* was a collection of articles, brought out by the *Nassau Guardian* in 1917. These sketches were reworked and augmented for a more substantial book published twelve years later in London, entitled *The Fortunate Islands*.

The first volume includes some interesting quotations on The Bahamas from the nineteenth-century writers Washington Irving, Captain Frederick Marryat and the author of *Tom Cringle's Log*, as well as some contemporaries. More directly, it provides details of life in Nassau during the Great War, along with a lively account of JUNKANOO (then held on Christmas morning), descriptions of traditional songs and dances, and the almost obligatory demeaning account of the 'Holy Jumpers'.

Much more revealing are Miss Defries's accounts of her trips by mail sailboat (often the only woman aboard and sometimes through rough seas) to several Out Islands, including Andros, the Berry Islands and Abaco, but especially Grand Bahama – then one of the most undeveloped of all Bahamian islands. Most memorable is her account of Aunt Celia, the midwife and medicine woman of Eight Mile Rock ('Nobody never dies of my treatments! Dey dies of old age, or drowning, or sharks, or poison: consumption too when they will shut derselves in and tighten up de windows …').

Miss Defries did not hesitate to write a chapter in her second volume entitled 'The Mind of the Negro' (which made much play on 'superstitions') and to use such now unacceptable terms as 'niggers', 'coons' and 'darkies'. But she did gain a considerable, if still somewhat condescending, respect for the hardihood, cheerfulness and inherent politeness of ordinary Bahamian blacks, especially mariners. On the other hand, her derogatory remarks on the effects of 'in-breeding' on the poor Out Island whites were outrageous, even by the standards of the day.

Defries's remarks on Junkanoo (in 1917) were generous and indeed prescient: 'Instead of denouncing the natives' Christmas Masquerade, why cannot it be encouraged and developed? It can be turned into a Pageant or Harlequinade. With a very little help from skilled people the negroes could produce something *national*, which would interest people as much in its way as the Irish Players or the Sacred Play at Oberammergau.' Even more wisely, she wrote towards the conclusion of her second book (1929): 'The Colour problem looms less large than in the U.S.A., but it nevertheless exists, and will one day have to be solved. The local system of education is very out-of-date and quite unsuited to the place. There is a crying need for better transport and for a revised system of government, and the 'truck' system by which the spongers are paid should be abolished … I do not hesitate to say that the future of this and all the West Indian Colonies depends on *understanding the Negro*.'

Further reading: A. D. Defries, *In a Forgotten Colony*. Nassau, *The Guardian*, 1917; *The Fortunate Islands: Being Adventures with the Negro in the Bahamas*, Cecil Palmer, 1929.

DELANCEY TOWN Area just 'Over-the-Hilll' in NASSAU, bounded by the present Hospital Lane in the east and Nassau Street in the west, and by Delancey Street on the north and Meeting Street on the south. Like FORT HILL, it was one of the first districts settled by blacks and later favoured by the relatively prosperous and upwardly mobile non-whites. Originally referred to as an area of dense bush 'behind the hospital' (which was then on West Hill Street) it was notorious as a haven for slave runaways. In the 1780s it attracted some of the few free blacks who accompanied the white LOYALISTS from America and, while still regarded as a dangerous wasteland by the authorities, was where the first Bahamian Black BAPTIST pastors, Samuel Scriven and Prince Williams, preached to their fellows, at first from under a tree.

The area was given its name in 1789 when the Loyalist Chief Justice, Stephen Delancey, purchased the whole 150 acres, built a mansion called Buena Vista in the prime central site, and in due course divided the remainder into nearly a hundred sizeable building plots. On one of these, Scriven's congregation erected the first Baptist church in The Bahamas, Bethel Meeting House, on the lane thereafter called Meeting Street. Scriven ministered there until his death in 1822, when he was succeeded by his assistant, Prince Williams. Three years later, however, there was a schism in the church, and Prince Williams led his faithful followers 300 yards down Meeting Street, to build the proudly independent St John's Native Baptist Church on Delancey Town's lot 76.

Delancey Town developed as a pretty suburb of modest but well-kept homes, most with well-tended gardens. Typical was the house of the early black businessman David PATTON at the corner of Augusta and Delancey Streets, which L. D. POWLES described in *Land of the Pink Pearl*. Buena Vista was occupied for many years by British officials and then by an American couple who turned it into one of Nassau's most elegant restaurants. As opportunities for non-whites expanded in the twentieth century, many of the houses were upgraded, though none (except Buena Vista itself) rivalled the mansion called Poinciana Hill built by the prosperous black lawyer-politician A. F. ADDERLEY at the western end of Meeting Street in the 1920s.

Meeting Street retains some of its traditional ambience, but tourism and prosperity have largely changed the rest of Delancey Town. Delancey Street in particular has been given over to guest-houses, small restaurants and night-clubs, not always succeeding and often changing hands. The residence built in 1926 by Sidney Eldon, one of the most successful non-white civil servants, which was the early home to both the future Bishop of The Bahamas and the Principal of the COLLEGE OF THE BAHAMAS, was for a time 'Sidney House', Nassau's only youth hostel. A much more emphatic sign of the times, Poinciana Hill, having burned down, has been demolished and replaced by an office block.

DEVEAUX, Andrew Jr. (1758–1812) First and most famous of the Bahamian LOYALISTS, sometimes somewhat exaggeratedly called the 'Bahamian Liberator'.

Andrew Deveaux was the son and namesake of a planter of Beaufort, South Carolina, dispossessed for taking the Loyalist side in the American War of Independence. Commissioned by Lord Cornwallis to raise a regiment for King George grandly called the Royal Foresters, Andrew Deveaux Jr. assumed the title of colonel though still in his early twenties. The regiment did not fully materialise, but Deveaux enjoyed some success in the confused and savage guerrilla fighting in South Carolina after the surrender of Cornwallis at Yorktown (October 1781), until forced to take refuge in East Florida with the raggle-taggle remnant of his force.

After being involved in raids on Georgia and a plan to recapture Pensacola, Deveaux was persuaded to lead an expedition to rescue NEW PROVIDENCE from its Spanish captors by a group of Bahamian refugees headed by Robert Rumer of HARBOUR ISLAND. Deveaux was able to attract no more than 70 Loyalist veterans from Florida with promises of booty and free land if they were successful. But Rumer and his associates recruited four well-armed privateers previously based in Nassau, and persuaded almost all the able-bodied freemen of Harbour Island and ELEUTHERA to join up, along with their slaves.

Having left St Augustine on 30 March 1783, Deveaux's gradually expanding force – eventually numbering about 300 – approached Nassau by way of Abaco and Egg Island, Eleuthera, reaching Salt Cay, which guarded the eastern approach to the Bahamian capital, on 12 April. The wily guerrilla leader used numerous stratagems to convince Antonio Claraco, the Spanish governor, that his force was more numerous and formidable than it was and that resistance was pointless. Knowing that the native Nassauvians were just waiting for the chance to rise against the Spanish, Don Claraco ordered the scuttling of the Spanish ships in the harbour and the concentration of his forces around his headquarters on Mount Fitzwilliam. Deveaux successfully landed east of Fort Montagu, which he then captured without resistance, and established himself in a threatening position east of the town. Having negotiated a truce, he then contrived an excuse to break it, pushing his men and cannons on to the slightly higher slopes on each side of the Spanish position.

There was some firing and a few casualties, but what made the manoeuvres almost ridiculous was the fact that both sides probably knew that the preliminaries of peace already signed in Europe since January 1783 were supposed to come into effect in the Americas by 9 April. Deveaux, wanting the benefits of a victory, however, feigned ignorance and demanded a Spanish formal surrender, offering generous terms. These Don Claraco gladly accepted on 18 April.

By the peace treaty The Bahamas was returned to Britain in exchange for the cession of the Floridas to Spain. As much as for Deveaux and his companions, and for the swarm of other Loyalists forced to leave Florida in his wake, the alleged reconquest of the islands was vital in giving them a claim to free land on which to resettle. Perhaps fittingly, Andrew Deveaux and his family were among the

Andrew Deveaux

DILLET, Stephen

foremost of these Loyalist beneficiaries. Besides the booty seized from the Spaniards, Andrew Deveaux Jr. obtained large land grants in New Providence and CAT ISLAND, and the entire islands of Little San Salvador and Highborn Cay in the EXUMAS. Three brothers also received land grants, and their father, Andrew Deveaux Sr., unable to return and claim his estate in South Carolina, settled at Port Howe in southern Cat Island, where the shell of his impressive mansion may still be seen. He died there in December 1814 at the age of 79, having outlived his four sons and most of the other Bahamian Loyalist planters.

Perhaps surprisingly, Andrew Deveaux Jr. did not settle permanently in the colony which he claimed to have liberated, shifting restlessly between The Bahamas, England and New York, where he died in July 1812, at the age of 54.

Further reading: J. A. Lewis, *The Final Campaign of the American Revolution: Rise and Fall of the Spanish Bahamas*. University of South Carolina Press, 1991; S. Riley, *Homeward Bound: A History of the Bahama Islands to 1850, with a Definitive Study of Abaco in the American Loyalist Plantation Period*, Island Research, 1983.

DILLET, Stephen (1797–1880) Outstanding, understandably conservative, early upwardly mobile immigrant. Born in Haiti of a French army officer and a free black woman, he came to The Bahamas almost by accident in 1802 at the age of five. He and his mother had been seized by a British privateer while fleeing from Haiti to Cuba and carried into Nassau, where his mother decided to stay. Soon bilingual and relatively well educated, Stephen trained as a tailor and married Charlotte Williams, a fellow 'free coloured', in 1822. Intelligent and articulate without being a radical, he was a protégé of Sir James Carmichael SMYTH (1829–35) and favoured by succeeding Governors. In 1834 he became one of the first four non-white Members of the House of Assembly, in which he was to serve for 27 years. From 1846 to 1876 he was Postmaster, and for part of that time, sometimes concurrently, Inspector-General of Police, Assistant Adjutant General and a director of the Public Bank.

Of Stephen Dillet's two legitimate sons, Thomas William became the second non-white Bahamian lawyer, having studied at King's College and the Inns of Court in London in the 1830s and being called to The Bahamas bar in 1848. He was an MHA from 1857 to 1865, served as Queen's Advocate at Grand Turk, as a judge of the General Court and as Acting Attorney General. The second son, Joseph Eugene, apparently migrated to Sierra Leone. Stephen Albert Dillet (1849–1930) was an illegitimate son, who made a distinguished career in the Bahamian civil service despite lacking his half-brothers' advantages and being of a markedly darker complexion.

DISEASE Peter Henry BRUCE in the 1740s was probably the first to praise the general healthiness of The Bahamas, and as early as 1800 HARBOUR ISLAND was lauded as a resort even healthier than NASSAU. It should be noted, however, that this reputed healthiness was only relative – when compared with the 'white men's graveyards' of West Africa or the West Indies, or even the unsanitary towns of Europe or North America. Indeed, it was only in the twentieth century that modern medicine and sanitation combined with a salubrious climate fully to substantiate the tourist advertisements.

The aboriginal Lucayans are often portrayed as living a remarkably healthy life. But this ignores the facts that they suffered from endemic syphilis, from which they only had relative immunity, and had a low life expectancy even compared with Europeans. Far worse, they had no immunity whatsoever to European diseases, particularly smallpox and varieties of the common cold. This contributed far more than overt cruelty to their rapid and total demise. The fact that they passed on syphilis to Europeans who lacked any immunity to the disease and initiated a horrifying epidemic in the Old World is sometimes termed 'the Arawaks' Revenge' – though scarcely a full recompense.

As in all areas colonised from different directions in an age when communications were becoming more global, The Bahamas was to an extent a cross-road for world diseases, with its mixed population intermittently suffering from new pathogens until they had built up immunities against them. New slaves brought diseases from Africa (as well as the genetic malady of sickle cell anaemia), of which the vector-borne tended to die out but the contagious – including yaws, elephantiasis and LEPROSY – persisted and even spread into the general population. Afro-Bahamians were also subject to European and Asiatic diseases to which they had no acquired immunity. Smallpox, however, was never a major scourge because of inoculation (or variolation), which was practised in Africa even before it was 'discovered' in Europe and brought to the Americas, quite early in the slave period.

Mosquitoes and other INSECTS were as bothersome in The Bahamas as elsewhere in the tropics, and mosquito-borne YELLOW FEVER and malaria were far from unknown during the eighteenth century, especially among 'unseasoned' newcomers. Nassau and some of the chief Out Island settlements suffered severely from the waves of CHOLERA from Asia that swept many of the world's ports in the 1850s and 1860s. Tick-borne typhus does not seem to have occurred, but insanitary conditions bred TYPHOID, as well as such afflictions as neonatal tetanus, worm infestations, septicaemia and chigger infections. Venereal diseases were also fairly rife because of promiscuous intercourse, ignorance and lack of effective treatment. Less prevalent though probably most feared of all was tuberculosis.

Bahamian medical conditions began to improve quite rapidly after 1900 with better knowledge about the causes and spread of disease, more effective medicines and treatments, and steadily more rigorous government regulations. The formation of a Board of Health, improvements at the General Hospital (previously regarded as a place of last resort) and firm quarantine regulations (which isolated infected arrivers on Athol Island off Nassau Harbour) were useful initial steps. A Public Health Act in 1914 gave the Board of Health wide powers to inspect houses, yards and premises selling food, required doctors to report cases of a whole list of infectious disease, and included rules to compel the seriously ill to be confined to hospital, and to keep sick children from school and persons with chronic infectious diseases from working at trades that would infect others. That these innovations were more notable in the breach than in the observance was borne out by the serious outbreaks of typhoid – not only in slum areas but extending to downtown Nassau and even infecting tourists – that occurred in the later 1920s. This occasioned the strongly critical report by the eminent doctor and health scientist Sir Wilfrid Beveridge, published in 1927. Only then were the existing rules effectively imposed and new health regulations gradually tightened the system of safeguards. As a consequence there was a dramatic improvement during the 1930s and steady progress thereafter.

Today, medical knowledge and treatment are much more readily available so that the general prosperity and basic healthiness of the Bahamian environment are reflected in demographic conditions equal to or better than most developed countries. The average life expectancy at birth in 1990 was 68.3 years for males and 75.3 years for females. The birth rate in 1998 was 20.1 per thousand, the death rate 6.1 per thousand, and the infant mortality rate 13.9 per thousand live births. Today many of the most common causes of adult deaths in The Bahamas – such as heart disease, intestinal and lung cancer – are actually the product of improved living conditions rather than the reverse. The only exceptions occur in the conditions of poverty and deprivation such as those in which illegal HAITIAN immigrants live, or with those comparatively recently introduced diseases not yet fully understood. Two diseases in particular continue to cause concern at the start of the twenty-first century: types of tuberculosis which are resistant to antibiotics, and the assaults of HIV and consequent AIDS, for which there is as yet no certain cure.

DOMINOES An immensely popular and surprisingly rowdy table game, deprecated only by those ignorant of its skills or disturbed, night or day, by the staccato sound of its slapped-down pieces and the noise of its boisterous participants and spectators.

The Chinese invented a form of dominoes in the twelfth century AD and the Inuit of North America also had a variant employing as many as 148 pieces. But the familiar modern game seems to have been developed in France in the late eighteenth century and is thought to have been carried to England, and perhaps the Caribbean and North America, during the French Revolutionary and Napoleonic Wars. It does not seem to have really caught on in the Caribbean for another century, and only became a favourite pastime after West Indians acquired the taste for it as migrants to the United States. In The Bahamas it became the predominant table game – largely displacing checkers and overwhelming WARRI in popularity – only after the mid-twentieth century, spurred on both by agricultural migrants returning from the United States and by West Indians, such as Barbadian, Jamaican and Trinidadian policemen, who were already habitual and intensely competitive players.

The game of dominoes has a culture and conventions of its own, and can almost become a full-time activity. Sets of games in pubs or on porches in shanty yards, accompanied by considerable drinking and gambling, commonly carry on into the small hours, or even invade daytime working hours. More formal contests, no less competitive and scarcely less boisterous – such as the famous matches at the police barracks between West Indian and Bahamian

Dominoes

DRUG TRAFFICKING

policemen in the 1960s – have involved as many as ten pairs on each side, the winner being the first team to reach an almost incredible hundred complete games. Any visitor who might regard dominoes as mere child's play is soon disabused by the concentration, observation and calculation required, and by the rhythm and speed of the play. Once each round begins there is a brief interval of quiet, with intensely knitted brows (and perhaps significant surreptitious looks between partners), then a sudden deafening rat-a-tat-tat of slapped-down pieces, often followed after only half have been laid by one of the players conceding the round and sweeping up the pieces. All, including the counting, is over in a few minutes, leaving the spectator both bewildered and impressed.

DRUG TRAFFICKING The history of PIRACY, PRIVATEERING, WRECKING, blockade-running and liquor smuggling showed that Bahamians always tended to seize what fleeting chances Fortune offered, even if it meant morally sailing very close to the wind. This national characteristic resurfaced in its most extreme and dangerous forms during the drug trafficking phase of the 1970s and 1980s.

Geographically, the Bahamian archipelago was ideally suited to act as a conduit and entrepot for Colombian cocaine and Jamaican ganja runners targeting the hugely lucrative North American drug market. Largish ships could enter Bahamian territorial waters, and planes land at the many isolated airstrips with little oversight, and transfer their illicit cargoes to speedboats and light planes for the last stage of the journey to the US mainland. The profit margins of the trade were so immense that the traffickers were quite ruthless and could accommodate high losses of men and machines. But by the same token they could afford to spend millions to make their operations run more smoothly and efficiently. They could pay ordinary Bahamians hundreds of dollars for lending a hand or keeping quiet; police and other officials thousands for turning a blind eye; and lawyers and more senior officials (as high up in the government as necessary) hundreds of thousands to acquire cays or small resorts to act as bases, to 'launder' the ill-gotten gains, to stall proceedings for extradition to the United States, or even – potentially most delicate and expensive of all – to impede American agents from pursuing their anti-drug operations in Bahamian territorial waters.

Such connivance and corruption was never anything like general, but was sufficiently widespread to allow the drug barons a heyday lasting a decade from the early 1970s, to tarnish the reputation of the PROGRESSIVE LIBERAL PARTY government of Lynden PINDLING, and lead the United States to come close to interfering unilaterally in Bahamian affairs. Drug-running on a massive scale was a fairly open secret by 1974 but not made public (and then incompletely) until a Commission of Inquiry in 1983–4. The most blatant example of drug activity involved NORMAN'S CAY, at the northern end of the EXUMAS chain. Developed as a resort with its own airstrip around 1970, it was sold to an innocent-sounding company registered in Nassau fronting for the Colombian drug lord Carlos Enrique 'Joe' Lehder, in 1975. The resort was closed to visiting yachtsmen, the runway extended, two large hangars built and a tall radio mast erected. The Colombian compound was patrolled by armed men with dogs, and the few foreign homeowners on one end of the cay frightened away. Neighbouring islanders reported almost continuous air traffic and subsequent informers told of being paid $400,000 a trip for bringing in cargoes of 500 kilos of cocaine worth $50,000 a kilo wholesale in the United States. Four times between 1979 and 1982 the cay was raided by a police flotilla but nothing incriminating was found. It later transpired that a senior police officer at headquarters in Nassau had provided Lehder with ample advance warning of the raids. Rumour had it that the traffic continued even after a police detachment was permanently stationed on Norman's Cay, and did not cease there until Lehder was persuaded to return to Colombia in 1983 (in 1987 he was extradited to the United States and sentenced to life plus 135 years in jail).

The situation had reached crisis level by 1983. The Bahamian government reported large seizures of cocaine and marijuana, but the American authorities believed that this was only window-dressing. A series of exposés in the American press (almost certainly US government-inspired) climaxed with sensational articles in the *Miami Herald* in September 1983 entitled 'A Nation for Sale: Corruption in The Bahamas'. These described the narrow failure of an attempted 'sting' by US agents against a senior Bahamian Minister and pointed a finger directly at Prime Minister Pindling. Somewhat unwisely, Pindling agreed to appear live on NBC, where he cut an unconvincing figure when faced by unexpected allegations and questions and stormed angrily out of the interview. An immediate fall-out was the condemnation by The Bahamas of President Reagan's concurrent invasion of Grenada. This was equated with US interference in internal Bahamian affairs in a speech by Foreign Minister Paul ADDERLEY before the Organization of American States.

The elaborate and seemingly thorough Commission of Inquiry, which lasted almost a year from December

1983, was an obvious exercise in damage control. The Commission was not a court, but certain examined politicians and officials were specifically exonerated, while others were condemned, at least by implication. A senator and three Ministers resigned – one of them, Arthur HANNA, in disgust at the general findings rather than because of personal guilt. Pindling himself was cleared of specific misdeeds but one of the three commissioners, Bishop Dexel Gomez, cast a suspicious eye on the sources of his non-official income. The police, customs and immigration services got a mixed report at best, though the Inquiry resulted in very few criminal charges or forced retirements. Lawyers and bankers with dubious clients escaped almost scot-free. Opposition critics spoke of a whitewash. More realistic or cynical observers, though, suggested that the infection was so systematic – involving so many different levels of society, occupations private and public, and members on both political sides – that there was an implicit agreement to close the Pandora's Box altogether.

Besides Norman's Cay, there were notorious hot-spots, notably Hawk's Nest Creek in southern Cat Island, south Andros, the Berry Islands, and Gorda Cay near Abaco (where the local agent was a Pinder from godly Spanish Wells), while Bimini almost replicated its role during the Prohibition era as the transhipment point closest to the US mainland. Yet there was not an airstrip anywhere in The Bahamas which did not have its tell-tale evidence of wrecked or abandoned aircraft without markings in the adjacent bush. On almost every Family Island settlement tales were told of suspicious comings and goings by night, air-drops to waiting boats by day, huge hidden caches of baled ganja and cocaine in plastic sacks guarded by strange men with machine guns, and occasional violent fights over the possession of the contraband – involving Bahamian islanders as well as Colombians and Jamaicans. Apart from areas sealed off from inquisitive outsiders, the commonest evidences of drug-running activity nearby were the unaccustomed frequency of US $100 bills in local transactions, and the incongruous appearance of elaborate 'drug-runners' houses' (many of them never more than half finished) in the prime locations of settlements that previously boasted no more than modest traditional cottages. Fishermen and boaters also came quickly to recognise 'square groupers', the kilogram packets of cocaine lost at sea.

All this might have been little different from – some would say no worse than – the piracy days of three centuries earlier, were it not for its disastrous social side effects. Apart from the generally demoralising effects of tainted money obtained without hard work, the drugs that stayed within The Bahamas spawned a local traffic, addiction and increasingly violent crime. At the forward edge, drug-pushers were a lamentable feature of all tourist locations. Competition for controlling the traffic, along with the ready availability of guns, led to gang warfare. Worse than this was the spread of addiction, particularly to crack cocaine, with an escalation of crimes of theft to pay for drugs, often accompanied by shootings and brutal rapes. Worst of all was the spread of drugs into the schools, with juvenile addicts and even pushers. Of Bimini, where both drugs and money were readily available, it was said that virtually all children over the age of ten were drug users, and a majority fully hooked on crack cocaine. Towards the end of the 1980s, pessimists were even talking of 'a whole lost generation' of Bahamian youth. These sorry realities exploded the myths that the drug traffic was neither the responsibility of The Bahamas nor caused the country and its people any harm (economically, indeed, quite the reverse).

However, the later 1980s did see a much greater degree of cooperation between the Bahamian and US authorities (in conjunction with efforts to stem the tide of illegal Haitian immigration), and there was certainly a great diminution of the drug traffic through The Bahamas. This was largely due to the success of OPBAT (Operation Bahamas and Turks and Caicos Islands), a multi-agency operation based in Nassau. Since 1986 it has established bases with helicpoters at Inagua, Andros (at AUTEC) and Exuma, and for a while operated aerostat balloons armed with surveillance radar on Grand Bahama and Inagua. The later 1990s, however, showed evidence of a worrying revival of the traffic through The Bahamas. In June 1998, for example, the DEA reported to the US Senate Caucus that overall seizures in the first three months of 1998 already exceeded the total for the entire previous three years – expressing particular concern about the container ship terminal recently opened in Freeport, and arguing against a cut-back in the support for OPBAT.

Further reading: *Report of the Commission of Inquiry Appointed to Inquire into the Illegal Use of The Bahamas for the Transshipment of Dangerous Drugs Destined for the United States of America, November 1983–December*, Bahamas Government, 1985; S. D. Kirkpatrick, *Turning the Tide: One Man Against the Medellin Cartel*, Dutton, 1991; M. Craton: *Pindling: The Life and Times of Lynden Oscar Pindling, First Prime Minister of The Bahamas, 1930–2000*, Macmillan Caribbean, 2002, 293–348; Colin Archer, *Alcohol and Drug Abuse in the Bahamas in Modern Bahamian* Society, 1989; www.copvcia.com; www.fromthewilderness.com

DUNDAS, Governor Hon. Sir Charles (1884–1956)

Popular Colonial Secretary and Governor who helped to steer The Bahamas through the Great Depression without the social and political disruption common throughout the West Indies, and was disappointed to have to make way for the Duke of WINDSOR in 1940.

DUNMORE, Governor Lord

An impoverished aristocrat and career administrator, Charles Dundas came to The Bahamas as Colonial Secretary in 1929 after service in Kenya and Tanganyika dating back to 1908. While endorsing Governor CLIFFORD's moves to encourage upmarket tourism, he was very aware of the desperate state of the Out Islands and the political dangers of underemployment in Nassau. Even before his appointment as Governor in 1937, he encouraged the passing of a Minimum Wage Act, the setting-up by Percy Christie and other moderates of the first trade union, and the efforts by the middle-class Ballot Party to obtain the secret ballot in elections.

Once Governor, Dundas successfully dampened down the effects of the INAGUA riot of 1937 and the tumultuous 1938 by-election in Nassau that saw Harry OAKES defeat the radical populist Milo BUTLER. In facing the calamitous effects of the great SPONGE blight of 1938 Dundas especially welcomed the relatively well-paid work offered hundreds of unemployed men and women by Oakes on his many projects.

Governor Dundas appointed the capable expatriate John Hughes as the first Labour Officer, but his belief that the roots of proletarian unrest lay in the Out Islands (and his concurrence with the West Indian Moyne Commission that its solution lay in the revival of peasant agriculture) was signified by the fact that Hughes's main role was as Chief Out Island Commissioner. Even before the outbreak of World War Two further underlined the importance of Out Island agriculture, Governor Dundas had appointed a general Out Island Committee, a committee to organise agricultural marketing, and a dozen agricultural inspectors and teachers. The limits of his vision, however, were revealed by his confidential opinion that 'the Bahamas coloured people are by nature and inclination essentially employees and little fitted to be independent producers', and his plan, expressed to the writer Rosita FORBES, to set up in the Out Islands the kind of rich white settler estates – almost like feudal manors – with which he was familiar in the highlands of East Africa.

In his aristocratic way, however, Governor Dundas was paternalistically fond of The Bahamas and its people. He served out World War Two as Governor of Uganda and did not return to The Bahamas before his death in 1956. However, he is fittingly commemorated by the institute he founded on Mackey Street in 1931 while Colonial Secretary for the training of domestic staff, which developed into an important focus for cultural activities, especially plays and concerts, and is still called the Dundas Civic Centre.

DUNMORE, Governor Lord The first nobleman to be Governor of The Bahamas (1787–96); a relatively impoverished Scottish earl who was memorably described by one of his many political enemies as greedy and licentious, with a 'capacity below mediocrity, little cultivated by education, ignorant of the constitution of England … the Lordly Despot of a petty Clan'.

John Murray, fourth Earl of Dunmore, had already been the last royal Governor of Virginia. He was forced to flee the colony at the approach of the rebel Americans, but not before he had antagonised even those planters inclined to be loyal by the 1775 proclamation promising freedom for slaves who would take up arms on behalf of King George III. After a few years in Britain, Dunmore arrived in Nassau with his family in 1787, to take command of a troublesome population that included not just LOYALISTS already familiar with his arbitrary ways, but many 'Loyalist' blacks regarding themselves as free.

Dunmore reassured many of the white Loyalists by the firmness with which he put down slave unrest and returned to slavery those blacks who were not unequivocally free. Yet he soon aroused scandal by his exercise of patronage (favouring, it was claimed, 'his cronies and the husbands of his lovers'), the nepotism that included making one of

Lord Dunmore

his sons Lieutenant Governor, and the shameless way he rewarded himself and his family with grants of some of the prime land in many of the islands.

It was as a builder that Lord Dunmore made his most lasting impact upon The Bahamas – as well as sparking great enmity by the extra taxation needed to fund his public projects. His ventures as a cotton planter failed, the sole relic of which are the ruins of his plantation house overlooking the settlement in southern LONG ISLAND still called Dunmore's. In NEW PROVIDENCE, he added to the official Governor's residence on Mount Fitzwilliam another large house on the ridge close by called Dunmore House (it survived as an officers' mess for the garrison and a Catholic priory until the 1980s) and a spacious house on the eastern shore of New Providence called The Hermitage – which still exists as the official residence of the Catholic Bishop. He also built a summer getaway on HARBOUR ISLAND (later the residence of the Commissioner), laying out the island's township anew and predictably rechristening it Dunmore Town.

Given the tumultuous unrest that occurred in French Saint Domingue (Haiti) from 1789 and the outbreak of the last and greatest of the Anglo–French wars in 1793, Lord Dunmore's ever more extravagant fortress-building ventures had more justification – though they emptied the treasury and finally exhausted the patience of the Bahamian elite and the British government alike. Fort Fincastle (named for one of Dunmore's subsidiary titles) was built on Nassau's highest hill, and other fortlets were erected on Potter's Cay, Hog Island and Harbour Island. But Dunmore's (literal) *tour de force*, and most permanent memorial, is Fort Charlotte, which sprawls like a couchant lion (or recumbent Scottish laird) overlooking the western entrance to Nassau harbour. Begun the year that Dunmore arrived in The Bahamas, it was in fact not finally completed until 1819. This was four years after the Napoleonic Wars were over (during which none of the Bahamian forts had fired a shot in anger) and 22 years after Lord Dunmore had relinquished his troubled post and retired to his ancestral lands in Scotland.

Further reading: Craton and Saunders, *Islanders*, i. 199–212.

DUPUCH, Sir Etienne (1899-1991) Combative non-white journalist and would-be political leader; an entrant in the *Guinness Book of Records* as owner-editor of the Nassau newspaper *The Tribune* for almost seventy years. He might also have laid claim to a Bahamian record for being the unique holder of three different knighthoods.

Unlike most Bahamians with French surnames, the Dupuches were descended not from refugees from the eighteenth-century Haitian Revolution, but from a Napoleonic veteran of the Battle of Waterloo. This was Elias Dupuch (1794–1870), who migrated from Bordeaux to Nassau by way of Martinique in 1840 and became a British citizen in 1855. Etienne, with three siblings and a half-brother, Eugene DUPUCH, was a great-grandson of Elias, and son of Leon E.H. Dupuch (1870–1914), who founded *The Tribune* in 1903.

Educated at the old Boys' Central School and brought up as an unquestioning British patriot within the puritanical Brethren church, Etienne volunteered for the Bahamian contingent to the British West Indies Regiment to fight in WORLD WAR ONE, at the age of 17. As vividly recalled in his two volumes of autobiography, his experiences in the Middle East and France modified his loyalty for the British Empire, giving him a life-long antipathy to racism and sympathy for the cause of colonial subjects, while at the same he retained an admiration for British ideals and institutions, including the monarchy. Other personal landmarks were his conversion to ROMAN CATHOLICISM under the influence of American missionary priests in the early 1920s, and his marriage to a white girl from Pennsylvania, Marie Plouse, in 1927, whom he brought back to Nassau by way of New York and INAGUA, his parliamentary constituency.

Leon Dupuch had died in the first year of World War One and Etienne had taken over the struggling *Tribune* after his return from the Western Front in 1919. The paper narrowly survived financial crises and political opposition through its owner-editor's energy, enterprise and determination. It proudly maintained an independent

Sir Etienne Dupuch. A triple knight in his splendour

DUPUCH, Hon. Eugene Aubrey Pyfrom

progressive stance, along the lines of its Latin motto, *nullius addictus jurare in verba magistri* ('Being bound to swear to the dogmas of no master') – though critics often pointed out the irony that no one could have been more dogmatic and magisterial than the owner-editor himself!

Etienne Dupuch served 24 years in the House of Assembly (1925–42 and 1949–56), four years in the Legislative Council (1960–4) and four years in the Senate (1964–8). His perennial political ambition was to be recognised as the destined leader of a non-racialist liberal-democratic government. Accordingly, he opposed the emergent PROGRESSIVE LIBERAL PARTY as being dangerously addicted to Black Power ideology, as adamantly as he condemned the racial exclusivity of BAY STREET'S UNITED BAHAMIAN PARTY. His attempt to form a centrist party under his leadership called the Bahamas Democratic League (1955–6), however, was a miserable failure.

In retrospect, Etienne Dupuch's chief achievements (which he never tired of mentioning in his editorials) were the organisation of a successful war materials and food relief committee during WORLD WAR TWO, and the campaign that led to the formal resolution against racial discrimination in January 1956. Later, like his half-brother Eugene, he veered ever closer to the UBP.

Claiming such grandees as Lord Beaverbrook and Lord Mountbatten as personal friends, and the proud recipient of numerous honours, Etienne Dupuch was appointed a Knight of the Order of St Gregory by Pope Pius XII in 1953. This was said to be 'in recognition of his work in the field of education and charities, and his defence of the Catholic Church's doctrines on divorce and birth control'. In 1965 he was dubbed knight by the Queen 'in recognition of his work in the fields of heath, education and charities'. He was also knighted by the Grand Master of the Knights of Malta.

Disenchanted by political failure and conditions in Nassau, Sir Etienne Dupuch handed over the helm of *The Tribune* to his daughter Eileen Dupuch Carron in 1972, and went into self-imposed exile in southern Florida for more than a decade. As Contributing Editor, however, he continued to write pungent and eagerly-read articles almost daily for the paper for a further 15 years. He was accidentally burned to death when attempting to eradicate an ant nest in his garden at Camperdown, New Providence, on 23 August 1991, aged 92. Survived by his wife of 63 years and six children, he was the last surviving Bahamian veteran of the World War One.

Further reading: E. Dupuch, *The Tribune Story*, London, 1967; *A Salute to Friend and Foe: My Battles, Sieges and Fortunes*, Nassau, 1982.

DUPUCH, Hon. Eugene Aubrey Pyfrom

(1912–81) Brilliant only son of Leon Dupuch by his second wife Ethelinda (neé Pyfrom). He was educated at the Catholic St Francis Xavier Academy and Queen's College in Nassau, and at the Catholic University of St John's, Minnesota. Beginning as a reporter and cartoonist on the family's *Nassau Tribune*, he continued to contribute to the paper after he turned to a law career, coming to prominence by his scrupulous and exhaustive reports on the trial of Alfred De Marigny for the murder of Sir Harry OAKES (1943), and through the long-running and witty column in dialect called 'Smoky Joe Says'.

After World War Two, Eugene Dupuch studied law in Toronto and at the English Inns of Court, and was called to The Bahamas Bar in 1949. Proving to be the ablest of all Bahamian advocates, he was appointed chairman of the committee to revise the laws of The Bahamas in 1957–9 and took silk as Queen's Counsel in 1960. Politically, he was a moderate and something of a chameleon. From 1950 he sat as an Independent MHA for Crooked Island and was often critical of BAY STREET. But after the formation of the PROGRESSIVE LIBERAL PARTY (1953) he showed an increasing distaste for racist rhetoric. In the 1956 general election he was the only successful candidate for the centrist and and short-lived Bahamas Democratic League (his half-brother Etienne DUPUCH having been narrowly defeated).

A natural choice as a member of many important government boards, Eugene Dupuch was actively wooed by the UNITED BAHAMIAN PARTY, which was desperate for non-white recruits of his calibre and credibility. He formally joined the UBP in 1962, partnering Roland SYMONETTE in winning the two-seat constituency of East Central Nassau in that year's general election. With the coming of internal self-government in 1964, he became an important member of Cabinet as Minister of Welfare, and actually acted as Premier on four occasions when Sir Roland Symonette was out of the colony.

Had the UBP not been discredited and defeated, Eugene Dupuch might well have become Symonette's successor as Premier or Prime Minister, but the PLP's takeover in 1967–7 closed that avenue. Eugene Dupuch was appointed Leader of the Opposition in the Senate and was the UBP's chief legal counsel at The Bahamas INDEPENDENCE talks in 1972. But that was effectively the ceiling of his political career. Retiring to private practice in 1975, he died in 1981.

EDUCATION Great advances in education have marked and reinforced the changes in The Bahamas and the achievements of the Bahamian people since the coming of majority rule and INDEPENDENCE. Problems, however, remain, many of them common to the modern world and modernising nations in general, but some being special to The Bahamas.

In early colonial times The Bahamas was hardly better served in education than in religion; not just because neither was regarded as vitally necessary or relevant, but because ministers were virtually the only teachers and were in notably short supply. Even after the minor improvements during the LOYALIST era and the efforts spearheaded by missionaries in the early nineteenth century to initiate a system of general education that would turn the ex-slaves into useful and peaceable citizens, Bahamian education remained drastically backward. Underfunded and elitist, it provided pitifully few chances of a secondary schooling or practical training, and virtually none for tertiary education and training for the professions. Exacerbating a system that provided a descending scale of opportunity between whites, middle-class non-whites, and the black majority, there was also a shocking disparity between Nassau and the Out Islands.

The first record of formal day schools in The Bahamas dates from 1770, when the rector of CHRIST CHURCH reported that his school had 54 pupils (of whom 48 were whites and six FREE COLOUREDS) and that there were two other schools of more modest size. One of these was probably attached to St John's church in Harbour Island, and the other either secular or run by a dissenting minister. Five years later, a New England dissenter named P. Belcher Noyes (who claimed a degree from Harvard) was said to run a private school in Nassau which had 23 pupils, six of whom were said to be 'Latin scholars'.

The coming of the Loyalists in the 1780s increased the number and size of schools, though they remained limited to whites and the more prosperous non-whites, and, except for the few elementary 'dame schools', to boys. What local education the teenage daughters of the elite received they got at home, especially if they lived in the Out Islands. A few privileged youngsters were sent to school in England or, from the early 1800s, to the United States of whom an even tinier minority went on to further education.

The first educational facilities for the black majority were Sunday schools set up by Nonconformist missionaries in competition with the established ANGLICAN Church in the 1820s. The first day schools for black children resulted from the meagre efforts of the colonial government to 'ameliorate' the condition of the slaves as their EMANCIPATION inexorably drew nearer, and to provide at least a minimal system of general education once they were freed. In 1832, despite opposition from the ruling whites, the liberal Governor Carmichael SMYTH set up full-time schools in the LIBERATED AFRICAN villages of Carmichael and ADELAIDE and expanded and liberalised the Christ Church school. Rechristened the King's School, it was to provide free places for a hundred pupils, irrespective of colour or gender – for girls up to the age of 12 and boys to 14. However, under pressure from the Assembly the King's School reverted to its previous form when the embattled Governor Smyth was transferred to British Guiana just before Emancipation came into effect. Moreover, when The Bahamas was granted funds (albeit minuscule) out of the imperial Negro Education Grant in 1834 – with the expectation that it would be administered through the churches – the Bahamian legislature immediately set up a Board of Education to ensure that the money was spent to their liking.

There was a general concurrence on the Board that the purposes of popular education were to promote 'sound Christian principles' including 'good Christian behaviour' and 'habits of industry'. But there was heated debate as to whether these were best instilled through the established Anglican Church alone, by all churches including the Nonconformist, or even by a secularised system within a general Christian context. In 1839 the Board membership was made interdenominational, but this increased rather than quelled rancour, especially in response to the overbearing demands of the Anglican archdeacon John Trew. The conflict moderated (but was by no means quelled) when the Board was permanently laicised in 1847, following an even more fundamental crisis. This was the removal of the Negro Educational Grant in 1846, on the general *laissez-faire* principle that each colony should be fully responsible for funding its educational system, and the disingenuous grounds that the purpose of 'civilising' the ex-slaves had already been satisfactorily accomplished.

The result was a secularised government system of education that served the purposes of the regime far better than it did those of the black majority. It followed British models to the best of its ability, but was so underfunded that it lagged years, often decades, behind, was able to reach barely a majority of the eligible children and scarcely aspired beyond the most rudimentary level

EDUCATION

of teaching. For more than a century it also continued to be dependent on the church schools to fill in the gaps and lead the way towards secondary education.

An optimistic beginning was made with the Education Act of 1847. With the stated aim of establishing 'a system of Popular Education and Training' by 'superintending and regulating the existing Establishment', this set up an Educational Committee, including a permanent secretary and an Inspector of Schools, who was expected to double as a 'normal' schoolmaster to train local teachers. Within two years, 21 board schools were designated. Six of them were in Nassau, at the crown of which was the Boys' Central School opposite the garrison barracks, with a curriculum tellingly consisting of 'Arithmetic, Geography, Writing, Spelling, Grammar, Handicrafts (including shoe-making), Vocal Music and Prayers'.

Boys' Central School was something of a show-case, especially under the supervision of the relatively liberal white George Cole, headmaster from 1871 and Inspector of Schools from 1881. Under Cole, BCS was open to all boys who could pass the entrance examination and whose parents could pay the moderate fees, and was said to produce many civil servants and most of the board school teachers. But this was only a tiny all-male and predominantly white or near-white elite. Moreover, the method of teaching employed and taught was the pyramidical 'Lancaster' or 'monitorial' system, by which the head teacher taught only the top class of pupil-teachers, who then passed on their imperfect learning to the class below, and so on down through the school. This system, already discredited and phased out in England in the 1840s, survived in Nassau into the twentieth century and in the remotest Bahamian Out Islands till the 1960s.

In the 1860s there were almost 30 board schools in The Bahamas but fewer than 40 paid teachers, with their combined salaries totalling under £2,000 a year. Compulsory education for all children up to the age of 12 was theoretically introduced in 1878 (eight years after England), but imperfectly enforced, and in any case limited to Nassau until 1889. In 1883 a Special Commission on Education reported that of 10,000 Bahamian children of school age, only 6,000 attended school, 2,000 having no school to go to and a further 2,000 having a school which they did not attend. Fees were still collected for public school education until 1892, and the official school-leaving age not raised to the English level of 14 until 1897. Corporal punishment was an established (and quite legal) feature of Bahamian public education until the 1950s.

Though three senior schools for pupils beyond the primary level were established in Nassau in the early twentieth century, and the non-racial and co-educational (though still fee-paying) GOVERNMENT HIGH SCHOOL substituted for the Boys' Central School in 1925, the all-age (and often one-room, one teacher) school was the norm in the Out Islands until at least the 1960s. Given this, the fact that the level of basic literacy of the entire population rose from just under 25 per cent in 1870 to about 50 per cent in 1900 and over 75 per cent in 1950 is quite remarkable. The most glaring deficiencies of all, however, were the gross disparity between those with merely an elementary and those with a secondary education – said to have been 67 to one in 1957 and the lowest in the entire region, including HAITI – and the almost complete absence of technical education. A Boys' Industrial School had been established as early as 1874, to be considerably extended from 1928. But since this was in fact a reformatory for delinquent youths, it was scarcely an attractive model for either boys or their parents.

The situation would have been far worse but for the continuously competitive educational activities of the churches. At the forefront were the Anglicans, led by the dynamic but tragically short-lived Rev. W. J. Woodcock, who between 1849 and 1851 established and left as his memorial three flourishing schools in and around his Over-the-Hill parish of St Agnes. Though the Anglican King's School was dissolved by an act of the Assembly in 1849, it was essentially revived by the second Bishop of The Bahamas, Addington Venables, as the Nassau Grammar School (for boys) in 1864, to which St Hilda's School for girls was added in 1886. Neither flourished, fading out in the 1920s, having been superseded largely

All-white one-room school, Man O' War Cay, Abaco, 1940s

EDUCATION

by the work of the METHODISTS, who set up the Wesleyan Collegiate School in 1871, the forerunner of the co-educational but largely segregationist QUEEN'S COLLEGE, founded by a consortium of Methodists and Presbyterians in 1890. Stronger and longer-lasting Anglican high schools awaited the establishment of ST JOHN'S COLLEGE in the 1940s and ST ANN'S SCHOOL in the 1960s, by which time the ROMAN CATHOLICS had established a very strong educational presence through many parochial primary schools, ST FRANCIS ACADEMY for girls and ST AUGUSTINE'S COLLEGE for boys – not to mention sundry primary and secondary schools set up by BAPTISTS, SEVENTH DAY ADVENTISTS and other denominations.

With the coming of prosperity to The Bahamas in the 1950s more money was deployed on education, as the regime realised that the existing system was not just a reproach to their rule and a potential source of social unrest, but was almost totally unequipped to provide the personnel needed for a modernising nation. A qualified (expatriate) Director of Education had been appointed as early as 1947, but his authority was practically limited to the government's junior, senior and all-age schools. By the 1951 Education Act, the Board of Education was given wider powers as well as increased funding, and fairly rudimentary teacher training and technical teaching facilities were initiated. But secondary education continued to receive grudging attention. All secondary schools (including GHS) remained autonomous, though some private schools were beginning to receive grants-in-aid as long as they were not openly discriminatory. Even this was too much progress for the white elite, who founded the rigidly segregated ST ANDREW'S SCHOOL as a fully independent institution, run as a company owned by the parents, in 1948.

The cautious progress in Bahamian education got a jolt with the publication of the highly critical Houghton Report in 1960. But even the creation of a Ministry of Education with the achievement of internal self-government under the UNITED BAHAMIAN PARTY in 1964 did not lead to the necessary acceleration. The government's annual expenditure on education, though it had quadrupled between 1957 and 1964 to exceed a million pounds, still lagged behind the amount spent in the promotion of tourism. It was only once the PROGRESSIVE LIBERAL PARTY came to absolute power in 1968 that the long-overdue changes were made and the annual allocation for education soared into first place in the budget – exceeding $50 million in the 1970s, and reaching $180 million in 2000 (three times that for the Ministry of Tourism).

The new dispensation: C. C. Sweeting Junior High School, 1970s

Over four decades, the number and variety of educational facilities multiplied and divided. The number of government and government-aided schools approached 200, of which more than thirty were designated high schools (19 of them in the Family Islands). Along with greatly improved technical training and adult education classes, teacher training facilities were expanded and upgraded (with a second teachers' college operating in San Salvador for a few years). After an initial period when up to 400 students a year were expensively sent away for study abroad on government scholarships, the establishment of the COLLEGE OF THE BAHAMAS in 1974 and its slow but steady progress towards university status began to fill the yawning local gap in tertiary education.

However, all was not well with the new nation's educational system, and problems developed and intermittently approached crisis level in many respects. These problems stemmed from the rapidity of the changes and the way that expansion out-ran funding, material and personnel resources. But these flaws were accompanied by and led to crises of morale at every level, from students, through teachers to administrators and the government itself. Initially, prosperity came so rapidly and easily to Bahamians that for many a distinguished and higher educational record seemed hardly necessary for – even delaying – economic success. Then, as economic conditions deteriorated and opportunities declined in the later 1970s and 1980s, the relevance of what was learned was further questioned, at much the same time as the easy money and moral corruption that came from drug-running spread its malign influence from sections of the adult population down into the schools – bringing serious problems of indiscipline, gangs, violence, crime and drug-taking.

EDUCATION

As elsewhere in the world, teaching was neither so prestigious nor as well paid as it deserved to be. Despite a great increase in the number of teachers, at least halving the average class size, recruitment of Bahamians lagged behind and the system remained heavily dependent on expatriates, increasingly drawn from poorer countries in the region and elsewhere in the developing world. This suited no one: the Bahamian teachers resented the expatriates' somewhat higher pay (due to necessary living allowances): the expatriates themselves resented their relegation to the less favoured postings (especially in the Family Islands); and the pupils and parents found many of their teachers (including some Bahamians) lacking in commitment or cultural sensitivity. Dissatisfaction with pay and conditions led to increased militancy by the Bahamian Union of Teachers (spreading over into an organisation of the more concerned and responsible senior students called the Students' National Action Party) which led to strikes, acts of arson and vandalism, and serious confrontations with the government in the early 1980s.

These conditions were reflected in the extremely disappointing results obtained in an examinations system increasingly felt to be irrelevant to Bahamian needs. A major shake-up occurred in the late 1980s and early 1990s. Even more important than increased allocations for salaries and facilities were the provision of a national curriculum and examination system more attuned to Bahamian needs and conditions. Rejecting all overseas models, a revived Bahamas Junior Certificate designed to qualify for entry to high school, and a radically new and carefully indigenised Bahamas General Certificate of Secondary Education, aimed to qualify school-leavers for tertiary education, were optimistically introduced in 1993. In principle, the government's reforms were admirable, including a rational core of required subjects, emphasising practical as well as theoretical work rather than mere rote learning, and stressing Bahamian content – not least in the imaginative history syllabus. But the flaws in the government's educational system were emphasised by the continued relatively greater success of the private, especially church-oriented, schools, the preference for them shown by many parents, and by the way that even the government tacitly acknowledged their superiority by steadily increasing the level of their state funding. Though students at government high schools in the late 1990s outnumbered those privately schooled five to one, the total number of examination subjects taken was about equal. Moreover, the failure rate of the former, over 50 per cent, was almost double that of the latter – with three times as many private school students receiving grades in the A–B range than candidates from the government's high schools.

Private schools flourished and multiplied as the newly prosperous and greatly expanded middle class opted to pay the fees that more or less guaranteed a more disciplined environment and a superior education. This situation also satisfied the government, easing the pressure on its own school system caused by the population explosion and financial shortfalls. Consequently, the government found it cost-effective to provide grants-in-aid to reputable private schools, guaranteeing standards through periodic inspections and allocating grants in proportion to the number of qualified teachers in each school.

Of the private secondary and combined primary/secondary schools only the elitist St Andrew's, the Lyford Cay School and the Tambearly School at Sandyport neither received subsidisation nor – in the long-established Bahamian tradition – had a formal religious affiliation. Loosely organised by the Bahamas Association of Independent Secondary Schools (BAISS) from the 1980s, by 2003 these institutions, besides St Andrew's and the Lyford Cay and Tambearly schools, included the Anglican ST JOHN'S COLLEGE, ST ANNE'S SCHOOL and Freeport Anglican High School, the Catholic ST AUGUSTINE'S COLLEGE, St Aquinas College and the Grand Bahama Catholic High School, the originally Methodist-oriented QUEEN'S COLLEGE, the Baptist Jordan-Prince Williams School, the Seventh Day Adventist Bahamas Academy, and the Pentecostal or interdenominational Christian Heritage School, Westminster College and Kingsway Academy.

Looking back, the traditional educational system, including its instillation of religious and moral precepts along with the cane and strap, began to be viewed more generously. Despite the immensely better conditions and opportunities in the twenty-first century and the earlier material and curricular limitations of Bahamian education it is still remarkable what was actually attained. If not to the system itself, much credit remains due to the heroic nineteenth- and early twentieth-century teachers, especially in the all-age Out Island schools, who achieved so much against the odds – both for themselves and for their pupils. Such distinguished and rightly celebrated Bahamians as Sir Henry TAYLOR and Sir Clifford DARLING (the third and fourth Bahamian Governors-General), Timothy GIBSON (author and composer of the National Anthem), Talmadge Sands (the first Bahamian Minister of Zion Baptist church) and Rodney Bain (Secretary to the Cabinet) began their careers as monitors or as technically unqualified head teachers in small and isolated all-age schools. Less heralded, others dedicated their entire careers to school-teaching – only a minority having opportunities for upward mobility within the system once it changed, expanded and modernised.

Among the most outstanding of these largely unsung heroes were the white Abaconians Walter Sands of Cherokee Sound, his pupil Patrick Bethel (who became the first principal of the Teachers' College in the 1950s), Haziel Albury of Man-O'-War Cay, Nelson Major, the black head teacher of the mixed-race school at Deadman's Cay, Long Island (widely regarded as one of the best of all Bahamian schools in the 1940s) and the black Cat Islander Hugh Campbell (1922–78).

Further reading: Craton and Saunders, *Islanders*, ii, *passim*; G. Saunders, *Social Life in the Bahamas 1880–1920s*, Nassau, 1996; J. Trainor, 'Public Education in the Bahamas', in D. W. Collingwood and S. Dodge, *Modern Bahamian Society*, Caribbean Books, 1989.

ELDON, Rt Rev. Michael Hartley First Bahamian – and first non-white – to become Bishop of the Bahamas. Born into the topmost tier of the minuscule Bahamian coloured middle class in 1931, he was the son of Sidney Eldon, Assistant Comptroller of Customs, and his formidable wife Rowena. His younger only sibling, Keva Bethel, was to be the first Bahamian Principal and President of the COLLEGE OF THE BAHAMAS (1982–98), of which, coincidentally, Bishop Eldon was then Chairman of Trustees.

Educated (as was his sister) at the predominantly white QUEEN'S COLLEGE and at Cambridge University, Michael Eldon completed his theological training at Oxford and was ordained priest in Nassau in 1955. As a curate and parish priest combining pastoral duties with teaching in church schools, first in Nassau and then among the rapidly expanding population of Grand Bahama, he gained a reputation for efficiency as well as piety, and was immensely popular. He was made Rural Dean of the Northern Bahamas in 1965, Archdeacon of Grand Bahama in 1967, Suffragan Bishop in 1971, and Bishop of the Bahamas and the Turks and Caicos Islands in the following year. In this climactic role he served almost a quarter century, retiring in 1996.

As Bishop during a period of repeated crises and rapid change, Bishop Eldon was both a rock of conservatism and a reformer. While sustaining the dignity of CHRIST CHURCH Cathedral as the traditional home of the Establishment, he did much to heal the rift between its traditional Low Church rituals and the Anglo-Catholicism practised in the parish churches and preferred by most black Bahamian Anglicans. Personally celibate, he was resistant to radical innovations such as the ordination of women and charismatic worship. But he energetically pursued a policy of BAHAMIANISING the traditionally expatriate clergy, ordaining some 50 black Bahamians during his episcopate (most of whom were married), besides establishing 20 new congregations and confirming over 20,000 persons in the Anglican faith.

Even more importantly, Bishop Eldon involved the Anglican laity much more in the running of the church – especially in restoring its shaky finances – and involved the church itself much more in social and educational projects. Besides being the Chairman of the College of the Bahamas from its planning stage in 1974 until 1997, he oversaw the financial rescue and expansion of the Anglican high school, ST JOHN'S COLLEGE.

ELEUTHERA Named by the Lucayans Segatoo and rechristened by the first English settlers from the Greek word for 'freedom', this bow-shaped island fronting the Atlantic was (with its offshore settlements of HARBOUR ISLAND and SPANISH WELLS) long regarded as only marginally second in importance to Nassau's island of NEW PROVIDENCE.

A hundred miles in length (160 km) but less than 200 square miles (520 sq km) in extent, Eleuthera widens somewhat at each end, but is mainly a mile (1.6 km) wide ribbon with a central ridge, its northern part almost split in two by the pounding ocean at the famous Glass Window between Upper Bogue and Gregory Town.

The flat triangle of north Eleuthera is fronted by the infamous 'Devil's Backbone' reef, graveyard of innumerable ships since the days of the Spanish galleons. The original colonists were wrecked on this reef in 1648, taking refuge in what is called 'Preacher's Cave' on the nearby mainland. From there they soon transferred to more promising locations, Harbour Island, Current settlement, and Governor's Harbour claiming priority. North Eleuthera, however, remained the place where 'Brilanders' farmed on common land granted to them for their part in the recapture of Nassau from the Spaniards in 1783, and where the white inhabitants of Harbour Island and Spanish Wells settled many of their black slaves upon their emancipation (1838). This is today the location of the airport serving north Eleuthera and the two important offshore islands.

Just south of the Glass Window are Gregory Town, a picturesque settlement clustered around a small, semicircular cove from which the best Bahamian pineapples were once shipped, and Hatchet Bay, the former site of the flourishing dairy farm founded by Austin Levy in 1936. Sadly, Levy's 2,000 acres of pasture have long reverted to bush, along with most of the formerly extensive pineapple fields in recent years. Hurricane Floyd (1999) capped the decline by destroying the custom-built harbour which Levy built – once the base of his plantation's famous shuttle-boat, the

ELEUTHERIAN ADVENTURERS

Fifty-Two Miles (named for the sailing distance between Nassau and Hatchet Bay).

Twenty miles (32 km) south, Hatchet Bay's Alice Town is the second of Eleuthera's three airports – built by the Americans for their early space programme but later given up. This is some 8 miles (13 km) north of Governor's Harbour, the administrative 'capital' of Eleuthera. With its gaily painted clapboard houses along the shore and the harbour-forming small peninsula called Cupid's Cay, this village vies with Tarpum Bay, 20 miles (32 km) further south, for the title of most picturesque settlement on Eleuthera proper. This stretch of the island, containing the villages of Palmetto Point and Savannah Sound, indeed, has proved in the past the most attractive to foreign investors and rich expatriate homeowners. Of the latter, the earliest and most influential was the English writer and socialite Rosita FORBES in the 1930s, who set a trend that culminated in the development of Windermere Island (where Prince Charles and Princess Diana honeymooned) and the establishment of a CLUB MEDITERRANÉE just over the hill on the ocean side of Governor's Harbour.

Southern Eleuthera is served by the airport named for the sizeable settlement of Rock Sound. Formerly called Wreck Sound because the main pursuit of its inhabitants was combing wrecks for a livelihood (if not, as slanderous rumours held, actually luring them on to the rocks), Rock Sound was later the site of a pineapple canning plant, the shipment point for the produce of the largest citrus and mango farm in The Bahamas, established by Arthur Vining Davis, and the home of many of those working at the ultra-deluxe resorts on nearby Winding Bay, and at Cotton Bay about 8 miles (13 km) further south.

Far southern Eleuthera, though, was always the least prosperous part of the island, and many of the settlements formed by ex-slaves on former COTTON plantations have long been ghost villages. Recent years, moreover, have seen south Eleuthera suffer most from the setbacks that have led to the decline of Eleuthera as a whole, and only as recently as 2004 have plans to reopen Windermere Island and Cotton Bay, and to replace Club Mediterranée, materialised. One modern development has been the creation of 'Princess Cay' (actually on the mainland) as a cruise-ship destination.

Further reading: E. Young, *Eleuthera, the Island Called Freedom*, London, 1966; C. Dean-Burrows, *Bahamian Folklore: The Eleutheran Paanorama from the Native Perspective*, Vantage Press, 1966.

ELEUTHERIAN ADVENTURERS The original English settlers of The Bahamas, who began a colony in northern ELEUTHERA that was an offshoot of Bermuda and an incidental by-product of the English Civil Wars.

In the 1640s, certain Puritan republicans felt constrained by political and religious restrictions and the lack of space in Bermuda. As early as 1644 they prospected The Bahamas and decided that the island which the Lucayans had called Segatoo (and they were to rename Eleuthera after the Greek word for 'freedom') was the most suitable place for an alternative colony. In 1647, under the leadership of William SAYLE, a sea-captain who had already served twice as Governor of Bermuda (1640, 1643), 25 dissidents formed a partnership called the Company of Eleutherian Adventurers, whose idealistic republican 'Articles' received the approval of the English Parliament which had recently deposed and was soon to execute King Charles I.

By the Articles the would-be colonists recognised the suzerainty of England, but were to be almost autonomously ruled by an elected governor, an advisory council of 12, and a legislative senate of up to 100, chosen from the chief male landowners. Each Adventurer (shareholder) was to receive 300 acres plus 35 acres for each dependent in the main settlement, plus up to 2,000 acres elsewhere. There was to be freedom of worship (that is, no established church), and while slavery was apparently condoned (for Africans, as in Bermuda), no native Amerindians were to be kept in bondage – the framers seemingly being ignorant of the fact that the Lucayans had been exterminated or transported by the Spaniards more than a century earlier. William Sayle was chosen Governor of the projected colony in October 1647.

Takers were fewer than expected, but in the early spring of 1648, some twelve families, 70 persons in all, set sail from Bermuda for Eleuthera in Sayle's 50-ton ship *William* and a 6-ton shallop. Misfortune dogged the enterprise.

House in Eleuthera

Preacher's Cave, north Eleuthera, said to be the first refuge of the Eleutherian Adventurers

Discord immediately broke out between the strict Puritan majority and those who believed that freedom of worship meant that they need not worship at all if they so willed. Two separate settlements might have been formed, but while choosing the place to land, the *William* was wrecked on the north Eleuthera reefs and almost all stores and provisions lost – leaving the settlers marooned on the nearby mainland. This was almost certainly at the small cove still called Governor's Bay, near what is said to have been the Adventurers' refuge and first place of worship, today called Preacher's Cave.

The intrepid William Sayle went off in the shallop to Virginia and brought back life-saving provisions. The original settlers were also soon joined by a second shipload of Puritan refugees expelled from Bermuda by outraged Royalists on hearing of the execution of the King. The settlement only survived, however, with help from the Puritans of New England led by John Winthrop, who in the spring of 1650 sent further provisions and supplies worth £700. In gratitude, the Eleutherian pioneers sent back to Boston a cargo of 10 tons of BRAZILETTO dyewood, which realised £124 and formed a substantial portion of the initial endowment of Harvard College.

The Eleutherian colony, falling far short of expectations, only gradually succeeded. As religious and political conditions eased in Bermuda many of the refugees returned there. Even William Sayle did not settle permanently, though this did not prevent his sons later claiming (in vain) that they had inherited the proprietorship of Eleuthera. Those settlers who did persevere, though, found more practicable locations than the original site.

These included HARBOUR ISLAND, near the original landfall, the Current, Governor's Harbour, in central Eleuthera, and NEW PROVIDENCE, originally called Sayle's Island, some 50 miles (80 km) to the west. These scattered pioneer settlers made a tenuous subsistence from farming, fishing, woodcutting, collecting AMBERGRIS and WRECKING, and were slowly augmented by further optimists and exiles from Bermuda. Though the ideals of the original Eleutherian Adventurers had faded, these families and their descendants – among them the 'white' Adderleys, Alburys, Bethells, Davises, Sands's and Saunders's – along with the few slaves whom they brought with them and who mostly assumed the same surnames, can rightly claim to be the true founders of the English colony of The Bahamas.

Captain William Sayle himself retained close connections with The Bahamas, but roamed widely between the English settlements of Barbados, the Leeward Islands and the American mainland from his base in Bermuda. He was chosen Governor of Bermuda for a third time (1658–62), successfully weathering the Restoration of King Charles II. As a distinguished coda to an influential career, William Sayle was appointed the governor and commander in chief of the expedition that first settled the Carolinas in 1670. Approaching 80 years of age, he died at Albemarle Point, South Carolina, in March 1671, but not before he had successfully petitioned the LORD PROPRIETORS of the Carolinas to have The Bahamas included within their grant.

Further reading: Craton and Saunders, *Islanders*, i. 74–91; H. C. Wilkinson, *The Adventurers of Bermuda: A history of the island from its discovery until the dissolution of the Somers Islands Company in 1684*, 2nd ed., Oxford University Press, 1958; E. Young, *Eleuthera, the Island Called Freedom*, London, 1966.

EMANCIPATION

EMANCIPATION Though now regarded as one of the most important milestones in Bahamian history and celebrated by an official annual public holiday on the first Monday in August, the freeing of Bahamian slaves between 1834 and 1838 was a transition feared and bitterly resisted by the Bahamian white plantocracy, which characterised it as the idea of well-meaning but ignorant English zealots working through a dictatorial imperial parliament.

Since the decline of COTTON plantations in the first decade of the nineteenth century, Bahamian owners had more slaves than they needed for the available work, and the under-employed slaves were increasingly restless as they became aware of the increasingly vocal movement for their emancipation in England. Having already opposed without success the abolition of the British transatlantic slave trade, the registration of Bahamian slaves, the ban on shipping slaves to more profitable colonies, and the liberation in The Bahamas of recaptured slaves, the Bahamian slave-owners were adamantly opposed to freeing their slaves, for financial and security reasons. They were quite prepared to let the few reliable slaves who had somehow managed to raise the necessary money, purchase their freedom. But they feared the sudden and arbitrary freeing of the 'slave property' which constituted for many of them the bulk of their remaining capital. The majority of Bahamian slave-owners also opposed the imposition of measures for the 'amelioration' of slave conditions which was gathering momentum from the mid-1820s – though a few favoured them to a degree, in the hope of delaying Emancipation by showing that Bahamian slavery was less harsh and repressive than depicted by the abolitionists.

Conflict between Bahamian slave-owners and the imperial authorities flared during the tenure of Governor Charles Cameron (1804–20) and the term of William WYLLY as Attorney-General (1815–22). But slave-owner resistance came to a head during the rule of the liberally-inclined Governor James Carmichael SMYTH (1829–33). There had been rising local opposition to the ameliorative laws passed between 1822 and 1828, and the crisis occurred over non-compliance in the matter of the punishment of recalcitrant slaves, specifically the flogging of females. When Smyth sacked a pro-slavery judge and the local police magistrate and demanded the suspension of a notoriously cruel Member, the House of Assembly (supported by the *Bahama Argus* newspaper) became abusive and rebellious and was twice dissolved. A petition to London for Smyth's dismissal was rejected, though he was judiciously promoted to be Governor of British Guiana in June 1833.

The Assembly's last act of resistance, however, had little or no effect on the outcome. During the year and a half that Smyth and his Council ruled without the Assembly, the British Parliament went through the last stages of the imperial legislation freeing the slaves. When Acting Governor Blayney Balfour met with the reconvened Assembly he presented it with a virtual *fait accompli*: the Emancipation Act passed at Westminster on 1 August 1833, to come into effect at midnight on 31 July one year later. Technically the law did not operate until echoing legislation was passed in each of the self-legislating colonies. But the Bahamian legislators had no real choice. Either they complied or they would lose the two generous concessions proffered by the imperial Parliament. These were that the former slaves would be compelled to serve a term of apprenticeship for six years (subsequently reduced to four years), and that the owners would be compensated for the loss of their slave property out of a fund totalling the then immense sum of £20,000,000 – which in due course meant the payment of an average of about £20 for each slave previously owned.

These terms were of course far more considerate of the economic and financial needs of the former slave-owners than of the welfare of the ex-slaves. It was much to the relief of the master-class and the abolitionist churchmen that the celebrations on 1 August 1834, and again exactly four years later when apprenticeship ended, were genuine but comparatively muted, channelled into religious thanksgiving rather than unrestrained tumult. Emancipation Day celebrations actually

The people celebrate Emancipation Day, Harbour Island, 1930s

grew more elaborate and jubilant as years went by. Most modern commentators would explain this by stressing that Emancipation itself was not such a dramatic and obvious change, and that it did not lead to true freedom for the black majority for 130 years. Some of the more cynical have claimed that credit for Emancipation was unfairly appropriated by the metropolitan philanthropists, downplaying purely impersonal causal factors, let alone crediting agency to the slaves themselves. Nonetheless, Emancipation Day is still celebrated each year, both as representing a vital and (in typically Bahamian style) peaceful transitional phase in Bahamian history – as well as a welcome excuse for a day-long jump-up.

Further reading: J. M. Wright, 'History of the Bahama Islands, with a Special Study of the Abolition of Slavery in the Colony', in G. Shattuck (ed.), *The Bahama Islands*, Geographical Society of Baltimore, 1905; Craton and Saunders, Islanders, i. 213–32, 358–96; M. Craton, *Sinews of Empire: A Short History of British Slavery*, Temple Smith and Doubleday, 1974, 239–93; G. Saunders, *Slavery in The Bahamas*, Nassau, 1985.

ENEAS, Dr Cleveland Wilmore (1915–1999) The first Bahamian black to qualify as a dentist; a dedicated reformist, social historian and famous raconteur. Proudly claiming direct descent from Yoruba LIBERATED AFRICANS, Cleveland Eneas was born in Bain Town, Nassau in 1915. He was the only son of Bishop Wilmore Venable Eneas (1883–1961), a Public Works Department foreman, mason and builder, who helped found the Bahamas branch of the pentecostal CHURCH OF GOD in 1910 – and whose own church building was located on the street popularly called 'Eneas Jumper Corner'.

A bright student whose parents could by then afford the modest fee of 10 guineas a year, young 'Cleve' was one of the early pupils of GOVERNMENT HIGH SCHOOL (1930). Inspired by the example of the first black Bahamian doctor, Claudius Roland Walker (graduate of Howard University and Meharry in the 1920s), his ambitious father sent Cleve to finish high school and obtain a BSc at Booker T. Washington's Tuskegee Institute in Alabama (1932–7). From there he earned a place at Meharry Medical College in Nashville, Tennessee. He graduated with a degree in dentistry and after a few years of internship returned to Nassau to practise in 1947, having met his future wife Muriel ('Phinny') at Nashville's other black institution of higher learning, Fisk University.

Besides his professional work, Cleve Eneas became tirelessly involved in public service organisations and progressive causes, as lobbyist, speaker and writer. In these respects, his wife – a teacher who became headmistress of ST ANN'S Anglican High School – was his perfect partner for more than 50 years. In 1950 Cleve Eneas was one of the founders of the Citizens' Committee and editor of its broadsheet, the *Citizen's Torch*. Formed to promote black pride and to counter local discrimination and segregation practices, the Committee's most notable achievement was to reverse the censorship of certain films, including Sidney POITIER's first starring vehicle, *No Way Out*.

Following the ideals of Booker T. Washington, Cleve and Phinny Eneas believed that the cause of the black majority would be better served through education, hard work and the generation of mutual respect, rather than by Black Power politics. They did not join the PROGRESSIVE LIBERAL PARTY either in its years of emergence or its 25 years in power, Cleve Eneas's only direct involvement in politics being a single term as a Senator for the short-lived Bahamas Democratic Party, led by Norman Solomon (1977–83). Somewhat paradoxically, given his parental background and the traditional racialist exclusivity of that church, in his middle and later years he became a pillar of the Presbyterian kirk. Cleve and Phinny Eneas had three children, one a dentist, the other two MDs.

Further reading: C. Eneas, *Bain Town*, Nassau, 1975; *Let the Church Roll On*, Nassau, 1985.

ENGLISH HERITAGE It is a common jest that while English visitors find The Bahamas a heavily Americanised version of the West Indies, American visitors relish the islands for their quaint Englishness. Bahamians admit that their character and culture have been subtly influenced from many directions, but proudly assert that the end product is nothing but Bahamian, a unique blend resulting both from the ingredients readily accepted and those rejected. This is particularly true of the remaining strands of the English heritage.

Genetically, no more than 10 per cent of Bahamians can claim predominantly 'Caucasian' origins (compared with the almost 90 per cent whose deepest roots are in Africa),

Bewigged Chief Justice inspects police guard of honour at annual ceremonial opening of Supreme Court sessions

but of that European tenth the great majority originated in England — even if arriving in The Bahamas by way of Bermuda or the North American mainland. They brought with them England's greatest gift to the world, the English language. But that is a heritage shared by many other parts of the former British Empire (and even more widely). Bahamian English, though more attuned to the English ear than, say, Jamaican creole or the lingua franca of the Indian subcontinent, is at least as distinct from that spoken in the former 'motherland ' as are the US or Australian variants.

The assumed superiority and exclusiveness of the English colonial civil servants made many Bahamians (particularly poor whites) anglophobes, and determined that the expatriate English lifestyle would not readily be copied. Though the customs of referring to England as 'home', calling cards, ballroom dancing and afternoon tea had their brief day among Bahamian snobs, they did not become engrained, or last. England provided no architectural, agricultural or boat-building models to The Bahamas, unless these were derived by way of other English colonies. England, the seedbed of most of the modern world's organised sports, introduced many to the Bahamian people, who in modern times have shown remarkable sporting talents. But competitive SAILING, ATHLETICS, TENNIS and SOCCER had already become worldwide sports before they caught on in The Bahamas. CRICKET and even RUGBY, introduced from England, have had some success, but in recent times have lost out in popularity to the US-dominated sports of BASEBALL (and SOFTBALL), American football and BASKETBALL.

Colonialism imposed or insinuated many English institutions. Some of these have been rejected or faded, but those which have been inherited and consciously retained are the most important aspects of the English heritage in The Bahamas. The ANGLICAN Church was a potent cultural force, and retained much prestige and influence long after it was disestablished in 1869. An educational system based on English models and principles — as well as using textbooks and examinations that were resolutely anglo-centric — was also influential right up to modern times, when Bahamian nationalists insisted on curricula and texts with much more local and relevant content, and alternative school systems emanating from the US began to compete.

Far more indelible have proved the British monarchy, the legislative, executive and judicial systems and customs, and, more important, the principles behind them. There are elements of snobbery and pure sentiment in the preference of the Bahamian majority for having ELIZABETH II as their Head of State. But it is also a rational choice when one compares having a constitutional monarch — that is, one with no legislative powers — who is the focus of pomp and source of honours (not to mention the symbol and presiding chairperson of the Commonwealth), with having a nominated or elected local president, however distinguished. Bahamians are still awarded, and accept, honours from the Queen on the Queen's birthday and New Year's Day.

Even more hallowed by custom and reason are the English traditions of parliamentary democracy, the bicameral legislature, the two-party system (with its safeguards of the rights of the Opposition), regular elections, responsible government, public accountability, the separation of powers between legislature and judiciary, non-elected judges, an independent and professional civil service, and an apolitical police force and army. Some of the customs and ceremonies involved — such as the wearing of traditional robes in court and chamber, the Speech from the Throne, the Changing of the Guard, the reverence for the national flag and the parliamentary mace — may seem to be picturesque at best, comic at worst; but they might be seen as symbols and reminders of systems and principles that have been proven, in an imperfect world, to be infinitely preferable to those in an ever-increasing number of other countries.

EVE, Joseph (*c.*1765–1825) The most versatile and accomplished of the Bahamian LOYALISTS; planter, inventor, editor, poet and architect. Born and brought up in Pennsylvania, he took the Tory side in the American War of Independence and emigrated to the Bahamas with his father Oswell Eve in 1783, hoping to set up as a COTTON planter. His invention of a wind-driven mechanical 'gin' which could clean up to 400 pounds (180 kg) of cotton a day (ten times what could be done by hand) would have set the local industry on its way to success were it not for poor soils, drought and the depredations of the cotton boll weevil. Settling in Nassau, Joseph Eve became the second editor and chief writer for the first Bahamian newspaper, the *Bahama Gazette*, after the death of John Wells in 1800. One of the founders and sustainers of the Nassau public library, Eve was the architect of the elegant ST MATTHEW'S CHURCH, consecrated in 1802, now the oldest extant church building in Nassau. Like many Bahamian Loyalists disappointed by the decline of economic prospects and the institution of slavery, and by the dearth of social and cultural amenities, Joseph Eve remigrated to the Southern United States with his family after the end of the Napoleonic War, dying at Augusta, Georgia in 1825.

EXUMAS A jewel-like chain more than 140 miles (125 km) in length, of which the conjoined islands of Great and Little Exuma are the multi-carat pendants. According to the authoritative *Yachtsman's Guide to The Bahamas*, the Exumas 'form what is probably the most exquisite cruising ground in the Northern hemisphere'.

The Exuma Cays are said to number one for every day of the year (of which 50 are sizeable and about 25 inhabited). They extend from the Sail Rocks, 35 miles (56 km) south-east of NEW PROVIDENCE, about 110 miles (177 km) in the same direction, to Rat and Pigeon Cays at the northern end of Great Exuma. On their windward side they stand on the precipitous edge of deep, dark blue Exuma Sound, and they serve as a natural breakwater for the shallower, crystalline and far calmer cruising waters on the lee. The *Yachtsman's Guide* gives the best general description, and perfectly conveys their fascination: 'The cays themselves vary considerably in size and shape. Some are low and barren; others such as Highborne have rolling hills and are covered with dense vegetation and small trees. Almost all have beautiful beaches and most have snug anchorages. The water in the Exuma Cays is crystal clear and the vivid colours, on a normal bright day with a moderate trade wind ruffling the surface, quite unbelievable – unless you can see them for yourself.'

Yachts and the MAIL BOATS running to and from Nassau make as much of the journey as they can on the smoother leeward side, threading the swirling cuts from one side of the chain to the other only when they can or have to. Mailboat passengers on the way up, almost invariably made queasy on the rolling waters of the Sound, experience first a gush of excitement as the seemingly perilous passage is made through Galliot Cut, and then a wonderful sense of release and relief – being immediately ready to tuck in to lunch as the boat anchors in the quiet waters of Little Farmer's Cay.

Many of the Exuma Cays are privately owned, some with their own airstrips (there are a dozen airstrips in the Exumas altogether). The most notorious of the private islands was NORMAN'S CAY in the north, which was taken over by the Colombian Carlos 'Joe' Lehder in the 1980s and turned into a major drug trans-shipment point (it has since returned to respectability). There are three considerable villages in the Cays, whose people make a good livelihood from fishing, piloting, and servicing visiting yachtsmen. They also include some of the most renowned and accomplished Bahamian sailors, who virtually live from regatta to regatta. The largest settlement is Black Point (300 people), at the northern end of the longest cay, 12-mile (19-km) long Great Guana Cay. Off the southern tip of Great Guana is the much smaller settlement of Little Farmer's Cay, in the pretty harbour of which can often be seen some of the prize-winning native sailboats. Though it has scarcely a hundred inhabitants, the unofficial capital of the Exuma Cays is Staniel Cay, almost in the exact centre of the chain. A neat and proud little place, with church, school, post office, library, and a clinic (named for St Luke) which the people built themselves – as well as a thriving marina and grocery stores – it is the birthplace and home of Rolly GRAY, the most famous of all Bahamian sailboat captains.

Besides its own wondrous Thunderball Grotto, where scenes in the James Bond epics *Thunderball* and *Never Say Never Again* and the movie *Splash* were shot, Staniel Cay is the best jump-off point for a visit to the Exuma Cays Land and Sea Park. This ecological treasure, covering all the cays in an area 22 miles (35 km) long and 7 miles (11 km) wide, was set up in 1958 as the first national park in The Bahamas and provided the initiative for the founding of The Bahamas National Trust in 1986. Fishing and any form of extraction was banned, and the Park thus became one of the earliest protected marine areas in the world. Protected by laws with severe monetary penalties, it is scrupulously managed by the Bahamas National Trust. Said to be an excellent location for forays by kayak, it is the home of several subspecies of IGUANA, colonies of relocated Bahamian AGOUTIS, freshwater and other TURTLES, and many species birds, insects and birds elsewhere rare or endandered. The park ranger station, open every day of the year, is on Waderick Wells Cay, in the centre of the Park.

Typical Exuma Cays

EXUMAS

Well populated by the Lucayans, Great and Little Exuma (plus the tail-end Hog Cay) were enthusiastically resettled in the 1780s by the LOYALISTS, who were optimistic about the islands' potential for growing sea island COTTON and producing salt for the Newfoundland cod fisheries. By 1792 the entire 30,000 acres had been divided into 115 parcels, allocated to more than 50 slave-owning planters. A township was established in the centre of Great Exuma named GEORGE TOWN after the English king. Plans were even mooted to make Exuma the capital of The Bahamas, both because of its central location and the magnificent roadstead between the mainland and Stocking Island – christened Elizabeth Harbour – which, it was claimed, would comfortably hold all the ships of the Royal Navy.

These dreams faded with the failure of cotton. Almost all of the planters left with their families, leaving the slaves they could not sell to fend for themselves. This they did so successfully that, in contrast to slaves in the sugar islands, they increased rapidly in numbers. The most notable of the ex-planter absentees was Lord John ROLLE, whose father Denys Rolle had migrated from his east Florida plantation with his 150 slaves when that province had been given back to the Spaniards by the treaty that ended the American War of Independence (1783).

By the end of slavery (1838) the Rolle slaves had increased more than twofold, distributed over five of the most fertile (or least infertile) sections of Great Exuma. These were then or later called (from north to south) Rolleville, Steventon (after the Rolle domain in Devon, England), Mount Thompson, Ramsey's and Rolle Town. Because Rolle had been unable to sell either his slaves or his land, these parcels became the ex-slaves' own by squatters' rights, and held in common. By the end of the nineteenth century they had become formal commonages, of which all of the Rolle slaves' descendants (who had every one taken their owner's surname) could claim a piece to work or build on, though not in perpetuity. Perhaps luckily, not all do, for today half the 3,700 people living in Exuma – and at least as many others scattered elsewhere – bear the surname Rolle.

In the nineteenth century Great and Little Exuma were notable exporters of people as the population grew faster than the means of their subsistence, and in the twentieth they have developed more slowly as a tourist and retirees' destination than their multiple attractions would have seemed to warrant. For many this was a positive feature. Exuma was a place to get away from the modern world without falling entirely off the map; a place that was characterised by the name of its most famous small hotel, George Town's *Peace & Plenty Inn* – built around what was formerly a sponge exchange, and before that, perhaps, a slave market. Only during the annual May frenzy of the National Family Island Regatta (see OUT ISLAND REGATTA), when all Bahamian sailors and sailing aficionados, and hundreds of foreign yachtsmen, descend on George Town, does Exuma seem a crowded, even overcrowded, place. Today Elizabeth Harbour and its many bays, notably on Stocking Island, fill with up to 600 yachts for the winter season.

Exuma's normal delightful laid-back ambience – some of the world's best and least trodden beaches, shelling, scuba-diving, sailing and bonefishing – may soon be changing. In 2000 three luxurious hotels, two 18-hole golf courses, a casino and several luxury condominium projects were under construction or in the planning stages. Exuma may be destined to become what ELEUTHERA once set out and failed to be, and what GRAND BAHAMA'S Freeport and Nassau's PARADISE ISLAND in fact became.

A curiosity, of no practical significance, is that the Tropic of Cancer bisects Great Exuma just south of George Town (eastwards it also passes through northern LONG ISLAND near STELLA MARIS)

Further reading: A. Vincent-Barwood, *This Sweet Place*, Nassau, 1998; C. Ray, 'Bahamian Protected Areas', *Bahamas Journal of Science*, 6 (1), 1998.

**FAMILY** Family and kinship, along with community and island identity, have traditionally been of great value to the people of The Bahamas. They were of central importance throughout the colonial period, and, in contrast to most West Indian colonies, this was at least as true for the black slave majority as for the island whites and other free persons during slavery days. The gradual loosening of family and kinship ties which has adversely affected modern Bahamian society – as it has most peoples in the modern world – is therefore a consequence almost entirely of aspects of modernisation, especially migration, urbanisation and the general erosion of moral standards.

Cohesive nuclear families, interlocking kinship and a strong sense of local community are common features of a peasant or quasi-peasant lifestyle, especially when a people is widely and thinly spread, as in the islands of The Bahamas during colonial times. This was especially so for the isolated all-white communities of the offshore cays of northern ELEUTHERA and ABACO, in whom the proud determination to retain their ethnic distinctiveness while avoiding the consequences of in-breeding additionally led to an almost obsessive concern with genealogy. Such characteristics were shared to a somewhat lesser degree among communities of near-whites and free blacks in other parts of The Bahamas. However, what surprises social historians accustomed to regard chattel slavery as inimical to family cohesion and destructive of traditional kinship patterns (and thus an explanation for disrupted families among contemporary Afro-Americans) is that nuclear families and cohesive kinship groupings within long-established local communities were quite common even among West Indian plantation slaves, and for economies like that of The Bahamas were almost the rule.

Recent analysis of the Bahamian slave registration returns (1821–34) has disclosed that not only were the slaves increasing naturally at the same healthy rate as modern Bahamians, but that just about as many were living in two-headed nuclear or extended family households, and no more in single female parent households, than is the case today.

There remains debate as to whether such a prevalence of nuclear families depended on the will of the slave-owners or that of the slaves, but the answer seems to be that it was to mutual advantage, particularly in the last phase of slavery, and therefore the outcome of a kind of tacit agreement. Even before it was forbidden to shift slaves from colony to colony or to separate slave parents from their children, slave-owners were bound by law to guarantee food and clothing, at a time when the decay of cotton plantations meant that their slaves were no longer producing an income for them. Accordingly, it was to the masters' advantage to encourage their slaves to subsist – and even to sell and buy – for themselves as quasi-peasant farmers, living in the pattern of nuclear family households within the former plantation community which was both the most efficient mode of production and that preferred by the slaves themselves (see William WYLLY).

This scenario, though, underplays two undoubted factors: that from the available evidence Bahamian slaves were organised in nuclear families from slavery's beginning in The Bahamas in the early eighteenth century; and that family and kinship formation and community identity actually grew stronger among Afro-Bahamians after slavery ended. One model was exemplified by the Exumian ex-slaves of Lord ROLLE and their descendants. Already living in tightly knit family groups, working sections of Rolle's land as virtual peasants, they were the most community-conscious and independent-minded of Bahamian slaves. Though not all genetically related, all of Rolle's slaves voluntarily took the surname Rolle after EMANCIPATION, and they and their descendants retained a permanent tie to their home island, however far they migrated, through sharing the commonage land in Exuma inherited (if informally) from their former owner.

One of the best close-up pictures of a typical traditional Afro-Bahamian family is to be found in the autobiography of Sir Sidney POITIER, born in 1927 of CAT ISLAND parents who moved with their family to NASSAU in 1937. The Poitiers, like most Cat Islanders, were originally peasant farmers, growing tomatoes for export to Nassau and even the United States. A close-knit family, all toiled together, with the mother sharing work in the fields as well as around the house, and the children assigned domestic chores from an early age. The father was the undoubted head of the household, but his absences while shipping produce to market meant that the mother's normally indispensable role was even more important while her husband was away.

Strong elements of this family pattern were retained even when bad economic times induced the Poitiers to transfer to Nassau. At that time, Over-the-Hilll Nassau still had much the character of an overgrown Out Island settlement – or rather, of a collection of mini-communities, many of which had specific Out Island affiliations. The close family lived and worked as a unit and pooled their resources, sharing and combining to a degree first with uncles, aunts and cousins, and secondarily with fellow migrants from their former home island. At the hardest of times, Sidney's mother not only ran the household but broke rocks by hand for paving roads, while his father even tried to farm an untenanted area of rocky bush land south of town, to help feed his family and augment his tenuous wages. For his part, from a toddler young Sidney fetched water and helped clean the yard, and later delivered groceries for pennies. He left school at the minimum leaving age (14) and began work as a labourer, but migrated to join family members and try his luck in Florida before he was 16. Yet his early experience of hardship and family self-help was to be remembered by the future Hollywood superstar with affectionate nostalgia, a surprisingly happy time of traditional family values.

However, it was migration and urbanisation, along with the other effects of modernisation which inexorably undermined the traditional Bahamian family and its established values. Leaving the family land in the Family Island for the Bahamian metropole was an uprooting which neither nostalgia nor periodic revisits could fully repair. Even more damaging were the prolonged absences in the United States of male household heads – in the early twentieth century as part of the 'Miami Craze', but even more as a consequence of the demand for labour in both World Wars and during the post-war 'CONTRACT' of the 1940s and 1950s. While this did have the beneficial effect of an inflow of much needed cash and necessarily strengthened the familial role of the wives left behind, it had the corresponding negative effect of weakening the traditional role of Bahamian fathers – particularly where they made other affective attachments and even established second families while abroad.

The steady erosion of traditional family values is a fairly general feature of modernising societies, but the trend applies with particular force to the modern Bahamas. It was obviously mainly due to the migration from the Family Islands and the increasingly urbanised lifestyle. The process accelerated as gradually rising material standards both made the interdependence of families progressively less vital and contributed to a creeping materialism and hedonism that amounted to a form of moral decay. For men, increasing prosperity was accompanied by increasing irresponsibility. Often absent or philandering, they not only abrogated their traditional authority in the home but tended to become almost marginal figures within the family context. For women, greater opportunities for wage employment gave them more financial independence, but at the cost of less time to maintain the home or exert parental discipline. For children (growing up ever faster in the street world), less parental supervision and shakier role models left them open to greater temptations. And for all town-dwellers there was an ever more pervasive ethos of self-serving promiscuity, occurring despite a seemingly contradictory growth of popular religion. Also, ironically, the increase in social welfare which accompanied the rising national prosperity from mid-century onwards, obviated the need for interdependent self-help on which the traditional family was based, as much as it mitigated the hardships of broken families – contributing to a descending spiral of deteriorating family values.

Whether or not this analysis of cause and effect is entirely fair, the existing situation in respect of Bahamian families is fairly dire. To cite just two telling statistics: by the year 2000 no less than 57 per cent of Bahamian children were born to and living with single mothers, of whom more than 25 per cent had their first child while still teenagers. While these statistics have not yet fallen to Jamaican levels (and are little worse than recent trends in the United Kingdom) they are far removed from those that existed when seven-eighths of Bahamians lived a peasant lifestyle in the Family Islands, and even those that characterised black Bahamians during the days of slavery.

Further reading: Craton and Saunders, *Islanders*, ii, *passim*; K. Otterbein, *The Andros Islanders: A Study of Family Organisation in the Bahamas*, University of Kansas Press, 1966; G. Saunders, *Social Life in the Bahamas 1885–1920*, Nassau, 1996.

FAWKES, Hon. Sir Randol F. (1924–2000) Dynamic but volatile and unpredictable labour leader, whose career resembled the trajectory of a faulty rocket, falling far short of his self-proclaimed achievements and ultimate goals. Son of a stonemason father and a mother who kept a small shop, Randol Fawkes showed early promise and followed his sister to GOVERNMENT HIGH SCHOOL. From there he articled (for a premium of £150 a year) with T. A. Toote, one of the only two black Bahamian lawyers. He was called to the Bahamas Bar in 1948 at the age of 24.

According to his memoirs, young Randol, on the occasion of his calling to the Bar, pledged himself to free Bahamian black people from oppression. He certainly became enthusiastically involved in progressive causes, including the Citizen's Committee (1949) and People's Penny Savings Bank (1951), and gained a reputation as a fiery and charismatic public speaker. In 1952, however, he himself fell foul of the law (in his own version on account of racial persecution, but in fact for forging a will) and was debarred for two years. This 'exile' he spent in New York, imbibing Black Power and labour ideology, and polishing his rhetoric and organisational skills.

FERGUSON, Amos

Hon. Sir Randol Fawkes

Returning to Nassau in 1954, Fawkes made an immediate popular impact, helping to form and lead the Bahamas Federation of Labour and joining the emergent PROGRESSIVE LIBERAL PARTY. In the 1956 general election he was, with Lynden PINDLING, one of the two successful PLP candidates for the constituency of Nassau South, out-polling his partner, who always acknowledged that at that time Fawkes was undoubtedly the people's 'main man'. Fawkes clearly had ambitions to lead the PLP, but having failed to have its name changed from a 'Liberal' to a 'Labour' party, he lost out to Pindling in the leadership contest. Falling out with many PLP supporters over the conduct of the General Strike in 1958, he left the PLP to form his own Labour Party.

As a labour leader, Fawkes retained an ardent if limited following, was instrumental in having Labour Day proclaimed a public holiday (1961), claimed success in sundry strikes, and contested with the two major parties the credit for the passage of rather more progressive labour legislation. His greatest moment, however, came when he was persuaded to break the deadlock between the UNITED BAHAMIAN PARTY and PLP in the 1967 election by accepting the post of Minister of Labour in a PLP–BFL 'coalition'.

Fawkes, though, proved an uncooperative and unpredictable colleague, and the mésalliance did not long survive the PLP landslide victory of 1968. The PLP won the support of an increasing number of labour unions, and even the non-PLP unions became split by ideological differences and rival ambitions. In the 1972 general election Fawkes and his Commonwealth Labour Party were humiliated, and though he did make a final unsuccessful attempt to be re-elected in the 1974 St Barnabas by-election (receiving a mere 88 votes), his active political career was effectively over. That for the remaining 23 years of his life he was a spent force was poignantly underlined by the consolation prize of a knighthood, awarded on the advice of Lynden Pindling's government in April 1977.

Further reading: R. Fawkes, *The Faith That Moved the Mountain*, Nassau, 1979.

FERGUSON, Amos The foremost Bahamian 'intuitive' painter, whose work was on permanent display first in the Pompey Museum on downtown Bay Street from 1993 to 2002, and from 2003 in the National Art Gallery. Though he is sometimes glibly referred to as 'the Bahamian Grandma Moses', Amos Ferguson's paintings in fact are more attuned to the folklore and religious visions of such untutored artists as the Jamaican Mallica 'Kapo' Reynolds or the Caymanian 'Miss Lassie' Bush. However, his works are not in any sense derivative, and are distinctly and uniquely Bahamian.

Born in Exuma in 1920 and with the barest local education, Amos Ferguson migrated to Nassau as a young man and took up the trade of house and sign painter. Spontaneously (under what he termed 'divine instruction') he took to painting scenes and themes in his spare time, using cardboard, plywood and ordinary house paints. He continued to use these simple media even after he was 'discovered' in the 1980s, when his work was exhibited in famous American galleries such as the Wadsworth Atheneum in Hartford, Connecticut, and began to command high prices.

Amos Ferguson

FIRES

Ferguson's simple genius was not corrupted by success. Following his inspiration, he continued to paint themes from folk life, folklore and the Bible in which the mundane and the spiritual were intertwined, often with descriptive subtitles. As one commentary described Ferguson's work in 1997, 'Many of his paintings display Old and New Testament characters and incidents translated into familiar Bahamian figures and locations ("Somebody is nocking at your hart door it nock like Jesus"); others showed remembered folk dances and tales ("Mamaid halfish and half people live in jumphole … come out to catch the sunshine"), or the Cowhead and Pitchy-Patchy Junkanoos of his youth. Though they can be described as two-dimensional, crudely drawn, and repetitive, Ferguson's paintings are magical, combining invention with formal simplicity in a way that is as unexpected and thrilling as his colours are brilliant.'

Further reading: A. Ferguson, *Under the Sunday Tree*, Harper and Row, 1988; P. Glinton et al. *Bahamian Art*, FINCO, 1992.

FIRES With buildings and outside kitchens built mostly of wood, open fires, kerosene stoves and lamps, and, in later years, sub-standard electrical wiring, domestic and commercial fires have always been a natural hazard in The Bahamas. However, to the point of notoriety, Bahamian fires have not always been accidental. Apart from burnings by marauding Spaniards in early colonial days, fires have often been set by arsonists; rarely out of personal maliciousness but more commonly, it is believed, for claiming insurance.

For example, at least until insurance investigators became more sceptical and sophisticated, any fire on commercial premises (particularly at night when the property was empty) was taken by the ordinary run of cynical gossipers as prima facie evidence either of business failure, or of plans to renovate and expand.

The three most celebrated fires in downtown Nassau, in 1922, 1942 and 2001, ran the whole gamut of Bahamian incendiary cause and effect. Much the most spectacular and memorable was the three-day blaze that destroyed H. M. Flagler's ColoniaL Hotel at the end of March 1922. The fire began in a storage building fronting Marlborough Street some time before dawn, and the few guests had barely time to escape before the flames spread to the main six-storey wooden edifice. The single city fire engine, manned by policemen and volunteers, arrived fairly promptly, but was able to do no more than limit the fire to the hotel itself and 18 houses on the south side of Marlborough Street. Probably the whole town was saved, however, by the good fortune that the prevailing breeze from the north-east carried the flames and sparks in the opposite direction. Almost miraculously no one was killed or even injured, though the conflagration produced a spectacle of surging flames and dense black smoke that was likened to a major volcanic eruption. Almost immediately, the event was an item in Bahamian folklore – the subject of innumerable tales and at least one anonymous Goombay song:

De hotel burn down smack and smooth.
De white man run and lef' he shoes.
Hey, hey, do Aun' Nanny do …

Chemical engine ain' worth a hang.
All it could do, go Bang, Bang, Bang!
Hey, hey, do Aun' Nanny do …

Fire at the British Colonial Hotel, 31 March 1922

No one was implicated in the Colonial Hotel fire (which was blamed on faulty electric wiring and lack of fire-proofing) but many regarded it as suspicious that Flagler's 20-year old hotel was already outdated and said to be losing money. It was also remarkable how quickly the site was acquired by another American, Allen Munson, and the New Colonial Hotel raised upon the ashes of the old with the help of a loan from the Bahamian government – well in time for the start of the next tourist season and the beginning of a decade of PROHIBITION-spurred prosperity.

The timing and the cause of the second great Nassau fire was (as it transpired, correctly) regarded with even more suspicion – and its location, on BAY STREET itself, made it potentially even more dangerous. On 28 June 1942, less than four weeks after the serious 'BURMA ROAD' RIOTS, a financially struggling white Bahamian small businessman set his shop alight, with the intention of obtaining insurance money for a fire that might plausibly be attributed either to accident or to a disgruntled veteran of the recent riots. Feeding on tinder-dry wood and fanned by the wind, the fire quickly spread over a whole block of the oldest commercial area of downtown Nassau, between Bay and George Streets. It might have gone much further but for the availability of extra fire engines from the wartime bases and the heroic efforts of servicemen and civilian volunteers, with Governor WINDSOR leading the way. Shocked by the consequence of his crime, the arsonist was easily apprehended, confessed, and was sentenced to seven years in jail – resuming a much more successful business as a famously reformed and chastened character after his discharge.

As recently as 2001, hugely improved fire-proofing and precautions, and far more, and more efficient, fire-fighting forces, proved that Nassau still remained far from invulnerable to major fires. In the early afternoon of Tuesday, 4 September 2001, a 27-year-old Rastafarian peanut-vendor named Cordney Gardiner suddenly poured kerosene over the goods on a stall in the Bay Street STRAW MARKET and set it afire, declaring 'I am tired of this. This is judgment day. Y'all are going to punish.' The fire and panic spread with alarming speed. It completely destroyed the two-story straw market and all the goods within it, gutted several shops and offices on the north side of Bay Street, including those of the Ministry of Tourism, and threatened the Pompey Museum in the historic VENDUE HOUSE, before it was brought under control by the combined resources of the entire Fire Department.

The Bay Street fire of September 2001 was an obvious and immediate blow to the TOURIST industry, most of all to the hundreds whose livelihood depended on straw-vending. Yet the determination of the government to make repairs, and of the resilience of the straw vendors themselves was expressed by the rap-poem called 'Fire on Bay' published on the internet by Dennis Arthur Dames some months later:

> The tourists' dollar will be missed
> All because of an arsonist.
> The tragedy has united the nation
> People coming together for re-creation.
> Bigger and better is the talk …

After being moved into temporary quarters next to the Hilton British Colonial Hotel, it was announced that a new building for the straw vendors would be completed by late 2005. Arrested and charged as early as 7 September 2001, Cordney Gardiner exhibited, or simulated, insanity and was not declared fit to stand trial until early in 2003. Despite outlandish behaviour while in the dock, he was found guilty by a jury vote of 9 : 3. Liable to a prison term of up to 20 years, he was more likely to serve his time in Sandilands Mental Hospital than the Fox Hill Jail.

Further reading: V. M. Moss, *Reminiscing: Memories of Old Nassau*, Ronald G. Lightbourn, 1999, 29-40.

FISHING Ninety-five per cent of the area of the Commonwealth of The Bahamas consists of sea, whether of huge shallow banks or submarine canyons and deep ocean. Bahamian history might authentically be written as the story of man coming to terms with, and subsisting on, a marine environment. From the time of the first inhabitants, through the era of early European venturers and settlers, right down to the present, the shallows, creeks, reefs and deeps have provided essential food and a livelihood. Probably no more than 10 per cent of Bahamians now go fishing regularly. But far more would if they could – moreover, knowing how to bait a hook and how and where to cast a line, almost as if it were a natural inheritance. Consciously or not, all Bahamians are still dependent on their surrounding element and its denizens – for their own diet and feeding the tourists who annually outnumber them by ten to one, for profitable exports, and to provide sport for the select few of their myriad visitors who can afford it. The government's chief concern today is to find a sustainable balance between maximising this wonderfully rich and varied resource and conserving it for the future.

A basic distinction is often made between fishing for food and fishing for sport, though in The Bahamas the borderline is indistinct. Many food fishermen actually enjoy the pursuit and challenge as if it were a sport; and many game fishermen consume their catch, or even sell it, somewhat to defray the cost of their fervent avocation. Probably a more useful separation – involving types of fish as well as the methods used – is between safari-type big game fishing in the deeps, fishing for smaller but equally challenging game on the shallow banks, and the more general fishing around the reefs. Offering superb opportunities in all three respects, The Bahamas can justifiably claim to be one of the world's premier fishing grounds, and certainly the finest and most varied fishing area close to the United States.

FISHING

Game fishing caters to rich men's machismo. Confronting the giants of the sea is inflated in Melville's *Moby Dick* or Hemingway's *Old Man and the Sea* into something grandiose: man's grappling with primal forces, even challenging God. Why else is it an essential feature of game fishing that the prize is traditionally photographed with its catcher alongside, as if the man is measuring himself against his proud but defeated adversary? Venturing into the deep blue waters for the mighty bluefin tuna or the scarcely smaller bill fish – blue and white marlin, sailfish and swordfish – requires a substantial motor boat, fully fledged rods and tackle, and a fighting chair. Trolling along the reef edge will almost certainly bring lesser game, such as wahoo, kingfish or grouper. On a fortunate day, fishermen may encounter a school of mahi-mahi (commonly called dolphin, though quite distinct from the much loved and carefully protected mammal of the same name), which are both feisty and regarded as the tastiest fish to eat.

Seeking the larger game requires special expertise, luck and an ability and willingness to fight, sometimes for hours. Each game species has its favoured migration routes and timetables, with the tuna and marlin most plentiful between April and August. The scarce and most-prized bluefin tuna is mainly found in May and June, and mostly in or near the GULF STREAM, close by Hemingway's favourite base on BIMINI. Wahoo, sailfish and amberjack are most plentiful in the winter months and mahi-mahi in winter and spring. Innumerable non-game fish, including barracuda and grouper, however, can be found close to the reefs at any time of year.

Fishing the shallows is a more modest endeavour than trolling the ocean. But challenging the Bahamian bonefish, like river fishing for salmon with rod and fly, still represents to its aficionados a contest between man's skills and cunning and the will of a canny and explosive creature to remain alive and free. Almost every major island has its bonefish flats and its fishing lodges – varying from the fairly spartan to the luxurious – bragging of their 20-pounder world record bonefish still waiting to be caught, along with rich pickings of barracuda and tarpon. Like some of the more competitive of the game-fish outfitters, many of these lodges are so confident of successful fishing that they advertise 'no splash, no cash' (though usually with a small-print footnote that the free fishing offer only applies to at least half-day charters and to any type of fish caught).

Charter-boat and guided fishing is only for the extremely well-heeled – costing as much as $5,000 a week or $500 per person by the day. Bahamian fishing, however, is not solely a rich man's sport. Only crawfishing is organised commercially on a large scale; most commercial fishermen fishing from small motor or sail dinghies. Amateurs, local or visitors, however, find plentiful opportunities with the simplest equipment, fishing with hand lines from reefs, docks or rowing boats, or pursuing jacks, snappers or grouper with snorkel and Hawaiian sling.

The Ministry of Agriculture and Fisheries encourages commercial fishing but in practice limits it to Bahamians. Their literature states that commercial fishing by foreigners is only permitted to the nationals of countries with whom The Bahamas has reciprocal fishing treaties. But it is not clear that any such countries actually exist (certainly they do not include either the United States or Cuba, the two countries most wishing to fish Bahamian waters on a commercial scale). The Ministry of Tourism, however, strongly promotes sport fishing as an attraction for visitors. There are at least 20 important fishing tournaments a year (in every month except October and December), more than half of which are held in Bimini or neighbouring CAT CAY – with the remainder spread around the Abacos, Berry Islands, Eleuthera and Exumas.

At the same time, though, the government protects the national fishing patrimony with enough restrictions and regulations to fill a sizeable book. First, there are Marine Protected Areas (MPAs) in which no fish may be taken at all. The chief of these is the Exuma Cays Land and Sea Park, but together they amount to some 120,000 acres and will eventually include 15 separate areas. Second, there are strict limitations on the size and number of fish that can be caught, with seasonal restrictions on some species. For example, no more than six of the smaller game fish (or 20

Fish for sale, Potter's Cay, Nassau

bonefish) may be brought in by any one person, and the larger game fish are all required to be released unharmed, with licensed exceptions only during official tournaments. Third, there are strict regulations governing the methods of fishing permitted. Apart from the more obvious prohibitions, such as the use of firearms, explosives and bleach, no one may fish while using scuba equipment or long-lines with ten or more hooks, and there are detailed restrictions on the use of nets and traps. Fourth, there is a complex system of licensing, both for local commercial fishermen and for visiting sports fishermen. For the latter, permits cost a quite reasonable $20 per trip, or $150 for an annual permit; but for game fishing boats with more than six reels aboard the annual permit costs $10,000.

Punishments for infringements of the Fisheries Resources (Jurisdiction and Conservation) Act of 1993 are officially draconian, amounting in some cases 'to a fine of not less than $50,000 or to imprisonment for a term of one year, or to both such fine and imprisonment'. Such penalties, though, seem more of a statement about the importance of conservation than practically enforceable. In 2001 the Department of Fisheries added to its handful of inspectors monitoring the major docks two 26-foot (8 m) patrol craft (one stationed in New Providence, the other in Abaco). But these resources could scarcely police an archipelago of hundreds of islands and cays and 100,000 square miles of ocean. Much more important for the preservation of Bahamian fishing resources at large are the fisheries protection activities which the patrol boats of the ROYAL BAHAMAS DEFENCE FORCE carry out in addition to their surveillance of illegal immigrants and drug-runners. These were of vital importance, for example, in curtailing the fishing for crawfish by Florida-based Cubans during what were termed the 'LOBSTER WARS' of the late 1970s.

Further information: Department of Fisheries, East Bay Street, Nassau, PO Box N-3028.

Further reading: S. K. Farrington Jr., *Atlantic Game Fishing*, Garden City Publishing, 1939; I. F. Took, *Fishes of the Caribbean Reefs*, Macmillan, 1980; J. Ramsay, 'Hooked on Fishing', in *Insight Guide: Bahamas*, Apa Publications, 2000, 248–57; Department of Fisheries, Nassau, *Annual Reports*; E. Hemingway, *The Old Man and the Sea*, Scribner's, 1952; *Islands in the Stream*, Scribner's, 1972.

FLAMINGO An elegant but sensitive bright pink wading bird that continues to flourish in remote INAGUA, thanks largely to the efforts of the BAHAMAS NATIONAL TRUST.

Though hunted by the Lucayans for food and their feathers, the gregarious West Indian flamingo (*Phoenicopterus ruber*) was found wherever there were large natural salinas throughout The Bahamas in the first century of English settlement. Early visitors marvelled at the pink clouds of birds on their daily morning and evening flights, and were enthralled by their noisy and frenetic annual mass courtship and mating rituals in March, which one ornithologist said appeared at a distance 'like a blazing prairie fire'.

Flamingos survived attacks from natural predators by adapting their feeding habits to salt marsh environments where few other animals could live, filtering insect larvae and tiny aquatic organisms from the soupy mud through their uniquely permeable beaks. Pairs of flamingos construct mud nests like miniature volcanoes in which the females lay a single egg. Both parents share in the incubation and feeding of their drab brown chick (with a regurgitated 'milk') during the weeks before they can feed themselves, though they then leave them for the rest of the three months before they are fully fledged and can fly. During the autumn and winter, most of the mature flamingos were accustomed to fly off to alternative locations, mainly in Cuba and Hispaniola, increasing their vulnerability.

Such fragile creatures had little protection against the spread of human habitation in The Bahamas, particularly since poor Out Islanders relished the 'fillymingo' for food and could find at least a small market for their plumage. Hunting parties with dogs took immature chicks and eggs as well as grown birds. As late as 1940 there were still colonies in ABACO, southern ANDROS and ACKLINS as well as Inagua. But almost the last straw was the establishment of flight training and air patrol bases in NEW PROVIDENCE in World War Two – pilots taking delight in strafing the rookeries to provoke spectacular mass take-offs by the alarmed birds.

By 1950 the Bahamian flamingo, now limited to a small rookery on Lake Windsor in Inagua, was on the verge of

Flamingos

FLAMINGO INCIDENT, 1980

extinction. This trend was reversed with the formation of a Society for the Protection of the Flamingo in 1952, and especially by the heroic efforts of its two Inaguan wardens, Samuel and James Nixon and American ornithologist Sandy Sprunt IV. In the early 1960s the Bahamas National Trust took over, acquiring 287 square miles (743 sq km) of Inagua as a National Park, obtaining protective legislation, and maintaining a 'birders'' camp, research station and several permanent staff. By the late 1970s the BNT could boast the guardianship of by far the largest remaining breeding colony of West Indian flamingos – its more than 25,000 birds probably constituting half the world's surviving population of the species. Another colony was spontaneously established in Acklins in the 1970s. Fittingly, in 1973 the flamingo was chosen as the national bird of The Bahamas.

Further reading: D. G. Campbell, *The Ephemeral Islands: A Natural History of the Bahamas*, Macmillan, 1978; R. P. Allen, *The Flamingoes: Their Life History and Survival*, Audubon Society, 1956; 'Flamingos Flourish at our Farthest Island', *Bahamas Handbook and Businessman's Annual, 1984*, Dupuch Publications, 1984, 44-57; P. Zahl, *Flamingo Hunt*, Bobb-Merrill, 1952.

FLAMINGO INCIDENT, 1980 This was the sinking of a BAHAMAS DEFENCE FORCE boat patrolling the Bahamian water boundary by Cuban MIG fighters, with the loss of four servicemen. The extraction of an apology and reparation from Cuba signified a successful assertion of Bahamian territoriality, while the state ceremonies mourning the dead were regarded as symbolising a national 'coming of age' following INDEPENDENCE.

With the creation of a marine branch of the BDF, The Bahamas was for the first time able to patrol its claimed boundaries against Cuban and other foreign trespassers. The Cuban air force countered by frequently 'buzzing' BDF patrol vessels performing their duties. A climax occurred on the evening of 10 May 1980 when Cuban MIGs twice strafed HMBS *Flamingo* as it was towing two Cuban fishing boats arrested for poaching towards the nearest settlement, Duncan Town, RAGGED ISLAND. On the second run, *Flamingo* was sunk with a rocket and its crew machine-gunned in the water, four marines being shot and drowned and others wounded.

The BDF survivors escaped to Ragged Island in one of the Cuban boats, but the Cuban airmen did not desist, making dummy attack runs on the settlement, attempting to rescue the arrested fishermen with a helicopter, and threatening BDF reinforcements as they flew in two days later in an unarmed DC3 aircraft. Despite this, the Bahamian forces managed to carry the Cuban poachers back to Nassau for trial.

The Bahamian government acted impeccably. The poachers were released on a cash bond of $80,000. No military aid was accepted from a very willing US government, but strongly worded protests were made to the United Nations as well as to Cuba. After considerable bluster and some delay, Castro's government, clearly concerned about driving The Bahamas more firmly into the US camp, made a formal apology for what they termed 'an unfortunate mistake', and paid up $4 million to replace the *Flamingo*, plus $400,000 to each of the families of the dead marines.

The *Flamingo* incident provoked patriotic demonstrations by all sections of the Bahamian people, and all parties save the minuscule Cuban-funded VANGUARD NATIONAL SOCIALIST PARTY. The state memorial service for the four victims – Fenrick Sturrup, Austin Smith, David Tucker and Arnold Williams – held at CLIFFORD PARK on Sunday 1 June 1980, was clearly an expression of the new nation's self-consciousness and resolve. This was signified by the almost immediate reinforcement of the BDF Marine Division by four new armed patrol boats named after each of the dead marines, and, some time later, symbolised by the theme of the nationalist opera written by Cleophas Adderley, Winston Saunders and Phillip Burrows called *Our Boys*, first performed in 1987.

Further reading: M. Craton, *Pindling: The Life and Times of Lynden Oscar Pindling (1930–2000), the First Prime Minister of The Bahamas*, Macmillan Caribbean, 2002, ch. 7.

FLORA The climate of The Bahamas is ideal for the growing of flowering trees, bushes, ground plants and epiphytes, and in places where there is sufficient soil and fresh water, luxuriant gardens can be quite easily cultivated. The sight and scent of flowers throughout the year in public and private gardens have been celebrated features of Nassau since at least the time of the painter Winslow HOMER and the poet Bliss CARMAN, a century ago. But what is not generally recognised is the degree to which the most spectacular and beautiful flowers are exotics, brought in for display by a proud and comparatively leisured elite. Many exotics, such as the poinciana, found Bahamian conditions so congenial that they eagerly colonised adjacent areas without cultivation and have long been regarded as natives. The truly indigenous Bahamian flora, though often beautiful, interesting and useful, are generally more modest in appearance, just as the cultivation of gardens for mere effect was not a priority for ordinary Bahamians in earlier and harsher times.

Most visitors simply enjoy the colours and scents of Bahamian flora that they encounter by chance around their hotels and in private and public gardens. Some visitors are sufficiently curious to pick out those flowers with which they are unfamiliar, and wonder how they got there, how they are cultivated, and whether they can be introduced back home as a permanent reminder of the Isles of June. For the comparative minority of serious eco-tourists, floral experts, flower hobbyists and dedicated local gardeners, however, The Bahamas is an almost endlessly rich area for exploration and study.

A comprehensive guide is beyond the scope of the present book, but there are several handbooks of Bahamian flora in print, of which the most recent and helpful for the ordinary reader is by Kathleen McNary Wood. Unusually, but usefully for identification, the author chooses to categorise Bahamian flora initially by their colour (white, yellow, orange, green, blue and purple, pink or red). With equal thoughtfulness, she gives flowers their popular as well as official Latin names, as well as subdividing each colour group into their main scientific categories. She also gives sufficient information on botany in general and Bahamian floral habitats to show non-experts what to look for, and where to look. As a bonus, Ms Wood even gives enough information on the medicinal uses of plants and flowers in the 182 individual entries to enable a systematic reader to compile at least a partial catalogue of Bahamian BUSH MEDICINES.

There are at least five further systems of categorisation beyond those used by Ms Wood. Valid distinctions can be made between those flowers which are cultivated in gardens or grow in the wild, and between exotics (such as the spectacular bougainvillea, frangipani, hibiscus, jacaranda, poinciana, poincettia and poui), natives (including the more modest but still beautiful national flower, the YELLOW ELDER and the bright blue flower of the national tree, the LIGNUM VITAE) and, rarest and most prized of all, the endemics (found naturally nowhere else, such as the rare and protected Inagua Orchid, *Encyclia inaguensis*). Though the subtropical Bahamian CLIMATE has minimal season variations, it is still possible to divide Bahamian flora by the time of year they usually flower (such as the endemic Bahamas passionflower, *Passiflora bahamensis*, which like the other eight species of passionflower owe their popular name to their custom of blooming at Easter-time). A separate category might even be made for aromatics (such as the corallita, honeysuckle, jasmine, morning glory, night-scented cereus and passionflowers). Finally, orchids, as enthusiastic specialist explorers, collectors and cultivators might testify, deserve a whole study to themselves. Besides, on the specific subject of Bahamian orchids (of which there are at least 40 endemic species) there is not yet a published study, either popular or specialist.

Altogether there are eight public gardens with displays of local and exotic flowers in The Bahamas, either free to enter or charging fees ranging from $2 to $8. In Nassau, the oldest and once most sumptuous is on Shirley Street south of Parliament Square, in the grounds of the former ROYAL VICTORIA HOTEL (now less well tended than formerly). On Village Road to the east are the 11-acre gardens of the BAHAMAS NATIONAL TRUST called The Retreat, while to the south and west of Fort Charlotte are both the 'lush but poorly maintained' Botanical Gardens, and the trimmer and more commercial ARDASTRA GARDENS and zoo. On PARADISE ISLAND the suitably named 35 acre Versailles Gardens – a favourite location for elegant weddings – are a reminder of the regal aspirations of their millionaire creators, Axel Wenner-Gren and Huntingdon Hartford.

In FREEPORT-Lucaya, three public gardens similarly celebrate the vision of two of the founders of 'the second city of The Bahamas' – the 100-acre Rand Memorial Nature Centre on East Settlers Way (the Grand Bahama headquarters of the Bahamas National Trust), the 11-acre Parrot Jungle and Garden of the Groves, and the Hydraflora Gardens, both a few miles to the east of downtown Freeport. Though elegant and restful places, neither of the two public gardens in ABACO have notable displays of Bahamian flora, the Byrle Patterson Memorial Garden in HOPE TOWN because it is too small, and the only slightly larger Loyalist Memorial Sculpture Garden in GREEN TURTLE CAY because almost all the space is taken up by the 25 sculptures which are its *raison d'etre*.

Further reading: D. and H. Correll, *Flora of the Bahama Archipelago including the Turks & Caicos Islands*, Lubrecht and Cremer, 1983; K. McNary Wood, *The Flora of The Bahamas and the Turks and Caicos Islands*, Macmillan Caribbean, 2003; M. Light, *Growing Orchids in the Caribbean*, Macmillan, 1995; L. Huber, *Flowers of the Bahamas*, Nassau, 2002.

Poinciana

FOLKLORE

FOLKLORE Bahamian folklore is so tied into the telling of 'Old Story' that the two terms are practically synonymous. Nobody could possibly better describe the custom, form and content of traditional Bahamian storytelling than the CAT ISLAND-born Patricia Glinton-Meicholas does in the introduction to her magnificent *An Evening in Guanima* (1994):

> *Unfortunately, few people 'talk ol' story' or even remember one nowadays. Like many 'people intensive' activities, storytelling has fallen prey to modernisation. Electronic and other forms of entertainment are anaesthetising the creativity of our oral storytellers and the need which produced them.*
>
> *As a result, few fully developed traditional stories are still told. In many cases, vague recollections of central characters, perhaps the basic plot line, or a brief song or incantation are now the only memorials to tales full of incident, metaphor and special sound effects. Unless storytelling receives a fresh injection of creativity and recaptures its audience, the tradition will be lost to us . . .*
>
> *Bahamian folktales, like Junkanoo, are primarily a part of this country's African heritage. Our main characters – the trickster Rabbi and his foil Bouki appear as Leuk the hare and Bouki the hyena in the stories of the Wolof people of West Africa. Antillean counterparts Compere Lapin or Ti Malice and Bouki cavort in tales throughout the islands of the Caribbean, to which Africans came mainly as involuntary immigrants from the 17th century to the era of Emancipation.*
>
> *The European legacy has also made a contribution. The Bahamian hero Jack, rescuer of maidens in distress and formidable adversary of demons and giants is surely grandson to Jack of 'beanstalk' fame. Stories of princes and castles, such as 'The Girl on the Gallows', are echoes of a European past. The story of Jack and the Magic Eggs has a close cousin in the Danish storytelling tradition. The Haitians, the most recent wave of immigrants to The Bahamas, have also brought stories to this country. 'The Master Trickster' is an adaptation of a Haitian tale.*
>
> *Bahamian oral stories are theatrical productions, in which the storyteller is actor, musician and stage manager. The creative performer makes use of mimicry (e.g. 'sperrits' always speak with a nasal voice), onomatopeia and gestures. He or she further enlivens the presentation by using handy items as musical instruments and by singing. Bahamian tales are nearly always punctuated by a brief song (called 'sing') …*

Bahamian folktales also have traditional opening and closing formulae:

> *Once upon a time, was a very good time*
> *Monkey chew tobakker an' spit white lime….*
>
> *They lived in peace and died in peace*
> *And were buried in a pot of blue whale grease.*

Further reading: P. Glinton-Meicholas, *An Evening in Guanima: A Treasury of Folktales from The Bahamas*, Guanima Press, 2nd. ed. 1994; C. L. Edwards, *Bahama Songs and Stories*, Strechert, 1942; M. Tertullian, *Old Stories and Riddles*, 2nd ed., Nassau, 2003;. M. Tertullian, *Old Stories and Riddles*, Bahamia Culturama, 1977.

FOOTBALL (SOCCER) In The Bahamas, football played with the round ball did not supersede RUGBY in popularity until the mid-twentieth century, and has not become anything like the national obsession it is, for example, in Brazil and many other Latin American countries. Yet there has been a Bahamas Football Association, operating at least intermittently, since 1928 and the game has gained much impetus since the 1950s from the participation of expatriates (especially HAITIANS and other West Indians). From 1967, when the BFA formally joined FIFA, a regular league and national championship were instituted and soccer began to spread more widely in the schools. In the 1980s The Bahamas, having joined the recently formed Caribbean and Central American Federation (CONCACAF) played its first representative games, if without much success. Since the 1990s, however, largely in response to soccer's rapid growth in the neighbouring United States, the game in The Bahamas has moved to new levels of organisation, participation and player skills.

The BFA had the latest of its periodic major reorganisations in 1996. By 2000, there were 14 adult teams in New Providence in a league with two seven-team divisions, playing a season running from November to April. In Grand Bahama, where the season only ran from January to April, there was another league with five teams, one of which was entirely made up of HAITIANS and another, Abacom United, based on Marsh Harbour, Abaco. At the end of each season there was a play-off for a national championship between the winners of the New Providence first division and the Grand Bahama league (the championship was won by Abacom United in 2000). Soccer was now played in nearly all high schools, including by a few girls, and besides inter-schools competitions, there had been the first representative Bahamian Under-19 and Under-15 teams entered in international tournaments, and even talk of a representative girls' team.

Three of the limiting factors were the shortage of adequate playing and training facilities and the lack of professional coaching. Even in New Providence all league games were played at Clifford Park until the late 1980s, with practice sessions held on any available scrap of flat ground. As late as 2003 the special problems faced by Abaconian players were underlined when a crucial league match was cancelled because the only field had been requisitioned for a visiting circus and funfair. Conditions in general, however, were already greatly improved. Among the innovations of the new regime of 1996 were the hiring of a full-time executive director and a technical director, and the setting up of special player development relationships with the USL 'A' League Richmond Kickers in Virginia, and with the youth division of Southampton FC of the English Premier League.

An important turning point had occurred on 16 February 2002, when Jack Warner, President of CONCACAF (and also vice president of FIFA) presided over the ceremonial opening of the first phase of a splendid new National Centre for Football Development at Oakes Field. In a stunning display of Bahamian sporting self-confidence in response to Jack Warner's encouraging speech at the opening, Alvin Smith, the permanent secretary in the Ministry for Sport – probably thinking more of the Golden Girls of Athletics than the reality that The Bahamas was currently ranked 193rd of the 204 member nations of FIFA – expressed the hope that the BFA might so continue their efforts as one day to bring the World Cup home to The Bahamas. Nothing ventured, nothing gained!

FORBES, (Joan) Rosita (1893–1967) Wealthy English traveller and writer who gave a fascinating outsider's account of The Bahamas and the building of her dream home in ELEUTHERA in 1940.

A notable beauty and chic socialite, Rosita Forbes was twice married and restless, craving a life of adventure, and seemingly as much at home visiting and writing about strange places and peoples as patrolling the cocktail circuit. She drove ambulances in World War One, and wrote several successful books about her ventures to Africa, the Middle East and many other places during the 1920s and 1930s.

In 1937 she met Charles DUNDAS in Lusaka, Northern Rhodesia, who persuaded her to visit and promote – even to settle in – The Bahamas, to which he had just been appointed Governor. The result was the enthusiastic potboiler *A Unicorn in the Bahamas* (1939), which disguised Forbes's dislike of Nassau and its elite society, but gave a romanticised view of Out Island life and history and strongly endorsed Governor Dundas's plans to revive the quasi-manorial lifestyle of the white LOYALIST settlers.

After rejecting Andros as too flat and backward, Rosita Forbes and her second husband (Col. Arthur McGrath) selected a prime site on a hilltop near Palmetto Point, Eleuthera for themselves. There (as described in the 1949 book *Appointment with Destiny*), they built a charming house called Unicorn Cay, with the help of the future Premier Roland SYMONETTE as foreman builder, and the black Nassauvian T. A. Toote as lawyer.

Despite the distractions of World War Two and continuing travels, the McGraths seem to have been happily based at Unicorn Cay for the rest of their lives. However, the dream of living as lord and lady of the manor – as for others who followed their example – never materialised, in the face of the proud independence of the local black Eleutherans.

Further reading: R. Forbes, *A Unicorn in the Bahamas*, Jenkins, 1939; *Appointment with Destiny*, Cassells, 1949.

Rosita Forbes

'FORT HILL'

'FORT HILL' The name given to the steep slope immediately south of that part of Nassau's ridge (formerly called Bennet's or Society Hill) on which Fort Fincastle was built in the 1790s and the landmark water tower added in 1928. In slavery days, it was the first of the areas inhabited by free blacks and those domestic slaves no longer permitted to live in their white owners' yards in downtown Nassau, and therefore one of the chief places where urban blacks sustained a culture essentially their own. One indication of this is that it was the location of the church of the pioneer black BAPTIST pastor, Frank Spence. After slavery ended, because it was closest to town and in an elevated location, what was now known as Fort Hill was a mini-district favoured by the relatively prosperous and ambitious black elite. Among these were such families as the Backfords, Bethels, Burnsides, Fawkeses, Foulkeses, Francises and Norths, who were to produce many distinguished Bahamians in the second half of the twentieth century, in the realms of business, politics, the professions and the arts.

With the migration to the suburbs beginning in the 1960s, Fort Hill, like the rest of 'Over-the-Hilll' Nassau, suffered something of the fate of 'inner city' areas in the United States. In July 1983, however, Senator Clara Rose King and other former residents initiated a reunion to revive the former community spirit of the area and to celebrate its famous sons and daughters. This was called the *For-mas-bur* Reunion because its compass was expanded to the whole half square mile south of *For*t Hill, bounded by East Street and the former Collins' Wall, as far as *Bur*ial Ground Corner, which includes *Mas*on's Addition – of which last the most notable alumni were Prime Minister Sir Lynden PINDLING, Governor-General Sir Milo BUTLER, and Senator Dame Doris JOHNSON.

Apparently, the reunion was a great success, but it does not seem that Senator King's admirable hope that it would be repeated on a regular basis and emulated by other Nassau districts has yet come to pass.

FORTS For more than half the years between the PROPRIETORS' acquisition of The Bahamas in 1670 and the defeat of Napoleon in 1815, Britain was at war with the Spanish, French or their own American colonists. So close to Spanish Cuba, French Saint Domingue and the North American mainland, NASSAU was both a strategic naval and PRIVATEERING base and vulnerable to enemy attacks. Consequently it needed forts and fortifications, which grew in size and strength along with the size and importance of the town, but were never really sufficient until just before the need for them had ended. Nassau's army garrison too was generally inadequate during the war-time era (more reliance being placed on the Royal Navy and privateers), being strongest during the peaceful reign of QUEEN VICTORIA. The garrison was withdrawn in the 1890s, but three of the four main forts exist to this day, preserved as picturesque curiosities for tourists.

The one fort of which no trace remains was the first, and for more than a century the most important. A rudimentary fortification was constructed on the waterfront at the western edge of what was then Charles Town as early as 1672. This was upgraded by 1697 and named Fort Nassau – soon after the town itself was renamed in honour of King William III (Prince of Orange-Nassau). Woodes ROGERS, the first Royal Governor, was not impressed with its fabric or firepower and did his best with limited resources to strengthen it and make it a suitable barrack for his tiny garrison. A print of about 1730 shows a fairly formidable stone structure perhaps 300 feet (91 m) square, surrounding a courtyard, with a gatehouse bravely flying the royal ensign, bastions at each corner and mountings for 28 cannon. A stout palisade of mastic logs provided an outer line of defence.

Having deteriorated during an interval of peace, Fort Nassau was almost completely rebuilt during the War of the Austrian Succession by the Prussian-born military engineer Peter Henry BRUCE. When it was completed in December 1744 Bruce proudly described it as mounting no less than 54 cannon and 26 mortars, with accommodation for 600 troops, a head gunner, armourer, surgeon and chaplain, and an apartment over the gateway for the Governor 'with a view of the whole town and harbour'. The fort had another restoration on the eve of the American War of Independence – though it was not effective in deterring either the invasion of the Americans in 1776 or that of the Spanish in 1782 – nor for that matter did it prevent the recapture of New Providence by Andrew DEVEAUX in 1783.

Superseded by the two fortresses built on Nassau's ridge, Fort Nassau was razed in 1837 and replaced by two substantial barracks for the West India Regiment garrison troops, facing a tree-lined open drilling space called the Parade (also known as Fleeming Square). When the garrison was withdrawn in the 1890s, this whole area was sold to the American Henry Flagler, whose massive Colonial Hotel covered the whole historic site. Today's guests of the British Colonial Hilton have a somewhat fanciful statue of Woodes Rogers in the forecourt to remind them of the past. But probably few of them are aware that they are sleeping and eating over the site of the well from which BLACKBEARD watered his ship, where Rogers read his commission, tried and hanged a dozen pirates, and which for more than 200 years echoed to the drums, fifes and marching feet of Nassau's soldierly defenders.

The oldest surviving Nassau fort, commanding the eastern approach to Nassau harbour, is the much photographed Fort Montagu. Though on the site of a previous fortification (which might have been almost as old as Fort Nassau) it was totally built in its present form by Peter Henry Bruce between 1742 and 1744, and sycophantically named for the Duke of Montagu, then Britain's Master of the Ordnance. A mere footlet just 60 feet (18 m) square and of suspect strength (one wall was blown down by the 1929 hurricane), Fort Montagu was little more than a guard-house and barrack for the eastern detachment of the garrison. Much more formidable was the nearby Bladen's Battery, the half dozen cannons of which effectively deterred ships from sailing up the harbour to Nassau and compelled would-be invaders to land their forces further to the east. In none of the three invasions of the American War, however, did Fort Montagu offer any real resistance once the invaders had landed – and Fort Nassau was then powerless to prevent the taking of Nassau town.

This flawed defence was remedied by the construction of Nassau's two most impressive fortresses by the grandiose Governor Lord DUNMORE (1787–96). In compensation for his demotion from the governorship of Virginia, Dunmore set out to build a monumental fortress to rival any in the West Indies. In 1787, while Britain was still at peace, he purchased the vacant 100 acres immediately to the west of Nassau, and built the massive main bastion on the crown of the ridge, commanding both the town and the main entrance to the harbour. This he named Fort Charlotte, after the consort of King George III. Already there had been cost over-runs. But the revolution in Haiti and the outbreak of war with France in 1793 gave Dunmore the pretext to add a second and a third segment to the fortress to the west (named respectively after one of his own titles and the army inspector sent to check on his expenditures) and a large, detached stone-block magazine to the east. When completed in 1794, the whole fortress, armed with as many as 85 large cannon, had cost eight times the original estimate.

Yet Fort Charlotte (as the whole fortress became called) was only the centrepiece of Dunmore's elaborate defence plans. Learning from the way that Deveaux's men had been able to dominate Nassau and force the Spaniards to surrender in 1783 by dragging guns to the top of Bennett's Hill, the highest point of the ridge, to the east of GOVERNMENT HOUSE, he had another smaller fort built there. Named Fort Fincastle after another of his family titles, this is often likened to a stranded paddle-steamer in shape, with its rounded stern and sharp-pointed bow mounting cannons, carronades and howitzers which effectively covered the harbour, Hog Island and the eastern approach to Nassau by land. Besides this, Dunmore ordered the construction of a half dozen subsidiary gun batteries: on the shore between Fort Charlotte and town, on POTTER'S CAY at the eastern end of the harbour, on Winton Heights near the eastern tip of NEW PROVIDENCE, on the Blue Hills south of Nassau, at Clifton Point at the far western point of the island, and at HARBOUR ISLAND – where he had built a summer retreat for himself in the township which he magnaminously allowed to be called Dunmore Town.

None of Lord Dunmore's fortifications were ever called on to fire a shot in anger, and once the century of international

Lord Dunmore's expensive monument, Fort Charlotte, guarding Nassau Harbour

peace began in 1815 they became redundant for defence purposes, changed their functions, or were allowed to decay. Fort Charlotte was the site of the barracks of the garrison of black soldiers of the West India Regiment from their arrival in 1802 until the new barracks was erected on the site of the dismantled Fort Nassau in 1837. It continued to be guarded (with daily ceremonial) by the troops in their colourful *zouave* uniforms until the garrison was disbanded in 1891. Not just because its masonry was too massive to be dismantled, it was retained by the government, along with its surrounding 100 acres down to the present day.

The area south of Fort Charlotte which was formerly the kitchen garden for the garrison became the government's horticultural and botanical gardens. The fort itself was already a tourist attraction when the first guidebooks were published in the 1880s and 1890s, and the open space between fort and sea was a popular public recreation area from the early twentieth century. These grounds were successively the first Nassau golf course (run by the Colonial Hotel), a polo ground initiated by Governor Sir Bede CLIFFORD in the 1930s, public playing grounds (now called Clifford Park) and finally, from the 1960s, the chief location for important national ceremonies – most memorably the celebration of INDEPENDENCE in July 1973 and its 25th Anniversary in 1998. As tourism developed the fort was intermittently commercialised and periodically spruced up – the most ambitious operation being a *son et lumière* programme in the 1970s, and the most controversial decorative move to paint the whole structure an eye-catching white.

An even more obligatory tourist venue is the well-preserved Fort Fincastle. The most traditional visitors' approach is by horse-drawn SURREY to the head of Elizabeth Avenue and up the 67 steps of the QUEEN'S STAIRCASE. The fort itself has little to show, but its ramparts have always provided a splendid panorama of Nassau and its harbour to the north. In the nineteenth century the fort was most important as a lookout point and signalling station. Its flagpole carried a complex code of signal flags, both to send messages to incoming ships and to inform Nassauvians of the imminent arrival or departure of different types of vessel. Since 1928, however, Fort Fincastle has been literally out-topped by the adjacent 125-foot (38 m) water tower, which not only provides an even better view extending over almost the whole of New Providence but a revolving beacon visible many miles out to sea.

Further reading: H. G. Malcolm, *Historical Memorandum relating to the Forts in New Providence*, Nassau, The Guardian, 1913; *Historic Forts of Nassau in the Bahamas*, Nassau, The Development Board, 1952.

FOX HILL A settlement 4 miles (6 km) south-east of downtown Nassau that retained the form of a rural village and a strong African character up to modern times.

Maps as early as the 1750s show a Fox's Point on the north-eastern shore of NEW PROVIDENCE, close to settlements of poor white and free black fishermen called The Creek and New Guinea respectively. Tradition has it that Fox was a freed slave called Samuel Fox (perhaps Fawkes), who owned a small property a mile inland named Fox Hill, which he subdivided into house-lots for fellow free blacks around a central giant silk cotton tree. From the 1820s, these black freemen included some LIBERATED AFRICANS, drawn to the area by its relatively fertile soils, and because it was close enough to Nassau for the sale of produce, yet far enough distant to be beyond close supervision by the authorities.

Thus Fox Hill Village was born as an independent Afro-Bahamian community long before the end of slavery. It owed its later development, however, to the enlightened self-interest of a white landowner far more affluent than Samuel Fox, and to the enterprise of many more newly arrived native Africans just after formal slavery ended. Chief Justice Robert Sandilands (an Englishman) was well aware of the government's concern to accommodate the influx of Liberated Africans. He also owned 1,200 acres in the Fox Hill area. In 1840 he subdivided much of this into about a hundred lots of between one and ten acres apiece which he sold for $10 an acre, payable in cash, produce or labour. The labourers he set to building a carriage road through his property the whole 4 miles (6 km) between Bay Street and Pipe Creek on the southern shore of the island (now Fox Hill Road).

Judge Sandilands called the people of Fox Hill – and especially the Liberated Africans – a 'fine body of industrious and contented people … upon whose labour one can always depend … for wage of one shilling a day.' They also proudly retained their AFRICAN HERITAGE and ethnic identity. The area subdivided by Sandilands developed three distinct mini-districts named Congo, Nango and Joshua Towns according to the separate parts of West Africa from which its people hailed, to which was added the tract laid out by Surveyor-General John Burnside specially for those blacks born in The Bahamas who had been liberated in 1838, called Burnside Town.

The name of the whole area was officially changed to Sandilands Village in 1849, but it has continued to be known popularly as Fox Hill to the present. Fox Hill – where African languages could be heard and authentic customs (especially OBEAH) observed well into the twentieth century – has always been regarded as the

The wide-spreading silk cotton tree at Fox Hill village square

authentic African heart of The Bahamas. Though this was once the cause of considerable ambivalence, Fox Hill has always come into its own as the location of a linked pair of annual celebrations: Emancipation Day on 1 August, and Fox Hill Day on the second Tuesday of the same month. The coincidence of names may also help to explain the apparent anomaly of the enthusiasm with which Bahamians continue to celebrate the burning of Guy Fawkes with fireworks and dancing on the night of 5 November. The spirit of Fox Hill was well captured by musician-entertainer Eric Minns with his ever-popular song, 'Fox Hill Gal'.

FREE COLOUREDS This is the term applied to those inhabitants of The Bahamas down to 1834 who were of mixed race but not enslaved. Lesser further distinctions were made according to the degree of African admixture, and between those born ostensibly free (sometimes called freemen) and those freed during their own lifetime (freedmen). The distinctively evolving status of such non-slave non-whites in the earlier days of the colony of The Bahamas had an effect on Bahamian class and race relations and attitudes long after slavery itself ended in 1834 – lasting, indeed, until the coming of full democracy in the 1960s.

There were free coloureds as well as a few slaves among the very earliest settlers of The Bahamas in the 1640s and 1650s, particularly since Bermuda saw the islands as a place to which it could extirpate such an unwanted element in its population (along with the most troublesome of its slaves). The early free coloureds may have lived somewhat apart from the whites. But their lifestyles were similar and largely interdependent, there was little practical discrimination between them, and a considerable degree of miscegenation – if mostly outside formal marriages. This easy-going attitude among the earliest settlers was epitomised by the selection of the mulatto Read Elding by the PROPRIETORS' Governor Nicholas Webb as his Deputy in 1699 – the only non-white to occupy such a post for more than 260 years.

Bahamian laws governing slaves and free coloureds were more or less copied from those of the true plantation colonies in the West Indies, irrespective of substantially different local conditions. By the Bahamian laws of 1748 and 1767 free coloureds were subjected to far more prohibitions and far harsher penalties than whites, including the threat of losing their own freedom if they were implicated in rebellion, or harboured slave runaways. In order to limit the achievement of free status by slaves, not only was it a law that the offspring of slaves took the status of the mother not the father (miscegenation almost invariably involving a non-white slave mother and a white or light-skinned free male, not vice versa) but no slaves could be manumitted except by their owners or by a special act of the legislature. Besides being ineligible for the vote or to sit in Parliament, free coloureds, though ostensibly with access to the courts and with the privilege of trial by jury, could not testify against a white (save in cases of debt) or in practice find a jury of their peers. To reinforce these discriminations, an act of 1756 (not repealed until 1824) carefully limited whites to those persons who could prove themselves to be 'above three degrees removed from a negro ancestor', as well as being both free and Christian.

FREE COLOUREDS

Despite the laws of 1748, 1756 and 1767, the proportion of free coloureds in The Bahamas reached as high as 20 per cent by 1780. Though they proportionately declined to about 10 per cent of the total population with the large influx of LOYALISTS and their slaves in the late 1780s, they were specially regarded as a potential social and political threat when non-whites were deeply involved in the French and Haitian revolutions between 1789 and 1804. By an act of 1789, all Bahamian free coloureds were required to be registered, to wear a distinguishing badge, and to perform demeaning public works. Regulations against free coloureds were further tightened in 1797 after the disclosure of a serious slave plot in 1797, though they were also given the opportunity of showing their loyalty by serving in the militia – the purpose of which was not only to defend the colony from external attack, but to police those still enslaved.

The situation changed subtly once the French war was over, as COTTON plantations declined, and as the EMANCIPATION of the slaves inexorably approached. For one thing, the proportion of free coloureds increased once more, thanks in large part both to the relaxation of the rules governing manumission and to the eagerness of many owners to capitalise on their slave property by allowing the slaves to buy their own freedom. By 1833 free coloureds (including the few hundred LIBERATED AFRICANS landed in The Bahamas since 1809) amounted to 23 per cent of the total population, almost half the number of remaining slaves and not far short of the total of 'reputed whites'. As the imperial government progressively enforced slave amelioration laws upon the reluctant Bahamian legislature, the embattled whites conceived a bold strategy to sustain their hegemony once the slave majority were nominally freed: to win the free coloureds to their side, or failing that, to make them into a buffer class. Their first move was to pass in January 1830 the law that gave the vote to coloureds who had been born free and were not Africans. The first general election after the change in 1832 was tumultuous and even counter-productive. Accordingly, the legislature passed a far more sweeping civil liberties bill in September 1833 – a full year before the Emancipation Bill came into effect and five years before the Bahamian slaves were fully freed. By this act, all coloureds and blacks born free were immediately to 'have and enjoy all the rights, privileges and immunities whatsoever to which they would have been entitled if born of and descended from white ancestors'. Slave-born freedmen were to wait two years to enjoy the same privileges, and the African-born, six years.

In the event, and over a very long period, the strategy of the white ruling class was brilliantly effective. It had already avoided the dissolution of its self-legislating Assembly by complying, however reluctantly, with the imperial government's directives concerning slave amelioration, emancipation and apprenticeship. Now, by ruling The Bahamas reasonably efficiently and peacefully it was allowed – along with only Bermuda and Barbados – to keep its self-styled 'representative system' intact and not become, like all the other colonies in the region a directly ruled 'crown colony'. White Bahamian legislators were even able to claim that their legislature was not only truly representative but even democratic. This, of course, was a myth and a sham.

The few non-white freemen with sufficient property were given the vote as early as 1830 and the first non-whites, including the Haitian-born Stephen DILLETT, were elected to the Assembly as much as five years before the full emancipation of the slaves. Property qualifications were steadily lowered after Emancipation until by the early twentieth century non-white voters were actually in a majority in some constituencies, and as many as a third of MHAs were non-whites. However, while the poorest in the society had no voice in the legislature, the very few non-whites who could afford to campaign and stand as MHAs (who were not paid until 1967) were almost exclusively of that conservative, self-serving stratum of society that aspired to the norms of the upper class, while seeing itself – either as the descendants of free coloureds or Liberated Africans – as being superior to the descendants of slaves.

Coupled to this was the carefully maintained pattern of representation that gave an increasingly disparate weight to the Out Islands over burgeoning Nassau. Non-whites found it even more difficult to contest for Out Island than for Nassau seats. The purchase of votes – exacerbated by the system of open voting – was common in Nassau, and almost the rule in the Out Islands. The advantage that this gave to Nassauvian whites with deep pockets was made worse by the mind-set of inferiority and dependency left over from slavery days – convincing the ordinary non-white voter that even if it was not the white man's permanent destiny to rule, it was better to regard election bribes as all-too-infrequent windfalls than to militate against the status quo. This retrogressive legacy – castigated by Lynden Pindling as the BLACK CRAB mentality – was not to be expunged, even from Nassau, until the 1960s.

Further reading: Craton and Saunders, i, *passim*; G. Saunders, *Slavery in The Bahamas*, Nassau, 1986; H. Johnson, *Bahamas from Slavery to Servitude*, University of Florida Press, 1996, esp. ch. 4.

FREE NATIONAL MOVEMENT (FNM)

FREE NATIONAL MOVEMENT (FNM) The political party formed in 1971 that gradually united the opposition to the ruling PROGRESSIVE LIBERAL PARTY, evolved a coherent and distinctive ideology, aligned itself firmly with United States, and upset the stagnating and tainted PLP in 1992. Winning re-election in 1997, the FNM government itself lost momentum and credibility, suffered from ambivalent leadership and economic woes beyond its control, and was overthrown by a surprisingly large margin in May 2002 – perhaps consigning The Bahamas to a politics of tentative centrism and electoral 'swings and roundabouts'.

Broadly speaking, the FNM was put together from three disparate elements: disgruntled and frustrated black refugees from the inner circles of the PLP, middle-class (and largely mulatto) aspirants who sought a middle way between radicalism and reaction, and the few moderate and uncompromised whites who comprised the rump of the UNITED BAHAMIAN PARTY (the BAY STREET party), defeated by the PLP in 1967. Naturally, the FNM represented itself as a party for all Bahamians, and constantly accused the PLP of 'playing the race card'. Increasingly it also proclaimed itself as dedicated to the free market and privatisation principles commonly associated with Ronald Reagan's American Republicans and Margaret Thatcher's British Conservatives – condemning the PLP's retention of government control over 'essential services' as inefficient if not socialistic, and its BAHAMIANISATION programme as a recipe for economic disaster. At the same time, the FNM set up an ever closer relationship with the US government, involving mutual respect and support – some of it allegedly undercover.

The chief problem for the FNM however was finding a leader who would command the respect and support of the Bahamian majority, while at the same time having the toughness to countermand the wiles and subterfuges of Lynden PINDLING and his PLP machine. The first FNM leader, Kendal ISAACS, was widely respected, but lacked oratorical power and the necessary ruthlessness, and indifferent health caused him to drop out of politics altogether between 1977 and 1982. His successor in 1987, Cecil WALLACE-WHITFIELD, who had led the initial breakaway from the PLP to form the 'Free PLP' in 1970, had great oratorical powers and grew wiser and less abrasive in his maturity, but cruelly succumbed to cancer within a few months of assuming the leadership. It was not until the former PLP Minister (and Pindling protégé) Hubert INGRAHAM was handed the reins in 1990 that the FNM had the right man in the right place at the right time to bring victory for the party.

However, it was extraneous factors rather than who led each party which determined when and why the FNM succeeded the PLP. The FNM was outmanoeuvred over the question of INDEPENDENCE in 1972–3, and the PLP and its leader were able to weather the worst of the drugs crisis of the 1980s through a series of well-publicised coups (such as hosting the Commonwealth Heads of Government meeting in 1985) sufficiently well to win a sixth consecutive general election in 1987. But it was one victory too many. A world-wide economic down-turn exacerbated internal Bahamian woes, and the PLP was no longer able to shrug off the soaring national debt and poverty and CRIME statistics, or to fend off accusations of unfulfilled promises, mismanagement and outright corruption – let alone maintain its worn-out claim to be the God-ordained party of the people.

For the first seven years after its victory in 1992, the FNM under Hubert Ingraham enjoyed a honeymoon period – that is, an era of golden-hued expectations not necessarily bound to be fulfilled. Diplomatic relations with the US immediately improved and many new forms of cooperation were established. A series of commissions of inquiry more or less convincingly accorded blame for all Bahamian ills to the PLP. Free market principles were officially adopted and plans were announced for the privatisation of all public corporations. Many of the rigours of the PLP's policy of Bahamianisation were relaxed, and investors (notably Sol Kerzner of Sun International) were welcomed with open arms.

The euphoria, though, did not last. The national debt continued to rise, as did inflation. Despite increased expenditures on the police force, the level of crime did not decrease, and there were worrying indications that drug-running – greatly reduced in the PLP's last phase – was again on the rise. The plans for the privatisation of the BAHAMAS ELECTRICITY CORPORATION and BATELCO led to serious industrial unrest and there were also demonstrations against some of the work regulations imposed at Sol Kerzner's ATLANTIS complex, hitherto the FNM's proud showpiece. Cut-backs in subsidies to MAIL BOATS and the national airline meant that the Family Islands, contrary to promises, were further isolated, underdeveloped and depopulated. A second and third serious hurricane during the decade caused huge damage in the Family Islands, some of it seemingly irreparable.

A further serious blow was the serious decline in tourism that followed the events of 11 September 2001 in the United States. But nearing the election the FNM created its own problems. Once the intention of the Prime Minister not to stand for a third term was

FREEPORT

known, an internal fight for power developed, leading to the departure of two Ministers, Tennyson Wells and Pierce Dupuch. The difficulties were compounded by the ineffective public presence of Tommy Turnquest, the leader designate. A final ignominy was the sound rejection of the government's attempt to reform the Constitution, which was soundly defeated in a public plebiscite.

Prime Minister Ingraham, who had seemed the FNM's trump card, indeed, appeared to have run out of steam and he and the party made a grievous tactical mistake when they decided that he would only hand over power to a successor after the FNM had achieved its expected victory in the May 2002 general election. Thus, the electors were being asked to support a prime minister who had no intention of leading them further, on behalf of an unproven heir-apparent chosen by the party caucus and not at the polls. In the event, Hubert Ingraham was one of only six successful FNM candidates (compared with 33 for the PLP), while his designated successor, Tommy Turnquest, son of the Governor General, was rejected by his own constituents.

Whether the PLP would be able, or even willing, to turn back the clock and revive and fulfil the ideals and hopes of the Pindling era, yet remained to be seen. Much more likely, it seemed, was that Bahamian politics would be less polarised than ever before, with the chief distinction being simply between the party enjoying the rewards and responsibilities of power, and the party in Opposition, waiting for the next turn of the roundabout, swing of the swing.

Further reading: C.A. Hughes, *Race and Politics in the Bahamas*, University of Queensland Press, 1981, 159–229; M. Craton, *Pindling: The Life and Times of Lynden Oscar Pindling, First Prime Minister of The Bahamas, 1930–2000*, Macmillan Caribbean, 2002, *passim*.

FREEPORT Freeport-Lucaya, the 'second city' of The Bahamas, was initially the brainchild of the American entrepreneur and lumber baron Wallace Groves. As his Abaco Lumber Company began to run out of suitable trees to cut down and sell at the beginning of the 1950s, Groves found partners and backers – Charles Hayward the English industrialist, the American shipping tycoon D. K. LUDWIG, and, it is believed, Meyer Lansky, the Mafia kingpin – and persuaded the British imperial government and the BAY STREET regime to parlay the original lumber concession into the first Hawksbill Creek Agreement (1955). Groves's company was given almost autonomous powers over a huge swathe of Grand Bahama east of Hawksbill Creek, along with tax and customs exemptions and the right to bring in workers and settlers as it wished – provided only that it achieved certain development goals within an allotted time.

The basic plan was to build the deep-water free port at Hawksbill Creek (after which the whole project got its name), an adjacent industrial park, a luxurious complex of hotels, CASINOS and marinas along the splendid stretch of beach to the east, and many square miles of upmarket home-sites, collectively called Lucaya, clustered, Florida-style, around golf courses, artificial lakes, and boat canals. Progress was spectacular. By 1960, Freeport-Lucaya boasted a port that could accommodate liners and tankers, a giant cement works, chemical factory, oil refinery and offshore bunkering operation, an airport capable of taking the largest jets, a network of the best roads in The Bahamas, and the makings of a city, with the electricity generating power and underground water resources enough for a population of at least a half million. Besides this, hotels were mushrooming, there were two casinos, three golf courses, a waterway with radiating boat-slips sliced right across the island, and an exotic duty-free shopping centre called the International Bazaar (sometimes called Bizarre). As a reward for this progress, Bay Street's UNITED BAHAMIAN PARTY government, in the last year of its power, more than doubled the acreage of Freeport-Lucaya by the second Hawksbill Creek Agreement (1966).

Severe troubles, however, were brewing. Workers, including Turks Islanders and HAITIANS, flocked in their thousands, but they could not live within the sacred boundaries of Freeport-Lucaya. Instead, they crowded into South African-type shanty-towns to the west of Hawksbill Creek or in the tiny enclaves near the harbour which the company had not been able to incorporate. Bahamians, especially blacks, were angry at the denial of chances to live and set up businesses within Freeport-Lucaya, and the favour shown to white expatriates, including many from the Jim Crow areas of the American South. At the same time, there were revelations about the involvement of Mafiosi in the casino business and of the wholesale bribing of UBP politicians over the matter of casino licence grants.

The crisis peaked when the populist and Bahamianist PROGRESSIVE LIBERAL PARTY came to power in 1967–8. Wallace Groves announced his retirement and the controlling company, the Grand Bahama Port Authority, was sold to a shadowy corporate giant called Benguet Consolidated, based in the Philippines and closely related to the notoriously corrupt Marcos regime. In 1969, the new Premier, Lynden PINDLING, threw down the gauntlet with his famous 'Bend or Break' speech. An official inquiry was held (the Wooding Commission) and, despite the attempted 'revolt' by the disgruntled original licensees, the Hawksbill Creek Agreement was amended. The company retained all of its land, but lost much of

FREEPORT

its exclusionary power and most of its exemptions, being forced to share responsibility for public services with The Bahamas government – which became a minority shareholder in the company with the right to nominate members to the board.

This first wave of BAHAMIANISATION marked the end of the boom period for Freeport-Lucaya, and the PLP government, rather than the general world economic downturn, was widely blamed for the subsequent failure of Freeport to quite live up to its initial promise. Ironically, as the PLP government moved closer into partnership with the Port Authority, most of the Bahamians in Freeport and the rest of Grand Bahama became resolute supporters of the free market ideology of the Opposition FREE NATIONAL MOVEMENT.

But if the dizzying pace of progress slowed, Freeport steadily gained in stature as the metropole of Grand Bahama and the second city of The Bahamas, with its own distinctive character. Today it boasts of having all the facilities of Nassau with a far better infrastructure, being quieter and with much more space, and having far fewer problems, including much less crime. Thanks to dedicated citizens such as 'Union Jack' HAYWARD, son of the chief of Groves's original partners, Freeport sees itself as a city that while proudly Bahamian and thoroughly modern, is cosmopolitan too – with a decided slant towards those British traditions and styles which conservative Bahamians like, and even American visitors and homeowners find attractively quaint. Besides its annual New Year's JUNKANOO and the sailing, scuba and fishing events common to all Bahamian resorts, Freeport-Lucaya actively engages in many distinctively British and international sports including cricket, rugby, tennis, squash and golf . It has also hosted major golf, tennis, motor racing and road running tournaments, and even international 'iron man' contests.

Freeport-Lucaya has three splendid botanical gardens. Close to the centre of town are the Hydroflora Gardens and the 11-acre Garden of the Groves, which displays 5,000 species of trees and plants from around the world. Just outside town is the Rand Memorial Nature Centre, home of the local branch of The BAHAMAS

Central Grand Bahama Island

FRIENDLY SOCIETIES

NATIONAL TRUST, which shows off 130 types of plant indigenous to The Bahamas, including 21 orchid species. Most worth an excursion, however, is the 40-acre Lucayan National Park, on both sides of the Grand Bahama Highway, a dozen miles (20 km) to the east of Freeport-Lucaya. On the surface are fascinating nature trails, but the true wonder is underground. This is what is claimed to be the longest underwater tunnel and cave system in the world – at least 6 miles (9.5 km) of which have so far been explored. One connecting sink hole was discovered to have been a Lucayan burial ground; and in another part was discovered a previously unknown class of tiny blind crustacean, the *Speleonectes lucayensis*.

Further reading: P. Barratt, *Grand Bahama*, 2nd ed., Macmillan Caribbean, 1982.

FRIENDLY SOCIETIES From slavery times until the mid-twentieth century the ordinary black people of The Bahamas were neglected where not oppressed. They were not encouraged to form organisations of their own, either religious or secular, and in most cases were actively discouraged from doing so. Quite remarkable, therefore, was the widespread success of the secular 'friendly societies' for mutual self-help set up by the ex-slaves and LIBERATED AFRICANS from the 1830s.

The friendly societies initially helped to preserve African identities and customs, but their most important and lasting purpose was 'to provide benefits for the sick, aged, widows and orphans, and, above all, a fitting and stylish burial for each of their members'. They owed their success not just to the services they provided but because they offered almost a parallel alternative society for black Bahamians, complete with their own hierarchies, regalia and rituals. By the same token, though regarded by the ruling whites with scant respect, they were at least tolerated because they both spared the regime much of the cost of social welfare and provided the black majority with a harmless and apparently non-political diversion.

The first officially recognised Bahamian friendly society dated from the year after formal slavery ended, but such organisations existed informally somewhat earlier among those already free. In October 1835, a petition signed by 152 men describing themselves as 'natives of Africa' petitioned Governor Colebrooke to give sanction and support to the friendly society already existing in GRANT'S TOWN, and to all other 'Christian African organisations'. Colebrooke's response was to arrange for the incorporation of the Grant's Town Friendly Society and that of a Bahamas Friendly Society two years later, under an act of 1825 which required each to elect a board of directors, to keep funds for benefits and expenses clearly separate, to have accounts properly audited, and to keep all monies in the recently established Nassau Savings Bank.

Whether formally incorporated or not, friendly societies proliferated, originally for the most part along 'tribal' lines. For many decades there were separate Ibo, Yoruba, Egbar, Fulani, Hausa and two Congo societies, of which the last-named (combined and formally incorporated in 1864) proved the most successful and longest-lasting. In 1910 a foreign missionary admiringly remarked, 'Among themselves, the negroes are charitable and even provident … they all belong to the mutual help societies which provide funds for burying the dead, for relief in sickness and act as savings banks. The affairs of these benefit associations are conducted with remarkable shrewdness and honesty. Noteworthy among them is the Congo United Society. It has an adult membership of more than 690, besides a juvenile branch. It was founded by Congo slaves towards the close of the slaving period. Although many of its members are illiterate, the affairs of the society are administered honestly and fairly.'

With the passing of the African-born and the general creolisation of the black population, the close African affiliations of the original Bahamian friendly societies faded. But the societies themselves, and similar organisations, actually grew in number and strength until the mid-twentieth century – with many persons being active members of several more or less parallel organisations. Although the Congo and Yoruba societies (along with the Bahamas Friendly Society) kept their original name and something of their original identities through the 1970s, the separate Ibo, Egbar and Fulani societies had long disappeared and their membership dispersed. The Hausa Society followed another pattern, changing its name to become the Knights of King George Society at the beginning of the second decade of the twentieth century. This title, along with the name of the Royal Victoria Union, founded in 1904, reflected the conservative and loyalist tendency of the Bahamian friendly societies of that era. Another characteristic of the Bahamian friendly societies was the increasing participation of women, exemplified in particular by the local success of two black organisations emanating from the United States; the Order of Good Samaritans and the even more grandly styled General Grand Accepted Order of Brothers and Sisters of Love and Charity, originating in Washington DC in 1847.

The indigenous Bahamian friendly societies were, indeed, greatly reinforced from the beginning of the twentieth century by the spread from the US of branches of similarly generated but much larger black fraternal (and sororal) organisations, particularly the Elks and Oddfellows. Black Bahamians were also attracted by offshoots of those American-based MASONIC LODGES which, far from being exclusively white like their British-based forerunners, had a predominantly black membership. Though regarded somewhat askance for being both foreign and Afro-American, these societies were still considered essentially conservative and politically harmless, despite the secrecy of their rituals and the spread of such radical ideas as those of GARVEYISM during the 1920s.

This changed substantially during the ferment of the Civil Rights movement in the United States during the 1950s and 1960s, when the Elks and other American black fraternal organisations became closely involved in political demonstrations, and their stance and tactics became transferred to The Bahamas under the leadership of the radical black Androsian (and Elks potentate) Clarence BAIN. It was patently obvious, however, that it was the climactic political and racial situation in The Bahamas that was leading the Bahamian friendly societies at last to take up a radical stance, rather than vice versa.

In the days following black majority rule and political INDEPENDENCE the Bahamian friendly societies both reverted to their traditionally apolitical stance and lost much of their traditional *raison d'etre*. Many of the societies and lodges lingered on and still occasionally paraded in public for the funerals of their declining membership. But their social, ceremonial and philanthropic functions survived increasingly through the activities of such SERVICE CLUBS as Rotary, Kiwanis and Lions. The more widespread success of these organisations, in fact, signified the fundamental changes in Bahamian society from the mid-twentieth century onwards, if not its Americanisation. Originating exclusively from the United States, these fraternal service clubs were designed to allow businessmen and professionals to meet regularly in order to discuss and perform service for the good of society at large. Thus they were at first predominantly a white preserve. But from mid-century they gradually extended to include ambitious and upwardly mobile blacks – so that by the century's end the membership of all of the local service organisations (even most of the Masonic lodges) were cross-ethnically democratic. Indeed, it could be maintained that the failure of the traditional friendly societies correspondingly to attract whites indicated that their time had virtually passed. *Sic transiunt tempora*.

FUNERALS For all Bahamians, but especially those of African descent, funerals have always been the most vital of the rites of passage. Celebrations of birth and christening are comparatively low-key; there is no general ritual to celebrate the attaining of adulthood; and weddings, though often extravagant, are more for family and friends than community occasions. Though the obsequies for the grander members of society are proportionately splendid – even state occasions – the community strives to give its humblest members a distinguished send-off. To ignorant outsiders it may seem ironic that a person's passage out of life is often grander than anything he or she enjoyed while alive. But the tradition in fact signifies motives both deep and touching: the determination to accord the deceased a dignity and status perhaps denied in life, in order that he or she might be suitably prepared to cross the ultimate threshold and join the ancestors in the spirit world.

Bahamian funerary rituals are shared by the extended family circle and the particular FRIENDLY SOCIETY or lodge to which the deceased belonged, within a formal structure ordained by the state and churches and, in modern times, with the ancillary help provided by professional funeral services. Throughout The Bahamas down to the twentieth century, and until much later in the Family Islands, everything was an immediate concern of the entire community, constrained by the statutory ordinance that a body had to be buried within 24 hours of death. Particularly where there was a shortage or absence of churches or ministers, it was very much a folk affair, extending over the days both before and after the actual death and interment. 'The strangest of their customs,' wrote the pioneer folklorist Charles Edwards in 1895, was to hold a pre-death wake at night at the house of a person thought to be on the point of dying. 'The singers, men and women, and children of all ages, sit about on the floor of the larger room of the hut and stand outside at the doors and windows while the invalid lies upon the floor in the smaller room. Long into the night they sing their most mournful hymns and "anthems", and only in the light of dawn do those who are left as chief mourners silently disperse.'

As soon as the expected death occurred, either family members or (as in Nassau or a sizeable settlement) delegated members of the deceased's friendly society or lodge, fashioned a simple plank coffin and dug a grave in the limestone rock of the nearby cemetery. After the last viewing of the body and the solemn closing of the coffin, the actual burial, accompanied by whatever church service and parade could be mustered, was attended by virtually the whole community and followed by a more common type of wake. The folksong recordist Samuel Charters described typical wakes he witnessed in ANDROS as recently as the 1950s. 'The women sing early, and the men stay outside drinking until about midnight, when they slip into the room and begin singing the loud "rhymed"

FUNERALS

spirituals. The women sing the slower hymns, often leading the songs from a hymnal. An older woman will sit in a reading chair, singing from her tattered book, reading by the light of the lantern.' In earlier times, and especially with the passing of notable community members, the mourning went on, in a diminuendo of night-time wakes, as long as the nine nights traditionally regarded in Africa as the time it took for a soul fully to pass over into the realm of the ancestral spirits.

Today, and especially in NEW PROVIDENCE and the larger settlements, the process has been considerably elaborated and extended, thanks mainly to the ability of morticians to embalm and preserve the body for a week or more and the availability of churches and ministers to be involved in the process. Traditional funerary elements, however, survive strongly, particularly in the involvement of the friendly societies and lodges and the rituals followed by the mourners. A modern Bahamian funeral process, indeed, can be analysed as the intertwining of four almost rival elements, in an ascending order of sociological importance: the formal requirements of the state; the services provided by the commercial undertakers; the involvement of the churches and their ministers; and the deep-seated folk traditions of family, community and people at large.

As soon as a person dies the death has to be officially notified, certified and recorded. Ministers are already involved but now professional undertakers (a specially prestigious and prosperous class in The Bahamas) are contacted and the scale and order of arrangements discussed and negotiated. It is a matter of family pride to have the most elaborate church ceremonies and funerary accoutrements affordable: an ornate coffin and the body expensively embalmed, clothed and cosmeticised for viewing over several days; swathes of flowers; a corps of elegant, black-clad professional attendants; and an impressive hearse and carriages for the chief mourners – now gleaming black Cadillacs rather than the former horse-drawn hearse with black plumes or the trundled bier, followed by the family and other mourners on foot.

Long provided for and still taken for granted in many cases, however, is the involvement of the deceased's friendly society or lodge. Although the open-coffin visitations are now more commonly at the funeral home than at private houses or lodge halls, the church and committal services are usually of central importance, and many burial wakes are held in church halls or elsewhere, a society or lodge parade with a band from church to cemetery, and back to the lodge hall for an elaborate meal, speeches celebrating

Funeral procession

the deceased, and general socialisation, are still optimal features, if less invariable as time goes by.

An article in the 1970 edition of the *Bahamas Handbook* memorably described what was then still a common weekly spectacle in downtown Nassau:

> *Except for the band which headed the procession rendering* Onward Christian Soldiers *with a particularly loud (but mournful) thump on the bass drum, there wasn't a sound from the five hundred-odd men, women and children in the funeral procession. Walking solemnly in pairs, little girls in white with huge butterfly bows anchored to their pigtails and little boys in spanking clean shirts carried immense wreaths of plastic flowers. Following the women in their white uniform dresses marched a man carrying a lodge banner of one of the fraternal orders in the same bright colours as the women's sashes. Proudly, the banner-carrier stepped out leading the lodge members who were making the last walk with the brother. A tightly-knit group of men in black, friends of the deceased and high in the ranks*

of the lodge, pushed the coffin on a bier towards its final destination. The family – the widow and her small children – followed behind in an isolation that nothing could touch.

At the same time, coming up the hill on Cumberland Street was another procession, also led by a band. But this band was jauntily playing When the Saints Go Marching In. The people were dressed the same, but their lines weren't as orderly. In fact, there was a real strut to their step. And there was no bier. They had left that in the cemetery with the deceased, the anguish, the wailing and the family. The two processions passed on the hill of Cumberland Street just above the Sheraton-British Colonial Hotel, one enveloped in a mood of heavy sorrow, and the other on its way to a party.

The most splendid of all Bahamian funerals was that accorded in September 2000 to former Prime Minister Sir Lynden PINDLING. Yet, despite the unparalleled pomp and circumstance of the occasion, by the wishes of the family and of the great populist himself, the whole process, from death-bed to the end of the official mourning period, essentially followed a recognisably traditional pattern.

Pindling's death-bed presented almost a set traditional tableau. Family, close associates (even former political foes) and ministers from several churches were gathered round the dying chief. Prayers were recited and hymns sung. Soon after death the morticians took charge and plans for the lying-in-state, funeral and burial were broadcast. Pindling lay in an open coffin at the House of Assembly for three days, while an endless line of people filed by to pay their last respects, and a group of women kept a continuous keening vigil in Parliament Square. On the last evening the drums, cowbells and bugles of a huge, almost impromptu, JUNKANOO parade bade the leader's spirit farewell.

During the entire period of official grief all negative assessments of the dead man were locally stilled. *Nil nisi bonum*. The day of the funeral itself, nine days after the death, was a majestic and moving national celebration. Following Pindling's own wishes, the funeral service was interdenominational and held neither in his own church nor in the Anglican cathedral downtown, but in the Church of God of Prophecy in the heart of Over-the-Hill Nassau. The solemn mile-long cortege from Parliament Square to the church, and the three-hour service were flawlessly enacted, with the people's raw emotions reaching a climax as the bier was then carried two miles across town through the teeming streets for interment in the Pindling family plot in the Western Cemetery. In the traditional manner, widow, family and chief mourners, however distinguished, followed the coffin on foot. As Pindling's official biographer wrote: 'The cemetery was roped off for the family, prelates and VIPs. But so dense was the crush that, in the words of the ZNS commentator, the police wisely allowed the people to break through the barriers and symbolically take over the interment ceremony. Fervent hymns accompanied the military salute, Masonic funeral honours and simple prayers as Sir Lynden was laid to rest. The hymns included the lovely song of hope, "Amazing Grace", the elegiac "It is Finished", and the triumphant chorus of "Come we that love the Lord".'

Further reading: 'The Bahamian Way of Death', *Bahamas Handbook and Businessman's Annual, 1970-71*, Dupuch Publications, 1971, 94–107; M. Craton, *Pindling: The Life and Times of the First Prime Minister of The Bahamas, 1930-2000*, Macmillan Caribbean, 2002, 406–21; S. Charters, *The Day is So Long and the Wages are So Poor*, UK, 1999.

GAMBIER VILLAGE A small settlement on north-western NEW PROVIDENCE 9 miles (14 miles) from NASSAU, founded by Governor Sir James Carmichael SMYTH in the 1830s (like Carmichael, Adelaide and FOX HILL elsewhere in the island) as a home for LIBERATED AFRICANS. However, its name was derived not from the West African Gambia River (as some guidebooks say) but from the fact that the area had formerly been owned by one of the Gambier brothers who had been Acting Governor and Vice Admiralty Judge during the 1750s.

The village was originally laid out as some thirty quarter-acre family house plots, extending in a narrow strip a half-mile (0.8 km) from the coastal road over its backing ridge. As in the other settlements, the inhabitants worked their garden plots and the surrounding untenanted land as subsistence farmers, carrying their surplus produce to Nassau by donkey or dinghy. A church and school were built, and by the early twentieth century the more successful inhabitants (who included Elisha Morris, one of the leaders of the famous uprising on the slave ship *CREOLE* in 1841) had obtained title to all the adjacent land.

The inhabitants retained a strong sense of village identity, but Gambier remained a poor and isolated place until modern transportation made it feasible for its people to work in town, and piped water, electricity and the telephone made it a more comfortable place in which to live. Substantial modern homes have replaced most of the wooden houses, but development has been somewhat held back by the fact that the village lies directly under one of the flight paths of aircraft coming in to land at Nassau International Airport.

GAMBLING Gambling in many forms still holds attractions for ordinary Bahamians, despite the opposition of the churches and the strictures of the law. Since the beginning of the twentieth century, Bahamians found ways to follow and participate in foreign lotteries, particularly the Cuban National Lottery and, rather later, the Florida and New York State lotteries. Horse racing in The Bahamas, organised between the 1920s and 1960s, was sustained as much by local punters as by wealthy sponsors, promotion by the Development Board and tourist bettors. The tradition of local betting on sporting events was carried on in sailing events, boxing contests and soccer matches, and even, it is credibly reported, in secretive cock-fights – introduced and run by Haitians but patronised by inveterate local gamblers.

The most controversial and longest-running Bahamian gambling issue has involved the legalisation of CASINOS. Though from their beginning in the 1920s they have officially been barred to Bahamian participants, and since the 1970s have ostensibly come under Bahamian government supervision and control, casinos have continued to be censured and their proliferation condemned by the churches – even those that condone raffles and other games of chance at charity functions – as a moral danger. The impropriety of seeking a reward without honest labour, and the fear that the gambling-prone poorer Bahamians will wager more than they can afford (as well as the thought that the net proceeds will be up for government disposal and eat into the income from church collections) explain the even less well-founded opposition to a Bahamian national lottery. A greater danger might be identified in the recent increase in international betting on the Internet, which is virtually impossible to control by churches or government alike.

One form of gambling that has survived over more than a century despite its technical illegality, and is probably more popular then ever, is the so-called Numbers Game. As in the parallel (but quite legal) ASUE savings system, its success depends on the efficiency and complete reliability of the central banker. Traditionally each banker's 'house' had a network of runners to sell tickets and pay out to winners. But today the houses are more likely to be static – fairly covert but widely known – with the transactions almost impersonal, even involving computer terminals and the internet. The method of operation varies from house to house, but there is a general pattern. Typically, tickets (or rather, written receipts) are sold for as little as 50 cents a number. Bets may be laid for a single two-digit number, or for three or four numbers, the latter either as straight or 'boxed' – that is, in all possible combinations. As in all similar betting cultures, great store is popularly laid on the significance of particular numbers on particular days or in particular circumstances, with well-thumbed 'numbers books' to give guidance.

Bets are normally daily, with evening payouts. But inveterate gamblers are accommodated with up to three separate draws each day in some houses. The winning numbers are determined from those in a specific US state lottery – most commonly those based in Chicago, Miami or New York. The odds vary from one in a hundred for a single number (50 to one if also reversed) up to one in ten thousand for four digits (though much less if 'boxed'). Pay-outs return roughly 70 percent to the successful punter,

GARVEYISM

POLICE have always more or less turned a blind eye to the Numbers traffic, not, as is sometimes said, because they are bribed to protect the operators, but because they find prosecution more trouble than it is worth, and like to indulge in 'playing the Numbers' themselves.

GARVEYISM Marcus Massiah Garvey (1887–1940) was a charismatic black Jamaican whose United Negro Improvement Association (UNIA) had an important if temporary and ambivalent impact on The Bahamas and Bahamians in the 1920s.

Inspired by the ideas and rhetoric of the Bahamian-born episcopalian minister and doctor Robert LOVE (1839–1914), Garvey founded the UNIA in Jamaica in 1914, but had his greatest impact in the northern United States in the restless aftermath of WORLD WAR ONE. Among the Bahamian migrants who reached prominent positions within Garvey's movement in the United States were Frederick Toote (brother of the black Nassauvian lawyer-politician T. A. Toote) who became the UNIA organiser in Philadelphia, and the Androsian Josiah Cockburn, one of the few blacks with an international master mariner's licence, who was the captain of the only steamship in Garvey's ill-fated Black Star Line.

Gambling on a hermit crab race

The most active and ardent of Bahamian Garveyites, however, were the members of the migrant community that made up a large proportion of the black population of Miami, Florida. Of Miami's 10,000 blacks, 7,000 were said to be West Indians, of whom at least two-thirds were from The Bahamas. Bahamians dominated the several UNIA chapters established in southern Florida from 1917. Generally ambitious though not overtly militant, the Miami Bahamians saw Garveyism as a way of countering the Jim Crow practices of white Southern Americans and fostering self-reliance. They were already well-attuned to the ethos and rituals of the UNIA from their experience of ethnic Friendly Societies and Lodges in Over-the-Hill Nassau, and wished to revive the Pan-African pride and self-help ideals that had inspired the likes of David PATTON and James C. Smith, with his moderately radical *Freeman* newspaper, in the late 1880s.

leaving 30 per cent for the banker. These odds seem both to satisfy the bettors and provide a substantial margin for the kingpin, at least on the average. However, to cover the risk of pay-outs exceeding the average on the short term, the Numbers operators have to maintain a large reserve, making some of them reputedly very wealthy indeed.

Apart from the obsessive grip it is said to hold on some of the poorest, the arguments against the Numbers Game are that it is run by gangsters and breeds violence and corruption. These fears are certainly exaggerated. The great majority of the populace regard the Numbers Game as a harmless diversion, a tradition that is almost a right. The Numbers kingpins have always been not only well known but accorded almost the status of popular heroes. Their invulnerabilty is both a consequence of the system's continued popularity and the cause of its success. The

Given the vicious opposition which the UNIA faced in the United States (from government agencies as well as from racist bigots) it is not surprising that UNIA adherents returning to The Bahamas promoted Garveyite ideas in their homeland with greater optimism than abroad. Returning enthusiasts, such as Samuel McPherson, Reuben Bethel and Oscar E. Johnson, were at the head of a wave of influence, which became stronger as US immigration restrictions, culminating in the Reed Act

GARVEYISM

of 1924, reversed the flow of migration between The Bahamas and the United States. Garveyite ideals attracted all blacks, but in the relative boom years of the 1920s they were especially attractive to two types of non-whites: those in the middling ranks who simply looked for better economic chances and a louder political voice, and those members of the non-white elite who saw in the movement the chances of leading the black majority, economically and politically.

From 1919, two UNIA chapters were established in New Providence, in GRANT'S TOWN and GAMBIER. Secret government reports to London estimated (probably with some exaggeration) that together they had a thousand members. BAY STREET and the Bahamian official establishment were sufficient alarmed by the threat of Garveyism to pass the Seditious Publications Act (1919–24) which was specially aimed at preventing the circulation of the UNIA's weekly newspaper the *Negro World* – though in this they were far from completely successful.

In 1920, Bahamian Garveyites inspired by Garvey's ideals of race-pride and self-reliance attempted to form a Union Mercantile Association (UMA), whose major project (based on Garvey's plans for the Black Star Line) was to finance a black-owned motorboat to carry goods and passengers between Nassau and Miami that would both undercut white shippers and merchants and spare non-white travellers the normal indignities inflicted upon them. Like the Black Star Line, the UMA had more propaganda than commercial success, provoking much attention and investigation from the Bahamas Police.

Rather less objectionable to the Establishment was the Bahamas Rejuvenation League, founded by Bahamian Garveyites in New York in 1920, with a branch in Nassau. The chief aim of the League was to improve educational opportunities for black Bahamians. Its first meeting in Nassau was attended by the white Anglican Bishop, Roscow Shedden, and even by the white editor of the *Nassau Guardian,* Miss Mary MOSELEY. In July 1921 the League's Ladies' Committee held a highly respectable garden party in aid of a scholarship fund – one of the beneficiaries being Claudius R. Walker, who completed a high school education with uncles in New York and went on to obtain a BSc at Howard University and qualify as a doctor at Meharry University in 1929.

During the 1920s, Garveyites and sympathisers formed the core of the relatively radical but informal Ballot Party in Nassau which, while it failed in its main political aim (the secret ballot), did achieve the setting-up of the non-racialist GOVERNMENT HIGH SCHOOL in 1925.

In 1926 Garveyites were also closely involved in the creation of a Citizen's Union, brainchild of the non-white Postmaster of The Bahamas Charles O. Anderson and the black lawyer T. A. Toote, which combined the educational aims of the Bahamas Rejuvenation League (BRL) with the economic aspirations of the moribund UMA. Plans to establish a limited form of banking in competition with the Royal Bank of Canada, almost inevitably, failed. But, largely through the energies of the recently returned Dr Claudius Walker and another black college graduate, Charles Weir, the Citizen's Union formed an adult education division in 1930. This held night classes for hundreds of illiterate men and women before fading away in 1931, and prompted Dr Walker's subsequent plans for a Bahamas Technical Institute.

By then, however, the direct influence of Garvey and the UNIA had already waned. The morale of UNIA members had been shaken by Garvey's imprisonment in the United States (on charges of mail fraud) between 1925 and 1927. But resolute efforts were made by the most ardent Garveyites to revive the UNIA chapters in time for Marcus Garvey's much heralded first (and only) visit to Nassau in November 1928. This one-day stopover was both a climax and a turning point for the Garveyite movement in The Bahamas. A large crowd turned out on the Southern Recreation Ground to hear the black hero's hour-long speech. Much of Garvey's rhetoric was loudly applauded, though the crowd was puzzled when he praised whites for what they had achieved and condemned blacks as lazy good-for-nothings who needed to reform themselves, and there was such obvious disagreement when he referred to Captain Josiah Cockburn as 'a damn scamp' that he quickly changed tack. Even more significantly, when Leon Walton YOUNG, the black MHA in whose house Garvey had stayed overnight but who was widely regarded as too closely associated with Bay Street politicians, followed Garvey to the podium, his speech was interrupted by murmuring, heckling and the tooting of car horns.

By the 1930s three things had contributed to undermine and devitalise the Garveyite movement. The Great Depression, far from inciting revolutionary activism, had changed the era of optimism in the 1920s to one of pessimistic torpor. Coupled with this, the entrenchment of 'Bay Street' and the increase in the number of white tourists, residents and investors from the United States led to the development of a pattern of race relations closer to 'Jim Crow' than the easier-going and familiar Bahamian tradition. In this economic and social climate, there had come about a division among the non-white majority, not so much in regard to aims as to political tactics.

The potential black leaders (most of whom had always had reservations about Marcus Garvey), such as Walton Young, Thaddeus Toote, A. F. ADDERLEY and Etienne DUPUCH, now looked mainly to their own interests and counselled moderation, even accommodation.

Significantly, in the Bahamian general election of 1935, the number of successful non-white candidates fell from nine to an all-time low of five. Marcus Garvey, hounded even from his native Jamaica, died in obscurity in London in 1940. The ideals of Garveyism did not entirely die but became submerged. It needed the catalytic events of WORLD WAR TWO and the subsequent economic revival to inspire a resurgence of the people's aspirations and actions – with former Garveyites playing at least a minor part in the 'BURMA ROAD' RIOTS of 1942, the GENERAL STRIKE of 1958, and the other events that led up to black majority rule in 1967 and INDEPENDENCE in 1973.

Further reading: E. D. Cronon, *Black Moses: The Story of Marcus Garvey and the Universal Negro Improvement Association*, University of Wisconsin Press, 1969; A. Martin, *Race First: The Ideological and Organizational Struggles of Marcus Garvey and the Universal Negro Improvement Association*, Majority Press, 1976; R. Hill (ed.), *The Marcus Garvey and Universal Negro Improvement Association Papers*, 6 vols., University of California Press, 1983–1995; G. Saunders, 'Garveyism and the Growth of Racial Consciousness in The Bahamas, 1920-1940', ACH Conference paper, Nassau, April 2001.

GENERAL ELECTIONS The periodic general re-election of representatives to the lower house of a bicameral legislature was a hallowed British tradition adopted by all settler colonies, including The Bahamas almost from the beginning. However, despite the claim of their beneficiaries that they were truly democratic and ideally designed to air and resolve important issues, Bahamian general elections were in fact a travesty of democracy, only rarely concerned with general issues, right down until true party politics emerged in the 1950s.

As described elsewhere (see PARLIAMENT) The Bahamas had some form of elected deliberative body even before the Assembly was formalised under Governor Woodes ROGERS in 1729 – to consist of 24 Members elected by the male free white freeholders of the colony. An Act of 1784 redistributed the seats and added one, giving eight to New Providence, three each to Harbour Island and Eleuthera, distributing a further 11 between Abaco, Cat Island, Long Island, Exuma and Andros. Except for minor adjustments (raising the number of seats to 29, drawn from 15 constituencies) this remained the pattern into the 1950s.

At first there does not seem to have been a fixed term for each parliament, Governors alone having the prerogative right to prorogue or dissolve the Assembly and to call for a new general election when they saw fit or were persuaded to do so. In 1794, however, following much Loyalist dissatisfaction and lobbying, a maximum term of seven years was fixed after the autocratic Governor Lord DUNMORE had kept a compliant parliament in being for more than nine years. This provision remained in effect until the maximum term was reduced to five years in the new constitution of 1964.

On the surface, the Bahamian electoral system emerged from the great transition of EMANCIPATION in a relatively liberal form. By 1864 there were a considerable number of non-whites among the 5,949 qualified electors – roughly a sixth of the total population of The Bahamas and three times the proportion of voters in any West Indian colony before the 1930s – elections, especially in New Providence, were avidly contended, and up to a third of those elected were non-whites (see FREE COLOUREDS).

Three quotations illustrate the farcical nature of the 'old representative system' in The Bahamas. As the first historian of the Emancipation period remarked about the first general election in which non-white candidates stood (1834): 'The elections in some of the Out Islands were nominal. In some of these only a few electors would assemble to vote and the poll was easily controlled. In closer settlements the poor inhabitants were dependent on the merchants for their necessities and were generally indebted to the latter, who could control their votes.'

Fifty years later, the disenchanted visiting magistrate L. D. POWLES wrote in *Land of the Pink Pearl* (1888):

> This mockery of representation is the greatest farce in the world. The coloured people have the suffrage, subject to a small property qualification, but have no idea how to use it. … The elections are by open voting, and bribery, corruption and intimidation are carried on in the most unblushing manner under the very noses of the officers presiding over the polling-booths. Nobody takes any notice, and as the coloured people have not yet learnt the art of political organisation, they are powerless to defend themselves. The result is that the House of Assembly is little less than a family gathering of Nassau whites, nearly all of whom are related to each other, either by blood or marriage. Laws are passed simply for the benefit of the family, whilst the coloured people are ground down and oppressed in a manner that is a disgrace to the British flag.

Even as late as 1948, Jack Ford, an English schoolteacher, could echo Powles in his description of a general election in Abaco (where the victims still included the poorest and most ignorant of the 'CONCHY JOES' as well as the non-whites):

> *The candidates arrived before election day on a charter boat and distributed bottles of liquor to the whole of the male population. Speeches were made with the usual impossible promises and then the politicians disappeared, leaving the rest to their agents. One had to own property in order to vote. A vote was worth five pounds and a new dinghy sail. On voting day each voter was asked who he wanted to vote for, and their choice was recorded. Nothing was secret for the whole township was gathered around to hear the pronouncement. When the voter left the polling area he openly received his reward from the agent.*

The power of money and patronage in Bahamian elections, even in Nassau, was illustrated by the decisive victory of Sir Harry OAKES over the black radical Milo BUTLER in the 1936 by-election for one of the seats for Nassau South, in which Oakes never appeared on the hustings. In June 1942 it was a matter of general relief – for the conservative middle-class non-whites as much as for the white oligarchy – that the general election held, as scheduled, just two weeks after the serious 'BURMA ROAD' RIOTS, passed off uneventfully, leaving the House of Assembly virtually unchanged. It was not until the PROGRESSIVE LIBERAL PARTY was formed in 1953 and fought the 1956 general election on a moderately radical party platform that general elections began to be fought on real socio-political issues.

The success of the PLP in getting six of its candidates elected in 1956, forming an organised Opposition in the Assembly, led the BAY STREET oligarchy to form itself into the UNITED BAHAMIAN PARTY and prepare itself to fight the 1962 election, deploying modern partisan as well as traditional electoral tactics. Despite women exercising the vote for the first time and the addition of two more two-seat New Providence constituencies (bringing the ratio to the Out Islands up to 12 : 21) the PLP was soundly beaten. The consequence was all-out – expensive though not bloody – political warfare, with the PLP targeting the Out Islands and resorting to mass demonstrations and symbolic actions, while the UBP relied on the kudos of having led The Bahamas to limited self-government in 1964, discrediting its opponents through the media, and the calculated strategy of retaining three-seat constituencies in Abaco and Eleuthera and two-seat constituencies in Harbour Island, Long Island and Exuma, while splitting New Providence into 17 single-seat constituencies. The result was desperately close, but brought about the crucial breakthrough victory for the PLP, which it cemented with a landslide triumph when Premier Lynden PINDLING called another general election in the following year.

Each of the seven quinquennial general elections since 1968 has been fought on rival slates of issues, but so far only four have been concerned with central issues of the magnitude of those between 1956 and 1967. These have been the 'INDEPENDENCE' election of 1972, that of 1987 which determined that the people wanted Pindling and the Bahamianist PLP to continue in power despite the revelations of the Ellicott Drug Commission, the 1992 election which overthrew the PLP after 25 years, and that ten years later, in which the people decided that the FREE NATIONAL MOVEMENT's counter-ideology was qually ineffectual – leaving a revitalised PLP perhaps to seek an effective middle ground.

Further reading: C.A. Hughes, *Race and Politics in the Bahamas*, University of Queensland Press, 1981.

GENERAL STRIKE, 1958 First serious and largely successful action by the black Bahamian majority against the entrenched white 'BAY STREET' regime.

By the late 1950s, long-delayed prosperity was coming to The Bahamas. But it was not matched by advances towards economic equality or political democracy. The PROGRESSIVE LIBERAL PARTY, formed in 1953, had achieved enough success in the 1956 elections to persuade the dominant forces in the legislature to formalise themselves as the UNITED BAHAMIAN PARTY. But the PLP had not yet consolidated all the Opposition elements, particularly those of the working classes, and looked for a dramatic and catalytic event that might bring worldwide attention and trigger necessary changes.

The opportunity came with the decision of the well-organised Taxi-Cab Union to protest Bay Street's attempts to monopolise transport facilities, by closing down the newly opened Nassau International Airport on 1 November 1957. Encouraged by this move, but determined to move beyond the concessions offered to the taxi-men, the PLP and the rapidly expanding unions in key sectors of the economy decided to call a general strike to coincide with the official opening of Parliament on Tuesday, 13 January 1958. Inspired by the rhetoric of their black leaders – especially Milo BUTLER, Randol FAWKES and Lynden PINDLING – the response was dramatic, involving such key personnel as hotel workers not allowed to unionise under the current legislation because they were classed as domestics.

Deprived of their staff and threatened by the closure of essential services, the hotels shut their doors, planes went back to Miami and the airport closed down. This, at the height of the tourist season, was bound to have an impact on the world media, as well as creating panic in the local commercial oligarchy. Alarmed at the possibility of a repeat of the 'BURMA ROAD' RIOTS of 1942, Bay Street shopkeepers boarded up their premises as if expecting a hurricane. Even more precipitate, and probably critical, was the decision by Governor Sir Raynor Arthur – shocked to be booed by a large and angry crowd when officially opening Parliament and worried by the current political unrest in Guyana – to send for military and naval aid from the British forces stationed in the Caribbean.

A company of the Royal Worcester Regiment was flown in from Jamaica on 14 January, and a Royal Navy frigate arrived in Nassau harbour a few days later. Neither was necessary, and their presence served the cause of the strikers far better than it did the UBP. Besides publicising in dramatic fashion conditions in Nassau and drawing a flood of support from unions in Britain, the United States and the British West Indies, it allowed the Opposition forces (which in any case had disowned violence from the start) to claim that they were themselves the victims of a repressive regime.

The strike (which was never absolutely general) petered out within ten days. But it had convinced the British government and the UBP alike of the need to make at least minimal concessions and changes. In April 1958 Colonial Secretary Alan Lennox-Boyd paid the first-ever official visit of a British Secretary of State to The Bahamas. He held full and frank discussions with all sides and he was backed up by senior officials of the British Trades Union Congress. Within the following three months, trade union and industrial conciliation legislation brought The Bahamas in line with developments in Jamaica, Trinidad and Barbados. This satisfied all but the extremists in the labour movement, who included their dynamic and ambitious chief spokesman, Randol Fawkes.

Other Opposition leaders were disappointed by the failure to address the salient needs for constitutional and electoral change. They were encouraged however by the way that the general strike had both publicised social, economic and political conditions in The Bahamas and demonstrated the way that changes could be achieved by efficiently concerted, but essentially peaceable, action by the black Bahamian majority.

Further reading: D. L. Johnson, *The Quiet Revolution in The Bahamas*, Nassau, Family Islands Press, 1972, 29–48; R. Fawkes, *The Faith That Moved the Mountain*, Nassau, privately published, 1979, 69–126; C. A. Hughes, *Race and Politics in the Bahamas*, University of Queensland Press, 1982, 62–94; M. Craton, *Pindling: The Life and Times of Lynden Oscar Pindling (1930–2000), First Prime Minister of The Bahamas*, Macmillan, 2002, 77–88; C. Darling (as told to P. B. Roker), *Sir Clifford Darling: A Bahamian Life Story*, i. *The Years of Struggle, 1922–1958*, Nassau, privately published 2002, 204–440.

GEOLOGY

Put in simplest terms, the Bahama islands (along with the Turks and Caicos islands) are scattered fragments barely emerging above sea level from a massive limestone platform, which is itself split by fractures that constitute deep water passages. The basic limestone was laid down over aeons by the deposit in warm, shallow sea waters of the broken down remains of calcareous organisms and the biochemical precipitation of calcium carbonate, progressively depressed by its own weight until it formed a subterranean layer over 3 miles (4.8 km) thick.

Bahamian geological history is best divided into two widely unequal phases: that which saw the formation of the underlying structure up to 200 million years ago, and the (geologically speaking) comparatively recent and still continuing phase which has seen the shaping of the islands and their surrounding seas over the last million years or so. The first is imperfectly understood and still a matter of debate. The present Bahama platform is clearly the product of vast tectonic activity following its original formation. The most commonly held theory is that it is the western half of a much larger limestone platform split apart by the gradual fissure that divided middle America from Africa and created the South Atlantic, rotating some 25 degrees to the north-east in the process. The fractures which formed the three deep channels along the axis of the Bahama platform and the half dozen crosswise sea passages are thought to be a product either of this major rift, or of subsequent more localised shifts. In either case, the outcome was the creation of one huge, six large and more than a dozen smaller banks, that were mainly dry land or very shallow sea according to the fluctuation in ocean levels due to global temperature changes and the relative extent of polar glaciation.

The observable geologic structure and present surface features of the Bahama islands are the result of processes that occurred during the four ice ages and interglacial periods of the most recent geological epoch (called the *Pleistocene*), over the last million years. Reef formation in the shallow tropical waters surrounding each island was a constant feature, accounting for the existence of fossil corals in the most recent limestone strata. Parallel general processes have been the build-up of limestone sands and sediments within the reef-edged banks (called *oolitic* if formed by calcium carbonation, *skeletal* if from calcified organisms, or *peloidal* if derived from untold trillions of faecal pellets), and the gradual deposit over millennia of wind-borne dust from the Sahara, which accounts for thin patches of reddish soils in areas not inundated in recent geological times.

Equally important, however, have been the action of waves and winds, differing in their effects (and perhaps their intensity) between low-water, large-island ice ages, and high-water, small-island interglacial eras. This has perhaps been best described by geologist Dr Paul Hearty:

GEORGE TOWN, EXUMA

Oolite sand banks

Once the sediments accumulate in shallow water, they must be transported first to the beach area, and subsequently onto the islands as sand dunes, resulting in island growth. Paradoxically, much island growth occurs during destructive hurricanes (destructive in the human sense). These powerful storms, perhaps of even greater power during warmer interglacials of the past, provide all the needed energy to mobilise the shallow water sediments and transport them to the coastlines. They also generate the wind necessary to whip the sand into large dunes that now form ridges on the windward (hurricane-ward) sides of Bahamian islands. Queen's Staircase in Nassau reveals the anatomy of these ancient coastal sand dunes, now cemented into limestone rock.

As Dr Hearty and other geologists have described, this explains the low ridges that run parallel to the coasts or form the spine of narrower Bahamian islands, and the strata and planing to be observed in exposed rock surfaces (including cliffs and quarries), as well as other features of the existing topography of Bahamian islands. Much modification, however, has occurred subsequent to deposition, due in part to faulting, but mainly to the effect of weathering, particularly the action of rain water on limestone rock. This has produced the surfaces of brittle and sharp-edged 'honeycomb' rock, 'banana holes', sinkholes, caves, interconnecting subterranean caverns, and submarine 'BLUE HOLES'.

In sum, the geology of the Bahamas is much more interesting and significant than it may seem at first glance. Not only does its study help in understanding the form and formation of the land to which Bahamians have adapted over time, but it displays processes that are constantly changing at a pace and in ways that are both perceptible and measurable. Not least, it includes features and processes still not fully understood, and is therefore a subject that calls for much further theorisation and research.

Further reading: N. E. Sealey: *Bahamian Landscapes: An Introduction to the Geography of The Bahamas*, Collins Caribbean, 1985; P. J. Hearty, 'On the Evolution of the Bahamian Islands: An Excerpt from Nature's Anthology', *Bahamas Handbook and Businessman's Annual, 1994*, Dupuch Publications, 1994, 44–56.

GEORGE TOWN, EXUMA Situated in the heart of the Bahamian archipelago, exactly on the invisible line of the Tropic of Cancer, and fronting one of the most splendid natural harbours in The Bahamas, George Town, EXUMA is among the most interesting and picturesque of Family Island townships. Though today it has fewer than 1,000 permanent inhabitants, it is often claimed that it might at least have equalled NASSAU in importance had not history passed it by.

Loyally named after the English monarch (George III) like many other notable colonial townships, George Town was specially laid out by a parliamentary act of 1792 to be the administrative centre for the LOYALISTS who first settled Exuma with their slaves after the American War of Independence. To Governor DUNMORE and officials of the Admiralty however, its location promised it even greater significance. Situated on the sheltered but strategic harbour between the Exuma mainland and Stocking Island, George Town was visualised as a safe and potent naval base against Britain's French, Spanish and American enemies (to whom Nassau was painfully vulnerable), and the commercial hub for the huge COTTON industry which the Loyalists optimistically anticipated. The era of international peace which followed 1815, along with the complete failure of Bahamian cotton plantations, punctured these plans hugely in Nassau's favour, and George Town grew only at a snail's pace.

However, before the end of slavery were built (not necessarily in this order) a church and parsonage, a courthouse-cum-jail, a government dock and market square, a warehouse or two, a slave vendue house (much later converted into a hostelry still called the 'Peace and Plenty') and a few 'town houses' for the meagre local gentry. These buildings were all located on the small ridge and peninsula between Elizabeth Harbour and the circular lake connected with it, later named Victoria Pond. After slavery ended, a steady trickle of former plantation slaves and their descendants migrated to George Town, settling mainly around the BAPTIST church on the opposite side of Victoria Pond.

George Town, Great Exuma

George Town's tidal pond was a centre for ship careening and repair and some ship-building in the early twentieth century. The township had minor surges of activity when small US bases were established during WORLD WAR TWO and for anti-drug surveillance in the 1980s, and it has remained the administrative and modest commercial centre of Great Exuma. But despite the six-fold increase in the Bahamian population and the twenty-fold increase in the size of Nassau, George Town's population has not doubled since 1906, when it consisted of 534 persons in 119 families, living in 125 houses – making it probably the fourth-largest Bahamian Out Island settlement, after Dunmore Town, Harbour Island, New Plymouth, Abaco and Matthew Town, Inagua. Once a fairly somnolent place, George Town has become a metropolis for yachts in the winter season, culminating in the National Family Island Regatta (see OUT ISLAND REGATTA) in May, when hundreds of competing or cruising sailboats and thousands of carousing visitors temporarily transform it.

Further reading: A. Vincent-Barwood, *This Sweet Place*, Nassau, 1998.

GIBSON, Timothy (1903–1979) Teacher, musician and composer of the Bahamian National Anthem. Born to the leading family in Savannah Sound, Eleuthera, Timothy Gibson was educated largely by his older brother Charles, headmaster of the public school at Deadman's Cay, Long Island. After a long teaching apprenticeship, mainly in the Out Islands, he was for 20 years headmaster of Western Junior School, Nassau, where among his pupils was Lynden PINDLING (whom he also taught piano). In 1955 Gibson was appointed Supervisor of Music for Schools and in 1962 an Assistant School Inspector. Besides dozens of popular songs, in retirement he wrote the music and words of three entries in the 1972 competition for the Anthem of the newly independent Bahamas: 'Beautiful Bahamas', 'Fairest Land on Earth', and 'March on Bahamaland' – of which the third was chosen the winner:

Timothy Gibson

GOLF

Lift up your head to the rising sun, Bahamaland;
March on to glory, your bright banners waving high.
See how the world marks the manner of your bearing!

Pledge to excel through love and unity.
Pressing onward, march together to a common loftier goal;
Steady sunward, though the weather hide the wide and treach'rous shoal.

Lift up your head to the rising sun, Bahamaland;
'Til the road you've trod lead unto your God,
March on, Bahamaland!

GOLF Regarded as essential adjuncts to upmarket TOURISM and prestigious residential developments, golf courses abound in The Bahamas. However, though golf is increasingly popular among middle-class Bahamians, members-only courses and green fees on those open to the public as high as $110 ensure that it remains essentially a pastime for the leisured and wealthy.

The very first Bahamian golf course was a somewhat unkempt but 'interesting' nine-holes laid out in 1900 at Fort Charlotte as an amenity for visitors to the new Colonial Hotel. Guides in the 1920s also refer to several 'pitch and putt' or 'clock golf' courses in the Colonial Hotel grounds or private gardens, even claiming that this miniature version of the game was originated in Nassau by a Dr Cassellberry.

The first 18-hole course – still in use after almost 80 years – was that of the Bahamas Country Club, laid out by the American course architect Devereux Emmett in 1925 2 miles (3 km) to the west of Nassau, between Goodman's Bay and Prospect Ridge. It was glowingly described by Mary MOSELEY in the *Bahamas Handbook* (1926):

There are holes close to the beach where the sea takes the place of the rough; there are water holes, long holes and short holes; a hole along the top of a ridge fifty feet above the rest of the course, and a hole in a coconut grove. There are holes to make a golfer use every shot in the bag, but although it is not an easy course to play there is nothing unfair or freakish about the layout. … The sand dunes and the white sandy rough, in contrast with the green grass of the fairways, and most of all the beautiful water of Delaporte Bay beyond make of these links a wonderful tropical beauty spot as well as a first-class golf course.

The Bahamas Country Club course (now the Radisson Cable Beach Golf Course) survived the Great Depression and World War Two as the only facility in The Bahamas. But golf courses proliferated as a function of the post-war tourism and offshore residential boom. The two most visionary pioneers were the founder of Grand Bahama's Freeport-Lucaya, Wallace Groves, and his financial partner Daniel K. LUDWIG – both, as it happened, far too busy to be golfers themselves. Almost before any hotels, roads or houses were built, no less than five golf courses were planned. Under the direction of the course designers Dick Wilson and Robert Trent Jones, the flat pine forest was artfully bulldozed into rolling vistas, with luxuriant fairways dotted with picturesque freshwater lakes (and kept verdant by the island's plentiful fresh water). The Lucayan Country Club course was ready in December 1963; the second, centred on Ludwig's King's Inn Resort (and later called the Bahamia Golf and Country Club), within a further eighteen months. By 1967, both clubs had added a second 18-hole course, and a fifth course had opened as the Fortune Hills Golf and Country Club.

The golf-course explosion in Grand Bahama was probably over-optimistic, especially given the downturn in Freeport-Lucaya's fortunes that occurred during the Pindling era. The Freeport model, however, was emulated with almost every major development, leading to the creation of splendid courses on Paradise Island and at Lyford Cay (both private), South Ocean Beach, New Providence, West End, Grand Bahama, Cotton Bay, Eleuthera, and Treasure Cay, Abaco (voted by *Golf Digest* in 1999 as the best of all Bahamian courses). Even the Berry Islands boasted a nine-hole golf course as an adjunct of the Great Harbour Yacht Club and Marina. Not all succeeded, and almost all went through hard times in the 1970s and 1980s. The later 1990s, however, saw a resurgence This was epitomised by a revamping of the Ocean Club course on Paradise Island under the direction of the popular golf star Tom Weiskopf. The reopening in December 2000 was celebrated by a father/son tournament including (with their offspring) Jack Nicklaus, Ray Floyd, Tom Kite, Johnny Miller and Hale Irwin. On Grand Bahama too, the hoped-for renaissance of Freeport-Lucaya has been aided by the great success of an annual Pro–Am tournament, held each January on Bahamia's refurbished Emerald and Ruby courses. At the time of printing, The Bahamas boasted no fewer than nine active 18-hole and two nine-hole golf courses, on six different islands, with several more under construction.

GOMEZ, Archbishop Drexel Wellington Born in the Berry Islands in 1937, Drexel Gomez had a vocation for the Anglican priesthood from his time as a student at GOVERNMENT HIGH SCHOOL and acolyte in the High Church parish of St Agnes, Nassau. A brilliant theological student in Barbados and England, he early came to the notice of the Caribbean hierarchy. After curacies in Nassau he was put in charge of the parish of Governor's Harbour, Eleuthera on his ordination as priest in 1962. Between 1964 and 1968 Father Gomez was lecturer in theology at Codrington College, Barbados, his former seminary, returning to be parish priest at Eight Mile Rock, Grand Bahama and become secretary/treasurer of the Bahamas diocese two years later.

Losing to Michael ELDON in the competition to be the first native (and non-white) Bishop of the Bahamas on the eve of Independence, Drexel Gomez landed an even more glittering prize when he was chosen Bishop of staunchly Anglican Barbados in 1972, at the early age of 35. Successfully serving the Barbados see for 21 not entirely trouble-free years, he returned to be Assistant Bishop of the Bahamas in 1993, succeeding Michael Eldon as Bishop on the latter's retirement in 1996. The crown of a distinguished career came in October, 1998, when he was made Lord Archbishop of the West Indies at the age of 61.

Theologically conservative in the High Church tradition and a strict moralist, Bishop Gomez was also an advocate of political and social change. He made a significant footnote to Bahamian history in 1984 when as a member of the three-man Drugs Commission of Inquiry he gave a minority opinion that whereas it had not been proved that any of Prime Minister Lynden PINDLING'S income had come from drug-running sources, it had not been conclusively proved to the contrary. In a eulogy delivered at Pindling's state funeral in September 2000, however, Archbishop Gomez referred to Pindling unequivocally as 'a pioneer of change who had united the people and set the nation on its path out of Egypt'.

GOOMBAY Goombay is the generic word for the distinctive traditional music of The Bahamas – involving drumming, dancing and singing – as it has evolved mainly from African roots, but with European secular and religious influences.

The word itself derives from a West African word meaning simply 'rhythm'. More specifically, throughout the slave societies of the New World goombay (in various spellings) was both the name given to the predominant type of medium-sized goatskin drum and to the avid celebrations of drumming, music and dancing performed on special occasions (when allowed by their masters) by the Afro-American slaves and their descendants.

In The Bahamas (as to a lesser extent in Jamaica and elsewhere) goombay music became inextricably related to the year-end festival of JUNKANOO. 'Rushing' to the heady music of drum, rattles, scrapers, cowbells and bugles is the primeval basis of both Bahamian rhythm and dance. On more frequent, and somewhat more formal, occasions small RAKE N' SCRAPE bands provided music for dances, in lodge halls or out in the open, which would include both Bahamian versions of European quadrilles and ring and jump-in dances with origins in Africa. From the early nineteenth century, singing at these and other functions would be heavily influenced by religious spirituals (or 'ant'ems'), derived at least in part from the American South – especially the 'Gullah' culture of the coastlands of Georgia and South Carolina. Such music remained strongest in the islands slowest to modernise, such as ANDROS and CAT ISLAND, so that musical folklorists came to refer to them as 'the real Bahamas'.

In the twentieth century, the purely secular aspects of goombay developed to provide both dance-hall music, and songs for popular and tourist entertainment. Composer-performers proliferated and gained wide – if at first localised – popularity. Significantly, such creative artists over the years included not just blacks, like Phillip Brice, 'Shorty the Serenader', George SYMONETTE and Alphonso HIGGS ('Blind Blake'), but Bahamian whites, such as Charles Lofthouse and Eric Minns. Some of their catchier songs – 'Hoist Up The John B Sail', 'Brown Skin Gal' or 'Bahama Mama' – gained a wide currency when adopted by American singers from the 1950s on. But by the end of the twentieth century Bahamian entertainers, such as 'Exuma' (Tony McKay) and Baha Men (originators of the Grammy-winning 'Who Let the Dogs Out?') themselves began to spread goombay music to a wider audience.

However, perhaps a majority of goombay vocal numbers had a narrower and more temporary application. They commemorated famous local events and successes, or disasters such as HURRICANES, FIRES or wrecks, or they commented with sly wit upon politicians and political scandals, or Bahamian characters and characteristics in general. In these respects, Bahamian goombay had similarities (was even influenced by) West Indian calypso. To the musically attuned, and those aware of the subtleties of Bahamian culture, however, goombay music remains essentially Bahamian – as distinct in its way as the Bahamian Junkanoo differs from the Trinidad Carnival, and a Bahamian rake n' scrape band from a Trinidadian STEEL BAND.

Goombay or 'Junkanoo' music has come to be a Bahamian trademark. It is performed wherever and whenever

GORDA CAY

Bahamians are putting on a show or sporting performance, abroad as well as at home. With or without a Bahamian connection, goombay festivals are celebrated in various centres of the Afro-American diaspora. In Bermuda, the 'Gombays' variant of Junkanoo has been celebrated around Christmas time since slavery days and still flourishes as a tourist attraction. Curiously, Asheville, in the mountains of North Carolina, has an annual Goombay Festival in August, which in recent years has featured costumed stilt dancers and expert drummers brought across from West Africa. But the most Bahamian of these foreign celebrations is that held annually in Key West, Florida. As befits a city with a close affiliation to The Bahamas since its founding days, Key West's October Goombay Festival regularly invites the band of the ROYAL BAHAMAS POLICE FORCE and authentic Bahamian junkanoo groups, as well as stalls selling Bahamian STRAW-WORK, CONCH and various other Bahamian delicacies.

Further reading: C. Bethel, 'Bahamian Music: From Quadrilles to Junkanoo', *Bahamas Handbook and Businessman's Annual, 1983*, Dupuch Publications, 1983, 81–95; 'Music in the Bahamas: Its Roots, Development and Personality', MA Thesis, University of California, Los Angeles, 1978.

GORDA CAY Gorda Cay is situated midway between Moores Island and the south-western tip of ABACO, on the edge of the deep-water Providence Channels leading to the Atlantic. A thousand acres in extent, it gets its name ('Gorda' means 'fat' in Spanish) because it is not the usual sliver shape, but round. Deserted except for a few seasonal farmers from nearby Sandy Point and occasional visiting yachtsmen and treasure hunters until the 1970s, it was then transformed, first by drug-runners and then by the Disney cruise-ship operators.

Being on a lee shore, Gorda Cay was avoided if possible by home-going Spanish galleons, though at least one was unlucky. In 1950, two white Abaconians announced the discovery of a 72-pound silver ingot and sundry gold coins off the Gorda Cay reef – though rumour has it that this was only a fraction of what was actually found, then and later. Though possessing two shallow harbours and excellent beaches on its leeward side, the potential of the cay itself aroused little interest from developers for a further two decades. In the early 1960s it was bought by a self-made millionaire from Trinidad settled in Freeport, ostensibly as a private getaway – though his construction of an excellent 2,400-foot (730-m) paved airstrip immediately dispelled the projected image of a barefoot refuge.

Whatever the original purpose intended, the airstrip was soon an active entrepot for the running of marijuana and cocaine. Alarmed by this unstoppable traffic and its unsavoury operators, the original owner sold out in the late 1970s, through Bahamian lawyers based in Nassau, to an American millionaire from Delray Beach, Florida. This was Frank Barber, who claimed plans to develop a resort, but ended his life in an American jail as a convicted drug-runner. At the height of the Barber regime in the early 1980s, Gorda Cay was guarded by ugly customers with guns and dogs, while large vessels and twin-engined planes daily transshipped narcotics into light aircraft and speedboats for the onward journey into the US. Apparently the traffic continued even after Barber was arrested and tried, when a native of Spanish Wells leased the Cay ostensibly to develop it as a citrus plantation, but in fact to reap a fortune by charging huge landing and trans-shipment fees.

Gorda Cay's development as a tourist centre occurred in the 1990s, but in an unexpected form. With its excellent natural facilities and ideal location, it became the most notable and successful of a handful of cruise-ship stop-over islands. The Disney Company spent millions making Gorda Cay accessible and attractive to their thousand-foot (300-m) liners with 2,500 passengers apiece. They dredged a deep-water dock and used the dredged sand to extend the already splendid beaches, planted shade trees and built paved pathways between bars, cabanas and recreational facilities served by miniature trains and young American employees dressed up as Disney characters. Ironically, this periodically frenzied hive of tourist activity was renamed Castaway Cay – and given an entirely spurious ethos in the public relations handouts. The visiting hordes were invited to imagine themselves castaways blessed with tropical comforts.

The transformation of a deserted and pristine island into an offshore adjunct of Disney World is largely a matter of taste. Other effects are incontrovertibly negative. Apart from the actual and potential ecological damage, The Bahamas and Bahamians gain only minimal economic benefits. Almost all of the money spent by the cruise-ship tourists is garnered by Disney, while most of the handful of Bahamians employed on Castaway Cay are relegated to 'sanitary duties'.

Further reading: R. Antoni, 'Blackbeard Doesn't Come Here Anymore', www.outsideonline.com/magazine/0199/9901blackbeard.html

GOULD, Steven Jay (1941–2002) Brilliant Harvard palaeontologist and popular scientific essayist, whose theory of 'punctuated equilibrium' revised Darwinian evolutionary theory, and whose own research involved 20 years' painstaking study of the snails of the Bahamian Family Islands.

Steven Jay Gould, like Darwin studying the varieties of finches on the different Galapagos Islands, accumulated the evidence that he hoped would make clearer the process of evolutionary change from a study – with the help of numerous graduate students and his own children – of the humble *cerion* land snails of NEW PROVIDENCE, ELEUTHERA, CAT ISLAND and INAGUA. Though not to the satisfaction of all specialists, this research reinforced his belief (and that of his chief collaborator, Niles Eldredge) that variation and speciation in nature were not strictly evolutionary and certainly not in a steady progressive sense. Some creatures scarcely changed over aeons, and most changes were successful adaptations to genetic modifications or even more obviously accidental – the result of climatic shifts or sudden cataclysms such as that which is thought to have wiped out the dinosaurs. This theory of a general natural equilibrium punctuated by sudden revolutionary changes (rather than steady, inexorable evolution) was dismissed by scientific opponents as simply a product of the politically radical Gould's inherent Marxism. In the heated scientific debates, Gould's theory was sometimes referred to as 'evolution by jerks' – to which the ever-genial Gould responded by calling the conservative counter-belief 'evolution by creeps'. Gould's theory was grasped at by creationists as disproving evolutionary theories altogether. However, Gould himself demolished creationism with as much force and disdain as he attacked the pseudo-scientists who misused Darwinism to support theories of racial inequalities.

Gould died shortly after publishing the most definitive of his many books, the 1,400 page *Structure of Evolutionary Theory*. He surely deserves to be as proudly honoured in The Bahamas as in his native United States, not just because he chose the islands as the proving ground for the most important revisions to evolutionary theory since Darwin's *Origin of Species*, or because he came to regard them as his second home, but for his lifelong advocacy of the superiority of scientific research over bigoted beliefs – especially those that would deny a fundamental equality to all mankind.

Further reading: S. J. Gould, *The Mismeasure of Man*, Norton, 1996; 'Evolution and Systematics of Cerion (*mollusca pulmonata*) on New Providence Island', *Bulletin of the Americn Museum of Natural History*, 182, 1986, 389–490; 'Punctuated Equilibrium Comes of Age', *Nature*, 366, 1993; T. Beardsley, 'Punctuated Equilibrium: Darwin Survives as the Debate Evolves', *Scientific American*, 262, 1990; L. P. Masur, 'Steven Jay Gould's Vision of History', *Massachusetts Review*, 30, 1989, 467–84.

GOVERNMENT HIGH SCHOOL

GOVERNMENT HIGH SCHOOL Founded in 1925, GHS was the first government high school, and for 40 years the only one. Open to all Bahamian boys and girls regardless of colour and class, with places awarded solely on the results of a competitive examination (provided parents could find the modest fees of ten guineas a year), it earned prestige and a reputation for classless and non-racialist elitism that was only eroded with the multiplication of high schools from the late 1960s. Today, the name GHS survives, as that of one of the 35 ostensibly co-equal government high schools throughout The Bahamas – a democratisation which only the alumni and alumnae of 'the old GHS' regret.

Physical forerunner of GHS was the Boys' Central School, set up in 1864 and located in the former Methodist Town Chapel in Nassau Court, opposite Fort Nassau (and after 1900, the British Colonial Hotel) in downtown Nassau. Though Boy's Central School was regarded as the best government school and trained a fair number of boys who distinguished themselves later, it did not teach beyond the junior level or take in many pupils from the Out Islands – besides not admitting girls at all. A product of the boom years of the 1920s, GHS was the result of a campaign by political progressives (mostly, but not exclusively, non-whites) to have a government school offering a level of education equal to that of the private QUEEN'S COLLEGE (founded 1889) to talented youngsters kept out either by QC's relatively high fees or its policy of not admitting non-whites.

Not that GHS was ever very radical. In the beginning, it took children only from the age of 13 to 16 (forms three to five), up to the level of the Cambridge Overseas School Certificate. Entry was only lowered to age 12 in 1940 with the addition of a second form, and no teaching was done at the sixth form levels until the late 1950s. The intention was to train only up to competence for the lower ranks of the local civil service, or, at most, to provide (for the more affluent and most ambitious), a grounding for further education and a professional training abroad.

The former West Methodist chapel in Nassau Court that successively housed the Boys' Central School, Government High School (1925–60) and government offices.

GOVERNMENT HIGH SCHOOL

Most important to the BAY STREET regime that had voted for the school in 1925 was that GHS pupils should be firmly taught – preferably by 'old school' whites – respectable conservative and 'British' values, especially that of knowing one's 'proper place' in society.

The first three head-teachers of GHS were British: Albert Woods (1925–42), Alfred Deans Peggs (1942–60), and Hugh Davies (1960–4). Of these, Peggs was the most outstanding in all respects. A stickler for discipline and an undoubted racist, his favourite saying (from Shakespeare's *Merchant of Venice*) was 'I am Sir Oracle. And when I ope my lips let no dogs bark.' Yet under Peggs the school developed a strong *esprit de corps*, quadrupled in numbers, expanded its curriculum, and produced a generation of groundbreaking professionals and politicians – those who were to lead The Bahamas out of the era of Bay Street dominance towards black majority rule and national independence.

Contemporaries at GHS in the 1940s, among others of both sexes scarcely less distinguished, included the young Paul ADDERLEY, Randol FAWKES, Arthur HANNA, Kendal ISAACS, Lynden PINDLING, Orville TURNQUEST and Cecil WALLACE-WHITFIELD.

One of Peggs's most remarkable achievements was to have GHS recognised as an autonomous body, independent of the Ministry of Education. Yet the very trend that the golden generation of GHS graduates led was bound to topple GHS from its lofty status. Under Peggs the school spilled over from the original building (with five classrooms, headmaster's office and crammed staff-room) into the neighbouring Good Samaritans' Hall and a range of new classrooms tacked on to the back. Under Peggs's successor, GHS moved into spacious new quarters at Oakes Field in 1960, with 300 students, a thriving sixth form, and an evening institute for adults. In 1964, the year

Government House at the head of George Street, Nassau, fronted by the marble statue of Christopher Columbus

GOVERNORS

The Bahamas attained internal self-government, GHS got its first Bahamian head-teacher, the much respected Cecil Valentine BETHEL.

However, the primacy of GHS as the elite secondary school for non-whites was already challenged by the Anglican ST JOHN'S COLLEGE and the Catholic ST AUGUSTINE'S COLLEGE (for boys) and ST FRANCIS XAVIER'S ACADEMY (for girls) – as well as by a liberalised Queen's College (now state-aided as well as coeducational). In 1965, the Ministry of Education suddenly upgraded all schools with any senior students to secondary status, and as soon as the PROGRESSIVE LIBERAL PARTY came to power in 1967, under Minister of Education Cecil Wallace-Whitfield initiated a vigorous campaign to set up genuine high schools, especially in the Family Islands. Inevitably this led to the relative decline of GHS. Almost the last blow was the decision in 1972 to transfer the Oakes Field campus to the newly established COLLEGE OF THE BAHAMAS, and to move GHS into newly built but inferior and less well-located quarters even further out of town.

GOVERNMENT HOUSE The palatial residence of the Governors and Governors General of The Bahamas, suitably overlooking the town from Nassau's ridge. The site is known as Mount Fitzwilliam, after the Governor who first placed his residence there in 1737. No trace remains of that original building, which was replaced by a large but somewhat plain two-storey house with wooden balconies between 1803 and 1806. From this vantage point Governors could look due north down George Street, past CHRIST CHURCH and the VENDUE HOUSE, to the harbour and the harbour bar, and across to the reassuring presences of FORTS Charlotte and Fincastle to west and east.

The grandest feature of the nineteenth-century Government House was the wide, steep stone staircase by which visitors approached, in the middle landing of which was placed the statue of a swashbuckling Christopher COLUMBUS – designed by the explorer's American biographer Washington Irving and presented to The Bahamas by Governor Sir James Carmichael SMYTH in 1832. Surrey drivers giving tourists the guided tour are reputed to claim that the great Discoverer not only landed on NEW PROVIDENCE but had been the first Governor of The Bahamas and lived in a house on that very spot.

Decidedly rickety, Government House was almost demolished by the 1929 hurricane but was completely remodelled by 1932. Though some of the old wooden interior was kept, the building was given an imposing Georgian facade, with shuttered widows, a pillared portico and elegant central cupola – the whole painted almost Bermudian-style in a fetching white and pink. Outward appearances, however, were not enough for Governor WINDSOR and his Duchess, who in 1940 insisted on an expensive renovation of the fusty interior before they would move in.

During the colonial era, Government House was the social focus for the British and Bahamian white elite. A visitors' book was kept in a sentry box at the gate, which prominent Bahamians signed whenever they left and returned to the colony, and which visitors (if they were of the right complexion) signed in the expectation of an invitation to one of the Governor's social functions. The only time that the ordinary people came close (except as servants or humble petitioners) was during the annual RED CROSS Fair in the extensive gardens on the reverse slope of the ridge – initiated, to their credit, by the Windsors during their war-time tenure. Though Government House is still at the centre of formal state occasions – ceremonially guarded round the clock by smart members of the ROYAL BAHAMIAN DEFENCE FORCE and with the Bahamian standard proudly flying from its flagstaff whenever the Governor-General is in residence – social protocol has naturally eased greatly since INDEPENDENCE, showing that 'Government Hill' is no longer the symbol of the rule of a governing elite, but an essential part of the people's patrimony.

Perhaps the ultimate sign of the times – combining democracy with endorsement of the country's most important industry – is that as part of the Ministry of Tourism's PEOPLE-TO-PEOPLE programme the Governor-General and his wife invite up to 120 fortunate visiting tourists to come and share afternoon tea with them at Government House on the first Friday of each month between January and August.

GOVERNORS Though no formal documentation exists for such titles, some authorities call the leader of the ELEUTHERIAN ADVENTURERS William Sayle and his son Nathanial the first Governors of The Bahamas (1648-61). It was the LORD PROPRIETORS who made the first formal appointments, between 1670 and 1716 – though some of those listed below were actually deputies, temporary, or even nominal appointees who never actually served. The line of 49 royal Governors ran from 1717 to INDEPENDENCE in 1973, when the local representative of the Crown as Head of State was re-styled Governor-General.

GRAND BAHAMA

Proprietary Governors
1670 Hugh Wentworth
1671 John Wentworth
1676 Charles Chillingworth
1677 Robert Clarke
1682 Robert Lilburne
1687 Thomas Bridges
1689 Cadwallader Jones
1693 NIcholas TROTT
1696 Nicholas Webb
1699 Read Elding
1700 Elias Haskett
1701 Ellis Lightfoot
1703 Edward Birch
1716 Roger Mostyn

Royal Governors
1717 Woodes ROGERS
1721 George Phenney
1728 Woodes Rogers
1733 Richard Fitzwilliam
1738 John Tinker
1759 Sir William SHIRLEY
1767 Sir Thomas Shirley
1774 Montfort Browne
1779 John Maxwell
1787 Lord DUNMORE
1797 William Dowdeswell
1801 John Halkett
1804 Charles Cameron
1820 Sir Lewis Grant
1829 Sir James Carmichael SMYTH
1835 William Colebrooke
1837 Sir Francis Cockburn
1844 George Matthew
1849 John Gregory
1854 Sir Alexander Bannerman
1857 Charles Bayley
1864 Sir Rawson Rawson
1869 Sir James Walker
1871 Sir George Strachan
1873 Sir John Pope-Hennessy
1874 Sir William Robinson
1880 Timothy Callaghan
1882 Sir Christopher Lees
1884 Sir Henry Blake
1887 Sir Ambrose Shea
1895 Sir William Haynes-Smith
1898 Sir George Carter
1904 Sir William Grey-Wilson

1912 Sir George Haddon-Smith
1914 Sir William Allardyce
1920 Sir Harry Cordeaux
1926 Sir Charles Orr
1932 Hon. Sir Bede CLIFFORD
1936 Hon. Sir Charles Dundas
1940 HRH Duke of WINDSOR
1945 Sir William Murphy
1950 Sir George Sandford
1951 Sir Robert Neville
1953 Lord RANFURLY
1957 Sir Raynor Arthur
1960 Sir Robert Stapledon
1964 Sir Ralph Grey
1968 Sir Francis Cumming-Bruce
1972 Sir John Paul

Governors-General (from 10 July 1973)
1972 Sir John Paul (retired 31 July 31, 1973)
1973 Sir Milo BUTLER (retired 22 Jan. 1979)
1979 Sir Gerald CASH (Acting, 2 Sept. 1976–23 Sept. 1979, retired 25 June 1988)
1988 Sir Henry TAYLOR (Acting, 26 June 1988–1 March 1991, retired 1 Jan.1992)
1992 Sir Clifford DARLING (retired 2 Jan. 1995)
1995 Sir Orville TURNQUEST (retired 31 Oct. 2002)
2002 Dame Ivy Dean-Dumont (retired 30 Nov. 2005)
2005 Hon. Arthur D. Hanna

GRAND BAHAMA A large, almost completely flat island (539 square miles, 1,396 squ. km) fronting the North West Providence Channel and backed by the western half of the Little Bahama Bank. Formerly one of the least developed islands, it was transformed by the creation of FREEPORT, 'Second City of the Bahamas' from the 1950s onwards.

When Amelia DEFRIES visited and wrote about Grand Bahama before World War One she rightly described it as one of the least known and most backward parts of a forgotten colony. Thought unsuitable for growing cotton, it was never settled by white planters, and in 1900 its 1,800 black inhabitants scratched a meagre subsistence from farming and fishing. The first change came during American PROHIBITION (1919–33) when the settlement of West End – just 50 miles (80 km) from Palm Beach, Florida – became a frontier-like town of riotous rum-runners. In the later 1930s the island slipped back into sleep.

The next minor spurt of development came just after World War Two: first, the transfer of operations by the Abaco Lumber Company to Pine Ridge, 5 miles (8 km) east of Hawksbill Creek; then the ambitious project by the Englishman Sir Billy BUTLIN to set up a holiday camp for airborne tourists at West End; and thirdly, the development by the Americans of a missile tracking station at Gold Rock Creek, halfway towards the eastern end of the island. Their impact though was short-lived. The lumber company soon ran out of trees suitable for plank wood and got into financial difficulties; Billy Butlin's enterprise proved ahead of its time and went bankrupt; and the Gold Rock base, once constructed, closed its gates to outsiders and contributed no more to the island's development.

It was at this stage that the dynamic American visionary Wallace Groves more or less took charge. Already living in the BERRY ISLANDS, he had sunk most of his capital into buying out the ailing Abaco Lumber Company in 1946. Once the largest pine trees were gone, he negotiated a lucrative contract to supply pit props to the British coal industry. Then, having finagled permission from the Bahamas government to lop even smaller trees, he made a deal to supply pulpwood to the American National Container Corporation. With its own small railway and famously decrepit steam engines, the Lumber Company at its peak employed 1,600 workers, mostly migrant labourers from the TURKS AND CAICOS ISLANDS, making Pine Ridge a company town with a larger population than the rest of Grand Bahama put together.

In the early 1950s the lumbering operation (almost literally) ran out of steam. But for Groves this was only a stage in a dazzling upward ascent, which within a decade led to the creation of Freeport-Lucaya. Consequently, within a half century Grand Bahama was almost totally transformed. From being the eighth most peopled island with only a single parliamentary representative, it has become by far the second most populous, with its 45,000 people represented by five MPs – down to 2002 all of them belonging to the FREE NATIONAL MOVEMENT. Almost the entire population of Grand Bahama, however, lives in Freeport-Lucaya and the western end of the island, at least a third of them in the straggling string of settlements accurately known as Eight Mile Rock. The eastern two-thirds of the island is almost uninhabited pinelands, shading off into channels and sandy cays that still seem a thousand miles away from the modern world.

Further reading: A. Defries, *In a Forgotten Colony*, Nassau Guardian, 1916); P. Barratt, *Grand Bahama*, 2nd. ed., Macmillan Caribbean, 1982.

GRANT'S TOWN The core settlement of Over-the-Hilll NASSAU, founded in the 1820s and almost having taken shape by 1850. Grant's Town originated as a place to house the growing number of LIBERATED AFRICANS who were employed in and around Nassau but not allowed to live in the downtown area, and it expanded to the point of overcrowding as SLAVERY came to an end, being a location favoured successively by those slaves freed early, by Apprentices after 1834, and by the rest of the slaves once emancipated in 1838.

Grant's Town was named after its planner, Governor Lewis Grant, a former major-general in the British Army. Under Grant's orders, Surveyor-General John James Burnside laid out a geometrical grid of roads and quarter-acre house plots in the area bounded by the southward extension of Nassau's Blue Hill Road and East Street (with an extended Market Street as its central axis), from what was named Lewis Street in the north to Wulff Road in the south. At first the plots were allocated to Liberated Africans gratis, but without freehold title. By 1835, though, there was such a demand for secure title that occupants were allowed to purchase their allotments for the sum of 10 shillings for a quarter acre house lot or £2 for an acre garden plot. These bargain prices helped spur a host of other would-be residents, who when allowed to purchase lands by auction raised the average price as high as £6 an acre within five years.

By 1840, Grant's Town was an active satellite of Nassau, though still without many of the features of a proper township. As part of the colonial government's missionary impulse an ANGLICAN chapel was established as early as 1835, in which an infant school was started by two philanthropic sisters called Walker. In 1838 Wesley Chapel was also built by METHODIST missionaries as a

Entrance to International Bazaar, Freeport

subordinate offshoot of the West Chapel in Nassau Court downtown, on a plot of land granted by Governor Sir Francis Cockburn. This chapel was granted autonomous status in 1847. Not to be outdone, the Anglican Church made Grant's Town a separate parish, and its chapel was consecrated as St Agnes parish church by the Bishop of Jamaica in April 1848. Two years later, following local pleas over the previous decade, an Act of Assembly set up a separate public market for Grant's Town, exactly modelled on that in downtown Nassau. In 1852, during the tenure of Governor John Gregory, the arch named after him was built across Market Street on the crest of the ridge, forming a symbolic bridge and gateway between 'white' downtown Nassau and what had become undoubtedly the heart of the black Nassauvian community.

Thereafter, Grant's Town progressed steadily. By 1900, when its population was probably as great as the rest of Nassau, it possessed numerous small grocery stores and artisan workshops (as well as innumerable rum shops), a full range of churches, several fraternal lodges, a couple of night clubs, a large government school and several small private schools, a public recreation ground, its own post office, and even a branch of the main public library (situated on the second floor of the post office building). Significantly, it was also provided with a well-manned police station. As yet, however, Grant's Town's roads were not properly paved, let alone lighted; it was to be years before water-mains and standpipes were installed along the three north–south streets; longer still before water or electricity was supplied to individual houses. Least satisfactory of all was the state of public sanitation. Garbage disposal was a problem but even worse was the fact that well into the twentieth century earth privies were the rule at the same time that much of the water used for all purposes, including cooking and drinking, was drawn from shallow wells. As many visitors noted, one of the salient characteristics of Over-the-Hill Nassau was the incongruously mixed aromas of bodily wastes and tropical flowers. The situation was hugely improved from the 1950s, with public garbage disposal and regulations for the construction of efficient septic tanks, though a communal sewage system had still not been installed by the end of the twentieth century.

That Southern Police Station was the most obvious symbol of government authority was no accident; for overcrowded and independent-minded Grant's Town was long seen as a potential social fire-keg by the authorities who overlooked it from Government Hill. It appears that on at least three occasions their nervousness was justified. In July 1863 there was a riot between inhabitants of Grant's Town and soldiers of the West Indies Regiment in the garrison, in which three soldiers and a civilian were injured. In April 1893 a serious confrontation occurred between Grant's Towners and the police, during which the police station was burned down, and the Governor sent for a gunboat. These disturbances however were eclipsed when Grant's Town became the storm centre of the 'BURMA ROAD' riots of May 1942. In retrospect this outburst is seen as the last of its kind, the forerunner of the political, social and economic changes of the 1950s and 1960s in which the people of Grant's Town – as orderly strikers and voters – were to play an important participatory role.

GRAY, Captain Rolly Most celebrated inhabitant of Staniel Cay, EXUMA, and by general repute the greatest-ever skipper of Bahamian racing sloops.

Born in 1922, Rolly Gray received a rudimentary education in the tiny local school. But like all the menfolk in his native settlement of black fishermen and mariners, he got his most important schooling in the ways of the sea. From the age of eight he raced local dinghies as boys in Nassau might play football or cricket; his first boat was called *Calamari* after the native wood from which it was made, and had sisal string for rigging and sewn flour sacks for sails.

By the time of the first OUT ISLAND REGATTA at George Town, Exuma, in 1954, Rolly Gray was already recognised as a master sailor, with an uncanny command of wind changes and tidal flows. Successively skippering his three locally built sloops named *Marie*, *Lady Muriel* and (most famous of all) the custom-built *Tida Wave*, he was regatta champion for 21 years. In 1959 when Prince Philip attended the regatta, Rolly Gray took him for a private sail in the prize-winning *Lady Muriel* at the Prince's own request. The tiller of that sloop is still to be seen in the

Main street, Grant's Town, with silk cotton tree, from an early twentieth-century postcard

Captain Rolly Gray and his crew prepare to race *Tida Wave* at Exuma's Out Island Regatta

Royal Entertainer's Restaurant on Staniel Cay, where visiting yachtsmen hang out with local sailors

A family man who had to work for a living (married at 28 and with eight children), Rolly Gray rarely sailed outside The Bahamas during his prime years. Well-heeled white Bahamian yachtsmen travelled the world to race, winning many medals, including Olympic Golds. Yet all of them (and, more remarkably, even his black rivals from Long Island, Eleuthera and Nassau) acknowledged Captain Rolly Gray as the supreme master, and not just in Bahamian waters. Legend tells of an occasion when he was invited to participate abroad in a three-race series sailing identical boats allotted randomly, against crews of world class sailors. Despite never having skippered that type of boat before and being in unfamiliar waters, Captain Rolly Gray led the way all three times across the finishing line.

GRAYCLIFF This handsome former mansion on NASSAU's West Hill Street, opposite the western gate of GOVERNMENT HOUSE, has as ancient and interesting a history as any in The Bahamas. Probably dating from the 1720s, it was built on the site of Nassau's original church, destroyed in a Spanish attack in 1703. Alleged fragments of the church's ruins can still be seen next to Graycliff's kitchen.

Unsubstantiated legend maintains that Graycliff was built and named by a reformed PIRATE called Graysmith, who settled in Nassau after his ship the *Grey Wolf* was sunk in a fight with a vessel of the Royal Navy in 1726. The first authentic record of the house dates from 1844, when (under the name Victoria House) it was advertised in the *Nassau Guardian* as a guesthouse for 'gentlefolk and invalids', run by a Mrs Nathaniel French. In the mid-nineteenth century it was the private residence of the prominent merchant-politician R. H. Sawyer, before becoming an elegant guesthouse once more in the 1920s and 1930s, owned and run by a famous hostess called Miss Polly Leach.

The most illustrious but not the happiest of Polly Leach's guests was Winston Churchill, whose three-week stay in January 1932 occurred at the very lowest point of his tumultuous career. Churchill, aged 52, was in Nassau convalescing from quite serious injuries after having been knocked down by a car while on a speaking tour in New York. This was at a time when he was in the political wilderness and still trying to recoup his almost total losses from the great Wall Street crash of 1929. In the bleakest of his 'black dog' moods Churchill told his wife that 'he did not think he would ever recover completely from the three events'. Luckily history proved him wrong, though his feelings for Nassau and The Bahamas remained clouded, and he never returned.

Graycliff reverted to private ownership and its original name when purchased by the Canadian multimillionaire Killams in 1937, who sold it on to the Earl and Countess of Dudley as a winter home in the 1960s. For more than three decades under the Killams and Dudleys, the house became a getaway rendezvous for such royals and tycoons as the WINDSORS, Mountbattens and Beaverbrooks. Graycliff's aristocratic ambience was carefully maintained when it was purchased by the Cuban-Italian Enrico Garzaroli in 1974 and turned into Nassau's most exclusive (and expensive) hotel and restaurant.

Graycliff hotel-restaurant on the probable site of the first Bahamian church, West Hill Street, Nassau

GREAT GUANA CAY (Abaco)

Boasting of being the only member in the West Indies of the prestigious international *Relais et Chateaux* chain of hotels and the only restaurant with a five star rating in The Bahamas, Graycliff has been featured in practically every glamour magazine. Its guest book is almost a *Who's Who* of the rich and at least temporarily famous; from the Shah of Iran and Princess Grace of Monaco, to Michael Caine, Perry Como, Margaret Trudeau, Ringo Starr and the Bee Gees. Building on his success, Signor Garzaroli purchased the two adjacent properties to the west in the 1990s, turning West Hill House into his private residence, and Postern Gate (next to the site of the old garrison hospital), somewhat bizarrely, into a factory for making Cuban-style cigars and a second exclusive and 'cigar-friendly' restaurant.

GREAT GUANA CAY (Abaco)

Physically and in some other ways remarkably similar to the cay of the same name in the EXUMAS, the Abaconian Great Guana Cay is significantly different in at least one respect. The least populous of the five 'LOYALIST Cays', along with CHEROKEE SOUND, its 150 native inhabitants are almost exclusively white. Though once boatbuilders and seafarers and still engaged in lobstering, they now (like the Exumians) cater increasingly to American yachtsmen and tourists, and are even said to be negotiating with the Ritz-Carlton chain for the building of a 150-room luxury hotel. The northern end of the island was former Disney Cruise Line's 'Castaway Bay' in the 1950s before it moved to Gorda Cay. In the twenty-first century the entire island is under development by major corporations providing for expatriate communities.

GREEK BAHAMIANS

The Bahamian Greek community owes its origins to the SPONGE industry of the later nineteenth century, but it has sustained itself and retained much of its distinctive identity despite the sudden collapse of sponging just before World War Two.

The first Greeks were a group of poor sponge fishermen (mainly from the Aegean island of Kalymnos) introduced in 1887 by Greek sponge merchants eager to expand their operations from the Mediterranean to The Bahamas and the Caribbean. These migrant workers were bitterly resented by native sponge fishermen, could not find employment, and were withdrawn within a few months. This setback did not deter the Greek merchants (mainly based in London and Paris), who sponsored the migration of Greek islanders and their families to engage in sponge processing and packing and act as buyers and agents. Through hard work and their connections with the international market, and despite considerable animosity from Bahamian fishermen and competitors (who saw them as driving down raw sponge and wholesale prices) the Greeks came almost to control the buying, packing and exporting of Bahamian sponges by the 1920s. The migrants prospered and grew in numbers, both by having large families and by the immigration of more distant family members. Several families – notably the Christofilis, Maillis and Esfakis families – became sponge merchants on their own account, but others diversified into the bakery, vegetable and fruit retailing and restaurant businesses. These sustained them through the Great Depression and allowed the Greek community to survive the devastating effects of the sponge blight of 1938. Though in the 1920s there were no more than a dozen Greek families in The Bahamas (all in Nassau), by the end of the century there were said to be as many as seventy, totalling perhaps 750 persons altogether.

In 1932 the Greek community built a handsome Greek Orthodox church on West Street, Nassau, and since that time have paid to have their own Orthodox priest from the homeland, to conduct services in Greek, and to teach the language to Bahamian Greek children in Sunday school. Even more clannishly, Bahamian Greek children have been expected to find Greek spouses; if not within the local community or their own extended families, either from Greece or from the Greek communities in the United States and Canada.

Further reading: H. Johnson, *From Slavery to Servitude 1783–1933*, University of Florida Press, 1996.

Greek Orthodox church

GREEN TURTLE CAY

GREEN TURTLE CAY Once the second most populous and prosperous island in The Bahamas, and still the largest and most populated of the five 'Loyalist Cays' of ABACO, Green Turtle Cay is both topographically and socially one of the most interesting of all Bahamian islands.

Located 8 miles (13 km) north of Treasure Cay and 2 miles (3 km) off the mainland dock near Abaco's northern airport, Green Turtle Cay is 3 miles (4.8 km) long and up to 1 ½ miles (2.4 km) wide. It is relatively hilly (up to 83 feet, 25 m in elevation), has four distinct harbours on its leeward side and many fine beaches all around. The picturesque main settlement, called New Plymouth, is located on a hooked peninsula at the southern end. It has an Anglican church on the point, many well-preserved Cape Cod style clapboard buildings, the famous Albert Lowe Museum, and the fascinating Loyalist Memorial Sculpture Garden. This main part of New Plymouth, with its criss-cross lanes grandly named King, Crown, Victoria, Parliament and Bay Streets, is the preserve (almost sanctum) of the white descendants of the LOYALISTS.

Yet, unlike the other Abaco 'Loyalist' cays (though rather like HARBOUR ISLAND, off ELEUTHERA), Green Turtle Cay has equal numbers of Bahamian whites and blacks, and almost as many wealthy expatriates. Though living in concord, they reside in different areas, do not mix much socially and (at least as far as the Bahamian whites and blacks are concerned) miscegenate not at all. The blacks live in noticeably less prosperous housing at the lower end of New Plymouth's harbour, which backs on to Black Sound. The white expatriates live mainly around (perhaps also coincidentally named) White Sound in the middle of the Cay, the wealthiest of whom are locally known as 'the White Sound Society'.

This compartmentalisation is a product of Green Turtle Cay's history. If one excludes the Lucayans (of whom traces have been found) the Cay was first settled by a shipload of Loyalists from New York in 1783. They brought with them some blacks, freedmen as well as slaves. These they employed to farm the northern half of the Cay and the nearby mainland, to work in the boatyards, as sailboat crewmen, or as domestics, allowing them to live in their own segregated areas on the Cay. At its peak around 1885, Green Turtle Cay was a bustling place with 1,500 people, its prosperity based on boatbuilding and being a convenient stopping point for vessels sailing to and from the United States, exporting wreck goods, sponges, pineapples, and other produce. With the advent of larger and faster steamships a gradual decline set in, with many people migrating, to reach a low point at the time of the sponge blight of the late 1930s. From the end of World War Two onwards the economy recovered with the coming of

New Plymouth, Green Turtle Cay

GUAVA DUFF

tourists and expatriate settlers, though Green Turtle Cay is now home to no more than 500 permanent residents, and is no longer the administrative centre for northern Abaco.

The most distinguished native inhabitant of Green Turtle Cay is the artist ALTON LOWE, direct descendant of one of the Loyalist settlers of 1783, son of the sea-captain, inventor, musician and artist Albert Lowe after whom the Museum is named, and related to the hundred or so other white Lowes still living on the Cay. Even more lively than the annual regatta week in July are the year-end celebrations on the Cay. In mid-December a New Plymouth Historical Weekend commemorates the Loyalist legacy, and between Christmas and New Year there is a Concert under the Stars featuring traditional local music and entertainments. The most riotous and distinctive cultural displays, however, are the local version of JUNKANOO, held on the mornings of Boxing Day and New Year's Day. In this the distinctive main figure is 'Old Bunce', half object of fun, half bogey-man, who follows the parade wrapped up in a sheet and pushed in a wheelbarrow. No one seems to know the origin of Bunce (pronounced 'Boonce'), but he seems to be a combination of the Green Man of ancient English folklore and the masked spirit-men common in West Africa. His local significance though is that he is probably a syncretic figure, common to all sections of society, taking part in the chief – if not the only – festival which they fully share.

The most atmospheric place to stay on Green Turtle Cay is the nine-room New Plymouth Inn in the centre of town, which would not seem out of place in Plymouth on Cape Cod; but there are also nine upscale small hotels and resorts on the main part of the Cay.

GUAVA DUFF The fruit of the guava is delicious eaten raw or made into jelly or jam. But its most distinctive use in The Bahamas is as an ingredient for a favourite dessert: guava duff, with its essential accompanying hard sauce.

> Ingredients:
> a dozen medium-size guavas (one pound)
> 4 cups flour
> ¾ cup shortening
> ½ cup milk
> 3 teaspoons baking powder
> 1 egg, beaten
> 2 tablespoons sugar
> 1 teaspoon each salt, ground cinnamon, allspice

Method: Wash, peel and halve the guavas. Remove the seeds and strain them through a sieve. Set the juice aside. Cook the diced fruit gently with the sugar and spices until soft. Sift together the flour, baking powder and salt and cut in the shortening until the mixture looks like bread crumbs. Add milk and egg and mix to a soft dough. Knead the dough, roll it into a large rectangle and spread the fruit on top. Roll up the dough from the short end and wrap it in cloth or foil. Cook in a double boiler at least one hour. Serve hot with chilled hard sauce.

To make the hard sauce, cream a cup of butter with ¾ cup of sugar. Add two eggs one after the other, beating vigorously until blended. Beat in brandy or rum until the sauce is smooth. Chill and serve in sauceboat.

GULF STREAM The Gulf Stream and its extension the North Atlantic Drift is a huge 'ocean river' of warm water, forming one of the most notable geographical boundaries and climate-influencing forces in the world. Where it constitutes the Florida Strait it provided the easiest route for sailing ships from the Caribbean to North America and back to Europe, and it helped determine the pattern of shipping routes throughout the Americas and even shape the course of colonial history. For The Bahamas, it influenced the pattern of aboriginal settlement, gave the islands great strategic importance as well as a degree of protection during colonial times, and has been largely instrumental in providing the climate which has proved such a priceless asset during the age of tourism. Its mid-line in the Florida Strait also constitutes the political boundary between The Bahamas and its great northern neighbour.

The Gulf Stream is the gathering of sun-warmed tropical waters flowing westward across the Caribbean where they turn northwards to exit into the Atlantic through the comparatively narrow strait between Florida and The Bahamas. Constricted into a channel 50 miles (72 km) wide and 245 feet (750 metres) deep, this flow reaches a speed of 7 kph and amounts to a shift of 30 million cubic metres of water a second – hundreds of times greater than that of the mighty Mississippi. Steadily widening, slowing and cooling, and now renamed the North Atlantic Drift, it is yet potent enough to aid eastward navigation, to keep the climate of Britain temperate (though in the latitude of Labrador), and Norwegian and Russian ports 500 miles (800 km) north of the Arctic Circle permanently ice-free. The temperature anomaly it creates amounts to a difference of +40 degrees F (21 degrees C) for these northern latitudes.

The northward rush of the Gulf Stream made it virtually impassable for aboriginal canoes and therefore ensured that the pre-Columbian peopling of the Bahamas came from the south-east – that is, from South and Central America by way of the Lesser and Greater Antilles – and consequently later than might have resulted from a migration by way of Florida. COLUMBUS did not discover the Gulf Stream, or even realise that Cuba was an island. But as soon as the Florida Strait was discovered the Spaniards adopted it as the natural route out of the Caribbean back to Europe, making Havana of strategic focal importance for the trade and defence of their American empire.

Trade routes and more profitable colonies elsewhere made The Bahamas itself of marginal economic importance. But the rich flow of Spanish galleons and the merchant ships of other rival nations through the Strait, along with the numerous vessels that went ashore on its bordering reefs, made the islands an ideal base for PIRATES, PRIVATEERS and scavengers of wrecks. The Bahamian WRECKING trade, indeed, lasted well into the steamship age and TREASURE HUNTING is more flourishing than ever – the reefs of the Florida Strait and the branching Providence Channels being among the most fruitful combing grounds.

Shielded from cold northern waters by the Gulf Stream, which warmed up cold northerly streams of air, The Bahamas was early christened (at least by winter visitors) 'the Isles of Perpetual June'. TOURISM, however, depended on the coming of the steamship, and mass tourism waited on the aeroplane. Even after the steamship's advent, the Gulf Stream helped to keep the number of visitors few until the railroad reached southern Florida at the very end of the nineteenth century, and Nassau could be reached from Miami within a day. Up to that time, the passage to Nassau from Savannah or Jacksonville against the flow and notorious chops of the Florida Strait was a two-day ordeal, while the preferred route to and from New York or Philadelphia took seven or eight days in all.

Even today, the national boundary between the United States and the Commonwealth of The Bahamas represents a symbolic divide; not just between the colossus of the modern world and its far smaller nearest offshore neighbour, but between two very different histories and cultures. Some of the lingering magic of this transition can still be sensed through observing the Bahamian paintings of the greatest American artist Winslow HOMER – whose 1899 masterwork was significantly entitled 'In the Gulf Stream'; and in the words of Ernest Hemingway's *Islands in the Stream*.

GUY FAWKES' DAY Although no longer a public holiday, 5 November is still joyfully celebrated by Bahamian children with bonfires, fireworks, a parade, and the burning of a 'Guy', though few have a clear notion (or care) about its original significance.

Guy Fawkes' day commemorates the last-minute discovery of a Catholic plot to blow up the English Parliament along with King James I on 5 November 1605. It was actually led by Robert Catesby. Guy (or Guido) Fawkes was the man found virtually holding the lighted fuse, who was tortured to reveal the other conspirators. The grateful King and Parliament decreed the anniversary of their salvation a day of public thanksgiving in perpetuity – an ordinance that spread to each English colony on its foundation. Laws against Catholics were tightened after 1605, and lasted until 1829. Guy Fawkes' Day was a day of official thanksgiving for at least another century.

Anthropologists tend to attribute the popularity and persistence of the Guy Fawkes celebration in The Bahamas to its similarity to African fire and mask rituals – the Guy being akin to the central 'Pitchy-Patchy' figure in the traditional JUNKANOO. Others more prosaically attribute it to the fact that Bahamians (especially children) love any excuse for a celebration – pointing out that 5 November comes in one of the longest intervals in the year between official public holidays, the ten weeks between Columbus or Discovery (now National Heroes') Day and Christmas.

'The Gulf Stream', 1899 oil painting by Winslow Homer

HAITI The western half of the island of the Greater Antilles which the Spanish christened Santo Domingo. Being closer to the southern Bahamas than those islands are to Nassau, and situated to windward, Haiti has always had a greater influence on The Bahamas than vice versa – greater, indeed, than even more neighbouring Cuba.

The Lucayans who inhabited The Bahamas when the Spanish arrived had originally migrated from Santo Domingo, and it was to satisfy the demand for slaves for their mines and plantations in Santo Domingo that the Spanish had completely depopulated The Bahamas by 1520. Two hundred years later, once the English had colonised The Bahamas and the French acquired the western half of Santo Domingo (which they called Saint Domingue), imperial rivalry occurred over the control of the Windward Passage into the Caribbean between Saint Domingue and Cuba, and the prevention of smuggling contrary to the principles of mercantilism.

Much more serious, however, were the tensions that occurred following the Haitian Revolution and the subsequent wars with revolutionary and Napoleonic France (1789–1815). Many of the slave-owners and free mulattoes who fled with their slaves from what was in 1804 renamed Haiti passed through The Bahamas, and a few of them stayed, despite local fears of 'revolutionary infection'. This accounts for many of the 'French' SURNAMES still common in The Bahamas, including Beneby, Bodie, Bonaby, Deleveaux, Demeritte, Deveaux, Dillet, Duvalier, Laroda, Moncur, Moree, Poitier and Symonette.

Bahamians were always hesitant to accept refugees from the frequent political turmoils in Haiti, or economic migrants who might compete with native Bahamians (as well as bringing a culture regarded as alien). But the closest and least conflicted relationships between Haiti and The Bahamas did occur during the century and a half after Haitian Independence, when the two countries were almost equally poor.

Haitian and Bahamian sailors from the northern Haitian ports and the southern islands of The Bahamas ranged from Nassau in the north to Port au Prince in the south. The Bahamians brought salt, dried conch, fish and some American and British manufactured goods to exchange for vegetables, fruits, livestock and the technically illicit raw Haitian rum called *taffia*. They also engaged in more intimate relationships, so that there were probably as many children with Bahamian fathers in the Haitian ports as there were Haitian-fathered children in the southern Bahamian islands.

Living far closer to Haiti than to Nassau, merchants based in Matthew Town, Inagua and Long Cay established close trading ties with Port-de-Paix, Cap Haitien and Port-au-Prince, and down to the 1940s some sent their daughters to be educated in Haitian Catholic convent schools. In those days, when there was comparatively little disparity in wealth or development between independent Haiti and colonial Bahamas, hardly more Haitians were motivated to migrate to The Bahamas than there were Bahamians who chose to settle in Haiti. However, the few non-white Bahamians fortunate enough to visit Haiti as tourists returned with an enthusiasm for the vitality and authenticity of Haitian popular culture, and enviously admired both the Parisian elegance and the political clout of the Haitian brown middle and upper classes.

This situation changed in scale and seriousness from the mid-twentieth century once the economies of Haiti and The Bahamas diverged and a rising tide of migrants flowed from impoverished and overpopulated northern Haiti to the burgeoning, sparsely populated and labour-hungry Bahamas. To those migrating for economic reasons were added the refugees from the political turmoils, oppression and near anarchy that accompanied and followed the corrupt regimes of Francois Duvalier and his son Jean-Claude (1957–87). By the time of Bahamian INDEPENDENCE there were said to be 40,000 Haitians living in The Bahamas, the majority of them illegal immigrants. Although no more than a hundredth of the total number of Haitians (and perhaps a tenth of all Haitian emigrés) this influx represented at least a sixth of those inhabiting The Bahamas. Accordingly, the connection between The Bahamas and its black neighbour to the south-west had once more become 'the Haitian Problem'. (See HAITIANS).

Further reading: David Nicholls, *From Dessalines to Duvalier: Race, Colour and National Independence*, Rutgers University Press, 1995 (1979); M. Craton, 'The Bahamian Self and the Haitian Other: The Migration of Haitians To and Through the Bahamas, 1950–2000', *Immigrants and Minorities*, 13 (3), 1995, 265–88.

HAITIANS The cultural divide between the francophone blacks of Haiti and the more ethnically mixed anglophone Bahamians only became a problem after the mid-twentieth century, once the contrast between Bahamian prosperity and labour shortages and Haitian overpopulation, poverty and political turmoil led to a flood of illegal migration. By the end of the century, with first, second and even third generation Haitian residents constituting a sixth of all persons living in The Bahamas, the problems of economic, social and cultural interrelationships, and the degree to which integration was feasible, had become critical.

A complicating dilemma was that the modern Haitian migration was initiated and sustained largely through the need of Bahamian employers to find labourers for tasks which Bahamians were no longer willing to undertake. Rural Haitians, used to back-breaking labour just to eke a living, made excellent farm labourers, woodcutters, gardeners and construction workers – at least until they found alternative opportunities as artisans and entrepreneurs. Some were brought in as gang labourers on work permits. But the great majority were illegal immigrants, individually and casually employed for as long as they were wanted, could find no better work, and remained undetected. Masters of word-of-mouth networking (called *telediol* in Haitian creole), they gravitated by sloop, MAIL BOAT and on foot to where work was available, lived for the most part in shanties on wasteland, and once reasonably well settled, sent for their families.

The Haitian shanty towns in The Bahamas – such as the notorious Pigeon Peas and The Mud on the outskirts of Marsh Harbour, Abaco; Blackwood and Gene's Bay on northern Eleuthera; on the fringes of Eight Mile Rock in Grand Bahama; or off Carmichael and Fire Trail Roads in central New Providence – were enclaves of Haitian culture, where *kweyole* was the language of choice, VODUN was practised, and even cockfighting (accompanied by avid gambling) was found. A fair number of Haitians in The Bahamas were clearly transients, making what living they could until an opportunity opened up to migrate onwards to Florida, New York or Montreal. But many others from the beginning made determined efforts to assimilate. Adults learned English and children were strongly encouraged to excel at school. There was some intermarriage and children of mixed marriages (or liaisons) were resolutely brought up as Bahamians. Names were often anglicised. Even if the ambitions of first-generation migrants to move up the socio-economic scale were thwarted, their children and grandchildren were encouraged to seek more respectable and remunerative employment. Most remarkably perhaps (though seldom noted) is the fact that many Haitian *évolués* forsook their traditional religion – a syncretic mix of *vodun* and Roman Catholicism – in favour of fervent Protestantism, particularly of the Pentecostal type.

The Bahamian Haitians have shown great tenacity and ingenuity in staying in their chosen place, and have been able to take advantage of wavering government policies about their rounding up and deportation – not to mention the connivance of Bahamian employers or the rumoured susceptibility of police and immigration officials to well-placed bribes. But the lot even of those determined to become Bahamians has not been easy. Since the 1960s there have been four distinct phases of repatriation efforts, under three successive governments. As early as 1963, the BAY STREET government carried out what was rather crudely termed 'Operation Clean Out', in which 2,800 Haitians were rounded up and shipped off. This was followed by an even more thorough operation in 1967, which ten years later was still referred to by its survivors as 'the Big Trouble'.

In its early years, the PROGRESSIVE LIBERAL PARTY tried with only limited success to repatriate illegal immigrants through cooperation with the regime of 'Baby Doc' Duvalier. By the later 1980s – in the face of the increased flow resulting from the deterioration of Haitian conditions from dismal to disastrous – PLP Minister Loftus Roker pursued a more draconian policy, with much public support, until the cost was found to be insupportable. An even worse situation was inherited by the FREE NATIONAL MOVEMENT government in 1992, with political refugees added to those driven by poverty. FNM Minister Arlington Butler carried out the most rigorous round-up and deportation programme yet, costing $75 million in 1994 (involving the setting-up of a detention centre on Carmichael Road termed a 'concentration camp' by the Opposition). The government, however, received aid from the United States – currently even more concerned than The Bahamas to

Haitian boats off Arawak Cay, Nassau

restrict the Haitian flow. Helped by a United Nations Refugee Committee report that declared that the Haitian migrants were economic rather than political refugees, these efforts were continued resolutely – resulting in the forcible repatriation of no less than 6,400 Haitians from The Bahamas in 2001.

Except for the minority that deplored the conditions under which Haitians were forced to live and favoured helping those genuinely willing to assimilate, Bahamians remained divided between those who wished to exploit the Haitians and those who would have them all deported. One commentator spoke for many Bahamians in distinguishing between those Haitians who had earned the right to citizenship, those on work permits who performed useful work and expected to be repatriated when their terms expired, and the majority of 'illegal, sneaky invaders'. These were accused of bringing in diseases and crime and overloading social services for which they did not pay. Worst of all, they were characterised as outsiders and inferiors, intent on swamping, diluting or distorting the authentic Bahamian culture – though quite what that was seen to be was not defined.

From an outsider's point of view, the Haitian in The Bahamas seems to be the Bahamian's Essential Other – the person who defines and justifies his or her own self-image. Too readily, the Bahamian characterizes the Haitian Other as naturally inferior, primitive, backward, superstitious, normally submissive but capable of outbursts of mindless violence. Not accustomed to democratic processes, Haitians are held to be ripe for subjection, even worthy of verbal and physical abuse. Such self-serving myths are forcefully demonstrated in the four entries illustrating 'Hitian' in John Holm and Allison Shilling's *Dictionary of Bahamian English* (1982): 'He gotta be verkin Hitian vitch' (he must be using voodoo spells to achieve what he wants); 'She got two Hitian' (she is of such standing that she has two Haitian labourers to work for her); 'Git your Hitian to do it' (that is, the unpleasant work you disdain to do yourself); 'Carry your Hitian hip! Stop bugging me' ('Haul you inferior ass! Don't bother me').

That such representations are false caricatures with dangerous socio-political implications should be obvious. They ignore the will of many if not most of Haitians in The Bahamas to do as much as they can to assimilate, the common features that already exist between Bahamian and Haitian culture and, most of all, the very real contributions which the Haitian immigrants can and will make to the evolving Bahamian identity. Notable among the special gifts and shared attributes which the Haitians bring are the African spiritual heritage, the wide range and richness of craft skills and creole folklore, the ethic of hard work and endurance, and probably most valuable of all, the close affinity of family and kin, and the affective bond to the place where one is born and raised – be it the Haitian heartland or the original Family Island home.

Further reading: M. Craton, 'The Bahamian Self and the Haitian Other: The Migration of Haitians To and Through the Bahamas, 1950-2000', *Immigrants and Minorities*, 14 (3), 1995, 265–88.

HANNA, Hon. Arthur Dion

Stalwart democrat, Bahamian nationalist, and one of the pillars of the PROGRESSIVE LIBERAL PARTY. A Member of Parliament for 32 years, he was one of Prime Minister PINDLING's most important Ministers and closest ally between 1967 and the early 1980s.

Arthur Dion Hanna was born at Pompey Bay, Acklins, in March 1928. His father was a lighthouse keeper and the family spent most of Arthur's earliest years at various isolated postings in the Family Islands. Despite rarely attending a formal primary school, he won a place at the GOVERNMENT HIGH SCHOOL, where he became

A. D. Hanna, 1960s

a close friend of Lynden Pindling and other members of a golden generation of future Bahamian leaders. From GHS he went to Bristol University in England to study law, returning to The Bahamas after being called to the Bar in 1955.

Of all the non-white Bahamians who studied in England, including Lynden Pindling, Arthur Hanna was probably the one most attracted to socialist ideology, egalitarianism and anti-imperialist rhetoric – a stance in which he was strongly supported by his white English wife, the former Beryl Church. Joining the fledgling PLP immediately after his return, Hanna quickly gained a popular following with his radical speeches. He entered Parliament in 1960 when he won the by-election for the double-seat Eastern District in partnership with H. M. TAYLOR, being one of the few PLP successes in the general election of 1962. Now regarded as one of the stars of the increasingly radicalised party, he virtually erased the disaffected Taylor in 1967, and went on to victory in the five subsequent general elections (1968–87), usually by stunning margins.

Premier (later Prime Minister) Pindling rewarded Hanna with the Ministry of Education in 1967, moving him upwards to Trade and Industry in 1968, Home Affairs in 1969, and finally to Finance (with responsibility for the Public Service) in 1973, at the time of INDEPENDENCE. During his brief tenure at Education, Hanna instituted a scholarship scheme which sent many Bahamians abroad to universities. In his next two posts, now that the PLP was firmly entrenched, he spearheaded an increasingly rigorous policy of BAHAMIANISATION. He was the architect of the Nationality Act, which abolished the status of 'Belonger' which had been designed to reinforce the white minority.

In his resolute Bahamianisation policy, Arthur Hanna stirred up many a hornets' nest – in the political Opposition almost as much as among self-interested foreigners. Yet as Minister of Finance, his achievements were much less controversial and give him a claim to have been one of the most constructive and far-sighted of Bahamian politicians. Among other things, he was responsible for legislation that set up the Central Bank and the Bahamas Development Bank, for the Lotteries and Gaming Act, the Financial Audit Administration Act, and the External Insurance Act.

In the first decade of Bahamian Independence, Arthur Hanna was so powerful and popular, and so closely associated with the Prime Minister, that Pindling and he were almost regarded as a duumvirate. Pindling was often content to play the role of figurehead and mediator, while Hanna made the hard-line speeches. This was fine while the two men retained their friendship and mutual respect dating back to their schooldays. But it went quite suddenly sour once Hanna lost confidence in Pindling's leadership during the DRUG crisis of the early 1980s, and for his part Pindling began to suspect a plot by Hanna and his supporters to displace him as Prime Minister and party head.

In October 1984, when Pindling sacked two of his internal critics (Hubert INGRAHAM and Perry CHRISTIE) along with three other Ministers implicated by the Drugs Commission, Hanna announced his resignation both from the Cabinet and from the post of Deputy Prime Minister. Pindling later claimed that this was due to pique following his own decision to take over Hanna's much-cherished Finance Ministry. Hanna, with calculated vagueness, simply said that it was on 'a matter of principle', though this was widely interpreted as the climax of a deep dissatisfaction with the shadier aspects of Pindling's rule. Whatever the true situation, the old friendship between Pindling and Hanna, thus broken, was never fully renewed.

Arthur Hanna neither resigned from the PLP (where he retained much affectionate support among the rank and file) nor from Parliament – where he felt free on occasion to criticise the Prime Minister and his government from the back benches. In the 1987 election he was elected unopposed (by either party). But in the 1992 landslide victory of the FREE NATIONAL MOVEMENT he shared in the PLP's defeat and announced his retirement from active politics and a return to the practice of the law. However, Hanna retained a close interest in political affairs, and as a mellow and popular elder statesman now in his late seventies was chosen by the once-again ruling PLP to be the seventh Bahamian Governor-General in November 2005, in succession to Dame Ivy Dean-Dumont.

HARBOUR ISLAND A hilly island 3 miles (4.8 km) long and half a mile (0.8 km) wide, 1½ miles (2.5 km) off the coast of north ELEUTHERA, universally rated among the prettiest and most interesting in The Bahamas. Nestling on its leeward side is the quaint 350-year-old village of Dunmore Town, which many of its 1,500 inhabitants still regard as The Bahamas' 'second city', while along its Atlantic Ocean eastern side is the world-famous Pink Sands Beach.

Harbour Island was first settled by the ELEUTHERIAN ADVENTURERS from Bermuda in 1648 and for a century was at least as important as Nassau – as a centre for boatbuilding, fishing, combing for wrecks and, in wartime, for more or less licensed privateering. Its Anglican church,

Harbour Island

St John's, dating from 1768, can claim to be the oldest in The Bahamas. Dunmore Town, hitherto developed higgledy-piggledy along the shore, was formally laid out (and named after) the LOYALIST Governor Lord DUNMORE in 1791. Dunmore started a fashion by making Harbour Island a getaway resort, building a summer house on the summit of the ridge that was later to be the Commissioner's residence.

Living by the sea and shipping, Harbour Island was relatively unaffected by the decline of plantations and the ending of slavery, and its heyday lasted throughout the age of sail. In 1880, when its population – about 2,000 – was greater than ever again, it was accurately described by L. G. POWLES as 'a miniature Nassau'. A bustling place, its leeward shore was busy with boatyards, its harbour crammed with sailing ships, engaged in trade between the islands or with the United States.

Harbour Island, like Nassau, was dominated by whites – shipbuilders, shipowners and merchants – but there were equal numbers of non-whites, many of them of mixed ancestry. This indicated a considerable degree of miscegenation, though it remained covert, and social and residential segregation was rigidly established by accepted custom. As in Nassau, the prosperous whites lived in the best houses on the ridge, in the town centre, and along the bay-front. Blacks lived over the back of the hill or on the northern or southern outskirts, generally in one-room shacks raised up on stones. The intermediate 'coloured' class lived, in all respects, in between. Segregation in church was just as rigid in all but the blacks' BAPTIST chapels – there being almost a riot in 1885 when five non-whites purposely entered the METHODIST church by the wrong door.

Such tensions were always rare, and customs changed only gradually in the twentieth century. Harbour Island remained deeply conservative and a bastion of 'white power' until well after mid-century. It retained the right to send three members to Parliament until 1962 (when it had a mere 1,372 registered voters) and did not elect an authentic non-white until 1982. It was, indeed, its quaint, old fashioned character, as much as the pink sands and other attractions, that brought, and continued to bring, tourists to the island. Unlike the rest of Eleuthera, Harbour Island continues to be a favourite tourist destination, almost cornering the market for a special type of clientele: the discerning, conservative and very rich. There is no single grand hotel, but many small select establishments, of which the oldest, Pink Sands, was described in 2000 as 'one of the most unpretentiously chic resort hotels in the world'. Room rates in the winter season run up to $2,000 a night, though that admittedly includes breakfast and dinner in a restaurant the food in which has been called 'sublime'.

HARD BARGAIN Evidence of the hardship of the lives of Bahamian slaves and of their struggle to live as peasant farmers once slavery ended is the fact that no fewer than four poor black settlements in the Family Islands still bear the name Hard Bargain. These are on Moores Island south of ABACO, near Coakley Town in north central ANDROS, in southern LONG ISLAND, and in central SAN SALVADOR.

Of these modest settlements much the most interesting is the last mentioned, because of its direct connection with the only village called Hard Bargain in the British Caribbean, in distant southern Trinidad. Hard Bargain, in what was then called Watling's Island, was the chief settlement of the 450 or so slaves owned by a failed COTTON planter named Burton Williams, who with his sons judiciously transferred 330 of the slaves to Trinidad

Hard Bargain, Long Island

to set up sugar plantations between 1821 and 1823, before the British government stopped such trafficking between colonies. Because of the registration of all colonial slaves insisted on by the imperial authorities (despite colonial opposition), it is almost uniquely possible not just to trace the transfer but to gauge its effects – comparing the fate of those transferred with that of those left behind in The Bahamas.

Following the failure of cotton plantations, Bahamian slaves had largely been left to make a subsistence living for themselves. Despite the difficulties of subsisting (mitigated somewhat by the regulations that compelled slave-owners to provide minimal supplies and provisions) the Bahamian slaves, mostly living in nuclear family households, were remarkably healthy and steadily increasing in numbers. Imperial regulations insisted both that slaves only be transferred if accompanied by their owners to set up new plantations, and that no slave families be split up by the transfer. Consequently, the Williams slaves shifted to Trinidad initially exhibited marital and demographic patterns almost identical with those left behind in The Bahamas, as well as being under the oversight of an owner who had every incentive to keep them healthy.

Yet the rigours of setting up and working a sugar plantation, the tropical climate and disease, had a disastrous effect on the transferred slaves. Even Williams had to admit to an official inquiry in 1825 that the transferred slaves would have returned to The Bahamas had that been possible. By the end of slavery in 1834 their fertility rates were so low and mortality rates so high, especially among infants, that numbers had actually declined, with the proportion of children at a dangerously low level. In contrast, the Williams slaves left behind in The Bahamas continued to increase and exhibit an extremely healthy demographic balance over the same decade.

Hard Bargain was the name retained by the Williams ex-slaves of San Salvador for their familiar settlement once they became free peasant cultivators of their former owner's land. Other Bahamian black freedmen who set out to farm decayed plantations or undeveloped land in Long Island, Andros and Moores Island (some of whom may have been former Williams slaves) gave the same name to their new settlements. Similarly, the Williams ex-slaves in Trinidad who forsook the Williamsville sugar plantation for a peasant lifestyle nearby also called their main settlement Hard Bargain. In the Trinidad case, it is a matter of speculation whether this was a comment on the hardships of subsisting as peasants on plantation margins, or a somewhat romanticised nostalgia for their former island home 1,250 miles to the north-west. In either case, perhaps a better name would not be Hard Bargain, but Harder Bargain.

Further reading: Craton and Saunders, *Islanders*, i. 258–96; M. Craton, 'Changing Patterns of Slave Family in the British West Indies', in *Empire, Enslavement and Freedom in the Caribbean*, Ian Randle Press, 1997, 233–59.

HAYWARD, Sir Jack

One of the chief founders and shapers of Freeport, Grand Bahama, whose resolute espousal of all things British there has accorded him the nickname 'Union Jack'.

Born in 1923 at Wolverhampton in the English industrial Midlands, Jack Hayward was the son of Sir Charles Hayward (1893–1983) the millionaire founder and owner of the giant manufacturing Firth Cleveland Company. Educated at Stowe, a progressive private school, he joined the ROYAL AIR FORCE at 18 and piloted glider-towing Dakotas in Burma in WORLD WAR TWO. After tours in Africa selling industrial machinery in the late 1940s, he was posted to the Firth Cleveland offices in New York in 1951.

Not relishing either the life of a salesman or being desk-bound, young Hayward discovered The Bahamas, spent as much time as he could there and decided to make it his home. He eagerly endorsed his father's purchase (for a mere million pounds) of a third of Wallace Grove's Grand Bahama interests in 1955, and assumed a vital role in the promotion and development of Freeport-Lucaya by the Grand Bahama Port Authority and Development Company. Though he travelled widely – mainly between the Bahamas and the UK – and still owns a house in Sussex, he built his dream home on Sea Shell Drive on Freeport's splendid seashore and made it his base. On the retirement of Groves in 1976, Hayward became Chairman of the GBDC and joint Chairman (with Edward St George) of the GBPA, travelling less and less, and not retiring from an active role until the 1990s.

Jack Hayward (he does not sport his title as knight) emulated his father in being a notable philanthropist. The

HEATH, Sir Robert

Hayward Foundation, set up in 1961, has disbursed at least £20 million. His personal benefactions – even more in Britain than in The Bahamas – help to explain how he got his nickname. Among his projects have been the saving of Wolverhampton Wanderers soccer team from bankruptcy and returning it to the Premier League, the rescue of the wreck of Brunel's iron ship *Great Britain* from the Falkland Islands, the purchase of Lundy Island on behalf of English Heritage, the sponsorship of the English women's cricket team, and helping to finance the new British Empire and Commonwealth Museum in Bristol.

Though demonstrably a lover of The Bahamas and its culture, the vision of 'Union Jack' is of a country where the British heritage remains important, if not paramount. In Freeport, his determination to stem the inexorable tide of Americanisation has led him to make somewhat extravagant gestures towards retaining British symbols and influences. These have included the setting-up of Churchill Square (with a bust of the great man at its centre) and of the English-style Pub-on-the-Mall in downtown Freeport, the importation of red London double-decker buses, and the enthusiastic promotion of the very un-American game of CRICKET.

What he referred to as his proudest honour was the renaming of Freeport's first non-denominational secondary school the Sir Jack Hayward High School by Prime Minister Hubert INGRAHAM in January 1998.

HEATH, Sir Robert (1575–1649) Kentish-born English Attorney General, rewarded for his loyalty to King Charles I by the grant of the Carolinas and Bahamas on 30 October 1629. Though Heath never visited or did anything to develop his proprietorship, the date of his grant has always been taken to mark the establishment of The Bahamas as a British colony.

Despite its non-implementation, however, Heath's grant, written in Latin, is of interest both to illustrate the ideas that the early Stuarts had for the development of English colonies, and to suggest what might have happened to The Bahamas had Heath not been distracted by the Civil War and been able to carry out his colonisation plans. Much like the grant of the 'Caribbee Islands' (including Barbados) to Lord Carlisle in the same year, the proprietorship was to be held and ruled indirectly almost like a feudal fief. Its model in most respects was the Palatinate of Durham in north-eastern England. The proprietor was enjoined to summon all freeholding settlers to a kind of parliament and to follow the laws of England as far as possible. But he was allowed to award titles, given wide judiciary powers, and granted the right to issue ordinances whenever the need arose. Beside the sole right to allocate lands, he was empowered to levy taxes and duties as he saw fit (subject only to free trade between the colony and England), and was granted all royalties save one fifth of the precious metals mined. The supremacy of the monarch was to be symbolically acknowledged by the donation of a golden coronet inscribed *Deos Coronet Opus Suum* – but only if and when the King chose to visit the colony.

Most of these provisions were adopted by the LORD PROPRIETORS, who were given a similar grant of the Carolinas and The Bahamas by Charles I's son Charles II in 1670 – though without success. As the PIRATE era showed, the orderly development of the Bahamian colony required direct royal control rather than indirect rule by proprietors.

Though Heath's 1629 grant was presumably invalidated by his failure to do anything about it, largely over-ridden by the later grant to the Lord Proprietors, and totally expunged by the institution of direct royal government in 1718, several persons claimed in the English courts to have bought or inherited all or part of Heath's grant. Most of these claims were far-fetched and none was successful in the Carolinas or The Bahamas.

Further reading: M. Craton, *A History of The Bahamas*, San Salvador Press, 1986.

Sir Robert Heath: plaque on the wall of the House of Assembly commemorating Heath's grant of The Bahamas, 1629

HOBBY HORSE HALL The former Bahamian horse race-track situated behind CABLE BEACH, which survived from the mid-1930s to the late 1960s despite bitter opposition from churchmen and other moralists, and is remembered by many with affectionate nostalgia.

The founder of Hobby Horse Hall was the American-born former rum-runner and adopted member of the BAY STREET oligarchy, George Murphy. But the project had the full endorsement of Governor Sir Bede CLIFFORD (1932–7), who saw it as an important part of his programme to attract rich American tourists to The Bahamas once the era of Prohibition was ended. Prominent among the wealthy expatriates who avidly took part in the 'sport of kings' in the early days was Sir Harry OAKES, who in typically competitive style imported and bred some of the most notable horses but also encouraged local participation. Horse-racing, indeed, caught on even more keenly with Bahamians, at all levels, than with visiting tourists. Local breeders (such as Max Bowe of The Forest, Exuma), trainers (most famously, 'Fuzzy' Lightbourne of Carmichael Road), local owners (including blacks like Arnold Pindling, father of the future Prime Minister Sir Lynden PINDLING), along with stablemen and jockeys, formed a colourful subculture. As money grew more plentiful after World War Two, the racing also drew an ever-increasing and dedicated clientele of eager bettors – exhibiting the ordinary Bahamians' love of gambling of all kinds

Hobby Horse Hall enjoyed its heyday (and its notoriety) in the last two decades of Bay Street rule and rising prosperity in the 1950s and 1960s. It was ostensibly under the control of the politician and genuine racing aficionado Dr Raymond Sawyer, but in reality under the dynamic direction of another self-made millionaire expatriate (like Oakes, from Canada), Alexis Nihon. A typical poster from 1962 proclaimed racing of a thoroughly modern and sophisticated form. Meetings were held twice weekly, on Tuesdays and Fridays, with seven races, sizeable fields, and all the paraphernalia of electric starting gate, photo finishes and electronic tote, and such refinements for bettors as a daily double and 'quinfecta'. The whole operation was advertised as 'Government Supervised'.

By all accounts, however, the racing was not quite so sophisticated or straight as the advertisement suggested. Even at the peak, the reservoir of available horses was limited, and known form should have made for predictable and boring results. In fact, the crafty importation of animals of unknown and sometimes shady provenance, and suspicious riding tactics, led to frequent upsets and rumours of fixing between bettors, owners and jockeys. Amusing, if mostly apocryphal, stories abounded. One of the most common anecdotes (dating from the last days of Hobby Horse Hall) told of an alleged occasion when all five horses in a race had been fixed not to win. One after another pulled up as if lame, till not one was running, and none even walked past the finishing post.

Hobby Horse Hall closed down at much the same time that the Bay Street regime was succeeded by the Progressive Liberal Party, among whose most influential supporters were the Baptist and other churches dead set against all forms of gambling by Bahamians. However, it was not just moral opprobrium, or even public scepticism about the racing itself, but a combination of the sheer expense of keeping such an operation going and competition from the new casinos (sustained and controlled by the PLP) that led to the closure. As recently as 2002, the chairman of the Bahamas Christian Council, Bishop Sam Greene, looked back on the era of Hobby Horse Hall as the grimmest illustration of the moral and social evils of gambling. However, in the last year of his life, Sir Lynden Pindling privately took a much more tolerant and nostalgic view: 'Those were some days,' he reminisced with a typical chuckle. 'Those race-horses that Daddy and them owned were what saw me through school.'

HOGSTY REEF A snaggle-toothed atoll with uncertain tidal currents midway between ACKLINS ISLAND and INAGUA. Since it lies across a commonly

Hogsty Reef

HOLE-IN-THE-WALL, ABACO

used route between the Atlantic and the Caribbean, it has always been a graveyard for unwary vessels. The *Yachtsman's Guide* reports that its fishing is excellent and that its many wrecks may contain treasure, but advises great caution. It has a warning light on one its tiny cays but its most conspicuous landmark, a run-aground freighter, can lure the unwary by day because at a distance it may look like a ship sailing safely through deep waters.

HOLE-IN-THE-WALL, ABACO The far southern tip of mainland ABACO, crowned by a famous red-striped lighthouse built in 1836 (now automated). Those few who venture down the rocky road to the point – said to need a four-wheel drive vehicle – are well rewarded. Besides a spectacular sea-spanning arch and sundry nearby caves, the name presumably also refers to the fact that Hole-in-the-Wall is the northern portal of the 25-mile (40-km) wide North-east Providence Channel, the main passage between the North Atlantic and NASSAU. The splendid panorama seen from the lighthouse gallery includes the wide, deserted scrub of southern Abaco, the deep expanse of blue ocean between there and SPANISH WELLS off northern Eleuthera, and the frequent freighters, liners and ocean-going yachts, and the occasional grey warships, that pass by.

HOMER, Winslow (1836–1910) Greatest American painter – and one of the world's supreme watercolourists – whose visits to The Bahamas helped spur the final development of his technique and inspired his masterpiece, *The Gulf Stream* (1899).

A dour Yankee bachelor born in Cambridge, Massachusetts, Winslow Homer came to notice as a magazine artist at the time of the American Civil War. Permanently affected by that conflict, he attained fame as a brilliant observer of the natural world and of man's heroic but not always successful combat with the forces of nature, especially the sea.

Already famous, but living a reclusive life at Prout's Neck on the coast of Maine, Homer made several winter trips to the American tropics, including KEY WEST, Cuba and Bermuda as well as The Bahamas. Though he stayed only twice in The Bahamas (1885, 1898) the colours of the sea and flowers, the brilliance of the light reflected off Nassau's white houses, roads and walls, and the liveliness and grace of black Bahamians, acted as a catalyst for some of his most brilliant and spontaneous watercolours – in contrast to the more sombre tones of his mainland work.

Though in part and at one level the visual equivalents of the enthusiastic but superficial descriptive verses of the Canadian Bliss CARMAN (who was in Nassau at

Hole-in-the-Wall, southern Abaco

the same time as Homer in 1898), Winslow Homer's Bahamian paintings had intimations of something far more profound – in the depiction of palm trees battered by a hurricane, the skeletons of wrecked schooners on the shore, and the hint of suffering and endurance in some of the native blacks he depicted.

This marriage of the perennial theme of man's conflict with implacable natural forces and the exotic tropical context bore fruit in Homer's most famous oil painting (now in the Metropolitan Museum in New York) completed in 1899, when the artist was 60 years of age. At the centre of *The Gulf Stream* is the heroic and defiant figure of a black mariner, the sole survivor, aboard a dismasted and rudderless sloop, in the aftermath of a cataclysmic storm. In the still brilliantly coloured but disrupted sea around the battered boat, sinister sharks circle with gaping maws, while on opposite sides of the horizon a waterspout threatens and an almost spectral three-masted merchant schooner under full sail passes blithely on its way.

Further reading: G. Hendricks, *The Life and Works of Winslow Homer*, Abrams, 1979; H. Cooper, *Winslow Homer Watercolours*, National Art Gallery, Washington, 1986.

HONOURS SYSTEM AND NATIONAL AWARDS Bahamians are proud to do well both for themselves and for their country, and they take even greater satisfaction when their achievements are publicly recognised. Of public honours and awards, those associated with the Crown still retain much kudos, and may even have been long a potent motive for retaining the monarchy. But the fact that even ostensibly royal awards are now made on local advice, along with the steady addition of purely Bahamian tokens of recognition, are sure indicators of a maturing sense of a proud and untrammelled national independence.

In colonial times, the award of imperial honours was made solely on the recommendation of the Governor and with the approval of the Colonial Office. They tended therefore to be comparatively rare, with a well-defined hierarchy of relative importance, and the plums almost routinely going to senior officials who steered a successful and safely conservative course – most notably to Chief Justices, long-serving Speakers and Governors themselves. With the coming of internal self-government in 1964, and even more with the change of government and constitution four years later, the honours system became much more obviously subject to political patronage. By the time of INDEPENDENCE in 1973, however, though still firmly in the gift of the party in power, awards were becoming more genuinely and generally an indicator of valuable contributions to the Bahamian nation.

Twice a year, at the New Year and on the Queen's Official Birthday in June, The Bahamas, along with the United Kingdom, the remaining dependencies, and all those countries which still recognise the British sovereign as their Head of State, features in the list of nominally royal awards. Apart from those honours that do remain more or less within the royal prerogative, and titles of nobility formerly, but no longer, hereditary (none of which has

'A Wall, Nassau', 1899 watercolour by Winslow Homer

ever been awarded to a native Bahamian), the most prestigious of these emanate nominally from two ancient institutions or orders: The Most Distinguished Order of St Michael and St George, and The Most Excellent Order of the British Empire. Within the first Order there are two levels of award: at the top, Knight or Dame Commander (KCMG or DCMG) and, somewhat less exalted, Companion (CMG). In the slightly less prestigious but much more populous Order of the British Empire, there are three levels: Knight or Dame (KBE and DBE), Officer (OBE), and Member (MBE). Besides all the above there are also rather more awards made of the British Empire Medal (BEM) – mainly for long-time services to the community at a workaday level.

Although it is generally known that the former imperial awards no longer derive strictly from the monarch (though the Queen's imprimatur still serves to minimise any suspicion of political jobbery) there exists a growing feeling that the Bahamian nation no longer needs such ancient titles, especially when they still carry the long outdated label of the British Empire. This is surely signified in the growing number of purely local honours which have been instituted since the 1990s, almost all limited solely to Bahamians, and covering the whole spectrum of service to the nation.

By far the most important of purely Bahamian awards is the Order of Merit, instituted by the FREE NATIONAL MOVEMENT government in 1996 to recognise Bahamian heroes and heroines in three specific nation-building categories: business, civics and arts, and education. Admirably, these persons were chosen with little or no regard to their political affiliation. This virtual pantheon of Bahamian achievers was augmented before the year 2000 by three other national awards of much wider application. These were the Prime Minister's Above and Beyond Excellence Award, for 'superior service to customers, businesses and the community', nominated and voted for by customers through a Bahamas Quality Council; the Cacique Awards given by the Ministry of Tourism to recognise valuable contributions to the tourist industry in many separate categories, including photography, writing, transportation, sports and leisure, and eco-tourism; and the Governor-General's Youth Awards, consisting of gold, silver and bronze medals for activities over an extended period in four categories: skills, physical recreation, expeditions and community service.

At a more unofficial level there are many other annual awards and honours, offered by service organisations, professional associations, or bodies representing a particular branch of Bahamian public activity. Of these, two are particularly notable: the annual DANSA Awards recognising contributions (by residents as well as Bahamian natives) to plays, musicals and revues staged at the Dundas Centre for the Performing Arts, and the Caribbean Gospel Music Marlin Awards, presented every year for achievements in the ever more popular field of regional gospel music, in no fewer than twenty different categories, including outstanding song, outstanding solo and group performance, and outstanding new album.

HOPE TOWN (ELBOW CAY) Best known and most picturesque of ABACO's offshore settlements, 'Ope Town Habaco (as guidebook writers say the locals call it) lies 6 miles (9 km) across the sound from MARSH HARBOUR, on a 6-mile long islet, called Elbow Cay because it is at the midway point of Abaco's arm where it juts out eastward into the Atlantic. This location explains the existence of Hope Town's most distinctive landmark, the white and red-striped lighthouse, completed in 1863.

Though as a township Hope Town was founded by American LOYALISTS around 1785, it is thought to be built on the site of a Lucayan village at least a thousand years older. In 1990 a local inhabitant digging a pit for a new cistern uncovered a Lucayan skull and pottery shards. Those AMERINDIANS were long gone and forgotten, though, when the Loyalists came. Of these re-settlers, traditionally the South Carolina widow Wyannie MALONE and her four children were the very first, and provided the settlement's root stock. At the turn of the twentieth century virtually every inhabitant could trace descent from the matriarch Malone. This, however, is far from proof that she was the settlement's Eve, as some would seem to believe. Quite apart from the fact that Wyannie's four children all married into other families, it is well known that the original Loyalists were soon augmented by white migrants from the pre-Loyalist settlements of North ELEUTHERA, considerably diluting the gene pool almost from the beginning.

However, until tourists discovered the Abaco cays in the mid-twentieth century, Hope Town, like the other 'Loyalist' settlements, derived positive virtues from isolation: industriousness, family pride and a spirit of independence and self-sufficiency. Hope Towners farmed and fished for subsistence, and built their own houses and boats from Abaconian plank and hardwoods and from 'ships' stores' combed from wrecks near and wide. Dependence on 'WRECKING' – which along with some SPONGING brought the only commodities the islanders could exchange for goods they could not make or obtain by themselves – explained why the Hope

Main street, Hope Town, Abaco

Towners opposed and even sabotaged the erection of the Elbow Cay lighthouse, delaying its completion from 1838 to 1863.

Today, thanks to tourism and catering to foreign residents, Hope Town is a prosperous but relatively sleepy place. The well-tended and brightly-painted houses on the eastern shore of the snug harbour almost seem to be posing for a photo. This is where the descendants of the original settlers still live – all but for two or three black families true 'CONCHY JOES'. It is also where they proudly renovated and repainted one old house to make the fascinating Wyannie Malone Historical Museum.

The excellent *Lonely Planet Guide* beautifully conveys the ambience of Hope Town today: 'A few locals still make a living by fishing or boatbuilding, but most rely on the tourist trade. A town council maintains strict building and business codes. No cars are allowed in the village. The only sounds are the thrum of motorboats, chimes of church bells, echoes of hammers on wood, coos of doves, and the rustle of the breeze in the palms.'

To north and even more to the south of the township are small, laid-back hotels and the homes of foreign residents. As early as 1980, the foreign-owned homes outnumbered the native-owned on Elbow Cay by 115 to 79 – almost exclusively the property of wealthy white Americans.

Further reading: S. Dodge and V. Malone, *A Guide and History of Hope Town*, White Sound Press, 1990.

HURRICANES Still called by the name given them by the pre-Columbian Amerindians, hurricanes throughout history have been the most devastating of natural scourges affecting the peoples of the Caribbean region – with those living in The Bahamas among the most often and seriously afflicted.

The Atlantic hurricane is the western version of the Asiatic typhoon. Technically it is an immense tropical cyclone, originating in the doldrums off West Africa, picking up its energy from the convection of moist air from the warm sea, and gathering force as it moves steadily westwards towards and through the Caribbean. Towards the end of its transit it almost invariably veers northwards, and only fades once it has encountered the North American mainland or the cooler Atlantic waters beyond Bermuda.

A counter-clockwise spiral of fierce winds with an eerily calm centre, the hurricane at first is only a few miles in diameter, with winds of no more than gale force. But it can become a monstrous circular saw – up to 500 miles (800 km) in diameter and with winds approaching 200 miles (320 km) an hour. Places and persons directly in its path on its westward course are first assailed with howling winds from the north, then lulled by an hour or two of dead calm, followed by an onslaught of unimaginable ferocity from the south. Equally damaging can be the huge wave surges and rainstorms which accompany hurricanes, overwashing low-lying areas and dumping up to 30 inches (760 mm) of rain in a day.

Hurricanes follow a regular but not entirely predictable pattern, and before modern weather forecasting, usually struck without warning. They occur almost exclusively during the late summer and autumn, as suggested by the well-known mnemonic: 'June, too soon. July, stand by. August, you must … September, remember. October, all over.' On the average, four or five hurricanes of varying

Hurricane damage at Francis straw market

HURRICANES

magnitude strike the Caribbean region each year, but a given location, even within the main belt between 15 and 25 degrees north, is unlikely to undergo a major assault more than once every four or five years. However, some of the worst onslaughts have occurred when hurricanes have not obeyed folklore rules: attacking in July, October or even November, approaching from unusual directions, becoming stationary rather than marching relentlessly forward, or suddenly deciding to change direction. Sometimes they follow each other with unexpected frequency. For example, after experiencing no major storms for several years, The Bahamas was swept by three serious hurricanes in 1926 alone, and five within the four years 1926–9.

The Bahamas, moreover, is specially vulnerable on several counts. The islands lie within the median hurricane belt and are aligned along the normal hurricane axis. They do not constitute a land-mass sufficient to slow a hurricane's build-up, and being flat and with minimal soils are extremely susceptible to coastal wave damage, salt-water inundation and soil erosion. One of the comparatively minor but sad effects of hurricanes on the fragile Bahamian ecosystem is the way that they decimate – and in severe cases come close to eradicating – native bird-life.

In aboriginal and early colonial times, hurricanes would have erased all habitations and destroyed all crops, canoes and sailing vessels, even threatening the people with extinction through starvation. Even in later colonial times, hurricane damage could be devastating. For example, the 'Great Bahama Hurricane' of 1866 wiped several islands almost clear. Even in Nassau 600 houses were totally destroyed, an equal number seriously damaged, and a thousand people made completely homeless. Substantial buildings like Trinity Methodist Church had to be completely rebuilt, and of 200 ships in the harbour only one was said to have escaped destruction or serious damage. Accounts tell of the bodies of crewmen in ships caught out in the storm being washed up on Bahamian shores for weeks afterwards, some of them half-eaten by sharks. Photographs of the effects of the 1926 and 1929 hurricanes were almost as graphic: trees uprooted or stripped bare, roads washed out and coastlines altered, substantial vessels deposited half a mile inland, wooden buildings reduced to matchwood, stone buildings unroofed, and even one wall of Fort Montagu (designed to withstand cannon fire) tumbled down.

Often proclaimed by churchmen as a form of divine punishment for misdemeanours, and still referred to by insurance companies as 'Acts of God', hurricanes have traditionally inclined even the least godly Bahamians towards a stoical fatalism. Modern construction methods and materials are proof against all but the most extreme hurricane winds, and advances in meteorology allow ample time to take precautions. Today, lives are rarely lost, ships are more or less safely harboured, and planes diverted or flown off out of the storm's path. Yet the material and financial damage can still be immense. Comparatively narrow but exceptionally violent Hurricane Andrew in August 1992 (which superstitious supporters of the Progressive Liberal Party saw as a consequence of their party's cataclysmic defeat just three days earlier) wreaked great damage in northern ELEUTHERA, the BERRY ISLANDS and BIMINI before it hit southern Florida and the Gulf States and became the costliest hurricane in North American history (an estimated total of $30 billion).

For The Bahamas alone, Hurricane Floyd in September 1999 caused relatively even greater harm. Larger in extent and almost as fierce as Andrew, it cut a longer swathe in the central and northern Bahamas. Apart from the damage to houses, roads, bridges and boats, so great was the destruction to standing crops and resort facilities already financially struggling in the current depression, that some pessimists reckoned that neither agriculture nor tourism in the Family Islands would ever fully recover.

Further reading: J. Macpherson, *Caribbean Lands: A Geography of the West Indies*, 2nd. ed., Macmillan Caribbean, 1967, 6–17; V. Moseley Moss, *Reminiscing: Memories of Old Nassau*, Ronald Lightbourn, 1999, 46–51; R. Johnson Clarke, 'Raging Devils in Paradise', *Bahamas Handbook and Businessman's Annual, 2001*, Dupuch Publications, 2001, 157–73.

IGUANA A huge lizard (or small dragon) which once teemed throughout The Bahamas but was hunted almost to extinction for food, and now, though protected by law, is found only in a handful of uninhabited cays and deserted parts of ANDROS.

The 13 species of iguana (*Iguanidae*) are exclusive to the New World. Those found on islands like The Bahamas are rock iguanas (*cyclura*), distinguished from the more numerous and familiar tree iguanas found especially in Central America and the Greater Antilles. Three species and seven subspecies of rock iguana still exist in The Bahamas, yet in such scattered locations and small numbers that their disappearance is thought to be but a matter of time. In the opinion of experts, only on two islets – Guana Cay in the Bight of ACKLINS and Booby Cay off the east end of MAYAGUANA – are iguanas found in such numbers as to guarantee their extended survival.

The largest of all Bahamian iguanas was a species found in NEW PROVIDENCE, now extinct, that grew to 6 feet (1.8 m) in length. The Andros species can grow to 5 ½ feet (1.6 m) but is now very rare – not just through being hunted for food but because of the destruction of its habitat by logging and the rooting out of its eggs by feral pigs. The other indigenous subspecies vary from 2 ½ feet up to 4 feet (0.7 to 1.2 m) in length once mature. Rock iguanas, despite their sharp teeth and fearsome appearance (enhanced by puffing up a spiked crown when under attack), are not predators or even carnivores – living off plants and berries. Females deposit their eggs in soil-filled crevices in the rocks or in the sand dunes along the shore. As with turtles, the nests are left unguarded and the eggs hatch out in the sun. Iguana hatchlings, miniature versions of their parents, are immediately able to forage on their own.

The former profusion of rock iguanas is attested by the half dozen islands and islets called Guana Cay scattered throughout The Bahamas. That iguanas were facing an almost mortal enemy in man was indicated by the naturalist Mark CATESBY in 1725. He praised 'guana' flesh as tasty and easily digestible and noted that the early settlers made it a major food source regardless of the consequences. They scoured the cays in their sloops, using trained dogs to hunt the iguanas without killing them. Brought to bay, the creatures were netted, their jaws bound up to prevent them biting, and they were thrown into the sloop's hold until it was filled. Once the hunters were back home the iguanas were killed, to be eaten fresh or salted and kept in barrels for later consumption. 'They

Iguana

are sometimes roasted,' reported Catesby, 'but the more common way is to boil them, taking out the leaves of fat, which they melt and clarify; this they put into a calabash or dish, into which they dip the flesh of the guanas as they eat it.'

Two fascinating characteristics of rock iguanas (shared by their *anolis* lizard cousins) are the possession of a tail that breaks off when seized and subsequently regrows, and of a vestigial third eye (complete with lens and retina), located between the two normal eyes. The purpose of this organ, called the pineal eye, is still not fully understood. One theory is that it is used to measure the length of days in order to time the reproduction cycle. Unfortunately, as David Campbell wrote in 1978, it is by no means certain that the rock iguanas will survive long enough for scientists to unravel this mystery.

Further reading: C. Knapp *et al.*, 'Status and Empirical Field Observations of the Andros Rock Iguana', *Bahamas Journal of Science*, 1, 1999.

IMPERIAL ORDER OF DAUGHTERS OF THE EMPIRE (IODE)
Loyalist women's organisation originating in Canada, which flourished in The Bahamas for the first two-thirds of the twentieth century.

The IODE was founded in 1900 by Mrs Margaret Polson Murray of Montreal, in response to the wave of imperial patriotism which was generated by Queen Victoria's Diamond Jubilee and the British cause in the Boer War. Though in practice limited to 'educated, middle-class English-speaking women who were loyal to Britain', by 1909 it had 133 chapters and 9,000 members, most numerously in the Toronto area. It was especially active during wartime in providing comforts for the fighting forces but increasingly also provided material aid and scholarships for veterans and their families. By the end of WORLD WAR ONE it had reached a peak, with

INAGUA

750 chapters and 40,000 members, and it was just as active in WORLD WAR TWO. Into the 1980s, thanks to an ethnic and social widening of its membership, and despite the steady erosion of royalist and imperial loyalist sentiments, the IODE still boasted 15,000 members. However, though still raising $3,000,000 a year for its various causes, membership had fallen below 7,000 by the end of the century.

The Bahamas branch of the IODE was even more elitist and conservative than the Canadian mother organisation, and consequently did not long survive the coming of black majority rule and national INDEPENDENCE. Founded in 1903, it membership was strictly limited to white ladies who could prove descent from families that had fled the American Revolution in the 1780s or had been already established in The Bahamas at that time. Thus it was a small but relatively wealthy elite, scarcely ever exceeding a hundred members, but, by the principle of *noblesse oblige*, dedicated to what it regarded as good works. Very much along the same lines as the Daughters of the American Revolution (DAR) on the other side of the former political divide, it was also (if unofficially) dedicated to the principles of white supremacy and the promotion of its own version of local history.

The first notable achievement of the Bahamian IODE was the 1904 planting of the magnificent double row of royal palms on what was then called Culmer Street but was renamed Victoria Avenue. Even more symbolically, the IODE ladies were responsible for commissioning and paying for the statue of QUEEN VICTORIA in Nassau's Parliament Square, unveiled before a large and enthusiastic crowd on Empire Day, 24 May 1905. Both the royal palms on Victoria Avenue and the statue of the Queen Empress still proudly stand in the same places, more than a hundred years after Victoria's death.

The IODE ladies were tireless in raising funds, knitting socks and making up parcels for servicemen in both world wars. But they were equally concerned to provide healthy recreational facilities for men in the armed forces stationed in or visiting Nassau. A canteen was established and parties and dances (strictly segregated) held at the IODE headquarters. Such innocent diversions continued to be offered in peace-time whenever a Royal Navy vessel was in port, only falling out of fashion in the early 1960s as the original IODE members aged and their numbers declined.

In 1959, the elegant Georgian-fronted IODE Hall at the junction of Shirley Street and Victoria Avenue became the headquarters of the BAHAMAS HISTORICAL SOCIETY, which originally had a strong pro-LOYALIST bias. From 1987 it also housed a fascinating if eclectic museum of local history. As the home of a now much liberalised BHS and itself fittingly a museum, the Hall (retaining its original name) has survived the fading away of the IODE branch itself.

INAGUA Properly it should be the Inagua*s*, since it comprises both the 550 square miles of Great Inagua, with its single settlement of Matthew Town at its south-western edge, and the island of Little Inagua 5 miles (8 km) off its northern point, 50 square miles (129 squ. km) in extent but completely uninhabited.

IODE Hall, Shirley Street and Elizabeth Avenue, Nassau

The name is something of a puzzle. It sounds both Amerindian and Spanish. It might be both. The Spaniards may have picked up the Lucayan name because it sounded like the Spanish for no water (*in-agua*), which would have been appropriate for an island so lacking in fresh water. For a couple of hundred years the English called it *Heneaga*, which doesn't solve the problem one way or the other.

Fourth largest of Bahamian islands (after ANDROS, ABACO and GRAND BAHAMA), Great Inagua is both the most distant from Nassau and that most unlike all others. At the far south-east point of The Bahamas, it is 380 miles (608 km) from the capital and barely 50 miles (80 km) from the nearest points of Cuba and HAITI – the mountains of which can be seen to the south-west and south on an exceptionally clear day. It is much drier and hotter than the islands to the north-west, with half the rainfall of Nassau (27 inches, 686 mm or less per year) and up to 10 degrees F warmer at any time of year. Its climate produces a dessicated landscape of thorny scrub, cactus and briny ponds, unsuitable for agriculture but ideal for producing SALT.

Location and climate indeed have shaped Great Inagua's history. The Taino AMERINDIANS used it as a stepping stone for their migration towards the north-west, and none seem to have stayed long. The Spaniards and French likewise regarded it as of strategic importance and landed there during their wars with the British, but neither thought it worth making a permanent claim. Only in the nineteenth century, through free trade and steamships, did Great Inagua achieve importance. The world's rising demand for salt led to the creation of solar salt-pans at the seaward end of the shallow (and saline) Lake Rosa that took up a third of the interior. Inagua's location where the Mayaguana and Caicos Passages through the Bahamian archipelago converge on the Windward Passage into the Caribbean between Cuba and Haiti also made it a convenient stopping place for picking up and dropping off stevedores from the southern Bahama Islands. At the same time the increased steamship traffic made Matthew Town a minor entrepot for trade with Haiti and eastern Cuba.

Inagua's population (or rather, that of Matthew Town) was a mere 174 in 1847, but it had grown to 1,200 by 1871. The township was ambitiously laid out to be the second city of The Bahamas, with a geometrical grid of six paved and named streets west to east and 14 north to south. There was a serious slump in the 1870s and 1880s when the Americans laid a protective tariff on salt and LONG CAY became a rival stopping place, but a major recovery from 1890 when the German Hamburg–America line chose Matthew Town as their preferred port of call. Matthew Town's population reached an all-time peak of 1,500 in 1900, when its shops boasted the best of Cuban and Haitian produce and almost the latest in European and American goods. In these years the children of the wealthiest merchants and shipping agents were sent to be schooled in Santiago or Port au Prince rather than to far more distant Nassau. A less creditable connection with Haiti is the story that Matthew Town was the birthplace of the notorious dictator Francois 'Papa Doc' Duvalier (1907–71). Though this is almost certainly an unfounded rumour, there may well be some family connection, for the surname Duvalier is indeed well known in Matthew Town and elsewhere in The Bahamas.

World War One, which led to the disappearance of the German steamers, brought a much more serious and longer slump, which intensified with the coming of the Great Depression. Inagua's population slid steadily to less than 600, and the naturalist Gilbert Klingel, whose yacht was wrecked on the north end of the island in 1929, described Matthew Town as a ghost town in the later stages of ruination. Redemption however came once more from salt. When Klingel came back in 1938 he was able to report a transformation made through the efforts of three brothers called Erikson and their West India Chemicals operation. Matthew Town had become something of a company town but it had electric light, a decent water supply, adequate food stores, and full employment. Its houses were repaired and painted, the streets cleared of weeds and there was a clinic and even a public library. The increased use of salt in industrial processes during and after World War Two continued the improvement, especially after the giant Morton Salt Company bought out the Eriksons in 1954. By the year 2000, Great Inagua was producing a million tons of solar salt a year. Matthew Town's population was back to 1,200, and although still isolated from Nassau by infrequent air services and mailboats that continue to take up to a week round-trip, it was described by the *Lonely Planet* guide as 'one of the largest, wealthiest and most sophisticated settlements in the Family Islands'.

The true wealth of the Inaguas, though, is their natural life. Half of Great Inagua and a 35-mile (56-km) stretch of its northern shore is the largest of the Bahamian National Parks, under the direction and protection of the BAHAMAS NATIONAL TRUST. On the inner half of Lake Rosa (renamed Windsor after the Governor Duke) the once threatened remnants of the Bahamian pink FLAMINGO have built up to a flock of 50,000, which shows signs of repopulating other islands. The lake

INDEPENDENCE

is also home to numerous roseate spoonbills, while the surrounding bush teems with IGUANAS and Bahama Parrots, as well as herds of wild boar and semi-feral donkeys and goats. Undisturbed by all but determined eco-tourists braving the infamous clouds of mosquitoes and sand-flies, sea TURTLES of all four major types come to nest on the sandy stretches of the park's foreshore.

If Great Inagua is still rarely visited by tourists and incompletely known, Little Inagua is virtually *terra incognita*. Completely surrounded by reefs and with no sheltered harbour, it is only regularly visited by Windjammer Cruises' supply boat *Amazing Grace*. All the *Yachtsman's Guide* and other guidebooks can say about this largest of Bahamian uninhabited islands is tantalisingly meagre: that its comparative fertility is attested by the fact that it contains the only stand of Cuban royal palms in The Bahamas, and that it is rumoured to be the place where Henry Christophe, the king of neighbouring Haiti (1811–20) buried a great treasure.

Further reading: G. Klingel, *Ocean Island*, New York, 1940; M. O. Erikson, *Great Inagua*, New York, 1987.

INDEPENDENCE Each year 10 July is rightly celebrated as the most important date in the Bahamian calendar: the anniversary of the day in 1973 that The Bahamas finally ceased to be a colony and became a fully fledged independent nation. In retrospect, this is sometimes depicted as the pre-ordained culmination of an inevitable process. But closer examination discloses complexities and conflicts about the details and timing, and shows that not all the problems of independent nationhood were instantly solved on 10 July 1973.

From the broadest perspective, Independence came as a result of the confluence of Bahamians' will to govern themselves and the British government's loss of the ability and will to retain its colonies after World War Two. Despite WINSTON CHURCHILL'S assertion that he had not become Prime Minister to preside over the dissolution of the British Empire, his resignation in 1955 and the Suez debacle of 1956 revealed the emptiness of imperialist rhetoric and the futility of imperial gestures. The dismantling of the Empire was virtually announced in the famous 'Winds of Change' speech by Churchill's pragmatic Tory successor Harold Macmillan in 1961, to be more bluntly expressed by a Tory minister in respect of The Bahamas a decade later: 'We'd like to get rid of the colonies. . . .We just want to get rid of you.'

The ruling class in The Bahamas had always been proud of the degree of practical independence they enjoyed, retaining the power of self-legislation and having a degree of executive authority through the system of government boards. It was the UNITED BAHAMIAN PARTY of the dominant white BAY STREET clique that achieved internal self-government for The Bahamas in 1964, declaring it to be the preliminary stage before full Independence – a stance with which the Opposition PROGRESSIVE LIBERAL PARTY fully agreed. The UBP's position, however, changed immediately the PLP's victory in 1967 brought the black majority to power. The old regime had seen itself leading The Bahamas to full Independence. Now they maintained that the ruling black party was incompetent and that Independence should be indefinitely postponed.

Knowing that even some non-whites were sceptical of the newcomers' ability to lead an independent nation, Prime Minister Lynden PINDLING proceeded cautiously, waiting for a general consensus and the right moment. Still taking a chance – and hoping to distract voters from other problems assailing his regime – Pindling declared at the opening of the legislature in June 1971 that Independence

10 July 1973: Prime Minister Lynden Pindling displays the Independence document to the people at Clifford Park

would be sought if the PLP won the next general election – which was to be brought forward to September 1972. A Green Paper eloquently put forward the case for Independence and there were heated debates throughout the country. Many Abaconians and some Long Islanders were adamantly opposed and threatened secession, and the Opposition FREE NATIONAL MOVEMENT (the UBP's successor) continued to maintain that The Bahamas was not yet ready.

However, led by the statesmanlike Kendal ISAACS, who feared above all the fragmentation of the country, the FNM announced that the issue would indeed be decided by the general election. When the PLP won a landslide victory in September 1972, the only issues were settling the details of Independence and dampening down the remaining resistance, centred on ABACO. The government's detailed plans were laid out in a White Paper in October 1972, and the nuts and bolts of the changeover and the details of the Independence Constitution were hammered out with remarkably little discord at an all-party conference in London two months later. The Bahamas Independence Bill passed through both houses of the British Parliament with negligible dissent in May 1973.

The PLP made the most of the Independence celebrations of 5–11 July 1973, but they were truly national events. Included were church services, a regatta and other sporting events, parades, fireworks and a JUNKANOO. At one of the three formal balls, Prince Charles famously danced with Marguerite PINDLING, elegant wife of the Prime Minister. But the most moving and symbolic moments were the lowering of the Union Jack and the raising of the Bahamian flag to the singing of the new national anthem on Clifford Park at midnight on Monday 9 July, and the ceremony the following morning when Prince Charles handed over the Constitutional Instruments and Prime Minister Pindling held them out to the huge crowd like a trophy. Throughout the celebrations one of the major themes was the self-congratulation that Bahamians had achieved Independence in unity and, unlike so many other ex-colonies, without any bloodshed whatsoever.

Transcending all social and partisan divisions, the annual celebrations of 10 July have grown in scale and importance over the years, exceeding even those for EMANCIPATION in August and the coming of majority rule in June. Most spectacular of all so far were the parades, ceremonies, fireworks and Junkanoo which marked the twenty-fifth anniversary of Independence on 10 July 1998 – marked, among other things, by the institution of the Order of The Bahamas, the nation's highest honour.

Further reading: *The Constitution of The Bahamas*, HMSO 1973.

INGRAHAM, Rt. Hon. Hubert Alexander Former PROGRESSIVE LIBERAL PARTY Minister who switched to the FREE NATIONAL MOVEMENT in 1990, led that party to victory and became the second Bahamian Prime Minister in August 1992. Born of working-class parents in the lumbering centre of Pine Ridge Grand Bahama in 1947, Hubert Ingraham was brought up in Cooper's Town, northern Abaco. Following the example of his parents, he became and remained a staunch Baptist, and a lifelong strong supporter of family values. He showed great promise and commitment from an early age and was personally encouraged by Prime Minister Lynden PINDLING. An active member of the United States Junior Chamber (the Jaycees), he moved from modest clerking jobs into the law, was called to the Bar in 1972, and became the law partner of PLP stalwart Perry CHRISTIE.

Entering front-line politics in 1975, Hubert Ingraham's rise was meteoric. He was regarded as invaluable to the PLP, both because his personal reputation for honesty countered wavering confidence in the government in that respect, and for the way that his local popularity strengthened the PLP's shaky hand in Abaco and Grand Bahama. Elected to the General Council of the PLP in 1976, he was chosen Party Chairman within a year, being elected PLP Member for his home constituency of Cooper's Town in the 1977 general election. An efficient and scrupulous chairman of several important parliamentary committees (notably those dealing with privilege, public accounts, influence peddling and political contributions), he was appointed Minister of Housing and National Insurance by Pindling in 1982, at the age of 35.

Hubert Ingraham

The affiliation, however, did not last. In 1984 Ingraham was among those demanding a major shake-up within the party, including the resignation of the chief himself, in the wake of the disclosures of the Drug Commission. Though it is not certain that he harboured such ambitions, to many dissidents Ingraham was seen as the most suitable alternative Prime Minister. In the event, Pindling resolutely outflanked what he regarded as an attempted coup. Ingraham was sacked from Cabinet (along with others, including Perry Christie), and in 1986 he was expelled from the PLP.

Now unrestrained, Ingraham mounted a barrage of criticism against government corruption, nepotism and mismanagement. In more general terms, he proclaimed the failure of the PLP's policies of rigid BAHAMIANISATION, moderate socialism and support of nationalised industries, and veered ever closer to the Opposition's ideology of free enterprise and flexibility. Though he had been re-elected as a PLP candidate in 1982, he did not resign his seat on his expulsion from the party, merely switching his designation to Independent, under which label he was convincingly returned by his loyal constituents in the 1987 general election.

Hubert Ingraham officially joined the FREE NATIONAL MOVEMENT in 1990, just before the death of its leader, Cecil WALLACE-WHITFIELD, being almost immediately chosen to take over command of the party. After an overwhelming victory by the FNM candidate in the by-election for Wallace-Whitfield's Grand Bahama seat, Ingraham led the FNM to a convincing win in the 1992 general election – ending the 25-year ascendancy of Pindling and the PLP.

After a hesitant start, the FNM government, helped by a gradual worldwide improvement in the economy, grew in power, and its leader, though lacking Pindling's charisma, steadily gained in confidence and stature. Essentially a product of the grassroots of Bahamian society, Ingraham pragmatically saw the need for less rather than more expenditure on social services and closer ties with the business community, both local and international. His first term was characterised by a deliberate reduction in the size and cost of government, the restriction of government's direct intervention in the economy, and the vigorous promotion of new capital investments from abroad – the symbol of which was the creation of the ATLANTIS hotel and casino complex on PARADISE ISLAND.

A landslide victory in the 1997 general election, leaving the PLP with a mere six seats, seemed to vindicate the FNM's policies and Ingraham's leadership. Even the most diehard members of the Opposition could not have foreseen the dramatic reversal that saw the return of the PLP under Perry Christie in the following election in May 2002. The most general explanation was the public's dissatisfaction with the FNM's failure to deliver on its longer term promises or to counter the economic downturn that followed the events of 11 September 2001. The revitalisation of the PLP and the reassessment of its ideals which followed the national obsequies on the death of Sir Lynden Pindling in September 2000 clearly had an unexpectedly potent effect. But Ingraham himself can also be said to have contributed to the FNM's eclipse by making a serious tactical mistake – announcing that he would lead the party through the election but would hand over to a successor immediately following the victory he confidently predicted.

INSECTS Three insects have been notable pests in The Bahamas, as elsewhere in the region: mosquitoes, sandflies and termites. Even while praising the general healthiness of the islands, Peter Henry BRUCE in the 1740s complained of being tormented 'both day and night' by 'bugs, cock-roaches, musquitos, flies, sand-flies, ants and trigers [chiggers]', noting that the locals laboured in vain to reduce the nuisance by clearing swamps and bush and keeping smoking fires almost continuously.

Had Bruce and his contemporaries been aware of the way that different species of mosquito can carry and transmit the viral and parasitic vectors of deadly diseases they would have regarded them more with fear than mere annoyance. Male mosquitoes feed mostly on flower nectar and other plant juices, but females need human or animal blood to hatch their eggs, and travel far in hunting it. Different species of mosquito specialise in transferring particular diseases from one target to another. The malaria virus is carried by the *anopheles*, those of yellow fever, dengue and encephalitis by the *aedes aegypti,* and the microscopic organisms that cause forms of filariasis (including elephantiasis in humans and heartworm in dogs) by the *culex* species.

All of these diseases, quite common in The Bahamas in the seventeenth and eighteenth centuries, had virtually died out there by the end of the nineteenth century. But their decline was largely fortuitous, and due to other factors than the recognition of the part played by mosquitoes in carrying them and any programme to eradicate them. Such measures – especially spraying standing water near houses with oil or larvicides to kill the wriggling larvae – have more or less cleared downtown Nassau and the chief tourist areas. But many species, especially the ravenous salt marsh *taeniorhynchus*, continue to be a pest in the outlying parts of New Providence and most of the Family Islands. Mosquitoes are particularly troublesome in the rainy summer months, on windless days, and at dusk or daybreak. A century ago a visiting naturalist declared that their swarms rendered the southern islands almost uninhabitable in the summer, and quoted the claim of Inaguans that 'their horses were sometimes killed by them'. Conditions have been greatly improved by the widespread installation of house-screens, and the availability and use of insecticide sprays and repellents. Yet, still familiar sights in many Family Islands are smoking yard fires on the hottest days, children and adults with reddened eyes from the smoke, and islanders talking by the roadside performing an instinctive and almost continuous semaphore-like arm-dance to ward off, and if possible kill, their insistent assailants.

Sandflies, though far smaller and less likely to transmit disease than mosquitoes, have always been, and still remain, the most detested of Bahamian pests. No larger than a pepper-grain (hence their familiar nickname 'no-see-ums'), their females are just as dependent as mosquitoes for a blood meal for reproduction. Worse, they swarm in two main species, of which one (*Leptoconops becquaerti*) favours sandy beaches and hunts throughout the day, and the other (*Culicoides furens*) breeds and lives in salinas and swamps and hunts by night. Between them giving no respite over 24 hours, sandflies are active throughout the year (though with a peak during summer and fall rainy seasons). The beach-haunting *Becquaerti* species is particularly noxious because it can operate in breezes of up to 15 miles per hour, compared with its ferocious cousin's inability to counter breezes of more than 6 miles per hour.

The sandfly threat to Bahamian TOURISM is effectively curbed by larvicide sprays on the main tourist beaches. Untreated beaches on still summer days can still be as tormented by no-see-ums as inland areas by night – though perhaps not quite to the extent found elsewhere in the region. According to David Campbell, on one unnamed resort island in the Lesser Antilles, an unfortunate researcher reported an almost incredible 3,000 bites per hour on a single unprotected leg!

No visitor to the Bahamas is as concerned about the depredations of the third major insect pest, the termite, as are Bahamians living in wooden houses. Indeed, for those living in less vulnerable buildings as well as strangers to the tropics, the termite is one of the most fascinating and important creatures of The Bahamas. As Campbell enthusiastically explains:

> *termites are re-cyclers, reducing wood, living or dead, to its constituents, from which new plants can arise. In the inclement north, where termites are fewer, a log may take decades to decay. But in the termite-infested tropics, a log can be reduced in a matter of weeks and be rapidly resurrected. Termites have carried out this vital function for hundreds of millions of years. Kin to the equally ancient cockroaches [rather than, as is commonly thought, to ants], they are among the most primitive of insects. It is hard to believe that termites have endured over the ages … for they are weak, soft-bodied insects which are killed by even brief exposure to sunlight and by slight changes in temperature and humidity. The reason for the termite's success is society; a rigid caste system which has institutionalised the sterilisation of the masses, child labour and slavery.*

Further reading: D. G. Campbell, *The Ephemeral Islands: A Natural History of The Bahamas*, Macmillan, 1978, 10–18, 73, 76, 91–3; S. Anderson and T. Dierkins, *The Mosquito Book*, Dennoch Press, 1998; C. Coughlan, *Mosquitoes*, Pebble Books, 1999; M. J. Pearce, *Termites: Biology and Pest Management*, CAB International, 1998.

Termite mound

INSURANCE INDUSTRY

INSURANCE INDUSTRY Local insurance is big business in The Bahamas, and has been so since J. S. Johnson & Co., the first local insurance broker, was founded in Nassau in 1854. As of March 2002, there were nine indigenous and 47 foreign insurance companies licensed to do local business in The Bahamas, with 17 licensed agents, 35 brokers who were also agents, and four plain brokers. As far as the general economy of The Bahamas is concerned, however, local insurance business has been dwarfed since the mid-twentieth century by that carried on in The Bahamas by offshore companies (not allowed to trade in The Bahamas or even deal in Bahamian currency), and since the 1980s by those engaged in what is somewhat confusingly called 'captive' insurance.

The Insurance Act of 1969 laid down the structure which made offshore insurance company formation in The Bahamas attractive to foreign companies, especially those based in the United States. The 1969 Insurance Act was amended and augmented by new legislation in 1979 and 1983 (along with the setting up of an Office of the Registrar of Insurance Companies under the Ministry of Finance and Investments), mainly with the purpose of attracting to The Bahamas the rapidly expanding business of captive insurance. This system is basically a form of self-insurance by very large companies, corporations or conglomerates, especially those that operate internationally. A concern such as a global oil or transportation company, or any organisation with a very large number of employees, sets up its own tied (or 'captive') insurance companies, almost invariably offshore. The salient benefit, not often stressed, is that the parent company has access to the revenue from premiums, which it can use (within limitations) for its own investment purposes. The other advantages include lower (or more flexible) premiums, much lower operating costs, the avoidance of brokerage fees, and easier access to the international reinsurance field, as well as (at least initially) the privacy, lower requirements about publishing annual accounts, and the tax deductible benefits enjoyed by all offshore insurance companies.

Within a decade, over 700 captive insurance companies had been established in The Bahamas, almost rivalling banking in the benefits they brought to the Bahamian economy in the way of fees, employment and other local expenditures. Indeed, so serious was the loss of tax revenue to the participating mother countries that from the 1990s increasing restrictions and regulations were applied to offshore captive insurance companies (as indeed to all offshore enterprises). Particularly damaging were the attacks on the secrecy of operations and the lack of sufficiently detailed accounts, and the removal by the US authorities of the domestic income tax deductible privilege for companies based abroad.

Though the Bahamian monetary authorities and the Office of the Insurance Registrar did their utmost to adapt to changing conditions and make operations more transparent, and a new Insurance Law was said to be in preparation in 2004 as part of a rescue operation, the brief golden age of the Bahamian captive insurance industry seemed to be over, with its very future open to doubt.

ISAACS, Sir Kendal George Lamon (1925–1997) Highly distinguished and universally respected lawyer, who has been called 'the finest Prime Minister or Governor-General the Bahamas never had'.

Born the thirteenth child of poor but respectable non-white middle-class parents, Kendal Isaacs was the most gifted all-round student of his day at GOVERNMENT HIGH SCHOOL, of which he was Head Boy in 1942. At 19 he volunteered for service in the Bahamas Battalion of the North Caribbean Regiment, and became one of the very few non-white Bahamians to achieve officer rank, ending World War Two as a 20-year-old lieutenant.

In 1946, after brief employment in the Customs Department, Kendal Isaacs went to Queens' College, Cambridge on a veteran's scholarship, to study for a BA and LLB. An elegant and clever tennis player (often

Sir Kendal Isaacs

Bahamas singles and doubles champion) he was awarded a Cambridge tennis 'Blue' – noting wryly in later years that whereas he did not suffer overt discrimination at Cambridge, he was not asked to represent the Varsity until after he had convincingly won the University championship.

Called to the English and Bahamas Bars in 1950, Isaacs spent two years in private practice before becoming a stipendiary and circuit magistrate. Regarded as both highly talented and politically neutral, he was chosen to be Solicitor General in 1955, and in 1963 became the first Bahamian (let alone non-white) to be appointed Attorney General. After taking a key role as Governor Stapledon's legal adviser at the 1963 constitutional talks in London, he acted briefly as a Supreme Court judge, before returning to a highly successful private practice. He was made Queen's Counsel (QC) in 1968 and served two terms as President of the Bahamas Bar Association.

An Independent Senator from 1965, Kendal Isaacs was Vice-President of the Senate from 1968 to 1971. In that year he was persuaded to take an active role in Opposition politics by those who wanted a well-respected moderate and mediator. It was thought that he might forge an alliance between the remnants of the old UNITED BAHAMIAN PARTY, those who had broken with the PROGRESSIVE LIBERAL PARTY in 1965, and the more recent breakaways of the Free PLP, led by the fiery, ambitious and abrasive Cecil WALLACE-WHITFIELD.

Having won the Fort Montagu seat for the newly created FREE NATIONAL MOVEMENT in the 1972 general election (in which Wallace-Whitfield was defeated), Kendal Isaacs was immediately chosen as Opposition Leader in the House of Assembly. However, his decision to accept the PLP's victory as a mandate for immediate INDEPENDENCE disastrously split the Opposition forces once more, and he resigned from politics on the grounds of ill-health before the next election.

Driven by a belief that the PLP regime and Prime Minister Lynden PINDLING were both corrupt and incompetent, and that he might more effectively lead the Opposition than either Cecil Wallace-Whitfield or Orville Turnquest, Kendal Isaacs returned to the fray in 1982. Convincingly winning the new Delaporte seat, he now led a much stronger and united FNM and relentlessly attacked the regime, especially over the findings of the 1984 Drug Commission. However, his legalistic determination to pursue malefactors through the courts as well as in parliament and in public debates, coupled with his own rather weak voice and shaky command of populist rhetoric, meant that Isaacs was consistently outplayed by the more slippery and charismatic Pindling.

Though he lost his own seat through obvious gerrymandering, Isaacs nobly took the blame for the FNM's unexpected defeat in the 1987 general election and resigned again – this time for good. Worn out by front-line politics, his health steadily declined. After the FNM's eventual victory in 1992 he was knighted, but was obliged to turn down the offer to be Governor-General in succession to Sir Clifford DARLING by the onset of Alzheimer's disease, to which succumbed five years later.

Once widowed, once divorced, and with no children, Sir Kendal Isaacs wed his childhood sweetheart, Miss Patricia Fountain, in 1975, enjoying in his last two decades the personal happiness that had long eluded him. A distinguished person in her own right, Lady Isaacs, after her husband's death, often deputised for Governor-General Orville TURNQUEST when he was away, and is said to have turned down the offer to be the first lady Governor-General on Turnquest's retirement in 2001.

JEROME, FATHER (Monsignor John Hawes), 1876–1956 Accorded almost saintly status as 'the hermit of Cat Island' in his later years, Father Jerome had in fact travelled widely in earlier days, was wise to the ways of the world though not worldly, and was just as notable an architect as a missionary priest.

Born in England in 1876, John Hawes was trained and practised as an architect before discovering a priestly vocation. An Anglo-Catholic, he was ordained into the Church of England at the age of 26 in 1902. He first went to The Bahamas in 1908, serving as a missionary priest in LONG ISLAND for two years. During that brief time he rebuilt the hurricane-battered hill-top church of St Paul's at Clarence Town and designed and built four other Anglican churches in southern Long Island.

Attracted by the ideals of St Francis of Assisi, John Hawes was received into the Roman Catholic Church at the Franciscan friary of Graymoor, New York, in 1911. After a year in service as a layman in Canada, he went to the Beda English College in Rome and was reordained as a Catholic priest on Easter Day 1915. Sent out to the scattered diocese of Geraldton in Western Australia, he served there for 25 years as a missionary and diocesan architect. His work was so esteemed that Pope Pius XI raised him to the rank of Monsignor – a title which he never used, preferring his Franciscan name, Father Jerome.

In 1940, at the age of 64, Father Jerome was given permission by Rome to retire to The Bahamas and live the rest of his life as a hermit. Going to CAT ISLAND, he designed and built with his own hands the hermitage atop the highest hill in The Bahamas which, though tiny, stands out as a landmark along the inner bight of the island. The 204-foot (62-m) hill, formerly called Como Hill, Father Jerome renamed Mount Alvernia, after the mountain close to the home town of St Francis. Approached by a winding path punctuated by stone-carved Stations of the Cross, the hermitage is a beautifully designed miniature, with a conjoined chapel, bell tower, kitchen, study, cloister and sleeping cell all within a 60-foot (18-m) compass. It has been described as akin to hermitages on Mount Athos or in ancient Ireland, or even as a Tolkienesque or Arthurian fantasy; but it is in fact unique.

Father Jerome spent as much time as he could at Mount Alvernia but found himself in constant demand as a counsellor and religious architect throughout The Bahamas. He was loved not just for his wisdom and humility but his invariable sense of humour. Mason and hod-carrier as well as designer, he built a tiny church dedicated to St Francis of Assisi at Old Bight, Cat Island,

Hermitage built by Father Jerome on the highest point in The Bahamas, renamed Mount Alvernia, Cat Island

and the far grander St Peter and Paul's Catholic Church on the hilltop facing his former Anglican St Paul's Church at Clarence Town, Long Island. Most impressive of all, though, was the design and construction of St Augustine's Monastery and School, again on a hilltop, in eastern New Providence, which was ready for occupation by 1950. 'Had Father Jerome's total concept been completed, including the great central church,' wrote Robert Douglas, 'it would I believe have achieved recognition as a "world class" piece of architecture.'

In a manner that would have struck the unpretentious Father Jerome as amusing rather than disappointing, he did not die on Mount Alvernia as he had originally planned. Having broken his hip in a fall, he spent many months at St Augustine's Monastery, before being flown to St Francis Hospital in Miami Beach for an operation. He seemed to be recovering but suddenly took a turn for the worse. At the last still capable of making a joke about a hermit pegging out in the 'horribly unprimitive' surroundings of Miami Beach, he died on 26 June 1956. As he wished, however, his body was carried to Cat Island and interred in a cave on Mount Alvernia which he had long prepared for it.

Further reading: P. Anson, *The Hermit of Cat Island*, Kennedy, 1957; C. J. Barry, *Upon These Rocks: Catholics in The Bahamas*, St John's Abbey Press, 1973; R. Douglas, *Island Heritage: Architecture of The Bahamas*, Darkstream Publications, 1992, 86–96.

JEWISH BAHAMIANS Bahamian Jews are so few as barely to constitute a recognisable minority. This is no mere historical accident; but rather the result of commercial exclusionism abetted by unofficial but effective anti-semitism. Only in recent years has being a Jew been regarded as irrelevant to one's acceptability as a professional, business person or settler in The Bahamas.

Unlike many West Indian colonies, The Bahamas never had an influx of 'Portuguese' (Sephardic) Jews. The first Jewish arrivals were Ashkenazi (Yiddish-speaking) businessmen – most of them non-observant in religion – at the tail end of a migration that had carried them from eastern Europe through the northern United States to southern Florida between the 1880s and the 1920s. It was well known that influential persons – notably the owner of the British Colonial Hotel, Allen Munson – were determined that Nassau would not welcome Jews, whom they claimed had already almost taken over Miami. Yet some Jewish businessmen boldly attempted to extend their operations into The Bahamas, then enjoying the boom of the rum-running era.

Their pioneer was Moses Garfunkel, who opened a branch of his Miami-based Home Furniture Company in Nassau in 1923, being succeeded there by his son Joseph in the following year. The Garfunkels easily undercut both the Bay Street stores and local craftsmen, by taking advantage of their connections in the United States, by bulk buying and shipping, and by the power of aggressive advertising, promotional techniques and easy payment terms. Personally popular, especially among his poorer customers, for his cheerfulness, sense of humour and generosity, Joseph Garfunkel suffered bitter opposition from his Bay Street rivals – though they were very willing to learn from his methods of buying, shipping and selling. Garfunkel's cause was not helped by two less scrupulous Jewish firms that opened up in Nassau in 1926; one that advertised itself as 'the store with a conscience' and the other, a tailor claiming to be a branch of a London firm, that promised to undercut local tailors (mostly middle-class non-whites) by 50 per cent and looked set to put them out of business.

Restrictions were placed on all foreign businessmen as the boom period was succeeded by the Great Depression, and Joseph Garfunkel was one of the few Jews who survived in Nassau. Another who suffered discrimination yet persevered was Austin Levy, who made no progress in Nassau but was allowed to purchase 2,000 acres in Eleuthera in 1936 and developed Hatchet Bay Farms. Similarly, when the Bahamian authorities were compelled to accept two highly qualified Jewish doctors escaping from Hitler's Germany in the late 1930s, they were only given Out Island postings and were glad to move on as soon as they could.

Only after World War Two did anti-semitism fade and conditions for Jews improve. One of those who engendered greater tolerance was the brilliant doctor Meyer Rassin, who opened Nassau's first private hospital in the 1950s. Other Jewish professionals, businessmen and settlers felt relatively comfortable in the developing 'second city' of Freeport, which, unlike Nassau, had a Jewish place of worship by the 1980s. Perhaps a sign for the future is the fact that the creator and owner of the *ATLANTIS* mega-hotel in the 1990s, Sol Kerzner, is himself a Jewish South African.

JITNEYS Neither New Providence nor Freeport have official municipal transportation services. Instead, besides the taxis and tour cars mainly to serve the tourists, they have the remarkably effective free-enterprise system of 35-seater buses called jitneys. In the last twenty years, jitneys have become an indispensable feature of daily life in the two most populated Bahamian islands. In a novel way they also exhibit traditional Bahamian characteristics: they are ingenious, free-wheeling and cheerfully adaptable to needs, with the operators and drivers showing something of the *élan* of the old buccaneers.

No one seems to know quite how many jitneys there are, but it is several hundred. Ostensibly, each is licensed by the Ministry of Transportation and assigned to a particular route (numbered and listed on the jitney's front) and the Ministry holds itself responsible for checking such matters as insurance and safety. In practice, though, it seems that anyone who can raise the capital to buy a Toyota or Nissan bus (as much as $75,000 for one spanking new or as little as $7,500 for one already somewhat worn and torn) can enter the business, so that competition is fierce, especially on the most travelled routes.

Everyone calls them jitneys, but the word jitney scarcely ever appears on the side of the vehicle. Instead there is the name of the owner-operator (the great majority owning one or at most two jitneys), grander words such as Bus, Transport or Transportation System, and adjectives designed to promise something special in the way of service in an intensely competitive field: Economy (though the fare is everywhere the same), Reliant, Reliable, Rapid, Competent, Superior, even Classical or (our favourite) Ecstasy. Many jitneys are also inscribed with mottoes or words of advice, such as 'Jesus Saves' or the somewhat ambiguous intended pun, 'Have you remembered to pray?'

Car drivers (and there is now more than one car for every two persons in New Providence) complain that the jitneys clog up the traffic at the focus of most routes in downtown Nassau, and grumble about the way that their drivers jockey in and out of traffic and make sudden stops and darting starts to let down and after taking up passengers. The atmosphere inside each vehicle, except to the most nervous newcomers, is much more relaxed and sociable. Reggae, rock or rap (not often goombay) blares from the hi-fi system. Passengers loudly exchange news and gossip with old friends and pleasantries with strangers. Most congenially of all, as each new passenger steps into the vehicle, whether regular customer or not, he or she almost invariably calls out 'good day' to those within, calling 'goodbye' and 'thank you' to the driver as they leave.

The jitney driver, as on a Family Island mail boat on a larger scale, is captain and chief character of his four-wheeled ship. With eyes wide open for every fleeting crevice in the traffic and any chance passenger on the sidewalk, and ears cocked for a sudden cry of 'bus stop' from a passenger, he yet has a spare hand to collect the standard one dollar fare or to give change, and even enough concentration left over to carry on a conversation or give directions to an alighting tourist. Very few of them are owner-drivers. Nearly all must work every angle to pay the owner a pre-determined minimum return each day, keeping the surplus. But notwithstanding the discontent of those with private cars, without the jitney people-movers, their determined drivers and their enterprising owners, not only would downtown Nassau and Freeport become even more hopelessly traffic-clogged, but the whole economy of which they are the heart might soon expire from a kind of congestive cardiac failure.

Dame Doris Johnson

JOHNSON, Dame Doris L. (1919–1998) Redoubtable feminist and political progressive; the first woman to run for the legislature (1962), and the first female Cabinet Minister (1968–73). Third in a family of ten children, Doris Johnson (née Sands) taught 17 years in public schools before she was able to go abroad to study for a degree and formal teaching qualifications. In between obtaining a BA in the United States and an MEd in Canada, she was the most dynamic and effective member of the WOMEN'S SUFFRAGE MOVEMENT, which won the vote for women in 1960.

An ardent supporter of the PROGRESSIVE LIBERAL PARTY, Doris Johnson stood for the party in the 1962 general election, coming fifth in the poll in the three-seat ELEUTHERA constituency. In the same year, she completed her studies for a PhD in Education at the University of New York, but was unable to find a job in a government school in the Bahamas. In 1965 she was the only female member of the PLP delegation to the United Nations, and took up a teaching appointment at Southern University in Louisiana for two years. With the PLP victory in 1967, however, she returned to Nassau and was appointed the first female Senator. In the following year she was made Government Leader in the Senate and Minister without portfolio in Premier Lynden PINDLING'S second Cabinet.

In 1969 Senator Johnson was appointed Minister of Transport when Warren Levarity was forced to resign with an alleged drinking problem. This move was not popular with ambitious backbenchers in a House of Assembly that was still exclusively male, though Johnson remained in Cabinet until 1973. She was then President of the Senate until her retirement in 1979, at which time she was awarded the title of Dame (DBE) by the Queen. Besides being the most notable pioneer of Bahamian women's rights and the highest woman achiever during the PLP years, Dame Doris Johnson was the objective historian of the phase in Bahamian history which she herself memorably christened 'the Quiet Revolution'.

Further reading: D. L. Johnson, *The Quiet Revolution in the Bahamas*, Family Islands Press, 1972.

JOHNSTON, Randolph W. (1904–1992) Charismatic and idealistic Canadian-born sculptor, who in mid-life found refuge from the modern world in Little Harbour, ABACO, overcame the difficulties of a Robinson Crusoe existence, recovered a flagging inspiration, and in the following three decades produced work of increasing distinction and relevance to The Bahamas.

In the winter of 1951, Johnston threw up his job and moved with his wife and three young boys to isolated MAN-O'-WAR CAY, where they rented a white-painted clapboard house for a few pounds a month. Sinking all their savings into the purchase and refurbishing of one of 'Uncle Will' Albury's schooners, the *Langosta*, the Johnstons roamed the islands as far south as the EXUMAS looking for a place of their own to settle, and an agreeable way to make a livelihood. In 1952 they found their Eden on the Abaco mainland 20 miles (32 km) south of MARSH HARBOUR and a few miles north of CHEROKEE SOUND. Little Harbour is a semicircular, beach-fringed anchorage approached between two scenic headlands, with an entrance which is narrow and shallow but safe in all winds. With no access by road, it was uninhabited except for the keeper of the light on the southern point, and in those days all the land could be bought for less than a hundred pounds an acre.

For almost two years the Johnstons lived in a cave, fishing and attempting to grow crops for subsistence, but only surviving by chartering the *Langosta*, collecting and selling shells in bulk, and making what they could from the sale of driftwood carvings and ceramics, fired in a home-made kiln. At times their efforts seemed hopeless, and Johnston had periodically to retreat to the States to seek and complete sculpture commissions. At first this was merely a necessary chore. But as time went on, both Randolph and Margot Johnston found a renewed enthusiasm and inspiration from their adopted home. Their work took on a new maturity and began to be in demand – at steadily rising and eventually high prices. By the mid-1960s, the Johnstons had almost achieved their ideal: a self-contained artistic community, with comfortable though not luxurious quarters and its own self-made but effective pottery kilns and bronze-casting foundry, in which the Johnston family and a shifting circle of apprentices and acolytes could work and learn without unwanted intrusions from the outside world. They did, however, maintain a bar, which they opened for visiting yachtsmen. It was in this ambience that Randolph Johnston produced the figurative works of his prime, such as the joyous depiction of a naked young couple called *Springtime* (1967), the stark *Death and Everyman* (1968) and the stunning *Nine Ages of Man* (1971) – originals or copies of which are still displayed at Little Harbour. At the same time, his wife Margot, son Peter, and daughter-in-law Debbie were producing their almost equally accomplished ceramics, carvings and castings of local birds, fishes and people.

Just as Randolph Johnston's work owed much to the Bahamian environment, so it became increasingly admired and respected locally in The Bahamas. From the late 1960s he received several commissions for the decoration of new government buildings, and for two bronze figures for JUMBEY VILLAGE at the time of Independence. His most notable Bahamian work – perhaps his masterpiece – is the poignant life-size bronze figure of a black woman cradling her naked child, to be seen in Nassau's Rawson Square, placed on a plinth of brain coral from the Little Harbour reef. Entitled simply *Bahamian Woman*, this was commissioned by the Bahamas government and unveiled by Prime Minister Lynden Pindling in July 1974.

Randolph Johnston, in his last years an impressive though unassuming white-bearded patriarch, died in 1992. His work at Little Harbour is still carried on by his son Peter and a former pupil, Richard Appaldo (who finished the bust by Johnston of Sir Milo Butler, also to be seen in Rawson Square). Though advertised and run as 'Pete's Pub and Gallery' the operation is not commercialised to a degree of which Johnston and his wife would have disapproved. Their spirit and achievements live on in the museum, studios and unique bronze foundry – of which guided tours can be had on request.

Further reading: R. W. Johnston (assisted by D. Johnston), *Artist on His Island: A Study in Self Reliance*, Little Harbour Press, 1975; E. M. Dahlgren, *Randolph Wardell Johnstone: Feel Intensely, Imagine Vividly, Control Purely*, Magazine Street Press, 1997; www.villasetc.com/petes

Mother and Child sculpture by Randolph Johnston

JUDICIAL SYSTEM

JUDICIAL SYSTEM Even more than the system of legislation, the Bahamian judicial system is the most obvious and important inheritance from England. The structure of courts, the personnel, dress and rituals, along with the hallowed principles of the separation of judicial powers and non-elective judges, are the same. Practitioners' qualifications are mutually recognised, and a direct connection between the two legal structures remains in the continuing role of the Privy Council in England as the ultimate court of appeal for The Bahamas. Most importantly, the laws applied are identical and interchangeable, with the exception of the local statute laws specific to The Bahamas.

From the earliest days of the Empire the English judicial system was extended to England's colonies as far as possible. In The Bahamas from the time of the Lord PROPRIETORS (1670–1718) there was an appointed Chief Justice and subordinate appointed magistrates (Justices of the Peace), exercising both criminal and civil jurisdiction. The Governor acted as an appeal judge, a judge in the frequent chancery and far rarer ecclesiastical cases, and as Vice-Admiral appointed the Judge and officials of the vitally important Vice-Admiralty Court. One deviation from English practice was that as slavery developed, special slave courts were constituted, to accommodate the legal fiction that slaves were property, not persons, and therefore could not act in their own defence.

As in England and all other colonies, respectable local gentry were chosen to be unpaid Justices of the Peace, though three stipendiary circuit magistrates were added to the roster towards the end of slavery, ostensibly to protect the interests of the slaves. These paid justices were retained when the special slave courts were abolished upon the emancipation of the slaves (1834–8), and their numbers and powers gradually increased as the JP system relatively declined. Before the end of the nineteenth century, in another small deviation from metropolitan practice, the men appointed to be Out Island Commissioners were given extended magisterial powers, civil and criminal – a function that is still accorded to Family Island Administrators.

During the nineteenth century, as the volume of judicial business increased and became ever more vital, the local judiciary gradually expanded and became more sophisticated. The number of courts below the Supreme Court multiplied, and with it the number of practising and qualified attorneys and solicitors. By 1900 there was a proud and flourishing local Bar, with its own training system recognised as nominally (if not quite in prestige) equal to qualification through English universities and the Inns of Court in London.

This steady expansion was eclipsed by the huge changes made necessary in the twentieth century by the six-fold increase in the population and the even greater expansion and complication of legal and judicial business. By 2000, the Bahamian judicial system was commonly described as the largest, busiest and most efficient of any country of similar size in the world. The highest tribunal in the country is the Court of Appeal, which sits permanently throughout the year. Its five judges are appointed by the Governor-General and include a residing president, two resident and two non-resident judges. Generally, three judges sit to conduct hearings. Customarily they are leading judges drawn from all over the Commonwealth and they need have no formal ties with The Bahamas.

The Chief Justice or one of the other eight Justices who are appointed by the Governor-General preside in the Supreme Court in Nassau, which has general, civil and criminal jurisdiction. In addition, there is a Supreme Court with two resident Justices in Freeport, Grand Bahama, dealing with the northern region of The Bahamas, comprising Bimini, Abaco and Grand Bahama. The two Supreme Courts hear civil and criminal matters throughout the year, beginning on the second Wednesday in January.

New Providence has no less than fifteen magistrates' courts – including a coroner's court, a drug court, a firearms court, a night civil court and two night traffic courts. Grand Bahama (with its population now almost 50,000) has three magistrates' courts – two in Freeport and one in Eight Mile Rock. The magistrates' courts are presided over by stipendiary and circuit magistrates, who include a chief magistrate, a deputy magistrate (in Freeport) and two senior magistrates as well as a dozen subordinate – including one stationed in Abaco. These magistrates exercise summary jurisdiction in criminal matters and in civil matters involving amounts not exceeding $5,000. In addition, all Family Island Administrators exercise summary jurisdiction in criminal matters of a less serious nature and in civil matters involving amounts not exceeding $400. There are also sixteen Justices of the Peace appointed to hear minor offences in New Providence.

In 2000 the Bahamas Bar Association consisted of more than 500 members – its numbers especially boosted by those lawyers specialising in the profitable area of commercial law. An Inner Bar, besides judges and senior government law officers, included five Queen's Counsel (QCs), eminent local lawyers appointed by the Governor-General on the advice of the Prime Minister after a rigorous selection process, who are qualified to represent the Crown in court. Though legal training and a calling

The Supreme Court, Nassau

to the Bar in England still carries much prestige, it is even less than formerly the common route to being called to the Bahamian Bar. A majority of lawyers now obtain their law degree and other qualifications through the no less rigorous but more convenient law schools of the UNIVERSITY OF THE WEST INDIES in Barbados, Jamaica and Trinidad, and at the local Law School opened in 1998 and named after the distinguished Bahamian lawyer and statesman, the Hon. Eugene DUPUCH QC.

Despite this apparent devolution, the Bahamian judicial system, its customs and rituals, remain resolutely traditional. Judges, court officials and lawyers wear the customary wigs and gowns and observe the age-worn punctilio. The Chief Justice remains an august and respected figure, virtually equal in his own sphere to the Governor-General and Prime Minister. This is symbolised in one of the most impressive and popular annual events, the formal opening of the Supreme Court in January – when most of the members of the Bahamas Bar appear in their finery and the Chief Justice inspects a guard of honour, while the band of the ROYAL BAHAMAS POLICE FORCE plays and a large crowd cheers.

JUMBEY VILLAGE A visionary project designed at the time of INDEPENDENCE permanently to celebrate the authentic Bahamian cultural heritage, which unfortunately failed but left seeds for future developments.

Jumbey Village was very largely the brainchild of the ardent nationalist and populist MP Edmund Moxey. It originated in an annual Jumbey Festival started by Moxey in his impoverished Coconut Grove constituency in 1969. In 1973, when Moxey was Permanent Secretary responsible for Culture, a permanent site was acquired quite far south on Blue Hills Road, on which houses, craft shops and a Bahamian museum (with exhibits purchased from the private museum on downtown East Street owned by Allison Dean) were constructed. However, a combination of a badly chosen location (too far south for tourist traffic and with unattractive surroundings), mismanagement, and, above all, the fact that Moxey fell out with the PLP over its financial support for a rival Goombay Festival and on more personal grounds, doomed the enterprise. Within a couple of years, craftsmen and artists abandoned the site, the buildings deteriorated and were eventually demolished, being replaced by the grandiose main office of the National Insurance Board.

Fortunately, the majority of its historical artefacts were rescued from Jumbey Village by the Department of ARCHIVES, which planned to use them for their own displays and as the nucleus of the long-planned national heritage MUSEUM. Other aspects of Jumbey Village have also been retained in more favourable locations; with the help of government in the permanent JUNKANOO display on Prince George Wharf, and with the commercial impetus of ordinary Bahamians in the craft markets on downtown BAY STREET, CABLE BEACH and PARADISE ISLAND, and, most spontaneously of all, in the thriving cultural village which has developed just west of Nassau City at ARAWAK CAY.

JUNKANOO

JUNKANOO A popular year-end festivity derived from slavery days, with roots in Africa. Found in Afro-American communities in several countries (including Jamaica, Belize and North Carolina) for several reasons it has gained and retained its strongest hold in The Bahamas, where it is the distinctive national festival – now for all sections of the population.

Strictly a masked and costumed parade with GOOMBAY drumming and strident music to a pulse-beat rhythm, Junkanoo has affinities with the masked rituals of West Africa. It developed during slavery as the 'legitimate catharsis' encouraged by the masters around Christmas and New Year, between the rigours of planting and harvesting cane on the sugar plantations. Though essentially secular and with few if any affinities to European customs, it has similarities to the pre-Lenten and crop-over festival of Carnival found in Trinidad and many other former colonies with a Catholic tradition.

Explanations for the origins of the word Junkanoo vary. Some authorities say that it is a corruption of the French *gens inconnus* (unknown persons); others that it derives from an actual person who lived in West Africa, called John Conny or John Canoe. Most likely, though, is the derivation suggested by Frederic G. Cassidy, the Jamaican etymologist:

> *Any etymology proposed for John Canoe must recognise that the dancer so named was always the central figure in the celebration –* the *leading dancer, grotesquely dressed, wearing a mask or some other disguising but distinctive headdress, who, with his train of followers, leapt about acrobatically and fearsomely as they wound their way through the village collecting contributions. The most likely source was the Ewe language, in which* dzonc *means a magician or sorcerer, and* kunu *means something terrible or deadly, a cause of death. Dzonco is also the name by which a sorcerer calls himself, and* nu *means a man – thus, 'sorcerer-man' or 'witch-doctor'.* (Jamaica Talk: Three Hundred Years of the English Language in Jamaica, Macmillan, *1961, 256–80)*

In the non-plantation Bahamas, Junkanoo developed a special significance, especially after slavery ended, being not just the joyous letting off of steam during the year-end holiday season, but the only time in the year that the mass of the people living Over-the-Hill in NASSAU boldly descended on the white bastion of down-town BAY

Twenty-first century Junkanoo on Bay Street

212

JUNKANOO

STREET and virtually took it over. Though the white elite and authorities did their utmost to regard the parade as no more than a picturesque spectacle (originally only on New Year's morning but later Boxing Day morning as well), their enjoyment had an edge of panic, as they became aware that the celebration verged ever closer to a political demonstration, or even riot.

Consequently, at times of social or political tension Junkanoo was banned, and only allowed back under strict regulations – as to the organisation of the groups, the type of costumes and music, and the timetable and route that the parade should follow. This regulatory trend developed further as the Development Board adopted Junkanoo as a means of attracting tourists, and commercial businesses increasingly sponsored Junkanoo groups. By the late 1950s and early 1960s, the formerly almost spontaneous festival had became a major competition, involving much money and months of preparation. Ever larger rival groups – representing different sections Over-the-Hill – competed with ever larger and more elaborate costumes and musical ensembles, presenting themes as seemingly irrelevant as 'Cops and Robbers' and 'Cowboys and Indians'. Only a few 'scrap gangs' of more or less impromptu 'rushers' with tattered costumes and basic drums, scrapers, cowbells and conch shells (or bugles) sustained the authentic spirit of the original Junkanoo – in which the key personage was the semi-mysterious, semi-sinister, prancing figure of Pitchy-Patchy, alias the sorcerer, *dzonkunu*.

Yet Junkanoo grew stronger even as it changed. It was co-opted by the ruling PROGRESSIVE LIBERAL PARTY as the People's Festival, with Prime Minister PINDLING himself declaring 'I am a Junkanoo' and enthusiastically taking part. This has injected a greater relevance, if at some risk of overkill. No longer is Junkanoo almost a male preserve, as more and more women and girls take part. More remarkably, it is no longer an exclusively black festival, as Bahamians of all colours and classes participate, rather than just watch from the outside. Major Junkanoo parades are held in all the chief islands at year's end, and Junkanoo groups, with their goombay music, pop up at every special occasion throughout the year, adding a truly national spice and fervour to such events as the competition for the Davis Cup in tennis, or the Carifta Games.

Further reading: E. C. Bethel, *Junkanoo: Festival of The Bahamas*, Macmillan Caribbean, 1991; M. Craton, 'Decoding Pitchy-Patchy: The Roots, Branches and Essence of Junkanoo', *Slavery and Abolition*, 16, 1, 1995, 14–44.

'Junkanoo Magic': acrylic on canvas by Brent Malone, 1987

KEY WEST Now a tourist destination proclaiming the distinction of being the southernmost city in the contiguous United States, Key West might also claim without undue exaggeration to have once been the westernmost outpost of The Bahamas.

Its name a corruption of the Spanish *Cayo Hueso* (Isle of Bones), Key West is the pendant of a necklace of islets extending a hundred miles (160 km) south and west of the Florida mainland. Sitting at the northern edge of the entrance to the Florida Strait, it lies a mere 90 miles (145 km) from the coast of Cuba and is just as close to CAY SAL, the nearest island of The Bahamas.

Just after Spain sold Florida to the United States in 1819, Cayo Hueso was sold to John Simonton of Mobile, Alabama, Admiral Matthew Perry occupied it, and a US naval depot was established. But it was the 'CONCHY JOE' mariners of Abaco who saw Key West's potential as a base for WRECKING and SPONGE FISHING and flocked to the area from the mid-1820s. Many migrated with their families in the 1830s and 1840s through fear of and distaste for the consequences of the EMANCIPATION of the Bahamian slaves, setting up in the still slave-holding US a community in appearance and lifestyle very much like that which they had left behind on the Abaco Cays. By 1849 it was said that two-thirds of the Abaco whites had either migrated to Key West or had close family connections there.

Being pioneers in such a favourable location, many of the Conchy Joe migrants prospered; none more so than William Curry of GREEN TURTLE CAY. Migrating to Key West in 1837, he became the uncrowned king of the wreckers and in due course built up a large shipyard, and owned the first ice factory and electricity generating plant. He was said to be the first Florida millionaire when he died in 1896. Other successful pioneers included the Sawyer who became the most prosperous local merchant, Richard Kemp, who exported the first sponges from Key West to New York, and John Lowe Jr., who owned what was said to have been the largest sponging fleet in Florida.

In 1892 it was reported that 8,000 of the 25,000 inhabitants of Key West were Bahamians. But by then the town and the racial composition of its people had substantially changed. With the ending of slavery in the US in 1865 many Bahamian non-whites had chosen to join the migration, attracted by employment opportunities in sponging, wrecking and various craftsman trades, as well as by the fact that their wages were paid in cash rather than by the TRUCK SYSTEM. In the 1880s there was a further wave of migration as the civil war in Cuba (and the opportunities offered by the US market) persuaded Cuban cigar manufacturers to move to Key West – attracting non-white Bahamian as well as Cuban workers. So many emigrated from New Providence, Harbour Island, Eleuthera and Bimini to Key West around this time that the Registrar General gave this as the main reason for the decline in the rate of population growth in The Bahamas between 1881 and 1891.

Into the twentieth century Key West retained its character as a Bahamian-Cuban-West Indian rather than American city. However, the balance changed steadily once H.M. Flagler's railroad linked it to mainland Florida in 1915, and even faster once the railroad was replaced by the Overseas Highway (with its 42 bridges) in 1938. Key West is now thoroughly Americanised, and much more akin to the rest of Southern Florida than to an Abaco township, or even NASSAU.

Yet more than a hint of the Bahamian connection remains. Native Key Westers proudly call themselves 'Conchs' and deny the title to mere residents. The conch in several of its traditional manifestations is served in many restaurants. The local phone book is still full of people with Bahamian (especially Conchy Joe) surnames: Albury, Curry, Kemp, Knowles, Lowe, Pinder and Sawyer. Most impressive of all, there are still many Bahamian style wooden houses surviving, lovingly restored and maintained, and proudly displayed.

Further reading: J. B. Browne, *Key West: The Old and New*, St Augustine, 1912; 'The Conch Connection. Key West: Almost in the Family', *The Bahamas Handbook and Businessman's Annual, 1986*, Dupuch Publications; R. Pierce, 'From the Bahamas to Florida', *Florida Genealogist*, 11, 1987, 19–24; H. Johnson, 'Late Nineteenth and Early Twentieth Century Labour Migration to Florida', in *The Bahamas in Slavery and Freedom*, Ian Randle Press, 1991, 163–80.

KNOWLES, Sir Durward Champion yachtsman. Born in 1925 and educated at QUEEN'S COLLEGE, Durward Knowles followed his father to become a Nassau harbour pilot. A life-long sailor whose exceptional talent was recognised early, he came to specialise in the two-man Star class boat introduced to the Bahamas by the playboy Alfred De Marigny in the early 1940s. Knowles's first notable success was a third place in the 1946 World Championships in Cuba. This was equalled when he and Sloane Farrington won the first Bahamian Olympic medal (a bronze) in the Melbourne Olympics of 1956, and eclipsed when he and Cecil Cooke won gold in the Tokyo Olympics of 1964. Though continuing to sail for pleasure, Durward Knowles devoted much of his spare time to good causes, especially the welfare of the disabled.

He was knighted by the Queen in 1996. The Cheshire Home for the disabled established by the Rotary Club under his auspices, was renamed the Sir Durward Knowles Cheshire Home.

Further reading: D. Hanks Jr., *Driven by the Stars*, 1992.

KWEYOLE (Haitian Creole Language)

Kweyole, or Haitian Creole, is the authentic French and African-based language spoken as a first language by 95 per cent of all Haitians (and the only language of perhaps 80 per cent of those) – which means that it is spoken by as many as one in ten of all people currently living in The Bahamas.

Kweyole (sometimes spelled kreyole) originated as a pidginised form of French spoken in the western half of Hispaniola (Haiti) when it was colonised by the French from the mid-seventeenth century and large numbers of African slaves were imported. Though Haitian Creole is said to be no closer to French than Italian is to Latin, clearly it has a French base, but with extensive borrowings from the lexicon and structure of African languages, especially Wolof, Fon, Mandingo and Ewe.

Kweyole was declared an official language only as recently as 1961 and attempts to make it the official language of instruction in Haitian schools during the 1970s failed. Since then, though, it has been at least a parallel language in the media and the chosen medium of several distinguished creative writers.

If there are difficulties for kweyole in Haiti itself these are magnified for the third of all Haitians who now live abroad, not least for the 30–40,000 living in The Bahamas. Speaking kweyole exclusively among themselves maintains a strong sense of Haitian identity. But this is two-edged. Far from enriching the common culture of the adopted country, it highlights and reinforces differences and promotes distrust.

Both sides would clearly benefit by a wider knowledge, if not general acceptance, of kweyole. Progress in this respect is slow and not without controversy. With more competent and respected interpreters available, Haitians get a fairer day in the courts (and the stereotype of the Haitian as a criminal is gradually eroded). There is not yet a Bahamian kweyole newspaper, but at least one Bahamian paper has regular articles in kweyole. The churches, of most denominations, have led the way in catering to (and recruiting) Haitians by holding services in kweyole, with bilingual ministers, usually of Haitian extraction. This trend, however, is opposed by those (not necessarily all racial bigots) who believe it fosters separation rather than integration. Similarly, the suggestion that schools in the areas of densest Haitian settlement should hold at least some of their classes in kweyole has not yet come close to implementation.

To give some notion of the printed appearance and sound of kweyole, and of the distance it has moved from French – as well the common fund of proverbial language between Haitians, French and English, here are a couple of Haitian proverbs, with translations:

Haitian: *Balai neuf balai bien*
French: *Un balai neuf balaye bien*
English: *A new broom sweeps clean*

Haitian: *Boef pas janm bouqué pòte còne li.*
French: *Un boeuf n'est jamais fatigué de porter ses cornes.*
English: *An ox never gets tired of carrying his own horns.*

And, a test for the linguistically adept (and biblically literate), four familiar verses from different books of the Bible, without translations:

Nan konmansman, Bondye keye syèl la ak late a. (Genesis 1: 1)

Se yon sòm David. Seyé a se gadò mwen, mwen p'ap janm manke anyem. (Psalms 23: 2)

Anvan Bondye te kreye anyem, Pawòl la te la. Pawòl la te avèk Bondye. Sa Bondye te ye, se sa Pawol la te ye tou. (John 1: 1)

Menm si mwen ta konn pale tout kalite lang moun pale ansanm ak lang zanj yo pale, si m' pa gen renmen nan kè m', bèl pawòl mwen yo pa pi plis pase yon tanbou k'ap fè anpil bwi, pase yon klòch k'ap sonnen. (I Corinthians 13: 1)

Further reading: W. R. Turnbull, *Creole Made Easy: A Simple Introduction to Haitian Creole for English Speaking People*, Mountain Maid, 2000; N. Shapiro et al. (eds.), *The Oxford Picture Dictionary: English/Haitian Creole: Angle/Kreyole Ayishyen*, Oxford University Press, 2000; www.kreyol.com/dictionary.html; www.kreyole.com/creole-bible/bib-la.html

LAKE CUNNINGHAM Some 2½ miles (4 km) long and a third of mile (0.5 km) wide, this scenic lake is located between the two highest ridges in the interior of NEW PROVIDENCE. Though it is well over a mile from the sea with no visible connection, its brackish waters rise and fall slightly with the tide, indicating a circulation that keeps them free from the odour that characterises more stagnant Bahamian ponds. Technically speaking, Lake Cunningham is a textbook example of the linear or crescent-shaped Bahamian *ridgeland lake*, formed wherever the land between two ridges falls below the level of the water-table – as distinct from a *rockland lake*, occurring in shallow, saucer-like depressions in the flat rockland, such as New Providence's LAKE KILLARNEY to the south-west, or Harrold Pond to the south-east.

Named after the LOYALIST general who owned most of the adjacent land (and many slaves), Lake Cunningham was until the early twentieth century a remote spot for picnickers and duck shooters. This changed after the 'inter-field road' between Oakes and Windsor airfields was built along its southern shore in World War Two, and luxurious mansions gradually filled the slope of the ridge to the north. Its ducks long chased away by the flow of road traffic and the occasional use of the lake by small seaplanes, the lake still provides one of the most attractive vistas in the New Providence interior, especially when viewed from the top of the southern ridge – which, at 123 feet (37 m), is the island's highest point.

LAKE KILLARNEY Probably named by a homesick and somewhat myopic Irishman, this body of shallow brackish water is by far the largest lake of NEW PROVIDENCE island. Its 4,000 acres are exceeded only by INAGUA's Lake Rosa, the serpentine Great Lake on SAN SALVADOR (which COLUMBUS noted), and some of the sea-connected lakes of northern ANDROS.

In common with Lake Rosa, the Great Lake on southern CAT ISLAND and the considerably smaller Harrold Pond on New Providence, Lake Killarney is a textbook example of the Bahamian rockland lake. Formed in shallow depressions in rock tableland since the time of the last Ice Age, even more than Bahamian ridgeland lakes, rockland lakes are characterised by islands and margins of mangrove growth, and are surrounded by marshland. Though rockland lakes expand temporarily during times of heavy rains, their general tendency is to shrink before the steady encroachment of mangroves and other plants, and silt build-up, to become permanent marshes.

Lake Killarney lacks the scenic attractiveness of nearby LAKE CUNNINGHAM. The adjacent Nassau International Airport inhibits house-building and has driven away the majority of the wildfowl that attracted hunters before World War Two. Of its nature, the lake and its surrounds remain difficult to access or traverse. However, this gives the area the distinction of being an almost pristine wetland wilderness, of great scientific interest, in almost incredibly close proximity to Nassau's teeming residential build-up.

Lake Killarney, New Providence

LAND TENURE Entitlement to land in The Bahamas has always been, and still is, a complex matter. Historically, it has been affected by the interplay of many different factors: by the ratio between the amount of usable land and the number of inhabitants; by the conflict between, on the one hand, aboriginal and African customs of tribal distribution and common use, and on the other, European concepts of real estate; by competing customs and laws governing the acquisition of land by Crown grant, purchase, inheritance or squatters' rights; and finally by the different and subtly changing concepts of absolute freehold, leasehold, family (or 'generational') land, and commonage. In modern times, when land has come under pressure from the expanding population, development, and the will to make profit through land transactions, the need to have clear title has become paramount. Yet even today there is still no absolutely uniform, effective or compulsory system of land registration, or an accurate and complete national survey of land ownership. The one constant since the achievement of majority rule and INDEPENDENCE, and the concomitant expansion of the principle of BAHAMIANISATION, is the determination that the land of The Bahamas is the national patrimony, not to be easily, and, if possible, not permanently, alienated to non-Bahamians.

The pressure of an expanding population in the Greater Antilles was the main cause of the migration of the 'Sub-Taino' Lucayans into The Bahamas. There seems to have been territorial demarcation between different kinship groups of Lucayans, and some competition, even conflict, between them over land. But in general there was more than sufficient for all groupings, with the land of each held in common and distributed by chiefs (*caziques*) according to each family unit's need.

European imperialism overrode this by arrogantly assuming that lands which it claimed (whether by right of alleged discovery, papal grant, conquest or effective settlement) were extensions of their own sovereign territories. New lands thus were *real estate*, that is, belonged basically to the crown, and were to be sub-granted, either to lordly tenants-in-chief in the feudal manner, or to the companies increasingly becoming involved in the imperial enterprise. The Spaniards had no use for The Bahamas once they had found more fertile lands, and especially once they had emptied the islands of their native people. The earliest English settlers, the Eleutherian Adventurers, regarded the land as common property and, with their few slaves, worked the best spare land they could find, for timber and subsistence crops.

During the regime of the Lord Proprietors (1670–1718), though the more able and energetic of their governors attempted to organise and record the distribution of lands on a more formal basis – at least for the island of New Providence and its offshore satellite, Hog Island (now Paradise Island). Following the model of other colonies, a distinction was made between land reserved for the Proprietors, estates granted to settlers on the payment of a nominal quit rent (to indicate that it was still technically leased), house-lots in the embryo township (christened NASSAU in 1695) granted on a basis much closer to absolute freehold, and lands available to be worked in common. This attempted system fell apart, however, partly through a dispute over Hog Island (which Governor Trott had allocated to himself but the settlers regarded as common land), but mainly because on the advent of the PIRATES the colony descended into near-anarchy.

Things did not immediately improve with the royal takeover of The Bahamas in 1718. Governor Woodes ROGERS's first registrar, Samuel Gohier, himself a notorious land speculator, absconded with all the records to England, where they were lost. Starting with an important Act for Settling Claims and the Payment of Quit Rents among the first raft of Bahamian laws in 1729, the system was gradually improved and regularised, though complicated by the fact that the residual land rights of the Proprietors were not bought out until 1787. Governor Thomas SHIRLEY in 1773 reported that only a fraction of the land was occupied with any sort of formal title (and that only in Nassau, New Providence, Hog and Rose Islands). For the rest, there was a confused mixture of four types of claim: original Proprietary grants, grants by Proprietary delegates and different Governors, and by what were called 'warrants of survey' – that is, claims based simply on uninterrupted possession and recognised development over a period of years. Much 'waste' land was simply worked for a period of years without title or claim (or even clear boundaries), before its occupier moved on somewhere else.

The situation changed radically once the American LOYALISTS descended upon The Bahamas after 1783 with their slaves, trebling the population and settling many islands for the first time. Land was freely granted to ostensible planters on a 'headright' basis – 40 acres for each white family head, and 20 for each dependent, family member or slave, for an annual quit rent of two shillings per hundred acres. The most promising islands – such as EXUMA, LONG ISLAND, and CAT ISLAND, as well as New Providence – were completely divided up, with almost no unallocated Crown Land left over. Though all government land grants were theoretically conditional on development and still subject to a nominal quit rent, in practice they could be bought and sold, bequeathed and inherited under the rules of English common law. As long as COTTON-growing and salt-production prospects remained optimistic, and even while slavery lasted (and slaves, themselves defined as real estate, could be tied to the land), there was a ready traffic in land, and considerable speculation – in which prominent Loyalist figures, including Andrew DEVEAUX and Governor Lord DUNMORE, were notable front-runners.

The successive failure of cotton plantations, the remigration of many planters, the reversion of most neglected and abandoned estates to the Crown, and finally, the decline and abolition of slavery, led to the next phase in the history of Bahamian land tenures. Though slave-owners received one last bonus in the British government's payment of compensation for their 'slave property', Bahamian land outside of Nassau became virtually unsaleable. The ex-slaves for the most part became subsistence peasant farmers, working what land they could find as best they could. A few, along with many of the LIBERATED AFRICANS landed in The Bahamas between 1809 and 1860, obtained title to small-holdings and house-plots by grant or purchase. Others became share-croppers on the decayed estates of those local white owners who had retained title to their estates. The great majority, however, worked land without either formal title or payment that had either been abandoned by its ostensible owners, or was technically Crown Land.

In 1846, the important Commutation Act abandoned the system of quit rents (now hopelessly in arrears), allowing owners the transfer of lands from quit rent leaseholds to absolute freeholds on the payment of overdue back rents. Yet while there was an immediate surge and steady increase thereafter in the number of freeholds – including house-plots in townships – the general effect was actually to increase the amount of Crown Land, while bringing little change to the condition of impoverished Out Islanders. 1846 also saw the first appointment of a Surveyor General, whose functions were to preside over the evolving Department of Lands and Surveys, to oversee the management and control of Crown Lands, and, if possible, to exercise some control over land entitlement procedures in general.

Slavery had been followed by fairly draconian laws for the eviction of illegal squatters, but these proved hardly worth the trouble and expense of enforcement. The ex-slaves benefited from a species of benign neglect, reinforced by the transfer of English common law provisions governing squatters' rights and commonages. As a consequence, large areas of 'casual cultivation' adjacent to Out Island settlements came to be regarded first as customary commonages and then gradually through squatters' rights as individual families' private property – inherited, bequeathed, and even bought and sold.

One of the two most notable Bahamian commonages were those lands in Exuma formerly belonging to Lord ROLLE which his slaves and their descendants – all tactically assuming the surname Rolle – effectively claimed (without documentary proof) had been bequeathed to them in perpetuity. The other was the 2,000 acres on the mainland of northern ELEUTHERA which (having already been worked in common for 130 years) were formally granted to the people of HARBOUR ISLAND for having assisted Andrew Deveaux in the 'recapture' of The Bahamas from the Spaniards in 1783. These and other customary commonages (mainly in Eleuthera) were brought under a general Bahamian Commonages Law in 1896. This represented a victory for the ordinary Out Islanders, spoilt only by the problems of multiple joint ownership, of management, and the inevitable restrictions on sale and development, even for mutual benefit.

Similar problems also derived from the widespread custom – known throughout the West Indies and almost certainly derived from Africa – of regarding land as belonging not to single individuals but to all members of entire families, equally. Such 'generational' land might derive from an original individual entitlement, but over generations might be claimed equally by many – theoretically hundreds – of family members, each with equal ownership and usage rights and an individual veto on sale or development.

These problems were not serious while land was plentiful and commercially of little worth. However, the situation changed as soon as the government saw opportunities of exploiting Crown Lands by concessions to foreign investors, and realtors and lawyers realised the profits to be made from selling Bahamian land to private individuals and development companies. Such generous concessions as were given to foreign SISAL planters in the 1890s and lumber companies from the early twentieth century were unobjectionable when they were in largely uninhabited islands such as ANDROS and ABACO, could be argued to be of general benefit, were hedged around by fixed requirements, and were of specified and relatively short duration. They became deeply troublesome, however, when they came into conflict with local counter-claimants – as, for example, Rosita FORBES found when she tried to set up a version of the Kenya 'white highlands' in central Eleuthera in the 1930s.

These operators had far readier access to the legislative process and the law than did the ordinary Bahamian Out Islanders. Lawyers argued that such customs as squatters' rights and generational entitlement were retrograde if not ridiculous, and found allies among ordinary islanders who wished to sell their birthright. It was not until the passing of the Quieting of Titles Act of 1959 that the rules and process by which unimpeachable freehold title to Bahamian land could be established were laid down, incidentally limiting the number of persons who could claim joint title to three. This, not coincidentally, immediately preceded the period when the BAY STREET regime was presiding over the most rapid phase of land dispersion in Bahamian history, between 1959 and 1967.

Though the PROGRESSIVE LIBERAL PARTY, which came to power in 1967, continued to welcome responsible foreign investment, and the lawyers who made up a fair proportion of the PLP's politicians relished the conveyancing and other land transaction business that naturally flowed their way, the party's BAHAMIANISATION policy ensured a gradual tightening of the regulations governing the holding of Bahamian land by non-Bahamians. This policy was most forcefully propounded in the Immovable Property (Acquisition by Foreign Persons) Bill of December 1980 – though its provisions did not come into effect until 1983. In future, land would not be sold to foreigners unless it was either to be used for purely residential purposes by approved individuals, or was to be used 'for approved industrial or other approved development purposes, having regard to the contribution that might be made to the development of the Bahamian economy and in accordance with development goals'.

In general, Bahamian land, both private and state-owned, was to be regarded as a resource for the national benefit, and not to be alienated without official approval. More specifically, land transactions made without approval were to be invalidated, and speculative purchases of land outlawed. Particular care was to be taken to monitor proposals to subdivide land into housing estates, and to veto buildings and other developments that too closely impinged on existing settlements or their potential future expansion. Not only would the realty business be reserved entirely for Bahamians (or companies a majority of whose principals were Bahamians), but foreign purchasers would be closely examined as to their intentions, their financial means, and even their character. Land transactions would also be much more rigorously taxed than before.

Concerned that such restrictions went too far, the FREE NATIONAL MOVEMENT passed a moderating land bill (called the International Persons Landholding Act) the year after it came to power in 1992. As the new century began, promotional literature could still laud The Bahamas as an ideal place for non-Bahamians to buy land, build and live an idyllic retirement – playing down the inevitable knots and expenses of acquiring irrefutable 'quiet title' or a freehold in perpetuity. However, the days were gone for ever when (as, for example, happened with The Forest estate on Great Exuma) whole sections of islands could be bought up cheaply by foreigners, their customary tenants evicted, the land crudely subdivided by bulldozed roads and sold to hundreds of other foreigners on a mainly speculative basis, with little prospect or intention of actual building.

The psychological even more than financial value for Bahamians of personally owning a section of their native land – and the continuing difficulties of obtaining absolute and unimpeachable title – were illustrated when an excited and proud government announced that the five 'Golden Girls' would be rewarded for winning the gold medal in the 4 x 100 metre relay at the 2000 Sydney Olympics by grants of Crown Land (as well as money). This form of reward was widely praised as symbolically significant. But it was almost two years before an appropriate site could be found and surveyed, titles searched, plans and deeds drawn up, and the actual presentation made.

Further reading: M. Craton, 'White Law and Black Custom: The Evolution of Bahamian Land Tenures', in J. Besson and J. Momsen (eds.), *Land and Development in The Caribbean*, Macmillan Caribbean, 1987, 88–114; Craton and Saunders, *Islanders*, i and ii, under 'Land Tenures', *passim*.

LANGUAGE What is spoken by Bahamians among themselves is something between a distinctive dialect of standard English and an authentic Creole language. Sometimes derided in the past as 'bad English' or, at best, regarded as quaint, it is in fact one of the most indelible indicators of a unique cultural heritage.

Bahamian is a form of English derived as much from the British North American colonies as directly from the homeland, and including African influences that likewise come mainly from the creolised language of the Afro-Americans of the coastal parts of the southern colonies, called *Gullah*. Despite the geographical proximity to French and Spanish colonies, the borrowings from French and Spanish are surprisingly few – and from French and Hispanic Creoles almost nil. There are some similarities with Jamaican Creole, but except for obvious modern borrowings, these (like the common fund of Africa-derived PROVERBS and the JUNKANOO) are thought to be the result of parallel histories of slavery and colonialism rather than derivation.

As the philologists Holm and Shilling note, many common creole features derive from the simplified *pidgin* language used by anglophone slave-traders to communicate with West Africans. Such include the abandonment of the

LANGUAGE

pluralising *-s* and its replacement by the reinforcing *–dem* (as in *two house, one teeth, de boy-dem*), simplification of tenses (such as *he go* for 'he went', *he did go* for 'he had gone'), or convenient syntactical shifts (as in *dat fish very stink, he very dunce, he big her*). New words or usages occurred, with great flexibility and inventiveness, to simplify, to fill gaps in the lexicon, or to accommodate conceptions peculiar to the language borrowed from (as *head-bone* for 'skull', *big-eye* for 'greedy', or *red* to mean a range of colours from tan, through orange, to scarlet).

Phonologically also, Bahamians, like Jamaicans and Gullah-speakers, tend to simplify both clusters of consonants (as saying *ak* for 'act', *gole* for 'gold') and adjacent vowels (as with *cheer* for 'chair', *feer* for fear, or *erl* for 'earl' – or even 'oil'). Bahamians change the consonants 'th' to 'd' or 't' at the beginning of a word and to 't' at the end – as in *dese* or *dose* (or more likely *dem*) for 'these' and 'those', *de* (or more likely *duh*) for 'the', *tree* and *truppence* for 'three' or 'three pence', and *rat* for 'wrath.' They also tend to exchange an initial 'v' for a 'w', and vice versa, or drop a 'w' altogether (as in *wex* for 'vex', *Spanish Vells* for 'Spanish Wells' and *ooman* for 'woman').

Syntactically and grammatically, Bahamian usage shows the influence of African forms, though not quite to the degree of out-and-out Caribbean Creoles. Examples include the non-standard deployment of the verbs 'to be' and 'to do' – as in *he bad, she did feel bad, she don't feel good, I can't sure, it don't worth nothing* – and the non-differentiation of tenses and voices (as in *That could eat?* for 'Can it be eaten?' or *I try to put out de fire but it wouldn't out* for 'I tried to put out the fire but it kept on burning.') The absence of pluralisation, of the possessive (as in *the boy uncle*) or gender differentiation (as in *he name Sally*) are said to be African in origin, as is the often non-English word order, particularly in asking questions (as in W*here he is? Ain't you is cousins? He tell me he say he sorry*).

A people's language is a key to its culture. How the language of ordinary Bahamians illustrates the essence, tone and wit of Bahamian culture (and a hint of how it sounds) is perhaps best conveyed by the following sample of Bahamianisms, in alphabetical order:

> **aunty** n.: a term of respect for a mature woman, whether related or not.
>
> **biggety** adj.: self-important, bold, brassy or boastful.
>
> **boonggy** n.: a slightly naughty but not abusive term for a sizeable female backside.
>
> **cuckoo soup** n.: an OBEAH potion said to be administered secretively to a man to cause him to fall in love with a particular female. Sometimes blamed by men for a marriage failure, as in *Your ma musse cuckoo me*.
>
> **cut-eye** n. or v.: a contemptuous look perfected by some women, accompanied by rolling eyes and a distinctive sucking of teeth.
>
> **dicty** adj.: (of men) dapper, concerned about social niceties.
>
> **filimingo** n.: the pink flamingo, national bird (*Phoenicopterus ruber*).
>
> **funny** adj.: not funny at all to most men so-called, meaning homosexual
>
> **grabalishus** adj.: greedy and acquisative.
>
> **hice** v.: hoist, as in *Hice up de John B. Sail*.
>
> **inside** adj.: (of off-spring) legitimate. Cf. **outside**.
>
> **jook** v.: a word of African origin, meaning to stab or cut with a knife.
>
> **kaprang** adj.: broken down.
>
> **kyan** v.: can't.
>
> **lady** n.: any female over about 35, even if not genteel.
>
> **monkey uncle!** Expression of surprise, equivalent to 'Well I never!'
>
> **nigger** n.: not a term of abuse in The Bahamas. A non-judgemental, even affectionate synonym for 'man'. Can even be used of whites, as (of a white footballer) 'That nigger could run!'
>
> **ogly-ogly** adj.: truly ugly. Such reinforcing repetition is common, as with **true-true** for absolutely authentic'.
>
> **people**: a pronoun used like 'one', usually of oneself, as in *People does get fed-up*.
>
> **potcake** n.: strictly the mixed encrustment in a cooking-pot. By transference, a specimen of the ubiquitous Bahamian mongrel dog.
>
> **quarm** v.: to walk in a mincing manner (men), seductively (women).
>
> **right here (among the strong)!** adj.: a common response to 'How do you do?'
>
> **scorch** v.: to score or chop, as in *scorch conch*.
>
> **scull** v.: to dance in a distinctively Bahamian way, with much hip movement, as in sculling a row-boat with an oar over the stern.
>
> **skylark** (pron. *skylack*) v.: to fool around or be kidding.

tingum n.: 'thingumajig' or 'that person whose name I can't remember'.

upstairs house n.: a two- or more storey house – comparative rarities in The Bahamas.

vimmen n.: plural of **voman** (or **ooman**).

wextation n.: annoyance.

yinna n.: Bahamian equivalent or synonym for **y'all**.

Further reading: J. A. Holm and Alison Watt Shilling, *Dictionary of Bahamian English*, Lexik House, 1980; P. Glinton Meicholas, *Talkin' Bahamian; More Talk n'Bahamian; How to be a True-True Bahamian: A Hilarious Look at Life in the Bahamas*, Guanima Press, 1992, 1994, 1995.

LAW OF THE SEA NEGOTIATIONS The successful involvement of The Bahamas in the United Nations Law of the Sea (UNCLOS) negotiations since achieving INDEPENDENCE (1973) has not only marked a national coming of age but pointed up some of the problems of being a small country neighbouring the giant United States.

The Bahamas inherited from Britain a weak and ill-defined definition of territorial rights and maritime authority – the symbols of which were the ability of foreigners to traverse, fish and otherwise exploit Bahamian waters without legal restriction. Accordingly, the new nation eagerly took part in the third series of UN negotiations attempting to establish a comprehensive set of maritime legal principles by international consensus (UNCLOS III), which began in 1973 and were not concluded until a convention was signed at Montego Bay, Jamaica in December 1982 – to come into full effect in 1994.

Following the lead of many maritime nations, The Bahamas had already extended its claim for territorial jurisdiction from the 3-mile limit inherited from Britain to 12 miles in 1969. In 1977, while UNCLOS III was proceeding on its leisurely course, The Bahamas also declared a 200-mile exclusive fishing zone under a Fisheries Resources (Jurisdiction and Conservation) Act. Of much greater general significance was the assertion by The Bahamas and certain archipelagic allies (notably Indonesia, the Philippines, Fiji and Tonga) of the so-called 'archipelagic principle' in 1973. By this, the boundaries of archipelagic nations were held to be a continuous base-line around the outermost islands. A rider of vital importance for The Bahamas was the definition of shallow banks as equivalent to dry land. The combined effect was to extend the territorial waters of The Bahamas (the dry land of which amounted to a mere 5,353 square miles, 13,864 squ. km) to something like 100,000 square miles (259,000 squ. km) – larger than any other Caribbean nation, including Cuba.

The final act of UNCLOS III, signed by 119 (and eventually 132) of the 151 participating nations, endorsed these principles and reinforced the 200 mile zone to make it apply to all economic activities, including the exploitation of sea-bed resources. This provision, along with concerns about free military access and other strategic considerations, explains why the US government (strongly backed by the oil and 'defence' industry lobbies) was the most notable nation not to sign the Montego Bay Convention of 1982. During the Reagan administration the US declared its own 12-mile territorial waters and 200-mile exclusive economic zones. Since 1982 the US has carried on a complex (some would say clumsy) minuet over the international Law of the Sea, making some concessions without actually signing the full UN Convention. As late as 1999, the Clinton administration unilaterally extended the limit of its territorial jurisdiction from 12 to 24 miles.

The Bahamas has willingly conceded that the major sea passages through its territory are international waters, subject only to restrictions on warships and the right of Bahamian authorities to control pollution and illegal trafficking. However, the effective defence and surveillance of its entire 100,000 square mile territory was clearly beyond Bahamian capabilities, and it was otherwise in Bahamian interests not too seriously to antagonise its all-powerful neighbour, potential protector, and possible benefactor, the United States.

Within the delicate parameters of this relationship, though, there remained considerable latitude for diplomatic negotiation, and in the outcome The Bahamas had grounds for pride in the way it established an independent but mature and responsible stance in regional affairs. The most telling examples of this relate to the qualified roles which US naval and coastguard forces play in Bahamian waters. Bahamian and US personnel cooperate actively in the interdiction of drug trafficking and illegal migration through Bahamian waters, but only within rules agreed in candid but friendly discussions between the two nations.

Further reading: G. L. Friday, 'Islands in the Stream: The Development of a Machinery for the Conduct of External Affairs and Bahamian Foreign Policy, 1973–1985', unpublished MA thesis, University of Waterloo, 1985; Craton and Saunders, *Islanders*, ii. 998, 367–384; J. C. Wang (ed.), *Handbook on Ocean Politics and Law*, Greenwood Press, 1992; www.globelaw.com/law_sea/isconts; www.iczm.org/unclos

LEBANESE BAHAMIANS A small group of distinctive migrants who found a niche and succeeded in The Bahamas in the late nineteenth and early twentieth centuries.

The Bahamian Lebanese (sometimes called Syrians) were part of a general diaspora – perhaps a million people in all

LEPROSY

– escaping from the economic hardships and oppression of the dying Turkish Empire into many parts of the still flourishing British and French empires. Nearly all Maronite Christians, with a vigorous entrepreneurial tradition and strong clannish networks, they were enterprising and hard-working. In The Bahamas, as elsewhere, they first appeared in the 1890s as itinerant pedlars, 'selling pins, buttons, cheap textiles, trinkets, even rice, sugar and grits, in tiny quantities at the lowest prices' on the sidewalks and wharves of Nassau, and in the Out Islands, where shops were few and far between.

Hoarding their tiny profits and with an international network of suppliers and backers, three or four Lebanese graduated to leasing and then owning shops on the fringes of central Bay Street. Concentrating on dry goods rather than groceries, they challenged the established businesses by means of their low profit margins and rapid turnover, and by introducing modern methods such as aggressive advertising, sales and payment by instalments. During the boom years of the 1920s the J. K. Amoury firm led the way by combining retail with wholesale business and becoming the commission agent for a whole range of business machines and luxury consumer items – from typewriters and adding machines to pianos and radios – helped by the fact that they were part of a family network stretching from New York to Brazil, effectively cutting out all middlemen. More provocatively, Amoury's entered the high-quality and tourist-oriented end of the market when they opened Nassau's first luxury boutique, called M. Sraeel, in 1926.

Though they suffered from some prejudice and opposition from Bay Street rivals, the Lebanese merchants also earned considerable respect for pioneering a more modern style of merchandising. It also helped that they were not very numerous, and that they were not JEWISH. The Amoury, Armaly and Moses families never entered the charmed circle of the 'Bay Street' oligarchy – almost certainly because they did not care to do so. However, that such a thing was possible was illustrated by the remarkable upwardly mobile Lebanese Ouwade family. The patriarch, born poor but with good connections, opened a Bay Street shop in 1894, changing his name to Baker. Within three generations the family had been admitted as full members of the Bay Street clique, with two brothers representing the traditional 'CONCHY JOE' strongholds of Eleuthera in the House of Assembly.

LEPROSY A severely disfiguring but not particularly lethal disease once quite common in The Bahamas, but now extinct. Caused by a bacillus, leprosy is contagious but slow-acting and not deserving of the fear and shame that it has generated since ancient times – when the leper was regarded as 'unclean' and treated as the ultimate outcast.

Leprosy was most common in The Bahamas in the nineteenth century, but the majority of sufferers remained with their families, usually secluded from public gaze, rather than housed in the leprosy ward of the Public Hospital in Nassau. Because of public reticence no accurate figures were available, but the seven lepers reported as patients in the hospital in 1911 were clearly outnumbered by those sufferers living at home both in Nassau and in various Family Islands, including Abaco, Acklins, San Salvador and Inagua. A special Leprosy Act in 1913 and the general Health Act of 1914 tightened up regulations concerning the notification of the disease and the non-employment of sufferers in various trades, and attempted to make hospitalisation compulsory. But there were no provisions either to bring Family Island lepers to Nassau, or to provide relief for sufferers who still had a family to support. As late as 1927 the general medical report by Sir Wilfrid Beveridge was equally critical of the fact that those lepers at the General Hospital were close to other patients and free to roam the town as they willed, as it was that so many of the Bahamian lepers remained in their family homes without proper attention.

As a consequence of the Beveridge Report a lazaretto was set up at Carmichael in what was then the scarcely inhabited interior of New Providence in 1928. By most measures, this establishment, which lasted until the late 1960s, was a notable success. Though isolated, the residents were not treated as pariahs. They were regularly visited by doctors and nurses and given the best available medications, but encouraged to run the place themselves. Though publicly supported, they were provided with plots of land to work and opportunities for money-making crafts. All in all, they formed an effective, almost self-supporting and surprisingly well-integrated small community – all the more remarkable given their diverse backgrounds. Some residents opted to stay when they were given freedom to leave, and there was even regret when it was decided that the lazaretto was no longer needed and should be closed.

LEWIS, Eloise (1927–1984) Renowned as 'The Bahamas Songbird', Eloise Lewis was perhaps the most outstanding Bahamian vocal performer from the 1950s to the 1970s, specialising equally in GOOMBAY, calypso and Latin American numbers.

Often described as bursting onto the Nassau music scene as a teenage prodigy, Eloise in fact trod a somewhat longer and harder road to success. Born in Jacksonville, Florida,

Eloise Lewise, the 'Bahama Songbird' in a nightclub performance, 1960s

she was brought to Nassau as a baby by her Bahamian parents. Though inspired by her older brother Freddy (originator of the famous goombay song 'Conch Ain't Got No Bone') she was largely self-taught, becoming an excellent guitarist and practising her singing by listening to records by Ella Fitzgerald and Dinah Shore After some success in local talent shows (where she often shared prizes with Berkeley 'Peanuts' TAYLOR), she made her professional debut in the late 1940s as guitarist and singer with the Lou Adams orchestra at the *Zanzibar* nightclub.

However, it was not until she formed the Eloise Trio (original members George Wilson on bass, 'Peanuts' on drums and 'Barbalou' on maraccas) and teamed up with the mellifluous and soulful singer Lionel Lottmore in the later 1950s that Eloise became an established star. Though appearing mostly in Nassau nightspots – notably Blackbeard's Tavern and the Drumbeat in the 1960s – she travelled widely in the United States and other countries and was a particular hit at the Sands and Flamingo in Las Vegas. She and her trio cut several 78 records for Decca and other labels.

Of her records, that most typically and memorably displaying Eloise's talent and range was the one made for Caribe in 1960, entitled 'The New and Exciting Eloise Trio'. Neatly sandwiched between the upbeat 'Come to the Caribbean' and the dreamy 'Bahama Lullaby' are perky and poignant calypsos and goombays like 'Lizzie Carry Basket on Head', 'Mango' and 'Yellow Bird', the sentimental ballad 'Lil' Darling' and the spirited spiritual 'Going Down Jordan', as well the staccato Latin American numbers, 'La Bomba', 'Anna Bacca' and 'Chi Chi Meringue', which were Eloise's most distinctive trademark.

LIBERATED AFRICANS

In her later years, overuse somewhat roughened Eloise's voice, though her dynamic stage persona long remained unimpaired. In 1975 she moved permanently to Freeport, performing at such places as the Bahamian Club and the Pirates' Den until ill-health forced an end to her career. She died in 1984 at the age of 57.

LIBERATED AFRICANS At least a fifth of Afro-Bahamians are not descended from slaves but from Africans freed from illegal slave traders and settled in The Bahamas between 1809 and 1860. These Liberated Africans and their descendants were consequently both proud of their distinctive non-slave status and naturally retained elements of their African culture more strongly than the majority of black Bahamians.

Following the imperial Act abolishing the British slave trade in 1808, a system was set up by which those liberated from illegal slavers who could not be repatriated would be settled in the nearest convenient British colony, and either enrolled into the armed forces or 'apprenticed' to local employers for between seven and 14 years. Because of the mixed origins of the captives and the circumstances of their capture, precise repatriation was rarely if ever possible, though the largest number of Liberated Africans were resettled in the British West African colony of Sierra Leone. Those who had already been carried across the Atlantic before recapture, though, were not sent back to Africa but relocated in British West Indian colonies – preferably those, unlike The Bahamas, where there was an ample need for labour, such as Trinidad and Jamaica.

Between 1809 and 1860 some 6,000 Liberated Africans (a quarter of the total) were landed in The Bahamas. These came from 26 slave vessels, mostly en route to Cuba flying either the Spanish or Portuguese flag, or wrecked on Bahamian shores. Their retention in The Bahamas was generally unpopular among the local ruling class on at least three grounds. Not only was there not a labour shortage and the arrival of fresh hands would decrease the value of 'slave property', but the greater degree of freedom enjoyed by the newcomers would exacerbate slave discontent – particularly among those creoles who regarded themselves superior to 'African barbarians'.

Sizeable influxes in 1811 and 1816 were accommodated with some difficulty, the Liberated Africans being distributed between the Second West India Regiment, ships of the Royal Navy, and domestic employers. But a larger wave in the 1830s, when the apprentice terms of the first arrivals were expiring and the emancipation of the slaves was fast approaching, intensified the problems.

The government's solution – carried out mainly under the forthright liberal Governor James Carmichael SMYTH – was to settle the newcomers in more or less supervised villages in the southern suburbs of Nassau, the more distant interior of New Providence, or on the nearer Out Islands.

This policy was followed until the last shipment of Africans was landed in 1860 and the post of Supervisor of Liberated Africans was discontinued shortly afterwards. By that time most of the Liberated Africans were well integrated into the Bahamian economy, while still retaining distinct characteristics and residential areas. Their culture remained strongly African in a generic sense, but coming from different parts of West Africa, they retained quite separate sub-ethnic identities. The two most numerous groups – making up at least half of the total – were Yorubas and Congoes. Cleveland ENEAS (himself of Yoruba descent), for example, claimed that Yorubas were dominant in Nassau's BAIN TOWN, regarding the Congoes of the adjacent area called *Conta Butta* ('Congo Borough') as inferiors. In the eastern village of FOX HILL, where many Bain Towners had relatives but one of the sections was called Congo Town, this situation may well have been reversed – though all of the inhabitants, including those of slave descent, got together each year to celebrate Emancipation and the ending of Apprenticeship on Fox Hill Day.

Several African languages were still spoken in The Bahamas in the 1880s, and the last surviving Liberated Africans did not die until the 1920s. African music, folklore and cultural practices – most famously OBEAH – lasted even longer than the separate Friendly Societies founded by and named for those of Congo, Yoruba, Ibo and Hausa descent. These had faded by the 1940s, though the Congo Society lingered on into the early 1970s. In more recent years, the AFRICAN HERITAGE of The Bahamas has been properly recognised and celebrated, but comparatively few Bahamians are aware of the distinct and important part played by the Liberated Africans.

One reminder is the poignant but little-known tale of those 171 Congoes who in 1888 petitioned the Belgian self-appointed King of the Congo to be repatriated from The Bahamas to their homeland. 'We were born in the Congo-land beside the great river and have families still living there,' they wrote. 'We were brought as slaves to the West Indies by the Spaniards, were freed by the Naval Power of England before reaching our destination, have been kindly treated by the Government, have become British subjects, speaking their language, and our children have some education therein. The lands given us, and those we have bought, are now exhausted. Owing to the lack of employment many of us endure great hardships – and we see no hope of future for our little ones. It is the desire of our hearts to return with our little ones, to our own land where the soil yields a return for labour.'

The response of King Leopold's functionaries was superficially favourable, but with worrying undertones. The Bahamian Congoes would be welcome, but only as long as their passage money was repaid by contract labour and they were prepared to pay rent in kind or labour for any land they might be given. If they agreed, the repatriation might go ahead as soon as the building of the projected railway between Matadi and Leopoldville was begun. In the event, the Congoes stayed in The Bahamas, which was almost certainly providential, given the atrocities inflicted on native and migrant workers in the grotesquely misnamed Congo Free State. However many hardships the first, second and third generations of Bahamian Congoes endured in their involuntarily adopted land, these were to be recompensed in subsequent generations, and were nothing to what they would have had to endure in King Leopold's private 'Heart of Darkness'.

Further reading: H. Johnson, 'The Liberated Africans, 1811–60', in *The Bahamas in Slavery and Freedom*, Ian Randle Press, 1991, 30–54; R. Adderley, '"New Negroes from Africa": Culture and Community among Liberated Africans in The Bahamas and Trinidad, 1810 to 1900', unpublished PhD thesis, University of Pennsylvania, 1996; A. Hochschild, *King Leopold's Ghost: A Story of Greed, Terror, and Heroism in Colonial Africa*, Houghton Mifflin, 1998.

LIBRARIES

The Bahamas has had public libraries of different sorts for nearly two hundred years. Their history is interesting and even has had its heroic aspects. Yet in general, libraries in The Bahamas have never kept pace with those in similar countries, let alone the United Kingdom and the United States. The besetting problem has always been the lack of adequate (and at first any) public funding.

The first library was that formed by the Bahamas Society for the Diffusion of Knowledge for the use of its members in 1837 and formally constituted as the Nassau Public Library by an Act of the Assembly in 1847. Located in two small rooms in the eastern wing of the Public Buildings, in 1850, it consisted of 1,500 volumes and had 50 subscribing members. In 1879 the Library was transferred into more elegant and comparatively spacious new quarters – the specially renovated former jail on the Shirley Street side of the Public Square – where it has remained to this day. Until 1930 it was also the *only* public library in New Providence and, while never formally segregated, very much the preserve of the more intellectually minded of the white elite.

LIBRARIES

The Grant's Town Library, opened in May 1930, was specifically intended to give the non-whites of Over-the-Hill Nassau their own public library. Located on the upper storey of the Grant's Town Post Office and next to the Police Station, it was accidentally destroyed when the two buildings were torched during the 'BURMA ROAD' RIOTS of May–June 1942. However, largely thanks to lobbying by the black MHAs Dr Claudius Walker and Bert Cambridge, the government was persuaded to finance a two-storey replacement. Located just south of Government House overlooking the Southern Recreation Ground – the favourite site for political meetings – it was opened in 1951 as the Southern Public Library. Under the benign chairmanship of Dr Cleveland ENEAS (who lived right opposite), and the long-time direction of librarian Mrs Lilian Weir Coakley (1955–92), it quickly became a hub of intellectual activity, research and discussion, to rival and then outpace its counterpart on the other side of Nassau's dividing ridge

In 1909 an Out Island Public Libraries Act was passed, with the expressed purposes of providing reading matter for all Bahamians, to encourage self-improvement, and to foster a sense of community identity. The budget allocation was pitifully small, but the more enterprising Commissioners in the less destitute islands were able to report some progress, and at least three of the most dynamic communities – Harbour Island, Governor's Harbour and Inagua – were able to build up libraries already in existence

On Grand Bahama, the Freeport Public Library, established in 1962, had outgrown its premises by 1966 and was rehoused in the John Harvard Building, where the major local philanthropist (and inventor of the dial telephone), James Rand, had established a small research library as early as 1958. In 1982 the John Harvard Library was taken over by the Grand Bahama Port Authority and renamed in honour of one of the first three major investors in Freeport, Sir Charles Hayward.

Of the private initiatives which sustained the exiguous Out Island libraries, however, the most important was the Ranfurly Out Island Library Service (1954–92). This was the brainchild of the remarkable Countess Hermione, wife of Governor Lord Ranfurly (1953–7). Books for children as well as adults were solicited from Britain and the more fortunate Commonwealth countries and distributed to Out Island schools and libraries, first from a small room at the back of Government House, then from a small building on Bank Lane, and finally from a former RAF warehouse at Oakes Field. Run by Sir Dudley and Lady Russell and a small band of volunteers after the Ranfurlys returned to England, the Service had handed on 200,000 books by 1975, three-quarters of them for children.

First Bahamian custom-built prison and guardhouse (1790) on Nassau's Shirley Street, housing the Nassau Public Library since 1879

Belatedly inspired (if not shamed) by the activity started by Lady Ranfurly and by the spontaneous development of libraries in Grand Bahama, the Bahamas government had indeed already begun to increase its expenditure on library facilities and move tentatively towards a rationally integrated national library system. Between 1973 and 1992 three new public libraries had been built in New Providence: in Coconut Grove (1974), in Yellow Elder (1987) and on Wulff Road (1988). Between 1992 and 2002 four more were added, specifically designed to be the focal point of community centres in disadvantaged areas of the island: on Kemp Road (1998), on East Street South, and in Elizabeth Estates and Flamingo Gardens (all in 1999).

Meanwhile, as new schools were built they were routinely provided with space for libraries (if not immediately adequate facilities or enough books), and under the COLLEGE OF THE BAHAMAS, several other libraries had come into operation to serve specific professional needs, receiving private and foreign aid as well as government support. At the forefront, in size, technology and professionalism, was COB's own main library, especially during the tenure of Canadian Paul Boultbee as Head Librarian (1974–81) and following substantial grants from the World Bank (doubling the library's size in 1984), and financial assistance from the Syntex Corporation, Rotary

LIGHTHOUSES

and the Lyford Cay Foundation, among others. By 2000, the COB (with easily the largest, most professional and best coordinated library system in the country) boasted three subordinate libraries: the Hilda Bowen Library in Nassau's Grosvenor Close for nurses in training and other medical professionals, the Northern Campus Library in Freeport, and the Exuma Resource Centre Library in GEORGE TOWN, EXUMA. Other public reference libraries have been developed more or less informally by the Sir Eugene Dupuch Law School and the Bahamas Archives.

Great improvements have taken place since the early 1990s, including integration of courses in basic library skills with a Diploma in Library Science course offered by COB. Equally important were the activities of a revived Bahamas Library Association and the appointment of Miss Nellie Brennen as Assistant Director of Education in charge of a separate Division of Library and Information Services. The creation of a National Library has been repeatedly discussed, but has so far failed to materialise.

Further reading: V. Balance and E. Bain, *Bahamian Public Libraries: An Overview*, Bahamas Library Publications, 1, 2000.

LIGHTHOUSES Even more than the coming of steam and improvements in cartography, it was the building of lighthouses that changed The Bahamas from being one of the world's most notorious graveyards for shipping, in which one third of its working population were engaged in 'wrecking.' Between 1836 and 1973 these lighthouses were built and maintained by the Imperial Lighthouse Service, being turned over to the Bahamas Government only with the achievement of Independence.

The first Bahamian lighthouse had actually been ordered and paid for by the local Assembly as early as 1817, in the most obvious place – showing the way to and through the entrance to Nassau harbour. At that time all British lighthouses were privately owned and only loosely under the control of the ancient guild of pilots called Trinity House. Private ownership was not finally ended until the Merchant Shipping Act of 1894. The crying need for more and more efficient lighthouses throughout the Empire, however, had led the British Parliament to create the Imperial Lighthouse Service in 1836, placing it firmly under a reformed Trinity House, with funding from a tonnage levy on all merchant shipping using British ports.

The tonnage levy was minuscule but the accrued total enabled the eventual building and maintenance of dozens of sturdy lighthouses throughout the British Empire. Under the control of a virtually autonomous body, these benefited international as well as British shipping. In The Bahamas five lighthouses were erected in the later 1830s and 1840s; at Hole-in-the-Wall, ABACO (marking the entrance to the North East Providence Channel), Great Isaac Rock (the North West Providence Channel), CAY SAL (at the junction of the Old Bahama and Florida Channels), Gun Cay (marking the dangerous eastern edge of the Florida Strait), and Grand Turk (then part of The Bahamas). To this rudimentary network were gradually added nine further major lighthouses over the next 40 years – not always without opposition from local licensed WRECKERS; on Cay Lobos (1859), Stirrup's Cay, Berry Islands and Elbow Cay, Abaco (1863), INAGUA and Castle Island (1868), Bird Rock and Sombrero Island (1876), and Dixon Hill, San Salvador (1887). By 1900, with progressively improved equipment and numerous intervening fixed lights, ships using all major Bahamian shipping lanes were never out of sight of at least one guiding beacon.

Though the Bahamian headquarters, warehouses and main dock of the ILS were in Nassau, the Service acted with proud efficiency completely independent of the Bahamas Government. Its Commander, an official under the authority of Trinity House, was invariably a retired or seconded Royal Navy officer. But his staff was exclusively Bahamian. Moreover, in marked contrast to the Bahamian civil service of the time, the entire staff, including

Candy stripe lighthouse at Hope Town, Abaco, the northeastern point of The Bahamas

head lighthouse keepers and captains of the flotilla of service vessels, were (with the one exception of George Thompson of CHEROKEE SOUND, Abaco) what the Service's historian termed 'of freed Negro slave-stock.'

The Bahamian branch of the ILS had a tremendous *esprit de corps*. But the life of its keepers was lonely, and in times of storm dangerous. Keepers and assistant keepers lived in neat houses next to the lighthouse with their families, but these locations were of their nature mostly very isolated, especially in the days before radio communications. Keepers served normally for two years at one place, then enjoyed two months' leave, before being posted to another lighthouse. Tenders came each month in good weather but less regularly when seas were rough. Those lighthouse children not fostered in Nassau received what schooling they got from their parents.

The success of the lighthouses (along with hugely improved ships' engines and navigational aids) was attested by the steady decrease in the number of wrecks after the 1860s, and their virtual elimination by the mid-twentieth century. When the ILS handed over its facilities to the newly independent Bahamas Government in 1973 – which placed them under the charge of the Nassau Port Authority – an era had passed. On the pleas of economy and reduced necessity, the Government gradually moved towards a completely automated system. Many of the fine historic structures were threatened by decay. Luckily, though, there were enough persons concerned about this to form a Bahamas Lighthouse Preservation Society, which aims to raise sufficient funds to 'preserve from automation the world's last three hand-wound, kerosene-burning lightstations, Elbow Reef and Hope Town, Abaco, San Salvador and Great Inagua'(statement from *The Lightstation*, newsletter of the BLPS, Spring 2004).

Further reading: R. Langton-Jones, *Silent Sentinels*, 2nd ed., Muller, 1950.

LIGNUM VITAE Appropriately chosen national tree of The Bahamas, of great value in boatbuilding and folk medicine, and with a pretty and fragrant violet-blue flower.

Found in undisturbed whitelands and rocky coastal coppices, this 'tree of life' (*guaiacum officinale*) seldom reaches 30 feet (9m) in height, with a gnarled and rarely straight trunk and spreading canopy that often bends away from the prevailing wind. Its wood is both the hardest and the heaviest known, sinking in the saltiest water and famously destructive of saws and axes. More important, lignum vitae timber is smooth-grained and contains an oily resin that makes it at least as good as metal for ships' bearings, pulley sheaves and deadeyes.

The flower of lignum vitae, the Bahamian national tree

Most remarkable of all are the lignum vitae's well-attested medicinal properties, the most important being the effectiveness of various parts of the tree in the treatment of syphilis. Medical science has shown that the guaiac resin actively destroys the spirochetes of the disease. This was pragmatically known to the Lucyans (in whom the disease was endemic) and eagerly adopted by the Spaniards and other Europeans once infection from 'the Arawaks' revenge' became endemic in the Old World. This, along with the development of boatbuilding in the colonies, led to a serious depletion that has scarcely been reversed now that boatbuilding has declined and modern medicine has produced more effective cures for syphilis. 'Teas' from the lignum vitae are still used in the Family Islands to treat a wide range of afflictions, from swollen glands and boils, to fevers and sundry aches and pains.

The tree's beauty is apparent when it bursts into a starry panoply of flowers. This occurs at different times of year and is usually associated with rains, though a given tree will tend to flower at the same time each year. According to botanist Kathleen McNary Wood, 'in addition to its appeal to humans, the lignum vitae has a high ecological value. Many insects and nectar-drinking birds prize the nectar of the fragrant flowers.'

Further reading: K. McNary Wood, *Flowers of the Bahamas*, Macmillan, 2000; W. Cutts, *Trees of the Bahamas*, Macmillan, 2004.

LITERATURE Bahamians have always been great talkers and good listeners, particularly when the medium is Bahamian dialect. Accordingly, the oral tradition is of prime importance in Bahamian literature and Bahamian writers have the most success in those forms of expression in which speech is most important: poetry, drama and storytelling. Whether simply retelling familiar fables, poking affectionate or satirical fun, or making strong comments about the problems and flaws in Bahamian society, Bahamian storytellers appeal to the national community using its common and everyday language in familiar contexts and situations. This was manifest in print at least as early as the 1930s in the popular series in the *Tribune* newspaper called 'Smokey Joe Says' by Eugene DUPUCH, and flowered in the 1970s with Jeanne Thompson's weekly column in the *Nassau Guardian* called 'Satirically Speaking', and her extremely popular Bahamian soap opera on ZNS Radio, *The Fergusons of Farm Road*.

In his seminal 1995 analysis of Bahamian literature, Anthony Dahl generalised from the rich resources of vernacular storytelling and plays, as well as from the best of the increasing flow of Bahamian poetry and from the handful of novels produced over the previous two decades, to stress the centrality of the family and its problems in the Bahamian literary consciousness. In addition he identified feelings of alienation or exile, and nostalgia for a Promised Land of an imagined past and a hoped-for future. Yet even these relate to an idealised vision of traditional family values and to the alienation that comes from illegitimacy, the absent father, and barriers of class and colour, as much as to the continuing need to migrate for an education and economic opportunities, and the tendency to look for cultural models everywhere but in the islands themselves. A look at more recent works, including the gritty novels of Ian Strachan and Keith Russell, discloses that these themes continue to occupy local writers, along with concerns about such social problems as violence, cultural mixing and the decline of ethical standards.

The 1980s and 1990s brought with them a new interest in the craft of writing, propelling an entirely new generation of writers on to the literary stage. Dahl presciently recognised the emergence of a new generation of self-confident women, a sense of national purpose and pride that transcended the traditional divisions produced by class and colour, and a growing sophistication that allowed Bahamian writers to select their modes, themes and archetypes from the artistic world at large. As Nicolette Bethel commented, by 2003 Bahamian literature had become perhaps the least segregated of Bahamian cultural domains. Bahamian writers were now drawn equally from both genders and all cultures and classes. Many of the most notable were women, such as Marion Bethel, a winner of the prestigious international Casa de las Americas Prize for poetry, and Lynn Sweeting, editor of *WomanSpeak*, a regional journal dedicated to giving a literary voice to women and including representatives of all cultural groups in The Bahamas.

The oral arts and vernacular tradition continued to flourish, and notable storytellers such as Patricia Glinton-Meicholas, Derek Burrows, Patricia Bazard and Kayla Lockhart-Edwards became more popular, abroad as well as at home. Poetry received a boost from the introduction of performance poetry and the success of 'slam' and 'rap' modes in the United States. According to Nicolette Bethel, literary high points have included the 1985 International Writers' Conference sponsored by the Nassau Poetry Society and the publication of its anthology, *Junction*, in 1987; the introduction in the 1990s of an imaginative literature syllabus for the Bahamas General Certificate of Education which encouraged young Bahamians not only to write but to publish; the founding of two local presses which loosened the stranglehold of foreign publishers; the University of Miami's Caribbean Writers' Workshop, which helped familiarise Bahamian writers with other writers and trends in the Caribbean at large; and, at the end of the 1990s, the establishment of the Bahamian Association for Cultural Studies (BACUS), which provided a much-needed focus, sponsoring three conferences and publishing two journals.

Perhaps with the exception of the production of stage drama (see THEATRE), Bahamian literature, in both its oral and strictly literary modes, seems to be in as flourishing, creative and expansive a state at the start of the new millennium as is its brother-and-sister venture, Bahamian ART.

Further reading: A. G. Dahl, *Literature of the Bahamas, 1724–1992: The March towards National Identity*, University Press of America, 1995; Patricia Glinton-Meicholas, *An Evening in Guanima: A Treasury of Folktales from The Bahamas*, Guanima Press, 1993; Nicolette Bethel, 'Thirty Years of Culture in The Bahamas', in W. K. Jones (ed.), *Bahamas: Independence and Beyond*, Jones Publications, 2003, 100–5; I. S. Cabrera (ed.), *From the Shallow Seas: Bahamian Creative Writing Today*, Casa de las Americas, 1995.

LIZARDS Of the surviving Bahamian reptiles, the rock IGUANA has cornered most interest. But the iguana's much smaller, more numerous and much less threatened cousins, the *anolis* and curly-tailed lizards and the gecko, are at least as interesting, amusing and worthy of study.

Curly tail lizard

The ancestors of some Bahamian lizards (such as the Key West anole) may have been accidental sea-borne migrants in comparatively recent times, but the existence of species paralleled in the Antilles, coupled with separate subspeciation between the major Bahamian islands, has argued for more ancient provenance. Most Bahamian species are likely to be surviving descendants of creatures antedating the tectonic movement that first split the North America from the Greater Antilles some 120 million years ago, with the separate subspecies representing evolutionary variations postdating the geologically much more recent oceanic cycles that split the Bahamas Platform into its smaller components.

Bahamian lizards have shown remarkable local evolutionary adaptability, so that up to four distinct species or subspecies are commonly found cohabiting peacefully within a comparatively small area, each having found and adapted to its particular habitat – from the sunbaked rocks of the foreshore, to the leaf-thick shrubbery and forest floor, the stems of bushes and crinkly barks of trees, to the higher reaches of woodland canopies.

Even for those without a scientific bent, lizard-watching can be a fascinating diversion, ideal for a lazy afternoon on the patio of a sun-baked Bahamian garden or in the leafy fringes of a beach. Bahamian lizards are harmless to humans, though deadly to the insects that constitute their main diet. They are capable of statuesque immobility, helped by the chameleon-like colour changes (mainly from whitish grey to darkish brown, but including tinges of green, red, yellow and black) which help them to blend into their surroundings. But when alarmed or ready to pounce they are capable of sudden bursts of speed, up to 15 m.p.h. (24 km.p.h.) – which when scaled makes them relatively as fast as any cheetah or bird of prey.

The lizards' ability to change colour in fact has a function even more basic than camouflage – acting as a temperature gauge and regulator. Being cold-blooded like all reptiles, they rely on the sun to warm them into activity on awaking. At this time their pigmentation is dark to facilitate the absorption of the sun's rays. Conversely, they are saved from being fried alive during the heat of the day by turning the lighter shade which reflects the sunlight. Lizards have several other characteristics which aid adaptation and survival, being able to subsist on a very low water intake and having powers of hibernation that allow them to live for long periods without food.

Other fascinating characteristics of many lizards have functional purposes. The *anolis* lizards are virtually mute, but have eloquent patterns of display. Most males, though of nondescript general colour, have a brilliantly coloured dewlap which they can distend, accompanying its deployment with an almost comical show of jerky knee-bending. This performance is both a territory-marker, designed to deter rivals or aggressors, and a display to impress the female of the species. An even more curious property of the curly-tailed and certain other lizards is the ability to discard their tail at will. This has the useful function of facilitating escape from predatory creatures (such as cats), particularly since the discarded tail continues spasmodic activity for a while, seeming to have a life of its own. Once the lizard has escaped it regenerates its tail quite quickly – though there does not seem to be research on how often this process can be repeated.

Probably no less common than the *anolis* lizards, the Bahamian geckos are less researched, not just because they are smaller, but because they are mainly nocturnal in their habits. This explains (if not accounts for) the facts that they have exceptionally sensitive eyes, uncovered by lids, and also, unlike other lizards, are variously vocal – making communication by 'clicks, chirps, cackles or tiny barks'. Their most outstanding and famous ability is to adhere to and walk on any hard surface, however smooth, including up vertical walls and across ceilings, upside down. This facility is widely thought to be made possible by suction pads on the soles of their feet. The fact is much more interesting. As David Campbell explains, geckos' under-soles are 'covered by numerous lamellae [scales]. Each lamella bears thousands (the total for all four feet may be in the millions) of bristles, each of which in turn, sprouts hundreds of microscopic suction cups. In effect, the gecko clings to smooth surfaces by means of millions of microscopic plungers. So small are the gecko's suction cups that they were described in detail only after the recent advent of scanning electron microscopy.'

Not regarded as either dangerous or (like the iguana) good for eating, Bahamian lizards are not under threat from Bahamians. They seem to be wily and swift enough to be relatively safe from animal predators. An additional danger, though, stems from their very charm. What makes them (especially the curly-tails) favourite pets in the United States also makes them vulnerable to the depredations of pet-shop supplying smugglers. As recently as 2002 a yacht impounded at George Town, Grand Cayman with hundreds of locally trapped lizards aboard for the American market was found also to be carrying 140 Bahamian curly-tails, worth perhaps US$100 apiece.

Further reading: D. G. Campbell, *The Ephemeral Islands: A Natural History of the Bahamas*, Macmillan, 1978; J. Roughgarden, *Anolis Lizards of the Caribbean: Ecology, Evolution and Plate Tectonics*, Oxford University Press, 1995.

LOBSTER

LOBSTER The great spiny lobster or crawfish (*panulirus argus*), still abundant despite ever more efficient harvesting, provides The Bahamas with its most valuable export commodity, amounting to 6.6 million pounds of tail meat, worth almost $90 million, in the year 2000. Two-thirds of crawfish exports go to the United States, and much of the rest to France.

The life cycle and behaviour patterns of crawfish are remarkable, and still not fully understood. They mate in the spring, with the females producing up to 2.5 million eggs, only a tiny fraction of which come to maturity. The minute larvae called *phyllosomes* feed on plankton, developing into fully fledged crustaceans after seven or eight annual moults. Each autumn – probably a habit from primeval times when it was seasonally necessary to seek warmer waters – mature crawfish travel in migratory swarms, commonly between 50 and 100 head to tail, but formerly sometimes in hundreds of thousands.

A fully mature crawfish weighs at least 10 pounds, but specimens can run up to 20 pounds and live for 25 years. Since the demand for lobster meat escalated from the 1940s onwards, however (with the preference being for succulent two-pounders), few have been able to grow so big or live so long, and the very survival of the species is only guaranteed by strictly observed conservation rules.

The traditional way of fishing for crawfish was 'tickling and scooping' by two men in an Abaco dinghy, no farther from their settlement than they could sail or scull in a day. Nowadays, large motor-boats (notably from the white settlement of Spanish Wells and the black settlement of Sandy Point, Abaco) with crews of up to a dozen and refrigerated holds, will roam distant grounds (such as the Little Bahama Bank, Berry Islands or Cay Sal) for a week to ten days, returning with 10,000 pounds of lobster tails worth $8–10 a pound. Most crawfish are taken from pre-planted wooden traps or artificial habitats known as 'condos' in 30 to 50 feet (9 to 15 m) of water by skin-divers using compressed air. It is a pursuit only for young and healthy men, though lucrative enough to allow many to have shares in their own boat as teenagers, build their own spacious house before marrying and turn to other occupations – or even a life of ease – in their thirties.

Overfishing is an ever-present danger. The crawfish are protected by heavy fines for illegal fishing methods, such as the use of bleach to force them out of their hiding places. The taking of any crawfish with a tail shorter than 5 ½ inches (140 mm) or any egg-bearing female is strictly forbidden, and there is an absolute ban on fishing them for four months between March and August. The worst danger, however, comes from pirate fishermen – mainly from Cuba or Florida Cubans – who ignore the 200-mile exclusion zone claimed by The Bahamas and are willing to risk the fishery protection patrols by the ROYAL BAHAMAS DEFENCE FORCE. An official report in the year 2000 concluded that Bahamian crawfish stocks were still healthy and self-renewing. But, as with other resources in the fragile Bahamian ecology, there is no certainty that this balance can be permanently maintained and that the crawfish will not go the way of green turtle under the pressure of demand by the voracious gourmets of the outside world.

Further reading: David G. Campbell, *The Ephemeral Islands: A Natural History of the Bahamas*, London, Macmillan, 1978, 128–9; 'Crawfish – the golden catch', *Bahamas Handbook, 2001*, Nassau, Dupuch Publications, 2001, 63–71.

LONG CAY (alias Fortune Island) This 5-mile (8-km) sliver of land, narrowly separated from CROOKED ISLAND and fronting the Crooked Island Passage, was formerly also known as Fortune Island. It might well be named Misfortune Island for the way that a once bustling place has become one of the most poignant ghost settlements in The Bahamas.

Long Cay, Crooked Island District

LONG ISLAND

COLUMBUS stopped there or passed close by when he named the whole area Isabella after his co-patron, the Queen of Spain. After the disappearance of the Lucayans the island was not settled until the early nineteenth century, when Albert Town (named after QUEEN VICTORIA'S consort) became a small maritime village based on the local SALT-pans, SPONGING in the Bight of ACKLINS, and combing the WRECKS that dotted the treacherous reefs of the Crooked Island Passage. In 1855 there were 350 people living there, of whom 15 were said to be whites.

Long Cay's days of fortune came when its location made it the chief stopping place for the steamships using the most convenient channel between the Atlantic, eastern Cuba and the Caribbean. American and European steamers stopped there mainly to pick up and drop off Bahamian stevedores, and this led to Albert Town becoming a minor entrepot for Bahamian produce and foreign goods. Albert Town took over from Pitt's Town, 20 miles (32 km) to the north on the western tip of Crooked Island, as a transshipment point for mails coming to and leaving The Bahamas.

At its peak in the first decade of the twentieth century, Long Cay was home to at least a thousand people. It was the base of the Commissioner for the entire Crooked Island and Acklins District. Albert Town boasted many shops and the second-largest church in The Bahamas – as well as places to serve the baser needs of transient mariners and labourers. It was said that Albert Towners were attuned to foreign fashions and news way ahead of Nassau, being able to read New York newspapers no more than three days old.

These glory days are now no more than third-hand memories. Modernisation, especially in transportation and communications, has long by-passed Long Cay. Its permanent population, over 500 as late as 1910, is now no more than a couple of dozen. Albert Town's hundreds of houses and stores are almost all piles of rubble in the bush, and the Anglican church, once unofficially called 'the Cathedral of the Southern Bahamas' is a roofless ruin.

LONG ISLAND Though not quite the longest or the narrowest Bahamian island, Long Island does live up to its name, being 60 miles (96 km) long in an almost straight line north to south, and nowhere more than 4 miles (6.5 km) wide. Its 230 square miles (596 squ. km), once the home of 5,000, now has only two-thirds as many, of whom about a third live in the piratical-sounding Deadman's Cay in the centre of the island.

Most guidebooks assert that the Lucayans called the island *Yuma*, but it is more likely that Yuma was Exuma, and that Long Island was the *Samana* which the AMERINDIANS first encountered by COLUMBUS pointed to as the major island of their people, where gold might be found. The explorer named the island Fernandina after his patron, the King of Spain, and found it well populated and pleasant, but without the sought-after precious metal. He immediately sailed on, as the canny islanders pointed him further to the south. Modern archaeologists have discovered that Long Island was indeed among the most populous and important of the Lucayans' islands. They too have found no gold, but numerous village sites, caves with petroglyphs, and innumerable artefacts, including ceremonial *duho* stools and religious ZEMIS.

A favourite rendezvous for pirates and fishing ground for the early settlers of ELEUTHERA and NEW PROVIDENCE, Long Island was first permanently settled by relatively poor LOYALISTS, mainly from the middle American colonies, who had few slaves and no grand plantocratic aspirations. The few would-be COTTON planters and SALT producers like Governor Lord DUNMORE soon failed, and the majority of the Loyalists who remained formed the small clan settlements which still bear their family names, living partly from the sea and small farming operations, but more distinctively from grazing scrawny cattle, horses and the goat-like local sheep for export to NASSAU.

Long Island has hills, rocky cliffs and splendid vistas, spectacular beaches, dive sites and fishing. But curiously it has not been transformed by TOURISM. The two chief resorts are at the north end of the island: the German-owned STELLA MARIS, near one of the two island airports for scheduled planes; and the luxurious and reclusive Cape Santa Maria Beach Resort, which lays claim to the very best beaches in The Bahamas, is difficult of access by road, but has its own airstrip for charter planes.

Ten miles (16 km) 'up south' (as Long Islanders say) from Stella Maris is the hamlet of Simms, formerly the administrative centre for the north of the island, with a neat Anglican church, post office, and tiny disused jail, still labelled H. M. Prison. The most notable descendant of the founding family of Simms is the artistic STRAW-worker Ivy Simms, whose work has been shown around the world and who now runs a small factory-workshop to produce straw hats, mats and bags for the discriminating visitor. The Simms family may well be *pre*-Loyalist, and descended from the mulatto ex-privateer and maybe pirate Benjamin Sims of New Providence, who left in his 1744 will a Captain Kidd-like treasure in golden guineas and doubloons worth altogether 1,500 pieces of eight.

LONG ISLAND

Another 15 miles (24 km) down the Queen's Highway is Salt Pond, where the Long Island Regatta is held each May. The next item of interest, 7 miles (11 km) further south on a deserted stretch of the road, is what is called even on the official Bahamas Survey map the 'Old Spanish Church'. This dilapidated building is the sole relic of a former settlement reportedly erased by a tidal wave some time in the nineteenth century. Local legend, however, gives it a much more piquant history. The settlement was said to have been founded by Spaniards from Cuba long before the first English settled The Bahamas. The chief evidence cited is the date 1609 allegedly engraved inside the church's bell-tower. Unfortunately, a sceptical examination reveals that the church is less than 200 years old, and that the indistinct inscription most likely reads 1809 – soon after the Loyalists came.

In typical Long Island fashion, both Deadman's Cay, the largest settlement and location of Long Island's main airport, and Clarence Town, the main stopping place for MAIL BOATS and administrative 'capital', a dozen miles further on, are scattered places without an obvious town centre. Clarence Town, though, is distinguished by two impressive white churches, facing each other on opposite hills. Both were the work of the architect priest Father JEROME. But one is Anglican, the other Roman Catholic. The former, along with three other churches in southern Long Island, was built while Father Jerome (then the Rev. Stephen Hawes) was still an adherent of the Church of England. The latter was constructed after his conversion to Rome, at the time when Catholic missionary clergy were busily proselytising Long Island and other Bahamas Out Islands.

The southern third of Long Island beyond Clarence Town is less scenic, more arid and more impoverished than the rest – belying the title the optimistic Columbus gave to its extreme tip: Cabo Verde. The ruins of Dunmore's plantation in the settlement that still bears his name set the tone of struggle and failure, as does the nearby hamlet called by disappointed ex-slaves HARD BARGAIN (a name, incidentally, shared by three other poor places elsewhere in The Bahamas). The curse of Lord Dunmore might also have been said to have blighted the extravagant project by the Diamond Crystal company to establish a huge solar salt plant nearby in the 1960s. Set up at the end of a spell of exceptionally dry years, it was ruined by a few years of unusually heavy rains. An attempt to transform the salinas into a colossal shrimp farm was an equal failure – though the word in 2002 was that Taiwanese Chinese were planning to step into the breach.

'Spanish' church, central Long Island

Long Islanders regard themselves as a distinctive people, as indeed they are commonly characterised by other Bahamians. Though there are settlements both south and north in which the people are the black direct descendants of African slaves, the majority of Long Islanders are mixed race 'Long Island whites'. Though proud of their descent from free LOYALIST settlers, they have never had quite the racial exclusivity of the 'CONCHY JOES' of the northern islands. Miscegenation – outside marriage as often as not – has always been a Long Island custom. Long Islanders, indeed, by vulgar repute are both handsome and famous lovers. Other Bahamians, perhaps out of jealousy, traditionally give a salacious connotation to both the physical endowments and the sexual stamina of 'Long Island Men' and 'Long Island Women.'

LOVE, Rev. Dr Joseph Robert

(1839–1914) Bahamian-born apostle of negritude and outspoken advocate for political and social change, who spent the last 30 years of his life in Jamaica and was the mentor of the 'Black Moses', Marcus GARVEY.

Born in Nassau in the year after the slaves were fully freed, to parents who had long been 'free coloureds', Robert Love attended St Agnes parish primary school and was one of the few black scholars taught at the CHRIST CHURCH grammar school. A bright and ambitious student, he was a teacher and Anglican lay preacher in Nassau for a few years, before looking for better opportunities in the United States just after the end of the Civil War. Ordained a deacon in the Episcopal Church in 1871, he worked for a time in Savannah, Georgia, before moving to New York, where in 1876 he became the first Afro-Bahamian to be ordained as a priest.

Following his ordination, Love attended medical school at the University of Buffalo, graduating as a doctor in 1879, at the age of 40. In 1881, he joined the Haitian Episcopal Mission under Bishop James Holly (the first African-American bishop in the Episcopal Church). Assigned to a congregation in Port-au-Prince consisting mainly of English-speaking West Indians, Love fell out with Bishop Holly over his plans to combine medical and pastoral work, and lost his position. He started his own church and accepted a post as physician to the Haitian army, but two years later was accused of inciting domestic discord by President Salomon and deported – choosing to settle with his family in Jamaica.

In his adopted country, Love soon added the role of journalist and political activist to his work as a doctor and minister. For twenty years (1885–1905) he was editor and chief writer of the *Jamaica Advocate*, which as the official publication of the Jamaican Union of Teachers gradually became more outspokenly radical and influential. Blazoning the achievements of such Afro-Americans as John Bruce, Edward Blyden, Sylvester Williams, W.E.B. Dubois and Booker T. Washington, and the work in Africa of black Baptist, Methodist and Episcopalian missionaries, Love's paper moved on from criticism of European colonialism in Africa to advocate improvements in popular education, land and tax reforms, and the return to representative government in Jamaica, along with the extension of the franchise – to women as well as all adult males.

In August 1898, Love organised a People's Convention to celebrate 'in a sympathetic and useful manner' the sixtieth anniversary of full freedom from slavery. This turned into a fervent forum for the discussion of popular political issues, and in the following year led to the formation of the Jamaican Association, which had the stated objective of protecting and extending the interests and rights of the ordinary Jamaican people. Now a widely respected figure (at least among the non-white majority), Love was elected to the Kingston City Council in 1900, was instrumental in the election of the first non-white to the Legislative Council in 1901, and was himself elected to that body in 1906. Serving until struck down by serious illness in 1910 (at the age of 71), he was noted not just for his articulate but non-violent radicalism but for being 'of all the black members of the Legislative Council the only one to hold a distinctly Negro attitude … a great exponent of racial pride, or negritude'. Perhaps his most notable declaration was one that was to be echoed by the black Bahamian populist Milo BUTLER half a century later: 'We love the white man because he is a brother; we love the coloured man because he is a son; we love the black man because we love ourselves.'

It was Robert Love's writings and political activity that largely inspired the young Marcus Garvey with pride in the African heritage, awareness of what Afro-Americans had already achieved against the odds, and their potential to improve their own lives and become politically influential once effectively organised and led. Love's work with the Jamaican Teachers' Union, People's Convention and Jamaican Association encouraged Garvey's own trade union efforts and the formation of the United Negro Improvement Association in the year that Robert Love died. However, after a brief false dawn in the early 1920s, it was to be at least another 40 years before the movement seeded by Robert Love and nurtured by Marcus Garvey came to full fruition – with the islands where Robert Love was born, ironically, almost bringing up the rear in the march to Jubilee.

LOWE, Alton Roland

LOWE, Alton Roland White Abaconian realist painter, largely self-taught, who equals BRENT MALONE in popularity and success and has even been called 'the national painter of the Bahamas' by his most fervent admirers.

A seventh-generation descendant of American LOYALISTS, Alton Lowe was born and bred in the maritime village of New Plymouth on GREEN TURTLE CAY, to which he returned as the most distinguished resident and benefactor once he had achieved success. His father, Albert Lowe, a noted boatbuilder who turned to making exquisite models when the industry declined, encouraged Alton to draw boats and local scenes from the age of eight and, at 12, to pick up the rudiments of painting from visiting American amateurs. Showing a precocious talent, when he left school at 16 he went to New York and Florida in the hope of pursuing an artistic career.

While abroad, Alton Lowe learned to paint in oils as well as other techniques. At first he concentrated on religious themes, mountain scenes and female nudes. But he was irresistibly drawn back to the subjects he knew and loved best: the seas, skies and traditional lifestyles of the people of his native Abaco – particularly the Conchy Joe mariners, their wives and flaxen-haired children. He held his first one-man show in Nassau in 1969 at the age of 25. Lowe's paintings found an avid market among those who were attracted by their colour, charm and verisimilitude. But to the discriminating viewer they struck a far deeper chord. To the authors of *Islanders in the Stream*, 'The patient ancient mariner, hand on tiller, quizzically gazing over the emerald shallows to the dark blue deep; the blond, blue-eyed young woman forever scanning the horizon for a returning sail', conveyed 'a more profound and complex mix of endurance, isolation, and poignant longing'.

Alton Lowe returned permanently to Green Turtle Cay in 1983 and built a substantial house in traditional Abaconian style on a high bluff, with views to the ocean in the east and over the inland 'Sea of Abaco' to the west. With the aim of preserving the heritage which was in his heart and had made his fortune, he created and endowed the Albert Lowe Museum (occupying a carefully restored traditional wooden house dating from 1826). Along with the sculptor James Masten he was also responsible for the creation of the Loyalists' Memorial Garden in his native New Plymouth.

LOYALISTS Term given to those white and free coloured refugees from the American War of Independence who, along with their slaves, reshaped The Bahamas; and, in more subtle and less freely acknowledged ways, were themselves reshaped by the islands.

The British imperial government, having kept The Bahamas while giving up Florida to the Spaniards as well as having lost the Thirteen Colonies to the Americans, freely offered the underpopulated and undeveloped islands as a refuge to those Tories who had opposed the Americans in the war and preferred to stay under the rule of the British Crown. Free land grants began in 1783 and lasted almost a decade. The resulting influx of newcomers to The Bahamas – some 1,600 whites, a few hundred free non-whites, and 5,000 slaves – constituted no more than 7 per cent of the total of post-war emigrants. Yet they trebled the colony's population, raised the proportion of slaves and free non-whites from a half to two-thirds, and increased the number of permanently settled islands from three to twelve.

The Bahamian 'Loyalists' were also a far more variegated influx than is traditionally described, with very different backgrounds and aspirations. The majority were categorised as 'white farmers and their slaves', who had been displaced from the southern mainland colonies, arrived by way of Florida or New York, and were expected to set up COTTON plantations on Bahamian Out Islands much like those they had left behind. Yet very few were in fact experienced planters with a large slave retinue, and cotton planting proved far more difficult than originally thought. Many more were either small-scale farmers with a handful of slaves, or displaced soldiers, officials and professionals, who much preferred to settle in the colonial capital than to tame an arid, rocky and bushy Out Island tract.

Even more complex were the varieties of non-whites who were part of the 'Loyalist' influx. Many were indeed plantation or domestic slaves, used to a life of toil and bondage, though for the most part creolised Afro-Americans rather than native Africans recently enslaved. Others (mainly arriving from New York) were ex-slaves promised their freedom in return for fighting for King George, or completely acculturated longer-freed blacks or coloureds, who were often skilled craftsmen, sometimes literate, and even owning slaves themselves.

In many ways, the newcomers did transform what they found. ABACO was the earliest island settled, though soon found less suitable for growing cotton than CAT ISLAND, LONG ISLAND, EXUMA, CROOKED ISLAND, ACKLINS and SAN SALVADOR, which (along with the Caicos Islands) were soon completely subdivided and cleared for plantations. When cotton proved an illusion, many of these plantations folded, but those that survived diversified into producing SALT, or became provision and stock farms for the Nassau market. At the same time, the slaves on decayed plantations who were not shipped

Shell of Loyalist grandeur: the remains of the Deveaux mansion, Port Howe, Cat Island

elsewhere turned themselves into a virtually independent subsistence peasantry. Their free descendants were either sharecroppers or worked land whose former white owners had long departed, which they held by squatters' right or in commonage.

The change wrought on NASSAU by the Loyalists was equally dramatic. The whites did their utmost to make the Bahamian capital like pre-war Charleston or even Philadelphia. They revivified the legislature and courts, added two new Anglican churches and a Presbyterian kirk and erected elegant public and private buildings on mainland architectural models. The lineaments of a polite society were created by setting up schools (for girls as well as boys), introducing the first library, print works, NEWSPAPERS, clubs, a literary and debating and an agricultural society, and theatrical entertainments.

Nassau became much larger and socially much more clearly subdivided. The richer whites lived downtown or on the ridge facing the harbour, while poor whites lived in humbler houses along the shore. Slaves no longer tended to live in their owner's yard and began to build up a black shanty-town Over-the-Hill. The small intermediate class of free non-whites appropriately lived mainly in between, on the reverse slopes of the ridge.

Tensions arose between the newcomers and the 'old inhabitants'. The established whites resented being outvoted in the reorganised legislature, while the Loyalists deplored, even despised, the easy-going society which they found. What caused most friction however was the sudden arrival of so many non-white immigrants, and differences over the way they should be treated. White former planters from the southern colonies naturally inclined towards strict control, applied to those non-whites claiming to be free, as well to the slaves. Alarmed by the black influx, many old inhabitants soon concurred. But the relatively large number of 'Loyalist' blacks and coloureds who claimed freedom resisted the tightening of regulations, finding allies first among the urban slaves and then, once plantations began to fail, among those slaves in the Out Islands who were either overworked or underemployed. This racial situation became especially severe once revolution broke out in neighbouring HAITI in 1791 and Britain went to war against Revolutionary France two years later.

All in all, the Loyalist-dominated Bahamas did not become an offshore replica of South Carolina but a subtle amalgam of the old colony and new features. Once cotton failed to produce the hoped-for bonanza, most of those Loyalists who could forsook The Bahamas altogether, going on to other islands in the region, to Britain, or even back to the United States. The poorer whites who never aspired to be planters had no option but to stay and adapted as best they could to Bahamian conditions, though in different ways. Those remaining in Abaco sundered themselves completely from non-whites, settled on the offshore cays, intermarried only with the existing white communities of HARBOUR ISLAND and northern ELEUTHERA, and established an almost entirely maritime way of life. Those settled in Long Island proudly retained their Loyalist heritage, but lived in more comfortable proximity to non-whites, becoming, indeed, gradually miscegenated – to form the distinctive type called 'Long Island White'. Much the same degree of racial mixing occurred in central and southern Eleuthera. Elsewhere in the Out Islands, however, the Loyalists' slaves and their descendants formed all-black settlements (and whole-island populations) of peasant farmer-fishermen, always poor and ill-served, and in times of drought and hurricane almost destitute.

Very different were the failed planters who chose to stay in Nassau, or had no choice but to do so. In the Bahamian mini-metropole, they reinforced the existing ruling socio-economic class, living by PRIVATEERING until the wars ended in 1815, and then building up a mercantile oligarchy based on wrecking, salt-production and a monopoly of trade. They commanded the land and labour as best they could, while proudly adhering to the traditional social patterns, legislative and legal machinery of the old regime. Well into the twentieth century the families descended from the Loyalist whites saw themselves as an ordained elite – a local aristocracy inferior to none – a stance

LUDWIG, Daniel K.

which even the families descended from the seventeenth-century Adventurers found it difficult to gainsay.

Further reading: G. Saunders, *Bahamian Loyalists and their Slaves*, Macmillan, 1983; S. Riley, *Homeward Bound: A History of the Bahama Islands to 1850, with a Definitive Study of Abaco in the American Loyalist Plantation Period*, Island Research, 1983; Craton and Saunders, *Islanders*, i. 177–357; M. Craton, 'Hopetown and Hard Bargain: The Loyalist Transformation in the Bahamas', in R. Bennett (ed.), *Settlements in the Americas: Cross Cultural Perspectives*, University of Delaware, 1993, 252–82; 'Loyalists Mainly to Themselves: The 'Black Loyalist' Diaspora to the Bahamas, 1783–c1820', in V. A. Shepherd (ed.), *Working Slavery, Pricing Freedom: Perspectives from the Caribbean, Africa and the African Diaspora*, Ian Randle Press, 2002, 44–68.

LUDWIG, Daniel K. (1897–1992) Billionaire American shipbuilder and entrepreneur who was one of the shapers of FREEPORT, GRAND BAHAMA in the late 1950s and early 1960s.

Born poor in South Haven, Michigan, Daniel Ludwig did not proceed beyond grade eight in school and started his own business at the age of 19. Making his way as a shipper of bulk molasses on the Great Lakes, he founded National Bulk Carriers in 1936 and accrued his first millions by building Liberty ships in World War Two, pioneering the use of welding in place of traditional rivets. By the end of the war D. K. Ludwig was already the fifth largest ship builder and owner in the United States. But it was in servicing the postwar demand for ever larger and cheaper shipments of oil and ores that Ludwig's business grew most spectacularly. His shipyards, first in Norfolk, Virginia and then in Kure, Japan, built over a hundred supertankers and large ore carriers, ranging up to 950 feet (290 m) in length and 107,000 deadweight tonnage. At its peak in the 1960s NBC was the largest single-owned shipping company in the world.

This did not exhaust Ludwig's almost manic quest for wealth, and among countless other projects he became a willing associate of Wallace Groves in Grand Bahama. By the Hawksbill Creek Agreement of 1955, Groves was bound to produce a deep-water harbour. This fitted in well with Ludwig's machinations. Currently in tough negotiations with the Japanese, he dredged the harbour while threatening to transfer his main shipyard from Japan to The Bahamas.

When the Japanese caved in, the Freeport shipyard plan was scrapped and Ludwig apparently regarded it as a loss leader and moved on. Not so. As it soon transpired, he had made a typically tough deal with Groves, exchanging the cost of excavating the harbour for much of the surrounding land and a thousand undeveloped acres close to downtown Freeport. In 1961, Ludwig sold the harbourside land to United States Steel to build a giant cement works, more than recouping his costs. In the following years, without personal publicity, he pursued much grander plans for his other acreage. In collaboration with the Grand Bahama Port Authority he helped build two major hotels, a casino and shopping centre, and on his own account an area of luxury homesites surrounding an 18-hole golf course, called Bahamia. With typical astuteness, it was only when he sensed that the Freeport bubble was about to burst in the later 1960s that Ludwig sold up and turned his attentions elsewhere.

Further reading: 'K. Ludwig: Industrial Typhoon', *Bahamas Handbook and Businessman's Annual, 1965-6*, Dupuch Publications, 1985, 356–67; P. Barratt, *Grand Bahama*, David and Charles, 1972, 94–5, 103, 145–9; J. A. Shields, *The Invisible Billionaire: Daniel Ludwig*, Houghton Mifflin, 1986.

MSC vessel entering Freeport's container terminal in 2002 in the harbour first dredged out by National Bulk Carriers D. K. Ludwig in the 1950s

LYFORD CAY

LYFORD CAY First and still foremost millionaires' enclave in The Bahamas, dating from 1958. Located on the previously almost uninhabited western extremity of NEW PROVIDENCE, Lyford Cay was created by Canadian tycoon Edward Plunkett Taylor (1901–89), with enthusiastic support from the three foremost members of the former BAY STREET oligarchy, Sir Harold CHRISTIE, Sir Roland SYMONETTE and Sir Stafford SANDS. It owes its continuing success in radically changed times, however, not just to its founders or to a maintenance of their policies of exclusivity based on social and ethnic grounds, but to the combined efforts of its managers, property owners and club members to maintain the highest standards of services, to rely on the natural segregation of sheer wealth (combined with snob appeal), and through a judicious exercise of *noblesse oblige* towards ordinary Bahamians through the philanthropic Lyford Cay Foundation.

Lyford Cay was named for its erstwhile owner, the merchant, privateer, sea-pilot and planter William Lyford Jr. (1719–94). He was born in Nassau at the time of Governor Woodes ROGERS and spent much of his life in Charleston, South Carolina and Savannah, Georgia, before fleeing first to Florida and then The Bahamas with other LOYALISTS in the early 1780s. According to the best-selling author Arthur Hailey (one of the most famous modern residents of Lyford Cay), William Lyford was a comrade-in-arms of the 'Bahamian Liberator' Andrew DEVEAUX in 1783, though the evidence is flimsy. What is more certain is that Lyford was one of the notable Loyalists receiving grants of Crown land and money in the late 1780s in compensation for his losses in the War of Independence. On condition of paying the routine annual quit rent of a farthing an acre, Lyford was given, besides 448 acres in western New Providence, 592 acres in southern CAT ISLAND (then called San Salvador), and was also granted £1,000 (typically, only a ninth of his claim) from the Loyalist Compensation Fund. With his few slaves, Lyford set out to grow cotton and guinea corn and to run stock on his two estates – on both of which he built small houses. But he had limited success as a planter. His lands were put up for sale on his death at the age of 75 in 1794, but found no immediate takers. For a few years the Lyford Cay acreage was owned by the chief West End proprietor William WYLLY (who bought it for £179 in 1808) though, like the rest of Wylly's land,

Lyford Cay

LYFORD CAY

it gradually fell into 'casual cultivation' or outright bush and swamp thereafter.

The small cay (formerly called West End Cay) which was the distinguishing feature of Lyford's New Providence estate was already almost joined to the mainland, and had become the rocky tip of a complete peninsula by 1840. For more than a century it and the beautiful curving beaches on each side were a favourite spot for picnickers, and before 1950 a few houses were built nearby by discerning expatriates. The person who visualised Lyford Cay's future most clearly, however, was the king of Bahamian realtors, Harold Christie (1896–1973), who used his unrivalled (often questionable) skills to acquire 2,800 surrounding acres, and built a house for himself on the point, which he hoped would be the focus of an exclusive, self-contained residential development for wealthy expatriates.

Land-rich but comparatively money-poor, and without the necessary management expertise to fulfill such a grandiose dream on his own, Christie more than met his match in the person of the richest Canadian entrepreneur, E. P. Taylor. While never becoming quite a tax refugee like Sir Harry OAKES, Taylor and his wife began to treat New Providence as a winter refuge in 1945, buying the elegant historic mansion *Jacaranda* in Nassau, and cementing friendships with the 'Bay Street' big-wigs and the titled and monied winter residents.

Taylor first viewed Lyford Cay in December 1945 as a guest of the American millionaire Allan Miller, one of the first to build there, and was pursued as a partner by Harold Christie. But after complex negotiations Taylor purchased the entire 2,800 acre property (and more) for himself in 1954, for $16 million, through a specially created Lyford Cay Development Company. Yet this was only the beginning of a colossal five-year transformation, costing at least $35 million before the first house-plots were sold.

Taylor's company was allowed to reroute West Bay Street, so that the Lyford Cay estate was totally cut off by a single security gate, effectively denying public access to the 'Cay' itself and its adjacent miles of superb beaches. From the beginning, no provision was made for the non-white workers to live within Lyford Cay's sacred precincts – an employees' village being constructed (according to official publicity, following the employees' wishes) on the eastern edge of the company's adjacent property. Not surprisingly, commercial outlets were also outlawed within the gated area – a tastefully designed small shopping mall and commercial centre being built just outside the guarded entrance.

A golf course, tennis courts, the first club house and a restaurant were ceremonially opened by Governor Sir Raynor Arthur on 1 December 1958 and within a further year the entire enterprise was a certain success – with the majority of house-lots already sold, for prices that would have paid for a mansion as well as a lot almost anywhere else in The Bahamas.

As far as the majority of residents wish, Lyford Cay is a totally self-contained community. Changes have come gradually and without disruption, with only a few of the oldest inhabitants expressing nostalgia for the almost total social exclusivity of the earliest years. The self-made wealthy now probably outnumber those with inherited money and hereditary titles. Besides such super-stars of page and screen as Arthur Hailey and Sean Connery (both born poor), there are working millionaires such as several members of the BACARDI clan – and perhaps a few of less reputable provenance. There are also now a considerable number of Bahamian property owners and Club members (the two categories are not quite synonymous) – and these are not just the sons and grandsons of Bay Street 'white knights' but also the more socially aspirant post-Independence non-white entrepreneurs. Gone are the days when the acceptance of the ultra-respectable Sir Kendal ISAACS as the first black member of the Lyford Cay Club (he never considered becoming a resident) was seen as shocking. Nowadays, almost all Lyford Cay residents contribute generously to the Lyford Cay Foundation, which performs many good works for Bahamian culture and provides scholarships for needy but worthy Bahamian students.

Lyford Cay has long been a benchmark and model within The Bahamas for communities of its kind. What is now almost forgotten is that it was, incidentally, the location of the event of greatest global significance ever to occur in The Bahamas. This was the three-power summit conference in 1962 between President John F. Kennedy and Prime Ministers Harold Macmillan and John Diefenbaker, which formulated the principle of Britain's (and Canada's) independent nuclear deterrent – the cornerstone of the 'free world's' alignment during the Cold War. Among the top level British participants was the Colonial Secretary Duncan Sandys, who took the opportunity of the Lyford Cay Conference to meet with local political leaders and discuss the changes that led to the achievement of internal self-government two years later.

Further reading: A. Hailey, *The Lyford Legacy: A History of Lyford Cay From 1788*, Lyford Cay Property Owners' Association, 2004; R. Rohmer, *E.P. Taylor*, Goodread Biographies, 1995.

MCKAY, Tony, 'Exuma', 'the Obeah Man' (1943–1997) Singer, songwriter, stage performer and painter, Tony McKay – better known as 'Exuma' or 'the Obeah Man' – did more than anyone else to publicise the more picturesque aspects of Bahamian culture, throughout the United States and further afield.

Despite his adopted stage name, Tony McKay was not an Exumian. Christened McFarlane Gregory Anthony McKay, he was born at Tea Bay, Cat Island and lived much of his life on Canaan Lane, off Shirley Street in Nassau. Though with minimal schooling, at the age of 17 he left for New York with ambitions to become an architect. Running out of money, he became an entertainer, cleverly catching on to the cult of folk music and spirit of protest current in the later 1960s and 1970s. Inventing a persona and adopting hairstyles and costumes that were extravagant if not bizarre, he drew on traditional Bahamian folk songs, the uniquely infectious rhythms of JUNKANOO and RAKE 'N SCRAPE, and the more colourful aspects of Afro-Bahamian folk culture, especially OBEAH. He was also fortunate in attracting capable and compatible sidemen for his style of music.

Tony McKay became something of a cult icon in Greenwich Village, performing alongside such contemporary stars as Bob Dylan, Richie Havens, Jimi Hendrix, Peter, Paul and Mary, and Barbara Streisand. He recorded *Exuma, the Obeah Man* and *Exuma II* with Mercury Records and four almost equally successful albums under contract with the Budda/Kama Sutra label. At the height of his popularity he opened the show for most of the top rock, jazz and reggae performers of the day, largely in New York and New Orleans, but also on tours to Jamaica, Holland and France. His music was performed by many other artists, notably the radical black artiste Nina Simone, who recorded 'Obeah Woman' and 'Dambala', among other songs.

In 1978, Tony McKay was awarded the British Empire Medal by the Queen for his contribution to Bahamian and Caribbean music. As his international fame receded during the 1980s and 1990s he spent more time back in The Bahamas, recording more exclusively local music on his own Nassau Records label; in recognition of this he was awarded a Bahamas Tourism Award. A growing proportion of Tony McKay's time, though, was devoted to developing his remarkable parallel talent as a self-taught painter. His subjects were the mundane but picturesque daily lives of ordinary black Bahamians, and more abstract representations of their inner souls and African heritage. Exhibiting with increasing success in Key West and Baltimore as well as Nassau from 1990, his work was said by one enthusiast in 1995 to convey 'the mystique and beauty of Bahamian life as stunningly in painting as in song'.

Not noted for an abstemious lifestyle, Tony McKay died in January 1997 at the age of 54.

Further reading: 'Exuma: The Obeah Man: A Bahamian Musical Icon', *Bahamas Handbook and Businessman's Annual 1996*, Dupuch Publications, 1996, 64-70; A. M. Sears, 'Exuma', Nina Simone website, www.boscarol.com/nina/exuma.html

Tony 'Exuma' McKay

MCKINNEN, Daniel An early travel writer, whose *Tour through the British West Indies* (1804) provides an invaluable account of The Bahamas and its inhabitants just after the LOYALIST influx. His most interesting statement is that contemporary Bahamians exhibited most of the (allegedly admirable) characteristics of the aboriginal Lucayans, despite the fact that the islands had been uninhabited for almost two centuries when the first white settlers came. Perhaps inadvertently, this assertion implies that it has always been the ecology and climate of the islands which has shaped their inhabitants, rather than vice versa

MAIL BOATS Despite what its boats are called, the regular government-supported shipping service between NASSAU and the Family Islands has never been entirely – or even mainly – devoted to carrying the mail. Laden with provisions, supplies and island produce, and crowded with passengers travelling to and from their home islands and places of work, Bahamian 'mail boats' have always been – and still remain – essential life-lines.

The Last Bahamian sail mailboat, Captain Sherwin Archer's *Arena*, 1950s

Regular mail services to and from The Bahamas began with the establishment of the West Indies packet boat route through the Crooked Island Passage (with a general Bahamas post office established at Pitt's Town on the north-western tip of CROOKED ISLAND) during the Napoleonic War, and took a substantial forward step with the formation of the Royal Mail Steam Packet line by James McQueen in 1842. Yet transportation *within* the islands – for passengers and cargo as well as mail – remained a matter of private enterprise and was haphazard throughout slavery days. A government-subsidised internal mail service was proposed as early as 1819 but not implemented until 1832, and never entirely regulated or regularised. The owners of boats serving the islands were simply paid a flat rate for carrying the mail, as long as they guaranteed a more or less regular service.

The first regularly scheduled mail boat was the fast-sailing former pilot-boat *Dart*, which began a service between Nassau and HARBOUR ISLAND in the 1850s. New routes were gradually added, but for fifty years mail boats were exclusively sailing vessels – the last of which, Captain Sherwin Archer's former sponge schooner *Arena*, serving ABACO, was not phased out until the 1950s. These heroic days – when mail schooners might be caught in sudden storms or becalmed for days, and the round trip to Inagua normally took two weeks – are admirably portrayed in the accounts by L. G. POWLES (1888) and Amelia DEFRIES (1917).

From the 1920s, however, the scattered islands were more firmly roped together by a heterogeneous flotilla of small motor vessels. Many of them were wooden-hulled converted sailboats, seemingly rickety and top-heavy, but still capable of negotiating the shoals and storms of Bahamian waters in the hands of their sea-hardened and expert captains and crews. Named after their owner's wife, children or a girlfriend, the owner or captain himself, or, in one case, even an eighteenth-century pirate (the *Stede Bonnet*), each vessel had its own character. Along with their captains and crew, they became respected, even loved, by the islanders whom they served year after year. Though most of the boats were owned by Bay Street merchants, some were still captained by their owners, and all captains, whether white, brown or black, were very important personages indeed in the islands which they serviced. Typical of these heroes was Frederick Bain, the towering grandfather of the future Prime Minister Lynden PINDLING, Captain of the Sawyers' *Alisada*, who owned shops and kept separate families in Nassau and LONG ISLAND.

The journalist Michael Mardon, who somewhat nervously ventured on the five-day voyage of the MV *Air Pheasant* to INAGUA in 1967, gave a memorable account of a typical mail boat of those now seemingly distant days: the chaotic loading and rush for cabins or deckspace before the evening departure from Nassau's POTTER'S CAY dock; the outward cargo of foodstuffs, drinks and other provisions, building supplies, hardware, appliances, gas cylinders, oil drums, and (last-loaded) a couple of cars or trucks; the moonlit or sunstruck chugging passage across glittering or multicoloured smooth waters; the rough and ready food, and passengers whiling away time with dominoes, cards, hymn singing and endless talk and arguments; the eager crowds and confused and prolonged transshipments at each stopping place (Long Island, CROOKED ISLAND, Long Cay and ACKLINS before Matthew Town, Inagua); the sudden storm and rough waters off Castle Island which produced wails and groans among the fearful and the seasick majority.

Michael Mardon spent much of the voyage listening to the sea yarns of the *Air Pheasant*'s Captain Anton Lockhart. Like his fellow Ragged Islanders, Lockhart had learned his sea skills in fishing the Great Bahama Bank and smuggling across the Old Bahama Channel into and out of Cuba. For more than 40 of his 56 years, though, he had been crew or captain of island mail boats. His most dreadful memory was of the night in June 1931 when his boat had been run down and cut in two by a liner off Castle Island, killing his first wife, brother and brother-in-law. He also told tales of great storms, other shipwrecks, rescuing shipwrecked and stranded mariners and Haitian migrants, and warning off Cuban fishermen poaching in Bahamian waters.

Michael Mardon enjoyed his experience (especially in retrospect) but flew back to Nassau from Inagua. He went down to Potter's Cay five days later to see the *Air Pheasant*'s return. The passengers were a different set but the same islander types, and the captain and crew greeted him almost like family. The vessel was nearly as laden as on the outward voyage. Besides the precious small canvas bags of mail, it unloaded cases of island produce, penned sheep, goats, pigs and a horse, a hundred crates of empty soda bottles and dozens of gas cylinders and oil drums for refilling.

Much of this former ambience is retained half a lifetime later, though now most of the vessels are steel-built, larger, somewhat faster and more efficient, and most of the mail and the comparatively wealthier passengers are now carried by BAHAMASAIR. Now that most Family Islands have abattoirs and packing houses and all mail boats have refrigeration, livestock is rarely carried and the produce is more neatly stacked. On many trips the majority of deck passengers are no longer Bahamians but Haitian migrants, travelling to different islands or returning to New Providence in search of work. With the decline of the Bay Street shipowners, most of the vessels are owned by syndicates of small businessmen (such as the MV *Bimini Mack*, owned by the Bimini Businessmen's Association) or island cooperatives (like the North Cat Island Cooperative Society, owner of the prosaically-named MV *North Cat Island Special*). Though dedicated to making it as much a self-sustaining private enterprise as possible, in order to maintain a reliable general service and sustain some of the less prosperous Family Islands, the government has been constrained to pump up to $20 million to operators through the Bahamas Development Bank since 1980, and to make subsidies totalling more than $2 million a year.

In return, the mail boat operators are obliged to carry free not just mail packages but all government supplies, and all officials (now very much a minority) who choose to travel by mail boat on official business rather then by air. Besides this, government continues the practice, dating back three-quarters of a century, of fixing the tariff for goods carried to the advantage of customers living in the Family Islands. Captains are strictly tested and licensed, and boats fairly rigorously inspected for seaworthiness and safety features, by the Nassau Port Authority.

Potter's Cay Dock (under the original PARADISE ISLAND bridge) remains the central hub of the entire system, involving almost 30 subsidised mail boats. But Nassau's metropolitan dominance is reinforced (as it always has been) by the fact that all services are simple out-and-back or round trips, with extremely limited opportunities to sail between the different Family Islands themselves. The Potter's Cay terminus (along with its adjacent fish and produce stalls) remains a restless and fascinating section of 'the real Bahamas', particularly during the August holiday weekend, when many of the boats are crowded with happy families off to the various Family Island 'homecomings', or in May when excursions are laid on to the OUT ISLAND REGATTA at George Town, EXUMA.

At all times of year, though, a mail boat trip remains a memorable experience for the most hardy and adventurous foreign visitors. Almost all guidebooks (whose authors may or may not have undertaken a trip themselves) give such excursions a glamorous spin. But, as always, it is the *Lonely Planet* guide that gives it a more cautionary evaluation:

> *It all sounds so Conradian and romantic, hopping aboard a beaten-up vessel – most are small general-cargo freighters, long on durability and short on luxury and, sometimes, seaworthiness – steered by a cheroot-smoking skipper surrounded by bales of bananas and sacks of letters. … A mail-boat trip does provide a unique sense of adventure and puts you close to Bahamians. But be prepared to have your carefully made plans shredded. All the vessels are slow and notoriously unreliable. You'll need to be flexible. Mail-boat travel can also be arduous. Many of the passages, such as the Crooked Island Passage and the crosscurrents in the New Providence Passage, are quite treacherous. Occasional (OK, make that frequent) rough seas and the smell of diesel can induce seasickness. … Accommodations vary from spartan to ultra-spartan. Often the only sleeping spaces are on wooden benches lining the narrow corridors… and you'll have to scramble for your spot before the savvy islanders. The losers get to sleep on the greasy floor. Sleeping on deck is usually better than suffering the fetid conditions below. This is not the Love Boat! You may be handed some fruit, a soda, and perhaps a tin of Spam on boarding but don't count on it. Take eats and drinks – especially a bottle of rum – to share with locals. A pack of cards comes in handy.*

Further reading: L. D. Powles, *The Land of the Pink Pearl: Recollections of Life in the Bahamas* (1888), Media Publishing, 1996; A. Defries, *In a Forgotten Colony*, Nassau Guardian, 1917; M. Mardon, 'A Passage to Inagua', *Bahamas Handbook and Businessman's Annual 1967*, Dupuch Publications, 1967, 36–48; 'Mail-Boats: Our Family Island Lifeline', *Bahamas Handbook and Businessman's Annual 1992*, Dupuch Publications, 1992, 150–3, 412–16.

MAIZE

Maize, alias Indian corn (*Zea mays*) is a gigantic, grain-producing domesticated grass originating in Mexico. Its cultivation accompanied – indeed, made possible – the development of civilisations throughout Meso-America, and facilitated the migration of the first peoples into other parts of the Americas, including the Caribbean and The Bahamas.

In colonial times, Bahamians – especially subsistence farmers in the Out Islands after slavery ended – were probably rather more dependent on corn than their Amerindian predecessors. But at the same time they did have the advantages of more varieties of corn, and metal mills as well as the age-old pestles and mortars. To an extremely limited extent corn growing for subsistence and the traditional methods of storage, preparation and cooking can still be found in some Family Islands. Bahamians as a whole still enjoy sweet corn bread, corn pone and corn dumplings, and boiled grits with fish remains a favourite breakfast. But little if any of the ingredients are home-grown any more, being imported, like the great majority of Bahamian foodstuffs, from North America. Some of the corn-flour recipes derive from elsewhere in the Caribbean (some originally from Africa) and even the relishing of hominy grits (an acquired taste if ever there was one) is a tradition that derives from the southern United States.

Further reading: R. J. Salvador, 'Maize', in *The Encyclopedia of Mexico: History, Culture and Society*, Fitzroy and Dearborn, 1997; D. Watts, *The West Indies: Patterns of Development, Culture and Environmental Change Since 1492*, Cambridge University Press, 1987, 53–77; www.maize.agron.iastate.edu

MALONE, Brent (1941–2004) The most distinguished and versatile of Bahamian artists, whose work joyously and proudly celebrates the culture and beauty of his native country.

Born in Nassau of 'CONCHY JOE' parents in 1941, Brent Malone demonstrated a precocious talent and by the age of 12 had made the brave decision to pursue a career in art. Obtaining an early grounding from local black artist Don Russell and his expatriate art teachers at QUEEN'S COLLEGE, Maureen Liddell, John Beadle and David Gill, he was the first Bahamian to obtain a distinction in Art in the Cambridge School Certificate.

Between 1957 and 1959, Malone, along with Maxwell TAYLOR, Kendall Hanna and the very young Eddie MINNIS, served an apprenticeship with the branch of the Chelsea Pottery set up in Nassau under the patronage of Sir Harold CHRISTIE and the direction of David Rawnsley. Encouraged by Rawnsley and David Gill, Malone then went to study at the Beckenham and Ravensbourne schools of art and design in England, acquiring a dazzling array of skills, in clothing design, etching and printing as well as pencil, crayon, pastel and oil paint media. After five years he returned to Nassau in 1964 when invited by Christie to take over the recently closed Chelsea Pottery – though this venture, renamed the Bahamian Pottery, failed within a year.

At that time it was not possible for an artist in The Bahamas to live entirely by his own work. For years, Brent Malone was torn between the compulsion to pursue his own muse, the need to run a series of galleries and boutiques to make ends meet, and the will to help out young artists less fortunate than himself. Through a series of successful group and one-man shows, however, his work gradually became famous and commanded first large and then astronomical prices. From 1972, thanks to the generosity of Lady Symonette, he had lived and had his studio and gallery in the elegant if somewhat faded gingerbread mansion on East Bay Street called The Temple, but in 1987 his business extended into the ownership of the upmarket Marlborough Antiques shop and gallery opposite the British Colonial Sheraton Hotel.

Success did not change either Malone's drive to paint or his encouragement of fellow Bahamian artists. Besides continuing to take on enormous commissions such as the mural for the foyer of the Swiss Bank building on Shirley Street, in 1991 he was the driving force behind the creation of the cooperative made up of six prominent Bahamian artists called B-CAUSE (Bahamian Creative Artists Unified for Serious Expression) – the stated aim of which was to promote the creation of a Bahamian National Art Gallery and school of art.

A dedicated, inventive and prolific artist, Brent Malone produced work that at opposite ends of the scale realistically portrays Bahamian people and life-ways (particularly those related to the sea), and symbolic designs on Bahamian themes that are most reminiscent

Brent Malone

of late nineteenth-century Art Nouveau. These seemingly contrasted styles came together in what became Brent Malone's almost trademark motif – the colourful and frenzied folk celebration of JUNKANOO. Still at the height of his powers, Brent Malone died of a heart attack in February 2004.

MALONE, Wyannie Legendary LOYALIST matriarch of the predominantly white settlement of HOPE TOWN, ABACO, after whom the local museum is named.

Although documentary records are scarce, family oral traditions attest that Wyanie Malone was a widow from Charleston, South Carolina who with her four children was among the founders of the settlement of Hope Town on Elbow Cay in 1785. Widow Malone is said to have moved on to Long Island, and one of her daughters to have run off with a Nantucket whaler. However, the other three children married and stayed – a daughter and namesake marrying a fellow Loyalist, Jacob Adams, and her two sons wedding girls from Harbour Island.

In 1902–3, purportedly scientific investigators from the BALTIMORE GEOGRAPHIC SOCIETY, using local oral testimony, drew up a vast genealogical chart to show that virtually all of the thousand white inhabitants of Hope Town could trace descent from the Widow Malone. Their purpose was clearly to show the adverse effects of genetic inbreeding. Yet, as the local resident historian Steve Dodge has conclusively argued:

> the scientists from Baltimore were so thrilled and excited to have discovered an experiment in human genetics that they misinterpreted, exaggerated and even fabricated the results. Further, recent studies seem to indicate that the deleterious results of inter-marriage, even of first cousins, have been grossly exaggerated, and that actually very few problems occur. The report of the Baltimore Geographical Society tells us more about the intellectual, social, and religious quirks of the 'scientists' from civilized Baltimore than it does about the people of Hope Town.

A century after it was published, the report was still a sore point with local whites. Yet rather than ignore or paint over the obvious flaws of the alleged scientists from Baltimore, they rightly celebrate and honour the Malone inheritance. Malone descendants – who included local entrepreneurs and promoters (notably the brothers Beltron, Ivor, Robert, Rudy and Vernon Malone), the most honoured of the surviving traditional boatbuilders (Winer Malone), and the foremost Bahamian artist (Brent Malone) – proudly combined to set up the fascinating museum bearing the name of their female forebear in 1975.

Further reading: G. B. Shattuck (ed.), *The Bahama Islands*, Baltimore Geographical Society, 1905, 410–14; S. Dodge, *Abaco: The History of an Out Island and its Cays*, 2nd ed. Decatur, White Sound Press, 1995, 179–82; S. Riley, *Homeward Bound*, Island Research, 1983.

MANATEE A slow-moving aquatic mammal of considerable charm once common in The Bahamas, the Caribbean manatee (*Trichecus manatus*) is now rarely seen. Though still to be spotted quite frequently in Florida, where it is protected because of its useful habit of eating greenery threatening to clog waterways, the last manatee seen for a long time in The Bahamas was one sighted in a canal in Freeport in 1975. More recently, however, manatees have again been seen in the Freeport canals and occasionally in the Berry Islands.

Growing up to 15 feet (4.5 m) in length, with a small, square head, tapering body and front and tail flippers, the manatee was either found singly or in family groups. Manatees communicate with each other by rubbing snouts, and emit chirping squeaks when alarmed. Perhaps surprisingly given their facial bristles, their appearance and languorous behaviour is said to have given rise to the legend of the mermaid.

Herbivorous, the manatee has no natural enemies, but is ill-equipped to coexist with man. Besides its lack of speed and poor eyesight, it has no offensive or defensive weapons. The Lucayans hunted it for its meat, but not to extinction. The early European settlers, who also valued its hide and oil, were far more predatory. Even the officially protected survivors in Florida are seriously endangered, not through hunting but from disastrous encounters with boat propellers.

MANGROVES Term loosely given to four distinct trees (red, black and white mangroves, and buttonwood) that together and in succession have a vital role in creating and expanding the flat dry lands of The Bahamas – a process that will continue as long as the plants are protected, not rooted out as unsightly by short-sighted developers.

The process (technically called ecological succession) began when the shallows in the lee of the limestone sand-dunes which emerged from the retreating ocean in the last ice age were colonised by the red mangrove (*Rhizoflora mangle*), a plant unusually well adapted to salt-water environments. A native to West Africa, the red mangrove produces seedlings capable of making long sea journeys, before resuming growth once they arrive at a destination with muddy shallows or rocky projecting crevices.

Once established, red mangroves spread, stilt-like, over the entire area shallow enough to allow their trunks and leaves access to the air, their tangled roots providing

MAN-O'-WAR CAY

a well-protected base for the build-up of a rich mulch of silts and vegetable matter. This, with the cooperation of micro-organisms, plant and animal inhabitants, very gradually fills in the tidal shallows originally colonised. Red mangroves are beneficial in other ways. They perform a vital role in the food chain of both land and sea creatures, providing food, such as marine fungi, for fishes and other marine creatures, and a habitat for crabs – which themselves become prey for raccoons and, in due course, human beings. In colonial times too, the red mangrove's leaves and bark provided a valuable red dye and tannin for curing leather, and its chemical-impregnated trunk wood proved valuably resistant to ship worms.

After the mixture of sediments and mulch colonised by red mangroves becomes a permanent mud, the black mangrove (*Svicennia nitida*) is ready to take over in the ecological succession. This tree is distinguished by the snorkel-like shoots (pneumatophores) sent up from the oxygen-starved mud towards the air – giving the mudflats something of the appearance of a bed of nails. Breathing in this way, the black mangrove roots grow strong and spread, holding the mud firm against erosion by waves or rain. Growing up to 40 feet (12 m) in height, the black mangrove has no commercial value in itself, but its fragrant white flowers are a potentially important source of bee honey.

As the mudflats colonised by the black mangroves gradually become hard ground, the white mangrove (*Laguncularia racemosa*) comes into its own. This taller tree (up to 60 feet (18m) in height and 2 feet (0.6 m) in girth), with succulent green leaves distinguished by salt-exuding glands at their base, is also said to be a honey source, as well as producing tannin from its rough, dark brown bark. On somewhat drier land, the white mangrove will give way to the buttonwood (*Conocarpus erecta*), also known as the button mangrove, another tall tree, producing a hard and heavy wood used in boatbuilding, as well as for charcoal and firewood. This tree, invariably found on the landward side of tidal mangrove swamps, in its turn yields to the areas of mixed coppice vegetation characteristic of flatlands that are permanently dry – thus ending what David Campbell has called 'the long march of the Bahamian mangrove'.

Further reading: D. G. Campbell, *The Ephemeral Islands: A Natural History of the Bahamas*, Macmillan, 1978; W. Cutts, *An Illustrated Guide to the Native Trees of the Bahamas*, Macmillan Caribbean, 2002.

MAN-O'-WAR CAY Third most populous of the five Abaco 'Loyalist Cays', rivalling SPANISH WELLS (off north Eleuthera) as the most traditionalist of all the 'CONCHY JOE' settlements.

Man-O'-War Cay – 3 ½ miles (5.6 km) long and about the same distance north of Elbow Cay – was named by the Royal Navy as early as the 1790s but apparently not settled until the 1820s. According to local oral tradition, the cay was first leased for farming to Benjamin Archer, a LOYALIST living at Marsh Harbour on the mainland. On a trip to the cay, Benjamin Archer's 13-year old daughter Eleanor met Benjamin Albury, a 16-year-old boy from Harbour Island, who had been wrecked and marooned there. They married and had 13 children, starting a tradition not only of extremely early marriages and large families but close consanguinity. In 1977, it was said that of the 235 Bahamian residents of Man-O'-War Cay, all but five could trace descent from Ben and Nellie Albury.

Fishing, farming and 'wrecking' were the mainstay of Man-O'-War, but after 1900 it became most notable for BOATBUILDING. This industry still continues, and flourishes, though mainly for the construction of fibre-glass boats rather than the traditional wooden Abaco schooners and dinghies. Compared with somewhat somnolent nearby Hope Town, Man-O'-War and its people seem constantly a-bustle.

According to Steve Dodge (who lives on Elbow Cay), Man-O'-War's 250 inhabitants are as different from their Hope Town neighbours as the Swiss are from Italians. The settlement does not live entirely in the past, but the inhabitants resolutely retain their age-old values. Some traditional 'Cape Cod' style wooden houses still line the tiny harbour, but most of the inhabitants live in modern bungalows fronted with trim lawns, and they get around on golf carts or motor scooters. They seem to be uniformly

Mangroves

MARKETING

prosperous but are deeply religious and teetotal and have welcomed neither hotels nor foreign residents. Until the 1950s, blacks were not even allowed to step ashore on the cay, and though today Bahamian-born HAITIANS are employed in the boatyards and as domestics, they are expected to leave the settlement by nightfall – either to go to their shacks at the north end of the cay (near the rubbish dump) or by boat to the mainland.

Though written 25 years ago, nothing conveys the ambience and charm of Man-O'-War better than the book written by its former native school-teacher Haziel T. Albury, *Man-O-War, My Island Home: A History of an Outer Abaco Island* (Holly Press, 1977). Coming close, however, is the wonderful collection of photographs displayed by the American Ruth Rodriguez in *Out Island Portraits, Bahamas 1946-1956* (Out Island Press, 1978).

MARKETING From the era of the peasant 'higgler' (itinerant vendor) to the age of capitalistic consumerism, the socio-economic history – if not the entire social history – of The Bahamas could be told through a description and analysis of changes in the patterns of marketing.

The situation and process were most clearly exemplified in the metropolitan island of NEW PROVIDENCE, as described in the general social history, *Islanders in the Stream*:

Black seamen land supplies from a mailboat on all-white Man O' War Cay, late 1940s

245

MARKETING

Unemployment and low wages meant that cash was short for food not grown at home, as well as for clothing and other imported goods. The balance of trade was heavily in favour of the importing wholesaler over the retailer and the retailer over the small producer. In the more distant settlements there was much peasant-like sharing and barter, but the nearer to Nassau a small producer lived the more necessary it was to enter the cash and market economies.

As in Africa, marketing played a large part in the lives of all black New Providence 'villagers', and most of the vendors were women. Some sold vegetables and fruits from door to door, other from small stalls outside their yards, at the end of their lanes, or in Grant's Town's small formal market. This market, petitioned for in 1840, was authorised and regulated by an act in 1850 that transferred the island's second formal market from Nassau's eastern suburbs and extended the monopoly of selling fish and fresh meat [from the downtown Nassau market]. . . . The original building, blown down in the 1866 hurricane, was rebuilt in 1873, but the Grant's Town Market never flourished and disappeared soon after 1900. It failed partly because local vendors were unwilling to pay rent for stalls in the formal market and were not constrained to do so, but mainly because downtown Nassau remained the predominant island mart, preferred by sellers and buyers from Grant's Town as well as the more distant settlements.

The majority of vendors went to downtown Nassau to sell in the streets or Market goods for which there was insufficient demand, or no sale at all, in the settlements. These included shell-work, hats and baskets made from plaited palmetto straw, or the African delicacy accara, made from cornmeal, as well as market garden produce. Many of the female vendors also purchased small items such as candies, peanuts, candles, matches, needles, mirrors and combs at downtown prices and sold them for tiny profits Over-the-Hill. The daily passage of market women up and down Market Street under the stone arch named after Governor Gregory, completed in 1852, was one of the picturesque Nassau sights. Some vendors walked great distances, their goods expertly balanced in flat wooden trays on their heads. The Fox Hill women usually walked all the way to town, ambling along with a swinging but stately gait, calling out their wares as they walked. In marketing, Bahamian women, like their Caribbean counterparts, exchanged news, ideas, and gossip. Such activities were vital forms of socialising and created information networks. Produce from the much more distant settlements of Adelaide and Gambier was usually brought up to Nassau Market on a donkey cart once or twice a week. If no carts were available, the vendor would walk – a round-trip of thirty-two miles for wares sold at both ends of the journey for scarcely a pound in all.

Haggling over prices, however, was, as in Jamaica and elsewhere, an essential feature of the higglers' mode of operation.

As time went on, shops became much more commonly the focus of retail trade, Over-the-Hill and even in the distant settlements, as well as in downtown Nassau. A vivid, if somewhat romanticised, vignette of such an establishment, called Morley's (situated either in Grant's Town or Fox Hill), was given by William Drysdale and L. D. POWLES in the 1880s. This shop was not only a general emporium, selling bottled beer, liquor and household goods as well as foodstuffs in small quantities (with a high cost-by-weight), but an important meeting place for the local community, open late into the night. Though it is not expressly stated, Morley was almost certainly a white Bahamian, fulfilling a vital intermediate entrepreneurial role between the local black community and the importing wholesalers and commission merchants.

The culmination of the capitalistic evolution of Bahamian commerce came in the era of economic prosperity that followed WORLD WAR TWO, and was characterised by the emergence of ever larger grocery and other retail businesses, and by the combination of different and novel business ventures, including TOURISM, tourist shops, transportation, fuel supplies, restaurants, bakeries, bottlers, brewers, the media, advertising and cinemas.

In The Bahamas today, direct selling by independent producers and the higgler market tradition do survive in at least two distinctive sectors of the economy: in the marketing of fish by fishermen at the dock, and in the sale of locally made STRAW products by straw-workers, predominantly women. At certain strategic street corners fruit and vegetable stalls are still to be found, but truly itinerant street vendors are almost a thing of the past. The two minor exceptions are the boys and young men who patrol the streets selling home-roasted and packaged peanuts and the daily NEWSPAPERS. Of far greater economic significance and carrying proportional political weight (on the male and female sides respectively) are the fish and straw-work sellers. Until recent years sales of fish were supposed to be limited to the official markets. But since the closing of Nassau's downtown fish (and turtle) market in the 1950s, flourishing informal markets for fish and conch have grown up where docking fishermen and local customers intersect – most notably under the Paradise Island bridge at POTTER'S CAY, at the Montagu boat ramp, and at ARAWAK CAY on Nassau's western

MARRIAGE CUSTOMS

Nassau market, Bay Street, 1890s

side. These outlets operate virtually outside government regulation or control.

Fish-sellers are almost exclusively male, but straw-work sellers not only represent the strongest survival of the female higgler tradition, but probably the most vigorous and vocal female pressure group in the modern Bahamas. The vendors in the main straw market on Bay Street or the satellite markets at other tourist centres expertly ply their picturesque trade by haggling potential customers with a combination of charm, aggression and guile. In doing so they sustain at least the appearance of strong competition between each other. But they have also frequently demonstrated an ability to combine whenever necessary to convince the government in power of their economic indispensability, and to win concessions.

Further reading: W. Drysdale, *In Sunny Lands*, Harper's, 1884; L. D. Powles, *The Land of the Pink Pearl: Recollections of Life in the Bahamas* (1888), Media Publications, 1996, 86–91; Craton and Saunders, ii. 105–11.

MARRIAGE CUSTOMS Traditional Bahamian courtship and marriage customs had a formality and importance which reflected not just a quest for respectability but the centrality of the nuclear family in Bahamian society. Even today, when 'family values' have been severely eroded by modernisation, weddings have remained important occasions for conspicuous display.

From the earliest colonial times formal church weddings performed and registered by a licensed minister were a crucial indicator of respectability, as well as of vital importance for such legal matters as legitimacy and inheritance. In the eighteenth century Bahamas they were, however, limited to Bahamian whites and the more respectable non-white free persons, ignoring the black slaves who made up the majority of the population by the third quarter of the eighteenth century – for whom, as legal chattel property, questions of respectability, legitimacy and inheritance were officially considered irrelevant. ..

The real situation among the slaves was, of course, different. Though precise evidence is sparse, the importance which Bahamian slaves (and even the more enlightened Bahamian slave-owners such as William WYLLY) attached to the formation of two-headed nuclear families strongly suggests that the slaves had their own protocols and ceremonies of courtship, betrothal and marriage – accompanied by the marital pair leaving their parents' houses to set up their own household. This process, if informal, seems to have more closely followed European rather than African practice (for example in not condoning polygyny), especially once the slaves had their own unlicensed 'Black Baptist' ministers towards the end of slavery.

That the marital customs of the black majority converged with those of persons never enslaved is also attested by the way that patterns of courtship, betrothal and marriage became generalised so soon after EMANCIPATION. The situation among islanders of all shades, from the mid-nineteenth century to the mid-twentieth, is summarised in the second volume of the social history *Islanders in the Stream*:

Courting for whites and blacks in the Out Islands was formal and not dissimilar to custom in Nassau. If he liked a girl, an Out Island man would consult his parents for their views even before making approaches to his intended and her family. Dowry was not a custom and wealth, not surprisingly, rarely a criterion. Far more important was respectability, health (that is, tacitly, nubility), and sufficient training in domestic skills. No young man would propose marriage with any hope of success who had not an independent competence in the way of land or boat or a house of his own completed, or nearly so.

Once a suitor's parents had approved of a match, he would write a letter to the girl's parents, requesting visiting rights. If he were illiterate, he would employ a competent scribe for this formal missive, as well as for any love letters he chose to send. Proposals were expected to describe to his would-be betrothed all the points in her moral character he particularly admired. Initially, virginity was highly valued; sexual relations were reserved ideally for those at least betrothed.

After some months, the man would send an engagement letter and ring to the girl's family. A courtship could last as long as three years (often delayed while the man completed his boat and house), though once an engagement was made, greater sexual intimacy was permitted. The wedding, arranged at a time or season when a minister and the

MARRIAGE CUSTOMS

maximum number of both families were available, though often hastened by pregnancy, was held in the nearest church, with the greatest affordable ostentation in the way of dress and ceremony. This was followed by a reception hosted by the bride's parents in their home, which included flowery formal speeches, refreshments of cake and wine for the women and children, and stronger liquor for the men in a back room. Usually there was dancing, much jollity, and some drunkenness, lasting late into the night, when the married couple was seen off to their new home – situated as a rule in the bridegroom's parents' yard.

Marriage gave both the man and woman a new status in the community, as well as a new household, especially when they began a family. Large families were admired as a proof of virility in the man, fertility in the woman, and perhaps the fidelity of both

Census returns showed the percentages of married couples to have risen to their highest levels by the end of the nineteenth century throughout The Bahamas. In 1891 over 65 per cent of Bahamians in the age range of 18 to 70 were, or had been, formally married, with the figures for all-black Andros and mixed-race Harbour Island alike around 70 per cent, and all-white Spanish Wells a remarkably high 77 per cent. In Nassau (where 23 per cent of Bahamians were living in 1891) the figure was already considerably lower (55 per cent), and the average incidence of formal marriages for the Bahamas as a whole gradually fell to this level, in tune with changing life-styles and mores (with up to 80 per cent of Bahamians coming to live in Nassau and Grand Bahama). The fact that up to half of all Bahamians chose never to get formally married, however, did not lessen the formality and ostentation of Bahamaian weddings, rather the reverse.

Patricia Glinton-Meicholas in *How to be a True-true Bahamian* pokes affectionate fun at the modern Nassau or Freeport wedding. In the author's inimitable style, a true (or *true-true*) picture emerges from her gentle satire. But what is patently clear to an outsider is that the grandiose and complex rite of passage that is described owes far more to North American customs than it does to the traditional life-ways of pre-modern Bahamians.

Wedding at Cable Beach, New Providence

To create a satisfactory facsimile of a real Bahamian wedding, ladies new to this country can follow these steps: First, establish a benchmark for expenditure and lavishness – usually the last wedding in your circle of family and friends. Your job will be to exceed this standard. … Entering gift selections at bridal registries is one of the hottest races in the Bahamian bridal sweepstakes … Family and friends generally aid and abet the bride in this genteel extortion by means of a ruse politely called the 'bridal shower' … You brides be sure to hire a photographer to capture your every moment from just after you don your undergarments to the time you enter the car that whisks you away from the party. …

For the reception, look to Hollywood for inspiration – wine, song and dance, of preference in a hotel ballroom. Let's have an emcee to introduce the main emcee, soloists and musical interludes, toasts to everyone who contributed to 'making this day possible'. … You can expect risque jokes about how the evening will end for the bride and groom; bouquets and garter throwings… and lastly, the cutting of a multi-tiered cake. Thankfully, somewhere in the midst of the excitement, a good meal is offered to reward the guests for their patient attendance.

The groom? You may have guessed that this is not his show. He need only turn up, appearing to be of sound mind, and make the responses that will satisfy the law. His shining hour comes the evening before the wedding, when, in the company of his mates, he casts a brief look back on Babylon.

MARSH HARBOUR, ABACO

Further reading: Craton and Saunders, *Islanders*, ii, *passim*; K. Otterbein, *The Andros Islanders: A Study of Family Organisation in the Bahamas*, University of Kansas Press, 1966; S. L. Brown, 'This is the Real Bahamas: Solidarity and Identity in Cat Island', Ph.D. dissertation, University of California, 1992; P. Glinton-Meicholas, *How to be a True-true Bahamian: A Hilarious Look at Life in the Bahamas*, Guanima Press, 1994.

MARSH HARBOUR, ABACO An extensive township in the geographical centre of mainland ABACO, once overshadowed by the offshore 'Loyalist Cays' but now Abaco's administrative 'capital' and mini-metropolis. What was first called Marsh's Harbour was a village of white LOYALISTS founded around 1785 on a narrow, T-shaped promontory jutting into Abaco Sound and forming a shallow harbour on each side. Further along the northern landward shore two exclusively black villages gradually grew up, called in the early twentieth century (after two Governors) Dundas Town and Murphy Town

Development came after World War Two with the building of Abaco's first airport 2 miles (3 km) south, the construction of the at first unpaved 'Great Abaco Highway', the beginning of a huge sugar plantation by the OWENS-ILLINOIS Company, and the rational decision by the Bahamian government to switch the local administrative centre to Marsh Harbour from Hope Town, 5 miles (8 km) off shore. Thanks to the growing popularity of Abaco with American tourists and the enterprise of Abaconian white entrepreneurs, Marsh Harbour's progress actually outstripped that of The Bahamas in general – though on a relatively much smaller scale.

As Steve Dodge recounted in the second edition of his excellent *Abaco: The History of an Out Island and its Cays*, Marsh Harbour, with its satellite villages, was home to more than 3,600, and could claim to be the third largest metropolitan area in The Bahamas. It boasted the first traffic lights outside of Nassau and Freeport, three supermarkets, at least five liquor stores, and several large hardware and auto-part outlets. These drew customers from fifty miles away to north and south. Besides government offices, a central post office, a large medical clinic and modern schools, it had good electricity, water and sewerage resources, at least three doctors, two dentists, and even a couple of lawyers. The only impediments to its own tourist development were the lack of good beaches nearby and the fact that its two harbours were too shallow to admit cruise passenger liners.

Formerly segregated, and with all of the major businesses (including the vital taxi and ferry-boat services) owned by whites, Marsh Harbour was once a focus of racial tensions. It was also the storm centre of the ABACO INDEPENDENCE MOVEMENT in the 1970s. Gradually since Bahamian INDEPENDENCE, and especially while the FREE NATIONAL MOVEMENT led by the black Abaconian Hubert INGRAHAM has been in power, commercial enterprises, if not housing areas, have become much more integrated and political tensions have subsided. A salient socio-racial problem remains, though, in the presence of hundreds of HAITIAN immigrants (many of them 'illegals'), who crowd into the slum sections of Marsh Harbour called Pigeon Peas and The Mud.

Marsh Harbour, central mainland Abaco

MASONIC LODGES

MASONIC LODGES Though it claims at least seventeenth-century origins in Scotland, Freemasonry dates its formal beginning in England to the establishment of the English Grand Lodge in 1717. With contributions from Scottish and Irish Grand Lodges, Freemasonry spread along with and actually survived the British Empire (remaining particularly strong in the United States). There were almost certainly Masons in The Bahamas from the time of Governor Woodes ROGERS, but Freemasonry formally began in the colony with the appointment by the English Grand Lodge of Governor John Tinker (who had been enrolled as a Mason since 1730) as Provincial Grand Master of The Bahamas 'and places adjacent' in 1752. It does not seem that Tinker and his immediate successors as PGM actually founded a local lodge (the records are obscure or lost), but there were certainly at least four lodges established or active in NASSAU during the LOYALIST period. These were Numbers 228 and 242, authorised by the so-called Atholl (or 'Ancient') English Grand Lodge in 1785 and 1787, respectively; Number 192, set up in 1749 by the Irish Grand Lodge as the regimental Lodge of the 47th (Irish) Regiment, which had fought at Quebec in 1759 and was in the Nassau garrison from 1790 to 1799; and Number 298, Union Lodge, authorised by the Scottish Grand Lodge in 1809 (and following the distinctive Scottish Rite).

The functions of these early Bahamian Lodges (and the fact that they saw their role as literally masonic) can be gathered from the newspaper reports of the time. They paraded in full regalia for an annual service at CHRIST CHURCH on the feast day of St John the Evangelist (27 December), and presided at the ceremonial cornerstone-laying for St Andrew's Kirk (1810), the Hog Island lighthouse (1816) and the rebuilt Christ Church (1837). From 1803, there were also both English and Scottish Lodges in the TURKS AND CAICOS ISLANDS – those islands being under the jurisdiction of The Bahamas until 1848. Even after Turks and Caicos came under the jurisdiction of Jamaica (1848–1963) and continuing to the present day, the 'English' Lodges in the Turks and Caicos (though not the 'Scottish') remained under the jurisdiction of the Provincial Grand Lodge of the Bahamas and Turks in Nassau at least until 1866, re-soldering the link a century later.

For one reason or another none of the original Bahamian lodges survive. The oldest still in existence was long the most important: Royal Victoria Lodge, Number 443, founded in 1837. The earliest masonic meeting-place in Nassau was a tavern, Webster's (exact location unknown), but by 1800 the lodges met in a room in the Public Buildings. Royal Victoria Lodge, and subsequent lodges had a Masonic Temple of their own on central Bay Street. This was replaced by the present building (still one of the most handsome on Bay Street) designed and built by Joseph Elias Dupuch, of which the cornerstone was laid in July 1882. At least six other masonic temples were built later, two in other parts of Nassau, and in other islands, including Grand Turk, Grand Bahama, Abaco, Harbour Island and Inagua (the last two now defunct).

Masonic Lodge Hall, central Bay Street, built by Joseph Elias Dupuch and dedicated in 1885

Originally restricted to white males over 21 (and with prejudices against Jews and other non-Christians), Freemasonry remained almost completely segregated on racial grounds, and denying full membership to all women, almost to the present. Although a few outstanding near-whites, such as Stephen DILLETT and his son Thomas, had been accepted as members in the mid-nineteenth century, by 1900 the Bay Street lodges seem to have become as segregated as the great majority of American lodges thereafter. There were, however, an increasing number of alternatives for blacks who wished to become Masons, originating in North America and spreading gradually to the rest of the world, including The Bahamas. The most authentic and successful of these were the so-called Prince Hall lodges. They are named after a distinguished black freedman, probably born in Africa around 1737, carried as a slave to Barbados, and from there to Boston, where he was freed in 1770. The first Prince Hall Lodge in The Bahamas – competing with the many active black FRIENDLY SOCIETIES already in existence – was constituted in 1863, graduating to a District Grand Lodge in 1883. Apart from the desire of American blacks for their own form of Freemasonry and the authenticity of the almost apostolic succession derived from Lodge Number 459, one of the chief reasons for the phenomenal spread of black American Freemasonry was the comparatively extensive (if parallel and mainly subordinate) role which it offered to black women and youngsters.

Today there are some 25 Masonic lodges in The Bahamas and Turks and Caicos Islands, separately organised under the English, Scottish and Prince Hall hierarchies, with considerable cross-membership and no more than a shadow of the old segregationalism.

In general, Freemasonry in The Bahamas, after something of a decline in the period of political, social and economic change of the 1960s and 1970s, seems to have enjoyed a renaissance since. This may seem especially surprising considering the competition by a proliferation of SERVICE CLUBS for many of the traditional charitable, social and comradely functions provided by Masonic lodges. The reason, though, is surely at least three-fold. Besides the novel opportunities, also provided by the service clubs, for men from all backgrounds to socialise and network, and (most admirably) to perform good works without ostentation, there are the perennial (if not atavistic) attractions of belonging to a selective and secret society; one that rewards its devotees with a steady progression through ever more exalted ranks and titles, while providing, even more than any Christian church, opportunities to perform arcane rituals and dress up in splendid regalia.

Further information: A. B. Sutton, 'Freemasonry in the Bahamas', c.1932; R. D. Seligman, 'Further Light on Freemasonry in the Bahamas, 1752–1882',1992, www.freemasonrybahamas.org; G. Draffen, 'Prince Hall Freemasonry',1976, www.freemasonry.org/phylaxis/prince hall.htm

MAYAGUANA This island, at the far eastern end of The Bahamas, is 26 miles long (41 km) west to east and 6 miles (10 km) across at its widest part. Considerably larger than Nassau's NEW PROVIDENCE with its 180,000 people, Mayaguana is now home to scarcely 300. It is one of the least poor Bahamian islands in respect of soils and fresh-water resources, but was always too far from potential markets to attract agricultural development. Without exceptional beaches and fringed with dangerous reefs, it has so far proved unattractive to hotel developers and visiting yachtsmen compared to the nearby Caicos Islands or Bahamian islands closer to the United States. Nevertheless, several major development projects have been proposed in recent years and undoubtedly Mayaguana's neglect will soon be a thing of the past.

A surveyor in 1857 praised the luxuriance of the food crops and the fine pineapples that the few settlers grew, and the potential of the interior savanna for grazing cattle and of the salinas for producing SALT for export. Yet despite an abundance of native hardwoods there was not a single boat on the island, and very few persons ever called there from other islands. A few subsistence farmers did settle from the impoverished and relatively overpopulated TURKS AND CAICOS ISLANDS, but Mayaguana at the turn of the twentieth century was regarded as the remotest, poorest and most backward Bahamian island.

The only development came fortuitously after mid-century, and did not last. When the Americans were developing their Apollo and Mercury space programmes in the wake of the Cuban Missile Crisis, Mayaguana became a link in the chain of tracking stations that stretched from Cape Canaveral through GRAND BAHAMA, ELEUTHERA, SAN SALVADOR, Mayaguana and Grand Turk as far as Ascension Island in the South Atlantic. Mayaguana became the temporary home of a sizeable crew of American technicians and their armed guardians, and the permanent recipient of an airfield large enough for jumbo jets. The three island settlements of Abraham's Bay (closest to the base), Betsy Bay and Pirates' Well hardly became boom towns, but drew people from other islands to help service the base and its personnel, in one way or another.

Mayaguana's population reached an all-time high of about 750 by the end of the 1960s. But when the US base was phased out and eventually closed down, more than half of these drifted away again. The island's inherited airport saw a BAHAMASAIR plane three times a week on its way to and from INAGUA, augmenting the weekly visit of the MAIL BOAT from Nassau. But the half-emptied settlements did not receive electricity or telephone services until 1997. In the year 2000 optimistic plans were announced for the creation of a vast eco-park, extending over the uninhabited half of Mayaguana. But this was expected to be at least a decade in the making, and by its very nature was planned to keep Mayaguana in its primal state, rather than developing it materially or boosting its resident population.

Further reading: J. Lurry-Wright, *Custom and Conflict on a Bahamian Out Island*, University Press of America, 1987.

MAYNARD, Hon. Sir Clement The only person who was a minister in every one of Prime Minister Lynden PINDLING'S cabinets over a quarter century (1967–92), Clement Maynard exemplified to a unique degree the qualities (other than good health) necessary for political durability during that tumultuous era. These were steadfast adherence to the PROGRESSIVE LIBERAL PARTY and its ideals, particularly an unswerving patriotism and support for the black majority; personal intelligence and an ability to suggest policies and debate without abrasiveness; a reputation for incorruptibility; the garnering of universal respect; and, perhaps most important of all, fidelity to the leader with never a hint of an ambition to take over from him.

Born in Nassau in 1928, Clement Maynard obtained training as a medical laboratory technician in the USA and UK. While working at the Princess Margaret Hospital, he was founder-president of the Professional Staff Union, joined the PLP, and was an active member of the ginger group called the National Council for Positive Action, formed in 1960. Though not selected to contest the crucial 1967 election, he was chosen to be Minister without Portfolio in Pindling's first Cabinet and nominated as an Opposition Member of the Senate. In the 1968 landslide, however, he was returned as MHA for GAMBIER by a large majority, retaining this and two other new constituencies in five subsequent general elections down to (and including) 1992.

Appointed Minister of Works in 1968, Maynard grew steadily in Pindling's esteem and took an increasingly important role in national affairs. He was an official delegate to the Independence Constitution talks in London in 1972. From 1977 he was one of the five members of the National Economic Council formed to promote economic nationalism. Also appointed Minister of Home Affairs in 1977, he was at the storm centre of the D'Arcy Ryan affair which proved the key test case in the CITIZENSHIP aspect of the government's BAHAMIANISATION policy – narrowly escaping going to jail for contempt of court in the process.

The apogee of Clement Maynard's political career, though, came during the troubled last decade of the Pindling regime. Specifically cleared by the commission of inquiry into the drug trade, he was a notable survivor of the great Cabinet reshuffle of 1984 (which saw the departure of Arthur HANNA, Perry CHRISTIE and Hubert INGRAHAM), becoming Minister of Tourism, Minister of Foreign Affairs and Deputy Prime Minister – for a time, all three at once. In all of his ministerial roles, Maynard was responsible for important initiatives, most of them accomplished without flourish or fanfare. For example, in tourism he approved the slogan 'It's Better in The Bahamas', and initiated the 'Goombay Summer', 'Bahama Host' and 'People-to-People' programmes. He was also involved in the creation of BAHAMASAIR and the Hotel Training School, and in the great extension of Nassau's cruise-ship docking facilities. As Foreign Minister, he was responsible for the expansion of diplomatic representation overseas, and chaired many important international meetings held in Nassau, including those of the CARICOM Foreign Ministers and the General Assembly of the ORGANISATION OF AMERICAN STATES in 1992. He also headed the delicate negotiations with the United State which led to the setting up the cooperative anti-drug OBPAT operation. He was knighted, to widespread acclaim, in 1988.

Though one of only six PLP contestants to be successful in the 1992 election, Sir Clement Maynard did not appear to share his leader's determination to carry on the fight. In 1993 he withdrew from the contest to be Deputy Leader of the party (from which Bernard Nottage and Perry Christie emerged as co-Deputies) and, having reached the age of 65, gradually and gracefully eased himself into a well-earned retirement from active politics.

MEDICAL SERVICES In early colonial days formally trained doctors were as scarce as ministers of the gospel, and the few there were seemed little if at all superior to the informal practitioners of BUSH MEDICINE on whom most islanders had to rely. In modern times, and especially since Independence, The Bahamas has had medical services as up-to-date and widespread as anywhere in the region – though, even with the large contribution made by the private sector, public health needs have constantly threatened to outrun the available material and financial resources.

The first hospital in The Bahamas was established for the army garrison some time in the later eighteenth century, located on a healthy hill-top site at the junction of West Hill Street and Hospital Lane in Nassau. It closed down and was demolished when the garrison was removed in 1892. The first public hospital was the combined hospital and poor house set up by an Act of the Assembly in 1809 and built just to the north-east of Fort Fincastle, on the site of the present Princess Margaret Hospital. Later called the Bahamas General Hospital, it remained a fairly primitive establishment. Combining the functions of lunatic asylum, leprosarium and work house with those of poor house and hospital, it was widely seen as a place of last resort, to be avoided as far as possible. As the memoirs of L. D. POWLES (1888), Amelia DEFRIES (1917) and Evans COTTMAN (1940s) disclose, proper medical care was virtually non-existent in the Out Islands.

Except for a quarantine station on Athol Island, 5 miles (8 km) to the east of Nassau, the BGH was the only public medical establishment in The Bahamas until well into the twentieth century. The closing of the workhouse shortly after slavery ended and the provision of a separate home for the indigent aged were definite improvements. But the creation of a separate 'lunatic' ward named the Jubilee Asylum at the time of QUEEN VICTORIA's sixtieth anniversary in 1897, and the renaming of the hospital in 1902 the Alexandra in honour of King Edward VII's consort, were little more than nominal changes. Almost within living memory, people were accustomed to see lepers walking the Nassau streets, and children looked over the wall of the Jubilee Asylum, to gape at the 'lunatics' allowed to roam the grounds (rather than strapped up in close confinement like the more difficult inmates).

The first significant improvements came slowly but steadily from the 1920s. The number of doctors (trained in the UK, USA and Canada) increased to a handful, including the first non-whites and one or two West Indians. As early as 1903, the Bahamas General Hospital had employed its first trained midwife, following this up with more or less formal training for local midwives and apprentice nurses in the mid-1920s. In 1928 lepers were isolated in a small facility at Carmichael, though by then their numbers had dwindled to a dozen or so. With the establishment of air training bases in WORLD WAR TWO, a modern small hospital was built on Prospect Ridge. This was exclusively for servicemen, but its doctors, medicines and equipment were to an extent available to the needy populace. During the War too, encouraged by the Duchess of Windsor, the BAHAMAS RED CROSS was revived and a good few Bahamian women served as volunteer nurses.

The pace of change, as in so many other respects, speeded up with the years of increasing prosperity following World War Two. A landmark year was 1953, when a considerably expanded main hospital was opened by, and named for, Princess Margaret, the sister of the recently crowned QUEEN ELIZABETH II. In the same year, Miss Hilda Bowen returned from England as the first trained Bahamian Sister, soon to be the first Bahamian Matron, Dr Francis Adderley came back from Edinburgh to be the first Bahamian medical officer working at the hospital, and the Polish Dr Henry Podlewski became the first qualified mental health doctor. Close on their heels came other nurses trained in the UK (among them, Patricia Fountain, later Lady Isaacs, Miss Bowen's successor as Matron) and the first doctors trained in the new teaching hospital of the UNIVERSITY OF THE WEST INDIES (notably the long-serving Cecil Bethel Jr. and John Lunn).

A major development was the separation of the psychiatric from the general hospital by the setting-up of the Sandilands Hospital south of Fox Hill in 1956. To this were later added a geriatric facility (1965) and a detoxification unit to treat drug addicts (1988). The entire complex in due course was rechristened the Sandilands Rehabilitation Centre. Equally important was the gradual transformation of the Princess Margaret Hospital into a teaching centre for Bahamian nurses. Classrooms first set up in 1958 were moved into larger, custom-built quarters in adjacent Sands Lane around the time of Bahamian Independence, and in 1987 a fully equipped School of Nursing was established in Grosvenor Close, being designated a unit of the COLLEGE OF THE BAHAMAS accredited to train nurses up to the level of the Associate Degree in Nursing. A full Faculty of Medicine in association with the University of the West Indies was initiated in 1997.

Private medical institutions include the 72-bed Doctors Hospital in downtown Nassau (formerly the Rassin Clinic, founded in the 1950s), the Western Medical Plaza and the Star Care Medical and Emergency Centre, both also in Nassau, and the 12-bed Lyford Cay Hospital and Bahamas Heart Institute. Proportionately, Freeport is even better served than Nassau. Besides the government-owned 77-bed Rand Memorial Hospital and the several government clinics throughout Grand Bahama, there are no less than a dozen small private hospitals, clinics and health-care centres in Freeport-Lucaya.

All in all, The Bahamas in 2003 could boast as many as 223 practising doctors, of whom no more than 20 were exclusively employed by the Department of Health, and the rest in private practice. Overall (and bearing in mind that Family Islanders usually go to Nassau to get the best medical attention), the ratio of qualified doctors to total population – one for roughly every 1,300 persons – rivals most countries in the developed world, and far exceeds any other country in the Caribbean region. Equally creditable, in 2003 The Bahamas as a whole was also served by almost 90 qualified dentists, a ratio of roughly one for every 3,300 members of the total population.

MEERES, Paul Sr. (1911–1971) A spectacularly handsome dancer who enjoyed a brilliant international cabaret career in the 1930s and 1940s but whose later years in Nassau were dogged by misfortune and whose retirement was cut short by a tragic death.

The son of an English Dean of CHRIST CHURCH and a coloured Bahamian woman, Paul Meeres had little formal training. But his natural grace and exotic looks led in a remarkably short time to head-line engagements at such renowned night-clubs as the *Folies Bergères* in Paris (where he sometimes partnered the world-famous American black Josephine Baker) and Havana's *Tropicana* – in the glamorous 'bad old days' long before Fidel Castro. Even the outbreak of World War Two

METHODISM

did not immediately stop his glittering progress with a succession of beautiful dancing partners, through the US and Canada, Central and South America.

Meeres returned to Nassau in 1945, confident of repeating his success in his home town with his own night club, called, with characteristic chic, *Chez Paul Meeres*. Tourism had not yet taken off and the local clientele, while in awe at Meeres's routines, preferred less sophisticated fare. Though he periodically returned to the international circuit in order to recoup his losses, he was no businessman. His first club burned down, and further ventures failed. In a bizarre turn of events he went to jail for a year as a stand-in for his aged mother, who had been convicted of harbouring a runaway criminal. Drinking to excess, he began to lose his looks as well as his dancing skills. One evening in November 1971, walking back to his home the worse for wear, he stumbled into the path of a government bus on Blue Hill Road, was knocked down and killed – at the age of 60.

Though too soon forgotten as a fallen star and a man before his time, Paul Meeres Sr. was happily recalled and honoured three decades later as one of 'the 100 Most Outstanding Bahamians of the 20th Century'.

Paul Meeres Sr.

METHODISM A nonconformist but relatively conservative sect formed when John Wesley (1703–91) reluctantly left the ANGLICAN Church in the 1730s. It spread to The Bahamas by 1800, both informally from the United States and through missionary activity from England by way of the West Indies. Originally targeting all those who were ignored by or dissatisfied with the established Anglican Church, the Methodists mainly attracted the non-elite whites and the free coloureds – two unmixable elements which were effectively segregated between or within the Methodist chapels for more than a hundred years. These ethnic divisions were scarcely healed, however, when Bahamian Methodists were divided even more sharply in the 1980s over the question of whether they should constitute an autonomous body or remain under the authority of the Jamaica-based Methodist Council for the Caribbean and the Americas (MCCA).

Methodism arrived in North America, gaining impetus from the wave of revivalism called the Great Awakening, when John Wesley sent missionary preachers from England in the 1770s, such as the dynamic Francis Asbury. One of the early non-white converts was the former slave, Joseph Paul (1750–1802), who with his wife and family migrated with the first ship-load of LOYALISTS from New York to Abaco in 1783. Soon moving on to Nassau, Paul attracted a small congregation and built the first Wesleyan chapel in The Bahamas in the western suburbs some time before 1793, along with the first day-school for non-white children. Paul, however, fell out with the earliest Wesleyan missionaries from England and the West Indies, on personal as well as doctrinal grounds, and (as Wesley himself had long wanted to do) rejoined the Anglican Church.

Although the Wesleyan Missionary Society was not formally constituted until 1814, the first semi-official Methodist missionaries arrived in The Bahamas in the 1790s following appeals by the great evangelist Dr Thomas Coke, who had been sent out to North America and the West Indies by John Wesley himself in 1784. The first comers were politely said to have been not worthy of their call, but rather more successful was William Turton, a Barbadian coloured man sent to Nassau in 1800 at Coke's behest and funded by the Manchester Methodist Conference in England. Turton established two modest chapels. One was on East Shirley Street (the forerunner of Ebenezer) and the other in Nassau Court opposite the ruins of Fort Nassau (superseded by Trinity chapel in 1864, it was later to house first the Boys' Central School and then the GOVERNMENT HIGH SCHOOL). Turton built up a sizeable following among the Nassau free coloureds. But he had less success with the black slaves, who preferred the Black Baptist preachers, and was quite bitterly opposed by the elite whites, not just on account of his own colour but because he had the temerity to convert and marry a local white woman.

William Turton's white successors from England, John Rutledge and William Dowson, had a much wider impact. Travelling quite widely throughout the islands, they made hundreds of ardent converts among the religion-starved poor whites of the northern ELEUTHERA and ABACO cays. Equally important, they converted a few of the white slave-owners (most notably William WYLLY the Attorney General), at the same time convincing them of the value of preaching Wesleyan doctrines and ethics to the slaves.

By the end of slavery, the Methodists had achieved respectability (cemented by the 1826 law that allowed officially licensed white nonconformist missionary ministers to perform and record baptisms, marriages and burials) and had established a strong niche among those who craved a dignified but simpler and more personal type of worship than offered by the Anglican Church. But, even more than the Anglican, it was already a church reflecting the racial divisions in Bahamian society – if never quite reaching the complete separation that occurred between white and black Methodists in the United States, which lasted from slavery times almost to the present day.

Sometimes glaring, more often subtle, divisions were displayed both in Nassau and the Out Islands. In the capital, Trinity took over as the major Methodist chapel from the 1860s, rivalling the nearby Anglican cathedral. Trinity's congregation was almost exclusively white (with a few ambitious near-whites) as were the children enrolled in the Wesleyan Nassau Collegiate School started in 1871 – forerunner of the equally segregated QUEEN'S COLLEGE, founded in 1890. In contrast, the mission chapel called Wesley set up in Grant's Town in 1839 as a branch of Turton's foundation in Nassau Court (usually called the West Chapel) had a congregation exclusively made up of recently freed blacks. Ebenezer, the former East Chapel, opened for worship in its present form in 1841, and is today regarded by many as the premier Methodist church in The Bahamas, from its beginning attracted a mixed, though informally segregated, congregation.

Naturally, in the all-white Out Island settlements, the Methodist congregations were exclusively white, not welcoming black visitors, let alone non-white pastors. This diehard separatism had probably its last expression in ultra-conservative Spanish Wells in 1990, when a group of local white Methodists left to form their own congregation after the Nassau Conference sent them a white minister who happened to be married to a black West Indian. In the nearby racially bifurcated settlement of Harbour Island, where the Wesley Methodist church dwarfs Anglican St John's, the customary apartheid did not last so long, but for many years non-white Methodists sat in different sections from the whites and were expected to enter and leave the church by a separate door. In 1885 a notorious incident (related by L. G. POWLES) occurred when five non-whites – with roots in Harbour Island as deep as those of any whites – were arrested, charged with disturbing the peace, found guilty and fined by the local magistrate for defying custom by peacefully entering their church by the door reserved for whites.

The unfortunate dissension that split and weakened the Bahamian Methodists at the end of the twentieth century had echoes of the divisive issues of the previous era. This time it was not so much a division between white and black Methodists as between nationalists who wanted an essentially Bahamian-governed church and those (including almost all Methodist West Indian residents) who sanctioned and welcomed the authority of the Jamaican-based MCCA.

The conflict was consonant with the general trend towards Bahamian Independence and became critical in the late 1980s when a Bahamian minister Rev. Colin Archer returned from an unrewarding stint in Jamaica and proclaimed the need for a separate and revitalised Bahamian church, under the banner of an Association for the Revival of Methodism in The Church Bahamas (ARM). After a couple of almost riotous synods, a majority of Bahamian (and Turks and Caicos) Methodists voted to

Ebenezer Methodist church, east Shirley Street, built 1839–41, on the site of an earlier bulding (1802), rebuilt after the 1929 hurricane and renovated 1957–62

MIGRATION

go their own way in March 1991 and to seek an Act of Parliament to set up a separate Methodist Church of The Bahamas (MCB) which would legally own all Methodist property (including churches, schools and funds) within the country.

The MCCA counterattacked, appointing a new Jamaican Superintendent and appealing to the Bahamian Supreme Court to block the Act. But it lost its case and the MCB legally came into existence in May 1993. Adherents of both sides naturally differ over whether or not the separation was beneficial to either. But what cannot be denied is that the net result of what was more an ideological than theological dispute has been an accelerated decline in total Methodist membership. Although the Methodists still claimed some 15,000 members in The Bahamas in 2000, this number was down by as much as 25 per cent since the 1970s, making them the fourth rather than the third largest Bahamian sect, behind the Baptists, Anglicans and ROMAN CATHOLICS.

Further reading: C.V. Williams, *The Methodist Contribution to Education in the Bahamas*, 1982.

MIGRATION Even more than with most other countries, migrations (both inward and outward, internal and external) have been a perennial feature of Bahamian history. But The Bahamas has been distinguished by the way that the ambience and lifestyle of the islands have been so affectionately engrained in its denizens that true Bahamians, however far or long they roam, have always exhibited an indelible nostalgia for the country – or even the individual island – where they were bred. This regard for The Bahamas as the true heartland significantly also overrides any affinity for the continent from which the ancestors originally came, be it Africa or Europe

That there has always been something special about the islands to engender affectionate feelings is attested by the fact that such sentiments were reportedly felt by the aboriginal AMERINDIANS whom the Spaniards found inhabiting the Bahamian archipelago at the end of the fifteenth century – who had no direct connections with later settlers. These Lucayan Tainos were quite aware of the Antillean islands and South American mainland from which they had migrated to The Bahamas, and felt some ancestral affinity for them. But according to Peter Martyr, some of the Lucayans who had been forcibly deported from The Bahamas to work the mines of Hispaniola escaped into the northern mountains, 'where they might breathe the air wafted from their native country. With extended arms and open mouths they seemed to drink in their native air, and when misery reduced them to exhaustion, they dropped dead upon the ground.'

It would be interesting to speculate as to when the Bermudian migrants who first settled The Bahamas in 1648 began to regard themselves as Bahamians (or Eleutherans), but it is worth noting that as early as 1686 a group of inhabitants who had been chased from NEW PROVIDENCE by the Spaniards voluntarily returned to what they regarded as their native place from the uncongenial shores of Jamaica. Such persons, and their descendants over four or five generations, were the true Bahamians who at first resented the immigration of the LOYALISTS from North America a century later, but who within a generation integrated with those who did not choose to remigrate and adapted to The Bahamas and its ways. It was also within this transitional period that the different mixes of whites, non-white free persons and slaves, and the subtle or marked differences between the ecology and economy of each of the dozen or more islands now settled, began to determine separate island identities and loyalties.

The history of The Bahamas over the subsequent century is the story of limited immigration outweighed both by circumstantial migrations between the islands and emigration to the United States, mainly Florida and New York. After slavery ended, the expanding non-white populations of many of the Loyalist-settled islands were driven to migrate within the island chain by local shortages of land for peasant farming, to undeveloped or abandoned areas, hitherto unpeopled islands, or the few islands which offered chances of wage employment. Over time, this accounted for the spread of settlement over empty or emptied parts of CAT ISLAND, LONG ISLAND, CROOKED ISLAND, and ACKLINS; for what was virtually the first settlement of GRAND BAHAMA and RUM CAY; for the settlement of Exumians and others in ANDROS, first as farmers and then as SPONGE fishermen and SISAL plantation workers; for the peopling of BIMINI and RAGGED ISLAND as bases for WRECKING and smuggling; and for the first settlement of INAGUA and LONG CAY, by workers at the SALT-pans and as stevedores recruited by passing steamers.

Towards the end of the century, mainland ABACO became fairly well populated for the first time by blacks migrating to work in lumbering and on the PINEAPPLE and sisal plantations. For the all-white settlements of the offshore Abaco cays, also quite rapidly increasing in population, however, the pattern of migration was significantly different, and more adventurous. From the last days of slavery, white Abaconians had been among the pioneer settlers of KEY WEST in far southern Florida. This had been motivated originally as much to distance themselves from the black majority as to seek a richer livelihood, though ironically, they were followed by a rising tide of black Bahamians once the cigar-making and sponge-fishing industries developed in and from Key West. In the second half of the nineteenth century the population of NASSAU was also substantially augmented for the first time by migrants from the Out Islands, though opportunities for wage employment there did not really expand rapidly enough to outpace the available workforce of former slaves, LIBERATED AFRICANS, their children and grandchildren.

The situation both for Nassau and in respect of Florida changed significantly from the beginning of the twentieth century, with a further surge during the decade of relative prosperity after World War One. As south Florida began to develop, large numbers of Bahamians migrated – either directly from the Out Islands or by way of Nassau – to work on the extension of the East Coast railway towards Key West, on the burgeoning truck farms and citrus groves, or the building up of Miami and other southeastern cities. This movement of people and money – with returnees sporting their dollar earnings, new clothing styles and adopted Americanisms in their speech – has been dubbed 'the Miami Craze'. The wartime demand in the United States for unskilled labour temporarily also increased the flow of Bahamians along with other West Indians, and despite the gradual tightening of US immigration restrictions, the two-way traffic continued vigorously through the 1920s.

During the era of American PROHIBITION (1919–31) not only did Bahamians forge closer links with the United States, but The Bahamas fared relatively better than the rest of the British West Indies. This led to a considerable immigration of West Indians to Nassau during the period, as skilled artisans, officials (especially policemen), teachers and other professionals, including doctors. In combination with the ideas generated among the Bahamian and West Indian communities in the United States – as well as among the veterans of overseas service during World War One – this caused a stirring of political consciousness among the ordinary black people, exemplified by the remarkable, if short-lived, success of GARVEYISM in the 1920s. Nearly all of this changed, though, during the Great Depression of the 1930s. The disappearance of wage opportunities in the United States and a virtually closed door against immigration stopped the outward flow, and many migrants returned to Nassau and the Out Islands, poor and dispirited. Symptomatically, Marcus Garvey himself was hounded by US authorities, discredited and deported from the United States and even his native Jamaica; he died in impoverished obscurity in England in 1940, with the once vigorous Garveyite chapters in Miami and Nassau faded away and almost forgotten.

However, the most dynamic and complex period of the movement of people and ideas was soon to follow, as a consequence of WORLD WAR TWO and the subsequent years of unparalleled prosperity. The war saw a temporary immigration of well-heeled refugees (with Governor WINDSOR and his Duchess at their head) and a much greater but rapidly shifting inflow of American, Canadian and British servicemen. Far more widely important was the scheme for the employment of thousands of unskilled Bahamian labourers in the United States commonly called THE CONTRACT, which began in 1941 and lasted until the early 1960s – coming to an end mainly because increased opportunities at home made it a less preferable option. Overall, though, The Contract had a vital impact; both culturally and materially. It greatly increased the amount of cash available for home improvements and starting small businesses, and also speeded the decline of the traditional subsistence farming and fishing economy and accelerated the migration from the Out Islands to Nassau. Not only did farms fade when left to be tended by women and old men by the absence of young men-folk in the United States, but returning migrant workers, understandably, found backbreaking toil for pitiful returns no longer acceptable.

The critical factor was the gradual fulfilment of rising expectations in the capital (and in Freeport from the late 1950s). The unprecedented bubble of prosperity that began to inflate during the last decade of the BAY STREET regime, and continued, with periodic leaks, through the subsequent twenty years, brought about other related demographic movements. The huge expansion of TOURISM, the development of The Bahamas as a major offshore BANKING centre, and its promotion as a paradise for rich foreign residents, brought a flood of foreigners to build and run the hotels and casinos, to man the financial sector and to occupy the new residential enclaves. The rapid and belated expansion of the school system also brought in a considerable number of non-Bahamian teachers. Most of these newcomers were whites, but a sizeable minority were opportunistic non-white middle-class migrants from the West Indies. But the largest influx of all, emulating the migration of black Bahamians to the United States in an earlier epoch, was the rising tide of black HAITIANS, mostly illegal immigrants, desperately eager to fill the need for unskilled manual labourers.

MILITIA

Broadly speaking, the Bay Street regime favoured both the immigration of whites who would boost their own influence, and at least the temporary immigration of low-paid blacks to fill the labour gap. The black majority PROGRESSIVE LIBERAL PARTY which succeeded to power in 1967, however, soon developed a different agenda. This can most simply be characterised as a policy of BAHAMIANISATION. As far and as soon as possible all prestigious and well-paid jobs would go to native Bahamians, with vigorous training schemes to help them fulfil such positions. Bahamians, however, would be encouraged to reverse the flow from the Family Islands and not to disdain farming, fishing and other forms of manual work. Foreigners, of whatever ethnicity or skills, would only be accepted as far, and as long, as their contribution to the country was sufficient and necessary. Those without the legal requirements for citizenship through birth or marriage who wished to stay permanently would have to demonstrate both their indispensability to The Bahamas and their willingness to fulfil all the criteria needed to become true Bahamians.

The ideal was, and remains, a stable nation with a clear sense of national identity, without the unplanned and often unsettling migrations of the past. However, the criteria for deciding when immigrants become Bahamians cannot be fixed by law, any more than a sense of belonging can be instilled by a calculated Bahamianisation policy. Bahamians include those who have not just got 'the sand in their shoes' but who (over a period of years or even a couple of generations) have sufficient material, familial and psychological investment in, and attachment to, the country to regard it as their true homeland. This cannot be precisely measured, and certainly not legislated.

Just as separate island identities are reinforced by meetings of the various island associations in Nassau and annual island 'homecomings', so Bahamians getting together in places like the UNIVERSITY OF THE WEST INDIES or the Bahamian High Commission in London, or at meetings such as those of the Association of Bahamians in Canada (ABC) or the Bahamian Association in New York, readily discuss and come to recognise the common links that bind together all true-true Bahamians Most significant of all is the often-noted phenomenon that Bahamians in such gatherings share food, music, news and reminiscences and tend to ignore the political, economic, social or ethnic barriers that often divide them back home in the islands themselves.

Further reading: P. Glinton-Meicholas, *How to be a True-True Bahamian: A Hilarious Look at Life in the Bahamas*, Guanima Press, 1994; M. Craton, 'A Recipe for the Perfect Calalu: Island and Regional Identity in the Caribbean', in *Empire, Enslavement and Freedom in the Caribbean*, Ian Randle Press, 1997, 439–57.

MILITIA In the former British Empire, militia service was obligatory for all able-bodied free male settlers. Colonial militias were limited to whites wherever possible, with ranks bearing a strong correlation to social ranking, from the Governor as local commander-in-chief downwards. In The Bahamas, the system was more or less initiated by the first royal Governor, Woodes ROGERS, who formed the white inhabitants into three militia companies to augment the 150 regular soldiers of the Independent Company which he had brought with him. This force was far from impressive, but served to deter a serious Spanish invasion attempt in 1720 with the aid of a well-armed vessel of the Royal Navy. It also helped to suppress the mutiny among the garrison troops which confronted Woodes Rogers's successor Richard Fitzwilliam in 1736.

Atholl Island, off Nassau, site of a former quarantine station and detention centre for illegal immigrants

With the coming of the LOYALISTS, the growing threat from revolutionary France and the rising fears of a slave insurrection, however, the Bahamian militia entered its period of greatest size and importance. As early as 1784, both to increase numbers and in an attempt to win over the middling class of free non-whites against the slaves, the regime extended the obligation to serve in the militia to all able-bodied non-white males aged 16–60 who had been free since 1768. These men were distinguished by having to wear a badge inscribed with the word FREE and their militia number. After an unsuccessful attempt to integrate the entire militia by assigning 40 non-whites to each company of 100 men, separate companies of non-white infantry and rangers were organised – though officered entirely by whites. Although, like the Bahamian militia as a whole, never called to active service, the non-white units were particularly tested in policing the slaves, proving their usefulness on night patrols and in helping to abort the serious slave plot of 1797.

The Bahamian militia reached its peak between the last phase of the war with Napoleonic France (and its American allies) and the end of slavery. According to historian Paul ALBURY, during the short war with the newly independent United States (1812-14), the militia in New Providence alone consisted of 500 men, organised into four separate infantry, dragoon, field and marine artillery units. Harbour Island raised three companies of infantry on its own, and there were other companies in Exuma, Long Island and Crooked Island (the last of which was also said to boast a unit of artillery).

Though an era of international peace began in 1815, the militia continued in full panoply for another two decades, mainly, it seems to overawe and control the slaves After the EMANCIPATION of the slaves, the militia lost its practical social purpose. As far as the ruling regime was concerned, external and internal security were adequately covered by the black troops of the WEST INDIA REGIMENT in the garrison and by a steadily expanded police force.

It was not until the Bahamian Home Guard formed during World War Two that The Bahamas again had a volunteer militia. Recruited from the very beginning of war in 1939 (originally as the Bahamas Volunteer Force), this eventually consisted of almost 500 men, mustered into four companies. They performed valuable guard, lookout and general service duties, especially once the American and British bases were established in New Providence from early 1942, being augmented by a locally recruited Bahamas Air Service Squadron in 1943. Though trained largely by white Canadian and British NCOs, and with a majority of white officers, these units were – like the British but not the American forces – officially fully integrated. Because they gave Bahamians of all shades equal opportunities to serve in home defence and at least a fair chance of advancement in rank, the Bahamas Home Guard and Air Service Squadron were important early forerunners of the truly national ROYAL BAHAMAS DEFENCE FORCE formed in 1976, three years after the achievement of INDEPENDENCE.

MINERAL RESOURCES With two exceptions, the Bahama islands are not rich in exploitable mineral resources. Though this could be regarded as an economic drawback, it does have the undoubted advantage of not seriously threatening ecological degradation or pollution.

What would almost instantly transform the Bahamian economy and ecology – as it has those of many otherwise resource-poor countries – would be the discovery of oil and gas resources in the underlying limestone. As late as the 1980s optimism prevailed among the several major oil companies carrying out surveys and exploration. But so far nothing has been found beyond a few non-viable traces. The reason for this is probably the geological structure of the Bahamas – a vast submarine limestone plateau split by mile-deep canyons.

Over the aeons, petroleum deposits will have been leached out by sea-water almost before they could be formed. There is some prospect that some oil and gas may still be found below the 20,000-foot (6,000-m) level already explored. But even if they are, under present conditions of world supply their extraction would scarcely be worth while.

Some Bahamian mineral resources are less utilised than formerly, or are of limited use. The AMERINDIANS used local clays for their pottery, adding crushed conch shells to temper the somewhat inferior raw material. These skills however have almost died. In the colonial period the native limestone was regarded as excellent building material, either as cemented freestone or as squared blocks (said to 'cut like cheese and harden like flint'). Today, though, there are no working stone quarries and few expert masons, concrete breeze-blocks having become the preferred basic building material.

Though it has the disadvantage of a high salt content, at least 150,000 tons of dredged sand is used annually in the Bahamian construction industry. In New Providence this most notably consists of material from dredging off Rose Island brought ashore near Nassau's Eastern Parade. Cement however remains one of the products which The Bahamas could produce from its native limestone but imports instead. The traditional skill of producing mortar from charcoal burning and lime-kilns proved far too arduous and time-consuming.

Apart from the production of solar SALT, the one success story relating to the exploitation of Bahamian natural resources is the extraction and export of the marine oolitic limestone called aragonite. Modern industries have an almost insatiable demand for calcium carbonate, and the oolitic 'sand' found on the Bahamian sea-banks is the purest form of that chemical found in nature – 97 per cent pure and of almost perfect granular consistency. Easily extractable reserves are said to amount to a hundred million tons – enough to supply the entire world's demand for a quarter century. There are four concession areas: the southern fringes of the TONGUE OF THE OCEAN, the western Bight of Eleuthera, the Joulter Cays off northern Andros, and the eastern side of the southern islands of the Bimini chain.

So far only the fourth and smallest of these has been exploited, which is just as well since even there the ecological disruption has been considerable. Preferred because of its closeness to the Florida Channel, this operation is centred on a sizeable island, Ocean Cay, which was virtually created as a byproduct of the dredging operations. It consists of no more than a large dumping ground for aragonite awaiting shipment, a dredged channel out to deep water, and an ugly small-company town for workers, with its own airstrip.

Aragonite royalties produce a useful income for The Bahamas – some US$5 million a year for about four million tons. Potentially, production and income could be multiplied many times over. The Bahamian government, however, is in something of a cleft stick in assessing whether the cost is worthwhile – caught between a company threatening to move elsewhere if royalties are raised too high, and conservationists who would chorus 'good riddance' if operations closed down.

Further reading: N. E. Sealey, *Bahamian Landscapes: An Introduction to the Geography of The Bahamas*, Collins Caribbean, 1985.

MINNIS, Edward A. ('Eddie') Painter, political cartoonist, and popular composer and singer of GOOMBAY songs, Eddie Minnis is not just one of the most talented of Bahamian all-rounders but one of the most significant proponents of traditional Bahamian values. His work celebrates the natural environment, and combines witty observation and narrative with pungent social and political comment.

Eddie Minnis was born in Nassau in 1947 and educated at ST JOHN'S COLLEGE and GOVERNMENT HIGH SCHOOL before going to Canada to study architecture, graduating from McGill University in 1971. His primary avocation, though, was art, and he never practised as a professional architect. Almost self-taught, he was already an adept worker in ink, watercolours and pastels, before developing a distinctive style of palette-knife oil painting.

Mining and shipping aragonite, Ocean Island, Biminis

He held his first one-man show in 1969, and three more to ever increasing acclaim in 1972, 1976 and 1986, as well as participating in numerous group shows. His bright and realistic canvases commanded first hundreds and subsequently several thousands of dollars apiece.

But painting proved only one of three important outlets of expression for Eddie Minnis. From 1971 he created the gently satirical cartoon called 'Pot Luck', which ran for seven years in the *Nassau Guardian* and a further five years in the *Daily Tribune* – only giving it up in 1983 when he decided that Bahamian politics and social conditions had deteriorated beyond the reach of his brand of subtle comment and satire. More lasting and perhaps more potent was his third career as a composer, writer and singer of calypso-style goombay songs, backed with traditional Bahamian 'RAKE 'N SCRAPE' instruments. Beginning with 'Der Real Ting', in 1971, over the next 30 years he created eleven albums, many of them in collaboration with Ronnie Butler and the Ramblers. All of them were in the distinctive Bahamian idiom and eminently danceable.

Further information: http//eddieminnis.com/bio.html

MISSIONARIES The transformation of The Bahamas from being 'almost a godless place' in early colonial days to one of the most ardently Christian countries in the world today was the work of waves of dedicated missionaries, not all from formal missionary societies, and sometimes competing bitterly with each other.

Once The Bahamas became a royal colony (1718) the Church of England was the offical 'established' church, as it was in England. Much reliance was placed upon the Society for the Propagation of the Gospel (founded 1701) and the Society for the Propagation of Christian Knowledge (founded 1698) for the provision of ministers, Bibles and other religious literature. But the SPG and SPCK were hopelessly over-stretched. The few Anglican ministers required for The Bahamas were indifferent in qualifications, zeal, and even morals. They were scarcely adequate to serve even the free population, and for the most part completely unconcerned about the religious welfare of the slaves – at least until the slaves' proselytisation by nonconformists became seen as socially dangerous.

The first missionary influences affecting the black majority – and even elements of the white population – were in fact a branching offshoot of the so-called Great Awakening in mainland North America in the second half of the eighteenth century. 'Loyalist' black preachers, including Joseph Paul, Frank Spence, Samuel Scriven and Prince Williams, who may have heard George Whitefield, Shubael Stearns or George Liele preach in America, set up Wesleyan and 'Black Baptist' congregations in Nassau long before the arrival of the first white nonconformist missionaries (see BAPTISTS). The first of these were Wesleyans sent at the urging of the zealous Dr Thomas Coke in the late 1790s (see METHODISM), followed almost two decades later by those sent by the Baptist Missionary Society (founded in 1814).

The spurt of nonconformist missionary activity emanating from Britain was a feature of the general evangelical revival of the late eighteenth century and its confluence with the growing movement to better the lot of the slaves and eventually to free them. Though Evangelical Anglicans took part in (in fact, pioneered) moves against slavery, in the Bahamian case they were more concerned with what they saw as a threat to the established order from a distorted version of Christianity. For their part, the Wesleyan and Baptist societies saw their role as taking advantage of the wave of enthusiasm for a simpler, non-establishment form of Christianity (with Methodism strongest among the poorer whites, Baptist Nonconformism among the blacks), while preventing its theology and practices getting out of hand. For Anglicans and nonconformist missionaries alike, 'civilising' the ordinary people was a vital, if not predominant, function of Christianity.

The chief effect of the early white missionaries' activities was simply to drive a wedge between white and non-white Methodists, and to draw an informal line between 'respectable' (that is, white-ministered) Baptist chapels, and those of the black majority. Though the Anglican Church did retain the most social prestige and respectability even after its disestablishment in 1869, it did far more to missionise the ordinary people as a consequence of the ritualist Oxford Movement in England, with its exclusively white clergy largely supported by donations from English Anglo-Catholics (see ANGLICANISM). However, this missionary activity was more effective in Nassau than in the Out Islands, both because Anglican resources were tenuous and local versions of Nonconformism were too deeply entrenched.

Some tension between Anglicans, Baptists and Methodists (indeed, within each sect) has remained to the present day. But since the early twentieth century The Bahamas has been notable as even more fertile ground for the missionaries of further competing forms of Christianity. Of these the Catholics from the United States were the earliest, most vigorous, and most successful, treating The Bahamas as a 'missionary diocese' from 1885 to 1953, during which time its number of adherents rose from 100 to 13,000 (16 per cent of the total population). The rise of Bahamian nationalism had a serious, if fairly temporary,

MOSELEY, Miss Mary

impact upon what was still regarded as an essentially US-based enterprise in the 1960s, but this introspective trend does not seem equally to have affected the many other missionary influences from the United States, both before and since. These have included the many fundamentalist, revivalist and pentecostalist churches (especially the many CHURCHES OF GOD) that have targeted mainly the black population, the SEVENTH DAY ADVENTISTS, who attract from a wide spectrum, and the Plymouth Brethren, who minister mainly to the lowlier whites. Such mainly US-based marginally Christian sects as Jehovah's Witnesses, Salvationists, Christian Scientists, Christian Spiritualists and Mormons have also enjoyed a modest but surprising degree of success.

Further reading: C. J. Barney, *Upon These Rocks*, 1973.

MOSELEY, Miss Mary (1878–1960)

Most notable Bahamian female journalist; long-time owner-editor of the *Nassau Guardian* newspaper, 'blue stocking' and life-long guardian of the LOYALIST version of the Bahamian past. Daughter of the part-owner and editor of the *Guardian* and granddaughter of the Englishman who founded it in 1844, she was educated at the girls' school attached to CHRIST CHURCH Cathedral. She took over the editorship on her father's early death in 1904 and bought out her uncle to become sole owner in 1907, at the age of 30.

Intensely patriotic, Miss Moseley was a charter member of the Bahamian chapter of the IMPERIAL ORDER OF THE DAUGHTERS OF THE EMPIRE, and took three years off from the newspaper to engage in war-work during World War One. For her chairing of the Ladies' Committee of the West Indies Regiment she became the first Bahamian recipient of the MBE, from King George V in 1917. Thereafter, she carried the *Guardian* through thick and thin until her retirement in 1952, always a strong supporter of the BAY STREET regime, but gaining universal respect for her own scrupulous reporting of parliamentary business.

Along with Harcourt Gladstone Malcolm (1875–1936) the long-time Speaker of the House of Assembly, Miss Moseley was an avid collector and publisher of historical memorabilia, especially as related to the Loyalist era. For many years it was reported that she was working on a definitive history of The Bahamas and this kept others from competing. But this work never materialised, and Miss Moseley's chief memorial remains the interesting and valuable *Bahamas Handbook*, published by the *Guardian* in 1926.

Further reading: R. Lightbourne, *Reminiscing*, Media, 2000.

MUNNINGS, Freddie Alfred (1921–1995)

Most popular band-leader and singer during the hey-day of the Bahamian NIGHTCLUBS in the 1940s, 1950s and 1960s. Born in Andros, Freddie Munnings grew to be a spectacularly handsome man with an exceptional musical talent and a warm, crooning singing voice. He was lucky to come on the scene at the right time, but he owed his success also to his zeal in polishing his instrumental and singing techniques in his spare time (studying at the New England Conservatory in Boston and Trinity College in London), and to his skillful entrepreneurship.

Freddie Munnings began his career in the nightclubs that blossomed in Over-the-Hill Nassau as tourism expanded after World War Two, especially the Zanzibar, Silver Slipper and Spider Web. But he reached the pinnacle of his success after he purchased and developed the Cat and Fiddle on Blue Hill Road in 1955. For two decades Freddie Munnings fronted an excellent dance band, popularised such songs as 'The Sloop John B', 'Bahamas Lullaby' and 'Come to the Caribbean', and drew just about all the top black American bandleaders, singers and entertainers to gigs in Nassau. These included Count Basie, Nat King Cole, Roy Hamilton, Dinah Wasington, Sam Cooke, Harry Belafonte, Aretha Franklin and (a perennial favourite) the comedian 'Flip' Wilson.

This golden age of the Nassau nightclub came to an end with the shift of entertainment to the hotels and cruise

Freddie Alfred Munnings

ships in the 1970s. When the Cat and Fiddle was no longer able to make money, Freddie Munnings went into a dignified but far from inactive retirement. A founding member of the Bahamas Musicians and Entertainers Union and an active member of the Kiwanis, he was not just a popular entertainer and promoter of local talent but a political activist and promoter of social causes.

MUSEUMS The remarkable number and variety of museums in Nassau and the Family Islands attests both to the abiding interest of Bahamians in their heritage and to the somewhat eclectic and selective (not to say unsophisticated) approaches to its presentation.

Of the five museums in Nassau, the oldest is appropriately housed in one of the oldest surviving public buildings, the former jail on the Shirley Street side of the Public Square that was transformed into a public library, reading room and museum in 1873. Its small display of pictures, documents and other artefacts was mainly put together under the auspices of Speaker Harcourt Malcolm (1875–1936), and closely monitored by his equally conservative historical collaborator, Miss Mary MOSELEY (1878–1960). Malcolm bequeathed his far more extensive private collection to the Library. But thanks largely to his widow, Miss Moseley, and the other library trustees, it was taken over by the BAHAMAS HISTORICAL SOCIETY shortly after its foundation in 1959. In due course it became the nucleus of the Society's museum, housed in the former IMPERIAL ORDER OF DAUGHTERS OF THE EMPIRE Hall, further down Shirley Street, into which the BHS moved in 1976.

The new ARCHIVES Department founded around the time of Independence in a building on Mackey Street included a small but wide-ranging and well-presented museum display. Much more important, though, was the designation during the 1980s of the Department of Archives as the organisation in charge of The Bahamas' entire material heritage. The Department's duties now included the encouragement of museums, as well as the protection of historical buildings and sites and the control of all archaeology and treasure hunting. In Nassau, this sweeping remit involved the Archives – along with commercial sponsors – in two significant museum projects: the POMPEY Museum of Slavery and Emancipation, housed in the historic VENDUE building on central Bay Street (with substantial help from the BACARDI rum company), and the restoration and refurbishment of the ancient BALCONY HOUSE on Market Street as the Balcony House Museum (thanks largely to its purchase by the Central Bank and help from the Ministry of Works and Utilities and the Antique Warehouse company). Both were opened to the public in 1993.

Further progress was anticipated by the passage through parliament of an Antiquities, Monuments and Museums Act in 1998, setting up a separate AMM Corporation. With its own premises on Hawkins Hill and professional staff under a qualified Director and Board, the AMMC was given the mandate, apart from the general oversight of archeological, preservation and other heritage matters, not only to create a consolidated national museum but to oversee and co-ordinate the operation and of all other museums throughout the country – thereby relieving the overworked Archives Department from many of its existing responsibilities.

Unfortunately, the Pompey Museum was badly damaged in the fire of September 2001 and by Hurricane Michelle two months later. Its contents (including the permanent display of works by the intuitive artist, Amos FERGUSON) were rescued, but the museum was forced to close down, pending repairs. The positive aspect of this setback was that a plan was soon announced to turn the museum into 'a modern interactive museum experience', incorporating 'more innovative and exciting exhibits'. This newly refurbished museum opened in 2004.

Of the ten museums of different sorts in the Family Islands, the Department of Archives, due to its limited personnel and budget, had so far been able to lend artefacts and expert help to only two. These are the small museum set up in the restored former Commissioner's office and jail in Cockburn Town, SAN SALVADOR (superseding the nearby collection of pre-Columbian artefacts called the Museum of the New World, privately owned by Mrs Ruth Wolper but closed since the 1980s), and the even smaller display constituting the LONG ISLAND Museum at the settlement of Petty's, just south of Deadman's Cay. Left almost entirely to their own resources and available expertise, the others (though all interesting and each well worth a visit) naturally concentrate on the history, lifestyle, folklore and achievements of their particular island and its people. Easily the most charming and informative are the two museums installed in beautifully preserved traditional wooden houses on the ABACO Cays: the Wyannie MALONE Museum in HOPE TOWN and the Albert Lowe Museum in New Plymouth on Green Turtle Cay. These provide a nostalgic view of a society so recently living in proud isolation, as well as invaluable details of the shipbuilding and sponge-fishing industries which sustained it.

Disappointingly, neither SPANISH WELLS nor HARBOUR ISLAND, though similar in history and importance to the Abaco Cays, have museums adequately illustrating and celebrating their storied past. The Spanish Wells Museum is described in the friendliest guidebook as simply containing 'a motley collection of photos and bric-a-brac in a venerable house' that is opened up only on request. The Harbour Island Museum merely consists of a 'meagre miscellany of faded photos' in a portion of the library named for the most distinguished local son of recent times, Sir George Roberts (1907–64), whose bust stands guard outside the front door. Rather better served, though also with a strong localised slant, are the other four Family Island museums. BIMINI's one-room museum, above the library opposite the straw market, concerns itself entirely with local history, with a collection of historic photographs and videos that give more than due prominence to sport fishing and Bimini's most famous part-time resident, Ernest Hemingway. At the opposite end of the archipelago, the occasional visitors to Matthew Town can also learn much about INAGUA's SALT industry and FLAMINGOS from the small Erickson Museum next to the library on Gregory Street, created and sustained by the Morton Salt Company. In the settlement of Knowles in the centre of CAT ISLAND, is the tiny but grandly titled Columbus World Centre Museum, the chief reason for which seems to be to proclaim the no longer defensible contention that Cat Island, not Watling's/San Salvador, was Columbus's landfall in the New World. Even more esoteric and eccentric (though engaging) is the 'museum' still run by Gloria Patience, the so-called 'Shark Lady' of The Ferry in Little EXUMA, which consists of her own simple clapboard house, stuffed with her own 'collectibles and other artistic creations, such as jewellery made from sharks' teeth and spines'.

Even though FREEPORT is almost too young to have a museum devoted to itself, it does house a small and well-presented museum celebrating the past and the culture of

Albert Lowe Museum, Green Turtle Cay, Abaco

the island of which it is a part. The GRAND BAHAMA Museum is a happy product of the fact that Peter Barratt, the original town planner of Freeport-Lucaya, is also the enthusiastic and sensitive historian of the island as a whole. Besides genuine Lucayan Indian and pirate-era artefacts and relics of the pre-Freeport lumbering industry, the museum contains a comprehensive marine exhibit and has excellent audio-visual facilities. Most telling of all, perhaps, in the garden outside the museum is a small native house of a century ago, reconstructed from local pine planks and shingles. This makes a poignant contrast to the modern Florida-style high-rises of the surrounding 'city of the future' – an impression not undermined by the sign which notes that this 'traditional' house was actually crafted from timbers cannibalised from the original, and already historic, Freeport airport terminal of the 1960s!

Further information: www.folklife.si.edu/unesco/saunders.htm

NAMES For historical reasons, common Bahamian surnames often indicate a special type of clannishness rather than a mere family affiliation. The most notable example is the several thousand persons who share the distinctively Bahamian surname of ROLLE – being descendants through the male line of the 300 slaves owned by Lord Rolle in the island of EXUMA. A similar sense of historical, regional or extended family identification is felt by black Bahamians sharing such surnames as Farquharson, Ferguson, Moss, Ingraham or Williams, or whites surnamed Albury, Higgs, Knowles, Lowe or Pinder. Quite the opposite process is at work, however, in the way that Bahamians of all sorts strive to give their children distinctive and distinguishing forenames. If Bahamian surnames by and large indicate group solidarity, Bahamian first names display a countervailing tendency to encourage a proud individualism.

Bahamian parents have always been inventive in choosing names for their offspring. L. D. POWLES noticed this tendency among the black population in the 1880s:

> *In the Bahamas there are innumerable Princes of Wales's, Prince Alberts and Prince Alfreds. There is a man named Tiberius Gracchus, a boy named Thaddeus de Warsaw Toot [later to make a mark], and a sergeant Duke of Wellington. … It is a common practice to call children after the month or day of the week on which they were born or christened, as 'March', 'July', 'Monday', 'Friday', etc. Scripture names are very common, so are names descriptive of a class, as 'Evangelist', and from some of the clergy I heard of parents who wished to have their children christened 'Iniquity', 'Miserere Lizzy', and 'Solomon's Porch'. Among female names I have met with Brinhilda, Clotilda, Cassandra, Savelita, Malvina, Eulalia, Denisia, Daphne, and a host of others, religious, classsical, ordinary, and Spanish, but every one of them high sounding.*

In modern times, parents are even more ingenious – to the point that it is a rare occurrence to find forenames duplicated in any sports team or school class list. As Patricia Glinton-Meicholas amusingly explains in *How to be a True-True Bahamian*, for every first name picked from the lexicon of common English Christian names, there are ten drawn from elsewhere; from biblical characters, however obscure, from historical personages (not necessarily heroes or heroines), from stars of the screen, TV, pop music world or politics, chosen for their poetic sound, or simply constructed by combining syllables or adding a prefix or suffix.

A kind of egotism frequently leads to Bahamian fathers passing on their own names to their offspring. As Patricia Glinton-Meicholas explains, Darren, son of Darren, is commonly called 'D. J. (Darren Junior), Li'l Darren or Li'l D, and the father becomes Big Darren or Big D.' Girls too are given reminders of their parents' names. 'Raymond has his Raymondessa, Carlton is father to Carlise and Stephen to Stevonya. Sometimes, mother and father's names are linked: Roger and Sharon call their daughter "Roshar", while Johnathon and Leona call their angel Johnnya Leonette. Paul and Rhonda named their boy Parhon.'

Most Bahamian parents however are even more inventively and eclectically original. Current fan magazines as well as history books and the Bible are combed for euphonious or distinguished names. At least since the 1960s, it has been fashionable for black parents to choose names from the African heritage, such as Amaya, Ayodele, Chike, Emelike, Ife, Kwame, Obadele, Malaike or Shaka. But great ingenuity is shown in coming up with completely new-minted forenames. For girls, Patricia Glinton cites the use of the prefixes La-, De- or D', the mid-word syllables sha-, shan, she- and shen-, and the suffixes -ae, -kera, -mae, -make, -nique, -nika, -tika, -tishka, -neisha, -teisha, -ette and -essa. Her 'Top Twenty' favourite girls' names (drawn from birthday lists and obituaries in the local press) are Daisunique, D'Andrea, Denae, Dekera, Laneisha, Lashan, Latishka, Latonya, Latoya, Llakel, Pastashia, Raynishka, Shakeitra, Shakera, Shameka, Shamond, Shanae, Shaquania, Shawna and Tamika. For boys she lists the same favourite prefixes as for girls, and the suffixes -ardo, -ario, -ero, -iko, -ron and -vaughn. Her list of favourite modern Bahamian boys' names is: Danardo, Danavio, Demark, Deron, Deshawn, Devon, Janero, Jimiko, Keno, Kevon, Lavardo, Leron, Shaun and Tameko.

Further reading: Louis Diston Powles, *The Land of the Pink Pearl: Recollections of Life in the Bahamas*, Media Publishing, 1998 (1888), 70–91; Patricia Glinton-Meicholas, *How to be a True-True Bahamian: A Hilarious Look at Life in the Bahamas*, Guanima Press, 1994, 27–32.

NASSAU Capital city of The Bahamas, on NEW PROVIDENCE Island; now home to almost two-thirds of the country's entire population. Founded by the earliest settlers from Bermuda led by Captain William SAYLE as Charles Town, it was no more than a clutter of huts along the shore until roughly laid out, given a fort, and renamed Nassau (one of King William III's Dutch titles) by the Lord PROPRIETORS' Governor Nicholas TROTT in 1695.

NASSAU

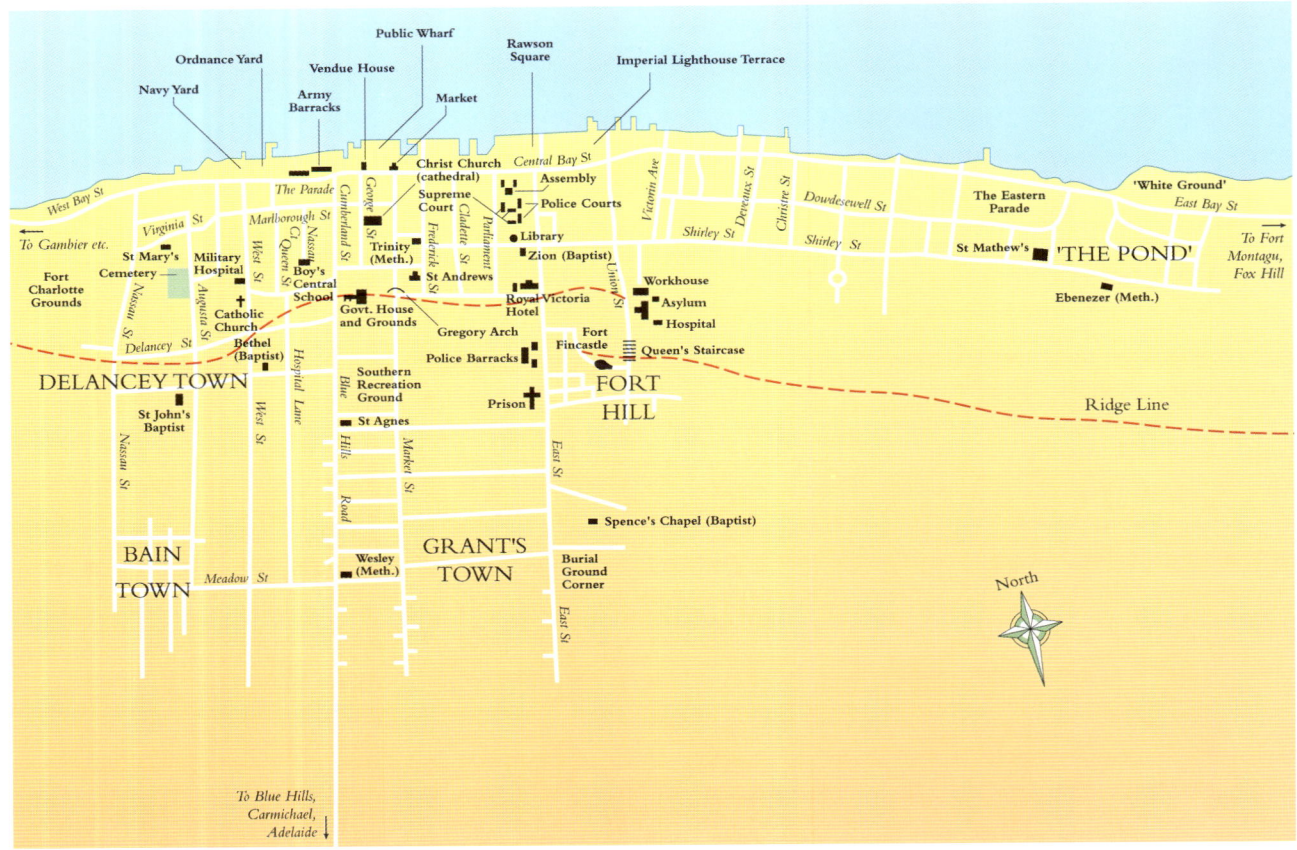

Nassau, Downtown and Over-the-Hill, c. 1900

Several times attacked and plundered by the Spanish and French (notably in 1684 and 1703), and for a couple of decades infested with PIRATES, Nassau attained respectability and began to grow under Governors Woodes ROGERS (1718–21, 1729–33), John Tinker (1738–58) and William SHIRLEY (1758–68). A visitor at the time of the American War of Independence, Johann Schoepf, described it as a modest collection of wooden houses (the largest still surrounded by gardens) along a single unpaved main road (BAY STREET) and a parallel lane named for Governor Shirley. The town boasted no more than a small fort, a tiny covered market (the VENDUE HOUSE or 'Bourse'), 'a church, a gaol and an Assembly house'. Its few hundred inhabitants – whites, free coloureds and domestic slaves – consisted, said Schoepf, of 'a few royal officials, diverse merchants, shipbuilders and carpenters, skippers, pilots, fishermen and what labourers are needed, with several families who live on the returns from their lands and work of their slaves'.

Nassau was virtually transformed after 1783 by the influx of American LOYALISTS and their slaves (who outnumbered them five to one). Within a quarter-century, the network of modern streets downtown was laid out and filled in with more substantial houses and shops. A central core of elegant stone public buildings was erected in and around three interlocked squares (Public, Parliament and Rawson) between ridge and harbour. The chief of these buildings (1805–16) were the cluster of three – said to be based on the palace of the royal Governor of North Carolina at New Bern – which since 1905 have faced the statue of QUEEN VICTORIA. These public buildings originally housed the House of Assembly, Council Chamber and Supreme Court (as they still do), the Treasury, Post Office, and the offices of the Colonial Secretary, Attorney and Solicitor General, Crown Surveyor and Provost Marshal. Nearby, then or later, were other offices and subsidiary courts, the police station, and the handsome octagonal jail, which housed a curfew and alarm bell (and in 1873 became the Nassau Public Library).

In the Loyalist era a new GOVERNMENT HOUSE and several private mansions sprouted on Nassau's 100-foot ridge, a second Anglican church (ST MATTHEW) and several Nonconformist chapels were built, and the grandiose Governor Lord DUNMORE (1787-96) oversaw the building of two FORTS worthy of Havana: Fort Charlotte, guarding the western entrance to the harbour, and Fort Fincastle, overlooking the town itself.

Meanwhile, Nassau developed distinct districts by function, class and colour – the essential elements of which continued well into the twentieth century. The mercantile and planter elite who no longer lived over their shops or in the few elegant residential streets downtown tended to move to the ridge outside of town that overlooked the harbour (especially to the east), leapfrogging the areas at the seaward fringes of town where the poor white 'CONCHY JOES' and some of the least impoverished non-whites lived, built and careened their boats, and cleaned, clipped and baled their sponges. The more prosperous coloureds lived mainly on the reverse slopes of Nassau's ridge, in the areas called DELANCEY TOWN and FORT HILL. The ever increasing majority of blacks gradually filled in the 4 square miles (10 sq. km) 'Over-the-Hill' bounded by East Street, Nassau Street and Wulff Road, swallowing up in the process the originally separate settlements of GRANT'S TOWN and BAIN TOWN. This whole area in itself became subtly subdivided, as Grant's Town and Bain Town retained something of their original character, and as people such as policemen and other petty officials and migrants from different Family Islands and the West Indies tended to congregate together. Until the late 1960s Over-the-Hill was also hemmed in like a ghetto on its eastern side by the notorious COLLINS' WALL, built in the Great Depression by unemployed blacks at the behest of a racist white rum-runner.

By 1900 the population of Nassau – designated a city since 1861 when CHRIST CHURCH was made into the cathedral church of the Anglican diocese of The Bahamas – was some 12,000 (a fifth of the Bahamian total). This had grown close to 50,000 by the mid-twentieth century – almost five-eighths of all Bahamians. Yet the most startling transformation came with the economic and political revolution of the 1960s onwards.

As money filtered down from BANKING and TOURISM and the opportunities and expectations of the black majority surged with the success of the PROGRESSIVE LIBERAL PARTY – and as roads were expanded and improved and all Bahamians came to regard ownership of a car as a necessity – a huge migration occurred to better houses in new suburbs in the hinterland to the south and east. By 2000, when Nassau's population had passed 175,000, the city and its suburbs had spread almost to cover the entire eastern half of New Providence, with more shops and businesses, and almost as many churches, as the town had had people two hundred years earlier.

The original area of Over-the-Hill, despite intermittent efforts by the government to revive and smarten it, assumed something of the decayed aura of an American 'inner city' – home of some of the least fortunate, including those illegal HAITIAN immigrants not living in the shanties hidden in the remaining remnants of bush on Nassau's outskirts.

Downtown Nassau is now given up almost entirely to business offices, banks and tourism. It is seriously crowded with traffic and has lost its traditional 'native' character. As cruise-ship business has proliferated (with up to a dozen ships docked in the expanded dock area) and central Bay Street's shops are now geared almost entirely to tourists, Nassauvians now mainly shop in the peripheral malls that have sprung up as part of the American-style suburbanisation process. The people's fish and produce markets, sailboat anchorages and MAIL BOAT docks have been relegated to the filled-in harbour area of ARAWAK CAY to the west and POTTER'S CAY to the east. Only on formal or celebratory occasions – important sessions of the legislature or courts, public demonstrations, state funerals, or the annual licensed mayhem of JUNKANOO – is the downtown area taken over once more by 'true true' Nassauvians.

Further reading: G. Saunders and L. M. Huber, *Nassau's Historic Landmarks*, Macmillan Caribbean, 2001; S. Dodge, *The Compleat Guide to Nassau*, White Sound Press, 1987)

NASSAU GROUPER This denizen of Bahamian reefs (*Epinephilus striatus*), recognisable by its dark vertical stripes and lugubrious fat-lipped visage, is the favourite fish food in The Bahamas. Caught either by spear or on long-line hooks, with other grouper varieties it accounts for almost 40 per cent of all scale fish landed and sold – some 350 tons a year – nearly all for local consumption. Its popularity leads to high prices, which encourages overfishing, threatening the depletion and virtual extinction that has overcome the species in nearby American and Caribbean waters.

The Nassau grouper, along with related kinds of tropical bass, has several distinctive characteristics. Carnivorous (even cannibalistic), it is solitary and territorial except in the winter spawning period, guarding its reef niche against intruders – though tales of huge specimens engorging unwary human swimmers are equally hard to swallow. Most interesting of all, the Nassau grouper is hermaphroditic, starting off adult life as a female and changing to a fully functional male once it reaches about 2 feet (0.6 m) in length. Spawning occurs during full-moon periods between November and March, when dense schools of grouper desert the reefs for nearby shallows (especially off southern Bimini, Andros, Long Island and Eleuthera), discharging untold billions of fertilised eggs that are wafted by ocean currents not just throughout The Bahamas but as far as Bermuda.

NATIONAL DEMOCRATIC PARTY (NDP)

Unfortunately for the conservation of the Nassau grouper, its spawning period (coinciding with the peak of demand for the tourist trade) is that when they are most easily and profitably fished – with the larger and older males being most vulnerable of all. Serious signs of depletion (exacerbated by the activities of poachers from the Dominican Republic) surfaced in the 1980s and 1990s. However, better late than never, in December 2003 the Bahamian Department of Fisheries began to emulate US authorities by declaring the first ever closed fishing season for Nassau grouper – placing an embargo on all fishing between December and March in a 'protected area' off one of the chief spawning areas off southern Andros, and placing a general ban on the 'taking, landing, processing, selling and offering for sale' of all fresh Nassau grouper throughout The Bahamas between mid-December and mid-February each year.

Further reading: D. Campbell, *The Ephemeral Islands: A Natural History of the Bahamas*, Macmillan, 1978, 141–5; R. Palmer, *Baha Mar, The Shallow Seas: An Underwater Guide to The Bahamas*, Immel Publishing, 1995, 125–27; Bahamas Department of Fisheries, Annual Reports.

NATIONAL DEMOCRATIC PARTY (NDP)

A short-lived (1965–8) third party of moderate reformists aiming to find a middle ground between the ultra-conservative and white racist UNITED BAHAMIAN PARTY and a PROGRESSIVE LIBERAL PARTY that they deemed to be leaning dangerously towards socialist and Black Power extremism.

The NDP was formed by three Members of Parliament who had been among the most popular of the eight winners for the PLP in the 1962 general election: Orville TURNQUEST, Paul ADDERLEY and Spurgeon Bethel. Correctly assuming that they would not approve an unconstitutional show of force, they were intentionally excluded by the more determined party leaders from the planning for the symbolically lawless events of 'BLACK TUESDAY' (27 April 1965). When the three refused to join in the PLP's subsequent boycott of Parliament (which lasted nine months), they were formally expelled from the party, almost immediately setting up the NDP.

Buoyed by the 8,311 votes their three leaders had received in 1962 (when they had actually out-polled their successful running-mates Milo BUTLER, Randol FAWKES and Lynden PINDLING), and with their own well-written newspaper, the *Bahamas Observer*, the NDP convinced themselves that they had a realistic chance of equalling if not topping the PLP in the 1967 general election. They campaigned strongly, but the outcome was, for them, a disaster. The 13 NDP candidates (all but two in New Providence) received a total of 833 votes. Much more important for the general outcome was that, with not one of the 13 out-polling a PLP candidate, the PLP was able to achieve a tie with the UBP and (with the help of Randol Fawkes and Alvin Braynen) bring majority rule to The Bahamas.

Though shattered, the NDP continued for a while, with Paul Adderley ardently counselling moderation to the Pindling government in the *Bahamas Observer*. Adderley became convinced that Pindling was heeding his advice, and the NDP leaders, arguing that they wanted to give the PLP the chance to sink the UBP for ever, announced that the NDP would not contest the early-called 1968 general election. With the PLP's landslide victory, however, it was the NDP even more quickly than the UBP that was scuttled. Its members, predictably, went in different directions. Orville Turnquest, after a phase in what was called the Bahamian Democratic Party (BDP), joined the rump of the UBP and those further defectors from the PLP initially called the Free PLP, as an important member and contender for the leadership of the FREE NATIONAL MOVEMENT. Paul Adderley, in due course (1972) rejoined the PLP, to become one of Pindling's most important Ministers, but never to challenge him as leader. Others, including Spurgeon Bethel, permanently disillusioned, left politics altogether.

NATIONAL INSURANCE

In former times, those poor Bahamians unable to work or to sustain their immediate family, looked first to members of their more extended family to come to their aid. If that was not feasible their only other option was to go cap in hand to a rich white patron – further entrenching the pattern of dependency and abnegation that was one of the most demeaning legacies of slavery days. Those without family to help and too proud to beg faced destitution, or even, in rare cases at the worst of times, death by starvation.

The process of modernisation in the twentieth century did not improve the situation, given the wholesale migration from the Out Islands to Nassau, the related decay of family and group interdependency, and the widening gap between the burgeoning numbers of the urban poor and the BAY STREET oligarchy. A national system of unemployment, sickness and retirement-age insurance was therefore an important plank of the PROGRESSIVE LIBERAL PARTY'S platform from the 1950s – and its steady implementation from the time of INDEPENDENCE was listed by ex-Prime Minister Lynden PINDLING in his retirement as one of the proudest and most satisfying achievements during his regime.

Further information: *Bahamas Handbook and Businessman's Annual*, Dupuch Publications; www.nib.bahamas.com

NATIONAL SYMBOLS In 1972, just before INDEPENDENCE, the British Blue Ensign with the badge of the Colony of the Bahamas was replaced by a new *national flag*. This consists of a black equilateral triangle on a background of three equal horizontal stripes, two aquamarine with a gold one in the middle. The symbolism of the flag was officially described as follows: 'Black, a strong colour, represents the vigour and force of a united people, the triangle pointing towards the body of the flag represents the enterprise and determination of the Bahamian people to develop and possess the rich resources of land and sea, symbolised by gold and aquamarine respectively; the colours of the flag are symbolic of the bright tropical region of our land of sea and sun.'

By a royal warrant dated 7 December 1971, the colonial coat of arms, with its Latin motto *Expulsis Piratis Restituta Commercia,* was replaced by one more suitable for a nation soon to be independent. A handbook for primary schools describes it thus: 'Our colourful coat of arms sums up the character of our island nation. Included in the coat of arms are the national bird, the flamingo; the national fish, the blue marlin; the ship of discovery; the ever-bright sun, and the popular conch shell. The motto of The Bahamas at the base of the coat of arms stresses our determination to succeed as a people: 'Forward, Upward, Onward, Together.' Subsequently, semi-official shields were designed for 18 separate Family Islands, each with appropriate symbols. These included a wooden native boat for Abaco, a billfish for Bimini, tomatoes for Cat Island, an onion for Exuma, a sheep for Long Island, and flamingos and salt for Inagua.

Besides the FLAMINGO as the national bird and the blue marlin as the national fish, The Bahamas has officially adopted the YELLOW ELDER (*Tecoma stans*) as its national flower, and the LIGNUM VITAE (*Guaiacum officinale*) as its national tree. For the Bahamian National Anthem, 'March on Bahamaland', see GIBSON, Timothy.

Further reading: H. Bain Jr., *Bahamian National Symbols*, Nassau.

NEW PROVIDENCE Called New Providence to distinguish it from England's former buccaneer colony off the coast of Nicaragua (OLD PROVIDENCE or Providencia), NASSAU's island is lozenge-shaped, some 21 (33 km) miles east to west and 7 miles (11 km) north to south at its widest extent, and 80 square miles (207 squ. km) in area. Its location makes it the natural site for the capital, chief port and largest town in The Bahamas. Sheltered by outlying islands, New Providence is situated in the heart of the northern Bahamas and is approached by the North West and North East Providence Channels which give access to the GULF STREAM and Atlantic Ocean. It is provided with a splendid natural harbour formed by PARADISE ISLAND on its northern side. There is an alternative deep-water anchorage on the lip of the TONGUE OF THE OCEAN at Clifton Pier on the south-western point, for the rare occasions when stormy winds blow in from the north, or for the delivery of such unglamorous cargoes as bunker oil.

The earliest English settlers soon found the island superior to ELEUTHERA as the centre of the new colony, and first named it Sayle's Island after their leader William SAYLE, former Governor of Bermuda and founder of South Carolina. The original township was called Charles Town after King Charles II (1649–82) but was given the name Nassau from one of William of Orange's titles when he took over as England's King William III in 1688.

For the first 250 years of settlement the development of New Providence was almost entirely limited to Nassau town and its immediate suburbs. During slavery days there were one or two plantations in the west of the island near the coast, but the interior beyond the east–west ridge called the Blue Hills was sufficiently a wilderness to provide a refuge for runaways. All the plantations had failed by the end of slavery, but scattered villages were established by the government for the LIBERATED AFRICANS saved from illegal slave-traders, and by the ex-slaves themselves; at FOX HILL in the east, Carmichael in the south, and GAMBIER and ADELAIDE in the west of the island. There was a rough carriage road (called the Eastern Road and West Bay Street) stretching along much of the northern shore, but the interior villages were connected to Nassau by no more than cart-tracks or footpaths and were almost as remote as the settlements in the nearer Out Islands. As late as the 1940s a picnic trip to South Beach, Adelaide or

Official Bahamian crest since 1971

NEW PROVIDENCE

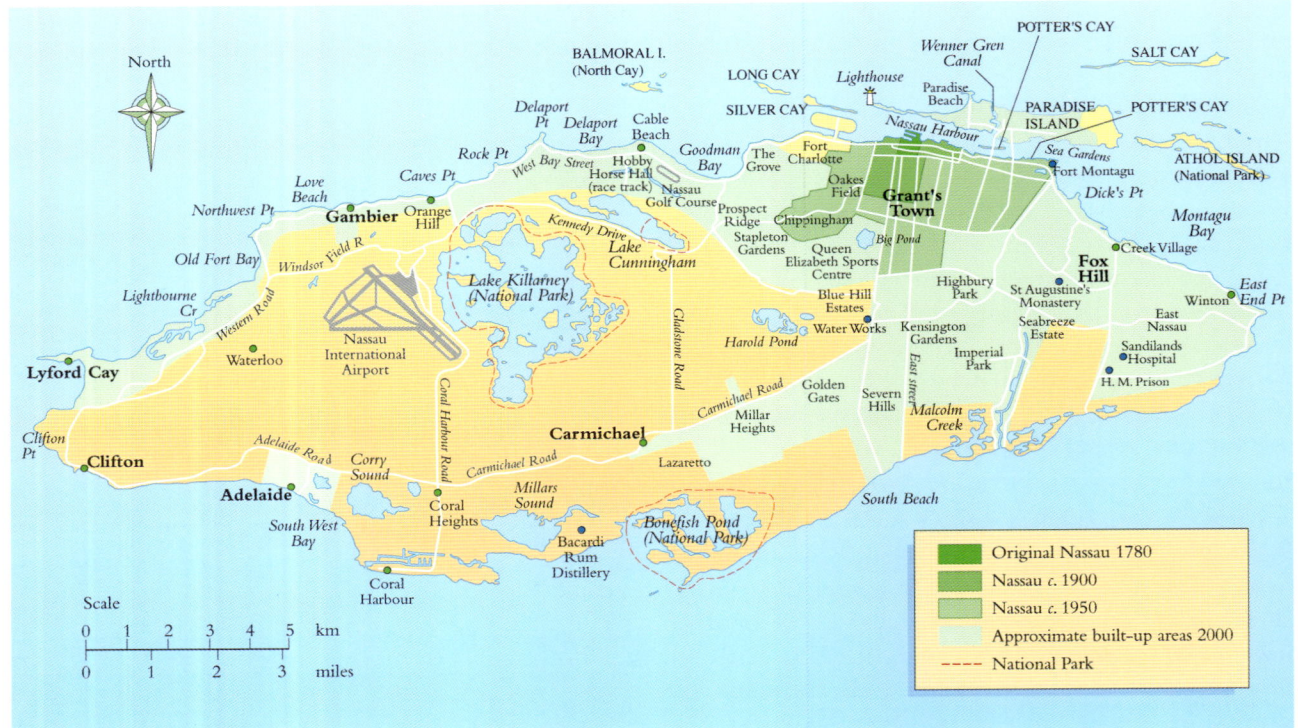

New Providence Island to 2000

the picturesque BLUE HOLE called Mermaid's Pool, was a day or weekend excursion for Nassauvians.

The first changes came with the southward and eastward expansion of Over-the-Hill Nassau, and the building during World War Two of the 'Inter-field Road' between the original Oakes airfield and Windsor Field in the unpopulated area to the west of Lakes CUNNINGHAM and KILLARNEY. After the War, however, development sped ahead of that of The Bahamas as a whole. For tourists and the wealthy, mansions and hotels sprang up along the scenic and sandy northern shore, quickly filling in the entire 5 miles (8 km) to East End Point, the incomparable sandy curve of CABLE BEACH to the west, and the ridge just to south, while in the far west, the Canadian magnate E.P.TAYLOR founded LYFORD CAY as the first and grandest of New Providence's millionaires' enclaves.

As Nassau's harbour was gradually widened and deepened until it could accommodate a dozen or more cruise liners at a time, Paradise Island was also developed as Nassau's equivalent of Miami Beach or West Palm Beach. At the same time, though, the socio-economic 'quiet revolution' from the 1960s onwards saw tens of thousands of less palatial homes built in the former bush to the south and east of Nassau by the upwardly mobile from the former slums Over-the-Hill and the flood of migrants from the Family Islands. Nassau has spread almost to envelop the entire eastern half of the island, making Fox Hill, South Beach and Carmichael mere outer suburbs (incidentally, almost burying the once magical Mermaid's Pool in the process).

By the year 2000, New Providence was home to more than two-thirds of the Bahamian population – perhaps 200,000 people if part-time wealthy residents and illegal HAITIAN immigrants are included. Curiously, 95 per cent of the population is concentrated in the eastern half of the island, giving it an average population density of about 4,750 per square mile, compared with no more than 250 for the other half. Though this relatively underpopulated area does include some vegetable and chicken farms, the BACARDI distillery, the giant generator plant and a brewery at Clifton Pier, and Nassau's massive international airport, it does still contain some areas of near wilderness: pine forest, palmetto bush, lakes, lagoons and mangrove swamp. How long this can last depends, firstly, on the finite resources of the island (particularly water supplies), and secondly, on the degree to which the government and conservationists can restrain the demographic and developmental tide. One significant issue in 2002 is whether or not a resort development near CLIFTON should be allowed to go ahead and erase the ruins of a Loyalist cotton plantation, slave quarters and the site of a Lucayan village, not found elsewhere on New Providence.

NEWSPAPERS The Bahamas has been relatively well served by newspapers since the coming of the LOYALISTS in the 1780s. Even during the nineteenth century, Bahamian newspapers provided a forum for political debate, though since prolonged success was dependent upon the award of government printing contracts, the official viewpoint tended to get the upper hand. The twentieth century saw great competition between two rival dailies, the conservative morning *Guardian* and the more critical evening *Tribune* – though even the latter never veered wholeheartedly to the left. An increasingly literate and news-hungry people were served by no less than four daily newspapers at the beginning of the twenty-first century – more than any other country the size of The Bahamas. All are of a technically high standard, though the need to be all things to all people in the quest for circulation tends them towards political uniformity.

Newspapers, along with facilities for general printing, were among the transforming innovations brought to Nassau by the American Loyalists. John Wells, a printer from Charleston, South Carolina, published the first issue of the weekly *Bahama Gazette* on 7 August 1784. He continued as editor till his death in 1800, when the paper was taken over by the versatile Joseph EVE. As its name implied, the *Bahama Gazette* – like the *Royal Gazette* which temporarily succeeded it between 1804 and 1814 – was mainly a vehicle for official notices and government proceedings, along with advertisements, a modicum of mostly outdated news, and even less commentary. A much stronger political role was assumed, however by the anti-government and anti-abolitionist *Bahama Argus* between 1831 and 1840.

The first genuine newspaper was the bi-weekly *Nassau Guardian,* founded in 1844 by an Englishman, Edwin Charles Moseley (1812–85), who had served his apprenticeship on the *Yorkshire Post* and London *Times*. To the still meagre items of news Moseley added lively editorials, a letters section, literary articles poems and even songs, complete with music. His critical achievement however was to obtain the government printing contract in 1845, which provided the regular infusion of cash that enabled the *Guardian* to outlast a half dozen potential rivals. Successively edited by Edwin Moseley's two sons (1885–1904) and by his redoubtable granddaughter Miss Mary MOSELEY (1904–48), this family paper became the bastion and mouthpiece of the Bahamian oligarchic white elite.

One fascinating but short-lived counter-voice was the comparatively radical *Freeman*, published by the non-whites James Carmichael Smith, Stephen Albert Dillett and David PATTON between 1887 and 1889. Though its motto was the decidedly unrevolutionary 'For God and Right, and Queen and Country', the *Freeman* was remarkably outspoken about the plight of the Bahamian black majority, and of the 'talented tenth' who aspired to be their leaders.

A more effective and much more long-lived critic of the regime was the *Nassau Tribune*, founded by the mulatto Leon Dupuch in 1903. Having left school at nine, Dupuch worked his way from paper boy to head of the job printing department of the *Guardian* and wrote for the short-lived radical *Watchman,* before acquiring a simple foot-treadle printer and producing his own four-page bi-weekly penny paper. Its bold Latin motto (*nullius addictus jurare in verba magistri*) and altruistic initial affirmation accurately outlined the policy followed by Leon Dupuch and (for most of his tenure) by his even more remarkable son, Etienne DUPUCH, owner-editor for 70 years (1919–89): 'For the establishment of popular privilege, for the uplifting and ennobling of our fellow creatures, for the improvement and education of the people, without which no country can enjoy the benefits of the great central Government under which it is our good fortune to live.'

With the installation of modern communications and technology, both the *Guardian* and the *Tribune* came to look like junior versions of metropolitan papers. Both became dailies in the late 1930s. In the 1950s and 1960s, though Etienne Dupuch continued to attack the white regime, it became increasingly a personal, even egotistical, crusade. Dupuch distrusted the black populist movement and bitterly attacked the PROGRESSIVE LIBERAL PARTY'S polemical bi-weekly *Herald*. As the *Guardian* was formally taken over by BAY STREET'S ruling UNITED BAHAMIAN PARTY, Dupuch's *Tribune* lost the will to be an effective counterweight; while for its part the PLP lacked the means and expertise to fulfil such a role. To some commentators, these factors contributed to the delay in the PLP's eventual victory between 1956 and 1967.

Even after the PLP came to power, it tended to rely on the media of RADIO and (somewhat later) TELEVISION, rather than a party-sponsored daily newspaper. As a symptom of the collapse of Bay Street's power, the *Guardian* itself became neutralised. Somewhat paradoxically, as Bahamian newspapers continued to flourish and take on a thoroughly modern appearance – with the *Freeport News*, a *Guardian* publication, first appearing in 1990 and the *Bahama Journal* joining the *Guardian* and the *Tribune* in 2000 – the Bahamian dailies became less distinguishable than ever before.

NIGHTCLUBS

At the start of the twenty-first century, the most notable innovations in the Bahamian press – indicating changing economic realities, needs and tastes – were that the *Nassau Daily Tribune* offered a reprint of sections of the *Miami Herald* and became a morning paper; that the *Nassau Daily Guardian* was returned to Bahamian ownership after a period of American control; and that the most successful competitor to the three dailies was a slick bi-weekly tabloid in the style of Rupert Murdoch called the *Punch* – complete with scantily clad male and female pin-ups and juicy scandals.

Further reading: E. Dupuch, *The Tribune Story*, Benn, 1967; H. S. Pactor, 'Communication in an Island Setting: A History of the Mass Media of the Bahama Islands, 1784-1956', unpublished PhD thesis, University of Tennessee, Knoxville, 1985.

NIGHTCLUBS

During their heyday in the mid-twentieth century Nassau's Over-the-Hill nightclubs were the favourite after-dark and weekend entertainment centres for visitors and locals alike. They were thus significant (and exciting) social and cultural crossing-points, the demise of which under the pressures of modern tourism is viewed with nostalgic regret by their now ageing former habitués.

As the writer L.D. POWLES described in the 1880s, the early tourists sought to spice their visit with 'native' entertainment. This was either provided by dancers and musicians on the terrace of the Royal Victoria Hotel, or more adventurously found on guided expeditions into the villages of the interior of New Providence. Just as the Afro-American entertainment found in Harlem became a magnet for adventurous white New Yorkers during the PROHIBITION years and later, so the 'native' night-spots and their entertainers catered for a similar taste among the gradually rising tide of tourists visiting Nassau.

Down to World War Two, much of the best entertainment was found on Bay Street downtown, in such white-owned 'taverns' as the *Bucket of Blood*, *Blackbeard's* and *Dirty Dick's*. But from the later 1940s to the mid-1960s several black entrepreneurs with experience in Miami and New York successfully developed nightclubs Over-the-Hill: *Weary Willie's*, the *Zanzibar*, *Silver Slipper*, *Spider's Web*, *Drumbeat* and, largest and most successful of all, Freddy MUNNINGS's *Cat and Fiddle*.

Though each of the nightclubs had its special character, they had a common format. Fronting the central dance floor was a stage and bandstand. Customers were seated at small tables on the edge of the dance floor, or, more discreetly, in booths behind. The clientele was mixed but not rigidly segregated. In most clubs there was an upstairs gallery, where white locals or tourists normally sat. Waitresses served the tables upstairs and down, but there was also an open bar downstairs, from where single males might eye the 'talent' or ladies of the night look for custom.

Though most non-white customers came to dance to their favourite band, the highlights of the evening were the two floor-shows; an 'early' one between 11 and midnight and another as late as 2 a.m. These were timed to coincide with the arrival of groups of tourists brought by taxis, or the hectic schedule of entertainers appearing at several clubs. They consisted of displays of fire-dancing, limbo dances or drumming, singing and comedy turns. Aimed mainly at visitors, these would be pretty familiar stuff to the locals, though they never seemed to tire of the voices of Freddy Munnings or Eloise LEWIS, the virtuoso playing of Harold McNair or 'Peanuts' TAYLOR, or the japes of 'Sweet Richard' DEAN. Less routinely, there were appearances by such black American entertainers as the bawdy stand-up comedian 'Flip' Wilson, singers Roy Hamilton, Harry Belafonte, Dinah Washington and Sam Cooke, or even world-famous big bands, including Count Basie's.

Nightclubs served food to go with the potent rum cocktails. But for the die-hard adventurers there were several less reputable last resorts. Such was the Conch Shell Club far out on Blue Hill Road, where the nightclub bands' sidemen sometimes played jazz for fun, an early breakfast of hamburger might be bought, or, for the desperate male, an assignation made with one of the HAITIAN or Dominican harlots.

The social geography and function of the nightclubs changed in the 1970s. As the numbers of tourists multiplied, the logistics of getting them Over-the-Hill became more complex. At the same time the increase in local crime gave the area an unsafe reputation. More important, the will of the hotels to monopolise tourists' entertainment combined with that of a more affluent local population to enjoy themselves in rather more glamorous surroundings. The consequence was the shift of nightspots towards the waterfront and into the hotels, as well as the substitution of imported American and West Indian music and forms of entertainment in place of the traditional local fare. Such a trend did not apply to Freeport, Nassau's rival as a tourist destination, since authentic Bahamian entertainment had not been firmly established there in the first place.

All the Over-the-Hill Nassau nightclubs had closed by 1975. Peanuts Taylor's Drumbeat Club bravely bucked the trend by relocating next to the British Colonial Hotel, but did not succeed for long. Other nightclubs, like Charley Charley's and the Pink Pussy-Cat on Delancey Street or that in Chippingham's ARDASTRA GARDENS, fell between several stools. Neither Over-the-Hill nor on the waterfront, they were more like French *boites* than the traditional clubs, and offered entertainment that was neither wholly exotic nor authentically Bahamian.

Although local musicians and entertainers had plentiful employment, by the end of twentieth century the only nightclub with anything like a traditional content and style was that of King Eric and his Knights, located at the Nassau Beach Hotel on CABLE BEACH. This hotel and its adjacent Johnny Canoe Café also featured regular RAKE N' SCRAPE and JUNKANOO-type performances. Other hotels offered excellent – even spectacular – music and entertainment, but of a type that would equally be found in Miami, Atlantic City or Las Vegas. Similarly, the nightspots most popular with youngsters, local and visiting alike, The Zoo and Club Waterloo, were almost indistinguishable from discotheques located in Florida or Hawaii, or on the French Riviera.

NORMAN'S CAY A 4-mile (6-km) long cay in the northern Exumas with a good harbour and 3,000-foot (914-m) airstrip which in the late 1970s and early 1980s earned notoriety as a drug transshipment point.

The southern end of the island, including a yacht club and the airstrip, was purchased by the Colombian Cali Cartel, who installed the sinister Carlos 'Joe' Lehder to run the operation. The club was closed to outsiders, a sophisticated wireless mast erected, and a fence put round the property. This was patrolled by armed Colombian thugs, who so intimidated the foreign residents on the cay that most of them left.

Planes carrying millions of dollars' worth of cocaine were said to have flown in almost nightly, either to pause before flying on to the United States, or to transfer their cargoes to motor boats or smaller aircraft. The police in Nassau were made aware of the traffic early in 1979, but repeated raids (nearly always delayed) drew a complete blank every time. This was because the drug runners had an inside line to at least one senior officer at police headquarters, if not also useful connections high up on the political ladder. Lehder himself was always conveniently absent in his yacht when the police descended, though he and his family continued to live on the cay intermittently until 1982.

The Drug Commission of Inquiry in 1984 was told that the traffic may even have continued into 1983 despite the presence of a permanent detachment of police on the cay, though it came to an end shortly afterwards with the entrapment of Lehder by the DEA, his extradition to the United States, his trial and sentencing to 25 years in jail. Norman's Cay reverted to duller but more licit activities. Visiting yachtsmen, besides sampling the famous bonefishing on the flats, can scuba-dive the wreck of at least one drug-running DC3 that misjudged the runway in the dark.

South end of Norman's Cay, looking southwards

OAKES, Sir Harry (1874–1943) Expatriate multi-millionaire, whose unsolved murder in Nassau in July 1943 has produced more theories and publications than any other event in Bahamian history except the landfall of Columbus.

Oakes was a complex and controversial character in whom a cultured upbringing, good taste and acts of generosity were combined with a preference for rough clothes and tough language, and sudden bursts of anger. He was born of middle-class but not wealthy parents in Maine, and educated at prestigious Bowdoin College. At first intending to be a doctor, he caught gold fever and spent two arduous and impoverished decades following one gold rush after another – from the Klondike, to Australia, New Zealand, Central Africa and the Yukon – before hitting the jackpot at Kirkland Lake in northern Ontario. In due course his Lakeshore Mine became the second most productive goldmine in the world. Contrary to legend, this was no mere stroke of luck, but the product of steely determination, applied geological expertise, and ruthless corporate organisation.

Finding himself one of the richest men in North America after years of privation, Oakes became a Canadian citizen, built or bought mansions in Maine, Ontario, London and Sussex, married an Australian beauty, and sired five handsome (though mostly ill-fated) children. In Canada he gained a reputation as a philanthropist, but took angry exception to what he regarded as discriminatory taxes, and in 1934 suddenly moved with his fortune to the tax-free Bahamas.

Oakes's arrival in Nassau at the height of the Great Depression was like the descent of a far from fairy-like Godfather. It is said that he was lured to The Bahamas by the wiles of the Bay Street realtor Harold CHRISTIE, and he certainly became Christie's closest associate and his best customer. Eventually he owned 10,000 acres, about a quarter, of the prime land in NEW PROVIDENCE. But this was no mere speculation. Oakes was responsible for countless projects, as often of general benefit as self-interested. Besides two palatial homes, he built the first airport (Oakes Field), bought the struggling British Colonial Hotel, financed a new wing of the General Hospital, and employed up to 1,500 out-of-work labourers at a time, at wages a dollar above the usual $4 a day.

Generally welcomed by the regime, Oakes became a British citizen, stood successfully for the Assembly against the young Milo BUTLER (without having actually to campaign), and was later appointed to the Executive Council. Completing his upward ascent, if not noticeably adding polish to his persona, he was made a hereditary baronet in 1939 (after making a princely donation to a London hospital). Upon the arrival of the Duke of WINDSOR as Governor in 1940, he became a golfing partner and close confidant of the former King Edward VIII.

The discovery of the battered and burned body of Sir Harry Oakes at his Westbourne home on the morning of Thursday 8 July 1943 (the day before he was due to join his wife at Bar Harbor, Maine for the summer) was therefore an almost all-round shock. The person charged with the murder and tried that November seemed to many the most likely perpetrator. This was Count Alfred de Marigny, a Mauritian playboy, who had recently married the Oakes's teenage daughter Nancy without her parents' consent. He was known to have had violent arguments with Sir Harry and was detested by many in the Nassau establishment, especially Governor Windsor and his wife.

There were shaky elements in Marigny's testimony but no obvious motive for such a brutal murder. What saved him from the noose, though, was the clear fact that emerged from clever cross-examination by the defence, that the two American detectives brought in to investigate, Melchen and Barker, had intentionally planted incriminating fingerprint evidence. In a sensational 9 : 3 decision, the jury acquitted Marigny, though at the same time it also recommended his deportation from The Bahamas. He left The Bahamas for Cuba, not to return for more than forty years, protesting his innocence in two widely spaced (and not entirely consistent) autobiographies. Nancy Oakes Marigny, having stood by de Marigny at his trial, divorced him a few months after it ended.

If it was not de Marigny, who then did kill Sir Harry Oakes? A number of alternative candidates have been proposed with varying degrees of plausibility. These have included some unknown disgruntled black employee, or an anonymous professional hit man, employed by BAY STREET, the official establishment, or even the Mafia.

The first has been considered possible because though Oakes was a benefactor to and popular with most black Bahamians, he was known to have treated roughly those who crossed him. Supporters of this theory made much of the alleged OBEAH elements at the murder scene – most of it sensational nonsense. Equally unlikely is the possibility that anyone in the official establishment could have had any motive stronger than jealousy or dislike that would have led them to propose Sir Harry's murder. It has been suggested, however, that by insisting on the employment of Melchen and Barker rather than the local police and experts among the wartime forces, Governor Windsor, along with others, had a motive or determination to set up Alfred de Marigny for the crime.

The Bay Street hypothesis, which strongly implicated Harold Christie and perhaps Stafford SANDS, was based on one or two undocumented suppositions. Superficially, it would seem incredible that Christie would have been party to the murder of his closest associate and best real estate customer. Yet, while he claimed to have spent the entire fatal night at Westbourne and slept the night through in the next bedroom to Sir Harry's, Christie asserted that he heard no suspicious noises or smelled any smoke. He also denied as impossible the evidence of a reliable witness that he was seen driving down Bay Street at midnight on that night. Christie's obvious discomfiture in the witness box and the evidence given has added fuel to the theory that Christie and others in the Bay Street circle were alarmed by information that Sir Harry was planning permanently to leave The Bahamas, along with his money, just as he had previously deserted Canada.

The remaining hypothesis – involving the Mafia and certain would-be Bay Street associates – is the most bizarre and yet in some ways the most plausible, especially given the subsequent history of CASINO tourism in The Bahamas. According to the supposition, Salvatore 'Lucky' Luciano and Meyer Lansky were already in the 1940s eager to establish hotels and casino gambling in The Bahamas, as a back-up or alternative to Cuba. This was very much favoured by Stafford Sands, and perhaps also by his fellow advocate of tourist development, Harold Christie. It was said to be adamantly opposed by Sir Harry Oakes – a non-gambler himself, who wished to keep The Bahamas from becoming another Havana, Las Vegas or Atlantic City, and had sufficient money and influence locally to get his way. Hence, so goes the hypothesis, Sir Harry had to be removed.

The Harry Oakes mystery will probably never be resolved, and for that reason it will almost certainly provoke endless, often heated debate. One of the best of the many books on the subject that has come closest so far to pouring cold water on the case is *Who Killed Sir Harry Oakes?* In 1983, while trotting out all the usual suspects and painting many a murky scenario, the English writer James Leasor came up with the distinct possibility that Sir Harry's death may, after all, have been an accident, which, for one reason or another, had to be covered up by the person or persons involved.

Further reading: A. de Marigny, *More Devil Than Saint*, Beechhurst Press, 1946; *A Conspiracy of Crowns*, Bantam Press, 1990; G. Bocca, *The Life and Death of Harry Oakes*, World Distributions, 1962; Marshall Houts, *King's X*, Morrow, 1972; 'Sir Harry Oakes: The Man Behind the Myth', *Bahamas Handbook and Businessman's Annual, 1976–77*, Dupuch Publications, 1976, 14–29; J. Leasor, *Who Killed Sir Harry Oakes?*, Heinemann, 1983; T. Findley, *Famous Last Words*, New York, 1995.

OBEAH Afro-Caribbean sorcery medicine, involving spells and fetishes administered by a shamanistic obeah-man (or woman). Its former prevalence and the fears that it generated explain why obeah was anathematised by the Christian churches and severely penalised under the law, in The Bahamas as elsewhere. Despite this opposition, obeah practices and beliefs covertly survived, and still persist. Male or female obeah shamans even advertise in the local Bahamian newspapers, under such transparent labels as 'spiritual healer, advisor and psychic reader'.

Though some authorities trace the roots of obeah to Ashanti (the modern Ghana), it is more likely generically West African in origin. The word obeah (or obi) itself is said to derive from the Efik word *ubio* – the Efik being a people from the Cross River area in the south-eastern part of modern Nigeria. Most West Africans, however, had a religion or system of beliefs that included a supreme creator, counterpoised forces of good and evil, and the potency of the spirits of ancestors and certain sacred places and things, such as water springs, caves and silk cotton trees (*ceibas*). Priestly shamans or the members of secret societies (such as the Leopard Men of the Efik) had the skill to communicate and intercede with the world of the spirits, and to exercise powers for good or evil, through the exercise of sorcery magic and the deployment of fetishes, charms and potions. In the Bahamas and British West Indies both the system itself and its apparatus are known as obeah.

Sir Harry Oakes (left) with his golf, bridge and drinking partner, Governor HRH the Duke of Windsor, 1941

'Obeah man' caricature at Junkanoo

The Efik word *ubio* means alternatively anything noxious, a charm or fetish to cause sickness or death, or a bad omen. This is consonant with the commonly held view in earlier times that obeah was exclusively 'black' or bad sorcery magic. Jamaican commentators have pointed out that in Ashanti there were opposing forces of good and evil, and argued that these were the roots of the well-known tension in Jamaica between obeah (Afro-Caribbean sorcery) and myalism (Afro-Jamaican quasi-religious ritual). Even more evident (and more apposite to Bahamian obeah) was the conflict between obeah and the Christian religion – Catholics, Anglicans and Nonconformists alike seeing obeah as communicating with the devil and the forces of darkness. Other commentators (particularly in recent times) have downplayed such a dichotomy, showing ways in which Afro-Caribbean religions (notably Haitian *vodun* or Cuban *santeria*) have syncretically assimilated Christian elements, and encompass principles of good as well as evil. Put another way, they incorporate (as all true religions do) 'white' as well as 'black' magic.

Obeah is by no stretch a religion (having no fixed creed, rituals or churches, no organised congregations, and its priests self-ordained) but it is a potent folklore force nevertheless and by no means entirely negative in its operation. In The Bahamas it has existed in some form since the foundation of the colony – the earliest colonists including black slaves as well as their white masters. Obeah's perceived potential for fomenting rebellion and poisoning led the Bahamian legislators to copy the draconian laws against it enacted by the plantation colonies more genuinely threatened. But the danger proved exaggerated and obeah flourished – despite the growing opposition of the churches – both in those 'all-black' islands deserted by white LOYALIST would-be planters, and in those parts of New Providence settled by LIBERATED AFRICANS who came directly from West Africa between 1809 and 1860 and were never enslaved.

Early white visitors and tourists such as L. D. POWLES, G. B. Shattuck, Amelia DEFRIES, or Hugh MacLachlan Bell saw obeah as little more than a quaint cultural phenomenon that reassuringly reinforced their sense of superiority over a superstitious and credulous people. H. M. Bell, for example, gave the following description in 1934:

The obeah man uses queer nostrums and relies on weird concoctions and effects to gain a livelihood. Old medicine bottles often are filled with simple drugs bought for a penny or two, then are sold, of course, for shillings. Dog's teeth, sharks' teeth, egg-shells, snake bones, skulls of cats and other animals, earth from old graves, miniature coffins and chicken feathers are used to cure almost any disease or avert any possible disaster. Our magician deals in love by supplying philtres, in revenge by putting curses upon enemies, and in cash by being paid on the barrelhead, so to speak, before he goes to work. Sometimes a female of the species develops quite a business before landing in police hands.

Such casual observations underestimated the popular status and spiritual importance of obeah-men and women – not to mention their value as psychiatric counsellors and practitioners of folk medicine. Such famous obeah-men as 'Pa Beah' (Zaccharias Adderley) of Fox Hill, New Providence, or 'Uncle Boy' of The Bight, Cat Island, seem to have had a genuine calling and to have performed effective cures and therapies – if not quite the miracles and mysteries popularly attributed to them. Their reputation, however, did them no harm. Any field, house or person known to have been 'fixed' by them with favourable obeah was almost guaranteed to be safe from theft, malicious damage or human attack. Innumerable tales are told of persons languishing, even dying, who knew themselves to have been placed under an obeah interdiction. There are many, if fewer, stories of persons bewitched into unsought liaisons, or horses on the race track performing either better or worse than expected. Apparently though, the record of obtaining bumper harvests, sudden treasure, predicting winning lottery numbers, or saving persons at death's door through obeah is no better than with any other form of necromancy or divination.

The laws against obeah are still on the books, but there have been no prosecutions for more than a century. This does not necessarily indicate obeah's decline so much as a more tolerant approach to folklore beliefs. In recent years obeah may even have gained ground in The Bahamas through the immigration of Jamaicans and HAITIANS – obeah having always been strongest in Jamaica, and Haitian *vodun* providing a potent crossover influence. It may only be a minority of Bahamians who still seek obeah potions and spells, but many more accord it at least some credence. Perhaps no more than one in ten Bahamians has ever resorted to obeah, but there is scarcely one of the remaining nine who has not encountered it and has an obeah tale to tell – nearly all in the category of 'I don't really believe this myself, but . . .'. As Patricia Glinton-Meicholas amusingly notices, many even of those educated and middle-class Bahamians who publicly dismiss and deride obeah should really place themselves in the category of agnostics, given their own tendency to hold superstitious beliefs and practise superstitious formulae. Some of these clearly have affinities to or roots in Afro-Caribbean obeah or its Christian antithesis – even if their practitioners do not go so far as to exorcise perceived malignant spirits by marking 'Xs', reciting 'Ten, ten, the Bible ten', or using the Bible itself as a talisman.

Further reading: T. McCartney, *Ten, Ten, the Bible Ten: Obeah in The Bahamas*, Nassau, 1976; Patricia Glinton-Meicholas, *How to be a True-True Bahamian: A Hilarious Look at Life in The Bahamas*, Guanima Press, 1994; S. Whittier (ed.), *Insight Guide: Bahamas*, APA Publications, 2000, 258–65; J. J. Williams, *Voodoo and Obeahs*, New York, 1932; 'Development of Obeah in Jamaica', www.sacred-texts.com/afr.

OFFSHORE BANKING AND FINANCE

Domestic BANKING has been dwarfed by the growth of offshore banking, which by the end of the twentieth century had made Nassau one of the world's top ten financial centres. With over 400 banks and trust companies licensed to operate in or from The Bahamas, it is an industry second in importance only to TOURISM, employing thousands of Bahamian men and women, and contributing some quarter billion dollars to the nation's Gross Domestic Product.

The rise of The Bahamas as an offshore financial centre, or tax haven, became established in the 1930s when it came to be a playground for wealthy visitors and winter residents attracted by the absence of personal and corporate taxation and death duties. Following World War Two the liberal policies of Sir Stafford SANDS expanded and formalised much offshore business of banking, company formation and trust companies, so that by the 1960s The Bahamas was a well-established offshore financial centre.

The continued growth of this financial sector at large was not achieved without difficulties and setbacks. The first problem was the continuing reluctance of the international financial community to trust the competence and probity of the Bahamian regime, especially following

Typical offshore banking and finance building, Price Waterhouse Coopers, West Bay Street, Nassau

OFFSHORE BANKING AND FINANCE

Independence. Coupled with the general down-turn in the world's economy, the number of banks and trust companies based or operating in Nassau declined from its first peak in the mid-1960s into the mid-1970s. Many of the companies moved to more 'reliable' (complaisant) places (such as Bermuda or the Cayman Islands), or threatened to do so as a form of blackmail. Prime Minister Lynden PINDLING had to exercise all his considerable powers of diplomacy and charm to reassure international investors and reverse the ebbing tide.

The second problem, which no amount of palliative speeches to international bankers could wholly dispel, was the undoubted incidence of shady operators among those setting up banks in Nassau, and the even shadier provenance of much of the money that was finding sanctuary or being routed through The Bahamas. The most notorious operator was the American Robert VESCO, who is widely considered to have bought his immunity from extradition through purchasing his own bank and spreading soft loans around in strategic places. In the 1980s, to the well-established practice of tax-evasion was added the 'laundering' of proceeds from drug-running through The Bahamas – complicated by the undoubted fact that the traffic did bring benefits to many Bahamians and to the Bahamian economy in general during a time of general recession.

This general situation in due course led to the worst problem of all: the pressure from the United States, the United Kingdom and other major capitalist countries to call a halt to illegal tax avoidance and the laundering of money derived from the drug trade and other criminal activities. With the change of government in 1992 there was a wholesale renewal of confidence in the Bahamian financial complex, and the number of banks and trust companies (along with offshore companies in general) reached an all-time high. In June 2000, not without warning, came a four-headed blow, when the G7 nations' Organisation for Economic Co-operation and Development (OECD) and Financial Action Task Force, and the US Treasury and Internal Revenue Service placed The Bahamas on a financial black list along with 34 other offshore financial jurisdictions.

The government was placed in a painful dilemma: how to satisfy the major capitalist governments without driving away business altogether. After much discussion, mainly behind closed doors, a whole raft of new legislation was passed later in 2000. This greatly tightened the regulations governing foreign banks and trust companies (especially in respect of naming their officers and reporting suspicious activities), increased the supervisory powers of the Central Bank, made much more precise definitions of what constituted money laundering and criminal tax evasion, set up a Financial Intelligence Unit, and laid out procedures for sharing information – short of breaching the confidentiality of legitimate offshore transactions. After a nervous interval, the government was able to breathe at least a preliminary sigh of relief. In April 2002, The Bahamas was taken off the OECD and FATF black list (along with all but seven of the previously listed jurisdictions), though this was virtually made conditional on the effectiveness of the recent legislation and the expectation that The Bahamas might go even further in making their financial business more 'transparent'. Around the same time, the US Treasury and IRS declared The Bahamas a 'compliant jurisdiction' – a category subject to review at six-year intervals.

At the end of 2002, there were just over 400 banks and trust companies licensed by the Central Bank of The Bahamas, of which at least 340 had fully complied with the provisions of the International Business Companies Act of 2000. Of these institutions, nine were defined as Commercial Banks, licensed as 'authorised dealers' to carry on all types of business, local and international, in all currencies, while a further 15, called 'authorised agents' could do likewise, subject only to going through exchange control. The remaining companies came under the general heading of 'other public licensees', with distinctions made between three sub-categories: 'resident' and 'non-resident' (dealing, respectively, mainly in Bahamian and foreign currencies), and 'restricted' (carrying on business with certain specified individuals).

By the beginning of the twenty-first century the Bahamian banking industry had become and remained a highly sophisticated system with many obvious advantages, including a good degree of discretion, if no longer an impenetrable veil of secrecy. The industry's publicity stresses not just 'the country's stable political system, modern and accommodating business legislation and skilled workforce' but points out that 'Bahamian law strongly protects the right to confidentiality and privacy of bank clients. Non-residents who do business in The Bahamas also enjoy freedom from exchange controls. The Bahamas has not entered into tax treaties with any other country. In addition, the country has no personal or corporate income, capital gains, estate, gift, or inheritance taxes.'

Further reading: A. Thompson, *An Economic History of The Bahamas*, Nassau, Commonwealth Publications, 1979; Neil Hartnell, 'Long Arm of the OECD', *Bahamas Handbook and Businessman's Annual 2002*, Dupuch Publications, 2002, 209–46, 340–7; www.centralbankbahamas.com

OLD FORT

OLD BAHAMA CHANNEL A geological cleft that forms the deep-water channel between the Great Bahama Bank and the northern shore of Cuba. It extends more than 300 miles (480 km), from just south of the Bahamian Cay Santo Domingo, where it is 35 miles (56 km) wide, narrowing to less than 10 miles (16 km) wide as it passes Cay Lobos and Guinchos Cay, and dividing into channels on each side of the CAY SAL Bank before joining the Florida Strait.

With a westward-flowing current and the prevailing winds from the east, the Channel appeared to be a useful alternative route from the Caribbean back to Europe, and its discovery by the Spaniards was one of the reasons for the establishment of Havana in 1519 as 'the key to the New World and rampart of the West Indies'. Negotiating the channel, though, was tricky even for the Spaniards (who intentionally kept their charts to themselves), and generally regarded as impractical for large fleets. The gamblers' decision of General Lord Albemarle and Admiral Pocock to use this route with their fleet of 20 warships and 30 transports and supply ships in their attack on Havana towards the end of the Seven Years War therefore provided the surprise that contributed to the capture of the 'impregnable' city, with its immense booty, in August 1762.

Had Britain retained Cuba rather than returning it to the Spaniards by the Treaty of Paris in 1763, the history of The Bahamas would have been completely changed, and the Old Bahama Channel become a new median waterway between two British colonies. Instead it became simply a water-boundary, used only by a few Bahamian and Cuban fishermen, wreckers and smugglers, and by the Cubans for local traffic. When sail gave way to steam, the Old Bahama Channel was no longer an advantageous through-route in either direction, and once Cuba became isolated in 1959 became almost deserted by large or foreign vessels. Its contemporary frontier role was dramatically highlighted by the incident in May 1980 when HMBS *FLAMINGO* was sunk by Cuban Migs while arresting Cuban fishermen poaching in Bahamian territorial waters. It is probably significant that Bahamian guidebooks, including the *Yachtsman's Guide*, ignore the Old Bahama Channel entirely.

OLD FORT A castellated and arcaded house built mainly of concrete in a vaguely Spanish style, next to Lightbourne Creek in western NEW PROVIDENCE. First constructed about 1912, it is often claimed to incorporate remnants of an early eighteenth-century fortification, or even, more implausibly still, those of a late seventeenth-century Spanish fort.

In fact, though they sometimes attacked, Spanish forces never occupied New Providence before 1782, and none ever constructed fortifications on the island. The only slim evidence of any old fort in the area is that it was the location 'where the Palatines dwell about five leagues West of Nassau' where in 1725 the second royal Governor of The Bahamas, George Phenney, established a private plantation and retreat and may have built a small gun battery to guard the western approach to New Providence.

In later times Phenney's old plantation was called Charlotteville. Around the turn of the twentieth century it grew SISAL before falling into decay. It was purchased in 1912 by a retired American professor called Dolley, who built the present structure, probably on the foundations of a former plantation 'great house'. From the 1920s the estate was owned by a succession of more or less wealthy Americans, including the grandfather of Nicholas Brady, Secretary of the Treasury under Presidents Bush and Reagan, and the well-known explorer Suydam Cutting; but in 1964 the house was vacated and gradually threatened with dereliction. The estate was bought as a long-term investment by a subsidiary of the New Providence Development Company in 1967, but not developed until the later 1990s. By that time the house had almost taken on the appearance of an authentic ancient ruin. By the beginning of the new century, however, it had been lavishly refurbished as the 'historic' centrepiece of Old Fort Bay, a millionaire's gated community, aiming to rival, if not outdo, neighbouring LYFORD CAY.

'Old Fort', built in the early twentieth century by an American resident in Spanish castellated style on the alleged site of an early eighteenth-century fortification (English)

OLDMIXON, John

OLDMIXON, John (1673–1742) Popular and prolific early eighteenth-century historical writer, whose rip-roaring account of The Bahamas in the age of the Lord PROPRIETORS and PIRATES (1741), reads as if written by the author of *Tom Jones*. Oldmixon's vignettes of the twelve Proprietary and the first three Royal Governors is a gallery of characters, mostly disreputable, and all larger than life. The early inhabitants of the colony he fairly convincingly describes as a maritime riff-raff, employed in WRECKING, PRIVATEERING or outright piracy, and spending their spare time in riotous living and litigation. Most, he claimed, were 'living a lewd, licentious Sort of Life … impatient under Government… every Man as he thought best for his Pleasure and Interest'.

'As for Wrecks,' wrote Oldmixon, 'the People of *Providence, Harbour Island* and Eleuthera dealt with them as it is said the good Men of *Sussex* do: All that came ashore was Prize, and if a Sailor had, by better Luck than the rest, got ashore as well as his Wreck, he was not sure of getting off again as well. This perhaps is Scandal, but it is most notorious that the Inhabitants looked upon every Thing they could get out of a Cast-away Ship as their own, and were not at any Trouble to enquire after the Owners.'

There was something of an Assembly in Nassau but it was just as corrupt and self-serving as the courts of law. 'Here were Courts of Justice of all Denominations, as in Westminster-Hall,' wrote Oldmixon for his English readers, 'and the Inhabitants were so litigious that not a Borough in Cornwall could compare with them; which is all the more amazing because they had not much to quarrel for or to spare for Law.'

Despite Oldmixon's tendency to write (like Henry Fielding) in simple terms of good and evil, his account is the best and most detailed we have of the period, being clearly based on first hand testimonies, including that of ex-Governor Nicholas TROTT. Oldmixon's account of The Bahamas, a substantial section of his *The British Empire in America* (two volumes, London, 1741), was abstracted by the Bahamian Jack Culmer as *History of the Isle of Providence,* published in London in 1949.

OLD PROVIDENCE (Providencia)

A small island off the coast of Nicaragua, now owned by Colombia, which was a colony of English Puritan buccaneers and planters between 1629 and 1639. Though it is 1,200 miles (1,930 km) distant and totally different (being smaller, mountainous and flamboyantly fertile) it was confused by the otherwise reputable nineteenth-century editors of the *Calendar of State Papers, Colonial* with the Bahamian island called *NEW* PROVIDENCE. Consequently, the earliest historians of The Bahamas sometimes attributed totally spurious events to the Bahamian Providence, including its alleged founding in 1629 by the Providence Island Company and its supposed eradication by angry Spaniards from Cuba ten years later. One hopes that these errors (corrected by the CSPC editors themselves some time later) have been expunged for good.

ORGANIZATION OF AMERICAN STATES (OAS)

The oldest and largest regional organisation for international cooperation in the world. It was formally chartered in 1948 but with roots dating back to the early nineteenth century. Though still regarded by sceptics as dominated by the United States, it now includes all 35 fully independent nations in the Americas. After some hesitation and with some remaining reservations, The Bahamas became its thirty-first member in 1982.

The Bahamas was wholly in favour of the general ideals of the OAS: 'strengthening democracy, advancing human rights, promoting peace and security, expanding trade and tackling complex problems caused by poverty, drugs and corruption'. Yet the nation hesitated for nine years after achieving INDEPENDENCE before signing up, mostly for the same reasons that kept Canada out of the OAS until 1990: unwillingness to fall completely under the hegemony of the United States, doubts about the wisdom of the continuing ostracism of Castro's Cuba, overlapping and perhaps conflicting commitments to other organisations (such as the Commonwealth and, in the Bahamian case, CARICOM), and persistent doubts about the drift towards hemispheric free trade. Enthusiasm for membership, however, steadily grew after the ending of the Cold War.

Further information: www.oas.org

OUT ISLAND REGATTA

Regattas including working sailboats had been held in Nassau as early as 1831. Yet by the 1950s the native work-boat had become a dying breed and competitive sailing a pastime almost exclusively for well-heeled white locals and visiting yachtsmen. From 1954 onwards the amazingly successful regatta held each spring in Elizabeth Harbour off George Town, EXUMA has radically changed this situation in both respects.

What old hands still insist on calling the Out (rather than Family) Islands Regatta was the brainchild of J. Linton Rigg (1900–75), the son of a bishop of Jamaica. A pioneer of yacht cruising in The Bahamas, Rigg retired from his New York ship brokering business in his forties to live on what was then isolated Goat Cay, Great Exuma, and indulge full-time his fanatical love of sailing. Rigg admired the boatbuilding skills and cheerful hardihood of the ordinary Out Islanders but regretted the decline of maritime employment and the traditional work-boat, and deplored the increasing gaps between both the different Bahamian classes and the widely scattered Out Island settlements.

Recruiting many friends in the international cruising fraternity and winning over several influential Bay Street yachtsmen-politicians (notably Speaker Robert Symonette, son of the first Premier, and Nassau's chief ship pilot, Captain Freddy Brown) Linton Rigg announced the first Out Island Regatta for working sailboats, to be spread over three days in April 1954. To general amazement, a heterogenous armada of 70 working sloops, schooners, fishing smacks and dinghies sailed down to Exuma from a half dozen islands, to join an equal number of shiny and elegant cruising yachts from Nassau and the United States. Divided into rough classes by size and following equally rough-and-ready rules and regulations, the work-boats engaged in avid but generally friendly – and sometimes hilarious – competition, each day's races being followed by convivial parties, afloat and ashore.

Filling an evident need, the Family Island Regatta, as it is now called, became an annual highlight for international as well as local sailors, from 1981 being preceded by a week-long Cruising Regatta for foreign boats. The regatta itself achieved an early coup when it was patronised by the 'Sailor Prince' Duke of Edinburgh, consort of QUEEN ELIZABETH II, in 1959.

The Out Island Regatta is indeed not a purely sailing event. Its spirit was admirably conveyed by the sailor-photographer Art Paine in the magazine *Wooden Boat* in January 1992:

> From the earliest days... plenty of shoreside activities emerged to entertain non-sailors. Parades, gospel singing, weight lifting, basketball and volleyball games, model boat races, sculling, and a beauty contest are examples. A hastily constructed midway of tin and plywood emporia takes shape just before the extravaganza begins, providing a variety of gustatorial and liquid refreshment and all sorts of crafts and mementos. 'The Shacks' are very much part of Regatta, providing a site for spectators and competitors to argue the merits of competing boats and crews, place a bit of lucre upon their convictions, and either celebrate their prescience or drown sorrows over the loss.

Exuberant team work in Elizabeth Harbour, Great Exuma

Over the years, the number of entrants and the number of islands participating escalated, with larger amounts of prize money, sponsorship, and an increase in sophistication – in the boats and their rigging and the rules and regulations, if not in the sailors' age-old skills. At the same time that customising racers became more and more common and 'work-boat' became a more elastic term, more than a dozen islands and settlements strove to copy the Exuma model with their own regattas. Far from being true working sailors competing in their spare time, many captains and even their crews became almost full-time racers. These conditions provided organising committees with endless headaches and provoked occasional acrimony – particularly, and perhaps symptomatically, between crowded and wealthy Nassau (which now had two or three regattas a year) and its Family Island competitors. All told, some 18 regattas on 15 islands are now held each year.

OWENS-ILLINOIS COMPANY

Yet despite the changes that have made 'work-boat' regatta sailing probably the major (and certainly the most distinctive) of Bahamian sporting events, the Out Island Regatta has retained both its primacy and its determination to hold on to its essential purposes: to sustain Bahamian boatbuilding and sailing skills and provide the spice of competition, but at the same time to occasion an annual party, at which Bahamians of all sorts and visitors from all over can mingle peacefully and in friendship. This ideal has been most strongly maintained by the American Howland Bottomley who, like Linton Rigg, gave up his profitable business in the US in favour of a barefoot sailing life in Exuma, and for four decades was (whatever his official title) referred to as 'Mister Regatta'. The spirit which both Rigg and his successor stood for was epitomised by Bottomley's declaration in 2000 both that he believed that the Bahamian Out Islanders were the salt of the earth, and that the two Bahamians he had most admired and regarded as his truest friends were the late 'Bobby' Symonette and his political opposite, Sir Lynden Oscar Pindling.

Further reading: A. Paine, 'The Family Island Regatta: A Personal Journey', *Wooden Boat*, Jan.–Feb. 1992, 66–77; 'Boats of the Shallow Sea', *The Boatman*, Apr. 1994, 16–25; Craton and Saunders, *Islanders*, ii. 468–70.

OWENS-ILLINOIS COMPANY

The forests of Caribbean pine found in the northern islands of The Bahamas have long been an attraction to lumber companies in the US, culminating in the massive logging operation conducted on all three islands by the Owens-Illinois Company from 1956 to 1973.

Owens-Illinois were pioneers in the manufacture of plastic caps and bottles during the 1930s. After World War Two the company aggressively diversified into the general packaging business (including cardboard and hardboard as well as glass and plastic) and expanded world-wide. By 2000 it boasted 60 factories in the US, employing some 15,000 persons, and another 80 operations overseas.

The Bahamas connection stemmed from the acquisition by Owens-Illinois in the mid-1950s of the pulpwood-processing National Container Corporation, which had itself recently acquired the unexpired portion of a 100 year logging lease on land in ABACO, GRAND BAHAMA and ANDROS. This lease already had a tortuous history dating back to the beginning of the century, and was originally granted on extremely generous terms to the specially formed Bahamas Timber Company, based in St Paul, Minnesota, in 1908. BTC set up an ultra-efficient mill and company town at what it called Wilson City in central Abaco, but pulled out in the middle of World War One once it had cleared all the substantial timber trees within an economic radius. BTC passed on its logging rights to another American outfit called Abaco Lumber Company which, based at Norman's Castle in northern Abaco but using more mobile felling and milling methods, likewise cleared most of the rest of Abaco before moving its operations to Pine Ridge, Grand Bahama in 1944.

In Grand Bahama, ALC was bought out by the dynamic Virginian Wallace Groves in 1946, and had a brief heyday (at its peak employing 1,800 low-paid Turks Islanders), thanks to a profitable contract for supplying pit-props for British coal-mines and the acquisition by Groves of a concession from The Bahamas government that allowed the harvesting of pine trees as small as 4 ½ inches (113 mm) in diameter. Astutely foreseeing the imminent depletion of economic timber in Grand Bahama, Groves then engineered a double coup; using the two million dollars made from the sale of the ALC's assets to National Container to obtain the Hawksbill Creek Agreement in 1955 and kick-start the dream city of Freeport-Lucaya.

By 1959, no longer constrained by the need for board lumber or even slender logs, Owens-Illinois turned to the virtual clear-cutting of Abaco for wood to be barged for pulping in Jacksonville, Florida. With awesome efficiency, the corporation dredged a deep-water channel to a new dock at its headquarters at Snake Cay, just south of MARSH HARBOUR, and bulldozed a truck-wide logging road the entire length of the island, which its publicity department promoted as the Great Abaco Highway. From the beginning the corporation knew that the lumbering operation would last a decade at most. But it promised lasting economic benefits for Abaco, ignoring the socio-economic problems of a temporary boom and the redeployment of transient workers (especially HAITIANS), and playing down the ecological damage. Most self-serving of all were the claims that a tree re-planting programme was not feasible and that simply leaving five mature trees per acre would be sufficient to re-seed and renew the pine forest within 20 years.

Once the Abaco pulpwood operation was over, Owens-Illinois turned to similar operations in Andros, but planned an agricultural project in Abaco in order to utilise its infrastructure and labour force. Castro's revolution and the subsequent US trade embargo on Cuba caused a five-fold jump in world sugar prices in the early 1960s and promised a huge boost to sugar-producing countries that enjoyed a quota for entry into the US market. In deals that were and remain obscure, Owens-Illinois negotiated an annual US import quota of 10,000 tons for The Bahamas (though the country had never previously produced sugar commercially), and parlayed Abaco logging rights for a grant of 50,000 Abaconian acres of Crown Land for

OWENS-ILLINOIS COMPANY

agricultural purposes from the Bahamas government.

Setting up a subsidiary called Bahamas Agricultural Industries Limited (BAIL), Owens-Illinois went about their project with their customary efficiency. They brought in state-of-the-art rock-crushing, planting and harvesting machinery and set up a similarly up-to-date (and conveniently retransportable) cane-processing mill and refinery, said to be capable of producing 50,000 tons of sugar a year. Canefields extending over 42 square miles (109 squ. km) were levelled, fertilised and planted, and sugar first exported in 1969. However, yields per acre were below expectation from the beginning and showed signs of declining in subsequent years. Fifteen thousand tons were produced in 1969 and 19,000 tons in 1970. But in November 1970 BAIL suddenly announced that it would not be harvesting the 1971 crop and was closing down operations, citing losses of $10 million over the previous two years. According to one of BAIL's directors, the low rainfall during the early growing period reduced yields to an uneconomic level once prices fell. In any event, the canefields remained fallow, gradually returning to bush, and the factory was sold and shipped off to South America.

Most seriously (some would say symbolically) from the middle 1980s investigators became concerned about the toxic wastes and pesticides which still contaminated the former BAIL canefields. These included the notorious 'agent orange' deployed, for other purpose, in Vietnam. Organisations such as Global Response demanded that they be cleaned up. After much harrying, it was only in August 1992 that Owens-Illinois accepted responsibility and promised to take the lead in a clean-up, and it was not until November 1994 that the government and Owens-Illinois actually began what turned out to be a difficult, lengthy and expensive process.

Further reading: S. Dodge, *Abaco: The History of an Out Island and its Cays*, White Sound Press, 2nd. ed., 1995, 78–84, 97–105; P.W. T. Henry, *The Pine Forests of The Bahamas*, Land Resource Study no. 16, 1974; www.global response.org

Pine forest

PARADISE ISLAND The largest of the small cays fringing the north side of NEW PROVIDENCE; a 5 ½-mile (9-km) sliver of land that forms NASSAU's excellent natural harbour; it now surpasses CABLE BEACH and FREEPORT as the glittering focus of Bahamian tourism.

Originally it was called Hog Island, a not highly valued islet; some Nassauvians used to row across in order to cultivate provisions and run small stock, including semi-wild pigs. Its first buildings were a small gun battery, a quarantine station, and the lighthouse built on the western end in 1816 to indicate the harbour entrance to ships approaching Nassau.

From the later eighteenth century some boatbuilding was carried out on Hog Island, and during the second half of the nineteenth century a dockyard was built on the harbour shore for the careening and repair of the modest-sized local vessels. During the AMERICAN CIVIL WAR (1861–5), Hog Island had a brief heyday as a coaling station for Confederate blockade-runners – remnants of the wreck of one which missed the entrance to Nassau harbour are still to be seen on the island's north-western shore.

In the early twentieth century the splendid beaches on the north side began to attract the few upper-class Nassauvians who had the inclination and leisure time for sea- and sun-bathing. When tourism tentatively began before World War One, a dozen wealthy Americans built the ultra-exclusive Porcupine Club, facing Nassau but separated from it by the harbour, and during the Prohibition era which followed the War the American shipping tycoon Frederick Munson purchased the lovely cove then called Saratoga Beach and renamed it Paradise Beach – hoping to make it too into an exclusive resort. More prosaically, the ambitious young Bahamian businessman Roland SYMONETTE built up the almost derelict old dockyard on the southern side of Hog Island into Nassau's major shipyard and oil storage depot.

The first major developer was the Swedish owner of Electrolux, Axel Wenner-Gren, who bought the central 500 acres of Hog Island from its American owner in 1939 for $150,000, intending to make it into a palatial retreat for himself. He began in splendid style, using hundreds of unemployed Bahamian labourers to build a house appropriately named Shangri-La, formal gardens modelled on Versailles, a hurricane-proof harbour for his 250-foot (76-m) yacht, and a navigable canal across the island. But at the very least Wenner-Gren's timing was poor. WORLD WAR TWO began for the British in 1939 and for the Americans in 1941, and the Swedish tycoon's undoubtedly fascist sympathies and German connections made him a suspect alien. Rumours even maintained (in error) that the Hog Island canal was designed as a refuelling base for German U-Boats. From 1942 Wenner-Gren transferred his major interests to Mexico, though he did not sell his Hog Island estate until just before his death in 1960.

Wenner-Gren's successor was the visionary and spendthrift heir to the A & P grocery fortune, Huntingdon Hartford II, who bought four-fifths of the island for $10 million. Hartford's impossible dream was to build a resort that would combine the utmost in elegance and luxury with

Paradise Island, eastern end

the more vulgar appeal of a casino and sporting spectacles such as *Ben Hur* style chariot races. His achievements were notable. He created the ultra de-luxe Ocean Club and Café Martinique, added an imported medieval cloister to the Versailles Garden, and persuaded the Bahamas government in May 1962 officially to change the name of the whole cay from Hog Island to Paradise Island. In typical praiseworthy but impractical style, Hartford also ordained that there should be no building taller than the tallest tree on the island.

Huntingdon Hartford was no match either for more predatory developers or their canny accomplices in the Bahamian government. His applications for a casino licence and for a bridge from the New Providence mainland both fell on stony ground. Having poured $25 million into Paradise Island (along with similarly extravagant projects elsewhere) Hartford found himself quickly running out of money. In 1966 he sold a 75 per cent interest in Paradise Island for $13 million to an incongruous outfit called Mary Carter Paints, which, though with respectable front-men, was widely suspected of being Mafia-owned. Be that as it may, in the twilight of the BAY STREET regime the majority owners gained licences both for a casino and a bridge, and renamed themselves RESORTS INTERNATIONAL. Huntingdon Hartford, after years as a sleeping partner and complaints of being cheated, was bought out for a relative pittance in 1975.

Under the Resorts International banner, Paradise Island flourished. Hotels and condominiums were built, an 18-hole golf-course was laid out, and a direct air service from Florida by A. B. CHALK's Grumman flying boats was instituted. By 1981, it was announced that Paradise Island was attracting more tourists than its mainland island of New Providence. The later 1980s, however, saw considerable confusion about ownership as well as mixed fortunes. In 1987, Donald Trump bought Resorts' Paradise Island interests for $79 million, only to sell them less than two years later to Merv Griffin for what was a clearly inflated price of $400 million. Under Griffin, extravagant further expansion took place, including the building of an airport at the eastern end of the island and the creation of Paradise Island Airways in 1989.

By 1992, Griffin was in serious financial trouble and desperate for a buyer. Into the breach stepped the South African tycoon Sol KERZNER, whose Sun International Corporation, with the enthusiastic cooperation of the new FREE NATIONAL MOVEMENT government, began the fifth and most extravagant of the phases of Paradise Island's development. Buying out Griffin for no more than $125 million, Kerzner negotiated numerous tax and immigration concessions and the building of a second bridge across the harbour. The airport was closed and became one of several sites for luxury condominiums. But the cornerstone of the new dispensation was the construction of the ATLANTIS mega-hotel. The first phase, costing $160 million, was completed by December 1994, only to be dwarfed by the ultimate phase, costing even more and opening four years later. Allowed to ignore Huntingdon Hartford's precept about the maximum height of buildings (as well as rejecting his ideas of elegant style) its pink-painted central block soars 23-storeys high and is visible from almost every point on New Providence. Far beyond dwarfing its local competitors, Kerzner's 2,300 room Atlantis complex was said by its creator in 2000 to be 'the most-often visited of any single Caribbean-area destination'.

Further reading: P. Albury, *Paradise Island Story*, Macmillan Caribbean, 1984.

PARLIAMENT Almost as much as the JUDICIAL SYSTEM, the Bahamian legislative and executive systems are legacies inherited from the former imperial power. Even the important changes made since colonial times have followed and been modelled on those in Britain, so that the present Bahamian pattern of a democratic parliament, majority party rule, prime minister and cabinet, upper house with limited powers, and a monarch with little more than a ceremonial function, are almost a carbon copy of that of the United Kingdom. Most Bahamians, like most Britons, laud the system both as the hallowed product of a long evolution, and as one that seems to work better than any alternatives. Even the surviving rituals that might at first glance seem picturesque superfluities are treasured as symbols of important and historic principles.

Bahamas House of Assembly in session during UBP heyday, 1964

PARLIAMENT

Under the old colonial system, English settlers expected to benefit from the advances made by parliamentarians in England; that is, to have representation in an elected lower house and the right to discuss and approve legislation equal to that of a non-elective upper house and the monarch (or viceroy). Elected representatives of the early settlers of The Bahamas had a voice in their own government as early as the time of the PROPRIETORS (1670-1718), being formally granted an elective House of Assembly in 1729, at the start of the second term of the first royal Governor, Captain Woodes ROGERS. As in all colonies, the practical power of the Assembly was enhanced by the dependence of the Governor on the elected representatives to vote the taxes necessary to run the government. At times the Speaker of the House was almost a counterweight to the Crown's appointed Governor – and at all times tended to be regarded (or regard himself) as the first citizen of the colony.

In line with the other British colonies in North America and the Caribbean, the Bahamian House of Assembly saw itself as representing 'the people' and couched its discourse in democratic terms, despite the exclusion from membership and the vote of white men without property, male indentured servants and 'free' non-whites, and all women – not to mention the black slave majority. Somewhat contradictorily, the powers of the elected house against the Governor and his Council were forcefully asserted by the LOYALISTS who fled to The Bahamas after the American War of Independence – though their demands were always couched in disingenuously loyal terms. The Bahamian Assembly – made up almost exclusively of slave-holders – was particularly obdurate in its opposition to imperial moves to ameliorate slave conditions during the first third of the nineteenth century.

The first major practical change to the Assembly, however, came during this period. In a tactical move to win the middle class of substantial free non-whites to their side, the white Assembly voted to extend the franchise to them in advance of the inevitable emancipation of the slaves. The tactic worked, for though the first non-whites sat in the Assembly well before the slaves were freed (1834–8) and came to number as many as a third of MHAs over the following century, they remained a conservative group of aspirants more concerned with their own personal and class interests than in extending power to the black majority. Unlike the majority of West Indian colonies, which had their assemblies dissolved and were directly ruled as Crown Colonies following the emancipation of the slaves, The Bahamas (with Bermuda and Barbados) was one of the three colonies which were considered sufficiently under the control of their white minority to be allowed to keep their 'representative' House of Assembly.

Consequently, the Bay Street cabal was able proudly to sustain a charade of allegedly representative government – complete with the trappings of gowns, wigs, ornate mace, arcane rituals and a slate of special parliamentary privileges. The tone was set for the bicentenary celebration of 1929 by the self-congratulatory *History of the Bahamas House of Assembly* written by the long-time Speaker, Sir Harcourt Malcolm. The level of debate was never high (sometimes ridiculed by imperial officials), but it did not need to be while Bay Street continued to get its way. As Malcolm pointed out, the Assembly already exerted almost paramount power, both through its right solely to initiate financial bills, approve the annual budget and expenditure, and through the existence of public boards made up largely of MHAs, which gave the Assembly quasi-executive powers.

The control of Parliament by the Bay Street cabal, rather than the system as such, began to come under threat only with the emergence of the radical black PROGRESSIVE LIBERAL PARTY as a parliamentary force in 1956. With six MHAs led by Lynden PINDLING constituting an effective and vocal Opposition party, Bay Street was compelled to formalise itself as the UNITED BAHAMIAN PARTY and enter into the game of parliamentary party politics. For almost a decade, as the conflict rose to a heated climax, nearly all the advantages accrued to the established side.

Following a resounding (if tainted) electoral victory in 1962, it was the UBP, with Sir Roland SYMONETTE at the helm, that in 1964 was allowed by the fading imperial power to lead The Bahamas into the next stage of constitutional evolution: internal self-rule under the system of Responsible Government. The Assembly instantly became the crucial centre of power, with the leader of the majority party styled Premier at the head of a Cabinet of Ministers taking the executive role formerly exercised by the Governor's Executive Council. The upper house of the traditional bicameral structure, formerly the Legislative Council, was reconstituted as a Senate, with decidedly secondary powers. The Governor's functions, though he still retained certain reserved powers (foreign affairs, defence and internal security), were also reduced, to come closer to the purely nominal and ceremonial role of the monarch, whom he represented in The Bahamas.

Though the PLP basically approved the constitutional change, it was galled that it was Bay Street's UBP that still held the reins of power. On 'BLACK TUESDAY' (27 April 1965) the inner council of the PLP made the calculated gamble to challenge the very essence of Parliament as it was then constituted – symbolised by Pindling's throwing of the sacred parliamentary mace out of the window and leading his fellow party Members out of the House – a self-imposed exile that lasted nine months. This dramatic action split the Opposition party irreconcilably, but it paid off within two years. In 1967 a partially repentant Pindling led his party to victory over a discredited UBP and succeeded Symonette as Premier – to be redesignated as Prime Minister in May 1969.

The Bahamian parliamentary system was finally reconstituted at the time of INDEPENDENCE in July 1973. As much as ever, it is modelled on that of the United Kingdom. QUEEN ELIZABETH II is still the Head of State, represented in The Bahamas by the Governor-General. Though nominally appointed by the Queen and serving 'at Her Majesty's pleasure', the Governor-General is in fact chosen by the government and has invariably since Independence been a Bahamian. The Governor-General signs bills into law after they are passed by the House of Assembly and the Senate, opens Parliament, and gives the annual Speech from the Throne (prepared in fact by the Prime Minister), unless the Queen herself is present. He (or she) has no practical powers, acting merely on advice, and is not expected to express personal views.

The executive branch of government is the Cabinet, which consists of at least nine Members, including the Prime Minister and Attorney General. At least the Prime Minister and the Minister of Finance must be Members of the House of Assembly. If not appointed from the House of Assembly, up to three Ministers may be appointed from the Senate. Though all drawn from the majority party in the House, Ministers are responsible to the House of Assembly, and the Prime Minister and his government are required to resign if they lose their majority or if there is a vote of no confidence in the House.

The bicameral legislature consists of the Senate and the House of Assembly, of which the latter is much the most important. Both are physically located in Parliament Square in downtown Nassau. The House, which currently consists of 40 Members, serves for a five-year term, unless the Prime Minister for any reason dissolves it sooner. A law begins as a bill in the House of Assembly, where it is read three times, debated, and if passed is sent to the Senate. There it is also read three times and debated, and if passed is sent to the Governor-General, becoming law as soon as it has received his (or her) signature.

The Senate (similar to, but very much smaller than the British House of Lords, and with no permanent Members) has 16 Members. Nine are appointed by the Governor-General on the advice of the Prime Minister, four on the advice of the Leader of the Opposition, and three on the advice of the Prime Minister after consultation with the Leader of the Opposition. This arrangement is designed to provide the Opposition with no fewer than four Members of the Senate and to claim up to three more based on its numerical strength in the House of Assembly. In effect, however, the numerical composition of the Senate determines that it rarely does anything more than rubber-stamp the decisions made in the Assembly – in any case having little power but to refine or delay the legislation.

Further reading: H. Malcolm, *History of the Bahamas House of Assembly*. Nassau, 1921; *Constitutional Development of The Bahamas*, Public Records Office, Ministry of Education and Culture, 1979.

PATTON, David Willard (*c*.1845–1920) Famously enterprising and much respected early black businessman. Beginning as a market gardener on Augusta Street in Nassau, through hard work David Patton became the owner (or leaser) of a large acreage at what was later Oakes Field, which he farmed with the help of labourers from nearby BAIN TOWN. He was the 'full-blooded African' whom L. D. POWLES in the 1880s was shown by the coloured Assemblyman James Carmichael Smith as an exemplar of what 'a lazy nigger can do with a bit of coral rock'. Powles also graphically described Patton's Augusta Street house. Though small, it stood out by its neat appearance and its well-tended garden, with a front verandah, glass windows, painted woodwork and whitewashed plaster. Inside there was, wrote Powles, 'as much furniture as he can cram in, and the most showy coloured prints and ornaments he can get hold of are hanging on the wall or dispersed about the room. If you are admitted to view the bedroom, you will be struck at once with the snowy whiteness of the bed linen, and the remarkable stiffness of the starched pillow-cases, bordered around with lace.'

Though upwardly mobile economically, and himself an employer and occasional money-lender, David Patton was an ardent spokesman for his less fortunate fellow blacks. Largely self-taught, with James Carmichael Smith and Stephen Albert Dillett he was a founder and one of the chief contributors to the radical newspaper *The Freeman* (1886–9), which, among other causes, attacked the TRUCK SYSTEM and championed the oppressed black SPONGE fishermen and workers in the PINEAPPLE and SISAL businesses.

The radical cause faded in the 1890s, not least because Smith and Dillet were antagonists in a notorious sexual scandal (the former seducing the daughter of the latter and in his defence labelling her a prostitute). Patton,

PEAS N' RICE

though, continued to prosper. He moved into the livery business and is sometimes given the credit for building and maintaining the first of the distinctive Nassau SURREYS. In 1900 his Union Livery Stables by the VENDUE HOUSE on Bay Street was advertised as offering 'Fine Rubber & Steel Tired Phaetons and American Horses … at all hours, day and night' to be hired by the day, week or month, at 'reasonable prices'. Successfully facing competition from two rival firms owned by whites, David Patton's livery business only faded with the coming of the automobile and (like his farming and produce marketing ventures) with his own passing.

PEAS N' RICE This essential side dish is found in different forms throughout the Caribbean, where it is usually called Rice n' Peas. The Bahamian form is distinctive, with the name reversed, probably to indicate the importance of the pigeon peas normally used. and once locally grown.

> Ingredients:
> ¼ cup salt pork or bacon, diced
> 8 oz (250 g) can pigeon peas (or black eye peas)
> 1 cup rice
> 1 each of onion, minced, stick celery, green pepper, diced
> 4 tablespoons tomato paste
> 2 cups water
> thyme

Method: Fry the salt pork or bacon till crisp. Add the onion, green pepper, celery and cook till mixture is pulpy. Add tomato paste and cook till most of water in pan is evaporated. Add drained peas, thyme, salt and pepper and cook a further two minutes. Pour in rice and add water to cover. Cover pot tightly and allow mixture to simmer until all liquid is evaporated.

PEOPLE-TO-PEOPLE PROGRAMME An admirable initiative by the Ministry of Tourism designed 'to foster communication and exchange ideas and to advance international friendship' by bringing visitors and Bahamians from different walks of life into personal contact by mutual arrangement. A thousand volunteers in NEW PROVIDENCE, four hundred in GRAND BAHAMA, and many others in ABACO, ELEUTHERA, EXUMA, BIMINI and SAN SALVADOR, representing a wide cross-section of the population, have made themselves available to meet with visitors interested in participating, usually in the evenings and at weekends during their stay. The Ministry organisers do their best to match visitors and hosts according to age, interests and occupations. Contact having been made, volunteers arrange to meet at an agreed time and location. There is no charge to the visitors and the hosts are not expected to offer accommodation or spend much money in entertainment. No doubt some exchanges work out less than perfectly, but the overwhelming majority of reports on both sides have been extremely positive.

Judging from the number of applicants, on the visitors' side the most popular feature of the programme is the opportunity given to up to 120 visitors a time to enjoy tea with the Governor-General and his wife on the lawns of GOVERNMENT HOUSE, on the first Friday of each month between January and August.

Visitors wishing to take part in the People-to-People programme should contact (if possible, two weeks in advance) the Manager in Nassau at PO Box N-3701, telephone (242) 326-5371 or 356-0435, fax. 356-0434, or e-mail pwilliam@gobahamas.com, and in Grand Bahama at PO Box F-40251 or telephone (242) 352-8044/5.

PINDLING, Lady Marguerite Barefoot 'brownskin gal' from Andros who became the elegant consort and indispensable partner of the first Bahamian Prime Minister, Sir Lynden PINDLING – earning in the process, through a mixture of admiration, envy and unfriendly gossip, the widespread nickname 'the Champagne Lady'.

Lady Marguerite Pindling

PINDLING, Rt. Hon. Sir Lynden Oscar

Marguerite MacKenzie was born in the impoverished settlement of Long Bay Cays, southern Andros, at the height of the Great Depression of the 1930s. She was the fifth of the 11 children of a black mother by a white father, Reuben McKenzie from Exuma, who already had sired seven children by his previous wife (who was also black). The notably pretty but shy Marguerite went to live with an older sister in Nassau at the age of 14, just after World War Two. Completing her somewhat sketchy education at Western Senior School, she worked as a photographer's assistant on Bay Street, where she caught the eye of the fledgling black lawyer, Lynden Pindling. After a courtship opposed on both sides (Lynden being too black, radical and pushy for the McKenzies, and Marguerite too poor and uneducated for the Pindlings) they were married in a simple ANGLICAN ceremony at St Ann's, Fox Hill, in May 1956, with just eight people present.

During Lynden Pindling's years of political emergence, Marguerite combined the jobs of legal secretary for her husband, maintaining their modest home, and bearing four children. Throughout the 44 years of their life together, the Pindlings strove to keep their family life insulated from political affairs. But once Lynden Pindling attained power and grew in political stature his wife gradually emerged from her shy cocoon to become both the model political leader's wife and a paragon of stylistic elegance. She performed with increasing effectiveness on the hustings and in door-to-door campaigning, especially in her native South Andros (which her husband crucially switched to represent in 1967). She also became the dominant force in the PROGRESSIVE LIBERAL PARTY's women's branch. At the same time she turned herself into a gracious hostess at the pinnacle of Bahamian society, equally at home with movie stars, foreign dignitaries and the British royal family. The international kudos she achieved by dancing with Prince Charles at the INDEPENDENCE celebrations in July 1973 reached its apogee when she became Lady Pindling on her husband's knighting by QUEEN ELIZABETH II in the spring of 1982.

As the Pindlings' lifestyle became more lavish and ostentatious, malicious gossip among the Prime Minister's opponents pictured Lady Marguerite as the Bahamian Imelda Marcos. Not only was she said to be behind many of Lynden Pindling's most important, controversial and seemingly impulsive decisions, but, through her extravagance, to have led him into corruption. At most, these accusations were exaggerated; at worst, they were slanderous. That they were politically motivated was borne out by the way they declined once her husband fell from power, left politics and fell mortally ill. Lady Marguerite's heroic and impeccably stately demeanour at the time of Sir Lynden's death and state funeral in August and September 2000 earned her a universal sympathy and admiration.

Further reading: M. Craton, *Pindling: The Life and Times of Lynden Oscar Pindling, First Prime Minister of The Bahamas, 1930–2000*, Macmillan Caribbean, 2002.

PINDLING, Rt. Hon. Sir Lynden Oscar (1930–2000) 'The Little Fella from East Street' who became the first Prime Minister of the Bahamas, led his PROGRESSIVE LIBERAL PARTY to six successive electoral victories, and was in power for a quarter of a century (1967–92).

Born and brought up in Mason's Addition in Over-the-Hill Nassau, Lynden Oscar Pindling was the only child of Arnold Pindling, Jamaican-born policeman, shopkeeper and racehorse owner, and Viola (née Bain) from isolated Acklins Island. Receiving his early education in several different schools and serving as his father's delivery boy, young Lynden got to know all parts of Nassau and made a wide circle of acquaintances. He also became familiar with and to many Out Islanders, on summer trips to the southern Bahamas in his grandfather's mail boat *Alisada*, and to a smallholding his father had leased at Savannah Sound, Eleuthera to grow tomatoes.

From Western Senior School, Lynden Pindling won one of the 20 annual places at GOVERNMENT HIGH

Rt. Hon Sir Lynden Oscar Pindling

PINDLING, Rt. Hon. Sir Lynden Oscar

SCHOOL, where, alongside many who were also to make a mark in Bahamian affairs, he studied from 1943 to 1946. A zealous student but more notable as a runner and games player, in his last two years he was chosen *Dux* (class leader) by the expatriate headmaster, Dr A. Deans Peggs.

In 1948, after a brief stint in the Post Office, 18-year old Lynden was sent to London by his ambitious parents, at a considerable financial sacrifice, to study to become a lawyer. He had an active social life with other students from many parts of the Commonwealth (including a role in the dance troupe organised by the Trinidadian Boscoe Holder) but quite comfortably passed his law exams at King's College and the Inns of Court. He was called to the English Bar late in 1952 and to the Bahamas Bar six months later, having delayed his return to take a diploma course in constitutional law and to see the coronation of QUEEN ELIZABETH II.

Although in London he met many West Indians, Africans and Asians who were to have important roles in their emergent nations, and despite the fact that Arnold Pindling was one of the electoral lieutenants for the black lawyer-politician T. A. Toote, young Lynden did not take much interest in politics until his difficulties of finding work as a young black lawyer in Nassau made him more aware of the whip hand held by the white minority BAY STREET regime over the black majority. Nailing his flag to the mast, he joined the infant PROGRESSIVE LIBERAL PARTY as its legal adviser shortly after its founding in 1953.

Lynden Pindling owed his rapid rise in the PLP, and his durability once at the helm, not just (as he always maintained) to the luck of being 'in the right place at the right time', but to an extraordinary combination of idealism, ambition and pragmatic flexibility, the ability to communicate with and inspire ordinary people, to listen, think clearly and act decisively, and the cunning to outflank his rivals as well as political opponents. Above all, with his key allies, he was able to ride the groundswell that transformed the PLP from a moderate centrist party led by members of the coloured middle class, to a radical black populist movement, inspired by the current ideology of Black Power and the tactics of the civil rights activists in the United States.

In 1956, Pindling was one of the first PLP Members elected to the House of Assembly (the 'Magnificent Six'), and because the PLP's Chairman H. M. TAYLOR had been defeated at the polls, became the party's Leader in the House. He managed to survive the PLP's failure in the 1962 general election and the disappointment of having Bay Street's UNITED BAHAMIAN PARTY lead the Bahamas to self-government in 1964. Even more critical was Pindling's decision to take a leading role in the events of 'BLACK TUESDAY' (1965), which split the PLP but (along with revelations of corruption) led to the defeat of the UBP in 1967 and the PLP's landslide victory in the following year. When he became the second Premier of the Bahamas in 1967, he was still 36, the youngest in the Commonwealth.

In 1968, Pindling's title was changed from Premier to Prime Minister and both he and the PLP went from strength to strength. They survived the defection of Cecil WALLACE-WHITFIELD and the Free PLP in 1971 and steered the Bahamas triumphantly to Independence in 1973. Buttressed by electoral success, Pindling and the PLP were able to accomplish many, if not all, of their promised reforms and innovations. These included huge improvements in education, social services and communications, a national insurance scheme, a central bank, a greatly expanded (if not proportionately more efficient) police force, and an adequate (but not overtly bellicose) force for the island country's defence. More symbolic were the introduction of a new motto, flag and national anthem, and the redesignation of the Out Islands as the Family Islands (components of a freshly-named Commonwealth of the Bahamas). Thanks largely to Pindling's initiatives and travels on the country's behalf, the Bahamas became a force in such international and regional bodies as the UN, UNESCO, OAS and CARICOM, as well as in purely Commonwealth organisations – even on occasion taking a bold stand against the overbearing presence of the neighbouring United States.

Above all, Lynden Pindling and the PLP stood for equal opportunities for all Bahamians and the equitable allocation of all resources and job opportunities wherever and whenever feasible. For an essentially non-racialist person like Pindling himself this implied reconciliation with the white community as soon as the black majority had received its due share. A particular target was Freeport, Grand Bahama, which under the previous regime had become almost a foreign enclave. Pindling's most famous speech, warning the Freeport authorities to 'Bend or Be Broken' (1969) caused some panic and outflow of investment. But the moderation and flexibility of the government's actual policies considerably restored investor confidence, with offshore banking, captive insurance and ship registration business steadily increasing, and the total numbers of tourists gradually rising from under one million to almost three million during the PLP's long regime.

The highlights of Pindling's 25 years as Premier and Prime Minister included the outburst of national solidarity at the time of the *FLAMINGO* incident (1980), the receipt of his knighthood from the Queen in 1983, and the chairmanship of the Commonwealth Heads of Government Meeting (CHOGM) which led to the Nassau Declaration in favour of sanctions against South Africa, and of the ensuing Committee of Six, which helped to effect the release of Nelson Mandela from prison, majority rule, Mandela's Presidency, and South Africa's rejoining the Commonwealth (1990–5).

The poor performance of the PLP during its last term in office – coupled with a serious downturn in the world economy and probably a decline in Pindling's own powers – led to the party's comprehensive defeat in 1992. The chief's decision to listen to the pleas of the party faithful and stay on as leader until an acceptable successor was found, was probably a mistake. He retired from the PLP leadership and from the House of Assembly (in which he had served for 41 years) only after the party was roundly defeated once more in 1997 – by which time Pindling's health was already in decline.

Lynden Pindling had married Marguerite McKenzie, a brown girl from Andros as poor as she was beautiful, in 1956, just a few weeks before he was first elected to Parliament. Their four children were all born before the PLP came to power; Obafemi (Obi) in 1959, Leslie in 1961, Michelle in 1962, and Monique in 1967. Lady Marguerite PINDLING played an important role as the wife of the chief (its exact nature and extent being matters of debate), but as far as possible the couple shielded their four children from the political hurly-burly. Obi and Michelle became lawyers, but only Michelle attempted to follow her father into politics. After making one unsuccessful bid for election in 1982, she was appointed a Senator by the resurgent PLP 20 years later.

Almost as much a demon to his opponents as he was an idol to his supporters while in power, Lynden Pindling was showered with honours and voted the 'Bahamian of the Century' on his retirement in 1997. Probably aware that he had not got much longer to live, in his last years he was rebaptised into his mother's Adventist faith. Facing the onset of first prostate and then bone cancer with fortitude, he died with dignity, surrounded by his family, at 12.40 a.m. on Saturday 20 August 2000. At the emotional and splendid state funeral nine days later Lynden Oscar Pindling was justly eulogised as the Bahamian Liberator, who not only freed the black people from political and social oppression, but also gave wings to the Bahamian national spirit.

Further reading: M. Craton, *Pindling: The Life and Times of Lynden Oscar Pindling (1930-200), First Prime Minister of the Bahamas*, Macmillan Caribbean, 2002.

PINEAPPLES Succulent local grown pineapples are still available in The Bahamas, but the Pineapple Festival held each June at Gregory Town, ELEUTHERA, is the only reminder that The Bahamas was the first – and for a long time the major – exporter of the fruit to North America and Europe.

The pineapple (*Ananas comosus*) is the fruit of a hardy plant that grows well in rocky soils under a hot sun and is therefore highly suited to Bahamian conditions. A native of Central America, it was transplanted to The Bahamas. Christopher COLUMBUS noted it with admiration in other islands on his voyages – though it is quite likely that it was already known to the Lucayans and simply escaped Columbus's notice on his way through The Bahamas. It was certainly well established by 1722, when George Phenney, the second royal Governor, wrote that The Bahamas was already producing the best pineapples in the Americas.

Peter Henry BRUCE (1744) and Daniel MCKINNEN (1803) described pineapple cultivation in NEW PROVIDENCE. But the development of a major industry required an export market, and faster transportation to get the fruit to market before it perished. These came from the 1840s onwards, with the building of large, fast schooners and the opening up of steamship routes. A key event was the arrival and successful sale of the first cargo of Bahamian pineapples at London's Covent Garden in 1844 – though apparently pineapples had been successfully shipped to New York for two or three years already.

By 1858 pineapple cultivation was regarded as so important that Governor Charles Bayley proposed that a pineapple, along with a CONCH, should supplant the traditional image of Queen Victoria on the very first Bahamian

Pineapple canning, Nassau, late 1870s. Print from *Leslie's Illustrated Newspaper*, June 1879

PIRATES

POSTAGE STAMP (they were in fact retained, but alongside a portrait of the Queen).

Over the next fifty years, Bahamian sugar loaf and red pineapples were immensely popular in England and the north-eastern United States, and cultivation spread over much of New Providence, down the length of Eleuthera, throughout CAT ISLAND, and into central ABACO and southern LONG ISLAND. Though, as was customary, the major profits went to the large landowners, the merchant middlemen and shippers, prosperity filtered down to some non-white farmers and boat-owners, especially in Eleuthera, while thousands of ordinary black labourers were able to earn at least some wages in the harsh work of clearing, planting, weeding and harvesting.

An important parallel development was the canning of pineapples, which did away with the need for rapid transporting to market and greatly expanded the orbit of sales, while at the same time enabling the canners to take advantage of the annual gluts in production, when prices of the harvested fruit tumbled. Canning operations were the first really mechanised industry in The Bahamas, as well as among the first joint stock enterprises, involving American as well as Bahamian entrepreneurs – bringing The Bahamas from the very periphery somewhat closer to the centre of the developing capitalist world system.

Canning pineapples had been tried at Governor's Harbour, Eleuthera as early as 1857. But the first successful operation was the establishment in Nassau of what became the J. S. Johnson Company in 1876. First, a group of Nassau merchants and growers formed a joint stock company, bringing in a technician from Baltimore to set up a small factory at the corner of Union and Bay Streets in Nassau. The factory expanded and gradually J. S. Johnson (Member of Parliament as well as aggressive businessman) bought out the other Bahamians and moved into partnership with New York distributors and investors – one of whom became the president of the company, while Johnson himself managed operations in The Bahamas. The peak year was 1892, when the J. S. Johnson Company shipped 75,000 cases of cut and cored pineapples in syrup and pineapple juice, and The Bahamas also exported eight million fresh pineapples for a total value of £56,000.

However, 1892 also, almost literally, saw the sowing of the seeds of decline. Because Bahamian pineapples were regarded as the finest in the world, a million cuttings were shipped for planting in Hawaii, where American planters were moving in to take advantage of conditions for large-scale production which were much more favourable than in The Bahamas. Similar competition was also coming from Americans moving into Cuba and Puerto Rico. When Hawaii and Puerto Rico were annexed by the US and Cuba became an American dependency after the Spanish American War of 1898, the days of Bahamian pineapple exports were numbered. American protectionist duties and the over-working of Bahamian pineapple lands were the last straw. In 1923 Bahamian pineapple exports were still worth £7,000; but by 1927 they brought in a grand total of £7! The J.S. Johnson Company narrowly survived through diversification, but only until the 1940s.

The Bahamian (or rather, Eleutheran) pineapple industry made a small but temporary recovery in the 1950s and 1960s. The Bay Street merchant-politician George Baker operated a large farm and canning factory at Rock Sound (selling under the 'Bahamas Best' label), and the local Thompson brothers did likewise at Gregory Town (as the 'Sun White' brand). Both operations, however, had folded by the mid-1970s. Today too few pineapples are grown to satisfy even the local market and the Bahamian fruit at $5 apiece are easily undercut by imports from nearby Florida and distant Hawaii. As the *Lonely Planet Guide* commented in 2002, even at the self-proclaimed 'Bahamian Pineapple Capital' of Gregory Town, 'the industry is so atrophied that local farmers have difficulty mustering a respectable supply of their usually large and succulent fruits to display at the annual Pineapple Festival'. Nonetheless, visitors can still be reminded of the past and enjoy the selection and crowning of the winner of the 'Miss Teen Pineapple Princess Pageant', watch a swim–bike–run 'Pineathelon', compete in a 'Pineapple-on-a-Rope Eating Contest', and satisfy their thirst with pineapple smoothies and pineapple punch.

Further reading: *The Pineapple Industry of The Bahamas*, Department of Archives, 1977.

PIRATES Despite their often romanticised image, pirates were out-and-out sea robbers who were a menace to civilised society and legitimate commerce alike. For a brief period during the misrule of the Lord PROPRIETORS (1670–1718) The Bahamas was the chief base for the pirates of the Americas, and the colony and its commerce were not placed on a secure footing until these pirates were expelled by the first royal governor, Captain Woodes ROGERS. Some commentators, however, have maintained, at least half-seriously, that elements of the piratical ethos remained indelibly imprinted on Bahamian society.

The ideal sphere of operations for pirates was an area strategically close to the main shipping routes that provided a complex of islands, shallows and channels from which they could pounce and into which they could safely retreat. They also needed a safe base to which they could return to lick their wounds, find recreation, repair damaged vessels, re-provision, and restore depleted crews. Just as important (though rarely mentioned in the literature), it was essential for successful pirates to have access to a town which allowed them to exchange their ill-gotten gains for money and to filter both their cash money and themselves back into more respectable businesses and occupations when the time was right.

During the Proprietorial period, the Bahamian archipelago and its few settlements, especially the town of NASSAU, fulfilled all these criteria. The Proprietors' governors were at first weak and complaisant if not corrupt, and towards the end of the period powerless to prevent a virtual takeover by the pirates. Even the most active and competent of them, Nicholas TROTT (1693–6) notoriously harboured the great Indian Ocean pirate Henry Avery, and was said by a mainland official to be reputed 'the greatest pirate broker that was ever in America'.

The era of maximum pirate activity in The Bahamas, the Caribbean and the North American seaboard was comparatively short, but also, because it reached such an intolerable pitch, its ultimate phase. The ending of the War of the Spanish Succession in 1713 left so many PRIVATEERS unemployed that they had little alternative but to join up with the pirates – who at least offered them a more egalitarian life, with much higher potential rewards, than privateering, merchant ships or ships of the Royal Navy. Marcus Rediker has estimated that in the first decade of the eighteenth century there were as many as 2,500 pirates active in the western hemisphere, of whom a thousand were based in The Bahamas, in some twenty ships. This was the era that saw the activities of the colourful rogues who enliven the pages of *The General History of the Pyrates* by 'Captain Charles Johnson' (Daniel Defoe), such as Benjamin Hornigold, Edward 'BLACKBEARD' Teach, 'Calico Jack' Rackham, Charles Vane, Stede Bonnet, and the 'Lady Pirates' Anne Bonny and Mary Read (who escaped the noose by claiming pregnancy).

The end of the Spanish War of Succession, however, also brought in the long era of 'Walpole's Peace' (1713-39), during which the European nations were at pains to establish civil order and successful commerce in their American colonies. This clearly demanded the eradication of piracy. It was as part of this general impetus that Woodes Rogers was sent to be the first royal Governor of The Bahamas in 1718, with the express command to stamp out piracy there. Rogers acted with exemplary force and adopted the long-lasting motto 'Expulsis Piratis Restituta Commercia'. It was not until at least 1722, though, that the last pirate captain and his crew were rooted out from the islands.

How deeply and lastingly the pirate ethos had become entrenched is a more debatable matter. Not only rascally governors, but virtually all the early settlers had profited one way and another from the pirates' activities. At least one Bahamian captain sent to round up pirates turned to piracy himself. An untold number of Bahamian mariners may have served at one time 'under the banner of King Death' before retiring to more reputable occupations with their ill (and hard) gotten gains. Over subsequent centuries, some Bahamians have learned to compensate for a generally hard life by seizing whatever fortune offers, however 'close to the wind' the sailing required – be it through PRIVATEERING, WRECKING, running the blockade during the AMERICAN CIVIL WAR, rum-running during the PROHIBITION era, or even DRUG-TRAFFICKING during the 1980s.

Perhaps no more than misguided romanticism can explain the popularity of alleged relics of Blackbeard found throughout New Providence (a tower, a meeting tree, a well and a tavern). But what is one to make of the fact that one of the important Bahamian trading boats in the 1960s to 1980s was christened after the notorious pirate (born in Barbados but Bahamas based) the MV *Stede Bonnet?*

Anne Bonny, a famous 'lady' pirate

POITIER, Sir Sidney

Further reading: C. Johnson (Daniel Defoe), *A General History of the Pyrates*, London, 1724; H. C. Christie, *Blackbeard: A Romance of the Bahamas*, London, 1930; P. Gosse, *The History of Piracy*, Longman, 1932; M. Rediker, *Between the Devil and the Deep Blue Sea: Merchant Seamen, Pirates, and the Anglo-American Maritime World, 1700–1750*. Cambridge University Press, 1987; 'The Aura of Blackbeard' in Craton and Saunders, *Islanders*, i. 104–14

POITIER, Sir Sidney Bahamian-American film superstar, born in 1927, the seventh child of a poor and uneducated farming couple of Arthur's Town, Cat Island. Through no accident, Sidney Poitier acquired the right to American citizenship at birth, his father having taken his very pregnant wife with him on a voyage to sell tomatoes in Miami, Florida – then almost a Mecca for impoverished Out Islanders. There was no chance of the whole family migrating, so the infant was carried back to Arthur's Town, where Sidney spent the first ten harum-scarum, dirt-poor, but generally happy years of his life.

After struggling for subsistence through the years of the Great Depression, the Poitiers sought a marginally better life in Nassau in 1937, crowding into a tiny rented wooden house on Hay Street, Over-the-Hill. Reginald, the aging father, worked for starvation wages in a bicycle shop and tried with little success to grow food crops on untenanted land in the New Providence interior, while his wife did sewing and washing, and broke roadstone by hand for pennies a hundredweight. Sidney got a reasonably good education at Western Junior and Senior Schools, and contributed to the family resources as a delivery boy for the East Street shop owned by the father of Lynden PINDLING. But he also ran with a pretty wild set of boys and later reckoned that he was lucky not to end up, like several of his friends in the reformatory (the Boys' Industrial School). Whenever he could, he would sneak into one of the several movie houses without paying, acting out with friends on the street the parts he saw played, but not even dreaming of sharing the glamorous Hollywood life pictured on the silver screen.

Before he was 16, with World War Two still on, Sidney took the plunge and went to Miami on the mail boat *Ena K*, with 10 dollars in his pocket. Restlessly shifting from one odd job and place to another, winter found him homeless and foodless in New York. Lying about his age (though now with American papers) he joined the Army to get out of the cold. After a few months he decided that that life was not for him, and in his first great acting part, feigned a nervous breakdown to get his discharge.

Encouraged to think he was a natural actor, and also confident of his good looks, Sidney went for audition with the American Negro Theatre in New York in 1945. From walk-on stage parts he was soon given important roles, and by 1950, at the age of 18, was chosen to play in his first film, the social race drama *No Way Out* (which for a time was banned in Nassau). The rest of Sidney Poitier's career is an important slice of American cinema history, involving more than 40 films, nine of which he directed himself.

Beginning with straight dramas, musicals and shows involving black characters, including *Cry the Beloved Country*, *Porgy and Bess* and *Raisin in the Sun*, Sidney Poitier graduated to movies that specifically dealt with race relations or cast him as the acceptable black man in a white world, such as *To Sir With Love*, *Guess Who's Coming to Dinner* and *In the Heat of the Night*, to reach a point where he was a guaranteed box-office draw in thrillers, westerns and comedies where his own colour was irrelevant. The turning point was the winning of a best actor Oscar for his part in *Lilies of the Field* (1961), and the peak of his career the granting of a Lifetime Achievement Award in 1992.

During the 1960s, like his friends Harry Belafonte and Diahann Carroll, Sidney Poitier became closely involved with the Civil Rights Movement, and this is what led him to return to The Bahamas and play a part in the achievement of black majority rule. During the 1960s he and his then wife built a house at Winton Heights in Nassau's eastern suburbs, and he became a close friend and confidant of Lynden Pindling and a strong supporter of the PROGRESSIVE LIBERAL PARTY.

Sir Sidney Poitier

This however did not last. Dissatisfaction with what he felt was the indifference of the PLP government to the Arts, coupled with professional demands on his time and complications in his private life, led Sidney Poitier to sell up in Nassau in 1970 and move to California, returning to The Bahamas only occasionally. Though the Pindling government arranged for him to receive an honorary knighthood in 1990, it was the FREE NATIONAL MOVEMENT government of Hubert INGRAHAM which succeeded in persuading the greatest Bahamian actor to renew ties with the land of his parents and upbringing – by appointing him to the largely honorific post of Bahamian Ambassador to Japan in 1997.

Further reading: S. Poitier, *This Life*, Ballantine Books, 1980; *The Measure of the Man*, Random House, 2000.

POLICE As the practical arm of the forces of law and order, the Bahamian police can trace their origins almost to the beginning of colonial times. In 1729, during the second regime of the first royal Governor, Woodes ROGERS, a Constable was first appointed to serve as an official of the magistrates' court. But it was not until the Loyalists arrived that the need was felt for more general policing. On the model of the former mainland colonies, constables were appointed by the parish vestries and in 1789 placed under the authority of a colonial Provost Marshal.

In 1833 a permanent paid constabulary was established for the first time, when the Police Magistrate was authorised to appoint six constables in Nassau, and local JPs were ordered to enrol up to a dozen more as needed in the Out Islands. With the transition to 'full freedom' in 1838, and the Police Act of 1840, the first proper Bahamian Police Force came into existence.

Following the custom practised elsewhere in the British Empire, a commanding officer and police recruits were sought from other colonies rather than from The Bahamas. After the failure of a plan to recruit Sikhs from India, a new Inspector (a former captain in the 12th Royal Hussars) arrived with 42 recruits from Barbados in January 1892. These, and further recruits from Jamaica and Trinidad as well as Barbados, were required to live permanently in barracks and were kept carefully distinct from the Bahamians already on the force. The new recruits (who were generally better educated than the Bahamians they were replacing because they came from colonies that were poorer but had better education systems) were given a thoroughly militarised training and instilled with an almost English public school *esprit de corps*. This was aided by smart uniforms, marching drills, proficiency medals, promotion strictly on merit, and organised sports. The police band, in later times to be the force's internationally famous hallmark, was founded in 1893 – with musical ability being an important recruitment criterion from the earliest days.

As first traffic and then tourism increased, the smart policemen with their blue winter and white summer uniforms became a picturesque feature of downtown Nassau, as they patrolled the streets, directed traffic or paraded on ceremonial occasions. In less glamorous routines behind the scenes, however, they were less impressive, especially once the level of crime began to rise in the 1930s and 1940s, and when having to deal with serious unrest, as in the 'BURMA ROAD' riots of 1942. The force was also overstretched by its continuing role as the capital's fire service

Changes began with a new Police Act in 1955 and were accelerated by the alarm engendered by the GENERAL STRIKE of 1958. For the first time, new recruits were not required to be unmarried and to live at least their first year in barracks, being given the options of free accommodation or a housing allowance. In 1958 the old prison was moved from East Street to Fox Hill, and the police barracks were first upgraded and then, three years later, moved into new quarters on the former ROYAL AIR FORCE base at Oakes Field, outside town. Better conditions and higher pay, along with the prospects of speedier promotion for qualified entrants in a force that was obviously expanding, encouraged local recruitment once more.

The 1960s and the 1970s saw the most rapid and important changes to date, as greater prosperity led to more adequate funding at the same time that The Bahamas achieved Independence in 1973. All existing branches expanded and new ones were created as The Bahamas was made fully responsible for internal security and began to take responsibility for external defence as well. Moreover, the process of the Bahamianisation of the police force proceeded rapidly and was virtually completed by 1973. The story of the force during this period is one of uninterrupted expansion and progress, endorsed by its re-designation as the Royal Bahamas Police Force by QUEEN ELIZABETH II during her first official visit to The Bahamas in 1966. The CID, which traced its origins back to the appointment of the first detective constable in 1909, expanded rapidly and became much more scientific, as did the separate Security and Intelligence branch first set up in 1958. In that year the police Marine Division was created with a single patrol boat – to which four 60-foot (18-m) patrol boats were added in 1971, named after

POMPEY'S REBELLION (1830)

Honour Guard, Royal Bahamas Police Force

the islands of Acklins, Andros, Eleuthera and San Salvador. In 1964, an Air Wing was set up with a single plane and a Mobile Division was formed. Much more importantly, in the same year women were enrolled for the first time, six being chosen out of 112 applicants – eventually to rise to more than 200 by the 1990s.

Much the most serious crisis in the history of the Bahamas Police Force occurred in the mid-1980s, when the Commission of Inquiry into the DRUG trade implicated many policemen, including several senior officers. This suggested that the expansion had been made too rapidly and even called into question the BAHAMIANISATION of the force. The 16 recommendations for reforms made by the Commission (particularly regarding the Drug Squad and the CID) were a wake-up call for the RBPF. Though no direct charges were laid, several 'bad apples' were sorted out and most of the suggested reforms made.

In startling contrast to the original 31-member police force of 1840, the RBPF in 2002 numbered 2,023 police officers and a civilian support staff of 250. Besides the numerous stations and branch departments in New Providence, there were more than 30 police stations in the Family Islands, six of which provided service round the clock. The annual expenditure on police services exceeded $70 million – rather more than on TOURISM, and exceeded only by EDUCATION and MEDICAL SERVICES. Even the superbly trained and world-famous RBPF Band – the members of which, once they have completed their basic police training, do virtually nothing but march and play music – had twice as many members as the entire police force in 1840.

Further reading: C. G. Pratt and M. A. Simmons, *A History of the Royal Bahamas Police Force, 1840–1990*, Royal Bahamas Police Force, 1990; H. Johnson, 'Social Control and the Colonial State: The Reorganisation of the Police Force, 1888–1893', in *The Bahamas in Slavery and Freedom*, Ian Randle Press, 1991, 110–24; Craton and Saunders, *Islanders*, ii. 20–5, 375–6.

POMPEY'S REBELLION (1830) The largely successful protest led by the Exumian slave of Lord ROLLE called Pompey, after whom the Museum of Bahamian Folk Culture in the former VENDUE HOUSE in downtown Nassau is named.

Once settled as a virtually independent peasant community, Rolle's slaves in Exuma were prepared to resist by force any attempt by their owner to transfer them from their adopted homeland. In November 1828 they had responded to a leaked plan to ship them to Trinidad by refusing to work, performing martial drills, and firing their (strictly illegal) muskets. Their protest was only calmed by the sending of a detachment of the WEST INDIA REGIMENT from the garrison in Nassau, and the announcement that the Trinidad plan had been dropped.

A few months later, a small group of Rolle's slaves, after initially agreeing to be moved to GRAND BAHAMA, changed their minds and were transferred by force by another armed detachment of garrison troops. The most serious trouble, however, occurred early in 1830 when Lord Rolle's agent A. J. Lees (a Member of Council) concocted a plan to ship 77 slaves from Exuma to CAT ISLAND. Families were not to be split, but the slaves were given only three days' notice and no chance to harvest their crops. Under the leadership of the 32-year-old Pompey (his name was probably an anglicised version of the Akan *Prempeh*), the selected slaves adamantly refused and fled into the bush.

When the fugitives' provisions were running out, Pompey and 44 others seized Lord Rolle's salt boat and sailed to Nassau to lay their grievance before the Governor, Sir James Carmichael SMYTH, who was widely thought to be sympathetic to the slaves. Without informing Smyth, A. J. Lees and the magistrates had Pompey's group thrown in the workhouse, charged as runaways and the adults flogged, including the women. When word of this reached the Governor he was extremely angry and instituted an immediate inquiry. Not only was the flogging of female slaves already seen by imperial authorities as a disgrace, but Lees had perjured himself in stating erroneously that the slaves (destined to be used as a jobbing gang for another owner) were to be transferred from one of Lord Rolle's estates to another. Two magistrates were sacked, A. J. Lees dismissed from the Council, and Pompey's group released and sent back to Exuma.

Reaching Exuma, Pompey and his party were welcomed as heroes. All Rolle's slaves refused to turn out to work for the estate and threatened armed resistance. Regretting his leniency, Governor Smyth sent down the largest contingent yet: 50 soldiers in the armed schooner HMS *Skipjack* and the sloop *Lady Rolle*, accompanied by the Chief Constable, Patrick Grace. At Steventon, the slaves were rounded up and harangued by Grace, while the soldiers searched their houses and confiscated 25 antiquated muskets. Pompey, however, forestalled similar action at Rolleville by racing ahead of the troops along the beach, so that the Rolleville slaves ran into the bush with their weapons.

Pompey himself was captured and given a public flogging with the maximum 39 lashes. Only then did the slaves agree to go back to work on Lord Rolle's grounds. This, though, was a mere pretence. It only lasted until the soldiers returned to Nassau, claiming that they had pacified Exuma. Although Pompey and his fellow rebels had not yet won their claim that the land actually belonged to them (which was not formally acknowledged until the Commonage Law was passed in 1896), the amount of work they performed for their absentee owner had dwindled from little to nothing by the end of slavery in 1838. Most significantly, they had established the principle that even as slaves they would not be moved with impunity from grounds and houses which they had effectively made their own.

Further reading: M. Craton, 'We Shall Not be Moved: Pompey's Slave Revolt in Exuma Island, Bahamas, 1830', *Nieuwe West Indische Gids*, Spring 1983, 19–35; Craton and Saunders, *Islanders*, i. 381–6.

PONCE DE LEON, Juan (*c*.1460–1521) Early Spanish conquistador who sailed through The Bahamas allegedly looking for the legendary Fountain of Youth located on an island called BIMINI, and is credited with the discovery of Florida and the Gulf Stream.

Ponce de Leon

Most accounts of Ponce de Leon's life are vague or even contradictory. He may have served as a squire against the Moors in Granada, but is first certainly noted as accompanying COLUMBUS on his second voyage to the New World in 1493. Settling in Hispaniola, Ponce de Leon rose to be *adelantado* (governor) of the province of Higuey, before being entrusted with the task of subduing and governing the adjacent island of Borinquen (Puerto Rico).

Ponce de Leon successfully petitioned the Crown in 1512 ostensibly to search for the island of Bimini and the Fountain of Youth, but more likely intending to look for gold, silver and slaves. Fitting out three vessels at his own expense (the *Santa Maria*, *Santiago* and *San Cristobal*), he set out from San German, Puerto Rico on 3 March 1513 and sailed northwards by way of Grand Turk and SAN SALVADOR. On 27 March he sighted what he took to be a new island, which he named (for the approach of Easter) *Pascua de Florida* ('Feast of Flowers').

Most historians take this landfall to have been what is now known as the peninsula of Florida, but some have speculated that it was actually the island of ABACO. In either case, Ponce de Leon may or (more likely) may not have passed or stopped at the islands now called the Biminis. What is certain is that five days after his first land-sighting, he went ashore at a point on the north-eastern coast of Florida close to the later settlement of St Augustine, having for the first time encountered the rapid northwards drift of the GULF STREAM. From his landing place, Ponce de Leon tacked with great difficulty southwards around the Florida Cays, and explored part of the west coast of Florida (which he still considered an island). He then touched briefly at Cuba and sailed back to Puerto Rico, probably by way of ANDROS. He had found no gold or silver, let alone the Fountain of Youth, and if he was looking for slaves he was thwarted both by the fierce resistance of the Indians of Florida and by the discovery that The Bahamas had already been depopulated. Famously (if somewhat implausibly) he reported encountering only a single old woman in the entire Bahamian archipelago.

Despite his failures, Ponce de Leon made a claim to have discovered and claimed new lands and in 1514 successfully petitioned to be allowed to conquer and colonise them. Though he was granted the title of *adelantado* of Florida and Bimini, it was seven years before he was able to sail again – by which time other Spaniards had explored more of the coastline and AMERINDIAN resistance had further stiffened. In the summer of 1521 Ponce de Leon set out for the Gulf shore of Florida, reportedly with

POPULATION

two ships and 200 would-be colonists, including soldiers, farmers, artisans and priests. This expedition, however, was savagely repulsed by Calusa Indians, and Ponce de Leon himself was mortally wounded by a poisoned arrow.

Further reading: S. E. Morison, *The European Discovery of America: The Southern Voyages, 1492–1616*, Oxford University Press, 1974, 502–17, 529–32.

POPULATION

A demographically healthy population is one in which there is a balance between males and females and between the fertility and mortality rates. These conditions are facilitated by an absence of wars, invasions and wholesale emigration, a healthy environment, and, not least, by the existence of stable families. Such has been the case throughout most of Bahamian history, resulting in a population not only relatively healthy but steadily, sometimes rapidly, expanding. Since the first colonial settlements became firmly established, the only exceptions have been short periods of epidemic or emigration – the catastrophic fate of the aboriginal AMERINDIANS being a different case altogether.

From the number and size of village sites discovered by archaeology it seems that there may have been as many as 40,000 Lucayans living in The Bahamas when COLUMBUS arrived – more people than the islands were to hold again until the 1870s. A peaceable people living in family and kinship units, the Lucayans subsisted effectively and healthily from the products of their fishing and farming. They may not have enjoyed a very long life by modern standards, but seem to have had enough children at least to keep up numbers. Moreover, the fact that they were still in the process of onward migration and had not yet entirely filled up the Bahamian archipelago before the arrival of the Spaniards suggests that they were being constantly augmented by migrating groups from Cuba and the island which Columbus named Santo Domingo. This situation was drastically changed and the flow reversed after 1492. The Lucayans did not fight the Spaniards, but they could not combat the introduction of smallpox or European varieties of the common cold, and those who survived the first onslaught were rounded up and deported to work the mines of Santo Domingo, and perished there. When PONCE DE LEON sailed through The Bahamas in 1512 he reported the islands depopulated save for a single old woman.

The Bahamas remained without permanent inhabitants for almost 140 years and without a steady and increasing population for a further 60 years. In the first census taken, by Governor Phenney in 1722, the entire population was a mere 989, of whom 427 whites and 233 blacks lived in NEW PROVIDENCE, 150 whites and 34 blacks in ELEUTHERA, 124 and 5 on HARBOUR ISLAND, and 12 and 3 at CAT ISLAND. The population increased by 50 per cent during the 1730s, reached 2,000 during the 1750s and steadily doubled again by 1775. These 4,000 persons – of whom roughly 1,750 were whites, 800 free non-whites and 1,450 black slaves – were still no more widely distributed than before.

The first, and proportionately, politically and culturally the most important major population surge occurred with the arrival of American LOYALISTS and their slaves after the end of the War of Independence (1783). Almost at once the arrival of some 1,600 whites and 5,700 slaves and free blacks trebled the colony's population and raised the proportions of slaves and free blacks to three-quarters, while increasing the number of settled islands from four to a dozen. Even more significantly, over the following decades the remigration of many of the whites after the failure of cotton planting, coupled with the remarkable fertility of the now under-worked slaves, further increased the disproportion between whites and blacks. Despite the transfer of some slaves to other colonies down to 1826, and the early manumission of others, there were still 10,000 slaves left to be freed in 1834. At the time of 'full freedom' in 1838, the total population of The Bahamas was some 19,000, of whom no more than 25 per cent were whites, about half of mixed race, and the remaining quarter unequivocally black.

The total population of The Bahamas rose steadily in the second two-thirds of the nineteenth century, increasing from 20,000 in 1840 to 54,000 in 1900. The only slowdowns occurred in mid-century with CHOLERA epidemics. The generally healthy rate of growth was evenly spread across the population, but for several reasons the proportion of those classed as whites continued to decrease, falling to one-sixth of the total by 1900. The total of non-whites was augmented by the settlement of some 6,500 LIBERATED AFRICANS between 1809 and 1860 – the very last African-born Bahamians surviving until the 1920s. A degree of miscegenation also added to the numbers and proportion of the non-whites. The northern communities that remained resolutely all-white were also somewhat depleted by the migration of a considerable number of their families to Key West at the southern tip of Florida.

Emigration by all sections of the population, mainly to Florida, was the chief reason why the total of those living in The Bahamas increased at a much slower pace in the first 40 years of the twentieth century. It rose from 54,000 in 1901 only to 67,000 in 1943, and actually declined between 1911 and 1921. The chief motive for the migration was to escape from the desperate poverty of the Out Islands, where three-quarters of the Bahamian population still lived in 1900 – with NASSAU beginning to expand rapidly both with Family Islanders seeking marginally better opportunities and with returnees from Florida once US immigration restrictions began to tighten in the 1930s.

This 'metropolitan effect', whereby Nassau proportionally soared ahead while the Family Islands (with the exception of GRAND BAHAMA) declined, not just proportionately but in absolute numbers, was one of the most remarkable features of the huge increase in the total Bahamian population once prosperity began to weave its spells from the 1950s onwards. The total population in 1953 was 85,000 – of whom 46,000 (54 per cent) lived in New Providence, 4,000 (6 per cent) in Grand Bahama, 3,400 (4 per cent) in Abaco, 7,000 (8 per cent) in Eleuthera, Harbour Island and SPANISH WELLS, and 24,000 (28 per cent) in the rest of The Bahamas. The total had ballooned to 305,000 by the year 2000 – with 212,000 (70 per cent) living in New Providence, 47,000 (15 per cent) in Grand Bahama, 13,000 (4 per cent) in Abaco, 8,000 (3 per cent) in Eleuthera, Harbour Island and Spanish Wells, and only 28,000 (9 per cent) in all other islands combined.

This astounding growth, with its disparities, was the result of complex interlocking factors, and was characterised by other remarkable features – some of them with serious social implications. In contrast to previous hard times, burgeoning prosperity brought many Bahamian emigrés back to the homeland. Despite the encouragement of white immigration by the Bay Street government in the 1950s and 1960s, the actual proportion of whites continued to decrease until it fell below 12 per cent. This trend was speeded not just by a virtual population explosion among the majority population but by large numbers coming to the Bahamas from the West Indies – above all HAITIANS, who at their peak may have numbered 40,000, or roughly 15 per cent of the people living in The Bahamas.

Though there were difficulties in obtaining accurate figures (especially of the number of immigrants and birth statistics), The Bahamas clearly underwent an unprecedented population surge through natural increase in the economic boom period accompanying the political transition from internal self government and full Independence (1964–73). During this time the rate of natural increase alone may have been as high as 37 per thousand of the total population, and 190 per thousand women aged between 15 and 40 – as high as anywhere in the developing world. As a consequence, no less than 44 per cent of the population was under the age of 15 in 1970. This 'baby boom' could be attributed to a rise in economic expectations as well as great improvements in health, diet and work conditions. But there were less positive factors involved. These included the disruption of traditional family life and decline of moral standards, particularly through migration from the Family Islands to relatively well-paid jobs in New Providence and Grand Bahama – leading, for example, to a rate of illegitimate births and teenage pregnancies rivalling those of Jamaica. Of the 5,444 Bahamian women who had children in the 1980 census year, only 37.5 per cent were legally married (with a further 15.8 per cent in common law unions), and 21 per cent of the children were born of teenage mothers, who on average had their first child at the age of 16 ½.

The age imbalance of the 'baby boom' years inevitably evened itself out over the following two decades, and with it the soaring rates of natural increase, though this merely eased rather than solved all the demographic and social problems. By the year 2000, the proportion of the population under 15 years of age had fallen to 29 per cent, though 64 per cent were still under the age of 30. The birth rate, still as high as 28.3 per thousand in 1980, had fallen to 24.0 in 1990, and to 18.0 in 1999. Although infant mortality had fallen from 30.0 per thousand births in 1980 to 24.4 in 1990 and 15.8 in 1999, the overall death rate had not declined to the same degree, due largely to the incidence of AIDS, falling from 6.4 per thousand in 1980 to 5.0 in 1983, but averaging 5.7 between 1995 and 2000.

Nonetheless, the Bahamian population remains generally stable and healthy. It is also projected to continue to expand, but at a more manageable rate than between the 1960s and 1980s. The expectation of life at birth, which in 1980 was 64 years for males and 72 for females had risen to 68 for males and 75 for females by the end of the century. The rate of natural increase (the excess of births over deaths) had fallen from 21.9 per thousand in 1980 to 18.7 in 1990 and 12.7 by 2000. But even with the further small decline expected, a population still with a large proportion in the fertile age range was projected to reach half a million by the year 2050 and 750,000 by the end of the twenty-first century.

With more than 80 per cent of the population urbanised by 2000 (compared with a mere 25 per cent in 1900) this was a fundamentally different people from a century earlier. Improved communications as well as a much greater sense of integration and common purpose have helped to break down former geographical and ethnic divisions. Apart from the problems associated with the shift from traditional Family Island lifestyles to those of

POSTAGE STAMPS

city life, for individuals as well as families, there remains the overwhelming problem of reversing the depopulation of most of the Family Islands. However, thanks to the resolute control of both legal and illegal immigration through a rigid policy of BAHAMIANISATION and the proud achievements of the new nation over the 30 years since Independence, the population of the Commonwealth of The Bahamas does essentially consist of true-true Bahamians – that is to say, those with deep island roots or proven commitment to the country over at least a generation. The twenty-first century population of The Bahamas is without the former degree of racial, social and political tensions. Happily, it also lacks both the conflictive relationships between natives and expatriates, and the problems of establishing a coherent national identity which afflict some other emergent nations in the region, such as the Cayman Islands.

Further reading: Craton and Saunders, *Islanders*, i, *passim*; N. Abdulah, *The Bahamas and Its People: A Demographic Analysis*, ISER, 1987.

POSTAGE STAMPS Stamped postmarks – first with a simple BAHAMAS, then with an official crown and/or the exact date and place of posting – were introduced by the Bahamian Post Office around 1802, much later than in other more important and busier colonies. Stick-on stamps also came rather later to The Bahamas than some other colonies (Trinidad, Bermuda and British Guiana having their own 'postmasters' provisionals' between 1847 and 1850). The first adhesive stamps used on Bahamian mail were British stamps authorised for use in The Bahamas, cancelled by the local AO5 stamp, between 1856 and 1859.

The first letter with the first Bahamian adhesive stamp was posted on 10 June 1859. The stamp was the one-penny value, of 'reddish lake' colour, intended for 'interinsular mail'. Engraved and recess-printed by the firm of Perkins Bacon in London, it featured the beautiful 1837 portrait of QUEEN VICTORIA by the Swiss-born artist Edward Chalon, supported by a CONCH shell and a PINEAPPLE. There were only 2,000 stamps in the first two consignments (printed at a cost of 1s.4d. per thousand), examples of which now sell at auction for thousands of dollars apiece.

'Chalon Head' stamps, including the 4d. and 6d. values soon added for postage to North America and the United Kingdom, continued to be issued until 1884, when they were superseded by a set with a new (but still youthful) portrait of the Queen. These included 2 ½ d., 1s., 5s. and £1 values – the last two used almost exclusively for stamp duty payments. Of the Bahamian 'classics' (stamps issued before 1900), the £1 stamps, postally used or 'mint', now command prices about the same as for the 6d. 'Chalons' which were overprinted 'fourpence' when the stock of that value ran out in 1883. Sadly (perhaps surprisingly), the high-value stamps used fiscally, not for postage, are relatively worthless.

As the volume of mail multiplied in the twentieth century (and with the accompanying growth of the pastime of philately), both the numbers and varieties of stamps issued steadily increased – though at a more gradual rate in The Bahamas than elsewhere until the 1960s. The very first Bahamian 'pictorial', a depiction of the 'Queen's Staircase' in Nassau issued just after the death of Queen Victoria, was not added to until 1920, or superseded until 1930. Commemoratives were issued in 1920 to celebrate the ending of World War One and in 1929 for the combined celebrations of the tercentenary of the initial grant of The Bahamas to Sir Robert Heath by the English Crown, and the bicentenary of the House of Assembly. Yet the only pictorials added before World War Two were those of FLAMINGOS in flight with the image of King George V (1935), and of the SEA GARDENS and Fort Charlotte with that of his son, George VI (1938).

Since World War Two, the eagerness of the government to publicise The Bahamas and to benefit from the popularity of philately have led to a bewildering multiplicity of stamp issues. Almost a miniature guidebook in itself was the set of 16 pictorials issued in 1947 at the time of the tercentenary of the arrival of the ELEUTHERIAN ADVENTURERS. This series was reissued in 1954 with the image of George VI changed to that of his daughter,

Original proof copy of the first Bahamian postage stamp, April 1859, with 'Chalon' head of Queen Victoria supported by a pineapple and a conch shell

ELIZABETH II, and again in January 1964 to celebrate the achievement of internal self-government. Thereafter, political and economic changes were more than matched by changes in the stamps on offer, beginning with a completely new set of 15 pictorials in January 1965 and the whole range of new stamps required by the switch from sterling to decimal currency in May 1966. Since that time, thanks largely to the efforts of a Bahamas Post Office Philatelic Bureau set up in the 1970s, every conceivable royal, national and international occasion has brought forth new commemorative stamps, and not a Christmas passes without a colourful new seasonal set. The Bahamas has never been one of those colonies and countries dependent on philatelic sales to balance its budget, but these tangential sales have certainly been a bonus.

Further reading: H. G. D. Gisburn, *Postage Stamps & Postal History of The Bahamas*, Stanley Gibbons, 1950; M. H. Luddington, *Bahamas Early Mail Services and Postal Markings*, Alpha, 1982; E. B. Proud, *The Postal History of the Bahama*, Heathfield, 2000; *Stanley Gibbons Postage Stamp Catalogue. Part One: British Commonwealth*, 100th ed., Stanley Gibbons, 2000.

POSTAL SERVICES In the earliest times letters were carried haphazardly in private vessels as opportunities occurred. In 1702 the English Post Office established a regular packet-boat service between Falmouth in Cornwall and the West Indian and North American colonies, though The Bahamas continued to be serviced indirectly for almost the whole of the eighteenth century. In 1710, however, a landmark Post Office Act decreed the setting up of a general post office in all English colonies, and established the formal 'ship's letter' system, whereby all ships' captains were required to carry mail on request, delivering it to the general post office on arrival, whether or not for onward redistribution. It was an extremely expensive system, with the rates between London to the West Indies set in 1710 at a shilling and sixpence per folded page, payable by the recipient.

Since much Bahamian mail was carried by way of the North American ports (especially Charleston and New York), the loss of the American colonies between 1775 and 1783 disrupted the imperial postal network. However, the system was reorganised and made more efficient by the setting up of a packet-boat station and general post office for The Bahamas at what was named Pitt's Town, at the north-western tip of CROOKED ISLAND, on the main sailing route between Britain and the West Indies, between 1787 and 1843.

Though some mail for The Bahamas continued to be trans-shipped at Long Cay and Inagua, the Pitt's Town GPO faded out because of more fundamental changes. Rowland Hill's principle that a cheaper yet more efficient postal system might be achieved through economies of scale (tested by the introduction of the nationwide penny post in Britain in 1840) was successfully realised through the introduction of steamships and contracted mail services – coupled with the worldwide spread of free trade principles. As a result of the formation of the Royal Mail Line by James McQueen in 1841 and the competition from the Nova Scotian Samuel Cunard over the following two decades, Nassau became a vital part of a mail network joining the West Indies and the Americas with Britain, Europe and the rest of the world. From 1843, Bahamian postal rates were reduced to sixpence per half-ounce letter to Britain, fourpence to the US and West Indies, and a mere penny between the Bahama Islands themselves.

However, service to the Out Islands remained slower and less reliable. The local equivalent of the ship's letter was introduced between the islands in the 1840s and the very first Bahamian adhesive stamp was specifically for 'interinsular postage'. Yet it was not until the 1880s that Out Island settlements began to be provided with separate post offices – each with its distinctive postmark – where islanders could post and pick up letters, parcels and the occasional postal order. A notable bonus for Out Islanders was that at least until World War Two newspapers and printed books were carried to them postage-free.

As an index of the uncommonly scattered nature of the Bahamian population and the importance of the postal network in their steady integration, in the 73 years between the setting up of the first in Governor's Harbour, ELEUTHERA in 1886 and that in Freeport, GRAND BAHAMA in 1959, over 80 subordinate post offices were established in The Bahamas (by 1980 there were, or had been, a total of 124). As the postal historian Harold Gisburn wrote in 1950, 'No British colony of comparable size includes a larger number of post offices within its borders.'

Usually attached to the office of the local Commissioner (who almost always served also as the local postmaster) Out Island post offices were important meeting places, as people gathered for the arrival of the mail boat, exchanging local news while waiting and sharing fresh news from Nassau or the wider world once the mail had been sorted and distributed. This was the peripheral equivalent of the phenomenon noted, for example, by the female American visitors Dickinson and Dowd (1886) of the way Nassauvians and visitors eagerly watched with spyglasses from Fort Fincastle for the arrival of the New York mail, and with equal impatience awaited its sorting

POSTCARDS

and handing out at the main post office in the public buildings.

In the twentieth century the major innovation was the addition of airmail to sea and surface mail, first to the Bahamian capital in the 1930s and gradually to the Out Islands after World War Two – giving a two-tier system of rates (or even five-tier with express, registered and insured deliveries). Yet The Bahamas still did not adopt a system of home deliveries, or even a general system of postbox collections. Customers still have to go to a post office to post their mail or to pick up mail from their individual boxes. While this has no doubt served to keep the rising cost of mailing marginally below the rate of inflation, in a traffic-clogged and increasingly frenetic city the self-service system no longer has the compensating charms of providing a place for people to meet, linger and exchange news and gossip.

Further reading: H. G. D. Gisburn, *Postage Stamps & Postal History of The Bahamas*, Stanley Gibbons, 1950; E. B. Proud, *The Postal History of The Bahamas*, Heathfield, 2000.

POSTCARDS Picture postcards are one of the most fascinating and historically revealing by-products of TOURISM. Over more than a century of Bahamian tourism they have been eagerly bought and distributed to the rest of the world by millions of visitors. At least a significant fraction have been preserved. As documents they not only illustrate what has and has not changed in what tourists have found interesting and picturesque about The Bahamas, but provide for anyone interested in the Bahamian past incidental details of places, people and lifestyles long gone, which otherwise might have been forgotten.

Plain postcards, ideal for brief and non-confidential messages, were first sold by the Bahamas Post Office in 1881, their postage costing only a penny to anywhere in the world. From shortly after this, the American-born pioneer of Bahamian photography Jacob F. Coonley (1830–1908) was offering for sale 'Artistic Views of Nassau and Vicinity … Embracing all Points of Interest to the Strangers Visiting these Summer Isles', at his studio on Nassau's Bay Street. By 1900, Coonley's success was followed up by the Bahamian William Pinder (local agent for Kodak), who offered mounted or unmounted photographs of 'Native Characters, Costumes, Summer and Winter Sceneries, &c.' At the same time, the first Bahamian drug store crassly advertised: 'if you want to secure one of the most interesting Photos of some of the old Africans who were formerly slaves in the Bahamas, come and have a look at our collection of beauties.' Within the next decade, the finest and most perceptive of all early Bahamian photogaphers, the Eleuthera-born James Osborne 'Doc' Sands (1885–1978), had begun work, taking over Coonley's business and studio.

By this time, however, the mass-produced picture postcard had challenged and begun to supplant the studio souvenir trade. The very first Bahamian postcards, printed in Germany and distributed by the merchant Walter K. Moore, date from about 1900. But they were soon followed by much larger numbers and a greater variety, produced in the United States (particularly by the Detroit Photographic Company) and in the United Kingdom, and sold in all hotels and tourist outlets. Some companies used their own photographers, most notably the Detroit Company's famous William Henry Jackson, who made his first visit to Nassau in 1903. But most of the best images were produced by local photographers; first 'Doc' Sands and F. W. Armbrister, and much later, Stanley Toogood and Freddy Maura.

Naturally, picture postcards from the beginning concentrated on the standard sites, scenes and subjects, venturing (like the tourists themselves) rarely from downtown Nassau, and hardly at all to even the nearest and comparatively more prosperous Out Islands. The bulk of any collection is made up of oft-repeated images of the forts, public buildings, churches, statues, the Queen's Staircase, the sailboat-crammed docks, palm-treed and be-flowered side-streets such as Winslow HOMER painted, and an uncrowded Bay Street, with a few picturesque pedestrians and horse-drawn vehicles and fewer ancient cars – somewhat superfluously directed by black policemen in smart uniforms.

Yet, as Craton and Saunders summarised in *Islanders in the Stream* (1998):

when the camera's unbiased eye betrayed the photographer's caution, or the photographer ventured beyond the neat if unsophisticated downtown area and sought to depict the 'quaint natives' and their lifestyle, a harsher reality unconsciously obtruded. Shops in the photographs are smaller and shabbier than their contemporary advertisements suggest, the ordinary people are dusty, ragged, barefoot, and not always smiling. The meagre wares displayed by the market women suggest a few pennies painstakingly earned, and the fishing, trading and sponging vessels crowded at the market wharf are tatterdemalion, suggesting a lack rather than plenitude of employment, and desperate competition among those who sailed them. In memorable images, a sullen herd of black men and women clip sponges under the watchful eye of a white man in a solar topee, and similarly-hatted white owners proprietarily stand amid soldierlike ranks of sisal cactus or pineapples without a labouring black in sight. Pictures of 'Bahama natives' taken in their homes Over-the-Hill accurately show the varieties of house (wattle-and-daub, boxes of boards raised on boulders or sticks, or crude freestone constructions) but poignantly emphasise the hopeless poverty of the people and their home environment – more like the poorest Out Islands than the suburbs of Nassau City and closer to 'darkest Africa' than to any parts of the countries from which the tourists came.

Later postcards have, as yet, less historical value. Usually inscribed with variants of the simple message 'Look where we are!' and the only occasionally sincere 'Wish you were here!' they continue to concentrate on the standard sites and scenes and depict the very real natural beauties of the islands. Having a slickly cosmetic, almost posed quality that probably dismayed 'Doc' Sands as he aged, they present what the Ministry of Tourism most wish the tourists to see, and visitors themselves wish to remember. All very well, but less than half the true picture. It would be a brave, but valuable entrepreneur who would offer for sale a parallel, less Panglossian. series of postcards of 'the real Bahamas' of the early twenty-first century. These might show, for example, a decayed Family Island settlement, a Haitian shanty town, one of the less photogenic, and prematurely shabby modern office blocks or schools, a Nassau rush-hour traffic jam, hospital line-up, court or prison scene; as well, a religious tent revival, sea baptism, political march or labour picket, a typical funeral, wedding, dance or cook-out; and finally not just action pictures of sporting triumphs, in sailing, tennis and athletics events, but pictures of the crowds of ordinary Bahamians avidly watching, celebrating (even gambling on) the outcome.

Further reading: S. Boyd Malone and R. Campbell Roberts, *Nostalgic Nassau: Picture Postcards, 1900–1940*, Nassau Nostalgia, 1991.

POTCAKES The name colloquially applied to the almost innumerable and infinitely variegated breed of Bahamian mongrel dogs, which are variously regarded with distaste, exasperation and grudging affection. The label comes from the name given to the hard-baked and discoloured residue of PEAS N' RICE left in the cooking pot (called 'bun bun' in certain parts of the West Indies) which is the food traditionally reserved for a household's canine hangers-on.

The majority of potcakes are left to roam, scavenge and breed freely. Though tending to be quarrelsome, they often travel in packs, and at night engage in a chorus of competitive howling, especially at full moon. In the more remote areas they are almost as feral, and potentially as dangerous, as Australian dingoes. More fortunate

Potcake

potcakes have closer (and jealously guarded) affiliations with households. They are valued as yard-dogs, and even welcomed in the house as children's pets and protectors.

This wide-ranging degree of acceptability is reflected in the range of treatment which potcakes are afforded. Thanks largely to the activities of the BAHAMAS HUMANE SOCIETY they neither pose the threat nor receive the treatment reported from the Turks and Caicos Islands – where they are said to be culled with guns and poison and even the planned introduction of canine distemper. Instead, the BHS in Nassau and Grand Bahama counsels responsible ownership, prosecutes cases of cruelty, and provides free veterinary treatment, while at the same time offering spaying and neutering services, rounding up troublesome strays, and 'humanely' dispatching by lethal injection those left unclaimed.

Despite the problems there are those who wish to preserve the dignity and raise the status of the Bahamian potcake. Chief of these are the members of the prestigious Bahamas Kennel Club, founded in 1982. Each year on the second weekend in March they hold a well-attended International Dog Show and Obedience Trials at the Botanic Gardens in Chippingham. Among the classes of canine up for display and prizes, the most unusual and much the most popular is that for local potcakes.

Further reading and information: 'Kehoe Finds Her Niche in Bimini Love Program', www.vetmed.ufl.edu/pr/news ext/spsu02/kehoe.htm; www.pegasusfoundation.org; Bahamas Kennel Club, fax c/o Rita Hall, 242-363-3969.

POTTER'S CAY An important and interesting islet at the eastern end of NASSAU's harbour; at first the site of a small gun battery, traces of which can still be seen. Unglamorously, in the 1920s it became the location of what is still Nassau's only mains sewage disposal unit – discreetly hidden from sight and undetectable by smell. In

POWLES, Louis Diston

Potter's Cay

the late 1960s it became an anchor point for the first of the two bridges connecting NEW PROVIDENCE with PARADISE ISLAND – which changed from two-way traffic to become the exit route from Paradise Island in 1998.

Though overflown by the bridge, Potter's Cay was not overshadowed. It assumed importance in the 1970s when the increased cruise-ship traffic at Nassau's main docks compelled the shifting of all local sailboats and MAIL BOATS from the old Market Range downtown. Potter's Cay became the starting point and terminus of the seemingly haphazard but essential mail-boat services to the Family Islands, and the site of a colourful and clamorous market for the fish and produce still brought into Nassau by boat – including the ever-declining number of working sailboats.

POWLES, Louis Diston (1842–1911) An English stipendiary and circuit magistrate, whose mere eight months' service in The Bahamas (1886–7) was enlivened by one of the most notable racial controversies and led to the publication of easily the best social, economic and political account of the islands during that period: *The Land of the Pink Pearl* (London, 1888; Nassau, 1996).

Born in the City of London and educated at Harrow and Oxford, Powles was a playwright and editor as well as a barrister. Appointed to The Bahamas by the Colonial Office on a stipend of £500 a year, he arrived in Nassau with his wife in November 1886. More than a third of his time was spent on two judicial circuits by sailboat, during which he visited all the main islands except Exuma. While in the colonial capital he also explored and took notes on all sections of the population: whites, coloureds and the black majority living Over-the-Hill.

Powles claimed to have come to The Bahamas with an open mind and to have been shocked by the conditions he found. His prevailing impression was of the cheerful hardihood and vital culture of ordinary black Bahamians in the face of oppression by the white oligarchy of 'CONCHY JOES'. His most telling attack was on the iniquitous TRUCK SYSTEM by which Bay Street merchants kept poor black SPONGE fishermen and farmers in thrall. He also spoke up for the small intermediate class of educated and progressive but socially and politically ostracised non-whites, which included James Carmichael Smith and David PATTON, the ADDERLEYS and DILLETTS.

If an idealist, Powles certainly lacked discretion. His chief mistake was to sentence to jail without the option of a fine, one James Lightbourne, a pillar of the METHODIST Church, for an assault on a black female employee, Susan Hopkins. In the appeal case Powles was quoted as saying in public that he would imprison any man for assault on any woman, and that he would not accept the word of any Methodist even on oath. Though initially supported by Governor Blake and by a petition from more than 500 non-white Nassauvians, Powles felt compelled to resign, and was further punished by being refused his repatriation grant by the white-dominated legislature. *The Land of the Pink Pearl*, published within a year of his return to England, however, was far more than an act of revenge – opening a window to conditions in one of Britain's least known and most neglected colonies.

Further reading: L. D. Powles, *The Land of the Pink Pearl: Recollections of Life in the Bahamas*, Media Publishing, 2nd ed., with an introduction by Neil Sealey, 1996.

PRESBYTERIANS Spiritual descendants of the Calvinist Independents among the earliest English settlers and Scottish LOYALISTS who established their own church in 1810, Bahamian Presbyterians formed an influential and exclusive minority within a minority well into the twentieth century.

Scots constituted a significant proportion of those who fled America to settle in The Bahamas in the 1780s, of whom the most dynamic and god-fearing was Michael Malcolm, born in Kinross, Scotland, in 1754. Malcolm was among the 55 Scots who set up the St Andrew's Society in Nassau in 1798, and those who formed the Lodge of Freemasons following the Scottish Rite (rather than the English) around the same time. The Scottish Presbyterians held their first services in the former jail in the courthouse basement soon after the prisoners were moved to the new jail on Shirley Street in 1799, but they lacked both their own minister and kirk for a further ten years.

Thanks to the efforts of Michael Malcolm and other Loyalist Scots now prominent in local business and politics, an affiliation was made with the Edinburgh Presbytery, a Rev. John Rae arrived in Nassau in December 1809 and the cornerstone of St Andrew's Kirk on East Hill Street was laid in August 1810. An even more significant development was the passing of an Act in 1824 – largely through the instigation of the Scottish Loyalists now dominant in the Assembly – for the Kirk to be placed on the same footing in the Establishment as the ANGLICAN Church and financially endowed (as in the United Kingdom). With this endorsement, the Kirk became the iron-clad bastion of the most conservative and racially exclusive members of the local and expatriate white elite – attracting many on social rather than theological grounds. For example, the non-Presbyterian Englishman Edwin Moseley founder of the *Nassau Guardian*, was its long-time choirmaster, while Sunday school was attended by the children of families of different denominations as long as they were of the right complexion.

What seemed like a mortal blow, the disestablishment and disendowment of the Kirk along with that of the Anglican Church between 1869 and 1875, was however mitigated by the relative prosperity and generosity of the Kirk's congregation. The Kirk was enlarged and remodelled in 1864, with galleries placed at each end of the original structure and a northern transept (now the nave) added, along with the present front porch and bell tower. The Kirk Hall – to house plays and other secular functions as well as Sunday Schools – was completed in May 1874, and the first Manse, just to the south of the Kirk, in 1894.

These changes, however, did not yet extend to an alteration in the exclusionist spirit of the Kirk, despite a steady decline in its traditional membership. Though a school for black children was founded Over-the-Hill on Quarry Mission Road by white Presbyterians as early as the 1880s as an act of *noblesse oblige*, it was as late as 1948, during the tenure of Rev. Poole, that the segregationist ST ANDREW'S SCHOOL (later transferred to Shirley Street and later still to Yamacraw) was set up in the Kirk Hall in 1948. A fundamental change occurred, however, in tune with impending political changes in the country, in the 1960s. This began when the middle-class blacks Dr CLEVELAND ENEAS and his wife 'Phinny' (who had been strictly brought up as a Presbyterian in the southern United States) were accepted as members, and soon became popular teachers in a gradually desegregated Sunday School.

St Andrew's Presbyterian kirk

Mainly during the tenure of ministers from the United States and especially with input from the Presbytery of Tropical Florida a policy of outreach and liberalisation was instituted, along the lines of a mission statement of 'bringing all people closer to God through worship, ministry and service'. A church office was created, and a church staff of full-time secretary, custodian and youth worker were all employed. The congregation became more involved in the BAHAMAS COUNCIL OF CHURCHES, and the Kirk began to sponsor a tutoring programme in basic literacy at the C. R. Walker School, just behind Government House.

From 1967 a Presbyterian Kirk was established by local demand in the new city of Freeport, Grand Bahama, and in 1995, the Nassau Kirk launched a new congregation in Marsh Harbour, Abaco, christening it The Kirk of the Pines. At the beginning of the twenty-first century, though still one of the smaller Bahamian religious denominations, the Presbyterians had not only resolutely moved with the times but actually boasted more adherents than in its unregenerate, more influential past.

Further reading: V. Moseley Moss, *Reminiscing: Memories of Old Nassau*, Ronald G. Lightbourn, 1999, *passim*.

PRISONS There were references to peace-breakers and political dissidents – even a couple of Governors – being cast into jail as early as 1692 during the time of the Lord PROPRIETORS. Their place of confinement was almost certainly in the earliest Fort Nassau (located on the site of the present British Colonial Hilton).

PRISONS

The first proper jail was mentioned in the 1760s as being located in the basement of the building which housed both the Assembly and the Supreme Court, at the junction of Bay and Market Streets in central Nassau. This place was deemed inadequate and inappropriate by the Loyalist legislators, who in 1790 commissioned the first separate and custom-built jail. This was the handsome octagonal building on the Shirley Street side of the new range of public buildings which since 1879 has housed the Nassau Public Library. Besides an unlighted dungeon below ground and two dozen tiny but somewhat airier cells on the two floors above, the balconied top storey was the base and lookout for the Nassau night guard and housed the bell which tolled at noon and the curfew hour and raised the alarm in (the rare) times of emergency.

The Shirley Street jail was not used either for slaves or soldiers – and female free persons seem to have been so generally law-abiding (or so under the control of their menfolk) that no special provision was made to jail them. Since slaves were deemed chattel property, their owners had almost unlimited power to punish them (short of 'life or limb'), including whipping, placing them in irons and confinement in the lock-ups found on most plantations. However, the most serious and persistent slave offenders, and especially runaways, were consigned to a separate house of correction in Nassau, euphemistically called the Workhouse (its exact location is unknown). The soldiers in the garrison had their own code of punishment and were confined, if necessary, in the dungeons that can still be seen in Fort Charlotte – used until the garrison was withdrawn in 1892.

Important early reforms were the creation of residential Industrial Schools (modelled on the British Borstals) for male and female young offenders in the late 1920s and 1930s. In the 1940s, the first tentative attempts at rehabilitation and post-custodial supervision were made. However, it was chiefly the pressure of numbers and space constraints that led to the closure of the central prison on East Street and its transfer to a far more spacious, sequestered and secure facility at Sandilands (Fox Hill) in 1952, run by a prison service now entirely separated from the police. On a 130-acre site in what was then an undeveloped area of south-eastern New Providence were initially a main prison to house 224 male inmates, a separate building for 80 male first offenders, and a women's prison designed to accommodate 30.

Intended to be as nearly as possible self-contained, the Fox Hill compound included a farm for stock animals and horticulture, workshops and a central service area for cooking, laundry, stores and administration offices, as well as a barracks, married housing, recreational facilities and a canteen for the staff. In 1965 an annexe was built to house up to a hundred illegal immigrants, and in subsequent years a medium security unit and a new and considerably larger women's prison were added – the illegal immigrants being rehoused in the old one until a special detainees' camp was made for them on Carmichael Road in the 1980s. By the late 1990s the Central Service Area at Fox Hill included an education centre, but there were still only six prison buildings, with a planned total capacity of no more than 700 – now reorganised into maximum, medium and minimum security units, a first offenders' unit, a remand centre, and the prison for women.

The primary problems were those of overcrowding, inadequate staffing and underfunding; yet these led to, and compounded, many other problems. By 2000 as many as 2,500 persons were being admitted to the Fox Hill Prison each year, with the prisoner count at any one time exceeding 1,300 – almost twice the planned capacity. Standards of food, clothing and hygiene were no better than mediocre and medical conditions seriously deficient. Though in 2000 the budget for the prison service exceeded $10 million a year (an astounding 1,500 times greater than in 1868), it was not only inadequate but inefficiently deployed. Probably the worst effect was the failure to rehabilitate the inmates, despite the best efforts of some uniformed staff members, non-uniformed staff within, and other civilians outside the Prison. This resulted not from lack of effort or shortage of money alone, but from a damaging tension and difference in philosophy between uniformed and non-uniformed staff.

The facts and figures published from 2000 by the prison service itself largely told the tale. For more than a decade there had been an impressively styled Prison Technical and Vocational Institute. But lack of teachers and resources and the impediments placed in the way of recruitment by prison regulations meant that the efforts only reached a minority of inmates. In 2004 the prison management presented the most urgent of a perennial series of reports and pleas to the government about conditions, their causes and possible remedies. In more specific and practical terms, the Education Officer and her staff presented cogent, thorough and practical proposals for a greatly stepped-up educational programme, not just for the prison inmates, but also for the training of new 'correctional officer recruits'. However, given the traditionally low profile of prison matters in political quarters, and their low priority in budget allocations, it remains uncertain whether these cries for help and change will be answered adequately, or in time, to avert complete disaster.

PRITCHARD, Sir Asa H. (1892–1990) Highly successful merchant and long-serving Speaker of the Assembly (1941–62) who epitomised the most objectionable features of the BAY STREET regime and was its last survivor.

Born in Nassau ten years before the death of Queen Victoria, Asa Pritchard gained wide experience abroad before returning to take over the family's small general store in 1913. An abstemious workaholic, he built the business into one of the largest Bahamian commission agencies, while also pursuing an active political career, mainly as a Member for Eleuthera. Chosen as Speaker as much for his rigid conservatism as for his ability and probity, he distinguished himself by his implacable resistance to the threat of black majority rule and the rise of the PROGRESSIVE LIBERAL PARTY.

On one infamous occasion, Speaker Pritchard telephoned Government House from the House of Assembly after midnight so that Governor Lord RANFURLY could hear the chants of 'PLP All the Way' from the Square outside and be persuaded to impose police restrictions and set up barricades. During the 1958 General Strike (when his Bay Street store was picketed and one of his sons charged with ramming his car through the crowd) Pritchard was confidentially described by Governor Sir Raynor ARTHUR as 'the worst of those bubbling lunatics … who think purely in terms of "turn the machine guns on them"'.

Coming to be regarded as a political dinosaur even by his own UNITED BAHAMIAN PARTY, Pritchard was replaced as Speaker by the much younger and more flexible Robert 'Bobby' Symonette at the time of the UBP's last victory in 1962. Pritchard was knighted in 1965 at the beginning of his long retirement. In his own magnaminous retirement speech in 1997, PLP leader Sir Lynden PINDLING listed Sir Asa Pritchard among the important makers of the modern Bahamas. Pindling, however, privately acknowledged that Pritchard's main contribution was to provide an extremist right-wing benchmark, which aided the PLP in winning over the hearts and minds of the black majority in 1967.

PRIVATEERS Often confused with PIRATES (out-and-out sea robbers), both by those whom they attacked and by later writers, *privateers* were in fact private sea warriors legitimised by royal authority, serving only in times of official war. Privateers (the term was used both for the sailors and the ships in which they sailed) were licensed by the royal authorities in wartime to attack enemies of the Crown and those who traded with them, under what were called letters of marque. Prizes seized by privateers, along with those seized by the Royal Navy, were not shared out in piratical style, but adjudicated in colonial Vice-Admiralty courts.

Because of its strategic location, NASSAU was an extremely active base for privateers during the frequent wars against the Spanish, French, Americans and their allies over the course of the 'long eighteenth century' (1688–1815), and its Vice-Admiralty Court (established in 1697) was one of the busiest in the Americas. In each of the four major wars of the eighteenth century at least a hundred rich prizes were condemned in the Nassau court, nearly all of them having been brought in by privateers. Yet, thanks largely to much greater activity by the Royal Navy, this was eclipsed in the last wars against the French and the Americans (1793–1815, 1812–14) when more than 500 vessels were adjudicated by the Nassau Vice-Admiralty Court.

Privateering was popular among ship-owners and captains for the profits that could be made from taking prizes, but also among crewmen, because their shares of prize-money were more generous than on Royal Navy ships, and discipline and living conditions far less rigorous. Similarly, the appointments as judges or other officials in Vice-Admiralty courts were eagerly sought, especially in wartime, for the huge fees they awarded themselves – gaining a well-earned reputation for expensive delays and outright corruption, not only from the owners of seized vessels but also the captains and crews of privateers and Royal Navy ships.

Privateering was an essential expedient during the early phases of the British Empire, before the Royal Navy was large enough to serve all imperial purposes throughout the globe. It lasted from the times of Hawkins and Drake until the era of free trade and the worldwide dominance of the Royal Navy following the end of the Napoleonic Wars. Similarly, Vice-Admiralty courts developed to fill imperial needs in all maritime and international matters beyond the jurisdiction of national land based courts. These included the trial of pirates, the adjudication of wrecks and the application of the mercantilist laws of trade. The value of prize business in wartime, though, hugely outran all else. Once this source dried up, the mercantilist laws were repealed and piracy became a thing of the past, the Vice Admiralty Court atrophied, becoming merely a minor and unprofitable adjunct of the other courts – curiously linked, indeed, for the sake of convenience, with the almost equally quiescent division of the judicature that dealt with matters of divorce.

PROGRESSIVE LIBERAL PARTY (PLP)

PROGRESSIVE LIBERAL PARTY (PLP) Formed in 1953 to counter the political dominance of the BAY STREET oligarchy, the PLP became the first formal political party in the Assembly in 1956, with six Members. Establishing itself as unequivocally the party of the black majority, the PLP narrowly came to power under the leadership of Lynden PINDLING in 1967, winning a landslide victory in the following year.

Riding the populist wave, cannily eschewing harsh radical and socialist policies in favour of long-overdue liberal reforms (notably in education), the PLP relied on steady constitutional and economic advances, a growing sense of nationalism, and the continuing popularity of its programme of BAHAMIANISATION. Undoubtedly, it also benefited from the prolonged failure of opposition forces to cohere. With Prime Minister Pindling at the helm, the party – despite setbacks, defections and mounting criticisms – won four further elections, before running out of steam and losing to the FREE NATIONAL MOVEMENT under Hubert INGRAHAM in 1992. Seemingly sunk in the following election in 1997 (its steersman retired and mortally ill), the PLP was to make a remarkable recovery in 2002, under Pindling's chosen successor, Perry CHRISTIE.

The brainchild of a group of mainly light-skinned non-whites led by Henry TAYLOR, Cyril Stevenson and William Cartwright, the Progressive Liberal Party began moderately enough. Its first manifesto in October 1953 claimed that, as its name suggested, the party was intended to be truly representative and reformist, not revolutionary or racialist.

In an unprecedented show of popular unison the PLP returned six Members to the House of Assembly in the general election of 8 June 1956 (Bain, Butler, Fawkes, Stevenson, Pindling and Sammy Isaacs), forming the first truly concerted opposition in Bahamian parliamentary history. Under the almost accidental leadership of Lynden Pindling (chosen by a narrow margin over his Nassau South running-mate Fawkes, after Taylor, the party Chairman, had failed to win a seat) they proved so effective that within two years the 'Bay Street' majority felt obliged to formalise itself as the UNITED BAHAMIAN PARTY, under the leadership of Roland SYMONETTE.

Once installed in Parliament, the PLP assumed the slogan 'All the Way'. But its path proved rocky and difficult for more than a decade. The party was thought to have made considerable advances as a consequence of the GENERAL STRIKE of 1958, and from the extension of the vote to women, so it was crushed by its decisive defeat in the 1962 general election and the fact that it was the

Premier Pindling and Governor Grey with the first PLP Cabinet, 1967

UBP that led The Bahamas to internal self-government in 1964. Clearly, more systematic organisation and hard-line campaigning were called for, as well as luck. Inspired by the burgeoning Black Power movement in the United States – and spearheaded by the members of the ginger group called the National Council for Positive Action – PLP rhetoric became much more overtly racist and its tactics more dramatic, climaxing in the events of 'BLACK TUESDAY' (27 April 1965). This carefully staged public protest and attack on the tainted symbols of parliamentary democracy for a time seemed a failed gamble since it more seriously divided the PLP opposition than it upset the party in power. The support of organised labour for the PLP was also limited by the ambition of Randol FAWKES to lead a separate Labour party and to become the national leader.

Almost fortuitously, however, the UBP soon lost the moral high ground by the revelation of wholesale greed and corruption on the part of Stafford SANDS and other Ministers in the granting of casino licences and other concessions. The UBP still had a huge edge in campaign funding and the control of the media, and were confident that their traditional hold on the Out Islands was unassailable. However, in the climactic electoral contest of 10 January 1967, the PLP, reinforced by young zealots returning from study abroad and with considerable help from American liberal sympathisers, was able sufficiently to extend its campaigning from New Providence to the other islands to achieve a heart-stopping tie, 18 : 18. This deadlock was resolved in the PLP's favour by the award to Randol Fawkes (the sole winner for Labour) of the post of Minister of Labour, and by the appointment of the maverick Eleutheran independent Alvin BRAYNEN as

Speaker. Once the dam had been broken the next stage was deceptively easy. In a second general election, called just 15 months later, the PLP extended its majority from one to 21 in a 38-seat House.

The great turnaround of 1967–8 was a lasting thrill for the PLP's groundroots supporters and almost the death knell of the UBP. But it far from guaranteed a long tenure for the PLP itself or its leader. Though it immediately initiated electoral and social reforms, Pindling's government was assailed from all sides; from those who accused it of proceeding too slowly and from entrenched interests fearful of even moderate socialism – not to mention those who were sceptical of the ability or willingness of black legislators to govern efficiently, fairly and without corruption. Even more bothersome was the problem of defections, motivated by personal ambitions and jealousies as often as by ideological differences or high moral principles.

Even before 1967 the PLP had an excellent party organisation, with its annual conferences orchestrated publicly to discuss progress and problems, to finalise and endorse policy and tactics, to unite the leaders and their supporters, and to inspire both in the climactic run-up to the next election. Once it came to power the party made up for its comparative lack of newspaper support by ensuring it controlled and judiciously utilised radio station ZNS. Pindling in particular proved a master in making radio (and later television) a medium that reached out to all parts and all the peoples of The Bahamas. The PLP established active party branches throughout the islands and kept closely attuned to political opinions, allegiances and population shifts, ensuring that these, as far as possible, were reflected in the periodic changes in constituency boundaries. Rather less subtly, the party from the beginning (but increasingly) used the patronage posts and contracts that were at its disposal to reward its faithful supporters.

The most damaging attacks on the PLP occurred during the DRUG TRAFFICKING crisis of the mid-1980s. The 1984 Commission of Inquiry revealed widespread involvement at all levels of society, including among prominent members of the PLP (with even Pindling narrowly escaping direct implication). Clearly, the government should have been held responsible. But it managed to survive on three implicit, and scarcely creditable, grounds. The drug traffic (along with money laundering and the harbouring of dodgy 'offshore' enterprises) unquestionably benefited a wide swathe of Bahamians and the Bahamian economy as a whole. Secondly, the beneficiaries were not limited to the PLP but included many members of the opposition, especially lawyers and businessmen. Besides this, the PLP government was able to appeal to nationalist feelings by characterising the United States' anti-drug campaign as not only heavy-handed and hypocritical, but intended to destabilise The Bahamas and overthrow the PLP.

The PLP was resoundingly defeated in the 1992 general election, and five years later was almost swept away – coincidentally left with the same number of Members, six, as it had first managed to elect 42 years earlier. With the retirement of Lynden Pindling a few months after the 1997 election and disputes as to who should fill his shoes as leader, it seemed to many that the PLP might be gone for ever. This was not to be so. Ironically, the death of the former Prime Minister in August 2000 had much to do with the PLP's Lazarus-like revival in May 2002.

Further reading: D. L. Johnson, *The Quiet Revolution in The Bahamas*, Family Islands Press, 1972; C. A. Hughes, *Race and Politics in The Bahamas*, Queensland University Press, 1981; M. Craton, *Pindling: The Life and Times of the First Prime Minister of The Bahamas*, Macmillan Caribbean, 2002.

PROHIBITION ERA (1919–1933)

'Rum-Running' by Bahamians during the 14-year era of American Prohibition, in conjunction with the phase of general world prosperity of the 'giddy 'twenties', brought one of the most notable periods of temporary good fortune and optimism to a local economy historically all too familiar with economic cycles of boom and bust.

World War One was followed by a slump in the prices of Bahamian exports of SPONGE and SISAL, along with a labour surplus caused by the return of servicemen and migrant workers. The situation was quickly reversed, however, by the opportunities provided by the passing of the Volstead Act, which turned the United States 'dry' in 1919. Geographically, The Bahamas was ideally located to be an entrepot for liquor. It arrived in the islands quite legally and only became illicit once it entered US territorial waters. Those who made the greatest profits were the intrepid smugglers who carried the contraband the final dangerous leg of its journey across the GULF STREAM to Florida. Yet the profits spread much more widely. Perhaps the greatest net beneficiaries were the suddenly expanded numbers of Nassau liquor merchants. But comparative prosperity filtered down to the seamen carrying the liquor piled on Nassau's docks to the warehouses and anchored storage vessels of West End, Grand Bahama, Bimini and Cat Cay, to stevedores, and to the men and women engaged in bottling the rum, whiskey and gin from barrels and sewing the bottles into the five-bottle sacks which were found to be the most convenient way to carry the liquor onwards.

Casks and cases of bootleg liquor await shipment from Nassau dock, late 1920s

Prohibition also brought large numbers of free-spending American rum-runners to Nassau, as well as tourists eager both to drink legally and to enjoy an atmosphere of excitement not known since the blockade-running era of the AMERICAN CIVIL WAR. The most important and lasting benefits accrued, though, from the hugely increased revenue to the Bahamian government. Quite apart from officials willing to bend regulations for backhanders, the government itself was naturally inclined to turn a blind eye, to ignore American complaints, and to assert it was doing nothing wrong. Even though an 80 per cent drawback was allowed on re-exports from 1920 and the excise duty was reduced by 50 per cent three years later, the flow was so great (even without the liquor that evaded duty altogether) that the total of Bahamian revenue from the traffic, already multiplied ten times to £81,000 in 1919, soared to over a million pounds in 1923, and did not fall below half a million before 1930. At its peak, revenue from liquor was ten times greater than that from all other sources.

Despite exaggerated complaints from Jeremiahs in press and pulpit about the increase in crime, drunkenness and general demoralisation, and the obvious fact that those who profited most, as usual, were a small coterie of BAY STREET magnates, it was an era of general economic improvement and optimism. Besides the increase in TOURISM and land and house sales to foreigners, the 1920s saw great improvements in electricity and water supplies, the first sewerage system, better roads, improved medical services, and a great increase in such material indicators as motor vehicles, telephones, radios and refrigerators – even though all these were far more apparent in downtown Nassau than Over-the-Hill or in the Out Islands.

Though rum-running declined in the few years before Prohibition ended in 1933, its profits somewhat mitigated and delayed the onset of the Great Depression – which began in the United States in 1929.

Further reading: F. van de Water, *The Real McCoy*, Doubleday, 1933; H. McLachlan Bell, *Bahamas: Isles of June*, McBride, 1934, 183–221; B. Clifford, *Proconsul: Being Incidents in the Life and Career of the Honourable Sir Bede Clifford, GCMG, CB, MVO*, Evans, 1964; Craton and Saunders, *Islanders*, ii. 237–57.

PROPRIETORS, LORD Making colonial grants to titled proprietors was a favourite method of the English Stuart kings. During the reign of Charles I the Bahama islands had been included in the proprietary grant to Sir

Robert HEATH (1629), though no colonial settlement resulted. Much more important, though ultimately a failure, was the project which followed the Restoration of Charles II to include The Bahamas in the proprietorship of the Carolinas granted to eight of the king's lordly favourites.

Charles II made the grant of the huge province named Carolina (after his father, Charles I) as early as 1663. But even before the first settlement was made there, William Sayle and two other adventurers interested in The Bahamas, Hugh Wentworth and John Darrell, petitioned the Carolina Proprietors to take at least NEW PROVIDENCE under their wing – where, it was claimed, there were already 500 settlers, excluding slaves.

In the event, six of the Carolina Proprietors obtained a separate patent for the entire Bahamas in November 1670, with its more or less impracticable provisions echoing those of the 1663 Carolina document. As long as the Proprietors recognised the ultimate sovereignty of the king, they had great latitude to set up their own constitution – even to grant titles of nobility They were to control the distribution of land, 'to pass laws as long as they were consonant with English law, to administer justice, to collect rents and tithes (though not customs), to coin money, raise troops, exercise martial law, and even make war and peace.' At the same time, though, they were encouraged to allow some form of representation for all white male freemen, to allow freedom of worship, and to promote the settlement of foreigners, as long as they became British subjects.

Each of the Proprietors appointed a deputy or local agent, and together they tried, with little success, to form a company of Adventurers to finance and economically exploit their colony. At the same time they appointed Hugh Wentworth Governor, providing him with a detailed and largely impracticable commission and set of instructions, dated April 1671. These documents were largely concerned with the setting up of the form of government, the allocation of land, the collection of taxes, and the control of the economy to the Proprietors' advantage.

The most interesting aspect of the proposed constitution was the way that it was adapted from the English system of a separate executive, judiciary and legislature, and a bicameral parliament. There was to be a Governor's Council analogous to the House of Lords (its members even referred to as 'the nobility'), and an Assembly equivalent to the House of Commons, consisting of 20 elected representatives from New Providence, ELEUTHERA and any other settled islands.

From the beginning things began to go wrong, and the colony proved such an unprofitable investment that the Proprietors left it more or less to its own devices. Before he could take up his appointment Hugh Wentworth died, and he was succeeded by his brother John, whom John Darrell described as a debauchee and virtual buccaneer. John Wentworth was succeeded in turn by no less than ten proprietary Governors between 1676 and 1707, of whom the most notable was the Bermudian Nicholas TROTT (1693–6). As detailed in John OLDMIXON's colourful *History of Providence*, if some of the proprietary governors were capable, others were rogues, and the rest ineffectual. All had limited control over the troublesome colonists, and none whatsoever over the PIRATES who increasingly flocked to The Bahamas, and in time descended on New Providence itself.

Though from the fragmentary records and accounts that remain it seems that at least the vestiges and skeleton of a legislature and judiciary developed, this progress was not sustained. By the second decade of the eighteenth century, the situation had become completely anarchic, leading the British imperial government to rescind the Proprietors' charter, declare The Bahamas a Crown Colony, and appoint Woodes ROGERS to be the first royal Governor in 1718. The Lord Proprietors and their legatees, however, did not willingly give up all their rights, especially quit rents for lands, and were not finally bought out until 1787.

Further reading: Craton and Saunders, *Islanders*, i. 92–114; J. Oldmixon (J. Culmer ed.), *History of the Isle of Providence*, London, 1949.

PROVERBS Like all peoples with a strong oral tradition, and especially those with strong links to African culture, Bahamians possess a rich store of proverbial sayings. These are used to enliven verbal communication and are a treasury of wit and wisdom. Taken together, indeed, they constitute something much more valuable and profound: a compendium of folk philosophy.

Many proverbs current in the Bahamas are similar or identical to ones found in the West Indies or southern USA. This is not normally through Bahamians borrowing from elsewhere in the hemisphere, but because nearly all such proverbs have common African origins. Scarcely one familiar proverb does not have an equivalent in some West African language, having been brought to the Americas in the slave ships between the sixteenth and nineteenth centuries.

L. D. POWLES recorded some of the proverbs he heard as a circuit magistrate in the 1880s in his book, *Land of the Pink Pearl* (London, 1888). They included the following (all more or less self-explanatory):

PUBLIC HOLIDAYS

Hog run for him life; dog run for him character.

Cockroach nebber so drunk he crossy fowl yard.

Spider and fly no make bargain.

No trow away dirty water before you hab clean.

Patricia Glinton-Meicholas in *More Talkin' Bahamian* (1995) showed how proverb-talking is still customary by adding some modern examples – not all immediately clear to outsiders:

Biscuit and cracker come on the same ship but in different packages (Though two people may seem to have a lot in common, there can be class differences. A polite way of saying 'You are not my kind').

Even teeth and tongue will fight (You can expect disagreements in the closest of relationships).

Bahamian political discourse also finds rich proverbial material in marine analogies. The most famous was the one used by Prime Minister Lynden PINDLING in a rousing convention speech: *If you can't fish, cut bait. If you can't cut bait, get out of the boat.*

Others:

Don't mind the noise in the market, just mind the price of the fish.

Fish'man never call his own fish stink.

Keep man mas'head.

The last one Ms Glinton-Meicholas explains in the following way:

This cryptic utterance is a short way of saying 'Keep a man on the masthead', which is a fascinating allusion to Bahamian methods of navigation. Non-Bahamian sailors are often astonished by Bahamian mariners' ability to sail unscathed through the shallow and shoal-filled waters of the great Bahama Banks, using only the changing colour of the water as a guide. In days gone by, when sailing vessels were the chief means of transport in the archipelago, a man used to go up to the masthead to perform this function. The proverb simply means that your circumstances are potentially dangerous, so you should stay on the alert.

Further reading: the above, plus: M. Tertullian, *Bahamian Sayings*, Media, 2002.

PUBLIC HOLIDAYS The Bahamas enjoys the following ten national public holidays. Those that fall on a Saturday or Sunday are usually observed on the following Monday.

New Year's Day	1 January
Good Friday	The Friday before Easter
Easter Monday	The Monday after Easter
Whit Monday	Seven weeks after Easter
Labour Day	The first Friday in June
Independence Day	10 July
Emancipation Day	First Monday in August
National Heroes' Day	12 October (formerly Discovery or Columbus Day)
Christmas Day	25 December
Boxing Day	26 December

QUEEN ELIZABETH II

That the British monarch also remained Head of State of The Bahamas more than thirty years after Bahamian INDEPENDENCE is attributable to four factors hallowed tradition and an elective affinity for British constitutional ideals; the proven advantages of having a non-elected but politically neutral person as the titular head of state; the convenience of having someone who, through inheritance and long training, provided dignity to state occasions and was the official fount of honours; and, not least of all, the impeccable and revered character of the monarch who in 2002 had occupied the British throne and been Head of the Commonwealth for half a century.

From a Bahamian perspective it is not insignificant that Lynden PINDLING, who was to lead The Bahamas to majority rule and political independence, purposely delayed his return from studying in London so that he could enjoy the pomp and ceremony of Queen Elizabeth II's coronation in 1953. More widely significant is the importance which the Queen has always attached to her role as Head of the Commonwealth, particularly in respect of the eight of the 50 or so Commonwealth countries of which she is still officially Head of State. The Queen's five visits to The Bahamas between 1966 and 1994 – each of them on the former royal yacht HMS *Britannia* – have been mutually happy and successful occasions.

Four of the five visits were of special importance, spanning significant stages in the evolution of The Bahamas as an independent nation. Before 1966, the Speech from the Throne outlining the forthcoming agenda at the Official Opening of Parliament was invariably delivered by the Governor as the distant monarch's appointed viceroy. On her first visit in 1966 the Queen delivered this speech in person to the assembled legislature of a colony which had just been granted Responsible Government under the UNITED BAHAMIAN PARTY led by Sir Roland SYMONETTE. In the traditional Westminster style, the speech was delivered by the Queen sitting on the throne in the Upper House (then the Executive Council chamber) with the Councillors sitting and the elected Members dutifully standing. This procedure was repeated (now in the Senate chamber) on the Queen's next visit just after Lynden Pindling's PROGRESSIVE LIBERAL PARTY government had led The Bahamas into Independence, and on her subsequent three visits.

While the Queen lives there seems no doubt that The Bahamas will continue to be technically a monarchical state. There is no serious talk of republicanism from any segment of the political spectrum. There was widespread disappointment that the British Labour government's controversial retirement of HMS *Britannia* in 1999, if not the Queen's advancing years, would inevitably cut down her mobility within the Commonwealth and maybe preclude any further visits to The Bahamas.

QUEEN'S COLLEGE

The oldest surviving independent school in The Bahamas, with roots dating back to 1870, QC was established by Wesleyan Methodists as a coeducational establishment for the children of the white elite, 'to obviate the necessity of sending them to England for their education'. Effectively segregated until the 1950s and keeping its close Methodist affiliation even longer, the school retained its proud primacy and greatly expanded by moving with the winds of political and social change in the later 1960s; its completely open admission policy and continuing high standards of teaching were rewarded and guaranteed by increased financial aid from the state.

In the nineteenth century, Trinity Methodist church was a bastion of those white Bahamians not members of the Anglican Church, and it was Trinity's congregation (along with that of the nearby Presbyterian Kirk) who were behind the plans of Trinity's Rev. Henry Bleby that led to the opening in 1871 of the Bahamas Wesleyan Proprietary Institution to compete with the Anglican King's College. Neither school prospered, though the Wesleyan establishment somehow outlasted the Anglican, moving into the specially built Victoria Hall on Charlotte Street. It was renamed the Wesleyan Collegiate Institute in

Queen Elizabeth II, flanked by Prince Philip and Premier Sir Roland Symonette, receives future Prime Minister Sir Lynden Pindling and Lady Pindling, 1966

QUEEN'S COLLEGE

1885 and was formally reconstituted as Queen's College in January 1890.

QC, charging up to £10 a year for senior students and 5 shillings a month for juniors, began with 75 children on the roll. But chiefly through a lack of teachers, numbers steadily dwindled, reaching their lower point in 1904, when there were only five boys and four girls enrolled. At that point a steady revival began, supported by the Wesleyan Methodist Missionary Society and led by Rev. William Bleby, son of the original founder, which continued through World War One and the relatively prosperous Prohibition years (1919–33). A special financial boost occurred when the Assembly voted the first government grant-in-aid to QC to offset their creation of the coeducational, non-racialist GOVERNMENT HIGH SCHOOL in 1925. In this era, the school was not only exclusively white but staunchly loyal to the British Crown and culture. No fewer than 40 QC alumni volunteered for service in World War One. Through the 1920s and 30s most of the senior girls were enrolled in a Red Cross Club and almost all the boys were members of the school's (all-white) troops of Boy Scouts and Cubs. The chief sports played were the very English ones of cricket and soccer, and classes were held in English (not Bahamian or West Indian) folk dancing.

'Old QC' in downtown Nassau reached its high point under the long headmastership of Rev. Henry Dyer (1926–60), the most dynamic of the nine of the first 14 head teachers who were Methodist ministers. With English schools as his model, Dyer gave QC a crest and motto ('Henceforth!'), started a school magazine (*The Magpie*) and instituted a system of houses – Columbus, Heath and Rogers for the seniors, Barracudas, Dolphins, Marlins and Wahoos for the juniors – to generate an internal *esprit de corps* and competition as substitutes for competing with other, non-white schools.

A high proportion of the white oligarchs of the BAY STREET heyday received their education at QC. Of these perhaps the most outstanding student was Sir Leonard Knowles, later Attorney General, President of the Senate and Chief Justice, who was the first Bahamian to pass the English Higher Certificate of Education in The Bahamas – in 1934. As late as 1960, school photographs disclose that the overwhelming majority of QC students still were whites (all but two out of 80 in the junior school in 1951). The few middle class non-white exceptions included the future Bishop Michael Eldon, his sister Keva, future Principal of the College of the Bahamas, and the future historian and Chief Archivist Dr Gail Saunders.

Though deeply conservative, it was Headmaster Dyer who initiated the inevitable transformation and expansion of QC in the 1960s by purchasing its new site off Village Road in 1957, to which the school moved in 1962. With steadily augmented government funding, the brand new buildings included a hostel for Out Island students. By 1966 there were more than 400 children enrolled, with a staff of 30, and after the coming of majority rule and INDEPENDENCE these numbers steadily increased.

Despite the retention of school fees, by the mid-1970s, the student body (as well as the staff) was as overwhelmingly non-white as it had been the reverse less than two decades

Queen's College Junior School sports day

earlier. Symbolic of the new dispensation, in place of that once named after Christopher Columbus, a school house was named King – not after the English monarch, but for the martyred American black leader.

In spite of the preference of many die-hard white parents for the more exclusive and entirely private ST ANDREW'S, the *esprit de corps* and academic standards of the 'new' QC remained admirably high. Among the proudest achievements to date has been the selection of the QC graduate Desiree Cox as the first Bahamian Rhodes Scholar in 1986. The school now competes with considerable success with the other high schools in a range of old and new sports, including basketball, softball, swimming and athletics. An Early Learning Centre was added to the Junior School and at the other end of the spectrum a Centre for Further Education was established and links forged with the United World College system.

Further reading: C.V. Williams, *The Methodist Contribution to Education in the Bahamas*, UK, 1982.

QUEEN'S STAIRCASE A flight of 67 steps leading up to Fort Fincastle from a cutting in NASSAU's backbone ridge that has been an attraction for visitors since tourism began and was featured on the very first Bahamian pictorial postage stamp (1901).

The origins and purpose of the cutting and steps have given rise to much speculation and misinformation. They are variously said to have been designed as a protected access to the fort in the case of an enemy attack, and as a projected route across the ridge that was aborted half way when the ending of slavery cut off the necessary supply of rock-hewing labourers. The cutting was indeed the work of slaves, but was in fact Nassau's chief stone quarry – the source of material for the four FORTS from at least 1741 and for later public buildings and the larger private houses. The staircase itself was certainly named for QUEEN VICTORIA (who died the year that its image appeared on Bahamian stamps) but the story that there was one step for each year of her reign was clearly in error – she was on the throne for 64 years, not 67.

The Queen's Staircase, however, remains photogenic and well worth a visit. It is a favourite stop for Nassau's famous horse-drawn SURREYS. The cutting is adorned with luxuriant tropical foliage – shaded from the sun and well watered from springs in the rock – and the panorama from the water-tower atop Fort Fincastle Hill (the highest viewpoint in Nassau) is an ample reward for the climb. Almost needless to say, there are also ample opportunities to purchase mementos from the straw-work, wood carving and postcard stall-holding vendors along the way.

Queen's Staircase

QUEEN VICTORIA Longest-reigning British monarch and the only Queen-Empress (1837–1901). For The Bahamas, as for the rest of the Empire which she never visited, Queen Victoria was a remote, iconic and almost mythical figure. Remembered by the black majority (somewhat inaccurately) as the benevolent monarch who freed them from slavery, she was always visualised as the glamorous young woman portrayed on Bahamian POSTAGE STAMPS and coins long after she had grown old and squat. Queen Victoria was honoured

QUEEN VICTORIA

by the names given to the first Bahamian hotel (the ROYAL VICTORIA HOTEL, 1861, now demolished), to the Victoria Hall, built in 1887 to house the elitist QUEEN'S COLLEGE, and to Victoria Avenue, one of Nassau's most elegant new streets in 1890 – appropriately planted with royal palms by the IMPERIAL ORDER OF DAUGHTERS OF THE EMPIRE.

Most remarkably in a country that proudly achieved its INDEPENDENCE in 1973, the image of Queen Victoria – a 30-year-old enthroned in imperial majesty – still occupies a place of honour in the centre of Nassau's Parliament Square, in the form of the beautiful, twice life-sized white marble statue unveiled by Governor Sir William Grey-Wilson in May 1905.

Statue of Queen Victoria, Parliament Square, Nassau

RACCOON A prolific and adaptive mammal (*Procyon lotor*) common in New Providence and Grand Bahama, whose origins are still a matter of debate. Raccoon remains in aboriginal middens have led to suggestions that they were introduced by the Lucayans as a food stock, but if so these animals may have become extinct along with their domestic hosts. The German visitor Johann Schoepf reported raccoons as pests in New Providence in 1784, but was certain that they were descended from pairs recently imported as pets. David Campbell in *The Ephemeral Islands* (1978) stated with authority that those then found numerously in Grand Bahama were all descended from a single pair released at West End in the 1930s (along with a pair of opossums which did not survive) – remarking whimsically that 'Adam and Eve could have done no better'. As in cities throughout the Americas, Nassau's raccoons are noted for foraging in the garbage cans and dumps at night and holing up in deserted buildings and cellars by day.

Bahamas raccoon

RADIO A vital factor in bringing the islands of The Bahamas closer to each other and to the outside world in the twentieth century, radio (along with TELEVISION) has also been one of the most potent agents for cultural dissemination – as often contaminating and diluting as enriching the distinctive Bahamian culture in the process. In the 1990s, moreover, Bahamian radio (as in Britain a half century earlier) became a test case for the relative merits of state control and privatisation.

Radio communication began at the instigation of the government. Even before World War One the defunct cable between New Providence and Florida had been replaced by a primitive apparatus sending and receiving messages in Morse. By 1925, wireless telegraphy had been installed between Nassau and Harbour Island and Governor's Harbour, Eleuthera, Hope Town and Norman's Castle, Abaco, West End, Grand Bahama, Bimini and Inagua, as well as between most of the outposts of the Imperial Lighthouse Service.

The early 1920s also saw the first private radio receivers in The Bahamas, picking up signals from Florida and Cuba and occasionally further afield. The government soon moved in to exact a licence fee of a pound a year, though the number of licensed receivers only rose from 25 to 600 between 1925 and 1935. By that time, the first experiments in local transmissions had been made and the first official radio station was about to be set up. The pioneer was Harold Chipman, who set up a low-power transmitter using the call-sign VI BAX in December 1930, sending out music, commentary on a local rugby game and a Christmas message from Governor Orr.

However, it was not until the tenure of the progressive Governor Sir Bede CLIFFORD (1932–7) that an official radio station was set up, using the internationally assigned (and permanent) call sign ZNS. In 1936, the Assembly passed an act to create a quasi-independent corporation (modelled on the BBC), and voted £750 to set up a two-room station above the Snappy Hat Shop at the junction of East and Shirley Streets, Nassau, along with £500 a year to run it. An English Canadian, Kenneth Brown, was appointed manager, though he was soon joined and eventually superseded by the Abaconian white, Harcourt 'Rusty' Bethel, who remained 'Mr ZNS' until the eve of INDEPENDENCE.

The first important broadcast by ZNS was of the Coronation of King George VI on 11 May 1937. Even by the outbreak of WORLD WAR TWO in September 1939, the station was only broadcasting 850 hours a year, made up of some 500 hours of re-broadcasts from the BBC, 175 hours of local messages, news and weather reports, 80 hours of music, 60 hours of talks, and 45 hours of religious broadcasts – with no paid advertisements.

ZNS came into its own during the War, as its audience eagerly followed events in the world at large and as Governor WINDSOR (following his own and his father's example with the pre-war BBC) used official broadcasts to inform and encourage the Bahamian people. But the most rapid expansion came after 1945, as prosperity brought greatly increased funding (along with limited commercial advertising) and first the BAY STREET regime and then

RAGGED ISLANDS

the succeeding black majority government saw radio as the most effective medium for reinforcing political power. This doubtless motivated the rejection of offers to take over the facility by outside interests, most notably the Canadian mogul Roy Thompson.

As late as 1950, ZNS was only broadcasting nine hours a day, but soon thereafter it became a 24-hour service, transmitting clearly throughout The Bahamas and further afield with up to 50,000 watts of power. By the end of the century, ZNS was broadcasting simultaneously on four channels; these were mainly religious and music FM channels, with a channel mainly to serve the northern Bahamas being added to ZNS 1.

Following the 1992 change in government, no fewer than four commercial FM stations obtained licences and began operations: 100 Jamz in October 1993, Love 97 in September 1994, More 94.5 FM in December 1995, and Island FM in August 2001.

Though all stations made resolute efforts to maintain 'local content', this rapid shift to highly competitive and commercialised radio on the American model inevitably led to an acceleration of the process of cultural globalisation – some of the commentators and disc jockeys seeming hardly Bahamian at all. Though even ZNS was not immune to this trend, moves to privatise it, however, seem to have been stalled.

Further reading: H. S. Pactor, 'Communication in an Island Setting: A History of the Mass Media of the Bahama Islands, 1784–1956', unpublished PhD thesis, University of Tennessee, Knoxville, 1985.

RAGGED ISLANDS A chain of remote islets south of EXUMA and LONG ISLAND, at the eastern edge of the Great Bahama Bank, culminating in arid and windswept Ragged Island itself. This 4-mile (6.5-km) long cay should perhaps be known as Rugged Island, for its single settlement of Duncan Town is traditionally home to some of the most sturdy and proudly independent of all Bahamians. In part they owed their livelihood to salt-raking (itself a tough enough pursuit), but made more money in the hazardous and clandestine activities of combing wrecks along the nearby OLD BAHAMA CHANNEL in competition with the Cubans, and in smuggling untaxed rum and other Cuban produce into the Bahamian market. As recently as the 1950s it was said that a resident Commissioner from Nassau who was unwilling to turn a blind eye to the smuggling trade had dynamite exploded in his yard at night.

WRECKING faded out a hundred years ago, salt is no longer worth the toil of harvesting, and the Cuban traffic came to an almost immediate halt after the victory of Fidel Castro in 1959. Despite the statement by the *Yachtsman's Guide to the Bahamas* that cruising the Ragged Islands Range offers almost as many delights as the Exumas or ABACOS, few yachstmen or fishermen seem to venture so far out of their way. Once with more than 400 people, Duncan Town now has less than 90, eking out a meagre living from fishing. Ragged Island has a 3,000-foot (900-m) airstrip but no scheduled flights, depending on the weekly MAIL BOAT for supplies. The only time the islands have proved newsworthy in recent years was when they were at the centre of the Cuban attack that led to the sinking of the HMBS *FLAMINGO* in May 1980.

RAKE N' SCRAPE The traditional home-made method of making music in The Bahamas, illustrating not just the innate rhythmic and musical talent of Bahamians, but their ability to make compelling music out of unpromising materials.

Rake n' Scrape bands date back to SLAVERY times and were vividly described by Louis Diston Powles in the 1880s. Typically, rake n' scrape bands had a drum made from a barrel covered with a goatskin, a carpenter's flexible saw that was scraped with a metal file, maracas (or seed pods), rhythm sticks, and a primitive bass made from a wash-tub with a string through it tied to a 3-foot (1-m) stick.

In an example of the way that Bahamian music was a melange of African and European styles, rake n' scrape music was used to accompany the Bahamian versions of the quadrille and heel-and-toe polka. Modern rake n' scrape

Typical rake n' scrape instruments

bands use a variety of more sophisticated instruments – such as accordion, saxophone or even electric guitar – as well as the basic GOOMBAY drum, saw and other rhythm-makers. But they still retain the original rake n' scrape style.

Distinguished Bahamian musicologist Clement Bethel described a traditional rake n' scrape dance which he witnessed in the hall of the Cat Island Association on Vesey Street in Over-the-Hill Nassau in 1983:

In a corner of the room three musicians – a piano accordion player, a goat-skin drummer and a saw scraper – are all playing away with a zeal and energy that would do credit to any modern rock band. The accordion player churns out a catchy Bahamian ditty called 'Good Morning Mister Fisher,' while his right foot keeps time with indefatigable regularity on the stone floor. Beside him, the drummer, his barrel drum tilted outwards between his legs, beats out a syncopated pattern with his naked hands on the stretched goat-skin head. Beneath the drum a lighted sterno keeps the head taut. At irregular intervals, always on the off-beat, the drummer slaps the centre of his instrument with his open palm. Simultaneously, each male dancer executes a highly individualistic caper culminating in a resounding stamp on the floor with his foot. This particular action invariably elicits chuckles of approval from the crowd.

By far the most intriguing of the instruments, however, is the saw. It's an ordinary carpenter's saw, but in the hands of an expert player it becomes a musical instrument of great eloquence. With the handle firmly lodged in his left armpit and the blade gripped in his left hand, the player produces a steady, hypnotic rhythm by scraping the notched edge with a screw-driver held in his right hand. From time to time the instrument moans eerily as the player flexes the blade to and fro in his left hand, while continuing to scrape away with his right.

Further reading: C. Bethel, 'Bahamian Music: from Quadrilles to Junkanoo', *Bahamas Handbook and Businessman's Annual 1983*, Dupuch Publications, 1983, 81–95.

RANFURLY, Governor Lord (1913–1988)

Aristocratic but undistinguished Governor, notable chiefly for siding with the BAY STREET regime and helping to initiate Freeport, and for having a remarkable wife who encouraged him in a couple of important and lasting acts of *noblesse oblige*.

Daniel Knox, Sixth Earl of Ranfurly was the son of an effective Governor of New Zealand. During WORLD WAR TWO he served in the Middle East, where his wife followed him, against all the rules. When he was captured at Tobruk and made a prisoner of war for three years she became an active member of the Special Operations Executive (SOE). After the War, Ranfurly worked in insurance in the City of London and farmed in Buckinghamshire, before somewhat unwisely being persuaded to succeed the popular Sir Robert Neville as Governor of The Bahamas.

Ranfurly was out of his depth. He and his wife were dismayed by social conditions but Ranfurly did not pin them on the Bay Street regime and in confidential dispatches showed that he despised, and perhaps feared, such populist leaders as Milo BUTLER and Randol FAWKES. When protests threatened to disrupt Assembly proceedings he followed the advice of the ultra-conservative Speaker Asa PRITCHARD to have crowds banned from Rawson Square. In an official speech in 1955 he recommended moderate electoral changes and anti-discrimination moves, but did nothing to enforce them. He was no match for the wily Wallace Groves and enthusiastically endorsed the hugely generous Hawksbill Creek Agreement which set up Freeport – being rewarded a few years later when the central crossroads in Freeport City was christened (without ironic intent) the Ranfurly Circus.

Unequivocally on the positive side of the ledger were the moves initiated by Hermione, Countess Ranfurly. Finding the majority of schools, especially in the Out Islands, without any books, she sent out appeals to England and set up the Ranfurly Library Service. Even more importantly she solicited the funding that led to the Ranfurly Home for Children on Mackey Street, which went from strength to strength and did immense good over the following half century.

Lord Ranfurly was almost certainly relieved to give up his post as the political temperature approached boiling point with the emergence of the PROGRESSIVE LIBERAL PARTY as an effective force in the Assembly. He was not employed again in the colonial service, and returned to the City and his farming until his retirement. Countess Ranfurly, however, continued energetically active a whole decade after her husband died in 1988. Building on her experience in The Bahamas, she was the driving impetus behind the creation of Book Aid International, which sent out up to half a million books a year to needy Third World countries – work for which she was awarded the OBE and received the premier award of Rotary International in 1987. She also wrote a best-selling account of her life during the war called *To War with Whittaker*, and published an autobiography (entitled self-deprecatingly *The Ugly One*) in 1998, three years before she died.

RASTAFARIANISM

RASTAFARIANISM A millennarian 'Back to Africa' movement which began in Jamaica in 1930, and today has ardent adherents wherever Afro-Jamaicans are found, including The Bahamas. Though fundamentally non-violent, the movement was for decades mistrusted and even persecuted by the colonial regime, both because its ideology and lifestyle were misunderstood and, more realistically, because of the fear engendered by gangster elements using it as a shield. Similar feelings – reinforced by traditional antipathies towards Jamaicans – still influence Bahamian attitudes towards the 'Rastas' living among them, despite the facts that Rastafarianism has achieved official endorsement in its homeland, and its style, if not ideology, has been widely adopted throughout the western world, largely through the iconic status of the Rastafarian reggae superstar Bob Marley (1945–81).

The movement dates its inspiration to the prophetic utterance by Marcus GARVEY in 1920: 'Look to Africa, where a black king shall be crowned, for the day of deliverance is at hand.' It gained its name and ideology with the coronation of Haile Selassie (formerly called Ras Tafari) as Emperor of Ethiopia in 1930. The Emperor became an instant avatar and Ethiopia the promised land of Afro-Jamaicans exiled in the white man's Babylon. While awaiting repatriation, Rastafarians rejected all they could of the Jamaican state and its culture, wearing their hair in lion-like 'dreadlocks', working out their own rituals and scriptures (a partially derived equivalent of the Bible called the Holy Piby), developing their own version of the Jamaican creole lexicon, and smoking marijuana as a sacred herb.

Increasing tolerance of Rastas in Jamaica had limited resonance in The Bahamas. Bahamians' normally tolerant spirit allowed the few genuine resident Rastas to live and worship in peace. But the police were much less tolerant of the smoking of the holy herb, being convinced that the use of marijuana was bound to be connected with drug-trafficking at large, if not with more widespread criminal activity. Even more blatant stereotyping was exhibited by the equation of the wearing of dreadlocks with socially disruptive and possibly criminal activity. Such a distinctive hairstyle – so essential for the true Rastafarian – was, for example, for a number of years, totally forbidden in all Bahamian schools.

Further reading: M. G. Smith, R. Augier and R. Nettleford, *The Ras Tafari Movement in Kingston, Jamaica*, ISER, 1960; D. R .A. Mack, *From Babylon to Rastafari*, Frontline, 1999.

REGATTAS Sailing regattas were held in Nassau as early as 1831 and in Harbour Island by the end of the nineteenth century. Modern regattas, though, date from the establishment of the OUT ISLAND REGATTA by J. Linton Rigg, Robert Symonette, Freddie Brown and others in 1954. This event, held in Elizabeth Harbour, George Town, Exuma, each April, has proved so successful in fostering community spirit, reviving local boatbuilding and drawing visitors, that there have been spin-offs in many islands throughout much of the year. This has led the government to declare local sailboat racing the official National Sport. Currently there are at least 18 Bahamian regattas. Those in New Providence, Long Island, Andros, Eleuthera and Abaco are among the most important. But what is now officially styled the Family Island Regatta in Exuma remains the queen of all.

Besides frequent open sailing races, no fewer than three traditional regattas are held each year in New Providence, during the New Year, Easter and Independence Day holidays. The following are the regattas currently held in the Family Islands:

Bimini Regatta Blast	Last week in March
Family Island Regatta, Exuma	Last week in April
Long Island Regatta, Salt Pond	Mid-May
North Andros Regatta, Morgan's Bluff	June
Freeport Regatta, Taino Beach	late June
Marsh Harbour Regatta, Abaco	early July
All Andros and Berry Islands Regatta	mid-July
Regatta Week, Green Turtle Cay, Abaco	July
All-Eleuthera Regatta, Rock Sound	July or August
Cat Island Homecoming Regatta	First Monday in August
Homecoming Regatta, Great Harbour Cay, Berry islands	First Monday in August
Emancipation Day Regatta, Little Harbour, Andros	First Monday in August
Annual Regatta, Lisbon Creek, Andros	August
North Eleuthera Regatta	October
Columbus Day Regatta, San Salvador	12 October

Regatta sailing, New Providence

Family Island regattas are far more than occasions for sailing competition, often being held in conjunction with 'homecoming' excursions during public holidays. Good examples are the All Andros and Berry Islands Independence Regatta held in northern Andros, and the Emancipation Day Homecoming Regatta at the Bight, Cat Island. The sailboat races are the highlights, but there are also bonefishing contests, boatbuilding demonstrations, competitive sports and other diversions. As the *Lonely Planet Guide* says of the Cat Island Homecoming, 'There are domino tournies, fashion shows, sometimes a beauty contest, and plenty of deafening music while rake n' scrape bands scratch out narcotic tunes.'

RELIGION The Commonwealth of The Bahamas prides itself on being one of the most religious nations in the world – that is, having one of the highest proportions of *Christian* church attendees. Even sceptics who point out that the number of adherents claimed by all Bahamian churches added up greatly exceeds the entire population of The Bahamas, do not undermine the general assertion, since it well known that many Bahamians, in a literally 'catholic' spirit, cordially embrace more than one church. A considerable number are also more or less ardent followers of non-Christian faiths. Religious devotion, though, has not been a constant in Bahamian history, which has passed through decidedly ungodly phases, and at times has been dominated by persons of notably ungodly character.

As a consequence of the takeover of The Bahamas by the British Crown in 1718, the islands fell within the province of the Established Church of England (specifically the Diocese of London). But the affiliation was little more than nominal and formal. The entire colony was a single parish, with its only church in NASSAU, until the parish of St John was set up in ELEUTHERA in the 1740s. As in all British West Indian colonies (and even in England itself), the chief role of the parish was secular. Its elected vestry was responsible for local government and the ordering of parochial society, and the rector's clerical duties were as much administrative as ecclesiastical – including the registration of births, deaths and marriages. Despite the efforts of successive Governors and the Society for the Propagation of the Gospel to find worthy ministers, there was rarely more than one at a time and sometimes none, with the incumbents at best undistinguished, and at worst no more godly than their flock. Though there were intermittent attempts to impose baptism and church attendance on the SLAVES (then a minority of the population), they were generally left to their own African beliefs and practices – which had many coincidental parallels with those of the aboriginal Lucayans.

As in so many other ways, the coming of the LOYALISTS after 1783 changed the pattern and tone of Bahamian religion – largely as an indirect effect of the mid-eighteenth century revival in North America called the Great Awakening. As a function of the increased size and sophistication of the white population and its adherence to British colonial forms, the established ANGLICAN Church nominally gained in strength – with seven new parishes added under the ultra-Loyalist Governor Lord DUNMORE in 1795. Much more important, though, was the injection of Nonconformist Christianity, among the slaves as well as all sections of the white population. Some of the leading Loyalists with a Scottish background set up St Andrew's PRESBYTERIAN kirk, which, because of its adherents' influence in the legislature, for half a century enjoyed privileges and support almost equal to those of the established Church of England. However, a much larger proportion of the white Loyalists, including most of the less wealthy and influential, became enthusiastic METHODISTS, especially once white Methodist missionaries began to work in The Bahamas in the early 1800s.

Some non-whites were attracted to the 'respectable' Anglican and Methodist churches, despite the fact that all of them practised rigid segregation – traces of which lingered into the twentieth century. However, because they sought greater participation in church services and organisation, and rituals and beliefs more attuned to those remembered and retained from Africa, the great majority of Bahamian blacks were drawn to the BAPTIST faith. Their earliest pastors, such as Samuel Scriven, Sharper Morris and Prince Williams, were 'Loyalist' black slaves or freedmen who had been converted by the Great Awakening on the American mainland and set up 'Black Baptist' churches in The Bahamas – three decades before the first white Baptist missionaries arrived from England.

By the middle of the nineteenth century the Christian religion was a dominant factor in Bahamian life at all levels, with the three major denominations – Anglican, Methodist and Baptist – clearly divided and demarcated, and with fairly equal numbers of adherents. Thereafter, the three major denominations continued to dominate, but with internal variations and with an ever-increasing number of rivals – which between them attracted at least a third of all practising Bahamian Christians by the year 2000, as well as growing numbers looking for a religious life outside Christianity altogether.

These tendencies to fission, however, were nothing to the inroads of other varieties of Christian faith. First and most important was ROMAN CATHOLICISM. It started simply to serve foreign Catholic residents, but soon became a potent missionary force and by the mid-twentieth century had taken over from Methodism as the faith with the third largest following. Almost as successful, certainly in total numbers, have been those American fundamentalist and pentecostal churches that have energetically evangelised The Bahamas since the last years of the nineteenth century. Most famous were the predominantly black 'jumper' CHURCHES OF GOD. But almost as successful among different sections of the population were the SEVENTH DAY ADVENTISTS (drawing members from a wide spectrum) and 'Plymouth' and other types of Brethren (mainly poorer whites). The Salvation Army has a small but active membership, and Christian Scientists can at least claim an established presence. The Bahamian GREEK community has a thriving Greek Orthodox church on Nassau's West Hill Street, with its own salaried priest brought from Greece.

Because Judaism is largely based on ethnicity and has never been a proselytising religion, JEWS have never been numerous in The Bahamas. So potent is the demand for a distinctive religious affiliation among Bahamians, however, that there have been a fair number of converts to other non-Christian religions in recent years. These have included non-whites who have become Black Moslems or RASTAFARIANS, and Bahamians of all shades and classes who have been drawn to become Jehovah's Witnesses, Ba'hais, Mormons, or even Scientologists. At least among Bahamian HAITIANS, the cult of VODUN ('Voodoo'), with its incongruous relationship to Roman Catholicism, continues to flourish. There does not seem to be a formal witchcraft (wicca) sect yet established in The Bahamas, though given the insidious popularity of New Age cults elsewhere, and the persistent belief in aspects of OBEAH locally, it may simply be a matter of time.

C. J. Barry, *Upon These Rocks: Catholicism in the Bahamas*, USA, 1973; G. Lester, *In Sunny Isles*, London, 1897.

RIDDLES Casting riddles is a popular Afro-Bahamian pastime. Traditionally all riddles begin with the formula: 'Mer riddle, mer riddle, mer ranny-O. Mer fadder had a ting!' The riddle always ends with 'What is it?' Examples:

It has one eye in the middle of its forehead. Answer: a needle.

'Before service'

It has no end and no beginning. Find them if you think I'm funning. It is the model for a ring. And always goes round something. Answer: a circle.

It is said that adding zero does not change the value. Then tell me pray, what is zero added on the top of zero? Answer: the figure eight.

It is said that two ones only equal two. Then tell me pray, what is one with one behind it? Answer: the figure eleven.

Errytime de win' blow Brer Nancy coat tail tear. Answer: a banana leaf.

Further reading: M. C. Tertullien, *Old Stories and Riddles*, Bahamia Culturama no. 1, 1977, 2nd ed., 2003.

ROGERS, Governor Captain Woodes (1679–1732)

First and third royal Governor of The Bahamas (1718–21, 1729–32), more widely known as the PRIVATEERING captain who sailed round the world (1708–11), sacked Guayaquil, captured the Acapulco galleon *Disengano*, and rescued Alexander Selkirk, the real-life original of Daniel Defoe's *Robinson Crusoe*.

Born in the Dorset seaport of Poole before his family moved to Bristol, Woodes Rogers (the third in line of that name) learned his seacraft and captaincy from his father, himself a successful privateer in the Spanish wars of King William and Queen Anne. Married to a daughter of the distinguished Admiral Sir William Whetstone, Woodes Rogers III also found backers among the merchants of Bristol for his voyage of circumnavigation in the private warships *Duke* and *Dutchess* – which eventually made a profit of 500 per cent for its shareholders, but rather less for Rogers himself.

Though famous for his exploits, told in his own account, *A Cruising Voyage Round the World* (1712), Woodes Rogers was at something of a loss for what to do as a sequel once peace was declared in 1713. A plan to mount an expedition against the PIRATES of Madagascar and establish an English colony there did not materialise, but out of it naturally evolved a similar project to expel the even more dangerous pirates from The Bahamas, and place that English colony on a more reputable footing.

Though the Lord PROPRIETORS retained some of their rights and the new colonial project was in large part a private commercial enterprise, Woodes Rogers was the first Bahamian Governor to receive a royal commission and instructions, and his regime received support from the Royal Navy. Always a strict disciplinarian, he set up a council consisting equally of officers who had come with him and reliable inhabitants, proceeded effectively against the pirates, and defended Nassau successfully against a Spanish attack. But insufficient new trade was opened up, the few German settlers brought in either died or soon left, and the cost of maintaining Rogers's own ship, the *Delicia*, and an independent company of troops with other expenses, made the enterprise a financial failure. His own health suffering from recurrent fevers, Woodes Rogers gave up his post after less than three years.

Rogers was succeeded by the often underrated soldier-governor George Phenney, who rebuilt the fort, imported a prefabricated church (the first CHRIST CHURCH), put forward plans for an ASSEMBLY, and attempted, with limited success, to initiate plantations worked by African slaves. His salient flaw was being married to an imperious and greedy lady, who fatally antagonised the local inhabitants by meddling in government and judicial matters and attempting to monopolise both wholesale and retail trade – allegedly selling rum and biscuit out of the back door of Government House.

Imaginative modern statue of Woodes Rogers, in front of the British Colonial Hilton, site of the original Fort Nassau

ROLLE, Lord John

Meanwhile, the impoverished Woodes Rogers was narrowly saved from debtors' prison by his good connections in the naval and military hierarchy and the London literary scene. In 1728, largely through the influence of the writer-politician Joseph Addison, he was reappointed Governor of The Bahamas, with a formal military commission, a salary of £400 a year, and considerably augmented powers. He arrived back in Nassau in August 1729. Woodes Rogers found the town ravaged by a recent hurricane and a worse than usual onslaught of disease. But he immediately called an elected Assembly, which held its first meeting on 29 September 1729 and passed the foundation slate of Bahamian laws. It was at this time also that the motto *Expulsis Piratis Restituta Commercia* was inscribed on the colony's new coat of arms and engraved on the Assembly's mace.

Matters, though, did not proceed either prosperously or peacefully. Woodes Rogers found the fertility of the islands overstated, and both commerce and the flow of new settlers disappointing. Worst of all, for a man of choleric and authoritarian temperament whose health was increasingly precarious, he found the opposition within the Assembly, led by an ambitious troublemaker called John Colebrooke, insupportable. Rogers made a brief recovery after a holiday in Charleston, South Carolina, in the summer of 1731, but died quite suddenly in Nassau on 15 July 1732, aged only 53.

Besides being the first royal Governor, Woodes Rogers was to be the only one to die in the islands. The site of his grave is now unknown, and his swashbuckling statue in front of the British Colonial Hilton Hotel is a romanticised invention. A more realistic likeness is that in the portrait of Rogers and his two children painted by Thomas Hogarth in 1728, now in the National Maritime Museum at Greenwich. Rogers's wife Sarah is conspicuously missing. Since she did not accompany him on either of his terms in The Bahamas but did not die until 1732, they were presumably legally separated. Their daughter, also Sarah, died in England, unmarried, in 1743. Their son, William Whetstone Rogers, stayed on in The Bahamas after the Governor died, but perished at Whydah on the coast of Dahomey, West Africa, in 1735, presumably while on a slave-trading voyage.

Further reading: B. Little, *Crusoe's Captain: Being a Life of Woodes Rogers, Seaman, Trader, Colonial Governor*, Odhams, 1960; Craton and Saunders, *Islanders*, i. 115–36.

ROLLE, Lord John (1750–1842) Absentee English proprietor, whose land and slave holdings in EXUMA were the largest in The Bahamas at the time of EMANCIPATION, and whose ex-slaves subsequently both assumed his surname and effectively claimed his lands in common.

John Rolle was the son of the Devonshire Tory MP and landowner Denys Rolle (1720–91) who was the most ambitious and quixotic colonial promoter in East Florida in the 1760s. Obtaining grants totalling 80,000 acres, Denys Rolle founded a settlement on the St John's River near the present town of Palatka, which he named Rollestown. Failing to attract and retain enough white indentured labourers, Rolle was turning his holdings into a slave plantation, producing cattle, turpentine and some provisions, when the Floridas were ceded to Spain at the end of the American War of Independence (1783).

An ardent LOYALIST, Denys Rolle abandoned his Florida venture (for which he received £6,600 compensation) and carried his 125 slaves and other possessions with him to the Promised Land of the Bahamas – being granted five prime parcels of land in Great Exuma from 1784. With even less experience than most other Loyalist planters, he attempted to establish cotton plantations with the help of his son John. But the Rolles soon despaired of success and returned to the family estate of Stevenstone in Devon, leaving their Exumian lands and slaves in the hands of overseers and attorneys. Neither father nor son revisited The Bahamas. Denys died in 1791, and John pursued a political career, being raised to the peerage as the first Baron Rolle of Stevenstone for his faithful support of the Tory Prime Minister, William Pitt. His only claims to fame in England were that he was the pilloried subject of the satirical poem *The Rolliad,* and that he tripped over his robes and fell down when being presented to Queen Victoria at her Coronation (1837).

Far more notable were what happened to the Rolle lands and slaves in The Bahamas. Because they were more or less left to subsist for themselves as virtual peasants, and formed their own families, the Rolle slaves tripled in numbers within fifty years. Lord Rolle found the cost of providing the supplies ordained by law far outran his income from the estate. He therefore made many self-serving proposals: to move his slaves to more productive colonies such as Cuba, Jamaica or Trinidad, and even to make them semi-free share-croppers, earning money to pay for their full manumission.

For their part, the Rolle slaves (exaggerating the gist of Lord Rolle's proposals) claimed that they had been promised their freedom and bequeathed the Exuma lands in Denys Rolle's will. This was not true (no such will or codicil has ever been found), yet the Rolle slaves did forcefully demonstrate a strong affinity for Exuma as their home. When Lord Rolle and his agents proposed

Lord John Rolle

to remove some of the slaves to Cat Island in 1830, all the Rolle slaves refused to perform any plantation tasks, and a rebel leader called POMPEY led a delegation to Governor Sir James Carmichael SMYTH in Nassau which successfully petitioned that they not be moved.

The outcome had advantages for both Lord Rolle and his former slaves. With Emancipation, Rolle's obligations to supply his slaves ended and he was the largest Bahamian beneficiary from the slave compensation fund, receiving some £4,800 for his 376 slaves – almost twice as much as any other Bahamian owner. Far from bequeathing his lands to his ex-slaves, his will ordered that the five parcels – named Rolleville, Rolle Town, Steventon (after the ancestral home in Devonshire), Ramsey's and Mount Thompson – be sold with his other Bahamian assets.

Effectively occupied by the ex-slaves, Rolle's Exumian lands found no buyers and technically reverted to the Crown. However, Lord Rolle's ex-slaves, all of whom assumed the surname of their former owner, were able to sustain the claim (or myth) that these five tracts belonged in perpetual commonage to all former slaves and their descendants with the Rolle surname, or proven Rolle lineage. With the government either accepting this *fait accompli* or applying traditional squatters' rights, this claim was acknowledged by the Bahamian Commonage Act of 1896.

Ironically, though the title of Lord Rolle has long since expired, the Rolles of The Bahamas, with a strong traditional but no genetic link with Denys or Lord John Rolle, are today by far the most numerous of all Bahamian clans.

Further reading: B. McDermott, 'Lord Rolle', *Bahamas Businessman's Annual*, Dupuch Publications, 1981, 14–32; M. Craton, 'Hobbesian or Panglossian? The Two Extremes of Slave Conditions in the British West Indies, 1783–1834', in *Empire, Enslavement and Freedom in the Caribbean*, Ian Randle Publishers, 1997, 203–32,

ROMAN CATHOLICISM Though slow to challenge the dominance of the ANGLICAN and Nonconformist churches in The Bahamas, the Roman Catholic Church made tremendous inroads in the first half of the twentieth century through robust and well-targeted missionary activity. By 1953 it claimed 20 per cent of churchgoers in the colony (compared with the Anglicans' 24 per cent and BAPTISTS' 30 per cent). Even more than Catholicism at large, the Roman Catholic Church in The Bahamas went through a critical period in the 1960s, but at the century's end still claimed the loyalty of at least 15 per cent of the Bahamian population.

Though The Bahamas was placed nominally under the care of the diocese of South Carolina in 1858, the few local Catholics (mostly Cubans) had no resident priest until 1885, when the archdiocese of New York took The Bahamas under its wing as a missionary enterprise. The Irish-American Archbishop Michael Corrigan sent out Fr. George O'Keefe, soon backed up by a small detachment of volunteer nuns from Mother Seton's Sisters of Charity. Against considerable local opposition, adjacent properties were purchased at the top of Nassau's West Street. On the first plot was built the small church of ST FRANCIS XAVIER – eventually to be extended and become the Catholic cathedral. Next door, on the crown of the ridge, the historic but aged Dunmore House was in due course partially restored to become the Catholic Priory.

In 1891, the Abbot of St John's, Minnesota, allowed Archbishop Corrigan to send his most dynamic underling, Fr. Chrysostom Schreiner, for a term of service in Nassau. Having decided that he had discovered his true vocation, Schreiner stayed, was appointed 'vicar forane' (missionary priest in charge), and proceeded to set the pattern and tone of Catholic expansion in the colony. Alternating between Nassau, ANDROS and WATLING'S/SAN SALVADOR until his death in 1928, Schreiner persuaded his mother house virtually to adopt The Bahamas as its own venture, sending a succession of German and like-minded missionary priests, lay brothers and nuns in his footsteps.

ROMAN CATHOLICISM

Chrysostom Schreiner and his successors were deeply conservative and paternalistic to the point of authoritarianism. But they were also moved by the obvious material as well as spiritual needs of all Bahamian non-whites, especially those in the neglected Out Islands. Like their rival Anglo-Catholic missionaries, they discovered that many ordinary Bahamians were attracted to a religion that offered its adherents schools, medical and even mechanical help and advice, along with attractive, unsegregated churches, agreeable rituals and opportunities for participation. But the American Catholic missionaries were able to tap and focus much more financial aid from lay supporters in their homeland than were the Anglo-Catholics – whose alms-givers had the whole British Empire to consider.

Moreover, much more often than their rivals, the Catholic missionaries in the Out Islands were practical men. One typical missionary priest (Cornelius Osendorf, OSB) wrote 'I was doctor and midwife and carpenter and mason, mechanic and everything else.' Of such men, perhaps the paragon was the architect-hermit Fr. JEROME (Monsignor Stephen Hawes), who, besides building his own famous hermitage in CAT ISLAND, designed and largely built with his own hands eight churches in Cat Island and LONG ISLAND, and was the architect of ST AUGUSTINE's monastery and high school for boys in Nassau. Many of the Catholic nuns also did sterling service, as clinical nurses, visiting carers and teachers, in Harbour Island, Eleuthera and Andros, as well as Nassau.

The appeal of Roman Catholicism in Nassau was equally powerful, with more subtle social nuances. As candidly described in the autobiographical writing of Sir Etienne DUPUCH, quite apart from its intellectual attractions, it offered a non-racialist but not necessarily egalitarian environment, in which non-whites could satisfy hierarchical ambitions denied them by the larger society. Besides this, the Catholic Church gained an undoubted advantage through its educational offerings at every level. Its schools offered teaching more professional, more prestigious and more widely available than that in almost all government schools.

The expansion of Roman Catholicism in The Bahamas during its first half century was, according to Rome's own calculations, unparalleled in the world. In 1885, Fr. O'Keefe ministered to a total flock of under a hundred, men, women and children. By 1934, when Bernard Kevenhoerster became the first Bishop of the (still missionary) diocese of The Bahamas, local Catholics numbered 3,200 out of a total population of 55,000 (5.8 per cent). By 1953, when the second Bishop, Leonard Hagarty, presided over a non-missionary diocese, Catholics numbered over 13,000, out of a population of 83,000 (15.7 per cent), with a higher proportion of regular churchgoers than most other denominations. Under Bishop Bernard alone, more than twenty new churches or missions were established, while in some twenty schools nearly 5,000 pupils were being taught. In St Francis Xavier Academy for girls and St Augustine's College for boys (founded in the Priory grounds in 1945 and moved into the same complex with St Augustine's Monastery at Fox Hill in 1947) there were almost a thousand pupils by 1950, with more than twenty teachers who were either priests or nuns.

Much less impressive, however, was the record of recruiting Bahamians into Catholic religious orders. In the late 1960s, however, this trend was suddenly reversed. This was a fall-out not only from the general turmoil in the Church which saw the heated debates around Vatican II and the growth of Liberation Theology in Latin America, but from the political ferment in The Bahamas which accompanied the achievement of majority rule and the rise of an ardent Bahamian nationalism. Most Bahamian novitiates became deeply dissatisfied with the old guard of local priests (most of them elderly Irish- or German-Americans), who were not just ultra-conservative and non-Bahamian but seemed actively to be denying Bahamians the chance of taking parochial responsibilities. Beginning with Fr. Coakley himself in 1968, seven young black Bahamian Benedictine priests at St Augustine's, six black Bahamian nuns, and three white American Benedictine priests resigned from their vocations. Most of these left the Church, and some got married. This began a phase which Monsignor Preston Moss, the sole member of the 1960s generation of young black religious who did not defect, has referred to as 'a desert experience'.

Since the 1970s, the Catholic Church in The Bahamas has made strenuous attempts to move with the times, though it almost certainly has not regained all its lost ground. It has been notably successful in Grand Bahama, where several new churches have been built and a large and flourishing Catholic high school, Mary Star of the Sea, has been established (very much on the American model). General changes throughout The Bahamas have included much greater involvement of the laity in church organisation and the Catholic School Board, the gradual phasing out of the older generation of white foreign priests and renewed efforts to attract local blacks into the priesthood. There have also been serious attempts at ecumenical cooperation with other religious denominations, and even moves beyond Vatican II's advocacy of vernacular services to experiment with a GOOMBAY mass and charismatic worship. Particularly praiseworthy has been the missionary and social work among the HAITIAN migrants, in Grand Bahama and Abaco as well as New Providence – the majority of Haitians, of course, being already nominal if unorthodox Catholics (including the adherents of *VODUN*).

Further reading: C. J. Barry, *Upon These Rocks: Catholics in the Bahamas*, St John's Abbey Press, 1973; E. Dupuch, *The Tribune Story*, Benn, 1967.

ROYAL AIR FORCE The continuing link with the Royal Air Force is the most notable and noble remaining connection between The Bahamas and the events of WORLD WAR TWO.

Even in WORLD WAR ONE a few Bahamians, such as Sidney Farrington and Harold CHRISTIE, served in the Royal Flying Corps and Canadian Air Force. But many more chose service in the RAF or RCAF as their contribution to the Allied cause between 1939 and 1945. Reflecting the initial recruiting bias, the majority were whites, including all of what were called the 'Gallant Five' who were the very first to sign up: D. Lester Brown, John Maillis, John Maura, Ivor Thompson and Fane Solomon.

Among those who beat the odds and survived, the most outstanding was probably D. Lester Brown, who went on 210 missions over enemy territory. But equally remarkable were Basil Johnson, one of the few Bahamian blacks to serve as aircrew, who won the Distinguished Flying Medal and came back safely from 50 bombing missions, and Leonard M. Thompson (RCAF) who was shot down on his twenty-sixth mission in 1943 and spent the rest of the war in a German prison camp. Several Bahamian women served in the WAAF, including Rosemary Kelly, who, living in England, was probably the very first Bahamian to volunteer for service when the war began.

The closest connection with the RAF occurred, though, as a consequence of the setting up of two important training, patrolling and ferrying air bases on NEW PROVIDENCE in 1943. More than 600 air crews were trained in New Providence, and many thousands of airmen spent time or passed through The Bahamas before the end of the war. Servicing them involved hundreds of Bahamians, either in uniform as RAF auxiliaries or as civilian personnel. Those who were sick or injured were cared for in a special hospital at Oakes Field, while recreational needs were catered for in two canteens and at the dances organised by the IMPERIAL ORDER OF DAUGHTERS OF THE EMPIRE – not to mention sundry less reputable places. A sizeable number of non-Bahamians servicemen married local women, or so enjoyed their RAF service time in The Bahamas that they returned once the war was over. These included the distinguished doctors Meyer Rassin and Trevor Jupp, Peter Gardener, the founder of the gourmet restaurant *Sun And*, and one of the chief founders of Freeport, Sir Jack Hayward. For many years a local RAF Association branch kept wartime memories alive.

The most lasting and poignant reminder in Nassau of World War Two, however, is the Royal Air Force cemetery on Farrington Road, Nassau (named after the veteran flier of the earlier war), which is the focus of solemn ceremonies on each Remembrance Day. Here in a surprisingly quiet and peaceful corner of the busy city are the lovingly tended resting places of 52 fliers who perished in the wars, while in the lych-gate entrance are engraved their names and those of 56 others whose bodies were not recovered from the sea or are buried in some foreign field. Also written there are the moving words of Lawrence Binyon:

> They shall grow not old, as we that are left grow old:
> Age shall not weary them, nor the years condemn.
> At the going down of the sun and in the morning
> We will remember them.

Further reading: L. Thompson, *I Wanted Wings*, White Sound Press, 1995

ROYAL BAHAMAS DEFENCE FORCE When The Bahamas took full responsibility for its own security on achieving INDEPENDENCE in 1973, it was presumed that external as well as internal security could be adequately covered by an expanded and modernised Royal Bahamas POLICE Force. Having been regarded as a quasi-military force since the last colonial garrison left at the end of the nineteenth century, the RBPF had added a Marine Division and even an Air Wing during the 1960s and 1970s.

The question of The Bahamas providing an adequate defence against a military attack never seriously arose (such an assault was not considered a realistic threat). But events and developments in the later 1970s and 1980s pointed up the inadequacies of the RBPF and the need for a separate defence force. This was initiated in 1976 and formalised by the Defence Act of 1979, with the Force given the triple mandate of halting the transit of DRUGS and illegal immigrants through Bahamian waters, and stopping the poaching of fishing resources. The patrol vessels of the RBPF Marine Division were transferred, along with most of their personnel, and with the cooperation of the Royal Navy and US Navy a small naval base and training facility was set up at Coral Harbour on the south-western shore of NEW PROVIDENCE.

In May 1980 Cuban Migs sank HMBS *FLAMINGO* with the loss of the lives of four Bahamian marines. This disaster had at least two positive effects: the subsequent Cuban apology (accompanied by a full indemnity) constituted a recognition of the full extent of Bahamian territorial waters, and the consequent Bahamian national resolve encouraged the further expansion of the RBDF – the first four new patrol boats being named for the dead marines.

Under the new Ministry of National Security, the RBDF steadily grew and modernised over the following two decades, adding 'disaster mitigation, environmental response, search and rescue, peace-keeping, harbour patrol and port security' to its mandated duties. A two-plane Air Wing was added, used chiefly for 'reconnaissance, maritime patrol, search and rescue and passenger transport'. By the 1990s, Coral Harbour was the base for six British-built, 100-foot (30-m), 20-crew patrol ships, as well as smaller vessels for search and rescue operations in harbours and shallow waters. In 1996, a subsidiary base was established at Matthew Town, Inagua, close to the point of entry into Bahamian waters of drug-runners and illegal migrants.

However, the proudest acquisition by the RBDF, marking a quantum leap in its capabilities, occurred in January 2000. This was the delivery of two 200-foot (60-m), ocean-going, 62-crew patrol vessels (christened HMBSS *Bahamas* and *Nassau*) built in the United States at the cost of $13 million apiece. Too large for the facilities at Coral Harbour, they were based in Nassau Harbour – which at least had the advantage of giving the RBDF a more visible presence for the majority of Bahamians than previously. By 2002, the RBDF boasted a total of almost a thousand members, including 60 officers and 100 women. Its annual budget allocation was almost $30 million – compared with the $70 million cost of the Royal Bahamas Police Force, with its 2,300 personnel.

ROYAL VICTORIA HOTEL

NASSAU's oldest and most distinctive hotel; a sadly missed downtown landmark that closed in 1971 after more than a century of operation, and burned down some years later.

A byproduct of the first contract for a passenger steamship service between New York and Nassau signed with Samuel Cunard in 1859, the hotel was built with a loan of £25,000 voted by the legislature, and enjoyed an immediate heyday serving the influx of affluent blockade-runners during the AMERICAN CIVIL WAR. Situated on the north-facing slope of Nassau's ridge overlooking the main public buildings and the harbour, the 'Royal Vic' was for a long time Nassau's most imposing edifice. Four storeys high, with 90 bedrooms and spacious public rooms, its distinguishing feature was its three-tier, all-round piazza, which provided splendid views and leisurely exercise for its clients out of the sun. Its two acres of fronting garden, a green oasis in the middle of town with many of the oldest and largest trees in The Bahamas, still survives as the only reminder of the hotel's former splendour.

Though never repeating the *Gone with the Wind* ambience of the 1860s, and for much of the period only open for the November to March Winter Season, the Royal Vic was the central focus of the Bahamian tourist trade, and main meeting place between Bahamians and visitors, till the end of the nineteenth century. It was vividly described by William Drysdale and L.D. POWLES in the 1880s. 'In the hotel grounds are a billiard-room, bar, and barber's shop, all combined into one,' wrote Powles, 'around which hover, during a goodly portion of the afternoon, a medley of conchs and foreigners of the male sex, drinking, smoking, playing billiards and other games, and talking scandal.' On many afternoons a band played on the lawn, on every Saturday there were 'pleasant little dances', called 'the hotel hops', and once a year, on 22 February, George Washington's birthday, the American manager hosted a 'grand ball'.

'One end of the hotel is rounded off like the stern of a steamboat,' wrote Drysdale, 'with a stone-arched court in front, where a breeze always blows, and where from breakfast until bedtime a fair is always in progress. It looks like an Oriental bazaar. Coloured men and women, boys and girls filled the open archways. Twenty people had things for sale, and a hundred more stood in the background waiting to see something sold.'

Royal Bahamas Defence Force vessels

Royal Victoria Hotel, 1860s

'The court of the hotel generally presents a very lively appearance between meal-times,' added Powles. 'The broad piazzas, well supplied with comfortable chairs occupied by the visitors, form the auditorium. The rest of the court is filled with a motley crowd of performers. Captains of one or two sailing-yachts advertise their craft, the sea-gardens and the wonders to be done in the fishing line. Carriages – or rather sardine boxes on wheels – ply for hire, and the drivers keep up an incessant clatter of tongues while waiting. Coloured people of both sexes and all ages, with fruit, shells, shell-work, baskets, canes and all sorts of other wares, stand about waiting for chance customers … Coloured boys scramble for pennies upon the hard pavements and brick. Sometimes the crowd sing Shouter hymns for the amusement of the company.

As late as 1926 Mary MOSELEY described the hotel as 'a charming and comfortable hotel for those desiring a quiet and homelike atmosphere,' with 'a regular clientele that remains faithful to it.' However, it remained too small to make a large profit, went through several ownerships, and gradually faded, like an ageing but indomitably dignified dowager aunt. It barely survived the colonial era, for a time was used as a government storehouse, and when it burned in 1991 was completely razed and its site turned into a parking lot.

Further reading: L. D. Powles, *The Land of the Pink Pearl: Recollections of Life in the Bahamas*, Sampson Low, 1888, new ed., Media Publications, 1996.

RUGBY FOOTBALL A rugged minority sport with a devoted small following among expatriates and locals, who find it preferable to American football for its continuous style of play, smaller number of players, and much less expensive equipment.

RUM CAY

Originating in English 'public schools' in the nineteenth century as a winter sport, Rugby football was introduced to Nassau in 1963 with the formation of a club called the Buccaneers. Besides intra-club play they found opponents from occasional visiting Royal Navy vessels and more or less scratch teams of American collegians during their annual spring break. At first, the only practice and playing area was Nassau's Eastern Parade, where, as if tackling on the hard and rough pitch wasn't dangerous enough, the touch-lines on both sides were busy city streets.

Initially regarded by locals as a curiosity completely unsuited to the Bahamian climate and stony available playing areas, Rugby steadily grew in popularity, not just among British, Australian and other Commonwealth expatriates but among young Bahamians who had been introduced to the sport while studying abroad. By the mid-1970s there were four active teams in New Providence and a Bahamas Rugby Union was formed. In the 1980s a permanent ground was acquired and developed and a clubhouse built at Winton at the eastern end of the island. In Freeport, Grand Bahama, there was an equally enthusastic club and even better facilities. The BRU now oversees a continuous schedule of games throughout a season which runs from October to April. The four Nassau teams compete annually for the Nassau Cup, while all five Bahamian teams contest the Bahamas Cup. Significantly, the almost perennial champions of both contests over the last decade has been the Baillou RFC (founded in 1967) which proudly proclaims that its membership is almost 100 per cent native Bahamian.

Thanks to word-of-mouth as well as formal publicity, The Bahamas has become a favourite destination for more and better visiting teams. Particularly successful has proved the annual Easter Cup tournament run by the Freeport club. Through competition with such visitors, more expert coaching, and rivalry between the five Bahamian teams, the standard of play has grown steadily higher, and the aspirations of the players even higher. By 1997 The Bahamas was able to send a national team to compete in the Rugby World Cup qualifying tournament against Bermuda, Barbados and Uruguay (though they did not advance to the next round), and in 1998 the BRU was bold enough to enter a team in the seven-a-side tournament in the Commonwealth Games in Kuala Lumpur. Here they came up against such giants of the game as New Zealand, Samoa and Tonga, and were thoroughly beaten. But they did creditably well against Canada and even won against the far from incompetent Cayman Islands.

Winning is not everything – as the promoters of the original 'public school' ethos of Rugby always insist. Playing the game in the right spirit of hard but friendly competition is said to be more important. As in the main Rugby-playing nations, the game in The Bahamas fosters a convivial as well as macho image. Though it would doubtless shock the godly Dr Thomas Arnold, headmaster of Rugby School where the game was born, the bar is an essential adjunct to any modern Rugby clubhouse. What have been referred to as 'exaggerated precautions against the dangers of dehydration' are an essential feature of post-game celebrations. In Nassau, a favourite hang-out for players and supporters is the aptly named Australian-owned *Billabong Pub* on Cumberland Street (*Billabong* is Aussie-speak for 'watering hole') – which besides serving imported beer and steaks, shows international Rugby on TV.

RUM CAY An axe-head shaped island some 10 miles by 4 (16 by 6.5 km) in the south central Bahamas. It has good beaches, rolling hills and relatively fertile soil, but is surrounded by reefs and without a good natural harbour. Once it was home to almost a thousand people, but today its single settlement, Port Nelson, has no more than 60, mostly in government employment or serving the single small diving resort and marina.

Well populated by the Lucayans, the island was the second visited by Christopher COLUMBUS in October 1492. He named it grandly Santa Maria de la Concepcion. Archaeologist William Keegan has identified more than a dozen Lucayan sites, the most outstanding of which is the Hartford cave on the northern coast. This once contained the most distinctive petroglyphs yet found in The Bahamas, though sadly most of these were chiselled out of the wall by the owner of a private museum.

Rum Cay

The island's present name is said to be derived from a West Indiaman carrying a cargo of rum which went ashore on its tricky surrounding reef. No trace of such a wreck has been found, but there is an even more interesting actual wreck lying in 30 feet (9 m) of water just off Signal Point on Rum Cay's south-eastern corner. This is what is left of the almost new British 100-gun steam-and-sail warship HMS *Conqueror*, which lost its way searching for the Crooked Island Passage in a storm in 1861, and went aground with great loss of life.

Rum Cay was settled by LOYALISTS hoping to grow cotton with their slaves. When the cotton plantations failed, attention was turned to producing solar salt from the natural salinas, while the slaves, once freed, found the island almost ideal for subsistence and raising cattle, produce and pineapples for export. A visiting surveyor in 1856 reported that there were 900 inhabitants of whom 42 were whites. The majority of the people worked in agriculture and 150 at the salt ponds, which produced up to half a million bushels a year.

This comparative prosperity continued until the HURRICANES of 1908 and 1926 destroyed the salinas, and the people found it steadily more difficult to live by peasant farming through the years of the Great Depression. Migration to Nassau or further afield was their only recourse. In recent years a small private airstrip has been installed, but the limited attempts to establish tourist facilities have so far not succeeded. Rum Cay enthusiasts, however, continue to insist that the island possesses great potential.

RUSSELL, Oris Stanley, CMG, OBE, OM, JP

(1922–2002) An extremely capable and widely respected white civil servant, who exemplified the highest ideals of Bahamian patriotism and the principles of civil service objectivity by serving with distinction and unwavering fidelity throughout the transition from colonialism to independence, and from the last phase of the BAY STREET regime through the first two decades of black majority rule.

Son of a Bay Street merchant, Russell was educated at QUEEN'S COLLEGE, entering public service as a lowly clerk in the Colonial Secretary's office in 1940. Through his manifest ability he rose to be Assistant Colonial Secretary, before being sent on a scholarship to study for Bachelor's and Master's degrees in Agriculture at the University of Florida, Gainesville (1947–51). On his return he was appointed Director of Agriculture, going on to become Permanent Secretary in the new Ministry of Agriculture on the achievement of internal self-government in 1964. Over a 20-year period Russell made his mark by innovations in machinery and methods, the introduction of new species and strains of vegetables, fruit and farm animals, and the setting up of the Botanic Gardens in Chippingham, the Central Agricultural Station on Gladstone Road, and the Oakes Field abattoir.

With the onset of INDEPENDENCE in the early 1970s, Oris Russell was chosen by advisers seconded from London for a key role in making the difficult transition from colonial to fully independent status and Commonwealth membership. As Permanent Secretary in the Ministry of Foreign Affairs, he was crucially involved in setting up the machinery of a diplomatic corps, negotiating new treaties and renegotiating those inherited from the colonial era, and (notably in conjunction with Minister Paul ADDERLEY) engaging in such complex and delicate issues as the LAW OF THE SEA NEGOTIATIONS, the 'Lobster War' with the United States, the sinking of HMBS *FLAMINGO* by the Cubans, and the US invasion of Grenada.

One of the founders and most dynamic members of the BAHAMAS NATIONAL TRUST, Oris Russell continued to be extremely busy after his official retirement in 1984. Besides his work on the Council of the BNT and as a JP, he was much in demand as a member of important local committees and as the Bahamian correspondent for international scientific organisations. One of his last appointments was as a member of the Bahamas Economic, Scientific and Technology Commission (BEST).

SAILING For the traditional Bahamian Out Island farmer-fisherman, working the land was a back-breaking, unromantic necessity. But sailing represented comparative freedom, excitement and even competition. This was poetically conveyed by Elgin Forsyth, a white Bahamian Commissioner in Andros in 1931: 'Every boy longs to leave school and fly to [the sea] before he is twelve years old. He sees himself gripping the helm, eyes fixed on the taut luff and smoking lee, while far behind the foaming wake the sails of his rivals, hull down, are rapidly slipping below the blue horizon. With such a picture lit with the matchless colours of the Bahamian landscape dyed into every fibre of his being, what charmer can lure him to the hot briar-filled fields, the dull bovine existence of a farmer's life?'

Motor boats have virtually displaced the true Bahamian working sailboat, but the lure and romance and excitement of sailing linger for Bahamian natives in the many annual REGATTAS for traditional work-boats. These competitions draw Bahamians from all classes both as participants and as spectators. Competitive sailing of international class sailboats is also immensely popular among Bahamians, for the most part drawn either from the Royal Bahamian Sailing Club or its breakaway rival Nassau Yacht Club. Members of both clubs have taken part and won medals in many ocean races in different parts of the world. But white Bahamian sailors (mostly from the NYC) have done especially well in the skittish, shallow-draught, two-man Star Class boats – introduced into Nassau in 1941 by Alfred De Marigny (the Mauritian playboy accused of the murder of his father-in-law, Sir Harry OAKES). It was in such craft that the Nassauvian sea pilot Sir Durward KNOWLES won the first Bahamian Olympic medal at Melbourne in 1956, the World Championship in 1960 (both with Sloane Farrington), and the first Bahamian Olympic gold medal at Tokyo in 1964 (with Cecil Cooke).

The incomparable waters of The Bahamas are also enjoyed by thousands of visiting sailors. Their Bible is the *Yachtsman's Guide* originated by Harry Etheridge in the late 1940s and long edited and charmingly illustrated by Harry Kline. 'The only way to see the Bahamas as they really are is by sea, in a small boat which is capable of crossing the Banks and exploring among the cays and islands in shallow water,' it proclaims. 'Probably the most suitable type of craft for the purpose is the motor sailer, with enough canvas to take advantage of the usually fresh trade winds when they are fair, and with sufficient power with which to plug to windward on the passage east from Florida. While yachts drawing as much as 9 feet have made long and successful cruises on the Banks, 6 feet should be regarded as a maximum, while 4 ft. 6 ins. is better still.'

Etheridge and Kline nominated the six best Bahamian sailing grounds, starting from Florida or, better still, NASSAU. In respect of its proximity to Florida, its range of shore facilities and its safety (being protected from the ocean and requiring no sailing out of sight of land) first to be mentioned is the Sea of ABACO – the 100-mile (160-km) stretch of water between the Abaco mainland and its picturesque offshore cays. A minimum of a fortnight's sailing is suggested but a month recommended if possible. Most attractive of all, however, is the endlessly intricate and intriguing 100-mile chain of the EXUMA Cays, beginning a day's run south-east of Nassau, in which yachtsmen linger happily for months at a time. The other recommended destinations – all within easy reach of Nassau – are the cays of northern ELEUTHERA, the leeward bight of central and southern Eleuthera, the miniature archipelago of the BERRY ISLANDS (equally easy of access from Florida or Nassau), and the eastern shores and creeks of ANDROS, with their outstanding fishing of all sorts.

Thousands of private yachts visit The Bahamas each year, but sailboats of all sorts are plentifully available for hire or charter. Though small boats such as Sunfish are usually available at seaside hotels (even provided as part of inclusive packages), larger boats for longer terms are to be found at the innumerable marinas or through charter agents. Though rates are to a degree competitive and novices as well as expert sailors are encouraged, generally speaking the sailing clientele is clearly distinguished from the normal run of tourists by their expertise and wealth, as well as by their determination to enjoy some of the best experiences which The Bahamas has to offer.

Further reading: M. H. Fields (ed.), *Yachtsman's Guide to The Bahamas and Turks & Caicos*, Tropic Isle Publishers (updated annually); M. Wilson, *Bahamas Cruising Guide*, Dolphin-Nomad (McGraw-Hill), 2003.

SAINT ANDREW'S SCHOOL The first and foremost of the elite Bahamian preparatory and secondary schools. It triumphantly survived the ending of racial segregation, and almost uniquely continues to flourish and expand without any financial aid from the Bahamas government. Its highest aspiration is to fulfil and sustain its self-given title of The International School of The Bahamas.

Though never strictly denominational, St Andrew's had a PRESBYTERIAN beginning. It started in 1948 in the church hall of St Andrew's kirk with the Presbyterian minister, Rev. J.H. Poole, as its first head teacher. The initial enrolment was 24 – 13 boys and 11 girls. Ostensibly the school's purpose was to prepare pre-teen children for boarding schools overseas, but it owed its expansion to the growing concern of many white parents about the steady desegregation found even in the formerly exclusive QUEEN'S COLLEGE.

Within two years there were 70 pupils enrolled, including older children, and the kirk hall was far too small. Enterprisingly, the parents formed the school into a limited company, of which they were the shareholders, raised capital and purchased the splendid mansion on Shirley Street formerly owned by the rum-runner Ralph Collins – builder of the notorious COLLINS' WALL. Now a fully fledged all-ages school, with preparatory, junior and senior divisions, St Andrew's grew steadily over the next two decades, until its pupils numbered almost 600 – some of them expatriates, but all of them white.

Space constraints and the rapidly changing political conditions led to the school's final move in 1971 to a spacious and at that time secluded site at Yamacraw, on the south-eastern seashore of New Providence. Even more difficult than financing the new buildings and maintaining high academic standards while retaining independence was the problem of making the inevitable adjustments to a Bahamian society no longer divided strictly by colour but more on grounds of class. From its earliest years at Yamacraw, St Andrew's began to accept worthy and capable children of all parents able and willing to pay the high fees, attracting a steadily increasing number of the children (and grandchildren) of the new generation of black businessmen and politicians, including by the end of the century those of the populist Prime Minister Lynden PINDLING

St Andrew's School motto is 'Ethics and Excellence'. Perhaps symbolic of both its aspirations on the international scene and its social transformation since the 1970s is the thrilling picture displayed in its front office showing the crowning achievement of one of its alumnae – that of Debbie Ferguson, arms spread wide in jubilation, crossing the line to win the Olympic gold medal for The Bahamas in the Women's sprint relay on 30 September 2000.

SAINT ANNE'S SCHOOL Though now sharing ideals, regulations and many other characteristics with the other two major schools operating under the Bahamian Anglican Central Education Authority (SAINT JOHN'S COLLEGE in Nassau and the Freeport Anglican High School), Saint Anne's School has a history that is an exemplary success story – leading it from the humblest beginnings to rival in size and even challenge the primacy of Saint John's College.

It began in 1955 as a parochial all-age school for Saint Anne's Church in FOX HILL, which in those days was almost as isolated from Nassau and educationally neglected as most Out Island settlements. Legend has it that Fr. David Pugh, Saint Anne's Welsh-born rector, was moved by the plight of a tearfully illiterate Fox Hill teenager to set up a school in the church hall. So great was the demand that the hall was first subdivided into three classrooms, a fourth added in Fr. Pugh's garage, and the overspill taught in groups in the churchyard, under a now famed (still standing) sapodilla tree, and even in the church graveyard. Over the years, Saint Anne's has built up an excellent reputation for the quality and character of its graduates.

SAINT AUGUSTINE'S COLLEGE Though run separately from the many other Roman Catholic schools administered by the Bahamas Catholic Board of Education (seven in New Providence and six in the Family Islands), St Augustine's College can fittingly claim to be the flagship of Catholic education in The Bahamas.

Founded in 1945 by American Benedictine monks as a school for boys regardless of colour or class (and not necessarily Catholic to start with), Saint Augustine's moved two years later from its temporary quarters next to ST FRANCIS XAVIER Cathedral in Nassau, to a permanent home in the impressive hill-top monastery on the road to Fox Hill designed by the legendary hermit Father JEROME. In its first two decades almost all the teachers were missionary monks, the ambience was semi-monastic, and the curriculum strongly slanted towards the American system. But as the monks aged, The Bahamas ceased to be a missionary diocese, and political and social changes swept through the islands and the Catholic Church alike, the school gradually laicised, liberalised and became more attuned to a British–Bahamian curriculum.

In 1967, the year that majority rule arrived in The Bahamas, St Augustine's became coeducational by assimilating the entire senior half of St Francis Xavier Academy, which traced its roots back as far as the beginning of Catholic education in The Bahamas in 1889 (the junior half, still on West Bay Street, was reconstituted as Xavier's Lower School). In 1973, the year of Bahamian INDEPENDENCE, Leviticus Adderley, an old scholar of SAC and teacher there, became its first lay, black and Bahamian Principal. During this period, the school greatly expanded, setting up boarding facilities for Family Island students and spilling over into a range of new buildings on the flat land south of the monastery ridge, where excellent sports facilities were also installed.

SAINT FRANCIS XAVIER CATHEDRAL

While earning fame for its sporting prowess, the school sustained a consistently high academic standard, following a wide-ranging curriculum similar to that of an English comprehensive school.

When, along with the Bahamian government schools, SAC shifted to the BGCSE examinations, 75 per cent of its students achieved a minimum of five subject passes at grade C or higher – a standard very much above the Bahamian average. An impressive percentage of SAC graduates went on to the COLLEGE OF THE BAHAMAS or universities in the West Indies, UK, Canada and the USA.

Further reading: C. J. Barry, *Upon These Rocks: Catholics in the Bahamas*, St John's Abbey Press; *Catholic Education 100: 1889–1989: Gift to the Nation*, Catholic Board of Education, 1989.

SAINT FRANCIS XAVIER CATHEDRAL

Situated at the junction of West Hill Street and West Street in NASSAU, what became the Roman Catholic diocesan cathedral of The Bahamas in 1960 had been founded as the first Catholic church in the Bahamas 75 years earlier. Gradually enlarged to match the growth of a flock that was eventually to amount to 20 per cent of the Bahamian population, the picturesque original building was replaced by a much grander edifice in 2004.

The missionary church of St Francis Xavier had a slow and somewhat stormy beginning. It was the result of pleas and financial contributions from the tiny nucleus of local Catholics, and the efforts of an Irish priest, Fr. Charles O'Keefe sent to Nassau by Archbishop Michael Corrigan of New York for the sake of his health. Between February and August 1885, funds were raised, the site purchased (from a Presbyterian) and the foundation laid. Though the church was no larger than a chapel, with a capacity of 100, its building took more than a year. It was delayed by a lightning strike in September 1886 which started a fire and instantly killed one of the workmen, Thomas Mackey – occurrences local Protestants did not hesitate to attribute to the wrath of God.

The first mass was held at St Francis Xavier Cathedral on 7 November 1886 and the church was dedicated by Archbishop Corrigan on Sunday 13 February 1887. For the first few years local antagonism continued, and because of the difficulty of finding a permanent pastor, the church was only open during the winter season. It was only after the Benedictine Abbey of St John's, Minnesota took the Bahamas mission more or less under its wing, and especially during the long pastorate of Fr. Chrysostom Schreiner (1891–1928) that the enterprise began to take off. Fr. Schreiner cannily acquired further land and buildings on both sides of the church, notably Dunmore House, the former officers' mess of the garrison, which became a priory for other missionary monks and lay brothers.

The dynamic and somewhat abrasive Chrysostom Schreiner had been designated 'Vicar Forane' of the Bahamas Catholic mission, but in 1933 his successor Fr.

St Francis Xavier Cathedral (Roman Catholic)

Bernard Kevenhoerster OSB was made 'Prefect Apostolic' and raised to the rank of bishop. It was during the tenure of Bishop Bernard (1933–50) that both St Francis Xavier's and the Catholic mission to The Bahamas made their most dramatic strides. While the Catholic parochial system was extended throughout The Bahamas (seventeen parishes and seven missions being established under Bishop Bernard alone) St Francis Xavier's church was several times elongated, until its seating capacity reached 700. A tower was added and the interior more ostentatiously beautified, including a massive bronze eucharistic tabernacle dedicated to the memory of Fr. Chrysostom Schreiner.

It was apparent that even the often-extended building was inadequate, but it was not until the late 1990s that a fund was opened to raise the $6,000,000 needed to build its replacement. Begun in 2000, a handsome new basilica immediately adjacent to the west, with a capacity of 1,500 on two levels, was eventually completed and consecrated on 30 March 2004.

Further reading: C. J. Barry, OSB, *Upon These Rocks: Catholics in the Bahamas*, St John's Abbey Press, 1973.

SAINT JOHN'S COLLEGE Named after the patron saint of the Anglican diocese (St John the Baptist), St John's College is the pre-eminent Anglican school in The Bahamas. With preparatory, junior and senior high school divisions, it carries on the traditions of the former parochial primary schools, King's College for Boys, and St Hilda's School for Girls (see EDUCATION)

St John's College was founded as an independent high school in 1947 by the Anglican diocese under the direction of the American bishop, Spence Burton. Situated on Market Street just south of Gregory's Arch (on the present location of the Dean William Granger Outreach Centre), it initially consisted of 135 pupils and seven teachers, with Fr. Robert Llewellyn, a Welshman, as Principal.

Though from its early days noted for solid academic performance and sporting prowess, St John's (like the diocese as a whole) struggled financially, being especially hampered by lack of space to expand. The corner was turned, however, as part of the virtual reformation that occurred under the leadership of the first Bahamian bishop, Michael ELDON (1972–96). In January 1979, all three divisions of the College were transferred to a 28-acre site on what is now Bishop Eldon Drive in south-central New Providence. Here it steadily expanded its enrolment and facilities, until in 2003 it boasted 'among other things, three computer laboratories, two libraries, three fully equipped Science and Specialist rooms, an auditorium (seating capacity 1000), a clinic and a fully operational cafeteria. The sporting facilities include basketball, volleyball and netball courts, a softball pitch, a soccer field, and an eight lane 25 metre swimming pool.' The 380 pupils in the Preparatory Department, the 241 Junior and 226 Senior High Schoolers were taught by a teaching staff numbering more than 70.

The motto of St John's College is *Respice, Adspice, Prospice* ('Look to the Past, Present and Future'), and its crest bears the Latin for 'Behold the Lamb of God', the words uttered by John the Baptist on first meeting Jesus Christ. St John's College is especially proud of its scholars who have gone into the Anglican ministry, as well as the many alumni who have made distinguished careers in Bahamian politics and business, the professions and sports. Among the most renowned have so far been the sporting heroes Tommy ROBINSON and Andre ROGERS, after whom the national athletics and baseball stadia are named.

SAINT MARY'S CHURCH Picturesque Anglican parish church on Virginia Street in what was formerly the western fringe of downtown NASSAU. The history of the church is as interesting as its site. It is located where the Wesleyan Joseph PAUL preached to non-whites in the 1790s, before he became an Anglican deacon and a founder and teacher (along with his two sons) of what was known as Bray's Associates' School. The school building became a chapel-at-ease for Christ Church, and attracted a congregation of non-whites who disliked the segregation and low church ritual practised in the mother church and were natural converts to the more participatory and flamboyant rituals initiated by the Oxford Movement in England.

Shortly after Christ Church became the Anglican cathedral (1861), St Mary's was made a separate parish, and a proper church building was erected, almost entirely through the efforts of the parishioners. This building was destroyed by the 1866 hurricane, but within three years the undaunted congregation had financed a more imposing edifice, 120 feet long by 60 wide (36 by 18 m), with a small bell-tower. Under a succession of expatriate Anglo-Catholic incumbents (but again paid for by the faithful parishioners), a pipe organ was installed in 1879 and a chancel and Lady Chapel added in 1898.

Though no non-white or Bahamian was vicar until the 1980s, non-whites assisted at the altar, filled the choir stalls and made up all the officials of the church. St Mary's was especially favoured by the non-whites of the emergent middle class, many of whom lived in nearby DELANCEY TOWN, just as SAINT AGNES catered to

SAINT MATTHEW'S CHURCH

the lower class blacks who lived around its Over-the-Hill location. Both churches, however, were resolutely Anglo-Catholic (in the view of one Methodist, 'competing to out-Rome Rome'), celebrating high masses, requiring confession and the observance of fasts and holy feast days, reserving the Blessed Sacrament and – especially St Mary's of course – venerating the Mother of Jesus almost equally with Her Son. Elements of these social and religious nuances have survived the great spread of ROMAN CATHOLICISM over the last century and the general BAHAMIANISATION of the Anglican Church, into the present day.

SAINT MATTHEW'S CHURCH

Until the LOYALIST influx, CHRIST CHURCH was the sole Anglican place of worship in NASSAU. The eastward spread of the town, however, led to a demand for a second parish church, which the Assembly agreed to subsidise in 1800. The most elegant of Loyalist buildings, it was designed by Joseph EVE and consecrated in July 1802. Built in an eclectic but pleasing mix of traditional English, neoclassical and American colonial styles, it has a nave and side aisles under a single roof but with separate barrel vaulting, supported on Corinthian columns, a chancel and altar in an apse to the east, and a gallery and baptistery to the west – with fine windows all around. The landmark octagonal clock-tower and steeple were added in 1816, and a stained glass east window (in memory of Bishop Addington Venables) installed in 1887. The entire edifice was tastefully restored and painted pink and white in the 1990s.

St Matthew's remained deeply conservative until the death of Parson Richardson Saunders in the 1890s. It followed the austere rituals of the Edwardian Prayer Book long after the other parish churches had been transformed by the Anglo-Catholic Oxford Movement. The most substantial parishioners rented the high-backed pews at front centre, while the poorer whites occupied the rest of the nave and front side aisles, the more respectable non-whites the remaining downstairs pews, and the blacks the upstairs gallery at the back. These arrangements, of course, gradually changed during the twentieth century, as did the customary church ritual.

Since Christ Church (which became a cathedral in 1861) was completely rebuilt in the late 1830s, St Matthew's is Nassau's oldest extant church building. Its churchyard and the adjacent public park contain the remains of many Loyalists and some even earlier tombstones transferred from Nassau's original burial ground near the centre of town.

SALT INDUSTRY

With the arguable exception of fishing, the harvesting of solar sea-salt is the oldest Bahamian industry, and the only one that has been in continuous operation from the earliest settlements to the present day.

It is almost certain that the aboriginal Lucayans garnered solar sea-salt, though no evidence remains to show whether they constructed simple salinas or merely collected salt casually from seasonally dried-out ponds. From the earliest period of English colonisation the potential of the Bahamian archipelago (including the TURKS AND CAICOS ISLANDS) for producing salt – mainly for the fishing industry of Newfoundland and the New England colonies – was one of its chief attractions. As early as 1670, a Bermudian called John Darrell wrote to London that Exuma already was producing salt as well as BRAZILETTO and other woods, and this persuaded the Lord PROPRIETORS to make sure that salt royalties were included in their grant of the Bahama Islands from King Charles II.

From the late 1670s, Bermudians had settled the Turks Islands and developed them into one of the major salt producers in the Americas. It was as much to take over this valuable resource as to protect it from rival French and Spanish claimants that the Turks and Caicos Islands were formally annexed to The Bahamas and officially (though not always effectively) came under the control of Nassau in the 1760s. As yet, very few Bahamian islands were settled, but in 1781 a general Order in Council was made to regulate and control all aspects of salt production throughout the islands. This was later made into a law that set up commissioners in each of the salt-producing islands, to oversee the allocation of shares in the ponds, their orderly cooperative working, the storage, shipping and sale of the salt, and even the working conditions of the salt-rakers.

With the coming of the LOYALISTS in the later 1780s, salt production was extended to almost all the newly settled islands, especially when the failure of cotton made it the most profitable alternative way in which the owners could deploy their slaves. By 1802, there were no fewer than 25 productive salinas apart from those in the Turks Islands, producing together, it was reckoned, as much as three million bushels (or about 11,250 tons) a year. The three major producers (half a million bushels apiece) were Little Exuma, Crooked Island and (most surprising) Rose Island, just east of Nassau. Rum Cay with Watling's, Long Island, Ragged Island and 'Heneagua' (Inagua) produced 300,000 bushels apiece, and Norman's Pond Cay (just north of Great Exuma) 200,000. Small amounts were also produced from salinas in Eleuthera, Cat Island and the Berry Islands.

With the coming of the free trade era of the nineteenth century the demand for salt hugely increased, for manufacturing industries as well as the fisheries. The attempts of salina owners to increase production, however, were frustrated by the ending of slavery, since no labourers would toil at what was the most onerous and unhealthy of occupations if they could avoid it. Total Bahamian salt production fell below 350,000 bushels in 1834, though it rose again to 1,660,000 bushels in 1839 after some concessions were made to Apprentice and ex-slave workers. Another more serious blow for the Nassau merchants was the detachment of the Turks and Caicos Islands from The Bahamas in 1848. Great efforts were immediately made to expand the Bahamian salt ponds by using more modern and labour-efficient methods. The most notable effort was the formation of the Heneagua Salt Pond Company (the very first Bahamian joint stock company) in December 1849 by a group of Nassau merchant-politicians, with a capital of £10,000. In 1865 this company was reorganised by the Hon. Timothy Darling and four others as the Inagua Tramway and Salt Company, which among other innovations built the first railway in The Bahamas and improved the loading facilities at the Matthew Town dock. Production was now limited to Inagua and Rum Cay, but between them they produced up to two million bushels a year.

From the 1870s, however, the Bahamian salt industry was hit and almost crippled by competition from salt produced by steam pressure from huge underground reservoirs in the United States, and by American protectionist duties. Total Bahamian exports fell to 80,000 bushels in 1889 and to less than 12,000 bushels in 1910. The salt industry was referred to as 'an expiring trade'. Inagua became almost deserted and Rum Cay one of the most desperately poor of all Bahamian islands. Almost miraculously, though, the industry was revived at the height of the Great Depression when three American brothers named Erickson set up the West India Chemical Company in Inagua. By ultra-efficient management and mechanising all operations, the Ericksons were able to exercise economies of scale. Their enterprise was helped by the facts the impoverished Inaguans and other southern Bahamians were happy for any kind of wage labour, that Matthew Town was run along the lines of a company town, and, above all by the great increase in demand that accompanied and followed World War Two.

In 1954, the giant Morton Salt Company bought out the Ericksons, and made further improvements in production and shipping methods; by the year 2000 Inagua was exporting a million tons of solar salt a year (mainly for industrial use, winter road salting and water softeners) – more then 80 times the total Bahamian production at its nineteenth-century peak. Less successful, though, was the attempt of the Diamond Crystal Salt Company to emulate Morton Salt in southern Long Island from 1962. After investing more than $2 million they began harvesting in 1965, but a disastrous run of storms and unusually rainy seasons forced them to close down operations within ten years.

Further reading: *The Salt Industry of The Bahamas*, Nassau, Archives Department, 1980.

SALVATION ARMY The patriarchal founder and first General of the Salvation Army was William Booth (1829–1912), a former Methodist minister who started an outdoor mission in the slums of London's East End in 1865, and with his wife Catherine and oldest son Bramwell formally constituted the Army in 1878. The brilliantly successful Booth formula – open-air meetings with lively band music, hand-outs of food and clothing to the needy, participation and enrolment as soldiers with prospects of promotion – and the members of the Booth family were largely responsible for the rapid spread of the Salvation Army throughout the English speaking world by 1900.

Colonel Mary Booth (one of William's granddaughters and Territorial Commander for Bermuda and the Caribbean) first visited Nassau early in 1931, when the Great Depression was at its height. Sensing a great local need, she ordered Major Lewis, the Bermuda Commandant, to initiate a Bahamian mission, leaving a Captain Mottram to carry on the work. The first meetings were held in Rawson Square and the Oddfellows Hall on Meeting Street in May 1931, and within a few weeks more than a dozen women and a smaller number of men had pledged to be soldiers of the Cross. The Nassau mission proved so promising that Major Lewis returned to take charge, bringing his wife and family. Major Lewis recruited and trained the first local Army brass band, and by 1935 a permanent Army Hall had been built on Mackey Street (extended and renamed The Citadel in 1965, it remains the Army's Bahamian headquarters to the present day).

Under the Lewises' successors, Adjutant and Mrs Moffatt, the Army extended its operations from secondary bases in Grant's Town and at Palmetto Point, Eleuthera, though they had less success in missions to the 'CONCHY JOE' settlements of Cherokee Sound and Spanish Wells. Growth in Nassau, however, was steady and impressive. In classic Salvation Army style, the local forces took every

SAMANA CAY

opportunity to evangelise while seeking to identify and fulfil social needs – finding a particularly necessary niche in working on behalf of the blind. Beginning in a modest building on Meadow Street in Grant's Town in the late 1930s, the Army pioneered the teaching of Braille and training blind persons in useful skills – work that was to expand in the post-war years to become the Institute of the Blind and School for the Visually Handicapped on Mackey Street and culminated in the Erin Harrison Gilmour Home and Learning Centre for Blind Children on Blue Hills Road, dedicated in 1985.

By the 1990s, all four Salvation Army Corps centres (Nassau Citadel, Grant's Town, Palmetto Point and Freeport) were providing a full range of church and other services for all ages. Both Nassau Corps had a special weekly programme and hot meal for the elderly (called 'Silver Threads' on Mackey Street and 'Good Companions' in Grant's Town), and distributed regular food parcels to the most needy. Freeport alone was providing approximately 280 food parcels a month to needy families in 1999. Grant's Town had been operating an emergency shelter for women and children since 1987 and there were thrift stores in Nassau and Freeport where it was possible to purchase used clothing and furniture at very reasonable prices. Members of a Salvation Army League of Mercy regularly visited all places of detention, hospitals and other institutions to bring a 'caring touch' and to hold religious services. Individuals 'shut-in' through age or infirmity were also visited in their homes. As from the earliest days, collections were made to provide special gifts of food, clothing and other needed items at Christmas and Easter.

Further reading: R. Hattersley, *Blood and Fire: William and Catherine Booth and Their Salvation Army*, Doubleday, 2000; A. R. Wiggins, *History of the Salvation Army*, Nelson, 1965; www.religiousmovements.lib.virginia.edu/nms/ salvationarmy.htm; www.salvationarmy.org.uk/en/Library/publications/ salvationist/1999

Samana Cay

SAMANA CAY Also known as Attwood's Cay, this medium-sized, uninhabited and more or less featureless island 25 miles (40 km) north of Acklins gained a short-lived prominence in 1986 when the *National Geographic Magazine* decided that it, and not Watling's Island, was Christopher COLUMBUS'S true first landfall in the Americas.

National Geographic's decision was based almost entirely on a minute realignment of the explorer's route across the Atlantic and a questionable interpretation of his description of the islands he could see on the voyage onward from the first landfall. Determined to find what they were looking for, the magazine's staff magnified and distorted Samana's features to fit their reading of Columbus's log, and even employed Charles Hoffman, the archaeologist who had found the proof that Columbus had made contact with the Lucayans on Watling's Island, to try to do better for Samana Cay. Not surprisingly, Hoffman did find evidence that Lucayans lived on or visited the cay, but no evidence that Columbus and his crews had been there. Despite *National Geographic*'s resolute attempt to rewrite history in time for the Columbus Quincentennial, it was Watling's Island that was duly celebrated as the authentic Guanahani/SAN SALVADOR in October 1992.

Samana Cay produces one item of commercial value. It contains some of the best wild stands of CASCARILLA trees (source of a valued aromatic bitter bark) in the CROOKED ISLAND District. It is therefore visited seasonally by bark-strippers from Acklins, who plant crops and run small stock to sustain them during their subsequent visits.

Further reading: *National Geographic*, 170 (5), 1986, 564–99; S. E. Morison, *Admiral of the Ocean Sea*, New York, 1942.

SANDS, Hon. Sir Stafford Lofthouse (1913–1972) Self-made millionaire and controversial kingpin of the white BAY STREET regime during its most successful final years. Born in Nassau of a poor-white family dating back to the original settlers in Eleuthera, Stafford Sands was one of those patriotic 'CONCHY JOES' whose dislike of the British colonial elite was almost as great as their racist disdain for their non-white countrymen.

Poverty decreed that Stafford Sands was one of the very few white boys sent to GOVERNMENT HIGH SCHOOL shortly after its founding in 1925, though his parents soon transferred him to exclusive QUEEN'S COLLEGE and were later able to let him complete his education in New York. An extremely able student in all subjects, including

Sir Stafford Sands

mathematics, in 1931 he was articled to be a lawyer in the chambers of Sir Kenneth Solomon (1883–1954), then the most powerful politician of the ruling clique.

Called to the Bahamas Bar in 1935 and first elected to the House of Assembly for Nassau City in 1937, Stafford Sands had a meteoric rise to wealth and power, climaxing during the economic boom that followed World War Two. Along with the other two grandees who epitomised the 'Bay Street Boys', Roland SYMONETTE and Harold CHRISTIE, he realised the interconnection between the domination of local politics and the creation of a personal business fortune, and the financial benefits that came from privileged access to foreign investors.

As a politician, Stafford Sands was MHA for Nassau City continuously for 30 years. In 1945 he was appointed to the Executive Council, but soon resigned to take over the chairmanship of the Development Board, which he transformed into an immensely powerful and effective engine for developing tourism, offshore banking and financial services. As a corporate lawyer, Sands built up the biggest portfolio of foreign 'suitcase companies', and from his early days forged lucrative connections with those foreigners interested in setting up casinos in the Bahamas. As a businessman, he used his burgeoning wealth and influence to put together a personal empire that included the largest grocery chain, liquor wholesaling and retailing, and gas and fuel suppliers. Inevitably, he was a director of innumerable other enterprises, Bahamian and foreign.

The summit of Bay Street's power and Stafford Sands's influence came with the victory of their UNITED BAHAMIAN PARTY in the 1962 election and the granting of internal self-government to The Bahamas two years later. In 1963, Sands was knighted, and in the first Bahamian Cabinet in 1964 was Minister of both Tourism and Finance. In a brief three years of furious activity, huge sums were pumped into tourist promotion (more than was spent on either education or social services), FREEPORT was developed as virtually a foreign enclave, complete with luxury hotels and casinos, and a new dollar (on a par with the American) was installed in place of sterling.

In 1967, however, the whole edifice came tumbling down. Evidence accumulated that the creation of Freeport had been accompanied by bribery and corruption, and that Sands (and others) had been at least indirectly involved with Mafiosi in the granting of casino licences. Sands's own voracity and effrontery dismayed even some of his colleagues in the UBP.

Stafford Sands boldly stood to give evidence before the inevitable commission of inquiry; but the exercise proved foolhardy, convincing most Bahamians of both his guilt and his arrogance. Genuinely fearing the consequences of black majority rule (and already ailing), he sold up in Nassau and went into self-imposed exile in Spain with his glamorous Swedish second wife. He died of cancer within five years, just before The Bahamas became fully independent.

However, in a typical Bahamian turnaround, time has largely healed Stafford Sands's reputation. Execrated by his political enemies for his racism, greed and ruthlessness during his lifetime, in the 1990s he was rehabilitated as a Bahamian patriot and one of the founders of the modern Bahamas, especially in respect of finance, tourism and foreign investment.

SAN SALVADOR (alias Watling's Island) Despite claims of varied implausibility by eight other candidates, the island which since 1926 has been officially called San Salvador owes its chief distinction to being the indubitable first landfall of Christopher COLUMBUS in the Americas.

Called Guanahani by the Lucayans, the 50 square mile (130 squ. km) rectangular island with lakes covering

San Salvador. Celebrating the Columbian Quincentennial 1992 at the presumed landing site

almost as much of its interior as dry land, is situated at the south-eastern prow of the Bahamian archipelago, atop a sea-mount with deep water all around. Depopulated by the Spaniards, Guanahani had the name which Columbus had given it bestowed by an early Governor on Cat Island (along with the legend that the Spanish had settled there). For almost two hundred years the island assumed the name Watlings, after an almost certainly mythical pirate said to have claimed it as his personal property.

The first settlers of whom there is record were LOYALIST planters and their slaves. The grandest of the planter grandees was Burton Williams, who, with the failure of cotton plantations, managed to transfer most of his able slaves to the more profitable sugar island of Trinidad before Britain banned the practice in 1826. Those slaves left behind lived far longer on the average than those transferred, but the difficulties for slaves and their descendants of living in a failed plantation economy are conveyed by the name they gave to one of their settlements: HARD BARGAIN. A true picture of the normal life of a Bahamian slave-holding towards the end of slavery is conveyed by the only surviving journal of a resident slave-owner, that of Charles Farquharson for the years 1830–2. It was a hard life for master as well as slaves, with a great deal of give-and-take and more interdependence than found elsewhere. Farquharson had to steer a fine line between punishment and incentives, realising that he would be ruined without the co-operation of his slaves, while for their part the slaves recognised that the complete collapse of the plantation would make life even more difficult for themselves, especially in terms of clothing and food.

Today, the ruins of slave-owners' modest 'great houses' are swallowed deep in the bush. Many of the slaves' quarters became settlements of subsistence farmers after Emancipation, but they too have fallen into ruin as times and lifestyles have changed. Watling's Island first came to outside notice with the building of the Dixon Hill lighthouse to show the way towards the Crooked Island Passage into the Caribbean in 1887, and with the celebrations of the quatercentenary of Columbus's arrival in 1892. Of much greater local significance were the setting up of a submarine tracking base by the British and American navies in WORLD WAR TWO, and of a missile tracking station by the United States in the early 1960s, complete with a well-paved airfield. When these facilities were decommissioned in the 1970s, their buildings were transformed into the second Bahamian teachers' training college – sadly short-lived – and a scientific field station run by a consortium of New York universities, which lasted much longer, and still runs as a private enterprise.

San Salvador's excellence as a scuba-diving resort began to be recognised in 1975, but it was the Columbus Quincentennial in 1992 that injected a real burst of activity and optimism, reinforced when CLUB MEDITERRANEE in the same year decided to make it one of their premier resorts. The 285-room *Club Med Columbus Isle* was located on the leeward (western) side of the island, 5 miles (8km) north of the presumed site of Columbus's landing and a mile (1.6 km) north of the quaint 'capital' village of Cockburn Town (which shares its name with that of the capital of the TURKS AND CAICOS ISLANDS). With three gourmet restaurants,

12 tennis courts, splendid watersports and scuba-diving facilities, the all-inclusive resort spanned 80 acres and 3 miles (5 km) of magnificent sandy beach.

Unlike all other southern Bahamian islands, San Salvador actually reversed the steady decline in its population, which rose from a low of about 700 in 1950 to an all-time high of 1,200 in the year 2000. All was not plain sailing, however. The chief problem was that of communications. The government promised the extension and upgrading of the airport needed to bring in regular jumbo-loads of tourists and supplies for Club Med. But this took years longer than expected and was barely accomplished before Hurricane Floyd battered the resort in 1998. With the numbers of Club Med customers already in decline worldwide, the events of 11 September 2001 proved a severe blow to Club Med Columbus Isle, which temporarily closed at the beginning of 2002. Its reopening in 2003 was optimistically viewed by San Salvadoreans as the salvation implied in the name given to their island by Christopher Columbus.

SAUNDERS, Dr Gail Though she always gave credit to her faithful and hard-working staff, the development of the Bahamas Archives owed most to the person who in 2002 had been Chief Archivist for thirty years. Gail Saunders (née North) is one of the most versatile and talented as well as distinguished of modern Bahamian women. Born on Fort Hill, Nassau, in 1944, she was educated at QUEEN'S COLLEGE, where she excelled as a track and tennis star as well as scholar. Becoming a government employee as a pupil-teacher while still in her teens, Gail North was soon sent on a scholarship to the University of Newcastle, where she obtained an honours degree in history. While in Britain she was the female inter-university sprint champion,

Returning to Nassau in 1968, Gail North taught for three years at the GOVERNMENT HIGH SCHOOL, before being selected as an archivist and sent back to study in England. During this period she married the young lawyer, actor and playwright Winston Saunders, and was several times Bahamian tennis mixed doubles champion, in partnership with her maternal uncle Kendal G. L. ISAACS, Attorney-General and later Leader of the Opposition. This family connection, however, did not prevent Mrs Saunders and her husband from being supporters of the PLP and personal friends of the PINDLING family.

Besides her work for the Department of Archives, Mrs Saunders found time and energy for an almost incredible array of other activities, many of them involving Bahamian history. Apart from other also far from honorific posts, she has been President of the Association of Caribbean Archivists, the Association of Caribbean History, and the Bahamas Historical Society – serving as editor of its journal for two decades. Already the author of several books on aspects of Bahamian history, in 1985 she completed a doctorate at the University of Waterloo, with a groundbreaking thesis on 'The Social History of The Bahamas, 1890-1953'. Following this, Dr Saunders collaborated with her Waterloo supervisor, Michael Craton, in the writing of the two-volume social history of The Bahamas, *Islanders in the Stream* (1992, 1997) – the second volume of which won the prestigious Goveia Prize for Caribbean History.

Dr Saunders (who with her husband is a notable collector of Bahamian art) has been one of the people most closely associated with the long-term and not untroubled project to provide The Bahamas with a national gallery and museum. Located in the palatial Villa Doyle on West Hill Street in Nassau, this was opened as soon as renovations were completed, late in 2003.

SAYLE, Captain William (1600–1671) A prominent early settler of Bermuda who can lay claim to have been the chief founder of two other English colonies: The Bahamas and South Carolina. Sayle had already been Governor of Bermuda twice when, as one of the principal promoters of the Company of ELEUTHERIAN ADVENTURERS and an experienced sea captain, he was chosen to lead the first expedition to settle ELEUTHERA in 1648. When the colony almost foundered at the start, he carried out the heroic voyage to obtain aid from Virginia and Massachusetts. Sayle and his family lived for some years on the northern mainland of Eleuthera close to what is still known as PREACHER'S CAVE, but he returned to Bermuda in 1656 and was appointed Governor once more (1658–62).

However, William Sayle and his sea-captain sons Thomas and Nathaniel kept close contact with The Bahamas, sailing and trading regularly between Barbados, The Bahamas, Bermuda and England, and even sustaining something of a family proprietary claim over the Bahamian colony. Well-attested legend has it that what was later called NEW PROVIDENCE was originally called Sayle's Island because Captain William Sayle had discovered the excellence of its natural harbour and its potential for settlement while sheltering there in a storm.

In 1663 King Charles II made the grant of lands which were called the Carolinas after himself to certain of his favourite lords, and in 1670 these Lord PROPRIETORS

SEA GARDENS

appointed William Sayle to lead the first colonising venture there and be its Governor. Unfortunately, the now aged Sayle died a few months after landing. But as a person so closely connected with the islands, it was very likely that he was influential in the decision of the Lord Proprietors of the Carolinas to have the King add The Bahamas to their proprietary grant in November 1670.

Further reading: Craton and Saunders, *Islanders*. i. 74-94.

SEA GARDENS Underwater wonderland that was formerly one of NASSAU's most famous tourist attractions. Situated at the eastern end of the harbour, between Paradise Island and Athol Island, in an area of especially clear and calm water some 5 fathoms (30 feet) deep, it offered a spectacular array of multicoloured corals and fish. Rowing boats with waterglasses, and later glass-bottomed motor boats, plied from Nassau's downtown market range to the Sea Gardens on half-day excursions. Aspinall's *Pocket Guide* (1923) gave a typical description: 'The visitor gazes in amazement at a submarine garden decked with growing corals, some assuming the shapes of waving yellow feathers, and others those of purple fans, among which swim fishes of every size, shape and hue, as one writer has aptly said, "like butterflies in a garden of brilliant flowers"'.

The area is no longer especially visited. In part, this is because the hugely increased activity in Nassau harbour has somewhat degraded its submarine life, but also because there are a large number of alternative excursions available to extensive coral reefs, such as around nearby Rose Island.

SEASHELLS Seashells are the multicoloured and many-shaped calcareous outer casings of the almost infinite variety of invertebrate molluscs which have inhabited the margins of the world's waterways almost since the beginning of life on the planet. Molluscs outnumber all living vertebrates and are second in number only to insects. There are more than 80,000 different species of marine shells and, like all forms of marine life, they particularly flourish in warm waters. The subtropical Bahamas, with its myriad cays, reefs, shallows and mangrove swamps, and its thousands of miles of mainly unfrequented beaches, is both one of the world's most flourishing habitats for molluscs and a paradise for the shell-collector.

Historically, shellfish and seashells have been of great importance, as foodstuffs, tools and ornaments – with the most spectacular and useful of Bahamian molluscs, the CONCH, becoming an emblem of the islands. Bahamian seashells are still avidly collected because of their beauty and variety. Beachcombing for shells or diving the shallows and reefs for the living molluscs are fascinating tourist diversions, providing vivid mementos of holidays in the Isles of June. Seashells, and the molluscs living within them, however, are also rich and important subjects for scientific research into the evolution of life on earth

Bahamian seashells vary in size from delicate miniatures less than a quarter inch long (8 mm) when fully developed to the splendid and fascinating queen conch and emperor helmet, each of which can span more than a foot (30 cm) from lower lip to apex. Their variety of shape, colour and pattern derives from the peculiar strategies of adaptation to many different marine habitats and foods of the five of seven basic groups of mollusca which have developed protective shells. These five groups include the most ancient of all, the deep-water 'living fossil' neopilina, chitons and tusk shell molluscs. But most numerous and varied of all are the univalves (snails), which include limpets, conchs, whelks, winkles, cowries, tritons, helmets, murexes, volutes, cones, turrets, augers, top-shells, periwinkles, vases, olives, tulips, tellins, donaxes and seaslugs; and the somewhat less variegated bivalves (clams), including oysters, mussels, scallops, cockles and lucinas. Each species and subspecies has its distinctive varieties of colours, patterns, shapes and surface features – valued to modern collectors according to their beauty, curiousness or rarity. Apart from the varieties of conchs (which include rooster-tails, hawk-wings and West Indian fighters as well as queens), among those most prized are the descriptively named knobby keyhole limpet, bleeding tooth, chestnut turban, measle cowrie, flamingo tongue, baby's ear, king helmet, trumpet triton, music volute (with its pattern like a musical score), alphabet, crown and carrot cones, zigzag, lion's paw and calico scallops, and the multicoloured and flower-like leafy jewel box.

Many regional molluscs are nutritious and tasty (particularly those that are herbivorous rather than carnivorous) and provided essential foodstuffs for the earliest human inhabitants of The Bahamas. From the predominance of seashells in AMERINDIAN 'kitchen middens' (with the sand-burrowing, 3-inch (7-cm) tiger lucina or codakia the most numerous of all) some archaeologists have concluded that the aboriginals could not have maintained themselves in The Bahamas without this resource. Historians have also claimed that even in later times shellfish alone sustained life in remote islands during times of famine. The largest of Bahamian molluscs, the conch, has been of greatest and most lasting significance. It still provides, either raw or cooked, some of the favourite and most distinctive

Bahamian dishes, and is endowed with almost mythical qualities (especially as an aphrodisiac).

Though there is no direct evidence that seashells (especially cowries) were ever used as currency as in parts of Africa and the Pacific, Bahamian seashells have always had intrinsic value as tools and ornaments (not to mention as small utensils and musical instruments). The very first inhabitants fashioned durable knives and scrapers from shells, particularly those of the conch, and ancient shell middens, containing shaped shells but no traces of pottery, provide the firmest evidence that the islands were peopled in pre-ceramic times. By early Spanish accounts, the Lucayans crafted splendid ceremonial headdresses and tunics from shells as well as feathers and plaited cotton. Even more remarkably, they spent countless hours painstakingly grinding and drilling the minute shell disc-beads which were strung together into necklaces and bracelets (which, indeed, must have had commercial as well as ceremonial value, if not to constitute a formal currency).

Afro-Bahamians used conch-shells as horns and fashioned shell rattles for early versions of RAKE N' SCRAPE music, though it is not clear whether the inspiration came from Africa or America (or both). Throughout colonial times, conch shells were used to decorate roof ridges, wall-tops, garden paths and graves. In the nineteenth century there was a sizeable demand from Italy for conch shell to fashion into cameos, and even today there is a considerable business in various small and colourful shells for making into necklaces, bracelets and to decorate STRAW WORK, for the tourist market. Though the unsightly piles of discarded conch shells at the edges of all Bahamian harbours are telling indicators of the danger of overfishing the islands' paramount mollusc, a giant statue of a queen conch just outside Nassau's International Airport suggests that no visit is quite complete without a polished pink conch-shell souvenir.

The most high-minded form of tourism is eco-tourism with a scientific bent. As the ever-increasing number of university field trips indicates, few destinations for scientific study are more popular than The Bahamas. And no subject of scientific research there suggests itself more strongly than that of the evolution, adaptation and subspeciation of shellfish in what is an ideal (and in human terms, agreeable) archipelagic environment. The Harvard palaeontologist Steven Jay GOULD has already used the minute study of terrestrial snails in The Bahamas to substantiate his own (still controversial) evolutionary theory of 'punctuated equilibrium'. But surely, the systematic study of the co-existence of such 'living fossils' as *neopilina* molluscs (completely unchanged over the past 600 million years) with multitudinous offshoot species that have changed and adapted, either once or many times, under different ecological and climatic conditions over the subsequent ages, should present the key to a final understanding of the nature of changes to life on earth – though probably giving as little comfort to strict Darwinians as to diehard creationists.

Further reading: M. Humfrey, *Sea Shells of the West Indies*, Collins, 1975; L. Sutty, *Seashell Treasures of the Caribbean*, Macmillan, 1986; *Seashells of the Caribbean*, Macmillan Caribbean, 1990.

SEMINOLES The so-called Seminoles were an offshoot of the Creek Nation of inland Georgia, which resolutely resisted the encroachments of the white colonists, and welcomed runaway negro slaves to share their cause. A mixed people, in whom the African strain was at least as strong as the Amerindian, the Seminoles (who gained their name either from the Creek word for refugees, *simano-lo*, or the Spanish *cimarrones*, 'wild runaways') had already fled into the relative safety of Spanish north-western Florida by 1775. The connection between the Florida Seminoles and The Bahamas has often been mentioned in books, but hitherto as a story wreathed in legend. The real facts, though, are as fascinating as any fiction.

The first Seminoles to visit in The Bahamas were a party of 28 under the aged paramount chieftain Kenadgie, who arrived in Nassau in September 1819. They complained of being hunted down 'as wild deer' by Americans in Florida and pleaded with Governor Vesey Munnings for military aid and supplies. They were temporarily housed in the barracks, given provisions and a gratuity of £100 for past services, but were shipped back to Florida after ten days.

Bahamian seminole descendant, Red Bay Cays, Andros

A smaller delegation of ten led by two lesser chiefs in April 1821 received an even more meagre response from Governor Lewis Grant before being sent away. They were given a blanket, pot and pan apiece, knives, spoons, cloth and small mirrors, worth altogether no more than £10.

Meanwhile, unnoticed, many canoe-loads of refugee Seminoles had crossed the Florida Straits and established a settlement at low-lying, wooded and swampy Red Bay Cays, on the north-western side of Andros. Their presence went undetected for several years, though it did give rise to a rumour that a remnant of the descendants of the ancient Lucayan AMERINDIANS still lived in the Androsian forest. In 1828, however, they were discovered and the officious collector of customs had them seized in three batches (about 150 persons in all) and declared runaway slaves in the Vice Admiralty Court.

Further inquiries, however, determined that though a few were technically slaves, the majority were genuine Seminole refugees, including the veteran warrior Scipio Bowlegs and his family. Despite attempts by some traders to have them all shipped back to the United States or on to Cuba to be sold as slaves, they were allowed to return to Red Bay Cays, where most had been living quietly and in reasonable safety for seven years. In 1831, in answer to queries from the abolitionist Governor Sir James Carmichael SMYTH, the same collector of customs was bound to report: 'They are comfortable in their situation. … many of them have made considerable money by felling timber, cutting dye woods, gathering sponge and picking up wrecked property … several of them have through their industry and good management purchased themselves small vessels and one of them several slaves.' They had all becoming good practising Christians, had their children baptised and marriages solemnised at Christ Church in Nassau, and even built their own church.

Over the years, the Bahamian Seminoles integrated smoothly and almost completely into Bahamian society and culture. The Red Bay Cays settlement narrowly survived the hurricanes of 1867 (after which it changed its location by several miles), 1899 and 1926. But many of the descendants of the original migrants intermarried with black natives and moved into other settlements in northern Andros — a mixing aided by the fact that they were mostly of African colour and provenance themselves. Though he noted dug-out canoes drawn up on the shore, the archaeologist John Goggin reported in 1937 that authentic traces of Amerindian culture had otherwise disappeared. However, such now fairly widely scattered families with proven links to the original refugees as the Bowlegs, McNeills, Newtons and Russells, remain justifiably proud of their oral traditions and distinctive heritage as the only remaining Bahamians of at least partial Amerindian stock.

Further reading: D. E. Wood, *A Guide to Selected Sources for the History of the Seminole Settlements of Red Bay Cays, Andros, 1817–1980*. Nassau, Department of Archives, 1980; H. Flagg et al., 'Black Indians of Red Bays', *Bahamas Handbook 2000*, Dupuch Publications, 1999; R. Howard, *Black Seminoles in the Bahamas*, University Press of Florida, 2002.

SEVENTH DAY ADVENTISTS

A Christian sect emanating from the United States, distinguished by its millennarian beliefs, efficient organisation and internal discipline, and its practice (on biblical grounds) of celebrating the Sabbath on Saturday, not Sunday. First evangelising in The Bahamas in 1893 and establishing its first church only in 1914, by the year 1992 it claimed to be the fourth largest denomination in the nation, with more than 11,000 baptised members.

The Bahamian SDA Church has owed its success in part to an excellent organisational structure and to the efficient and scrupulous management of its income from tithes. But the chief reason that it has taken such a firm hold is the intrinsic attraction of its spiritual message and almost puritan ethos, in a materialist world beset by escalating dangers and fears. The Adventists are by no means alone in their fundamentalist approach to the Bible, their belief in the Second Coming or the primacy of God's elect. Yet the certainty of their belief in a day of judgement likely to come at any moment, when salvation and eternal life in a purified world will be limited to a 'remnant' of those already redeemed, gives the Adventists' version of Christianity a special immediacy and potency.

Seventh Day Adventist church and headquarters

Moreover, Seventh Day Adventists' singularity (symbolised by adherence to a Sabbath on a day regarded by the majority as a time for relaxation, if not dissipation) has undoubted social value. On biblical authority, Adventists are enjoined to regard the body as the Temple of the Holy Spirit (among other things they are to reject alcohol, tobacco and other stimulants), to observe the FAMILY as sacred, and to espouse the concepts of the brotherhood of man and stewardship, as well as the notion of donating at least a tenth of one's income to the cause. A final benefit promised by SDA theology is that redemption is possible at any time to the truly penitent, however late in life. This doctrine (at the risk of sounding flippant) may even have a special appeal to politicians. Notable converts to Seventh Day Adventism as they approached death were two of the greatest of all Bahamian politicians (often opponents in the political arena), Sir Lynden PINDLING in 1996 and Sir Randol FAWKES in 1999.

Further reading: G. Land (ed.), *Adventism in America: A History*, Eerdmans, 1986; www.bahamasconference.org

SHARKS Despite centuries of being fished for their oil and skins and hunted as hated predators, at least 15 species of shark are still to be found in Bahamian waters. Of these, the most common are the nurse, tiger, Caribbean reef, lemon and blacktip species. The sinister-looking hammerhead and the notorious great white are much rarer, and the huge whale shark – fiercest of all – is almost unknown.

Primitive creatures with cartilage instead of bone, who must keep in constant motion not so much in search of prey but to aerate their gills, sharks are the natural lords of the oceanic feeding chain and thus an essential feature of the ecological balance of the underwater world. It is perhaps for this reason that they have been both feared and hunted by man, much like the lords of the jungle and savannah that are the obsessive prey of rich game hunters. The symbiotic relationship between man and shark, however, has not yet attracted the portentous philosophising of Ernest Hemingway's African safari stories or the Nobel Prize-winning *The Old Man and the Sea*, let alone an equivalent of Herman Melville's great *Moby Dick*. Instead we only have Peter Benchley's book and Steven Spielberg's 1975 film *Jaws*.

With good reason, sharks normally avoid human beings. But being naturally voracious and equipped with low-power brains, they are quite easily attracted by cut and bloody bait, and even driven into a feeding frenzy so indiscriminate that they will savage each other. The *Lonely Planet Guide* insists that 'more people are killed in The

Reef shark

Bahamas by falling coconuts than by sharks', while at the same time avidly advertising the numerous shark dive operations that only exist because of tourists' will to flirt with the obvious danger.

The potential of feeding sharks as a tourist spectacle was discovered almost by accident when visitors were drawn to view the furious mayhem generated by the daily disposal of chicken entrails from the poultry farm at Hatchet Bay, ELEUTHERA in the 1960s. Gradually, close-up shark-watching by scuba-diving tourists became the Bahamian equivalent of extreme skateboarding, sky-diving and bungee-jumping. By 2000 there were such shark-viewing operations on every major tourist island. Most notable were those run by the STELLA MARIS resort on Long Island, by Coral Divers on western NEW PROVIDENCE, by the Underwater Explorers' Society (UNEXSO) at Freeport, GRAND BAHAMA (at $140 dollars a dive), and at WALKER'S CAY in northern ABACO. Much more responsibly, the Walker's Cay 'Shark Rodeo' is run in conjunction with serious scientific study of shark behaviour entitled the Apex Predator Project, under the auspices of the Aquarium of the Americas in New Orleans, the US National Fisheries Service, the University of Miami and the BAHAMAS NATIONAL TRUST. The University of Miami also undertakes important shark research at its oceanographic centre in BIMINI, which is the successor of the long-established Lerner Marine Laboratory.

Further reading: J. Stafford-Deitsch, *Sharks of Florida, Bahamas & Caribbean*, Aqua Press, 2000.

SHIP REGISTRATION Outdoing such long-established 'flags of convenience' countries as Panama, Honduras and Liberia (offering softer regulations and lower fees), The Bahamas by the year 2000 had the world's third largest registered fleet. Though usually portrayed as a dazzling success, and of undoubted financial benefit to the Bahamian treasury, this development is not without its questionable aspects and threatens even greater long-term problems.

Registration in The Bahamas of non-Bahamian ships was first made possible by the Merchant Shipping Act of 1976. But it really took off after the FREE NATIONAL MOVEMENT came to power in 1992. The key event was the creation of the Bahamas Maritime Authority, which started operations in July 1995. The BMA was described as 'a semi-autonomous, government-owned corporation, specifically designed to be responsive to the needs of the maritime market place'. Though emphasising the strategic location, excellent legal, banking, communications and port facilities of The Bahamas, the BMA was headquartered in London and headed by highly experienced professionals who were mainly British, with an international roster of licensed inspectors who eventually numbered 330, stationed in 200 ports throughout the world.

The advantages which the BMA offered international shipowners and operators included what were said to be highly competitive fees, the absence of most forms of taxation, efficient communications and speedy paperwork. The chief drawing cards, however, were inspection and licensing requirements that met but did not exceed internationally acceptable norms, and what was nicely described as 'crewing flexibility'. The latter allowed the employment of officers from anywhere in the world as long as they were certified by internationally recognised agencies, and positively encouraged the recruitment of crew from countries where wages were low and union membership not obligatory.

Ships accepted for registration had to be of at least 1,600 gross tons and were supposed to be no more than 12 years old – though in the latter case exceptions could be made subject to more frequent and rigorous inspections and approval by the Bahamas Ministry of Transportation. The initial registration fees were relatively higher than the competition, but annual fees were lower, and all fees were capped for vessels exceeding 25,000 tons. These factors not only skewed the registration towards very large vessels, but meant that the financial benefit to The Bahamas, while splendid during the period of expansion, was bound to taper off thereafter. Thus, while the FNM government could convincingly claim to have generated $48 million in registration fees between 1995 and 2000, the PROGRESSIVE LIBERAL PARTY which succeeded the FNM in 2002 could look forward to an annual income of no more than $6 million from that source.

By the year 2000, The Bahamas could boast a registered fleet of some 1,500 vessels, totalling more than 32 million gross tonnage. The ships carrying the Bahamian flag included many giant supertankers and ore carriers, some of the largest container and general cargo vessels, and a high proportion of the rapidly expanding number of passenger cruise liners – many of which were indeed plying Bahamian waters and stopping off at Nassau, Freeport and sundry small Family Islands.

In its publicity the BMA proudly claimed that its mission was 'based on its commitment to the ship owner, the safety of seafarers and ships, the marine environment, and service to the global maritime community'. While the first and last of these assertions were indubitable, the validity of the second and third was more open to question. This was cruelly borne out by three catastrophes involving Bahamas-registered ships that occurred in the single month of November 2002. The first was the loss of the huge single-hulled oil-tanker *Prestige*, which split in two and sank off northern Spain, depositing much of its 70,000 tons of crude oil along the fish-rich shores of Galicia. The second was the sinking of the Korean-owned but Bahamas-registered *Hual* off the coast of Japan, with the loss of its cargo of 4,000 cars and other vehicles, worth $82 million. Even more damaging was the simultaneous outbreak of gastrointestinal disease among hundreds of passengers on several of the cruise ships of two of the companies registering their vessels in The Bahamas. This not only led to the withdrawal of ships from service for complete disinfection but raised the tourism-damping spectre of possible terrorist instigation.

SHIRLEY, Governor William (1694–1771) With the exception of WOODES ROGERS, William Shirley was the most distinguished and forceful of the pre-Loyalist Governors of The Bahamas (1758–68). English-born and trained in the law, he migrated to Massachusetts in the 1720s. There he rose swiftly through the official ranks to become successively Governor of Massachusetts and New England and Commander-in-Chief of all British North American armed forces. During the Austrian Succession War he was responsible for the capture of Louisburg from the French (1745), and in 1754 with Benjamin Franklin and others came close to uniting the Thirteen Colonies in a confederation to remove the French threat altogether. On the outbreak of the Seven Years' War, though, he was held responsible for the loss of Fort Oswego, relieved of his post and demoted far down the scale to be Governor of The Bahamas.

Though already in his sixties, William Shirley brought all his energy and experience to bear in his lowlier post – as well as the zeal of a committed British imperialist. Thanks to the position of The Bahamas across the supply lines to Santo Domingo and Cuba, and Britain's command of the sea, PRIVATEERS and Royal Navy captains brought a flood of captured French and Spanish vessels to be adjudicated in Nassau's Vice Admiralty Court until the end of the War, reaching a peak after the British capture of Havana in 1762.

Thanks to the wartime prosperity, Nassau grew and flourished as never before. The population, including new slaves, increased by half. The town was resurveyed and swamps drained to east and west. New streets were laid out and new houses sprang up – most notably along the residential thoroughfare parallel to East Bay Street which Shirley planned and which still bears his name. Under William Shirley's masterful leadership many important laws were passed, most importantly the comprehensive social ordinance entitled the 'Act for governing of Negroes, Mulattoes and Indians' (1767).

William Shirley also had grandiose plans for the entire colony. He instigated the expulsion of the French from Grand Turk in 1764 and was behind the incorporation of the Turks and Caicos Islands under Nassau in 1766. The giving back of Cuba to Spain in the Treaty of Paris (1763), though, was a disappointment to staunch imperialists, and the inevitable postwar deflation affected both the colony and its Governor. Shirley had already made enemies on the mainland, if not in Nassau, when he sacked the Vice Admiralty Judge Samuel Gambier for being too kind to Americans involved in the clandestine Monte Christi trade with Britain's enemies during the war, and he shared in the unpopularity of the British authorities when the Stamp Act was imposed in 1766. This was mitigated somewhat when the Stamp Act was repealed and Shirley endorsed the proposal to make both Nassau and Grand Turk free ports in the following year. But by now William Shirley was both old and ailing. Pleading 'an inveterate scurvy', he retired, not to England, but to Roxbury, Massachusetts, where he died in 1771.

Further reading: Craton and Saunders, *Islanders*, i. 137–76.

SISAL The agave plant from which sisal hemp fibre is processed, mainly for making rope, is ideally suited to the subtropical climate and rocky soils of The Bahamas. For 30 years (1889–1919), sisal plantations promised a useful boost to the economy of the impoverished islands, only to prove one more disappointment, for reasons beyond local, or even imperial, control. As usual too, it was the ordinary black workers and small peasant cultivators who suffered even more than the large-scale planters.

The energetic Colonial Secretary Charles R. Nesbitt first argued for the potential of sisal and imported the first agave plants from the Yucatan, in 1845. But it was not until the governorship of the relatively progressive Sir Ambrose Shea (1889–94) that much was done about its systematic cultivation. A commission was set up, which explored methods of cultivation and processing in Mexico and conditions in the world market. It calculated that sisal hemp could be produced for £12 a ton, which suggested a handsome profit, given that the United States did not produce its own supply and charged no import duty, and that current market prices were between £20 and £25 a ton.

Sir Ambrose Shea realistically recognised that efficient production demanded large plantations and factories, and thus required substantial investors. But production was labour intensive at a time when the most suitable areas were underpopulated. Mills could strip the spiny leaves, speed the soaking ('retting') and drying of the fibrous cores, and comb and bale the resultant fibre. But each stage required a fair number of workers, not to mention the labour needed for clearing and preparing the ground, planting, tending the plants, and cutting and carrying the leaves to the factory and the bales of sisal hemp to the dock.

Perhaps disingenuously, Shea proposed an arrangement that, he claimed, would be beneficial to large investors and peasant farmers alike. At Shea's behest, acts were passed which set a stiff duty of 20 per cent on imported hemp and a bounty of a penny a pound on all hemp produced locally within the first five years. At the same time,

Agave (sisal) plantation, Andros, from a postcard, early 1900s

SLAVERY

outside investors were offered huge acreages of Crown land virtually free, provided they set up a factory, while 'small settlers' were offered 10-acre plots at 5 shillings an acre on adjacent land, as long as they grew agave plants for process in the nearby factory and provided labour for the plantation. This plan received strong approval from the dynamic Conservative Secretary of State for the Colonies, Joseph Chamberlain.

As sisal hemp prices soared during the Spanish–American War (which cut off supplies from Cuba, Puerto Rico and the Philippines) and the Boer War (which produced a surge in demand by the British army) a considerable number of investors took up Shea's invitation – the most notable being Joseph Chamberlain himself, who sent his son Neville (the future British Prime Minister) to manage the family's 20,000 acre plantation in northern Andros. By 1902 there were 14 processing mills in Andros, Abaco and Eleuthera, producing almost 1,000 tons for export, valued at more than £37,000.

Things then began to go wrong. Agave cultivation, processing and shipping proved more tricky than expected. Too few small settlers took up the offer of land, and those who did found little time or incentive to grow their own plants and felt exploited as labourers by the plantation owners. Worst of all, the price of sisal hemp began to fall as Cuba, Puerto Rico and the Philippines resumed production, now under the protective umbrella of the United States. In 1940, Neville Chamberlain told his successor Winston Churchill that the tribulations he had suffered as Prime Minister reminded him of the hard times and disappointments he had endured as a young man trying to make a success of his father's sisal plantation in Andros.

Prospects revived temporarily with the increase in demand and higher prices during World War One. But the postwar years reversed the trend, with strong competition ironically now coming also from other parts of the British Empire, especially India and East Africa. All Bahamian sisal plantations had closed down by the mid-1920s. A final blow even to small-scale production for export was the gradual substitution of synthetic for natural fibres in the making of rope from the 1930s onwards.

However, the disappearance of sisal plantations and the ending of a viable market for cordage hemp was not quite the end of sisal cultivation in The Bahamas. Grown on a much smaller scale, or more casually culled from the remnants of former plantations, it was processed for a long time by peasant farmers in the Family Islands to provide the raw material for sturdy bags, hats and mats – mainly for sale to tourists. By the 1990s though, few islanders were willing to engage in such strenuous and ill-rewarded work, the demand in the tourist market had far outstripped local supply, and nearly all sisal fibre now came in from Haiti.

SLAVERY Unlike the major British West Indian colonies The Bahamas never developed a successful plantation economy. Yet black slaves came to constitute three-quarters of the population before slavery ended in 1838. These factors determined that while The Bahamas exhibited most of the classic characteristics of a slave society (that is, a society that is essentially shaped by the institution of slavery, with a slave majority), it was one that was subtly distinct, not just in its form and degree of severity, but in its post-EMANCIPATION and modern legacies.

A few black slaves accompanied the first white settlers from Bermuda in the seventeenth century, and by the middle of the eighteenth century slaves were sufficiently numerous for the Bahamian Assembly to copy the slave laws of other colonies in the region, where slaves made up as much as 90 per cent of the population. These laws were based on the convenient fiction that slaves were chattels, things not persons, and that they could therefore be bought, sold, bequeathed or shifted without restriction, and could be punished inhumanely without legal recourse. Though miscegenation (almost exclusively between free males and slave women) was common, the door against manumission was almost closed by the provision that children took the status of their mothers, not fathers. Laws against any form of resistance were especially draconian; for example, threatening non-white freedmen who harboured runaways with re-enslavement.

It seems that the first Bahamian slave laws were stricter on paper than in reality. But controls tightened during the last two decades of the eighteenth century; first, as LOYALIST refugees arrived in The Bahamas with their slaves after the end of the American War of Independence and attempted to set up COTTON plantations much like those they had left behind on the mainland; and secondly, once the French and Haitian revolutions threatened to extend their influence to The Bahamas. Even when the cotton plantations failed, the threat of revolutionary insurrection faded, and popular anti-slavery sentiments began to carry weight with the imperial government, the remaining Bahamian slave-owners hung on to the vestiges of the slavery system and their slave property as long as they could, resisting all changes in the system through their proudly self-legislating assembly as adamantly as any true West Indian plantocrats.

Abolitionists' view of a slave sale (rare in The Bahamas)

Besides appealing to the almost sacred principle of property rights and their long-established right to make their own laws (and, more subtly, to the belief common among whites that Africans were natural slaves), the Bahamian slave-owners claimed that their version of slavery was relatively benign and that their slaves were generally content – myths, incidentally, long sustained by the slave-owners' descendants. The truth was very different, and far more complex. The factors that made Bahamian slave conditions less harsh in some respects than elsewhere were largely fortuitous and stemmed more from the owners' self-interest than from changes in imperial or local government policy. Bahamian masters did work their slaves hard whenever they could (notably at the SALT-pans), could be as cruel as their counterparts elsewhere, and used force whenever necessary to keep their slaves in order. They also carried out a 30-year, and ultimately successful, rearguard campaign to retain the essential status quo.

Once the Bahamian cotton plantations failed and many of the would-be planters left The Bahamas it became convenient for most of the remaining owners to allow their slaves to become virtually self-sufficient peasant farmers, and to enter the market economy and wage-market at least partially on their own behalf. Because the majority were not worked under the whip, grew much of their own food, lived in a relatively healthy environment, and (mainly through their own choice) stayed in close-knit family units, Bahamian slaves increased steadily in numbers and lived on the average much longer than those on West Indian plantations. Some owners also capitalised on their slave property by allowing those exceptional slaves who had earned enough money to buy their freedom, so that the last decade of slavery saw a substantial rise in the number of manumissions. Even this was turned to the advantage of the master class. In the very last stage of slavery Bahamian freedmen were awarded significant social, legal and political concessions, aimed at making them into a middling class to act as a buffer between the ruling whites and the soon to be emancipated black slaves.

For their part, the slaves did the best they could in the circumstances to make a life of their own. They inventively played on the masters' will to leave them to their own devices, while at the same time taking advantage of the provisions, clothing and other supplies which their owners were required by law to give them. Though adept at minor forms of non-cooperation, Bahamian slaves shied from open resistance. This was not just because of the difficulties of organising themselves but from the realisation that such action would be counter-productive. This was borne out even by the limited success of the most notable exception to the rule: the 1831 protest by the Exumian slaves of Lord ROLLE known as POMPEY'S REBELLION. The reputedly liberal Governor Sir James Carmichael SMYTH was prepared to concede to the slaves' main complaint and ensure that they would not be moved from their customary family homes and grounds. But he was unable to prevent Pompey and his followers from being imprisoned and whipped, and was so convinced by the regime's alarmism that he sent troops from the garrison down to EXUMA to keep the overly independent slaves of Lord Rolle in line.

The subsequent transfer of Carmichael Smyth from The Bahamas to British Guiana was locally seen as a victory for the white regime. Even more important was the tactical decision of the Assembly to accept the inevitable and pass the echoing legislation nominally emancipating the slaves. Thereby they not only obtained the proffered bait of financial compensation for the slaves and the transitional use of their labour under the system of Apprenticeship, but ensured the continuance of the right of self-legislation. As a consequence, as shown elsewhere (see EMANCIPATION) the Bahamian slave-owning class was able to manage the transition from slavery to ostensible freedom in such a way that they retained socio-economic power for another 130 years. The ex-slaves and their descendants were left politically powerless, educationally and economically neglected, and burdened with a psychological legacy that included political inertia, dependency and a form of inferiority complex that has been called the 'BLACK CRAB' MENTALITY. Though the Bahamian descendants of slaves demonstrated great

SMYTH, Governor Sir James Carmichael

endurance, adaptability and inventiveness, true freedom did not dawn until the coming of black majority rule in 1967, and the full liberation of the Bahamian spirit did not occur until after the achievement of national INDEPENDENCE in 1973.

Further reading: Craton and Saunders, *Islanders*, vol i; G. Saunders, *Slavery in the Bahamas*, Nassau, 1985.

SMYTH, Governor Sir James Carmichael (1779–1838) Soldier Governor (1828–33) during the stormy period preceeding slave EMANCIPATION.

One of ten children, Smyth made his own way in the world and earned distinction as an officer in the Royal Engineers. He was with Sir John Moore on his famous retreat to Corunna (1808) and on Wellington's staff at the Battle of Waterloo (1815). Made a baronet through Wellington's patronage and rising to the rank of Major-General, he did important work on the fortifications in the West Indies and the Canada–United States border before being appointed Governor of The Bahamas in May 1828.

Always a dutiful officer, Smyth arrived with instructions to ameliorate the conditions of the slaves and LIBERATED AFRICANS, but found the slave-holding planters and merchants who dominated the legislature in truculent mood. Crises occurred over the flogging of female slaves, especially those involved in the revolt led by the Exumian slave POMPEY (1830). Smyth sacked an assistant judge and the chief police magistrate, demanded the suspension of a particularly cruel Assemblyman, and twice dissolved the Assembly when it proved recalcitrant and disrespectful – ruling the colony without its assistance for the last year of his tenure. The Liberated Africans' settlements (the chief of which was named Carmichael after himself) he organised like military cantonments, providing them with schools and chapels and each head of household with a market garden.

Carmichael Smyth's regime sharply divided the colony, being as popular with the unfree as it was detested by the oligarchy. The Colonial Office was bombarded with counter-petitions, praising him and asking for his removal. The latter were officially rejected, but perhaps in the hope of pacification, Smyth was promoted to be Governor of British Guiana in June 1833, just a year before the slaves were scheduled to be freed.

In British Guiana, Smyth was much more successful than in The Bahamas, garnering respect on all sides for the firm but tactful way in which he oversaw the transition from slavery to emancipation. When he died suddenly of a fever in March 1838 (at the age of 59) he was universally mourned. A statue, by the well-known artist Chantrey, was raised in Georgetown in his honour, paid for by public subscription. No such commemoration was made in Nassau. Coincidentally, however, it was Governor Carmichael Smyth who in 1830 was responsible for raising the striking statue of Christopher COLUMBUS which still stands on the steps in front of GOVERNMENT HOUSE in Nassau.

Further reading: J. M. Wright, 'History of the Bahama Islands, with a Special Study of the Abolition of Slavery in the Colony', in G. Shattuck (ed.), *The Bahama Islands*, Geographical Society of Baltimore, 1905.

SNAKES

There is a fairly rich variety of snake species in The Bahamas, none of which are harmful and some of which are positively beneficial to humans. Their harmlessness and usefulness however have not prevented them having a bad reputation in folk mythology and being usually slaughtered on sight.

Snakes, like other fauna, colonised The Bahamas by way of land bridges during the last Ice Ages. Already divided into distinct genera and species, once isolated on separate islands they developed over the millennia into subspecies, some of them endemic to such small habitats as the BIMINIS, CROOKED ISLAND and ACKLINS, and the RAGGED ISLANDS. For example, the commonest, largest and most misunderstood of Bahamian snakes, the fowl snake (genus *Epicrates*), has three species, and no less than eight local subspecies.

Bahamian fowl snakes are boa constrictors, descended from ancient South American stock. Their long survival has been aided in part by the fact that their young are born live and soon forage for themselves, not hatched from vulnerable eggs. Left alone, fowl snakes can live for

Bahamian boa constrictor

decades and grow to 6 feet (2 m) or more in length, but few are so fortunate. Apart from cats and dogs, their worst modern enemy is humankind. Many Bahamians – infused with the biblical image of the Serpent or some deeper antipathy – believe that they can hypnotise, like to sleep with babies and steal their milk, are venomous, and most of all, evil! These beliefs, all unfounded, lead them to be savagely killed whenever possible.

A fascinating cousin of the Bahamian fowl snake, and somewhat less threatened because of its reclusive nature and diminutive size, is the foot-long (30 cm) Bahamian pygmy boa (*Trophidohis canus*). Found in concealed damp areas, like the fowl snake it has subspeciated over its wide but scattered range in The Bahamas, from CAY SAL and Bimini to INAGUA. The prettiest, as well as least threatening of Bahamian snakes, its adults have a distinctive black and grey checkerboard marking, while young specimens have conspicuous orange-tipped tails. Pygmy boas have the unique characteristic of bleeding through their eyes when under stress – thought to be a mechanism to convince predators that they are dead and not good eating.

Two other Bahamian snakes are of great interest. Smallest and most reclusive of all is the 5-inch (12 cm) Bahamian worm snake (*Tryphlops biminiensis*). Living under the soil or in rotten wood, and feeding on insect larvae, ants and termites, this tiny serpent is easily mistaken for the creature after which it is named. Though no faster moving than an earthworm, and with only vestigial eyes, it is so un-snakelike that some specialists have categorised it as a legless form of underground lizard. The swift-moving brown racer (*Alsophis vudii*) hunts insects and lizards in leaf-littered forested areas or backyards. This creature is distinguished by possessing rear-fangs and being the only venomous Bahamian snake. Though these attributes enable it to overpower its customary prey, they are virtually harmless to humankind, or even to the domestic cats and dogs which, along with humans, are, unfortunately, now their worst enemies.

Further reading: C. Mattison, *Snakes of the World*, Blandford Press, 1981; *The Encyclopedia of Snakes*, Blandford Press, 1995; P. J. Tolson, *A Natural History of West Indian Boas*, R. & A. Publishing, 1993.

SPANISH INVASION, 1782–1783

Though a comparatively minor episode in the last phase of the War of the American Revolution, the one-year occupation of NEW PROVIDENCE by the Spanish was a significant phase in Bahamian history. Not only was it the only interruption in British rule by that of a foreign power, but it incidentally led to the period of LOYALIST dominance that followed the American War.

Spain did not join forces with the rebel Americans until 1779, four years after fighting began and a year after the French had taken arms against the British. Even more than the French, the Spanish were more concerned about their colonial rivalry with Britain than with the cause of the American republicans as such. Though the capture of New Providence would extinguish a dangerous nest of PRIVATEERS and provide a much needed if minor victory, its taking was of much less importance than the retaking of Gibraltar and the Floridas, and the possible reconquest of Jamaica.

The attack on New Providence was planned as early as 1780, but the Spanish did not have enough spare troops until after the capture of Pensacola (capital of West Florida), or enough armed naval support until the arrival at Havana of the South Carolinian Commodore Alexander Gillon with a large frigate and a dozen other American privateers. The expedition, under the command of Juan Manuel de Cagigal, the Captain General of Havana, set out from Cuba on 22 April 1782, with 2,000 soldiers and 1,300 sailors carried in more than fifty vessels of all sizes, arriving off Nassau Harbour on 5 May.

The appearance of the Spanish/American armada thoroughly alarmed the far from bellicose Governor John Maxwell. Nominally, he commanded over 1,000 men and two forts with more than 50 guns. But his 250 regular soldiers were mainly invalids, and many of the local militiamen were fearful for their property and thought to be unlikely to risk it by putting up a fight. Governor Maxwell was therefore glad to take the advice of Commodore Gillon and the chief Nassau merchants and accept the generous surrender terms offered by General Cagigal.

The British troops were allowed to march out from the garrison 'with the honours of war', to be shipped off to the nearest convenient British port at Spanish expense. The inhabitants who chose to leave were permitted to do so with all their property and slaves, being given a year to settle up their affairs. The Bahamas was formally declared to be under Spanish suzerainty. But those British subjects who preferred to stay were to be guaranteed their accustomed laws and freedom of worship, and allowed to trade freely. Only arms and 'public property' were to be confiscated by the Spanish, and even privateer vessels were allowed to be retained by their owners, as long as they were disarmed and returned to peaceful pursuits.

Within a few days, Gillon sailed with his flotilla for the American mainland, and Cagigal with most of his troops left for Havana. Governor Maxwell and some of his officials were carried off as hostages, but soon released on parole.

SPANISH WELLS

New Providence was left under the governorship of Don Antonio Claraco y Sanz, with the help of a handful of Spanish officials, and under the protection of a garrison of some 300 regular soldiers, and 150 sailors in seven small armed vessels.

The following year, however, was an increasing time of tension and discontent for the Spanish occupiers and native Nassauvians alike. As the grip of the Royal Navy tightened on the Caribbean sea lanes after Admiral Rodney's great victory of The Saintes in April 1782, the Spanish in Nassau increasingly felt like a beleaguered and isolated garrison rather than the ruling power. The Nassauvians accused the Spaniards of reneging on the surrender terms, particularly in restoring prize property formerly condemned in the local Admiralty Court, and in imposing Spanish taxes. Local merchants found that the promised opportunities for trade (presumably with the Americans, Spanish and French) did not materialise. They gave the Spanish governor such a hard time that he referred to them as 'these wretched portions of mankind', and described Nassau as 'one of the miserable spots of the universe'.

The short-lived Spanish occupation of New Providence ended somewhat anticlimactically with the 'reconquest' led by Andrew DEVEAUX. Though this figures importantly in Loyalist mythology, it is undoubtedly deflated by the fact that it occurred some time after peace had been signed between Britain and Spain.

Further reading: J.A. Lewis, *The Final Campaign of the American Revolution: Rise and Fall of the Spanish Bahamas*, University of South Carolina Press, 1991.

SPANISH WELLS Proudly independent, prosperous and traditionally all-white settlement off north Eleuthera. Sigillians (as the inhabitants call themselves) are descended from ELEUTHERIAN ADVENTURERS and a few LOYALISTS who built up a small village on St George's Island, fronting the natural harbour formed by adjacent Russell Island and tiny Charles Island. With the late twentieth-century expansion of wealth (but not noticeably of numbers), the settlement spilled over from St George's to Russell Island, the two islands being joined by a bridge, built by the Sigillians themselves. No such link, however, was ever constructed across the narrow channel separating them from the Eleutheran mainland.

Though they held some slaves, Sigillians housed all on the mainland except a few domestics, who were expected to be off the cay by nightfall. This tradition lasted until the 1950s. Miscegenation was virtually inconceivable, and inevitably led to exile. This exclusivity was self-reinforcing. Sigillians claimed that their relative non-dependence on slavery contributed to their hardy self-reliance, and that, unlike the rest of The Bahamas, they suffered none of its legacies, including (paradoxical or even erroneous as it may seem to outsiders) racialism itself.

The late twentieth century has led to a considerable lessening of racial (or racialist) conservatism. But strong vestiges do remain. Very few blacks permanently live in the settlement, and the domestic and menial labour which prosperous Sigillians require but Bahamian blacks spurn, is now provided by HAITIANS – many of them illegal immigrants. The Haitians live in temporary shacks, either on the nearby mainland or in the least visited parts of Russell Island. When a considerable number of Haitian children showed up in the government school, some parents set up their own school. And when the Methodist synod sent a white minister who happened to be married to a black Bahamian, several of the congregation formed their own splinter church.

Historically, Sigillians have been the butt of mild mockery by other Bahamians, especially the inhabitants of nearby rival HARBOUR ISLAND ('Brilanders'). But in the late twentieth century they have had the joke on the jokesters. The prevalence of close-cousin marriage and the consequent shortage of surnames led to the story that if a visitor called out in the street for 'Pinder', a head would pop out of every door and window. Sigillians' alleged backwardness and naivete were the basis of the joke that they would purchase blocks of ice in Harbour Island and could never understand why it disappeared before they arrived back home, blaming the Brilanders for pulling a trick.

Sigillians were undoubtedly among the poorest and most backward of 'CONCHY JOES' before the turn of the twentieth century. But they proved as capable as any of taking advantage of their colour during the heyday of the BAY STREET regime, and showed great commercial acumen and adaptability in the hardest of later times. Some migrated to make money in Nassau, only to return home to invest their savings on retirement. Though Spanish Wells, along with Harbour Island, is now linked to Nassau by a high-speed hydrofoil, the settlement (with typical reticence) did not invest largely in the tourist business. Instead, Sigillians expanded their reputation as the most skilled, hard-working, wide-roaming and enterprising of Bahamian mariners.

At least one Pinder has been involved in the millionaire-making drug business, but for the majority of Sigillians this was neither acceptable not necessary. Lobster fishing has filled Spanish Wells harbour with million-dollar fishing boats, equipped with huge freezers and the latest

Spanish Wells lobster fishing vessels

electronics. Some are owned and run by self-confident youngsters who leave school at 16 and – in startling contrast to earlier days – are able to build palatial homes on Russell Island before they marry.

SPIDERS A similar range of spiders are just as common in The Bahamas as throughout the Caribbean. But the spider (or *anancy*) has not been personified in Bahamian folklore to the same extent as in other places of the African diaspora. Particularly in Jamaica, what are generically called 'Anancy Stories' celebrate a spider character as the ultimate trickster. Such stories originate in the area of modern Ghana (*ananse* is the word for spider in the Twi language) and their dispersion reflects the predominant area from which slaves came. In the Bahamas, as in HAITI and other places in the Antilles, the near equivalent (but rather more benign) trickster figure is the rabbit or hare, known in The Bahamas as Br'Rabby, who, with his comic foil Br'Bouki the hyena, has been traced back to the Wolof people of modern Senegal and The Gambia.

The Bahamian preference for a rabbit over a spider as a folktale hero may result from a general distaste for a creature that can spin webs that adhere to if not entangle unwary humans, can bite and sting, and in at least one common species inject a potentially lethal venom, the majority of Bahamian spiders are in fact almost harmless to humans. Beside the web-spinning crab and Santa Claus spiders of the woodlands, this includes the ground spider (generally but erroneously called a tarantula) found in gardens and vacant lots, which is unnecessarily feared because of its size. Technically a member of the family called hairy megalomorphs (alias bird spiders) this creature can attain a body length of 5 inches (13 cm) and a leg span approaching a foot (30 cm). Though half the size of their monster cousins found in the Amazon, Bahamian ground spiders include among their prey small lizards, baby birds and mice and large insects – in the process helping to control garden pests. Equipped with eight eyes and 360-degree vision, they are capable of scuttling quickly on their eight legs in any direction, like crabs. With wonderful acute senses, they prefer to hunt at night and lie low by day, which is just as well since they are unfairly bludgeoned on sight by humans. When confronting an enemy, including man, ground spiders squat down on their haunches, raise their abdomens and emit a faint feline sound. The erect hairs on their abdomens, if rubbed off, can cause skin irritations, but their bite is said to be 'no worse than a bee or wasp sting'.

Spider, Long Island

SPONGING

Much more dangerous is the so-called black widow spider (*Lactrodectus mactans*) quite commonly found in Bahamian gardens and farm plots – and recognisable by the red hourglass-shaped marking on its underbelly. Members of the so-called comb-footed *theridae* family, black widows get their name from the behaviour of the female. Three times the size of the male, they only mate once, usually eating their partner immediately after copulation. Even if he escapes, the male does not live long thereafter since he has lost the use of the fangs necessary for feeding and soon starves to death. Meanwhile, the female deposits up to 750 eggs in a silken pouch attached to her web, guarding it watchfully until the swarm of baby spiders emerge.

The feeding habits of the black widow are as seemingly sinister as its mating, and its bite can be a serious matter indeed. Black widows feast on other spiders as well as a range of insects and small crustacea. Normally they snare their prey with the same silken filaments with which they construct their webs, killing them with their fangs and sucking out their bodily fluids before discarding the carcass into a grisly pile beneath their webs. Their notorious venom is mainly for defence and is a powerful deterrent, not least for humans. A neuro-toxin, its first impact is no worse than a painful sting, which passes after an hour or two. But, as David Campbell vividly describes, this is gradually succeeded by 'weakness, tremors, cramps, rigidity of the abdominal muscles and sometimes excruciating aches in the limbs and soles of the feet. In severe cases there are delayed symptoms of reduced heartbeat, feeble pulse, laboured breathing, stupor, and delirium. There have been several authenticated human fatalities resulting from black widow bites in the Bahamas.'

Further reading: D. G. Campbell, *The Ephemeral Islands: A Natural History of the Bahamas*, Macmillan, 1978, 10–11, 42; F. G. Cassidy, *Jamaica Talk: Three Hundred Years of the English Language in Jamaica*, Macmillan, 1961, 275–6, 287, 394, 400; P. Glinton, *An Evening in Guanima: A Treasury of Folktales from The Bahamas*, Guanima Press, 1993.

SPONGING During the century following the end of slavery The Bahamas became the world's largest producer of natural sponges. With up to 600 vessels employed and 6,000 men and women engaged in fishing, cleaning, clipping and packing the six distinct grades of sponge, the industry dominated the Bahamian economy and shaped the lives of much of the population for more than fifty years. Unfortunately, though, few of the effects were beneficial. Even the major local players in the industry – ship-owners, outfitters and sponge merchants – suffered from the fact that The Bahamas was at the outer producing edge of a worldwide marketing system, while the actual producers, the black Bahamian sponge fishermen, were at the bottom of a descending spiral of dependency and exploitation.

Sponges had been fished from the eastern Mediterranean since classical times, and GREEK islanders continued to dominate the industry and trade through the mediaeval into the modern era. In the nineteenth century, however, as the Industrial Revolution hugely increased the demand for coarser varieties of sponge, it was noticed that the shallow subtropical waters of The Bahamas and western Florida offered a seemingly inexhaustible supply. Of these sources, much the most extensive was the 12,000 square miles (3200 squ. km) of the Great Bahama Bank on the western side of ANDROS, commonly called The Mud – though the Little Bahama Bank between ABACO and GRAND BAHAMA, and the Bights of ACKLINS and ELEUTHERA were other rich areas.

Gustave Renouard, a Frenchman wrecked in The Bahamas in 1841, is credited with discovering the potential of the Bahamian sponge beds; he set up a small export trade to Paris which was continued and expanded by his Bahamian son-in-law, Edward Brown. As early as 1843, exports for the year totalled 132 bales of 100 pounds apiece. The best-quality sponges, the so-called velvet and wool varieties, had a ready sale at the non-luxury end of the toiletry market, but there was an even greater demand for the coarser grass, hard-head, reef and yellow sponges for industrial purposes – particularly in Britain and the United States.

By the 1880s the industry was in full swing. Hundreds of sloops and schooners – each with a crew of up to ten and four or five attendant dinghies – dotted the expanses of The Mud, tended the watery 'crawls' on the shores of Andros, or crowded the Nassau docks as they unloaded the dried sponges and restocked for another trip. Voyages generally lasted six to eight weeks, with the fisherman paid not in wages but in shares of the outcome of the venture. The drawback of this system was that the chief shareholders were the ship-owners, who were also often sponge merchants themselves, as well as the general retail merchants who provided provisions for the voyage. They would advance goods to the ordinary sailors on credit against their eventual shares, being able to set both the prices of the provisions supplied and the amount of the shares. This TRUCK SYSTEM was eventually modified by an act of 1905 which decreed that all payments had to be in cash, though the custom of advances and merchant-decreed payments and the pattern of indebtedness continued. Given that Bahamian mariners and the sponge workers on shore were forced to compete with each other in an economy with scarcely any alternative jobs, and that the Bahamian merchants themselves were squeezed by the world marketing structure, the sponge fishermen and

Clipping and sorting sponges in a Nassau sponge-yard. From an early postcard

their families remained hopelessly poor, with no prospects of advancement.

They were also engaged in a desperately hard cycle of work, most of it under a pitiless sun. At the sponge beds, the dinghies were sent out to obtain suitable sponges with the aid of a water glass and a hooked pole called a 'grains'. The sponges were laid out on the deck and hung in the rigging so that their gelatinous covering and small creatures living within them might dry out and die in the sun. This was an extremely smelly process and the stink of sponge vessels extended for miles.

Once a week, the sponge vessels would visit the mangrove-staked crawls, leaving the new sponges to soak in the tidal sea-water, and beating and scraping the previous week's catch to remove the last of the odorous covering and any excess coral or sand. When a full cargo had been harvested and cleaned, the vessel and its rigging were loaded with chains of sponges (called 'beads') and sailed back to Nassau. There the sponges were delivered to the central Sponge Exchange, arranged in lots according to size and quality and sold by auction through licensed brokers to the main merchant-exporters. At first these were mainly Bahamians, some of them at the same time brokers, outfitters and ship-owners, as well as buyers and exporters. But by the 1880s the majority were Greeks engaged solely in buying and exporting, either migrants permanently settled in Nassau (such as the Christofilis, Esfakis and Damianos families) or agents of international firms. Of the latter, the most notable and aggressive was the Vouvalis Company, the largest in the world, with its head office in London and branches in Paris, Athens, Africa, Cuba and Tarpon Springs, Florida.

Once a merchant had purchased a lot, this was loaded on to distinctive two-wheeled donkey drays and conveyed to his own sponge yard to be prepared for export. The sponges were laid out in the sun to bleach, then clipped into neat shapes and sorted once more, before being compressed in a wooden screw press into the squared 100-pound (45-kg) bales, within burlap wrapping sewn by twine. All the work save the baling and loading was performed by women, who customarily smoked clay pipes as they worked.

The sponge fishing fleets suffered periodic disasters, such as the hurricanes of 1899 and 1926, though of course it was the ordinary fishermen and shore workers who suffered even more than the owners, outfitters and merchants. The industry reached its peak during World War One, when wartime demand raised prices to record levels. In 1917 exports totalled more than 10,000 bales, 27 per cent of world production, worth altogether over $400,000. Thereafter prices fell, especially once synthetic sponges began to erode the market. Frantic attempts to sustain high net income levels led to serious overfishing, despite the regulations (which had long existed) limiting

STANDPIPES

the size of sponges taken, and banning the use of trawls or fishing by divers.

Experiments to cultivate new sponges, successfully carried out by H. C. Christie in 1926, were never officially implemented. The years of the Great Depression were a period of serious decline, leading to even greater hardships among the sponge fishermen. Yet when a catastrophic fungal blight in 1938 destroyed 95 per cent of all Bahamian sponges within a year and brought the industry to an immediate close, there were few serious mourners. Twenty years later most of the varieties of sponge had revived, but except for two small and short-lived operations in the 1970s the industry itself has not made a comeback. In an era of expanding prosperity, the Bahamian sponge industry is now regarded as an unfortunate necessity of the bad old days.

Further reading: *The Sponging Industry*. Nassau, Public Records Office, Archives Section, 1974.

STANDPIPES As in many West Indian colonies provided with municipal water supplies in the early twentieth century, the standpipes providing free water to the public in Over-the-Hill Nassau and other poor suburban areas served much the same function as the traditional English parish pump or the public wells in colonial peasant villages, including those in the Bahamian Family Islands; that is, providing not just water but important places for women and children to meet and gossip, much as their men-folk did in the neighbourhood BARS.

Until the 1920s water used for all purposes was drawn from private cisterns or wells located in dangerous proximity to earth privies. Periodic outbreaks of TYPHOID and the need to reassure tourists encouraged the government to use some of the profits of the rum-running era to provide safer water supplies. For the first time sewerage was provided, though only for the prosperous parts of town north of the ridge. More generously, a well-field large enough to supply Nassau's entire population was tapped in an unoccupied area to the west of town, and filtration beds and a modern pumping station built. In 1928, Nassau's most prominent landmark, the white painted concrete water tower (126 feet (38 m) tall and its top 216 feet (65 m) above sea level) was completed, with sufficient capacity and pressure to provide water everywhere within a 2-mile (3 km) radius.

The houses in the prosperous (predominantly white) parts of town soon enjoyed individually piped water – for which they paid a modest water-rate. For at least thirty years the black majority Over-the-Hill were served simply by water mains running south down the four main streets, with a standpipe (that is, an upright cylinder with a faucet attached) located at almost every junction (or 'corner') where by-roads branched off at right angles. The standpipes, however, were rightly regarded as a major boon; for not only was the water clean and plentiful, but free.

What was written of the standpipes in Barbadian villages (which got piped water as early as 1900) was true also of the mini-neighbourhoods of Over-the-Hill Nassau three, four or five decades later. It was the task of children to fetch water before and after school, but housewives also visited the corner for water in the middle of the day. 'This was fetched in galvanised buckets and other containers, transported to the home in the hand or on the head, the latter method having been credited for the finely poised carriage which local women exhibited. It was then stored for further use in wooden barrels or large metal drums. … The standpipe was a point of social gathering for the village where the latest news was heard, children's games were played, young lovers chatted, and quarrels, even fights, occurred' (*A–Z of Barbados Heritage*). Such scenes and rituals sadly faded in the final third of the twentieth century, as the supply of water increased and virtually all houses throughout New Providence enjoyed the amenity (and could afford the expense) of piped water.

Street corner standpipe

Further reading: S. Carrington, H. Fraser, J. Gilmore, A. Forde, *A–Z of Barbados Heritage*, Macmillan Caribbean, 2003.

Stella Maris resort

STELLA MARIS ('Star of the Sea' in Latin) A German-owned residential complex and resort in a stunning location in northern LONG ISLAND, chiefly known as a base for scuba-diving and fishing.

The operators of Stella Maris have their own 4,000-foot (1219-m) airport, with scheduled BAHAMASAIR flights serving the whole of north Long Island, as well as chartered flights and private planes bringing guests to the resort. There is a fine restaurant, clubhouse, boutique and other amenities for residents and the more sedentary guests. But the key facility is the nearby marina on the leeward side of the island, with an impressive array of boats to service the more maritime-minded and energetic. Fishermen stalk bonefish on the flats, cruise the shores for reef fish, or venture in powerboats into the Atlantic for the plentiful tarpon, marlin and other game fish. There are innumerable opportunities for mere snorkellers, while scuba-divers have a variety of exciting options, including the far-famed CONCEPTION ISLAND 'wall', the rather more distant reefs of RUM CAY and SAN SALVADOR, several wreck dives, and the famous on-shore BLUE HOLE near Clarence Town.

Further information: www.stellamarisresort.com

STRAW WORK Weaving goods from the fronds of the native silver top palm is among the oldest of Bahamian crafts. The Lucayan AMERINDIANS probably wove straw baskets and items of clothing. They certainly made straw mats. These were used in their pottery process, providing the distinctive surface pattern for pots and griddles which gives them the name 'palmetto ware'.

From the earliest years of post-Columbian settlement, the islanders utilised the dried silver-top palm fronds to fashion hats, mats and baskets of all sizes (the most tightly woven said to be practically watertight), though apparently not the tough and water-resistant rope produced by Cayman Islanders. From the late nineteenth century, sun-dried fibres from the sisal plant were also used in what was still generically called straw work.

Though a well-established craft, straw work developed hugely as an adjunct of the TOURIST industry from the 1920s onwards. At its peak it employed countless Out Islanders in the preparation of the raw material and weaving the basic plait. Up to 3,000 people were involved in the manufacture of elegant decorated hats, bags, baskets, mats and other objects, and their sale from stalls on BAY STREET in downtown Nassau. Besides the basic straw plait, straw work incorporates native shells and imported raffia, as well as cloth linings. As a whole, the industry involves a complex network of wholesalers and suppliers, and some mass production by workshop owners. But unlike other Bahamian industries it never fell under the control of the white Bay Street oligarchy. Straw work has always been dependent on enterprising small businesspersons and individuals, of whom the key figures have been the skilled plait weavers, designers, craft workers and, above all, the street vendors – a vocal and well-organised sorority of black women.

Straw work depends on hard work and great skill at every level, and the independence of its workers was not won without some political struggle. The initial preparation of the palm and palmetto leaves and sisal fibre is a painstaking process, the rewards of which were in no way commensurate with the handiwork and time involved. The quality of the finished product is very dependent on that of the plait, of which there are up to 200 varieties, with names like Peas and Rice, Jacob's Ladder, Lace and Ric-Rac, Hole in the Wall, and Brickle Top. Some weavers and designers, such as Ivy Simms of Long Island, Judy Rolle of Bimini or Joseph Laroda of Abaco, attained almost legendary status.

Most of the earliest straw vendors (like many other black marketwomen) came from the village of FOX HILL to set up stalls where they could on Bay Street. By far the most enterprising was Florence Pyfrom, who operated a workshop on Charlotte Street in the 1930s. She employed up to 200 women and even exported to the United States, but was forced to close down in 1945, just as tourism was on the verge of its postwar expansion. Bay Street merchants, accustomed to regard all black vendors as a social nuisance, were slow to see straw vendors as a boon to tourism rather than competitors, and gave them no encouragement. As a bloc the straw vendors were therefore ardent supporters of the PROGRESSIVE LIBERAL

STROMATOLITES

Making straw baskets in a Grant's Town cabin, 1890s

PARTY and its populist leaders, especially Milo BUTLER and Lynden PINDLING. Actively campaigning through a Straw Vendors' Association formed in the early 1960s, they obtained their reward after the PLP's 1967 victory. In the 1970s they were provided with a covered Straw Market in Rawson Square, and in 1983 with even larger two-storey premises further down the street, on the site of the former main market.

The chief founder and later President of the SVA, Miss Telator Strachan, was appointed a PLP Senator. She was also involved in the planning of a New Providence Handicraft Cooperative and the setting up of a junior branch of the SVA. Though divisions arose on partisan lines after the defeat of the PLP in 1992, and the straw workers and vendors have had to overcome such setbacks as the failure of the projected cooperative in the late 1980s and the burning down of the Market Plaza in 2000, they remain a powerful lobby force in Bahamian politics. However, how long they can continue adequately to service the tourist industry while providing an acceptable standard of living for native workers, in the face of the increasing shortage and cost of raw materials and competition from cheap imports from Haiti, the Dominican Republic and elsewhere, remains a moot question.

Further reading: K. Knowles, *Straw! A Short Account of the Straw Industry in The Bahamas*, Media Publishing, 1998.

STROMATOLITES One of the least known distinctions of The Bahamas is that it is one of only three places on earth that is home to its oldest living creature, the original progenitor of life on the planet. Until recent years it was believed that the single-celled organisms called stromatolites, whose initiation of photosynthesis created the oxygen which enabled the development of higher life-forms, were uniquely to be found as the earliest of all fossils, dating back three and a half billion years. Then, incredibly, living colonies of stromatolites were found; first in a shallow subtropical salt lagoon at Shark Bay in Western Australia, at one other site in Australia, and then in a BLUE HOLE off Stocking Island in EXUMA – having somehow survived unaffected by evolution almost since the dawn of time.

This, of course, is a matter of wonder for visitors, and pride for native Bahamians. The exact location of such a living

Stromatolites

laboratory of life's origins, however, should remain a secret, save to selected and responsible scientists. This is not only because stromatolites are in themselves unremarkable to look at, but because the disturbance caused by visitors and souvenir-seekers would very likely soon undo the miracle of their survival over such an unimaginable stretch of time.

SUGAR The climate of The Bahamas is not ideal and its soils quite inadequate for the production of sugar on a large scale. Consequently, sugar plantations like those in most British West Indian colonies did not develop in The Bahamas during the colonial period – saving the islands from the most intensive, and one of the most oppressive, forms of SLAVERY. Sugar was produced on a very small scale purely for local consumption – as is attested by the few small and primitive wooden sugar mills that have survived.

One short-lived and ill-starred exception occurred in recent times, however. As a consequence of the US embargo on exports from Castro's Cuba in 1960, the international price of sugar suddenly soared to an unprecedented $600 a ton. The OWENS-ILLINOIS Company, having stripped its concession land in ABACO clear of trees, obtained a US sugar import quota for The Bahamas of 10,000 tons a year, parlayed its timber licence into a long-term lease on 50,000 acres of Crown Land, and set out to develop a huge sugar plantation, through a subsidiary called Bahamas Agricultural Industries Limited (BAIL).

An area south of MARSH HARBOUR 3 miles (5 km) wide and 17 miles (27 km) long was cleared, its rocky soil pulverised, and cane shoots planted. The latest mechanical harvesters were imported. A factory capable of producing 50,000 tons of sugar a year was erected at Snake Cay, along with excellent accommodation and facilities for workers and managers. Then things began to go wrong. At the same time that a Bahamian government less favourable to foreign companies came to power, the world price of sugar took a sharp and continuing downturn. The first sugar was produced in 1969 but yields proved disappointing. In the first year 15,000 tons were exported (far more than The Bahamas had produced in its entire history), but in the second year the total only reached 19,000 tons from an acreage almost half as large again. Reporting that it had already lost $10 million and could not foresee a profit, BAIL decided not even to harvest the 1971 crop, closed down the factory, laid off the workers and put the whole operation up for sale. The factory (conveniently designed to be easily dismantled) found a ready buyer, who shipped it off to a more promising location in South America – leaving the anomalous Abaconian canefields to revert over the years to their primeval state.

Further reading: S. Dodge, *Abaco: The History of an Out Island and its Cays*, White Sound Press, 1995, 100–3.

Sugar cane

'SUITCASE COMPANIES'

'SUITCASE COMPANIES' Nickname formerly given to companies nominally based in The Bahamas in order mainly to evade taxation in the countries where they carried on their real business. Constituting a lucrative source of income for the predominantly white lawyers during the BAY STREET era, such almost fictional entities – easily and speedily registered, with minimal details required, for the payment of comparatively modest initial and annual fees – came to be numbered in the tens of thousands by the early 1960s. Offshore companies officially based in The Bahamas continue to be a vital component of the Bahamian economy. But their operation has come under steadily more scrupulous vigilance and regulation from two directions over the last half century. The companies' real home countries have gradually closed up taxation loopholes and done much to enforce greater transparency. But equally important have been the trends in The Bahamas itself to require more rigorous documentation, to raise fees to more realistic levels, and to insist on greater local participation in the companies as part of a policy of progressive BAHAMIANISATION.

In the 1950s, following the example of such enterprising semi-independent jurisdictions as the Channel Islands, Isle of Man and Bermuda (not to mention the longer-established expertise of such neutral havens as Switzerland, Liechtenstein and Monaco), Sir Stafford SANDS and the other white Bay Street lawyers quite openly boasted of the advantages and ease of setting up a Bahamian 'suitcase company', blazoning their success by almost covering the outer walls of their offices with the plaques of companies officially headquartered within. As one investment adviser almost bragged in the late 1950s, 'Because no treaties provide for the exchange of financial information between the Bahamas and other governments, the accounts of such corporations carried on the books of a Nassau bank or stockbroker are not subject to scrutiny by foreign authorities.' Even in 1965 a European financial expert writing for the *Bahamas Handbook and Businessman's Annual* candidly admitted the four salient reasons, apart from freedom from local taxation, minimal bureaucracy and moderate fees, for a person to set up an offshore company in The Bahamas: 'A. To remain anonymous in a particular transaction while at the same time controlling the situation. B. To by-pass certain regulations to which he might be subject in his own country. C. To channel funds in certain directions without attracting attention. D. To take advantage of certain tax situations more profitable in other parts of the world.'

This easy-going situation obviously could not survive once it involved billions in annual business. Even during the last years of the Bay Street regime, banks and trust companies in particular were coming under increasing scrutiny and regulation. By 2000 the rules and regulations governing all companies registered in The Bahamas had become extremely complex, and almost as rigorous as anywhere else. There was special concern for those companies involved in BANKING and INSURANCE. But clear distinctions were also made according to whether a company's business was carried on within The Bahamas, between The Bahamas and other countries, or entirely outside The Bahamas, and according to the degree of actual involvement by Bahamians required or encouraged.

Within the regulations laid down by the 1992 Companies Act and its subsequent amendments, the government still strives to make the setting up of a Bahamian company as easy, expeditious and reasonable in cost as is feasible. To incorporate a company in The Bahamas it is simply necessary to file a Memorandum of Association with the office of the Registrar General, signed by a minimum of two subscribers, giving the proposed name of the company, its authorised capital (if limited by shares), and the proposed location of its office within The Bahamas. Subscribers who are not Bahamian must get permission from the Controller of Exchange, but this is normally a mere formality.

The nearest equivalents to the original 'suitcase companies' are what are termed International Business Companies

Suitcase companies: company nameplates on the front wall of a Bay Street lawyer's office, 1950s

(IBCs). These, in competition with other jurisdictions, have many attractive features, but are also hedged round with far more restrictions than formerly. They can be set up within a day, or in urgent cases with all the relevant documents presented, within less than an hour. Though they must have a local registered office and agent and are officially required to keep financial records, they are not required to employ a company secretary, to hold local meetings, or to file annual audited returns or accounts. In any case, no tax is payable in The Bahamas on offshore profits. At the minimum, IBCs may consist of a single shareholder (who may be anonymous or merely have a corporate identity) and just one director, who is not required to be a local. In many cases the most valued concession of all is that there is no requirement to disclose the identity of an IBC's beneficial owner.

On the downside, however, Bahamian IBCs are simply for trading carried on outside The Bahamas. They cannot sell their own shares in The Bahamas or solicit funds from the Bahamian public, may not own any real estate in The Bahamas, and are virtually forbidden to engage in any banking or insurance activities whatsoever. In this last respect the intention to separate the remaining 'suitcase company' activity from the much more important, and far more sensitive, financial sector is unequivocally shown by the following statement in an official brochure advertising the benefits of the International Business Company Act of 2000: 'Unless government permission is granted', IBCs 'cannot undertake the business of banking, insurance, assurance, reinsurance, fund management, collective investment schemes, trust management, trusteeship, the rendering of investment advice or any activity that would suggest an association with the banking or insurance industries.'

Further reading and information: *Bahamas Handbook and Businessman's Annual*, Dupuch Publications, annually from 1961; for relevant current legislation, apply to Government Publications, PO Box N-7147.

SURNAMES

Bahamian family names are useful, if imperfect, indicators of the national heritage. To a limited extent they can suggest when and why a family came to the islands, its ethnicity, and particular island connections. Precise genealogical research, however, is made difficult by the comparative shortage of names peculiar to The Bahamas (or not common elsewhere), by the amount of migration to, from and within the islands, by intermarriage and illegitimacy, and, not least, the custom of former slaves simply to assume the surnames of their erstwhile masters.

The surname closest to being unique to The Bahamas – and with the most distinctive history – is ROLLE. The name was assumed by all of Lord Rolle's former slaves and their descendants in order to enjoy commonage rights on Rolle's lands in EXUMA. The members of these families multiplied and spread throughout The Bahamas, until the surname Rolle became the commonest Bahamian surname and proportionately more common than 'Smith' in England or 'Williams' in the British West Indies. It is sufficiently distinctive that if encountered elsewhere in the world a Bahamian connection can be confidently presumed. The surname Rolle, no doubt for related historical reasons, is also one of the few that is held almost exclusively by blacks. No other Bahamian surnames enjoy such exclusivity or distinctiveness. But those that come close include: Bain, Bowleg, Edgecumbe, Hanna, Pyfrom, Rahming, Roker, Turnquest and Tynes.

For obvious reasons, even fewer family names are exclusively held by whites than exclusively by blacks (though there are families, such as the ADDERLEYS and Bethels, with separate 'white' and 'black' divisions). However, there are many surnames that indicate specific historic roots or original island connections. Those with the best claim to priority in The Bahamas are the six families whose surnames are found among the records of the first settlers in ELEUTHERA in the seventeenth century: Adderley, Albury, Bethel, Davis, Sands and Saunders.

Most exclusive were those white families who never had much to do with slavery and settled in the offshore cays of northern Eleuthera and ABACO, who inter-bred with each other but much more rarely with non-whites. This hermetic tradition accounts for the famous prevalence in the settlement of SPANISH WELLS of the surname Pinder (incidentally, the most distinctively Bahamian of all predominantly 'white' surnames). But much the same might be said of the Albury, Bethell, Curry, Higgs, Lowe, Malone, Roberts, Russell and Sawyer families of the offshore cays, if not quite of the Bethel, Braynen, Carey, Culmer, Sands and Symonette families of mainland Eleuthera. LONG ISLAND, with its easier-going attitude to miscegenation, has its own roll-call of distinctive names, shared today by persons of all complexions: Burrows, Cartwright, Darville, Dean, Fox, Knowles, Simms, Taylor, Turnquest and Wells. Much the same applies to the Forbes, McKenzie, Minns and Minnis families of EXUMA, and perhaps to the Hanna, Heastie and Tynes clans stemming from ACKLINS ISLAND.

NASSAU was much more of a melting pot, with successive waves of different immigrants. Apart from the centuries-old steady incursion of surnames from the British Isles, probably the most numerous are those that derive from (or by way of) the British West Indies, such as Alleyne, Brathwaite, Callender, Glover, Maycock, Maynard, Nottage, Phillips, Pindling, Walcott and Worrell.

SURREYS

Other ethnic groups still detectable by their exotic surnames were also drawn by historic circumstances and found significant niches in the Bahamian populace. Notable among these are the surnames of the ethnic groups separately mentioned elsewhere: the GREEKS (such as the Antonas, Christofilis, Esfakis, Klonaris, Maillis and Tsavousis families), the LEBANESE (including the Ageeb, Amoury, Armaly, Moses and Ouwade/Baker families) and the CHINESE (Cheas, Lees and Wongs). The last of these arrived by way of Cuba, which over the years donated a trickle of Hispanics to the Bahamian mix – providing such surnames as Cancino, Gomez, Gonzalez or Rhodiquez.

Since the mid-twentieth century, the flood of migrants from HAITI has led to probably the largest and most rapid incursion of distinctive new surnames – though comparatively few of the migrants have stayed long enough or become sufficiently entrenched for their surnames to have made a significant impact. Far less immediately obvious is the number of 'French' surnames that have found their way into The Bahamas over a much longer period. The French-sounding surnames Demeritte and Symonette appeared in a Bahamian census as early as 1740. A few such surnames, such as Deveaux and Delancey, came with the LOYALISTS by way of the American mainland, and the DUPUCH family at least claims that its antecedents came directly from France. But the great majority of the French-surnamed families came by way of Haiti, as a result of the turmoils of the Haitian Revolution or more peaceable later interchanges. The francophone provenance of some names is obvious. These include Duvalier (though no close connection with the notorious dictator family has ever been proven), Deleveaux, Bonamy (*Bon ami*), Moncur (*Mon coeur*), or even Levarity (*Le verité*). The French origin of some surnames may even surprise some of those holding them. These include such well entrenched Bahamian surnames as Beneby, Bodie, Dillett, Laroda, Moree and Poitier.

SURREYS The most picturesque and tenacious relics of the last century still to be found in car-clogged downtown NASSAU are the two dozen or so horse-drawn surreys plying for trade from tourists eager for a taste of the capital's quaint and more leisurely earlier days.

Nassau's four-wheeled, four-seat, sun-shielded surreys are survivors of days before the internal combustion engine, when tourism had scarcely begun. Owned by enterprising blacks living on the southern slopes of the town's ridge (most notably, David PATTON), they were hired out mainly to carry the Nassauvian white elite to market or church. None of these vehicles (for the most part imported from St Augustine, Savannah or Charleston) were built less than 75 years ago, and some may be twice as old. The surreys are kept in working order with great ingenuity, despite the absence of skilled carriage-makers, wheelwrights or blacksmiths (the horses are shod only on their rear hooves, if at all).

In spite of the descent of cruise-ship hordes, the multiplication of local car-ownership, and the transformation of Nassau into a high-rise banking centre, what was written by the present author in the *Bahamas Handbook* in 1966 (the year that QUEEN ELIZABETH II and Prince Philip rode a surrey during the monarch's first state visit) still remains essentially true at the beginning of the twenty-first century.

Surrey

*'They're corny; they hold up traffic,' complained the unsentimental locals as they sped to their air-conditioned offices in their glitzy new cars. But that is what the tourist comes to Nassau for. A little corn. A little slowing down of pace. A **rallentando**. You will find the surreys under the palms in Rawson Square or in Frederick Street by the Poinciana Restaurant – ancient carriages waiting as the world rushes by, with patient dobbins drowsing in the shade. The huge wheels and framework are painted with every preposterous shade of dazzling colour: canary, crimson, flamingo pink. On the back, in spindly letters, equally eye-catching names: Wells Fargo, Lightning Express, Cool Cadillac. 'One horse power. Air conditioned', barks out a venerable charioteer in a top hat he inherited from his daddy. 'Come take a peek at lil' ol' Nassau. Jus' one guinea for an hour in the cool.'*

George Symonette (centre) pianist and singer with Leonard White's 'Chocolate Dandies', performing before an all-white audience at Nassau Yacht Club, 1930s

SYMONETTE, George (1912–1988) Immensely popular pianist and troubadour, perhaps the first artiste to make a full-time career out of entertaining the tourists, but whose very success was based on his unfailing facade of geniality and a calculated determination not too obviously to rock the political and social boat.

An accomplished pianist, and a singer with a pleasing voice, George Symonette first came to notice as the piano driving force and chief vocalist of the demeaningly named 'Chocolate Dandies' dance band led by Leonard White in the 1930s. Contemporary photographs already show the 6-foot 5-inch (1.92m) George with the beaming grin (invariably referred to in the press as his 'piano-key smile') that was to be his lasting trade-mark – along with his later, almost Churchillian, cigar.

Though popular with the exclusively white clientele of the Nassau hotels, White's 'Dandies' were not encouraged to mix with the guests and could not even attend the hotels except when performing. Moreover, they were so meagrely paid that none of them could afford to give up their daytime jobs. George Symonette was trained and worked as a pharmacist, and it was not until tourism began to expand in the 1950s and he began to be a popular soloist in places like Chez Paul Meeres and Blackbeard's Tavern that he was able to become a full-time entertainer. Later, along with other similarly bland and safe 'native' talents such as 'Peanuts' TAYLOR and Eloise LEWIS, he became one of the favourite artistes used by the tourist board to showcase The Bahamas, on short tours of Florida and other parts of the United States.

Often billed as 'the King of GOOMBAY', George Symonette did write some of his own local songs, though never quite having the song-writing talent of 'Blind Blake' HIGGS, Charlie Lightbourne or Eddie MINNIS. Nevertheless, his piano skills did invariably infuse such Trinidadian and Jamaican calypso standards as 'Rum and Coca Cola', 'Matilda', 'Linsted Market' or 'Island in the Sun' with the authentic Bahamian goombay beat. The limits of his repertoire as a medium of social and political comment (so unlike the savagely witty calypso giants of Trinidad), and also the fact that 'showpiece natives' like George Symonette were never to gain fabulous riches from their trade, are perhaps conveyed – typically between the lines – in the refrain of one of his own songs, referring to the paramount leader of the 'BAY STREET boys': 'My name is Symonette; but I ain't R.T.' (see following entry).

SYMONETTE, Rt. Hon. Sir Roland Theodore (1898–1980) The most outstanding and contradictory of the 'BAY STREET boys' who dominated Bahamian business and politics in the middle half of the twentieth century. A ruthless and seemingly racialist self-made millionaire, he grew in stature and mellowed when he became the first Bahamian Premier, and ended his career almost universally honoured and admired as a founding father of the modern Bahamas.

Born in the tiny settlement of The Current, Eleuthera while Queen Victoria was still alive, Roland Symonette was the ninth child of parents so poor that almost the only asset they had to bequeath was the proud claim that they

SYMONETTE, Rt. Hon. Sir Roland Theodore

were white, and therefore in a privileged class, distinct from the Afro-Bahamian majority. What complicated young Roland's life was the fact that the claim was not absolutely true. He had darker kin, and his own features patently displayed a mixed ancestry. This seems to have given him a redoubled will to succeed, not just against all non-white Bahamians but also against the snobbish British colonialists, who looked down equally on blacks and poor 'CONCHY JOES' like himself. The symbol of this ambivalence was to be his creation, with others like himself, of the Nassau Yacht Club (itself racially exclusive) in 1931, to counter the Royal Nassau Sailing Club, which had denied him membership as a vulgar *nouveau riche*.

Roland Symonette received his only education in the local one-room public school, where he did sufficiently well to be a 'teaching monitor' for a dollar a week. He left school at 16, first carrying produce from his father's farm to market in Nassau, then migrating to Palm Beach, Florida to engage in fishing. By dint of hard work he purchased a small freighter to carry on trade between Florida and Nassau. Though, for obvious reasons, it was one of the most obscure passages in his career, he was among the boldest, most enterprising and luckiest Bahamian rum-runners during the era of American Prohibition (1919–33).

Having, it is said, made his first million from rum-running, Symonette moved naturally into the more legitimate wholesale and retail liquor business in Nassau. More profitably still, he bought up large tracts of land on Nassau's outskirts, went into building and became in time the largest *rentier* in the Bahamas. Through both enterprises, it was, in effect, ordinary black Bahamians who were the providers of his second fortune. This, however, was only the start of a wide-ranging business empire, which included ships, the largest Bahamian shipyard, and a whole range of important and lucrative construction projects in the Out Islands; roads, docks, dredging, bridges and airports.

These later developments were integrally connected both to the general economic expansion of the Bahamas after World War Two and to Roland Symonette's rise to political prominence. He was first elected to the House of Assembly in 1925 for his birthplace constituency of Harbour Island, moving on to represent Nassau East continuously from 1933 to his retirement in 1977. In his early days in Parliament, Symonette (himself a life-long workaholic) condemned black Bahamians as a whole as lazy, favouring the immigration of West Indian workers. Later, however, he was much more discreet and patriotic, building up a considerable personal following among blacks as well as whites, as much through mutual respect as by old style patronage.

With the formation and first successes of the PROGRESSIVE LIBERAL PARTY, Roland Symonette was the principal founder of Bay Street's political arm, the UNITED BAHAMIAN PARTY. Having been knighted in 1959, he became the first Premier of The Bahamas on the granting of internal self-government in 1964. Once at the helm he continued to profit from the lack of conflict of interest legislation, but also showed considerable statesmanship and political wisdom – for example, opposing his own party's stance over the granting of casino licences. He was unable, however, to prevent the coming of majority rule.

Untainted by the findings of the Freeport and Casinos Inquiries, Sir Roland Symonette, unlike Sir Stafford Sands, did not slink away; he continued to lead the UBP until it dissolved, and to represent Nassau East for a further decade – while continuing his business interests scarcely abated. He died in 1980 at the age of 82, three years after retiring from active politics.

Sir Roland Symonette was married three times and had five children. By his second wife he was the father of Robert Hallam Symonette (1926–99), Olympic yachtsman, prosperous businessman in his own right, and Speaker of the House of Assembly from 1962 to 1967. By his third wife, Sir Roland was father of Theodore Brent Symonette, who for a time in the early 1990s was Minister of Tourism in the FREE NATIONAL MOVEMENT government which succeeded the PLP.

Rt. Hon. Sir Roland Symonette

TAYLOR, Berkeley 'Peanuts' Popular entertainer and nightclub owner of the last third of the twentieth century, who came to notice in the late 1950s as a diminutive, pre-teenage peanut vendor with a charming demeanour and great dexterity on the goatskin drum and bongos. A favourite with tourists and photographers seeking picturesque and authentic Afro-Bahamian culture, he became a fixture in Over-the-Hill nightclubs during their heyday in the 1960s – his most celebrated turn being to play 'Mary Had a Little Lamb' on a tuned congo drum. In the somewhat disorderly world of 'native entertainment' he showed unusual business acumen, first starting the Drumbeat Club Over-the-Hill in the early 1970s and then transferring it to the downtown waterfront when the focus of night-time entertainment shifted there. This venture, however, did not survive the further shifts in entertainment fashions and locations in the 1980s, and with the decline and demise of Peanuts Taylor's Drumbeat Club, Taylor himself almost faded from the nightclub scene.

Berkeley 'Peanuts' Taylor

TAYLOR, Sir Henry Morton (1903–1994) 'Long Island white' who was the most important of the founders of the PROGRESSIVE LIBERAL PARTY, Henry Morton Taylor was later marginalised within the party and squeezed out, but ended his career as the third Governor-General of the independent Bahamas (1988–92).

Born illegitimate in Clarence Town, Long Island near the beginning of the twentieth century, young Henry took the surname of his adoptive parents, Joseph and Evelyn Taylor. Relatively well educated in the local public school, by schoolteacher aunts, and through correspondence courses, he spent his first ten adult years as a teacher in Long Island and Acklin's (1924–34). Appalled by the neglected plight of the Bahamas Out Islands during the Great Depression, he then became a political activist, while struggling to make a living as a bookkeeper. In 1949 he won one of the two Long Island seats in the House of Assembly and in 1953, with Cyril Stevenson, William Cartwright and others, founded the PLP as the first real political party in the Bahamas. Of all the founders, he was the most active and effective in setting up branches of the party in many Out Islands, especially those to the south and east.

For ten years (1953–63) Henry Taylor was unanimously elected as party chairman, but when he lost his own seat in the 1956 general election, Lynden PINDLING was chosen to be the party's parliamentary leader and steadily grew in power. More importantly, the youth now influential in the PLP reckoned that Taylor and the other founders (most of them, like Taylor, near-white, 'middle-class' and Catholic) were insufficiently radical or populist, and were completely untuned to the ideology of Black Power then sweeping the world, and which the black Bahamian majority needed in order to achieve the majority rule which was their democratic right.

As Chairman of the PLP Henry Taylor was a member of the party's first delegation of protest to London in 1956. After winning back a seat in a 1960 by-election, he led a delegation of women to London which was largely instrumental in obtaining the franchise for women. In 1961, however, he went against the party's policy of total non-cooperation and accepted the UNITED BAHAMIAN PARTY's poisoned bait of a seat on Stafford SANDS's all-powerful Development Board. By his own account, the loss of his parliamentary seat in the 1962 general election was the result of the PLP's withdrawal of practical support and a critical factor in the party's failure in the election as a whole.

On reliquishing his chairmanship of the PLP in 1963, Taylor was accorded the more or less empty title of Honorary Chairman for Life. But he ceased to play a part

TAYLOR, Maxwell

H. M. Taylor (on right) with his Chief rival for leadership of the PLP, Lynden Pindling, 1960s

in the events which were to lead to the party's victories in 1967 and 1968. In the 1967 general election, indeed, he stood as an Independent – unopposed by the UBP – against the PLP's A. D. HANNA, only to lose ignominiously by 187 votes to 1,126. For ten years Taylor went into virtual exile in Florida, ostensibly to write his memoirs. Partially reconciled, he returned in 1978, but politically he was a spent force. His appointment as the editor of the parliamentary record ('Hansard') in 1979 and his knighthood in 1980 were more or less consolation prizes, as were his appointments as Acting Governor-General between 1988 and 1991, and as Governor-General from then until the FREE NATIONAL MOVEMENT came to power in 1992. Sir Henry Taylor died on St Valentine's Day, 1994 at the age of 89, and was buried in his birthplace, Clarence Town, Long Island.

Further reading: H. M. Taylor, *My Political Memoirs: A Political History of the Bahamas in the Twentieth Century*, Nassau, 1987.

TAYLOR, Maxwell

Probably the most distinguished and among the most dedicated of black Bahamian artists. Uncompromising in his style – concentrating on the forms and lifestyles of the black majority, using mainly harsh and sombre images and colours, and eschewing literal realism – he had a much harder route to success than more accessible artists such as Brent MALONE or Alton LOWE. Unable to make a living by his art in Nassau, Taylor has spent most of his career in the United States, and even there had to work at humdrum and labouring jobs until he achieved recognition and substantial sales. This, however, never soured him or made him forget his Bahamian roots.

Born and educated in Nassau, Maxwell Taylor, like several other local artists of his vintage, got his start at Bahamian Don Russell's grandly styled Academy of Fine Arts and under the more sophisticated tutelage of the Englishman David Rawnsley at the Nassau branch of the Chelsea Pottery. In the 1960s he briefly travelled and studied in England, before settling more permanently in New York. There in his spare time he attended the Arts Students League and Pratt Graphic Center and also worked with the American artist Robert Blackburn. As a consequence, he became adept in a variety of media, especially print-making, etching, woodcuts and silk-screen printing, as well as ceramics. Over two decades his work became recognised as distinctive in its diversity and complexity, its raw emotive power and its social commitment – particularly towards the plight of the black poor and oppressed.

Maxwell Taylor returned to Nassau as often as he could. For eleven consecutive years he held an annual workshop in artistic techniques for young Bahamians, thanks to the generosity of FINCO. Over the years, his work was more widely exhibited, in New York, South Carolina, Georgia and Washington DC, so that he actually became better known in the US than in his homeland. This changed, however, when his work was prominently displayed at the exhibition 'Bahamian Art Today' held at Brent Malone's Matinee Gallery in 1977, and in a triumphant one-man show in Nassau two years later. By the time that he was the widely acknowledged star of the exhibition by ten local artists held to commemorate the tenth anniversary of Bahamian Independence in July 1983, Maxwell Taylor had achieved well-earned heroic status.

TELEVISION

The revolutionary change from radio to television broadcasting came relatively late to The Bahamas (the Coronation of King George VI in November 1936, the first major broadcast over ZNS Radio, was also the BBC's first important television transmission within the UK). But once established in the 1970s, television had dramatic effects upon communications, patterns of entertainment, and, indeed, Bahamian culture as a whole.

Largely for technical reasons, exposure to television was one of the areas in which Grand Bahama (and especially Freeport) was ahead of Nassau. It was in Grand Bahama, along with Bimini, that the first clear TV pictures were received in The Bahamas in the 1950s – transmitted from stations in Florida less than 100 miles (160 km) distant. American Cable TV was also made available to Freeport as early as 1965, more than a decade before ZNS began TV transmissions. This comparatively early exposure to TV from the US no doubt reinforced and accelerated the cultural Americanisation of the north-western Bahamas which many Bahamians (and British) deplored.

For The Bahamas as a whole, the first stage of the TV revolution came with the setting up of satellite transmissions from the middle 1960s up to the early 1970s. Once synchronous satellites proliferated, equal coverage of first dozens and then hundreds of transmissions was possible for every island in the archipelago – if at considerable cost. Even when transmitters evolved effective ways to tax receivers, Bahamians who could afford them rushed to install satellite dishes – while for bars and hotels they became almost a *sine qua non* of success.

The government and ZNS responded slowly to the implications of the change, and it was not until 1977 that it set up its TV facility – formally opened by the Queen on 20 October of that year. The delay did have the advantage, however, that ZNS was able from the beginning to use the latest technology and techniques – for example, transmitting pictures with a higher definition and sharper colour quality than used by the BBC, and leapfrogging altogether the relatively primitive 'visual radio' and 'talking heads and still pictures' phases of presentation. From the first day, Channel 13 transmitted with 50,000 watts of power, over an effective radius of 130 miles (210 km) – an area containing 95 per cent of the Bahamian population.

In 1994, a 15-year licence was granted to Cable Bahamas Ltd., who in 1995 purchased Grand Bahama CATV, giving them a monopoly of cable TV throughout the Bahamas. By 2001 they claimed that cable TV was available for 94 per cent of all Bahamian households, and that they already had 155,000 subscribers. They had also made available thoroughly up-to-date Internet and data services. In 2002, however, there remained considerable tension between Cable Bahamas and the Bahamas Broadcasting Corporation, particularly over the payment by the former to the latter for joint and reciprocal services.

By the end of the twentieth century, television watching had become at least as much a part of daily life in The Bahamas as anywhere else in the world. Globalisation is often described as of universal benefit. But inevitably it leads to the weakening of distinctive local cultures, such as that of The Bahamas, and can even act as a form of cultural propaganda. Luckily, those at the Broadcasting Corporation of The Bahamas seem well aware of such dangers. They stress that Channel 13 is independent of any external television network and that its programming is, above all, 'chosen to serve the national interest'.

TENNIS Next to track and field ATHLETICS, tennis is the sport in which The Bahamas now competes most notably at the international level. This was not a simple consequence of an ideal climate for year-round outdoor play, the growing availability of facilities, and the natural ability of Bahamians. More interestingly, the development of tennis from a pastime for the white elite to an authentic national sport occurred in parallel with – and exemplified – underlying social, racial and political changes.

The all-white Nassau Lawn Tennis Club was founded in 1879, only six years after the invention of the modern game by Walter Wingfield, and just two years after the first 'world' championship was held at Wimbledon. Tennis was a tourist attraction, and during the 1920s and 1930s, as a highlight of the tourist season, the Colonial Hotel held international tournaments that attracted such famous stars as Helen Wills Moody and Fred Perry. But the hotels' courts remained as out of bounds to non-whites as those of the NLTC. This was especially galling for the small middle class of aspiring 'persons of colour' who were attracted both to the game itself and to its social cachet. In the mid-1920s they got their own court next to the gym for women run by Nurse Florence Ward at the corner of Shirley and Charlotte Streets, and formed the Gym Tennis Club.

From its beginning, the Gym produced some highly skilled players. Most notable was the long-time champion, mother and teacher of other champions, Bertha Isaacs (much later awarded the title of Dame) who led teams to compete successfully in all-black tournaments in Florida. In the late 1930s the Gym moved to a four-court facility with a pavilion in Nassau's southern district, at the corner of Mackey Street and Wulff Road. Its 200 members were drawn almost entirely from the non-white middle class (largely because even the relatively small fees were beyond the means of the black majority) and the club differed from the others only in being more willing to host white players solely on the merit of their game, rather than the other way round.

This absurd system of sporting apartheid continued for another 25 years, even as tourism expanded, the number of public courts multiplied, and the Gym became

TENNIS

obviously the home of the colony's best players and the place where the most important local competitions were held. Along with other outstanding non-white players of that era, Kendal ISAACS, Attorney General as well as Cambridge University champion and 'Blue', did not play at the all-white clubs – though he might have refused if asked. Seeking to resolve the situation, in 1962 an expatriate player, Malcolm Hale, wrote to the Jamaican LTC asking that The Bahamas be allowed to participate for the regional Brandon Trophy. Receiving a favourable reply, Hale initiated the formation of the Bahamas Lawn Tennis Association on 5 June 1962. Only the Gym TC participated, but that was no longer really relevant. Bahamian national tennis was on its way.

In the first national championships held under the BLTA, a white Bahamian, George Carey (a member of the both the NLTC and the Gym), defeated the black Gym member Donald Archer to win the men's singles, while Kendal Isaacs and his brother Robert won the men's doubles. But it was two younger players who put the Bahamas on the regional tennis map, successively winning the Brandon Trophy, forcing their way into the Commonwealth Caribbean Davis Cup team, and being so regularly selected as to influence the decision to accord separate Davis Cup representation to several Commonwealth Caribbean countries, including The Bahamas. These forerunners were the diminutive Leo Rolle (b. 1947), who was first spotted as an eager barefooted ballboy at the Gym, and the Greek-Bahamian John Antonas (b. 1952), who was the first local boy to go to the US on a tennis scholarship (University of Alabama).

Progress was even more rapid in the 1980s and 1990s, as The Bahamas did so well in Davis Cup play as to come within one stage (albeit an away tie with the US) of gaining entry into the elite World Group, in October 1993. This was very largely due to the talents of two more brilliant young players. Roger 'Slinger' Smith, a black born in Grand Bahama in 1964, was number one in singles and doubles at Ohio State and twice 'Big Ten' singles champion, before spending a dozen years on the world professional circuit. During that time he had victories over Pete Sampras, Peter Korda and Michael Chang, and had his finest moment when he defeated Ivan Lendl, then World Number One to reach the quarter-finals of the 1993 US Open.

Even more distinguished has been the record of Mark Knowles (b. 1971), son of an English woman professional player and a white Bahamian father. He won a scholarship to the Bolletieri Academy in Florida at the age of ten and was for three years number one in singles and doubles at UCLA. Becoming a professional in 1992, he did well in singles but splendidly in doubles play. In 1995, he and his Canadian partner Daniel Nestor reached the number one world doubles ranking. After a comparative lull (while Nestor was constrained to play with another Canadian) they repeated the feat early in 2002 on winning the Australian Open. Knowles (who won an extra tournament with another partner) ended the year in sole possession of the top world ranking – at age 32 – an achievement repeated in 2004.

It is unlikely that other Bahamians will soon reach such dizzy heights. But just as the former and present stars have been the product of a confluence of national talents during an era of proud nationalism, an even stronger national programme has been developed as a result of the enthusiasm and optimism generated by their success. Rolle, Antonas and Smith all have tennis schools at major hotels, while Knowles since 2001 has been host of a glittering annual tennis invitational tournament at the ATLANTIS hotel. Even more important has been the creation by the BLTA since 1998 of a fine new National Tennis Centre at the Oakes Field sports complex – boasting a dozen state-of-the-art courts and matching off-court facilities.

Mark Knowles, World Doubles Champion (with Canadian Daniel Nestor) 1990s

THEATRE Given that Bahamians are natural dramatic storytellers and mimics, it is not surprising that so many have made successful acting careers – on stage and in radio, television and the movies. Yet what Bahamian performers from Bert WILLIAMS through to Sidney POITIER, Esther Rolle and Calvin Lokhart had in common was that their talents only found full expression once they had gone abroad, particularly to the United States. Until the last third of the twentieth century, social and economic factors severely limited opportunities for formal acting in the home islands for ordinary Bahamians. Following the economic boom and the liberation of the Bahamian spirit accompanying majority rule and national independence, however, indigenous Bahamian theatre quite suddenly flowered – to the point that the Jamaican cultural guru Rex Nettleford praised The Bahamas as a leader in the development of theatre throughout the region.

The first references to theatre in The Bahamas date from the later LOYALIST period when members of the white Nassau elite performed amateur theatricals for audiences of their own kind. Expatriates continued to dominate the theatre well into the modern era.

A literally dramatic change occurred from the 1960s, with the emergence of an impressive array of non-white players and playwrights, appealing for the first time to a national audience. The initial catalyst was probably the local radio station ZNS, which from the 1960s realised the potential audience for dialect-speaking advertisers, storytellers and locally oriented soap-operas, of which the most popular was Jeanne Thompson's long-running *The Fergusons of Farm Road*. Yet from the same well-spring in the 1970s and 1980s flowed an overwhelming flood of plays, both comic and serious, but mainly in the vernacular on locally relevant themes, by Susan Wallace, James Catalyn, Telcine Turner, Sam Bootle, Percy Miller, Winston Saunders, Ian Strachan and Nicolette Bethel as well as Jeanne Thompson. These were produced and performed with increasing sophistication by the Bahamas Drama Circle, the University Players and the repertory company based on the newly created Dundas Centre of the Performing Arts from 1981 onwards.

Central to this florescence was the annual Dundas Repertory season, which ran from 1981 to 1999. Founded by the DCPA chairman – playwright, director and actor Winston Saunders – the eagerly awaited annual season was for almost two decades under the artistic direction of Philip A. Burrows, an actor trained at the American Academy of Dramatic Art. Following the philosophy of the AADA (which sought to enrich American theatre by combining in its repertoire plays drawn from many classical traditions along with more strictly indigenous work) the Dundas season exposed Bahamian audiences not just to local and regional works, but also to prize-winning Broadway and West End plays.

In all, as Nicolette Bethel recounted in 2003, the Dundas season within two decades produced over sixty shows, at least half of which were original Bahamian works. 'Almost every Bahamian playwright of the Independence era had productions workshopped and produced by the Season, and the actors and technicians who received their training there could stand shoulder-to-shoulder with any in the world.' Under Burrows and Saunders, the season even produced two Bahamian operas; Cleophas Adderley's nationalist epic *Our Boys*, based on the sinking of HMBS *FLAMINGO* in 1980, and Clement BETHEL'S folk opera, *The Legend of Sammie Swain*, a reworking of a Cat Island folktale.

Yet, as Nicolette Bethel admitted, the Dundas season was not without its critics; both on the grounds that its repertoire was too wide-ranging, and that its members had come to represent a closed, elitist group. 'Notable dissidents included James Catalyn, whose group James Catalyn and Friends provided audiences with a more traditional diet of satirical skits, and Ian Strachan's Track Road Theatre, which aimed at a younger group of players and performers, and was established with the philosophy of taking theatre to the people, rather than bringing the people to the Dundas.' Partly as a consequence of such contrary winds, both Saunders and Burrows resigned, and the Dundas season and its invaluable infrastructure were dismantled in 1999.

The loss of the Dundas theatre facility was a grievous blow, making the cost of productions in alternative and temporary venues prohibitive. However, there remained some favourable glimmers. 'Theatre continues in pockets,' concluded Nicolette Bethel, 'thanks to the dedication of various independent companies. In addition to Strachan's Track Road, Helen Klonaris has created a feminist group, Wicked Sistah Productions, and the core members of the Repertory company have established Ringplay Productions, a theatre company committed to continuing Burrows' philosophy. These, together with the artists represented by Michael Pintard's Scribes Limited, represent the future of Bahamian theatre.'

TONGUE OF THE OCEAN One of the chief geological wonders of The Bahamas, the Tongue of the Ocean is a submarine chasm just as long and deep, and about the same width, as the Grand Canyon of the Colorado. Though certainly not formed, like the Grand

Tongue of the Ocean, viewed from space

Canyon, from aeons of river erosion, its exact origin remains mysterious. Like the parallel Exuma Sound and the four transverse channels which crisscross The Bahamas and the Turks and Caicos Islands, it was probably formed by a comparatively sudden shift and fissure in the basic limestone platform on which the whole archipelago sits.

Unlike the other channels, however, the Tongue of the Ocean is a gigantic cul-de-sac, looking on the map as much like a Christmas stocking as a giant ant-eater's tongue. Joined to the latitudinal North East Providence Channel between NEW PROVIDENCE and northern ANDROS (barely 20 miles (32 km) apart), it extends 125 miles (200 km) south and, with sheer sides, varies between 3,500 and 6,000 feet (1,400 to 2,000 metres) in depth. For almost its entire length it is fringed by the Androsian barrier reef to the west, and to the south and east terminates at the immense shoals of the Great Bahama Bank.

Because it is so close to the US seaboard, is not an international waterway and is almost totally enclosed, with an entrance easily put under surveillance, the Tongue of the Ocean was a natural location for the United States' Atlantic Undersea Testing and Evaluation Centre (AUTEC), set up by agreement with the British government when The Bahamas was a colony, and still highly active and secretive today, 30 years after INDEPENDENCE.

TOURISM Known since the eighteenth century as 'The Isles of June' and said to be blessed with 'one of the most serene, genial and delightful climates in the world', the Bahama islands were bound to draw large numbers of tourists once improved communications made them readily accessible. The earliest visitors made the slow journey from North America by sailing boat during the winter months. This trickle became a regular flow once sail gave way to steam in the second half of the nineteenth century. Yet it was air travel and the luxury of air conditioning which from the mid-twentieth century made the flow a flood and extended Bahamian tourism from the winter months throughout the year.

Recognising the benefits of tourism to a meagre economy, Bahamians always extended an eager welcome. But from the 1950s the government turned tourism into the dominant Bahamian industry, spent millions on advertising, licensed casinos and opened up new islands to tourist development – particularly GRAND BAHAMA. The Bahamas offered a dazzling array of diversions for a wide spectrum of visitors; not just sunning, swimming and watersports, night-clubbing, gambling and duty-free shopping, but serious golf and tennis, sailing, sport fishing, and eco-tourism. By the year 2000, The Bahamas Ministry of Tourism was able to boast that the country was hosting over four million visitors a year.

Not all was gain. The Bahamas suffers from all the problems – social and psychological as well as economic – common to countries dependent on tourism. They are magnified in the Bahamian case by the shortage of viable alternatives. This gives The Bahamas a weak bargaining hand and a definite advantage to external investors. Not least of the problems are that already more than half of the visitors to The Bahamas are cruise-ship passengers, who barely touch at the inhabited islands and leave very little money behind. Also, of the stop-over visitors an increasing proportion are on 'all-inclusive' packages in foreign-owned resorts, which naturally tend to expatriate all their profits.

The potential of The Bahamas as a health resort was first promoted by Peter Henry BRUCE in the 1740s. One of the first tourist visitors to The Bahamas was none other than George Washington. The future first US President stopped there in 1751 on his only venture outside the American mainland, while accompanying his older half-brother Lawrence on a vain attempt to cure his tuberculosis in the West Indies. Traffic increased somewhat after the coming of the American LOYALISTS in the 1780s, but it was intermittent and there were no organised local facilities until the government made a contract with Samuel Cunard for a mail and passenger steamship connection with New York in 1859 and built the first hotel, the 90-room ROYAL VICTORIA, in the following year.

Nassau and its hotel enjoyed a fortuitous boom through the blockade-running period of the AMERICAN CIVIL WAR (1861–5). But a real tourist trade was not established until NASSAU showed itself relatively healthy with the ending of its occasional bouts of cholera, yellow fever and malaria, and the steamships serving it proved absolutely safe. A particular blow was the fate of the SS *Missouri*, which caught fire and sank off ABACO in 1872, with the loss of 84 of its 95 passengers and crew – among whom was Lewis Cleveland, manager of the Royal Victoria Hotel and brother of the future US President, Grover Cleveland. The real founder of the Nassau winter tourist season was James E. Ward, who took over the mail and passenger contract in 1879. He provided first a fortnightly then a weekly service, taking three and a half days each way between New York and Nassau.

The Ward steamers (which also served Cuba) had a perfect safety record between 1879 and their discontinuance in 1917. But they encountered increasing competition from quicker and cheaper routes, bringing tourists from more widespread parts of the United States. Even in 1880 passengers had the option of taking the train as far south as Fernandina, near Jacksonville, and the two-day voyage across the (notoriously choppy) Florida Channel to Nassau. In the 1890s, however, Henry M. Flagler almost revolutionised the traffic. He extended the Florida East Coast Railroad (with its chain of luxury beach hotels) as far as Miami, from which fast steamers could reach Nassau within 24 hours. By negotiations with a willing local government in 1899, Flagler built the 200-room Colonial Hotel on the site of the dismantled Fort Nassau, and also purchased the competing Royal Victoria.

Over this period, interest in The Bahamas as a tourist destination for Americans was reflected in – and stimulated by – the first guidebooks: Charles Ives's *The Isles of Summer* (published by the author in New Haven, 1880), William Drysdale's *In Sunny Lands* (New York, 1884), *Stark's History of and Guide to The Bahamas* (Boston, 1891) and G. J. H. Northcroft's *Sketches of Summerland* (Nassau, 1900). Also, shortly after the turn of the century the first picture POSTCARDS were produced by the pioneer local photographers J. F. Coonley, W. Pinder and J. O. 'Doc' Sands, with the help of the Detroit Photograph Company.

Despite the creation of the Development Board in 1914, World War One soon brought the fledgling tourist industry to a complete halt. Its revival and expansion during the boom era of US PROHIBITION was symbolised by the phoenix-like rebuilding of Flagler's failing Colonial Hotel as the 250-room New Colonial Hotel after its destruction by fire on 31 March 1922 – with the help of a government loan of £270,000. In 1926, buoyant BAY STREET interests also financed the building of the 200-room Fort Montagu Hotel at the other end of Nassau. Though the majority of black Bahamians suffered cruelly during the Great Depression, its full impact was postponed by the continuation of Prohibition until 1933, and its effects on tourism were mitigated by the efforts of Governor Sir Bede CLIFFORD, the legislature and the Development Board to improve the facilities available to those eager and able to escape the asperities of the worldwide slump. The building of the new Prince George Dock (named after the future King George VI) in 1928 had already brought the first liners into Nassau Harbour and the first wave of cruise-ship visitors.

As the promoters proudly proclaimed, the number of tourists actually rose from some 10,000 in 1932 to 25,000 in 1935 and 48,000 in 1939 (exceeding the total population of The Bahamas for the first time). Yet it remained predominantly a seasonal winter traffic (between December and March), limited to Nassau and attracting mainly visitors described as being 'at the upper end of the international social scale, including a heady mix of celebrities of stage, politics and literature, American money, and British titles'. Even when World War Two broke out in Europe, Bahamian tourism did not immediately decline. Rich refugees from Britain mingled with hedonistic Americans until the United States was drawn into the War. As many as 28,000 visitors came to the Bahamas as late as 1941, though falling to 6,000, 3,000 and almost zero in the succeeding four years.

Prewar tourist figures were not exceeded until 1950. But thereafter there was an upward surge and the industry was transformed. There had been air flights through the 1920s and 1930s, but only by small and expensive seaplanes. Beginning with Pan Am's daily flights into Nassau's Oakes Field in the late 1940s, large land-planes belonging to competing airlines brought rapidly expanding numbers of tourists quickly and cheaply from ever farther afield – to a steadily increasing number of Bahamian airfields. Equally important was the first Hotels Encouragement Act of 1949 – which saw the first hotels built on CABLE BEACH – and the promotional activities of a revived Development Board under the aggressive leadership of the Bay Street lawyer and tycoon Stafford SANDS.

The visionary efforts of the Englishman Billy BUTLIN to bring mass tourism to Grand Bahama failed within two years, but between 1949 and 1955 annual tourist arrivals had multiplied ten times to 132,000 and tripled again to 342,000 by 1960. No longer was the traffic limited to

TOURISM

the winter season and the very rich. Drawn in part by budget rates in the summer (and 'shoulder' rates in fall and spring), but on the average with far more money and time to spend on vacations than during the prewar years, more and more Americans were persuaded to take holidays in a Bahamas advertised as near but exotic, and now easily affordable. Another factor was the closing down of Cuba as a tourist destination for Americans by the Castro revolution and US embargo from 1959.

By 1965, the Development Board's annual expenditure of £1,500,000 represented 12 per cent of the colonial budget (exceeding medical services and topped, narrowly, only by education), though its chairman was able to boast three-quarters of a million tourist arrivals. Added to the first major expansion of tourism outside New Providence was the opening up, initially on a modest scale, of hotels to non-white tourists, following the anti-discrimination resolution in the Assembly in 1956.

The greatest surge in Bahamian tourism, along with the first awareness of its major problems, in fact occurred in the later 1960s. The granting of virtual autonomy to the developers of Freeport, the highly controversial allocation of CASINO licences and, above all, the amended Hotels Encouragement Act of 1965 led to an explosion of building and tourist figures reaching a peak of one and a half million by 1970 – 400,000 of whom were visitors to Grand Bahama.

Besides the attempt of Freeport to rival Nassau, casino-hotels were built on Cable Beach and PARADISE ISLAND, and several large resorts opened in ELEUTHERA and mainland ABACO. However, the generous concessions given to developers – which included a 20-year tax holiday, the remission of duties on imported materials, and the unlimited right to employ foreign workers and staff – led both to over-building and opposition among the Bahamian workforce. Worse were the opportunities for bribery over the granting of building and casino licences – with well-attested rumours that the casino licensees had links to Mafiosi who had formerly operated in Cuba.

The revelations of widespread kickbacks contributed largely to the defeat of the UNITED BAHAMIAN PARTY in 1967 and the subsequent exile of Sir Stafford Sands. Yet Lynden PINDLING's PROGRESSIVE LIBERAL PARTY inherited serious problems, made all the harder by a general downturn in the world economy in the 1970s. The PLP government recognised the country's dependence on tourism and did not wish to kill the golden goose. But it was faced by declining standards caused by a demoralised workforce, and demands from its supporters for greater government oversight and control of hotel and casino operations, and the complete BAHAMIANISATION both of the workforce up to management levels and of the hotel-related concessions.

The problem of morale and poor service Pindling countered by explaining that service was not servility, and that good service was good business – even going so far as to dress up as a porter and carry luggage to illustrate his point. Meanwhile, his government steadily applied pressure to cut the numbers of foreign staff and increase the promotion prospects of Bahamians and the number of Bahamian concessionaires. The takeover of the casinos and their staffing entirely by Bahamians was more problematic, not just because of the opposition of their owner/operators but because some Bahamians opposed casinos altogether. However, in due course the virtually complete Bahamianisation of the staff was achieved and the operation of casinos and auditing of their accounts placed under a local Casino Management Board.

Most troublesome of all was government's role in respect to the hotels themselves, since several of them were close to failing altogether in the 1970s. A Hotel Corporation was created, ostensibly to oversee the running of the hotels and controlling new building. But it found itself more involved in bailing out struggling hotels, finding alternative buyers or lessees, or even buying and running hotels itself. The net result was to add to the already fast escalating national debt. As much as it was commended for saving the chief national industry, the Hotel Corporation – of which Pindling himself was long the chairman – came under fire for mismanagement and was accused of sweetheart deals and featherbedding, if not outright corruption.

The figures for tourist arrivals, including a growing proportion of cruise-ship passengers, increased only slowly through the 1970s and did not pass two million a year until 1983, when the share of New Providence and Paradise Island combined was barely greater than the total for Grand Bahama and the other Family Islands. The official total numbers remained steady over the last decade of PLP rule, though this disguised a serious decline in the popularity of Freeport and an even more rapid increase in the ratio of cruise-ship trippers compared with stopovers, mainly arriving by air. By the late 1980s, the further expanded docking facilities sometimes harboured ten cruise liners at a time.

The decade of rule by the free-market oriented FREE NATIONAL MOVEMENT saw at least an apparent further surge forward in the Bahamian tourist industry. Overshadowed by the *ATLANTIS* colossus, many new hotels were built and old ones renovated and extended, along with open-plan villa-type resorts and time-share apartments and villas. Paradise Island was transformed almost to become a Bahamian variant of Miami Beach or Palm Beach, and Freeport was revived by a massive injection of capital from the Hong Kong-based Hutchinson Whampoa consortium. By the year 2000, The Bahamas as a whole could boast no fewer than a hundred hotels and resorts, of which 40 had more than 50 rooms. The grand total of tourist rooms (for hotels of all sizes and time-share villas and apartments) was an almost incredible 13,500. Of these, some 4,400 were in 30 hotels and resorts on the island of New Providence, 3,800 in a dozen on Paradise Island, 3,750 in 22 on Grand Bahama, and the remaining 1,550 scattered in nearly 50 mostly small establishments throughout the Family Islands. The total of tourist visitors was computed to be 4,204,180 and their spending in The Bahamas a colossal $1.8 billion a year. Roughly 25,000 people, a sixth of the total Bahamian workforce, were employed directly in the tourist industry – of whom nearly 60 per cent were women. In Grand Bahama, the dependence on tourism was even greater, employing at least 30 per cent of the workforce.

However, despite upbeat publicity from the Ministry of Tourism, the situation was far from optimal. There were flaws and setbacks and the PLP government of Perry CHRISTIE faced a somewhat uncertain future when it returned to power in May 2002. The FNM government claimed that $2 billion had been spent on tourist infrastructure during their ten-year tenure, and they had certainly made strenuous efforts to clean up and beautify the tourist areas in New Providence. But CRIME, both petty and serious, remained a problem. Always susceptible to external economic factors, Bahamian tourism was at least as badly hit as its competitors by the fall-out from the events of 11 September 2001. This came on the heels of several hurricanes which especially damaged the Family Islands and pushed several struggling resorts in Eleuthera and the Abacos over the financial edge.

In a generally shrinking regional market, small Family Island operations whose running costs were inevitably high found it specially difficult to compete with cost-effective and more budget-oriented tourist destinations. Insufficient, unreliable and expensive airline connections compounded the problem. Moreover, what hurt the Family Islands relative to the 'big three' of Bahamian tourism (New Providence, Paradise Island and Freeport) affected The Bahamas as a whole compared with regional tourist destinations. These were able to offer 'better value', largely because they were less reliant on imported foodstuffs and necessary manufactured items. Already the hotels of Mexico's Yucatan and the Dominican Republic were out-drawing those of The Bahamas, and only the continuing US embargo on Cuba prevented Americans making it (as it already was to Canadians) their favourite 'island in the sun'. Even within the narrower orbit of the three main Bahamian tourist areas there was competition. Over-enthusiastic expansion coupled with the relative decline in stopover passengers had led to the problem of over-capacity. Visitors gravitated to those hotels which offered most and, even if not the cheapest, were best value – which in effect meant that the older Cable Beach hotels tended to lose out to the newer ones on Paradise Island, while Freeport lost out to both.

From the Bahamian perspective, however (though not from that of foreign tour operators), the predominant threat was that posed by the growth of cruise-ship traffic and other 'all-inclusive' operations. The method of such transnational operators as CLUB MEDITERRANÉE was to set up as near to a self-sufficient enclave as possible, contributing as little as possible to the local economy, and pulling up stakes if conditions or profits were unsatisfactory. Much the same applied to the Florida-based cruise-ship companies, whose passengers comprised nearly 60 per cent of official visitors to The Bahamas in 2000.

Though they found it convenient to have their ships registered in The Bahamas (a valuable increment to the Bahamian treasury), they tended to regard The Bahamas as a domain to be exploited. At most their teeming passengers were allowed to spend a few hours on Bay Street, mingling more with each other than with the locals and if spending anything at all, mainly patronising only the cheaper outlets – selling T shirts made in Taiwan and 'native' handicrafts made in Haiti or the Dominican Republic. By the Cruise Ship (Overnight Incentives) Act of 1995, cruise-ships remaining in Nassau for at least

Disney cruise ship

TRADE UNIONS

18 hours were allowed to operate their own shops and casinos and sell duty-free liquor in port.

The chief mitigation as far as the government was concerned was the payment of docking fees and a per capita port tax of between $5 and $15 dollars a person according to the number carried. Yet even these levies the cruise operators cannily avoided if they could. Even before some of the cruise-ships became so huge that they could not dock in Nassau's harbour, several of the major cruise-ship companies purchased their own small islands in The Bahamas, rechristened them with exotic names, set up tourist facilities ashore, and made them their sole destination in The Bahamas. The Disney Cruise Line, for example, renamed and remodelled GORDA CAY as Castaway Cay. Turning such hitherto pristine cays into miniature Disneylands ran in bizarre counterpoint with the activities of more sensitive operators and their clients who were concerned with conserving the islands and enjoying them through responsible eco-tourism.

TRADE UNIONS The lack of an organised proletariat as well as the political dominance of the ruling class meant that trade unions were even slower to develop in The Bahamas than in the rest of the region. Moreover, the maturation of Bahamian trade unions (along lines pioneered by the labour movements first in Britain and the USA and then the West Indies) was also retarded by at least three other factors. There was a general naivety about the function of trade unions within a labour movement, particularly a failure to distinguish general political from strictly labour aims and actions, and the divergent interests and ambitions of different labour unions and would-be labour leaders. Also, perhaps crucially, there was a failure of trade unions either to cohere as a unified force, or to adhere to one political party – particularly when what was formerly regarded as the most appropriate party, the PROGRESSIVE LIBERAL PARTY, became entrenched in power for a quarter century.

Because of inertia as well as repressive legislation against 'combinations', the first attempt to form a Workers' Union in Nassau in 1921 soon petered out. Likewise, the only faint echo of the industrial ferment affecting the British West Indies in the later 1930s, the formation of a short-lived Labour Association in 1936, had no more effect than the passage of a 1937 act setting the minimum wage for labourers at a paltry 4 shillings a day. Not until the serious 'BURMA ROAD' RIOTS of June 1942 was the colonial government sufficiently concerned by the threat of concerted labour unrest to raise the minimum daily wage by 25 per cent, to call a commission of inquiry, and to sponsor an Act in 1943 formally authorising trade unions, as long as they were properly registered, strictly regulated, and limited in their ability to strike, picket and negotiate.

Real progress, both in labour organisation and union legislation, awaited the postwar years and especially the outcome of the GENERAL STRIKE of January 1958. This was spearheaded by the somewhat awkwardly aligned forces of the Taxi-Cab Union, the recently formed Bahamas Federation of Labour led by Randol FAWKES, and the Progressive Liberal Party, of which Lynden PINDLING was rapidly emerging as the paramount leader. Though the strike itself was only a partial success, it aroused support from labour organisations in the UK, USA and West Indies, and led inexorably to the much more progressive union legislation that followed the visit of Secretary of State Alan Lennox-Boyd in April 1958. Even more importantly, the alliance of convenience between Pindling and Fawkes and their respective supporters in the emergent local labour movement lasted long enough to help ensure the narrow achievement of majority rule by the PLP in January 1967.

Fawkes, the only successful BFL candidate in the 1967 election, jubilantly became the first Minister of Labour. But the alliance did not long survive the PLP's landslide victory in the following year. Having failed to persuade the PLP to change its name to the Progressive *Labour* Party, Fawkes soon fell out of favour in the party, lost office and went his own way – though not before getting Parliament to declare the first Friday in June each year Labour Day. Fawkes and his BFL retained some support for a few years, but this simply divided the labour movement – the majority of unions joined under the umbrella of a Bahamas Federation of Trade Unions (BFTU) being strongly enough affiliated to the PLP to be given two seats on the PLP's General Council and to have three of its staunchest members coopted as PLP Members of Parliament.

Together, the PLP and the BFTU drafted an important Industrial Relations Act in 1970. With INDEPENDENCE approaching this was nationalistic in that it forbade foreigners to be officials of Bahamian trade unions and discouraged Bahamian membership in international trade unions. But it was also far too conservative for radical labourites; for example, in forbidding the closed shop, in its arbitration procedures, in restricting the rights of civil servants to unionise, and in denying workers in designated 'essential services' the right to strike. These conditions were increasingly crucial issues as the PLP became ever more firmly in control and resistant to change.

During the 1970s both the personal charisma of Fawkes and the potency of the BFL faded. But at the same time the BFTU became weak and divided – failing to revive by reconstituting itself as the grand-sounding Commonwealth of The Bahamas Trade Union Congress (BTUC). Instead, the former mantle of Randol Fawkes fell on the fire-eating Dudley Williams, whose radical Bahamas Workers' Council, targeting such workers as the employees of public corporations and longshoremen who by striking might effectively bring the entire country to a standstill, provoked the first serious confrontation with the PLP government in 1973–4. At his most splenetic, Williams complained that since 1967 'the only black people who have been able to move up are the upper class blacks and the English educated blacks. The real "grass-roots" demand the chance to move up also.'

This obvious appeal for class solidarity and political activism was firmly deflected by the then Minister of Labour, Clifford DARLING (ironically one of the heroes of the 1958 General Strike) who stated the principle (or opinion) that the best and most effective union was one that was 'confined to its own craft or industry'. Prime Minister Pindling was also at his most palliative in arguing that the functions of government and unions were complementary and should not conflict, while the majority of the populace demonstrated their preference for calm negotiation and compromise over violent confrontation. But the basic problems remained and relations between the PLP government and the labour movement steadily deteriorated throughout the 1980s. The chief thorn in the PLP's flesh was the activism of the Teachers' Union while under the dynamic leadership of Leonard Archer. But trouble arose over the conditions under which unions representing the workers in public corporations such as the BAHAMAS ELECTRICITY CORPORATION and BATELCO could act. A climax was reached once Leonard Archer became the President of the BTUC, and that regenerated organisation, and the majority of the 55 Bahamian trade unions now marching under its banner, began to place more trust in the FREE NATIONAL MOVEMENT than in Pindling's PLP.

During the decade of power that the FNM enjoyed after its victory in 1992, important legislation was indeed passed in respect of trade unions and labour relations in general. This included the establishment of an Industrial Tribunal in April 1997, the passage of a comprehensive new Employment Act and a new Minimum Wages Act in 2001, and of a Health and Safety at Work Act in 2002. The combined outcome was the provision for the first time of a virtual charter of workers' rights, and a fully comprehensive structure of relationships and negotiating machinery, between workers and employers and between labour unions and the government. Predictably, however, the package retained many conservative elements.

It remained illegal for a trade union to operate in The Bahamas unless it were properly recognised and registered. No person under 16 could be a member of a trade union. A union could not have foreign connections without a proper licence in writing from the Ministry of Labour. An employer was required to recognise a union as a bargaining agent as long as at least 50 per cent of its employees were members. An employer had just two weeks to accept or reject a union claim for recognition. No employee could be dismissed or adversely treated as a result of union involvement.

The resolution of all industrial disputes was primarily the concern of the employer and employees concerned, but ultimately of the Industrial Tribunal and the Ministry of Labour working in conjunction. All industrial agreements between employers and unions had to be sent to both the Industrial Tribunal and the Minister of Labour, with the Minister then having two weeks to make comments to the Tribunal. After taking the comments into consideration, the Tribunal was virtually bound to register the agreement as long as it was found to contain no illegalities. Properly registered industrial agreements were to be considered binding.

Any strike that had a purpose other than the furtherance of a trade dispute, or which was designed to coerce the government was declared illegal. The same principle applied to lockouts by employers. Pickets were required to be properly authorised by the relevant union, to be peaceful, and to be limited to 15 persons at any one time. Demonstrations on behalf of parties to an industrial dispute were only to be held in places other than the relevant place of work.

This was the structure of organisation, the machinery of negotiation and the rules which the PLP took over when it was returned to office in May 2002. But it was unlikely to make major further changes, at least in the short term. The PLP's philosophy regarding trade unions had already been almost written in stone by Prime Minister Lynden Pindling in the year following Bahamian Independence. 'The trade unions and the Progressive Liberal Party should respect each other's independence in organisation and terms of reference,' he told the PLP's Annual Convention in 1974. 'The trade unions cannot relieve the Party of the tasks of political leadership nor of the activation and mobilisation of members, supporters or the population as a whole. Nor can the Party relieve the trade union movement of its central task of mobilising and representing

TREES

workers for the improvement of their working conditions and standard of living.'

TREES Despite the general paucity of the soil, The Bahamas supports a rich variety of subtropical and tropical trees, both native and exotic, with 32 per cent of its land area still designated as forests and woodland. The original trees are said to have colonised the islands from the south and east, from seeds carried on ocean currents or in the crops of migrant birds. The aboriginal Amerindians made but a small impact on the natural forest cover, so that Christopher COLUMBUS was able to describe it in glowing terms. European colonisation, however, did make steady and substantial changes; by cutting out the main stands of dye-woods and timber suitable for boatbuilding, by savagely clearing the land with axe and fire for attempted plantations and subsistence agriculture, and by commercial timber cutting; as well as, on the positive side, by importing a wide range of exotic fruit, ornamental or otherwise useful tree species.

The chief victims of colonial development were the always rare tall trees from which the Lucayans fashioned their dug-out canoes. The huge silk cotton tree (*ceiba*) was imported in the early colonial period. The scattered Bahamian examples were, with various fig species, often shade trees at the centre of settlements. The largest and most famous, long called Blackbeard's Tree, a favourite gathering place outside the Supreme Court in Nassau's city centre, eventually succumbed to old age in the 1970s.

In The Bahamas, three distinct soil types produce their own distinctive tree communities, with or without human intervention. *Whitelands* are based on white limestone or coral sands. Found mainly along beaches and most commonly in the southern islands, these soils are low in nutrients and the ability to retain moisture. Distinctive trees include the cultivated coconut palm (*Cocos nucifera*) originally from the Indo-Pacific area, the CASUARINA (*Casuarina equesitifolia*) imported from Australia, and the native sea grape (*Coccoloba uvifera*). A beguilingly attractive but dangerous denizen of the shoreline, as of other parts of the islands, is the native manchioneel (*Hippomane mancinella*), a tree with sweet-scented flowers which produces a poisonous sap.

Blacklands are based on a dark loamy soil with considerable nutrients and water-retaining capacity. Most suitable for agriculture and gardening, they have thus been the areas most cleared of their native species and (in respect of trees) replaced by useful fruit trees and ornamentals. The former notably include many varieties of citrus, the sapodilla (*Manilkara zapota*), guava (*psidium*), the soursop, custard apple and sugar apple (*Annona muricata, reticulata* and *squamosa*) from Central America, the mango (*Mangifera indica*) from tropical Asia, and the breadfruit (*Artocarpus communis*), famously brought from the Pacific to the West Indies by Captain William Bligh to provide food for the slaves. Of the imported ornamental trees, the jacaranda (*Jacaranda coerulea*), originally from Argentina, with its violet-blue flowers, has escaped from cultivation and is now widely spread in the wild. The flamboyant red poinciana (*Delonix regia*), originally from Madagascar, has likewise flourished, and is so common as to be almost emblematic of The Bahamas – though at the same time regarded by botanists as something of a pest since it easily spreads and inhibits competing flora. The majestic royal palm (*Roystonia regia*) often planted in ornamental rows (as alongside Elizabeth Avenue in downtown Nassau) is usually regarded as an introduced species originating in Cuba, but the existence of a stand on uninhabited Little Inagua suggests that it is in fact indigenous to The Bahamas.

At least as common as the white and black soil areas of The Bahamas are the *coastal rocklands* – pitted and holed expanses of limestone, often stretching far back from the shoreline. It is a harsh habitat, where only the hardiest of species are able to exist, by sending their roots into the sparse

Once the most famous of all Bahamian trees: 'Blackbeard's' silk cotton tree outside the Old Post Office and Supreme Court, Parliament Square, Nassau, died and was cut down in the 1970s

pockets of soil in the crevices. Perhaps as a consequence of the struggle for survival, these unpromising areas can produce some of the most valuable Bahamian hardwoods, including LIGNUM VITAE (*Guaiacum officinale*), fittingly the Bahamian national tree.

By a categorisation almost distinct from that based on soil types, botanists identify three broad Bahamian habitats that produce their distinctive types and range of trees; the MANGROVE community, the pinelands (or 'pineyards'), and the Bahamian coppice.

The four species of mangrove (red, black white and buttonwood, in that order) serve an invaluable purpose in successively building up the Bahamian shoreline from sandy shallows to tidal mud and progressively drier land, which in turn is characterised by savannas, by pineland and by clumps or larger areas of Bahamian coppice. In all three of these habitats are found small stands or isolated examples of three palm or palmetto species which, along with the stumpier types of palmetto, have proved invaluable to the inhabitants of The Bahamas since the time of the Lucayans in providing thatch and straw for making into baskets, mats, brushes and hats. These are the thatch palm (*Thrinax radiata*), the silver top palm (*Coccothrinax argentata*) and, most important of all because of its tolerance of wet conditions and salinity, the pond top, sabal or cabbage palm (*Sabal palmetto*).

Pinelands, dominated by the Caribbean pine (*Pinus caribaea* var. *bahamensis*) constitute the largest areas of almost pure forest in the Bahamas, extending – at least until invaded by housing developments or logged out – over much of NEW PROVIDENCE, ANDROS, ABACO and GRAND BAHAMA. The Caribbean pine reaches 90 feet (27 m) in height with a girth 3 feet (1 m) in diameter elsewhere, but in the sandy and rocky flatlands of The Bahamas the local variant rarely exceeds 40 feet (12 m) in height and 18 inches (46 cm) in girth.

Better plankwood and mast timber could always be found elsewhere, but Bahamian coppices produced excellent hardwoods for the stems, keels, ribs and hardware of boats, for house frames, and handsome and long-lasting furniture and cabinetry. The chief native hardwoods are mahogany (*Sweitenia mahagoni*), which has retained its original Arawak name (though in The Bahamas usually called madeira from the Spanish word for wood, *madera*), mastic (*Mastichodendron foetidissimum*), horseflesh (*Lysiloma sabicu*), ironwood (*Krugiodendron ferreum*) and, most famous and versatile of all, LIGNUM VITAE (*Guaiacum officinale*). The Bahamian cedar (*Juniperus lucayana*) and the native wild tamarind (*Lysiloma bahamensis*) also made excellent building timber. Some of these trees attain great age and

Ficus (tropical fig tree)

height in first-growth stands in Cuba (horseflesh, up to 200 feet (61 m)) but they were never so lofty in The Bahamas and survivors are mainly second or third growths and comparative dwarfs.

Besides the hardwoods with other uses, the many trees valuable for cabinet-making included the coconut-scented satin wood (*Zanthoxylum flavum*), the easily worked reddish-brown ink wood (*Exothea paniculata*), the light brown saffron (*Chrysophyllum oliviforme*), the dark brown heartwood of the pigeon plum (*Coccoloba diversifolia*), and the light and dark fiddlewood (*Citharexylum caudatum* and *fructicosum*) used, as it name suggests, in making violins, among other things. Spanish cedar (*cedreta odorata*), with its distinctive aroma favoured for the making of cigar boxes, was probably imported from Cuba in the colonial period.

The barks of several Bahamian trees were used to produce tannin and/or dyes, notably BRAZILETTO (*Caesalpinia vesicaria*), the red mangrove (*Rhizophora mangle*) and logwood (*Haemotoxlum campechianum*) – though the last was never so abundant in The Bahamas as to challenge the huge industry that developed on the Logwood Shore of Central America. Two Bahamian trees were (and remain) favourite spice producers, the wild cinnamon (*Canella winterana*) which produces both a flavoursome bark and pepper-like berries, and CASCARILLA (*Croton eluteria*), which still supports a minor industry in the southern Bahamas to supply the bitter ingredient of Campari liqueur. Some other trees produce useful gums and resins, of which the most common and versatile is the gum elemi (*Bursera simarouba*). Not only is this a hardy and impressive landscape tree growing to 80 feet (24 m), producing a gummy resin used for making incense, varnish and glue, but its wood has been used for making bowls and drums, fishing floats, and carvings for tourists.

Besides trees of commercial value for export there are many others with domestic uses. Most importantly, they have provided wood for boat and house-building, straw for thatch and weaving, firewood and charcoal, fences and hedges. Yet almost as important are the very large number whose bark, sap, resin, boiled wood, leaves or flowers have been used as BUSH MEDICINE, claiming cures or alleviation for every affliction from constipation, diarrhoea and the common cold, through bruises and toothache, to syphilis and cancer. As well, many trees produce fruits, with or without medicinal value that are starch foods (like the breadfruit); deliciously edible (such as the guava or mango); can be made into jellies or jam (such as the seagrape or cocoplum, *Chrysobalanus icaco*), ice-cream (especially the soursop), drinks cold or hot, or even a potent local liquor (from the guana berry or gooseberry, *Byrsonima lucida*). So far though, Bahamians do not seem to have copied West Indians, especially Trinidadians, to make the refreshing drink mauby from the bark of the soldier wood (*Columbrina eliptica*), which is quite common in The Bahamas.

Additionally, there are trees whose wood makes serviceable torches, which produce specifics against insects (such as the crushed seeds of the necklace pod, *Sophora tormentosa*, or twigs of the bay berry, *Myrica cerifera*, used to keep fleas and cockroaches away), or which act as substitutes for soap, and provide wax for making candles. The calabash tree (*Crescentia cujute*), introduced from Central or South America and which may or may not have been known to the Lucayans, produces (as its name suggests) cups, bowls and containers from the shell of its seeds. One extremely versatile tree is the white ironwood (*Hypelate trifoliata*), which besides being used as boat timber, can be cut into blocks to act as holystones, shaved and steeped in water and wood ash to make a bleaching agent, and which also produces a leaf which will froth and clean like soap. The extremely common jumbay (*Leucaena leucocephala*), found in scrublands and thickets, is similarly versatile; not just a source of firewood and charcoal, but providing pulp for paper and rayon, leaves for fodder for cattle and goats (though not for donkeys and mules), timber for house-building, furniture, posts and poles, and shade for cultivated tree crops such as coffee and cacao.

Trees have been of vital importance throughout the history of the Bahamian people. Significantly, both the AMERINDIANS who first peopled the islands and the AFRICANS who were the ancestors of the modern Bahamian majority regarded trees as sacred. Beyond that, Bahamians as a whole can be said historically to have been as adaptively attuned to and dependent upon their terrestrial habitat as to the sea that surrounds their islands. These are aspects of the Bahamian heritage that deserve recognition, respect and, as far as possible, preservation.

Further reading: W. Cutts, *Trees of the Bahamas and Florida*, Macmillan Caribbean, 2002; D. G. Campbell, *The Ephemeral Islands: A Natural History of the Bahamas*, Macmillan, 1978; J. Patterson, *Native Trees of the Bahamas*, Bahamas National Trust, 2002.

TROTT, Governor Nicholas

(1658–1730) Most energetic and enterprising, and not the least rascally, of the Governors of The Bahamas appointed by the LORD PROPRIETORS (1693–6). A Bermudian merchant adventurer with useful connections, Trott claimed to have restored the Bahamian colony after it was laid waste by the Spanish, laying out the capital and renaming it NASSAU, building a fort, calling an Assembly, and passing laws regularising LAND TENURES. However, he set a precedent (notably followed by Governor Lord DUNMORE) by being himself the chief beneficiary of land grants. Most controversially he acquired Hog Island for 50 pounds and 8 shillings a year despite the inhabitants' claim that it was common ground. But he also obtained prime house lots in Nassau, plantations on NEW PROVIDENCE, and half of the entire island of EXUMA.

Nicholas Trott was accused by the Governor of Massachusetts of being 'the greatest pirate-broker that was ever in America'. His most notorious exploit was to allow the successful pirate Henry Avery to land his men and booty taken from the Great Mogul in Nassau in 1696 for a handsome levy in gold, on the unconvincing and contradictory plea that he was ignorant of who Avery was and that his ship outgunned Nassau's fort. Trott was relieved of his post by the Lord Proprietors and sailed to England to defend himself, but instead was briefly thrown into jail for illegally taxing a Dutch ship and appropriating its cargo. However, he recovered brilliantly by marrying Anne Amy, the daughter of one of the Lord Proprietors, going on to be one of the major early landowners in South Carolina – where his nephew and namesake was usefully, in succession, Attorney-General, Speaker and Chief Justice.

Further reading: J. Oldmixon, *History of the Isle of Providence*, Culmer, 1949; P. Albury, *Paradise Island Story*, Macmillan Caribbean, 1984, 15–22; Craton and Saunders, *Islanders*, i. 92–106.

TRUCK SYSTEM

Even more than by controlling farmable land, the Bahamian white ruling class was able to keep Bahamian blacks in subordination for a century after formal slavery ended by the manipulation of credit, especially the notorious truck system.

It can be argued that the control by the dominant class of the earning power of the employed dates back to slavery days, most directly in the way that owners appropriated the wages earned by hired-out slaves, save for the bare amount needed to sustain them. A more obvious forerunner of the post-slavery credit and truck systems occurred in the employment of LIBERATED AFRICANS in the SALT-pans which certain white entrepreneurs developed as alternative enterprises to the failed cotton plantations. Not only were the Liberated Africans compelled to this work, but the small wages they were legally entitled to earn were entirely deducted in payment for the necessary food and provisions they purchased from the stores owned by their employers.

Such a system was almost seamlessly adopted in the successive larger scale farming enterprises that the ruling class attempted to develop for a century after slavery ended, especially the growing of pineapples, tomatoes and sisal. In the most blatant instances, workers were paid only in tokens redeemable for purchases at the farm-owner's store. Credit was readily extended, as a form of virtual bondage. Such credit mechanisms to guarantee a supply of servile labour were also employed in sections of the ship-building industry, and in the stevedoring trade which long dominated the economy of the southeastern islands.

The most notorious example of the credit and truck system occurred in the Bahamian SPONGE industry, from the mid-nineteenth century onwards. This was memorably exposed by the outraged Stipendiary Magistrate Louis Diston POWLES, and his non-white friends who published the short-lived *Freeman* newspaper in the 1880s. The desperately poor sponge fishermen were caught in a vice because the boat-owners and outfitters and the sponge-buyers were effectively (and often literally) the same people. The situation is described in *Islanders in the Stream*:

> Since a sponging voyage normally took from six to eight weeks, the fishermen were willing candidates for advances from their employers, paid more often in truck goods [provisions, often of dubious quality] than in cash and credited against the proceeds of the voyage. Even had the returns been sufficient to free the mariners from an almost permanent cycle of debt, the payment of advances mainly in flour and other foodstuffs tempted the improvident to neglect farming while ashore and thus increased their dependence on the sponging trade. The most obnoxious feature of the fishermen's exploitation in the 1880s, though, was the final payment for the delivered sponges, which was not only rigged but secret. After the sale of the cargo [reported Governor Blake], the total amount of which was not known to the men, they were paid off in the merchant's office, each man receiving generally but a few shillings, which, he was informed, represented the balance due to him after the payment of the vessel's outfit, the amount of which he did not know, and of his private debt, of the items of which he knew nothing.

Though most of the abuses of the truck system were gradually corrected by legislation, the 'company store' syndrome continued to operate well into the twentieth century – particularly in the lumbering industry in Abaco and Grand Bahama – and the deleterious aspects of the credit system in general proved even more difficult to eradicate. The advancement of credit to ensure continuing patronage while tying the customer to the purchase of inferior goods at inflated prices, was the standard practice of Bay Street merchants (and, it must be said, of the more unscrupulous non-white shopkeepers too). Even more insidious was the fact that the liquor outlets, where many ordinary Bahamians became addicted, overspent and got heavily into debt, were almost monopolised by Bay Street merchants.

Further reading: H. Johnson, 'The Share System in the Nineteenth and Early Twentieth Centuries', 'Post-Emancipation Labour Systems', and 'The Credit and Truck Systems in the Nineteenth and Early Twentieth Centuries', in *The Bahamas in Slavery and Freedom*, Ian Randle Press, 1991, 55–109; Craton and Saunders, *Islanders*, ii. 34–45.

TURKS AND CAICOS ISLANDS Geographically a south-eastern extension of the Bahamian archipelago, and nominally under the jurisdiction of The Bahamas from 1764 to 1848, this chain of eight flat islands and 41 small cays is one of the few fragments of the former British Empire that have found it advantageous to remain a British overseas dependency into the twenty-first century. Though a fair number of Bahamians have roots in the Turks and Caicos Islands, connections are now more tenuous than ever – signified by the fact that only one plane flies each week and one ship sails each month between Nassau and Grand Turk.

Situated on both sides of the Turks Island Passage, which (being connected to the Windward Passage between Hispaniola and Cuba) is one of the major sea routes between the Atlantic and the Caribbean, the islands had considerable strategic value during colonial times and intermittently were pawns between Britain, France and Spain. Britain predominated because of the value of the Turks Island SALT-pans for the Newfoundland cod fishery and the importance of the islands as a way-station between Britain and her West Indian colonies, especially Jamaica.

The salt industry was developed by Bermudians and their slaves from 1670, and for almost a century the Turks Islands were virtually a subdependency of Bermuda. After the Seven Years' War (1756–63) Britain formally took control of the islands and placed them under the supervision of the Governor of The Bahamas. However, attempts to pass laws to regulate the salt industry and levy taxes had little success because of the difficulties of communication, the resistance of the Bermudian salt barons, and the insubordination of the agent appointed, Andrew Symmer. From time to time it was suggested that Turks Island be declared a free port, which acknowledged the reality that it traded as it willed. During the American War of Independence (1775–83) it became a notorious base for trading even with the American rebels. After 1783, however, as the outer fringe of the wave of migration that first populated many islands of The Bahamas, American LOYALISTS settled in the Caicos Islands to plant COTTON with their slaves. It was mainly this migration that led the British government to place the Turks and Caicos Islands more firmly under the jurisdiction of Nassau in 1799, despite continuing opposition from the older inhabitants.

From 1799 to 1848, representatives for the Turks and Caicos Islands sat in the Bahamian House of Assembly, though their attendance was irregular and their influence slight. The islands were also declared a separate Anglican parish (St George's) when six new parishes were created by the Assembly in 1795 – a fact that probably explains the apparent anomaly that the Anglican Church in the Turks and Caicos Islands fell under the jurisdiction of the first Bishop of The Bahamas (rather than of Jamaica) in 1861 and has remained part of the Anglican see of The Bahamas down to the present day.

As in the Bahamas at large, the cotton plantations failed even before slavery ended, and although salt production continued for a further century and Grand Turk became an important cable relay station in the 1880s, the islands themselves were desperately poor even by West Indian standards. Many of the islanders migrated for employment elsewhere, The Bahamas becoming the favourite destination once the Bahamian economy began to take off after World War Two. Black Turks Island labourers (employed especially in ABACO and GRAND BAHAMA) were regarded as hard workers and preferable to HAITIANS because they spoke English and were British subjects. But they were paid no more and treated little better – losing their preferential legal status as early as 1968.

Ruled as an impoverished sub-colony by Jamaica from 1848, the Turks and Caicos Islands (with a population of less than 7,000) resolutely decided to separate when Jamaica became independent in 1962. As The Bahamas itself became self-governing, there was considerable talk of it reincorporating the Turks and Caicos Islands. Most islanders favoured the move, but it was turned down by the BAY STREET regime in 1965 because the islands would be difficult to administer or develop from Nassau, and would be a drain on the Bahamian treasury for the foreseeable future. More far-fetched plans for the islands to become a province of Canada also came to nothing. With little choice but considerable enterprise, the islanders have made their own way – taking advantage of a constitution giving them internal self-government and the benefits of Britain's residual obligations alike. With several of the Caicos Islands becoming upmarket tourist destinations and Turks Island a moderately flourishing centre for offshore banking, the islands that might have become part of The Bahamas are now one of its regional competitors. This is despite the more than minor hiccup in 1992 when the Chief Minister was arrested and jailed in the United States for complicity in drug smuggling and Britain temporarily suspended the islands' constitution.

Further reading: C.D. Hutchings, *History of the Turks and Caicos Islands*, South Caicos, 1975; A. Dottis et al. (eds.), *Our Country: The Turks and Caicos Islands*, Macmillan Caribbean, 1989.

TURNQUEST, Hon. Sir Orville Alton

An able and eloquent lawyer who lacked the steely singlemindedness necessary to reach the very top in Bahamian politics, but became an effective and popular Governor-General (1995–2001).

Hon. Sir Orville Turnquest

Born of middle-class parents in Grant's Town, Nassau in 1930, Orville Turnquest was educated at GOVERNMENT HIGH SCHOOL, where from his small size he gained his life-long nickname 'Tiny' and was already somewhat in the shadow of his schoolmates Lynden PINDLING, Paul ADDERLEY and Cecil WALLACE-WHITFIELD. Articled in the chambers of the moderate black lawyer-politician A. F. ADDERLEY, he was called to the Bahamas Bar in 1953. He subsequently studied at the Inns of Court in London, and was called to the English Bar in 1960.

With Paul Adderley, Turnquest was one of the up-and-coming black professionals recruited by the PROGRESSIVE LIBERAL PARTY, being elected Secretary-Treasurer of the party from 1960 to 1962. In the 1962 general election he won a resounding victory alongside Lynden Pindling in the double-seat constituency of Nassau South Central, and seemed to have a bright future within the PLP. But he became nervous of the radical Black Power tendency within the party, and after the events of BLACK TUESDAY (1965), with Adderley, broke away to form the National Democratic Party. After a humiliating defeat in his home constituency of Grants Town in the 1967 general election that brought Pindling and the PLP to power, Turnquest concentrated on his legal career for some years, as junior partner to the distinguished conservative Eugene DUPUCH (1912–81). He then joined the united Opposition party calling itself the FREE NATIONAL MOVEMENT for the Independence election of 1972, only to suffer another electoral defeat.

Awarded the consolation prize of Opposition Leader in the Senate (1972), Turnquest now grew dissatisfied with the abrasive character and tactics of the FNM leader Wallace-Whitfield, and became a member of the splinter Bahamas Democratic Party. He lost his third consecutive election bid under that label in 1977. Only when the gentlemanly and moderate Kendal ISAACS was leader did Turnquest return to the FNM fold, sharing the party's gradual rise to power by winning the Fort Montagu seat for them in 1982 and holding it easily in 1987 and 1992.

Once Isaacs had retired and Wallace-Whitfield died, Orville Turnquest might have been expected to emerge as leader of the FNM. Instead, the party chose the PLP defector Hubert INGRAHAM, who led them to victory in 1992 and a landslide triumph in 1997. Turnquest instead was chosen to be the fifth Bahamian Governor-General in 1995, receiving a knighthood in 1997. He carried out his official duties with dignity and geniality, being notable for the way he made Government House accessible to all Bahamians.

TURTLES Aquatic turtles, freshwater as well as seawater, are still found in the The Bahamas. But like many other creatures valued by man for food or other reasons their survival is seriously threatened. All five species of sea turtle have been recorded in The Bahamas, though neither the huge jellyfish-eating leatherback (*Dermochelys coriacea*) nor the much smaller ridley (*Lepidochelys olivacea kempi*) were ever as common as the other three – which once roamed the whole archipelago in large numbers and laid their eggs on virtually every sandy Bahamian shore. Of these, the loggerhead (*Caretta caretta*) is the most common today, mainly because its shell has had no commercial value and its flesh is scarcely palatable. Rare specimens have been reported weighing 1,000 pounds (450 kg), with shells 7 feet (2 m) across, though most are less than half that size. Loggerheads, as their name suggests, have massive skulls and jaws, which can crunch open even a conchshell for the food inside.

Much more important commercially – and consequently more threatened with extinction – have been those sea turtles whose names are still recalled in two Bahamian locations where once they flourished: Freeport's Hawksbill Creek, and Abaco's offshore GREEN TURTLE CAY. The green turtle (*Chelonia mydas*), which alone of the sea turtles is a herbivore, was always much prized for its tasty steak meat and gelatinous 'callipee' (the basis for the traditional soup at the Lord Mayor of London's banquets) and for the way that the creature could be kept alive on deck to provide fresh meat on long sea voyages. Though the meat of the omniverous hawksbill (*Eretmochelys imbricata*) was not favoured, this turtle was highly valued for its mottled 'tortoiseshell', from which fashionable ladies' combs and other luxury items continued to be fashioned long after the coming of plastic substitutes. At

Green turtle female laying eggs

TYPHOID

the height of the traffic The Bahamas exported 20,000 pounds of tortoiseshell a year, though even by 1900 this had been reduced by two-thirds through overfishing.

Hawksbills, the rarest and smallest of Bahamian turtles, are now absolutely protected by law. There are heavy fines for killing them and fines with confiscation for persons attempting to import tortoiseshell products into the United States and some other countries. Unfortunately, there is not yet an absolute ban on the killing and eating of green turtles. But fishing them is forbidden in the four months between April and July, none less than 24 inches (60 cm) across may be killed, and none at all, or any of their eggs, may be taken from a nesting beach.

Turtle meat or soup is now an expensive rarity on Bahamian menus, but not expensive or rare enough. As the naturalist David Campbell wrote in 1978:

> *Anyone who has ever witnessed a green turtle, or any sea turtle, struggle onto a dark beach, excavate a nest and laboriously lay her eggs, one by one, or watched a giant wallowing in the sea, punctuated by occasional explosive breaths, must have sensed that these are truly primeval beasts, something very special in the animal kingdom. And anyone who has witnessed the slaughter of one of these reptiles in a market would be callous not to perceive the waste. The 'connoisseur' who sips clear turtle broth in a London restaurant, buys soon-to-be-forgotten knicknacks of 'tortoise' shell, or fantazises adventures in eating an overcooked turtle steak in a Nassau restaurant, is wasting a priceless biological resource. Sea turtles are objects of unique beauty which have evolved in accord with tides and currents and perhaps even the shifting of the continents. Their value is in their existence, not in the dollars, pounds and yen that, dismembered, they represent. (The Ephemeral Islands: A Natural History of the Bahamas,* Macmillan, 1978, p. 36)

Hardly less wonderful in their way than sea turtles are the two (perhaps two and a half) species of freshwater turtle still to be found in scattered Bahamian locations. As late as the 1930s the most numerous and widespread species, *Chrysemys felis*, was found in Andros, Eleuthera and Cat Island. Largely thanks to the islanders' taste for them (they call them 'peter') they are now found in only a few small freshwater ponds on Cat Island. The species *Chrysemis malonei* found in north-western Inagua (and named after a local commissioner) was not eaten by the natives, but was said to be almost extinct in the late 1970s because of repeated droughts. Around that time a curious third habitat was discovered not 3 miles (5 km) from downtown Nassau, in the freshwater ponds on the PARADISE ISLAND golf course – though it is thought that the turtles there were hybrids, sharing the genes of escaped pets as well as authentic Bahamian species.

Further reading: A. Carr, *So Excellent a Fishe: A Natural History of Sea Turtles*, Natural History Press, 1967; D. G. Campbell, *The Ephemeral Islands: A Natural History of the Bahamas*, Macmillan, 1978, 34–6, 72–4; M. E. Lightbourn, 'Conserving a Bahamian Heritage: The Mysterious Green Turtles', *Bahamas Handbook and Businessman's Annual, 1981–82*, Dupuch Publications, 1981, 106–15.

TYPHOID A debilitating, painful and sometimes fatal infection that as late as the 1920s challenged the reputation for healthiness which Nassau and The Bahamas wished to promote.

Periodic outbreaks of typhoid in Nassau were one of the motives for the Public Health Act of 1914, which attempted to reduce infections by cleaning up yards, latrines, drains and the public markets. But these measures proved ineffectual and led the government to address the major need: the provision of an adequate supply of clean and chlorinated drinking water. As Sir Wilfrid Beveridge's 1927 Public Health Report showed, typhoid remained endemic, and affected all quarters of the Bahamian capital. In a single eight-month period, no fewer than 81 cases of typhoid were reported. Predictably, the largest number, 34, were from Grant's Town and Bain Town, but at least as many were found in the crowded and insanitary suburbs to east and west, and even a handful in Nassau's downtown core. Worst of all, a few cases had occurred among tourist visitors.

Once the new waterworks were in full operation, along with the provision of Nassau's first sewerage system and the implementation of many of Beveridge's other health recommendations, typhoid epidemics soon became things of the past. Today, safe water supplies and well-observed health regulations (not to mention infinitely improved medical facilities) mean that visitors to The Bahamas have no reason to fear even those non-lethal but bothersome stomach upsets for which some other tourist destinations are notorious.

UNITED BAHAMIAN PARTY (UBP)

The formal party representing the white 'BAY STREET' oligarchy, formed to counter the emergent PROGRESSIVE LIBERAL PARTY in 1958. The UBP won the 1962 general election and led The Bahamas into limited self-government in 1964, but fell from office in 1967 and was almost blown away in the general election of 1968. Recognising that the days of 'white power' were over, the party was dissolved before the 1972 Independence election, with its few remaining active politicians joining forces with the FREE NATIONAL MOVEMENT in Opposition.

Before the formation of a party claiming to represent the black majority in 1953 and the election of six of its candidates in 1956, there was no need for the ruling white forces to play partisan politics. PLP activism inside and outside the House of Assembly – particularly the organised unrest that climaxed in the January 1958 general strike – compelled a change, and the UBP was formally constituted in March 1958. However, in the political escalation leading up to the 1962 election, the UBP held almost all the cards. The imbalances in the electoral system (with the Out Islands proportionately overrepresented, two and three-seat constituencies, and multiple voting) which had already helped the UBP obtain such a large majority were reinforced by the fact that the UBP had by far the larger financial resources. These enabled them to campaign more widely and efficiently, spending much money on propaganda and actually buying votes.

Added to this was the rapidly expanding economy, for which the UBP as the party of 'Bay Street' could claim the credit. A final intangible factor was the degree to which ordinary blacks, especially in the Out Islands, believed that politics, like business, was something special to white men, and that despite being the overwhelming majority of the population, non-whites had neither the experience nor the means to take over. Even the PLP's hopes that the recently enfranchised Bahamian women would feel differently and might tip the balance were destined to be dashed.

In the 1962 election the PLP could claim that they polled more total votes than the UBP but this was not reflected in the number of seats. The PLP won 6 of the 12 seats in New Providence but a mere 2 of the 21 in the Out Islands, leaving the UBP with a majority of 19 to 8 (with 4 UBP-leaning alleged Independents and a sole Labour Member). Accordingly, it was under the UBP that The Bahamas obtained internal self-government in 1964,

The core of the UBP; the almost entirely white composition of Parliament in the early 1950s

with a 'responsible' Cabinet headed by the first Premier, Sir Roland SYMONETTE. Buoyed by a generally booming world economy, the party presided over a phase of unprecedented expansion in tourism, offshore banking and foreign investment.

Though the Opposition proved to have its faint-hearts and the UBP went to great lengths with propaganda, gerrymandering and electoral bribery, PLP efforts and UBP misdemeanours were just enough to bring the government down in the general election of 10 January 1967. This time the PLP not only won 12 of the 17 New Providence seats but 6 of those in the Out Islands, exactly matching the total of 18 won by the UBP (4 and 14) – with the balance tipped by the one Independent, Alvin BRAYNEN, accepting the role of Speaker, and the one Labour winner, Randol FAWKES, siding with the PLP. The UBP was reluctant to accept its defeat, but Lynden Pindling's calm and canny leadership, the advantages accruing from being in power, and the landslide PLP victory that resulted from the tactical calling of a second election within 15 months, made it final.

On 10 April 1968, the UBP won only 4 Out Island and 3 New Providence seats to the PLP's total of 29 (13 and 16). Within a few months, one of the few remaining UBP Members, Basil Kelly, was announcing, 'We have to accept that white man's rule is finished in this country.' After failing to find credible black UBP candidates (with the sole exception of Cleophas Adderley, who filled the Nassau City seat vacated by the fugitive Sir Stafford Sands), the rump of the UBP sought to form a cross-ethnic alliance with other Opposition groups. Talks with the short-lived National Democratic Party occurred in 1969 but broke down over the question of leadership. By 1972 the UBP had officially dissolved and its remaining members merged with the fledgling FNM. Together they fought the Independence election, but with fairly disastrous results, though four white former UBP members (including the ageing Sir Roland Symonette) were among the nine successful FNM candidates.

The UBP was officially no more, but its spectre remained. The facts that the FNM espoused some of the political and economic principles of the UBP and did harbour some of its more liberal or flexible former members, for a long time allowed PLP zealots to claim that it was still the UBP in disguise and was even being manipulated by a cabal of 'white knights' behind the scenes. These myths gradually became threadbare, but it was not until 1992 that the FNM was finally able to topple the PLP.

Further reading: C.A. Hughes, *Race and Politics in the Bahamas*, University of Queensland Press, 1981; Craton and Saunders, ii, *passim*.

UNIVERSITY OF THE WEST INDIES Since its foundation as the University College of the West Indies in Jamaica in 1948 and its incorporation as a fully-fledged and autonomous university in 1962 the UWI has established and maintained itself as the premier tertiary education institution in the Commonwealth Caribbean. A durable relic of the abortive attempt to form a British West Indies Federation (1947–61), UWI is still a federal organisation, with its three main campuses at Mona, Jamaica; St Augustine, Trinidad; and Cave Hill, Barbados; and outreach facilities still serving all the former British colonies in the region with the exception of Guyana. However, the connection with The Bahamas, though initially useful, was never strong and since the 1980s has grown weaker, for two salient reasons: the lack of a compelling sense of political and cultural identity, and the steady progress of The Bahamas towards having an autonomous university of its own.

Just as the old BAY STREET oligarchy spurned any notion of joining the BWI Federation (a sentiment that may well have been mutual), it rejected the proposal of the moderately radical non-whites' Citizen Committee in the 1950s that The Bahamas should be a contributory participant in the new UCWI. This decision was reinforced as UWI became seen as a hotbed of young black radicals in the early 1960s. Nonetheless, UWI never closed its doors to Bahamians and in the mid-1960s appointed a Resident Tutor in Nassau to coach youngsters towards the University's fairly stiff, British-style entrance requirements. From the beginning, a trickle of non-white Bahamians, especially those studying law and medicine, preferred UWI to more expensive and distant options in the US, Canada and the UK. This flow was at its greatest as the PROGRESSIVE LIBERAL PARTY government provided many more scholarships for overseas studies during the 1970s. Close relations between UWI and The Bahamas climaxed with the establishment in Nassau of UWI's Centre for Hotel and Tourism Management (offering the last two years of a bachelor's degree and postgraduate diplomas in hotel and tourism management) in 1980.

Integration, though, did not proceed further. UWI had its own internal difficulties in the 1980s (which saw the three main campuses almost going their separate ways), at the same time that the growth of Bahamian nationalism saw the rejection of the Caribbean-oriented CXC examinations in the schools and a rising demand for the COLLEGE OF THE BAHAMAS (established in 1974) to move more quickly towards autonomy and university status. Ironically, this move was expedited not just by gradual disengagement from UWI but also by closer links with several American universities. Somewhat mixed signals were also displayed when the FREE NATIONAL MOVEMENT government in 1993 provided splendid new facilities for a Bahamian Tourism Training College in seeming competition with the UWI's well-established Centre for Hotel and Tourism Management. The situation was only partially resolved in 2000 when the BTTC was formally incorporated within the College of The Bahamas (as the School of Hospitality and Tourism Studies, SHTS), sharing the same Thompson Boulevard campus adjacent to the COB with the UWI's renamed Hotel Management Programme – officially still directed by the Social Studies Faculty in Mona, Jamaica.

Relations between the COB and UWI remain correct rather than cordial, and it seems unlikely that the connection will ever get closer again. Even the numbers of Bahamians studying medicine in Jamaica and Barbados and law in Barbados and Trinidad are yearly declining; the former through a preference for UK, Canadian or US schools and the gradual improvement of medical training facilities in The Bahamas, and the latter because of competition from the more convenient LLB and law diploma programmes offered by the COB and the Eugene Dupuch Law School (coincidentally both housed in the same premises as the BTTC and the SHTS).

College of The Bahamas School of Hospitality and Tourism Studies, affiliated with the University of the West Indies

VANGUARD PARTY Though carefully keeping the name of Marx and the label Communist out of its title, the Vanguard Nationalist and Socialist Party, which struggled in vain to gain a foothold in The Bahamas during the 1970s and 1980s, was a Marxist Communist group damagingly supported by Fidel Castro's totalitarian Cuba. It proved that however radical and suspicious of the United States and favourable to good relations with Cuba Bahamians might be, they were never likely to be attracted to a Communist ideology.

The VNSP originated in July 1971 as a splinter group of doctrinaire Marxists, led by John McCartney and Leonard Carey, which broke away from the idealistic radical organisation called Unicomm when a majority of its members decided to become more closely aligned to the ruling PROGRESSIVE LIBERAL PARTY. Impressively, if with discretion, the newly formed party declared: 'We call ourselves vanguard because we are the first party in the country that will address itself to the complete reconstruction of society. We call ourselves socialist because we believe that the wealth of the country belongs to the community and that there should be broader ownership of the means of production. We call ourselves nationalist because we believe that all principal institutions should be geared to suit the Bahamian people.'

Receiving financial aid from Cuba (which then meant indirectly from the USSR), the party brought out a well-written newspaper, the *Vanguard*. This was given away free at street corners to those unable or unwilling to buy it. Free 'fraternal visits' to Cuba were offered, along with student scholarships to Cuban schools and universities. These had a fair number of takers, but made few if any permanent converts. Those whom the party did recruit were as likely to be attracted by its support for Black Power in the United States as for the Castroite Revolution in Cuba. In the best Bahamian democratic tradition, the VNSP was tolerated. But its suppression was scarcely necessary. This was apparent in the party's dismal showing in the general elections which it contested. In 1977, for example, the VNSP's five candidates polled a grand total of 55 votes.

An indication of the VNSP's subservience to Cuba and the Communist International (Comintern), and a serious setback to its hopes of gaining Bahamian adherents, was its failure to condemn Cuba at the time of the sinking of HMBS *FLAMINGO* in May 1980. The party seized the chance to align with the PLP government when it protested the US invasion of Grenada in November 1983, but this show of solidarity was an embarrassment rather than an asset for the government. The drying up of external funding with the decline of Russian financial support for Cuba was almost a death blow – emphasised and probably accelerated by John McCartney's decision to return to the full-time teaching of political science in the United States. The VNSP nominally contested the general elections of 1982 and 1987 but these were no more than hopeless (some would say pathetic) gestures. Perhaps the crowning irony was that by 2003 the only current reference to 'Vanguard Bahamas' on the Internet was for a cruise-ship excursion from Baltimore to Nassau by a company called Van Guard Tours and Cruises.

Further reading: *The Struggle For Freedom In The Bahamas*, Vanguard Nationalist and Socialist Party of the Bahamas, 1980; J. T. McCarthy, 'The Influence of the Black Panther Party (USA) on the Vanguard Party in the Bahamas', *New Political Science*, 21 (2), 1999, 205–16.

VENDUE HOUSE Probably the oldest surviving public building in NASSAU, dating from 1769 and called 'the Vendue House or Bourse' by the visitor Johann Shoepf in 1783. Situated on the north side of BAY STREET facing up George Street towards GOVERNMENT HOUSE, it was originally a single-storey stone building much like the central market building in a typical small English town, with three open arcades at each end and five on the sides. As its name suggests, its most notable function was for sales by auction – of slaves as well as landed properties, ships and other goods. But it was also the hub of the 'huckstering' trade (informal daily marketing) until a larger covered market was built further down Bay Street shortly after the end of slavery. A focal meeting point for Nassauvians of all classes, the Vendue House was the

Vendue House at the northern end of George Street in one of the very first Bahamian photographs, early 1860s

chief place where public notices were posted (especially important before the coming of NEWSPAPERS) and also gained a reputation as the gathering place for the rowdier and less reputable elements among the populace.

By the end of the nineteenth century, Vendue House had lost most of its earlier functions and importance. Just before World War One, its arcades were bricked in, a second storey was added, and it became first the home of Nassau's telegraph office, telephone exchange and electricity department, and then the offices of the BAHAMAS ELECTRICITY CORPORATION. By the time BEC relocated in the 1970s, Vendue House had become seriously shabby. It was handsomely restored by the government with help from the BACARDI Company in the early 1990s and in 1993 became the POMPEY Museum. Named after the celebrated leader of one of the very few Bahamian slave revolts (1830), the museum concentrated on the history of those blacks who were once sold in the building. It also contained a permanent display of the work of the modern black intuitive painter Amos FERGUSON. Paintings and exhibits were fortunately saved from the effects of the serious Bay Street fire of October 2001, though the building itself was somewhat scorched.

VESCO, Robert Corporate swindler on a mammoth scale who made a considerable impact on the local economy (not to say morals) when he fled to The Bahamas in the 1970s.

Born the son of a Detroit auto worker in 1934, Robert Vesco left school at 16 and had his first job in an auto body shop. Moving to New York and New Jersey in the late 1950s he rose rapidly from being an engineer in a chemical works and an independent manufacturers' representative to become a high-profile whizz-kid in the risky world of company promotion, acquisitions and mergers. In the mid-1960s, by methods later called 'unscrupulous acts of financial legerdemain' he put together a portfolio of companies, the combined annual turnover of which he claimed to have increased from $1.3 million to $100,000,000 within three years. To many investors, large and small, he seemed a get-rich-quick magician.

Vesco's crucial coup was to parlay his insubstantial edifice of mainly manufacturing companies into the acquisition of the Swiss-based investment firm International Overseas Services in 1971, systematically stripping its assets and transferring as much as a quarter of a billion dollars into his personal accounts. Anticipating grand jury and US Security Exchange Commission indictments for this and for an illegal $250,000 contribution to the fund to re-elect President Richard Nixon, Vesco transferred his activities to The Bahamas in 1972.

In Nassau, Vesco bought up a local bank, Butler's, renamed it the Bahamas Commonwealth Bank, and said that he intended to make it the virtual national bank of the newly independent Bahamas. With or without direct bribery, he guaranteed himself against extradition to the United States (or Switzerland) by spreading around at least $25 million in local business investments and soft personal loans to key individuals. Among those involved was Prime Minister Lynden PINDLING, whose palatial new Prospect Ridge mansion was said to have been financed with Vesco money – though under investigation Pindling explained that the original loan had been made by Butler's Bank and that soon after he learned it had been transferred to Vesco's Bahamas Commonwealth Bank he made other arrangements.

While still based in The Bahamas, Robert Vesco was thought to have further padded his ill-gotten fortune through arms deals with rogue-state Libya and involvement with the Colombian Medellin drug cartel. It was only when the campaign against DRUG-RUNNING in The Bahamas began to heat up at the beginning of the 1980s that Vesco's immunity against extradition became tenuous, and he left The Bahamas. After similar but decreasingly secure stays in Panama, Costa Rica and Antigua, Vesco, somewhat bizarrely, found safe haven in Castro's Cuba in 1984. There he is said to live in far from socialist austerity, with his own luxurious mansion, yacht and plane.

VODUN The correct name for an authentic West African and Afro-Caribbean religion, that has been the official religion of Benin since 1996, is almost universal in HAITI, and is still practised among the thousands of HAITIAN immigrants in The Bahamas. Vodun should not be referred to as 'Voodoo' – the name given to the inauthentic and sinister version invented in the United States that is one of the staples of Hollywood and pulp fiction.

Vodun is an animistic religion with generally unacknowledged parallels to Roman Catholicism, which originated thousands of years ago among the Yoruba people of Dahomey (now Benin) in West Africa. It survived and flourished with gradual syncretic changes among the slaves carried to the New World. Variants are known elsewhere as *Candomble*, *Macumba*, *Obeah*, *Santeria* and *Umbanda*. But true Vodun is centred on Haiti, where the overwhelming majority of the people are black and the country has been proudly independent since 1804. Over the last 200 years, the only consistent outside influence has been the Roman Catholic Church, to which the majority of Haitians, including ardent Vodun practitioners, nominally belong. This adherence is clearly attributable to common beliefs in a supreme being, a pantheon of saint-like lesser spirits, forces of evil as well as good, the intercessionary and mystic role of priests, and ceremonies that include ritualistic consumption of flesh and blood.

The chief god of Vodun, whom the Yoruba called *Olorun*, is omnipotent, remote and unknowable. Communication, however, can be made through the hundreds of minor spirits called *loa*, each of whom has special attributes and powers and can be supplicated through sacrificial gifts, to avert catastrophe or achieve desired benefits. The *loa* who derived from Africa are termed *rada*; those added from the New World, often revered leaders now deceased, are called *petro*. Among the notably ominous or powerful *loa* are *Baron Samedi*, the guardian of the grave, *Dambala* the serpent spirit, *Erinle* the spirit of the forests, *Erzulie*, female spirit of love, *Mawu Lisa* spirit of creation, *Ogun* spirit of war, *Osun* spirit of healing streams, *Shango* spirit of storms, and *Zaka* spirit of agriculture.

Male Vodun priests are called *houngans* and female *mambos*. A vodun temple is called a *hounfor*. At its focus is a pillar called a *poteau-mitan* where the god and spirits communicate with the worshippers. There is also an altar, elaborately decorated with candles, pictures of Christian saints, and symbolic items related to the *loa*. The main purpose of Vodun ritual is to make contact with a particular spirit, to gain its favour by offering animal sacrifices and gifts, and to obtain help in the way of better crops, a higher standard of living, and relief from sickness. Rituals are also held to celebrate lucky events, to escape a run of ill-fortune, to celebrate the *loa* on its special day, or as rites of passage at times of birth, marriage and death. Ceremonies are preceded or may be followed by a feast, and consist of the creation of a *veve*, or pattern of cornflour on the floor special to the *loa* supplicated, music from purified rattles and drums, dancing rising to a climax in spirit possession, and the drinking of blood from sacrificed animals.

Almost invariably, *hougans* and *mambos* confine their activities to practising 'white magic' designed to bring good fortune or healing. Priests called *bokors* dedicated to evil sorcery or 'black magic' are far less common. However, there are at least two aspects of Vodun belief and practice that have uncomfortable features for outsiders. One is the belief that each person has a soul which consists of two parts; the inseparable *gros bon ange* ('big guardian angel'), and the *ti bon ange* ('little guardian angel') that leaves the body during sleep or spirit possession and can suffer damage, or even wander away. Another belief unique to Vodun is that a dead person can be revived as a *zombie*. This wandering soul has no will of its own, but is under the control of others, sometimes for evil purposes. Though most Haitians believe in zombies (just as Jamaicans believe in *duppies*) and many claim to have encountered one, the less credulous regard them simply as persons who have not actually died but have been put under the influence of powerful soporifics by priests exercising 'black' sorcery medicine.

The widely held view of outsiders that 'Voodoo' priests and practitioners exercise their evil arts by sticking pins into dolls representing persons they wish to harm, though it may be based on practices occasionally observed in South America, is a sensational and misleading invention. A product of centuries of bigotry and oppression inspired by fear, such misrepresentations distort and bring discredit to a genuine religion older than Christianity itself, still practised by some 60 million people – and at least worthy of sympathetic consideration, tolerance and respect.

Further reading: A. Metraux, *Voodoo in Haiti*, Andre Deutsch, 1959; W. Davis, *Passage of Darkness: The Ethnobiology of the Haitian Zombie*, University of North Carolina Press, 1988; 'Vodun and related religions', www.religious tolerance.org/voodoo.htm

WALKER'S CAY This tiny resort island has the distinction (and advantage) of being the northernmost scrap of habitable land in The Bahamas, 500 miles (800 km) in a direct line from Matthew Town, Inagua, at the country's south-eastern tip.

Probably named for Thomas Walker, the Lord PROPRIETORS' Vice Admiralty judge, who used it as a refuge from the Spanish and the pirates occupying Nassau in the early 1700s, Walker's Cay owed its success as a resort to its closeness to the United States, its convenience as a stopping place between Florida and the ABACOS, and for its superlative fishing of all types. According to its publicity, it has held more International Game Fishing Association records than any other resort in the world, as well as being the base for some of the finest casting for bonefish.

No more than a mile (1.6 km) long, Walker's Cay consists almost entirely of a two-runway airport on the northern half, a small artificial harbour in the centre, a 62-room hotel, and a clubhouse on a 50-foot (15-m) bluff at the southern end. It has two swimming pools (one with sea water, one with fresh). There are also two good beaches, but would-be swimmers from the resort have to be wary of small planes using the busy airstrips, including the thrice-daily service by A. B. CHALK'S airline based in Fort Lauderdale.

Walker's Cay was first developed as a fishing camp just before World War Two. It became an exclusive resort for wealthy Americans during the 1950s and 1960s, when two of its most famous (or notorious) frequent visitors were President-to-be Richard M. Nixon and his long-time friend and business associate 'Bebe' Rebozo. After a period of decline, the resort was revived and expanded for a slightly more popular market in the 1990s. The clientele, however, is still almost exclusively American. The Bahamian staff of the resort commute daily from populous Grand Cay, 3 miles (4.8 km) to the south-east.

WALLACE-WHITFIELD, Hon. Sir Cecil (1930–1990) A brilliant and dynamic but damagingly outspoken black politician, whose ambition to be Prime Minister disrupted in turn both the PROGRESSIVE LIBERAL PARTY (of which he was one of the earliest recruits) and the Opposition FREE NATIONAL MOVEMENT, which he helped to form but led only in defeat.

Cecil Wallace-Whitfield was born within the same week and in the same district as Lynden PINDLING, who was destined to be his chief political rival. Unlike Pindling, he was illegitimate, taking his surname from both his Whitfield father and his Wallace mother. Like Pindling (and many other future lawyer-politicians) he was educated at GOVERNMENT HIGH SCHOOL, but started a career in Customs before turning to the law and politics.

Wallace-Whitfield made a creditable showing in contesting the BAY STREET stronghold of Eleuthera in the elections of 1956 and 1962 and quickly rose within the inner circle of the PLP. After playing an important role in the events of 'BLACK TUESDAY' (1965) he was selected by the party to stand for his home constituency of St Agnes in Over-the-Hill Nassau in the crucial 1967 election. His resounding victory then (repeated in the following year) almost inevitably led to his selection as a Minister in Premier Pindling's first Cabinet.

As Minister first of Works and then Education Wallace-Whitfield demonstrated tremendous energy and enthusiasm and made impressive headway. But his overexpenditure and impatience with the pace of progress, coupled with his obvious ambition, his high profile, and even his very success as a Minister, led to serious friction with Pindling and the inner guard of the PLP. This grew steadily worse and climaxed at the PLP National Convention in October 1970. After an impassioned speech, Wallace-Whitfield resigned from the government, memorably quoting Martin Luther King's 'Free, free at last, my soul is free at last.'

Seven other dissidents joined Wallace-Whitfield in forming what they called at first the Free PLP, but which soon became the nucleus of repeated attempts to form an united and viable Opposition. The difficulty was welding together those who had left the PLP at different times for different reasons with the remnants of Bay Street's UNITED BAHAMIAN PARTY and others previously uncommitted to either party. But this task was complicated by the fact that while some would accept no leader but Wallace-Whitfield, others were unwilling to accept him at any price.

The Opposition fought and lost the 1972 election as the FREE NATIONAL MOVEMENT, with Wallace-Whitfield losing his own St Agnes seat by a wide margin. In 1977 with the Opposition split, the FNM lost again, with Wallace-Whitfield, this time standing for Marsh Harbour, Abaco, coming third in the poll. The Opposition reunited and did rather better in 1982 and 1987 when the leadership was virtually shared, between Kendal ISAACS as parliamentary leader and

WARRI

Wallace-Whitfield as party chairman. Capitalising on the widespread dissatisfaction with the PLP in Grand Bahama, Wallace-Whitfield achieved his last great electoral victories by winning for the FNM Pine Ridge in 1982 and Marco City in 1987 – the fourth and fifth constituencies he had contested in his 30-year career.

Kendal Isaacs resigned after the FNM's defeat in 1987 and Wallace-Whitfield at last became the party's parliamentary leader. By now though he was suffering from a mortal illness and his force was spent. In a move that was both generous and an indication that he was no longer a political threat, Lynden Pindling recommended his old rival and adversary for a knighthood, which he received from the Queen in August 1989. He died in May 1990, at the age of 60.

WARRI A once very popular 'pit and pebble' board game for two persons, midway in complexity and in the degree of skill required between checkers and chess. It originated in ancient Egypt some 3,500 years ago. Spreading to much of Asia and throughout Africa, it was brought to the Americas, including The Bahamas, by slaves from West Africa.

The West African word *warri* means 'houses', and each contest is a simulated war-game in which the winner is the first person to capture more than half of his (or her) opponent's houses. The rules for taking out opponents and capturing 'houses' are relatively simple, but the strategy and tactics involved to make a champion require immense skill and planning. An annual international warri tournament is held in Cannes, France, and there is a section for warri in the 'Mind Games Olympiad' held each year in London.

Until modern times Warri was one of the favourite pastimes of non-white Bahamians. It was not necessarily played on a wooden board; scooped holes and pebbles on a beach or piece of flat ground could serve. Incisions for playing warri have been found on a window-ledge at the late eighteenth-century ruins of Winton Fort guarding the eastern approaches to NEW PROVIDENCE – no doubt indicating how non-white sentinels whiled away the tedium of long fruitless watches. Some warri is still played in The Bahamas, sometimes on antique boards. However, the popularity of warri was gradually eroded by checkers among the ordinary people and by chess and backgammon among the middle classes, before being overwhelmed by the rage for DOMINOES (imported directly or indirectly from the United States) from the 1950s. Handsome wooden warri boards are still to be found on sale in Nassau and Freeport (generally carved by HAITIANS), but these are mainly for the tourist market.

WATER SUPPLIES With no rivers or streams (let alone snowfields or glaciers) and being made of extremely porous limestone, The Bahamas has no natural resources of surface fresh water. Its people traditionally relied on catching rainwater off roofs in cisterns or barrels, or on wells, which were often far from the house and sometimes went brackish with overuse. A mains water system was first introduced in Nassau in the early twentieth century (see STANDPIPES) and gradually extended to all substantial settlements by mid-century, though finding enough water to tap was always problematic and the cost relatively high (see COST OF LIVING).

In fact, The Bahamas, which for the most part has an adequate rainfall, does have large reserves of subterranean fresh water, because seeping rainwater does not readily mingle with the underlying seawater and lies as a freshwater 'lens' under the land surface, atop the layers of brackish and salt water. The chief problem, though, is that the most plenteous lenses do not necessarily lie in the areas of densest settlement, and for New Providence in particular the expansion of the population hugely outran the capacity of the island's well-fields. In contrast, Grand Bahama had easily tappable reserves that the early developers of Freeport claimed were sufficient for a population of a million – 25 times the population in fact living there by the year 2000. Andros – by far the largest Bahamian island – was even more richly endowed, with subterranean freshwater lenses up to 100 feet (30 m) thick extending over a quarter of its land area – to serve a mere 7,000 people.

Before 1945, Nassau was supplied almost entirely from the well-field called Perpall's Tract just to the west of town, but from then on water was drawn from farther afield, especially the area of BLUE HILLS and LAKE KILLARNEY. By 1971, when the population of New Providence had reached 100,000, the island's well-fields were being tapped to the extent of two billion gallons a year, but were already overtaxed, with the quality of water deteriorating. During the 1970s, means were urgently explored to augment supplies, with desalination plants being initially most favoured. The process of reverse osmosis – which had been privately adopted on a very small scale at CAT CAY and WALKER'S CAY – was soon rejected as far too costly. Instead, reliance was placed on a still experimental method of obtaining distilled water from steam-driven electricity generators. At their peak the distillation plants at Clifton Pier and Blue Hills produced 390 million gallons of pure water a year. But serious problems with salt-encrustation coupled with the multiplication of oil prices in the mid-1970s led to the complete discontinuation of this source by the end of the decade. By this time water supplies in New Providence were totally inadequate.

Andros came to the rescue in a way that should have been obvious from the beginning. From 1978, water pumped from the plentiful lenses of North Andros began to be barged from Morgan's Bluff to Nassau's ARAWAK CAY, where it was transferred into the New Providence water mains. In 1982 this relief amounted to no more than had been obtained from distillation. But within the following two decades, as the population of New Providence came close to a quarter million, the supply from Andros rose steadily, to more than double what was being produced from the local well-fields – for a total of more than four billion gallons a year. Besides this, several of the newest hotels, including the *ATLANTIS* complex, took advantage of improved technology, and installed their own reverse osmosis plants.

New Providence is adequately provided with water but the supply is carefully metered and not cheap (let alone free, as it was once to those who depended on standpipes).

There is a minimum charge of up to $122 per quarter with the first 3,000 gallons free. Above 3,000 gallons the charge is from $12 up to $20 per thousand gallons, depending on the total amount used. For the Family Islands with mains services provided by the Water & Sewerage Corporation (Abaco, Eleuthera, Exuma and San Salvador) the changes are about half those in New Providence. In Freeport-Lucaya and the other settlements served by the privately owned Grand Bahama Utility Company (which can provide up to nine million gallons a day from its four well-fields) the charges are a comparative bargain: $3.40 per month per thousand gallons for the first 10,000 gallons, and no more than $4.80 per thousand gallons for unlimited usage.

Freeport boasts that its piped water is perfectly safe to drink from the tap. Elsewhere, advice is more cautious. 'The Bahamas has its own natural purification system in its limestone base,' says the *Lonely Planet Guide*. 'Water is usually safe to drink from faucets throughout the islands, but this is not guaranteed. If you don't know for certain that the water is safe, always assume the worst.' Perhaps the best indicator is that almost every Bahamian who can afford it drinks and cooks with nothing but the freely available and reasonably priced distilled water.

WEST INDIA REGIMENTS Black regiments of the British Army first raised in 1795 and with a close association with The Bahamas, as garrison troops (1801–91) and as the units which many Bahamians voluntarily joined in WORLD WAR ONE (1915–18) and some in WORLD WAR TWO (1944–6).

The need to expand British forces in the West Indies to include black troops was greatly accelerated by the threat posed by the Haitian and French Revolutions, the extensive campaigns undertaken, and by the horrendous mortality suffered by troops sent straight from Europe. Arguing that army service was preferable to plantation slavery, and making promises (hardly ever kept) that soldier slaves would be freed once their service was up, the War Office raised no fewer than 12 regiments of black slaves between 1795 and 1798. These were recruited in part from creolised slaves whom the planters could be persuaded to spare, but mainly from slaves freshly brought from Africa. In all, the Army bought 13,400 slaves for military service before the slave trade was ended in 1808, at an average cost of £70, and spent almost as much in purchasing slaves from colonial owners before the wars ended in 1815. In all, probably 100,000 black troops served the British in the Caribbean during the last French wars, of whom perhaps half died while serving.

Water tower, the highest viewpoint on New Providence, built on Fort Fincastle (Bennet's) Hill 1928

WEST INDIA REGIMENTS

West India regiment Bahamas garrison soldier in *zouave* uniform, 1880s

Though there was a separate militia unit for non-whites in The Bahamas from the time of Governor DUNMORE (1787–96), the local whites professed satisfaction with their puny white garrison and were seriously alarmed when this was replaced by a detachment of 272 black soldiers from the 5th and 6th West India Regiment in May 1801. Since Britain and France were temporarily at peace they were regarded as unnecessary. The whites changed their tune once war was renewed and generally welcomed the recruitment into the local garrison, from 1881, of the most able-bodied of the LIBERATED AFRICANS released from illicit slave ships.

After slavery ended, the West India Regiment soldiers were rotated between Nassau and their base in Jamaica but not removed, becoming indeed more firmly established once an airy new barracks was built on the site of the dismantled Fort Nassau in 1837. Their parades and guard duties made them a familiar part of the Nassau scene (later, a picturesque tourist attraction). Though never fully trusted or appreciated by the Bahamian whites, they generally served as a neutral and disciplined back-up to the local police forces and an armed safeguard in cases of more serious civil disturbance. Accordingly, once they were removed in 1891, following the combination of the 1st and 2nd Regiments, it was considered imperative immediately to reorganise the local police – significantly making it a quasi-military force recruited from other parts of the British West Indies.

The Bahamian connection with British military forces was renewed, and reached its peak, in World War One. At the beginning of the war it was Britain's intention not to augment the existing non-white units (such as the West India Regiment) or to employ any of them in combat against European forces. The awful slaughter on the Western Front led to a revision of this policy by the beginning of 1915. The War Office created an entirely new unit called the British West Indies Regiment and put out a call for volunteers to serve 'King and Empire'. This elicited a huge response from every colony, not least The Bahamas, especially Jamaica. In all, 12 battalions were formed, trained in Jamaica and dispatched to the Middle East and the Western Front – though only three battalions saw active service and the remainder were employed in pioneer and supply line duties. In all, 397 officers and 15,204 other ranks served in the West Indies Regiment between 1915 and 1919, of whom no fewer than 10,280 were Jamaicans, 1,478 from Trinidad, 831 from Barbados and 486 (in eight separate drafts) from The Bahamas. Of the full total, 185 were killed and 697 wounded on active duty, and 1,071 perished from sickness. Of Bahamians, six men were killed in action, three died of wounds, and 28 from other causes.

The British West Indies Regiment was treated scarcely better than their forerunners a century earlier. At one stage there was a near mutiny when the War Office attempted to deny a 50 per cent pay increase awarded to white units, and in 1918 the 10th Battalion actually mutinied over conditions in their camp at Taranto, Italy. Other black soldiers in hospital or awaiting demobilisation were targeted in a race riot in Liverpool, England, early in 1919. The War Office clearly regarded the BWIR as a temporary expedient and was glad to disband it later in 1919. Many of its veterans, including Bahamians, came back to their homelands with their imperial patriotism dimmed and with hopes – not to be soon fulfilled – of effecting political change.

However, it was not the experience of the earlier war so much as other opportunities to serve, in home defence as well as by sea and air, that retarded the raising of a unit in World War Two similar to the British West Indies Regiment of World War One. It was not until 1944, more than four years after the war started, that a First Caribbean Regiment was formed out of homeguard units from various colonies. The Bahamas contributed volunteers from the Bahamas Defence Force set up in 1942, providing the nucleus of a Bahamas Battalion in the new regiment – some of whom saw service briefly in Italy and Egypt before the war ended. The Caribbean Regiment was disbanded in 1946, but not before it had demonstrated significant differences from its predecessor: both in its division into battalions by region and in having for the first time non-white commissioned officers. Among these were the Bahamian lieutenant Wenzel Granger, who led a detachment of the Bahamas Battalion in Italy and was later to head the Bahamian POLICE, and the 19-year-old second lieutenant KENDAL ISAACS – later to become the Attorney General and Leader of the Opposition in a self-governing and independent Bahamas.

The one final attempt to create a military force for the entire British Caribbean was an even more emphatic indicator of the political change accelerated in the region by World War Two. In 1959 the name West India Regiment was revived for the unit intended to serve the planned Federation of the West Indies. This, of course, did not survive the rapid dissolution of the Federation itself, being disbanded in 1961. As an inevitable indicator of the evolution of colonies into independent states it has been succeeded by a galaxy of separate defence forces. Among the last-formed of these – though not least in efficiency, smartness and even size – was the ROYAL BAHAMAS DEFENCE FORCE, instituted in 1976.

Further reading: R. N. Buckley, *Slaves in Redcoats: The British West Indic Regiments, 1795-1815*, Yale, 1979; F. Holmes, *The Bahamas in the Great War*, Tribune, 1924; www.lineone.net/bwir/regiments.html

WEST INDIES FEDERATION Promoted by Britain as the most convenient way to devolve responsibility for the West Indian colonies after World War Two, and the speediest, if not the only, way that such small units might be granted full independence with Dominion status within the Commonwealth, the West Indies Federation actually lasted a far shorter time (1958–62) than the period during which it was discussed and planned (1948–58). Old rivalries were not fully buried, particularly between the three chief participants (Jamaica, Trinidad and Tobago and Barbados). The climactic downfall came when Britain reversed its previous stance and allowed Jamaica to achieve political independence and full Commonwealth membership on its own in 1962 – to be rapidly followed by Trinidad and Tobago and Barbados.

Though some of the earlier proposals for a British West Indian federation included The Bahamas (as well as Bermuda and the mainland American colonies of British Guiana and British Honduras), there was little enthusiasm in the West Indies and even less in The Bahamas for the islands' inclusion in the preliminary negotiations. Progressive West Indians regarded The Bahamas as a politically backward outlier that was more attuned to the United States than to the Caribbean, while the white BAY STREET oligarchy then in control feared not only political and bureaucratic interference, but being financially drained and swamped by immigrants of a different colour and culture. The Bahamas did not participate in the federal negotiations even as an observer, and any subsequent adherence to the Federation was obviated by its demise long before the coming of black majority rule (1967).

Further reading: D. Lowenthal, *The West Indies Federation: Perspectives on a New Nation*, Greenwood Press, 1961; G. K. Lewis, *The Growth of the Modern West Indies*, McGibbon and Kee, 1968.

WHALES Once upon a time many species of whales, including the great humpback and sperm whales, swarmed in Bahamian waters. Fishing for them, as well as searching the beaches for their AMBERGRIS, were among the motives that drew the first English settlers to the islands. For several reasons, whale fishing never developed fully in The Bahamas. But the huge demand for oil and other whale products during the nineteenth and twentieth centuries led to such worldwide depletion that only a fraction of the former number of whales now visit The Bahamas. The comparative few remaining now that protective measures are at least partially in place, however, does allow for occasional sightings and scientific research on one of the natural wonders of creation.

In pre-Columbian times, Bahamian whales were more or less invulnerable to Lucayan fishermen because of their size. But the earliest English promoters of The Bahamas mentioned whales, and even more their ambergris, as among the islands' attractions. It was more than mere coincidence that Hugh Wentworth, the first Governor of The Bahamas for the Lord PROPRIETORS (1670–1) was also the managing director of the first Bermudian whaling company. The two most prized of the almost legendary leviathans were the plankton-filtering humpback and the toothed carnivorous sperm whale, also known as the great white. Both of these species migrated in huge numbers from the Newfoundland Banks to the Antilles in the spring-time, the humpback females to bear and suckle their calves mainly in the south-eastern shallows of the Bahamian archipelago before returning northwards, while the sperm whales roamed rather more widely and longer through the islands. In 1836 the Colonial Secretary Charles Nesbitt reported seeing a shoal of 30 to 40 great whites disporting in the ocean just off Nassau's Hog Island.

Both the humpback and great white whales (often 55 feet (19 m) long, weighing 50 tons, and capable of smashing or dragging down quite large wooden vessels) were too large and fierce for Bahamian whale-fishers, or even the better-armed and more daring Bermudians. It was the intrepid New Englanders, immortalised in Herman Melville's *Moby Dick,* who came to dominate the whaling industry, and in the process reduce the great whales to a rarity in The Bahamas and throughout the western Atlantic.

Bahamian whalers, based either in ABACO or in the south-eastern islands, fished mainly for smaller prey, including monk seals (until they were gone), bottle-nosed dolphins, and pilot whales. Harpooning even medium-sized whales (up to 20 foot (6 m) in length) from open dories could still be hazardous, and fishermen were not infrequently drowned or seriously injured. Operations came to an end in the early twentieth century, however, not because of the physical risks involved but because the shortage of prey and the unfavourable ratio between the cost of outfitting and processing the catch against the financial return made it no longer commercially viable.

In the late twentieth century, whale watching has superseded whale fishing in The Bahamas as in most of the world. Though the untold multitude of great whales once migrating through Bahamian waters each year are now reduced to less than a thousand, sightings still arouse excitement and awe – heightened by the continuing discoveries made by scientists about whale characteristics and behaviour. Even more awesome than the size they attain is the means the great whales have of communicating with each other. Such 'whale songs', still imperfectly understood, are messages far more complex than birdsong, lasting half an hour and with almost infinite modulations.

Curiously, humpback whales do not 'sing' while they are feeding on the rich fish and plankton grounds during the summer and autumn. During the winter calving period in The Bahamas and the West Indies only single whales sing. Mother whales keep silent, probably to protect their comparatively vulnerable offspring. Recent research has shown that whales can communicate over dozens, perhaps hundreds, of miles as they travel. This enables herds ('pods') to keep in touch and formation, passing on information and warnings. Though this wonderful attribute has served the species well for millions of years, it has not saved whales from the danger of extermination by modern human predators. Ironically, in The Bahamas, it has been man's own experiments with underwater sonar which pose one of the latest threats to whales' survival. When a half dozen disoriented pilot whales landed up on a beach and perished in Grand Bahama and Abaco in 2001, it was determined that their own sophisticated sonar apparatus had been disrupted by experiments carried out from the US Atlantic Undersea Testing and Evaluation Center (AUTEC) on Andros.

Further reading: H. T. Andersen (ed.), *The Biology of Marine Mammals*, London, 1969; L. Watson, *Sea Guide to Whales of the World*, London, 1981; K. Balcomb *et al.*, 'Mass Stranding of Cetaceans Caused by Naval Sonar', *Bahamas Journal of Science*, 8 (2), 2001.

WILLIAMS, Egbert Austin 'Bert' (1874–1922)

Bahamian-born entertainer of genius, whose art transcended the conventions of the 'nigger minstrel' show to bring him top-billing on Broadway and international fame.

Bert Williams was born in east Nassau in 1874, but moved with his family to California when he was 12. He showed such a precocious talent at high school as a dancer and mime that he decided on a stage career. In 1893, when he was 19, Bert teamed up with George Walker, the son of a black policeman from Kansas, starting a partnership that lasted until shortly before Walker died in 1909. Originally billed as 'The Real Coons' they developed a routine in which the black Walker was the artful schemer with an affected accent, who tended to be outsmarted by the light-skinned Williams, playing the part of a 'country bumpkin' with the accent of a 'Southern nigger'. Adding brilliant comic moves that were as much mime as dance, and a repertoire of catchy and affecting songs (in which Williams spoke rather than sang the lyrics), they were said to have added pathos and even dignity to the traditional degrading

Humpback whale

stereotypes. Within three years they were performing on Broadway in Victor Herbert's hit extravaganza *Gold Bug*.

Bert Williams survived the death of his partner and went on to greater heights as a solo performer. He starred in more than a dozen shows and recorded 70 of his songs on early records. Privately, like many great comedians, he was a depressive. He became an American citizen in 1918, but always felt that he never quite fitted, suffering both from white condescension and the envy of many blacks. He grieved that he and his wife had no children, drank far too much, and hankered for the one big dramatic role that would raise his stature above that of the politely domesticated clown. One of his most famous songs, 'Nobody', encapsulated his deep-seated melancholy. The crowning disappointment was said to have been his failure to be given the title role in Eugene O'Neil's great play *The Emperor Jones* (the part instead was a tremendous hit for the younger Paul Robeson). Bert Williams, weakened by liver cirrhosis, died of pneumonia in 1922, at the age of 48.

The great black American leader Booker T. Washington said, 'Bert Williams has done more for the race than I have. He has smiled his way into people's hearts. I have been obliged to fight my way.' A more poignant epitaph came from the great white comedian W. C. Fields (himself a depressive and an alcoholic): 'He was the funniest man I ever saw … and the saddest man I ever knew.'

Further reading: A. Charters, *Nobody: The Story of Bert Williams*, Collier-Macmillan, 1970; E. L. Smith, *Bert Williams: A Biography of the Pioneer Black Comedian*, New York, 1992.

WILLIAMSON, John Ernest

(1881–1966) English-born American pioneer underwater photographer and self-publicist. Developing with his brother a glass-fronted diving-bell suspended from a barge by an accordion-like access tube, 'Ernie' Williamson made his first submarine movie in Chesapeake Bay in 1914. Over the years he produced films with such titles as *The Submarine Eye* and *Wonders of the Sea,* and a moderately successful version of Jules Verne's *Twenty Thousand Leagues Under the Sea.*

Settling in Nassau soon after World War One, Williamson pioneered underwater colour photography as early as 1924. With a studio and dock near the eastern police station, he remained based in Nassau for the rest of his life, making films when he could and showing the wonders of the deep to tourists, from his 'Photosphere'. In August 1939, with the blessing of the Development Board, he set up what he proudly proclaimed to be the first Undersea Post Office. Letters stamped with its own postmark ('Sea Floor Bahamas') for the few months it operated, still have a

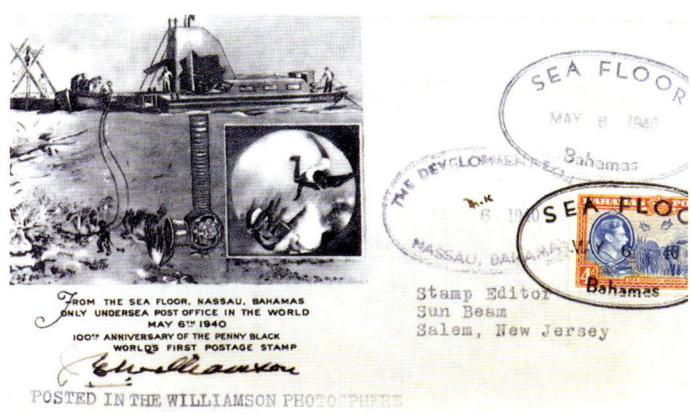

Commemorative first day cover from Williamson's Sea Floor Post Office, showing photosphere and stamp illustrating the famous Sea Gardens, May 1940

curiosity value among stamp collectors. Among the grateful recipients of first-day covers were the keen philatelists King George VI and President Franklin Roosevelt, to whom Williamson described himself as 'author, explorer, and originator of underwater photography'.

To the end of his days, Ernie Williamson proudly showed off the letter of thanks from President Roosevelt: 'I greatly appreciate your kind thought in writing to me upon the occasion of the opening of this most unusual and interesting post office. I am sure that this unique contribution to science will give immeasurable pleasure to those persons who are privileged to visit the Bahamas.'

Williamson published a fascinating autobiography entitled *Twenty Years Under the Sea* in 1936 and also wrote a book for children called *Child of the Deep*, based on the underwater exploits of his daughter Sylvia. After her father died in 1966, for the rest of her own life, Sylvia (now Mrs Munroe) proudly treasured the massive cast-iron Williamson Photosphere. Rumour has it that it is still to be found somewhere in Nassau.

WINDSOR, Duke of, Governor

(1894–1972) Christened Edward Albert Christian George Andrew Patrick David at a ceremony graced by Queen Victoria, and reigning briefly as King Edward VIII, the Duke of Windsor was Governor of The Bahamas from 1940 to 1945.

Blessed by good looks, the eldest great grandson of Victoria, grandson of Edward VII and son of George V, was bereft of parental affection, ill-educated, indolent and self-indulgent. Heir apparent to the throne and Prince of Wales for a quarter century (1911–36), he was accorded film-star popularity and status during his 'good will' travels throughout the British Empire between the world wars,

WINDSOR, Duke of, Governor

while living the life of a bachelor playboy behind the scenes. Dalliances with a succession of married women were hushed up or condoned, just as an amicable meeting with Adolf Hitler in October 1937 was only regarded as significant in retrospect.

However, a royal crisis erupted when the Prince of Wales, now in his forties, chose a twice-divorced American woman, Wallis Simpson, as the woman he wished to marry, at the very time that George V was dying and the Prince's accession to the throne was imminent. When he became King in January 1936, Edward VIII fully expected that his intended wife would be accepted as Queen. Not so. The political and religious Establishment closed ranks, preferring that Mrs Simpson remain the King's unofficial mistress, or at most be a 'morganatic' wife – that is, without the style of Queen and any offspring lacking title to the succession. This the King found unacceptable, and in the most gallant and decisive action of his life he gave up the throne on 10 December 1936.

Now simply styled Duke of Windsor, Edward left for France, where he married Wallis Simpson quietly in June 1937. When World War Two broke out two years later, the Windsors fled to Portugal. Though his personal loyalty to the British cause was never questioned, it was the revelation of an outlandish German plot to kidnap the former King and make him a puppet after the planned invasion of Britain that persuaded Winston Churchill to have him appointed Governor of the safely distant Bahamas in August 1940.

The Windsors lent glamour to the local social scene, especially among the well-heeled tourists who continued to flock to the islands until the United States entered the war in December 1941. Though the Duchess privately called Nassau a 'dump' and referred to local whites and blacks alike in terms of contempt, the Windsors made well-publicised contributions to wartime causes, such as the RED CROSS and the provision of recreation facilities for servicemen. They also figure-headed the creation of a sorely needed Infant Welfare Clinic on Nassau's Blue Hill Road. The Duke made patriotic broadcasts on ZNS radio (the first Governor to use that medium) and gained much popularity by what John Grigg has called his 'marvellous gift for making charming, impromptu speeches off the cuff'. He and the local calypsonian 'BLIND BLAKE' HIGGS formed a relationship of seemingly mutual admiration.

Governor Windsor was not blamed for the causes that led to the 'BURMA ROAD' RIOTS in June 1942 or for the harsh measures used in their suppression. He was accorded exaggerated credit for the way he turned out in his shirtsleeves to supervise the fighting of the great Bay Street FIRE a few weeks later. Perhaps luckily, he escaped public censure for the bungling way in which he handled the murder of his drinking and golfing associate Sir Harry OAKES in July 1943. Rightly overshadowing that were his part in the formation of the Economic Committee set up to study and improve conditions in the Family Islands and, most important of all, in the arrangements negotiated on his trips to Washington to organise the employment of migrant Bahamian farm workers in the United States, commonly called the CONTRACT – which lasted until the 1960s.

The Duke and Duchess left The Bahamas in May 1945 immediately the war in Europe was over. The Duke turned down (as he was probably expected to) the only alternative post he was offered, the Governorship of Bermuda. The couple spent the remaining 27 years of the Duke's life in France. He died of cancer of the throat in 1972 while still in exile in France, but was given a state funeral in England and buried at Windsor. The Duchess (who survived until 1986) was allowed to attend the ceremonies, but was never accorded the title of Royal Highness for which her devoted husband had long, and increasingly bitterly, campaigned.

The former King Edward VIII and his Duchess salute a parade passing Parliament Square

Further reading: M. Pye, *The King Over the Water*, London, 1981; M. Bloch, *The Duke of Windsor's War*, London, 1982; P. Ziegler, *King Edward VIII*, Collins, 1990.

WOMEN'S SUFFRAGE MOVEMENT Though as wives and mothers Bahamian women have always been of crucial importance within the family and home, their direct involvement in politics is a comparatively recent development. Women did not receive the vote until 1960, and the first woman was not elected to Parliament until 1982. Despite the huge advances made by women in education, the professions and business, only one woman obtained Cabinet rank during the 25 years of PROGRESSIVE LIBERAL PARTY government (1967–92).

In the 1920s the GARVEYITE movement promoted a significant political role for women, but this impulse faded with the movement itself during the 1930s. In the male (and white) dominated world of Bahamian politics, those women who claimed the vote and their few male allies were marginalised, and often disappointed. The pioneer suffragette was Mary Naomi Mason-Ingraham (1901–82), who with Eugenie Lockhart, Althea Mortimer, Georgianna Symonette and Mable Walker organised and unsuccessfully presented a petition with 550 signatures to the House of Assembly in 1950.

During the 1950s, the suffragettes obtained a dynamic and eloquent recruit in Doris L. JOHNSON (1919–98). In January 1959, they staged a demonstration and obtained an audience with visiting Secretary of State for the Colonies Alan Lennox-Boyd. They were given some encouragement, but told to remain patient. The subsequent new Elections Law gave the vote to all men over 21 but not to women. Undeterred, the suffragettes campaigned vigorously and produced a petition with 9,500 signatures, which was presented to the House of Assembly by the independent MHA Gerald Cash. Forbidden to present their case directly in the House, the suffragettes persuaded the parliamentarians to adjourn to a nearby court, where an impassioned speech by Doris Johnson carried the day.

Though opinion on both sides of the House was divided as to the political benefit of female suffrage, the vote was extended to women by an amendment to the law in 1960, first coming into effect at the 1962 general election. Following their disappointing performance in the election, the PLP made much more resolute efforts to win the women's vote, which bore obvious fruits in the victories of 1967 and 1968. Doris Johnson failed in her one attempt to win election (1962), but was made a Senator and became the first (and only) female PLP Minister in 1968.

While Lynden Pindling was in power women continued to play a very small role in front line politics. The first woman elected to the House was the staunch feminist Janet BOSTWICK, standing for the FREE NATIONAL MOVEMENT in 1982. In 1992 she became the first elected female Minister. By 2000, however, the political emancipation of Bahamian women had reached the point where five of the 35 FNM majority and one of the five PLP minority in the Assembly, along with six of the 16 Senators, were women – of whom three held posts in Prime Minister Hubert INGRAHAM's 15-person Cabinet. Of these, Dame Ivy Dean-Dumont became the first female Governor-General in 2001.

Members of the politicised minority of women supporting the PLP in the 1962 general election

WORLD RECORDS, BAHAMIAN Apart from such hard-to-measure claims as the country with the most and most impressive beaches, dive-sites or Spanish galleon wrecks; the obviously flawed statistics of the boast to have most churches per capita and the largest proportion of regular church attendees (something like 125 per cent of the entire population!); and ignoring such dubious accolades as the nation with one of the highest ratios of policemen to civilians and among the fastest-rising numbers of teenage pregnancies and unmarried mothers – there are at least ten authentic world records that have been established in The Bahamas and by Bahamians.

The oldest Bahamian entry in the *Guinness Book of World Records* is for the discovery of the world's largest marine sponge – a monster 8 feet (2.4 m) in circumference weighing 90 pounds (41 kg) once cut, dried and beaten, recovered from off western ANDROS in 1909. Despite its reputation for huge and feisty game fish, the Bahamas only holds one actual world record, for a wahoo weighing 155 pounds (72 kg) caught off SAN SALVADOR in 1990 (which superseded one of 149 pounds (67 kg) hooked off CAT CAY in 1962). San Salvador was also the island near which the deepest marine plant has been found, a primitive algae recovered from a depth of 884 feet (269 m). Of rather less scientific import, The Bahamas is also said to be the location where the strongest ever animal bite has been recorded – one of 132 pounds (59 kg) pressure exerted by a hungry shark – though quite how it was measured, and under what circumstances, is not made clear.

The Bahamas boasts two of the five longest CORAL REEFS in the world, several of the largest 'ocean holes', and arguably the most extensive system of underwater caves (in GRAND BAHAMA) and the largest coral atoll – though the last two claims are based on disputable definitions. Thanks largely to its clear warm waters, The Bahamas for a time held world records for free scuba diving (437 feet (132 m) for men and 325 feet (99 m) for women off Grand Bahama in 1968) – though these have greatly, and ever more dangerously, been superseded since. For a brief period also, an intrepid individual, now forgotten, held the world water ski-ing distance record by being towed the 200 or so miles (320 km) from Palm Beach to Nassau. As a curiosity this was on a par with the much-heralded establishment by John E. WILLIAMSON of the world's first underwater post office in 1939.

Far more worthy and notable are the records established by several other native or adoptive Bahamians. As described elsewhere, the airline founded by A. B. 'Pappy' CHALK to fly between Miami and The Bahamas in July 1919 and still flying in 2003 has a realistic claim to be the world's oldest and longest-running. Sir Etienne DUPUCH, owner-editor of the *Nassau Daily Tribune* from 1919 and still contributing editor at the time of his death in 1992, laid claim to being the longest-serving newspaper editor of all time. The yachtsman Sir Durward KNOWLES shared with two other yachtsmen and a fencer the distinction of competing in the Olympic Games over a period of 40 years (in his case, from 1948 to 1988). Most remarkable records of all, however, are those achieved in recent years by Bahamian track athletes, of whom the five women sprinters nicknamed 'The Golden Girls' were the outstanding but not the only stars. Between the Commonwealth Games in Perth in 1982 and the Sydney Olympics in 2000 these athletes have frequently earned the record of 'most medals per capita' for their proud nation.

WORLD WAR ONE (1914–1918) Britain declared war against Germany on behalf of herself and her colonies on Tuesday 4 August 1914. Thanks to the telegraph, this news arrived in Nassau the same day. Despite the obscurity of the real issues and the remoteness of the fields of conflict, the news was greeted by patriotic loyalty, especially among the white and near-white elite. The Assembly met immediately and voted emergency powers to the Governor and a contribution of £10,000 to the imperial cause (later augmented to £50,000). Committees were formed, to recruit volunteers, collect funds, gather useful war materials, and to increase farming production to offset a possible enemy blockade.

Volunteers came forward from all classes, but especially among those threatened with unemployment because of the sudden closing of the German Hamburg Amerika shipping line and the expected disruption of exports of SISAL and SPONGE. However, it was not until the war proliferated and became a bloody stalemate that Britain felt the need to mobilise forces other than those of the United Kingdom, the white self-governing colonies and India. Only from the middle of 1915 did Britain call on the British West Indies to provide reinforcements – and even then mainly support forces rather than combat troops. Though a considerable number of white Bahamians had already joined the British or Canadian forces directly, by that time, the initial enthusiasm of non-whites had somewhat faded, given that the war had had a positive rather than negative effect on the economy. Sisal and sponge prices had soared through wartime demands, the export of farm produce to the United States was unimpaired, and even the tourist trade remained buoyant until America was brought into the war in 1917.

Nevertheless, The Bahamas did make a notable contribution in manpower once recruitment was organised through the British WEST INDIES REGIMENT based in Jamaica. In response to a renewed recruiting drive in August 1915, 70 Bahamian men of all shades, occupations and ages offered themselves, from whom were chosen a First Contingent thereafter nicknamed 'The Gallant Thirty'. Kitted out and fed at local expense, given some rudimentary drilling and placed under the temporary command of one of the half dozen whites, William F. Albury, these were embarked on the sponge sloop *Varuna* and given a public send-off to Jamaica on 10 September 1915.

The Gallant Thirty were followed by further contingents of 105 and 87 men in November 1915 and May 1916, and by smaller (and declining) drafts of 78, 53, 51, 50 and 32 between August 1916 and September 1917. After training

WORLD WAR ONE (1914–1918)

'Gallant Thirty' Volunteers ready to embark for Jamaica on their to the Middle East, September 1915

in Jamaica, they were sent to Egypt and France. Though a machine-gun detachment formed from the Gallant Thirty did see combat in southern Palestine (and the British West Indies Regiment as a whole received official praise from General Allenby and Field Marshal Haig), the West Indians were engaged mainly in pioneer duties – building roads, trenches and gun emplacements. They shared the squalor of front-line conditions and many of the dangers, without the chance of performing heroic deeds or receiving the (admittedly parlous) rewards of combat medals.

For those who remained at home, the war brought few discomforts save, for some, in the last two years. When the United States joined the war in April 1917 the tourist trade came to an abrupt stop. Worse, American export restrictions followed German U-Boat activity in the Florida Straits. Late in 1917 stringent rationing restrictions were imposed, but this did not prevent serious shortages of flour, rice and kerosene, and threats of actual starvation in the south-western islands. Such hardships, though, were mitigated, by the wartime labour shortages in the US, which led to the employment of up to 3,000 Bahamians in the construction of port facilities in Charleston, South Carolina, at wage rates that were four times as high as those in The Bahamas, and even higher in relation to the shilling a day which Bahamians serving in the armed forces were paid.

This bonus came to an end with the cessation of hostilities. All the same, the Armistice was joyously celebrated in Nassau as soon as soon as the news reached the city on the afternoon of Monday, 11 November 1918. The first Bahamian contingent, though, did not return to Nassau until April 1919, by which time the jubilation was more muted.

In all, some 1,800 Bahamian men offered themselves for service in World War One (10 per cent of the adult male population), of whom about 700 served overseas. Besides the 486 who joined the five battalions of the West India Regiment in Jamaica from Nassau, more than 100 Bahamians signed up from Panama, Belize, the United States and United Kingdom. Overwhelmingly, these were non-whites. About 75 Bahamian whites (including no fewer than 36 scholars of QUEEN'S COLLEGE) joined the Canadian, British, or (from 1917) American forces. Compared with most of the forces (notably Australians, New Zealanders and Canadians), Bahamian casualties were light. Probably fewer than 50 of the 700 who served

WORLD WAR TWO

overseas died on active service. Of those recruited in The Bahamas, only nine were killed or died of wounds, and 28 died from other causes.

The most important effects of the war were psychological and, in the very long term, political. As the 1982 memoirs of Sir Etienne DUPUCH (the last surviving veteran) showed, for those who served the experience widened horizons and made many non-whites aware that they were asked to contribute to what was an imperial, even a white man's, war. They encountered prejudice and discrimination that made Dupuch declare, 'It was then for the first time that I realised that the lowest, dirtiest, scrubbiest Englishman was considered superior to the finest Indian.'

In talking to those from the Indian subcontinent such as Sikhs, Dupuch and his Bahamian fellows also realised that such imperial subjects were not just fighting because of a 'warrior tradition', and certainly not out of a simple loyalty to 'King and Country', but in the hope of recompense in the form of political concessions. Dupuch himself remained loyal to what he saw as British ideals, and even to the British Empire, but engaged in a lifelong crusade to ameliorate racial (if not class) distinctions in The Bahamas. A few others were more radicalised – joining the movement led by Marcus GARVEY in the immediate post-war years. Among these was the almost forgotten figure of Johnny Demeritte, who despite wounds which eventually led to the amputation of both legs, had been involved in a race riot in Liverpool, England, before his demobilisation.

Further reading: F. Holmes, *The Bahamas in the Great War*, London, 1924; E. Dupuch, *A Salute to Friend and Foe*, Nassau, 1982; *The Bahamas During the World Wars 1914–1918 and 193–1945*, Nassau, Department of Archives, 1986.

WORLD WAR TWO (1939–1945) The Bahamas was more directly involved in the second world war than in the first, though with even less bloodshed and with no dramatic effects. The news that Britain had declared war against Germany on behalf of its colonies as well as itself reached Nassau at daybreak on Sunday 3 September 1939. The immediate response was similar to that 25 years earlier. The Assembly loyally pledged itself to the imperial cause and voted loans and grants that eventually totalled £332,000 – about half the colony's annual budget. Though there was no active recruiting at this time, many Bahamians (nearly all whites) signed on in the armed forces in Britain or went to Canada to join up there.

Among the general population, still suffering from the effects of the Great Depression and the devastation of the SPONGE industry, however, there was less enthusiasm. Almost nothing changed during the year of 'phoney war' before Dunkirk, and there was no general involvement until after the United States was brought into the war in December 1941. TOURISM was unaffected for two years and was actually boosted by the arrival of well-heeled refugees – the chief and social focus of whom were the Duke of Windsor and his American Duchess, after Churchill's appointment of the Duke as Governor in August 1940. Churchill's more important action in donating bases in The Bahamas and elsewhere in the West Indies to the Americans in return for 50 ageing destroyers went almost unnoticed, until the US established a seaplane base in EXUMA in 1942.

Of much greater consequence was the construction from May 1942 of two major air fields on NEW PROVIDENCE by the Americans, for the use of their own forces and the Royal Air Force. The contractors spent over a million pounds in The Bahamas on what was locally referred to as 'the Project', and provided work for 2,400 chronically underemployed workmen – though at the same time differentials in wages provoked ugly rioting in June 1942. Once finished, Oakes and Windsor Fields served as bases for US patrols against U-Boats prowling Bahamian waters, air-sea rescue operations, an RAF Transport Command staging-post for ferrying bomber aircraft to the war zones by way of South America and West Africa, and an RAF Operational Training Unit which was to produce more than a thousand bomber air crews.

The temporary strategic importance of New Providence led to the reintroduction of a small army garrison – provided first by a company of British Cameron Highlanders and then by Pictou Highlanders from Canada. Reinforcing these soldiers were local volunteers; a Bahamas Home Guard organised and financed by the colonial government; a Bahamas Defence Force maintained by the imperial government; and a Bahamas Air Service Squadron that served as auxiliaries to the RAF bases. Unlike the previous war, there was very limited recruitment for overseas service, and none before 1944. In that year a battalion was formed from the Bahamas Defence Force for incorporation in the North Caribbean Regiment. After special training locally and in Jamaica, this body saw active service in the Mediterranean and Near East, being demobilised in January 1946.

In all (including those men and a few women who enrolled abroad in the British, Canadian and American forces) it was estimated that more than a thousand Bahamians saw service in uniform during World War Two, of whom about 25 died on active service.

Royal Air Force Victory march down Bay Street, May 1945

Of particular significance for the Bahamian economy as well was the initiation, in part through the efforts of Governor Windsor, of the large-scale recruitment of agricultural labourers for work in the United States. Popularly called the CONTRACT, at its peak the scheme employed 5,000 Bahamian men (and a few women). Though it had a damaging effect on agriculture in the Family Islands, it provided a most welcome boost to the general economy that continued for twenty years, uninterrupted by the ending of the war.

Further reading: *Bahamas Annual Report 1946*, HMSO, 1947; E. Dupuch, *The Tribune Story*, Benn, 1967; 'War Years in Nassau', *Bahamas Handbook and Businessman's Annual, 1978–79*, Dupuch Publications, 1979; *The Bahamas During the World Wars 1914–1918 and 1939–1945*, Nassau, Department of Archives, 1985.

WRECKING The salvaging of wrecks was an often misunderstood and somewhat unfairly maligned occupation that employed thousands of Bahamians during the age of sail.

The crossroads of many sailing routes, The Bahamas was notorious for its uncharted rocks and shoals, which multiplied the normal dangers of unexpected changes of wind and weather and the occasional storms of freakish power. The annual toll sometimes exceeded a hundred vessels. Disastrous acts of God to the victims, wrecks were positive godsends to the impoverished islanders. They offered chances of obtaining materials not produced in the islands, and the opportunity of selling rescued cargoes.

Almost as much as pirates, Bahamian wreckers gained a fearsome reputation, but were in fact victims of poverty and necessity rather than hard and callous brutes. As early as 1802, MCKINNEN described 40 wrecking boats permanently clustered along 'the Floriday shore' and quoted an Exumian wrecker as laughingly indifferent to the fate of wrecked sailors and bragging that rather than guiding vessels safely he and his fellows actually extinguished warning lights. Certain strategically located islands and settlements became notorious as bases for wreckers, such as BIMINI for the Florida Strait, RAGGED ISLAND for the Old Bahama Channel and north Cuban shore, LONG CAY for the Crooked Island Passage, and Rock (previously Wreck) Sound, ELEUTHERA for the Central Bahamas.

The imperial government had a constant battle to control wrecking, and to commandeer its profits, by making it obligatory to work through the local Admiralty Court, by passing progressively tighter salvage laws, and requiring all wreckers to be officially licensed. As traffic increased during the era of peace and free trade, the Bahamian wrecking trade reached its peak of activity. During the 1850s and 1860s between 60 and 100 sizeable vessels went ashore each year, and there were over 300 licensed wreckers and as many as 3,000 – a half of all Bahamian mariners – were crewmen on wrecking vessels. From 1855 to 1864, however, only 37 salvage cases were processed through the Nassau Admiralty Court, and an untold number escaped official notice.

Governors and other officials therefore carried out a determined campaign to condemn wrecking for its moral and social as well as its economic effects. In 1865, for example, the circuit judge after visiting Bimini reported: 'The wrecking system every day develops its sad depravity, and indicates the urgent necessity of more prompt and effective measures; if not for prevention of enormous plunder, for at least the recovery of some portion of the articles stolen.' Governor Rawson went even further in the following year, attributing the deplorable conditions at Rock Sound to the prevalence of wrecking, rather than the lack of alternative employment. The occasions when Bahamian mariners risked their lives to save people from wrecked ships – such as the Abaconian wreckers who received a gold medal from the Royal Lifeboat Society for rescuing the crew and passengers from a wreck on the Great Isaac Rock in 1853 – got far less prominent notice.

Government vigilance did have some effect, but at the price of occasional local unrest. One such case occurred in 1877 when the Admiralty Court decreed that a wreck at Long Cay was not legally salvage because the captain may have purposely run the vessel on the rocks and the Long Cay locals had done nothing to prevent the wreck. An even more serious case occurred at Port Howe, CAT ISLAND in 1882, when an officious local magistrate was clubbed with an oar when he denied salvage rights and tried to arrest a wrecker called Bowleg. A riot ensued and a dozen 'conspirators' were jailed or fined after a detachment of police was sent down from Nassau.

Wrecking had virtually died out by the twentieth century, but only in part because of vigorous government action. The substitution of steam for sail gradually reduced the chances of a captain suffering the nightmare of being caught helpless on a lee shore. But just as important were the improvement of charts, onboard navigational aids and, most important of all, the provision of more and better lighthouses and numerous strategically located navigational beacons by the Imperial LIGHTHOUSE Service. Laws for salvaging wrecks still exist, and there is still an Admiralty Division of the Supreme Court of The Bahamas. But no one today does, or could, live the life of a licensed wrecker.

WYLLY, William (*c.*1760–1828) A prominent LOYALIST lawyer, planter and slave-owner of Irish origin. Clearly of a contentious disposition, Wylly had successive confrontations with Governor DUNMORE on behalf of his fellow immigrants, and with his fellow planters in upholding the slave amelioration laws. Most importantly, he was the author of revealing accounts in his own defence, of conditions in The Bahamas in general, and of his own estate and slave management in particular.

Born in Georgia of parents who had migrated from Belfast in 1750, William Wylly was trained as a lawyer, fought for King George, and took refuge first in the Canadian Maritimes and then in The Bahamas. Appointed a King's Counsel and Solicitor General, he carried the case of the Bahamian Loyalists against the 'Old Inhabitants' and the oppressive Lord Dunmore to England in 1788, where he published anonymously a vitriolic but informative pamphlet entitled *A Short Account of the Bahama Islands: Their Climate, Productions &c to which are Added some Strictures upon their relative and political Situation, the Defects of their present Government &c.*

Back in The Bahamas, Wylly combined the role of planter with that of a law officer. He attempted without success to develop a plantation in Long Island before concentrating on his three estates of CLIFTON, Tusculum and Waterloo in western New Providence. His legal career seems to have become more important and changed direction once Lord Dunmore left The Bahamas in 1796 and following his personal conversion as an ardent Methodist. Under Governors Dowdeswell, Halkett and Cameron, Wylly served for a time as Chief Justice but mainly as Attorney General, making many enemies for his rigorous prosecution of the imperial government's new directives concerning the easement of slavery. His most controversial cases – occurring between 1815 and 1817 – concerned the prevention of the forcible movement of slaves under the laws against slave trading, the admissibility of evidence by free coloured persons against whites, and the prosecution of slave-owners for cruelty and for not supplying their slaves with the provisions and clothing ordained by law. Along with Governor Cameron, Wylly became especially unpopular with the plantocratic Assembly by attempting to compel the passage of a local law (as applied in Crown Colonies since 1812) for the registration of all Bahamian slaves.

Bahamian slave registration was delayed until 1822, after much turmoil and several suspensions of the Assembly. Wylly himself came much more directly under attack. On one occasion he was horsewhipped on Bay Street by an irate planter. In 1817, he was accused of contempt of the Assembly for corresponding with the abolitionist African Society in London, and his arrest was ordered by the Speaker. At the first attempt, Wylly was saved from being taken at his Clifton estate by the sergeant-at-arms by a show of force on the part of 20 of his slaves, armed with flintlock muskets and cutlasses. A couple of days later he was seized in town and only sprung from jail by a writ of *habeas corpus* taken out by Governor Cameron.

Wylly's reputation as a relatively liberal slave-owner – and his consequent popularity with most of his own slaves – was genuinely earned. As his locally printed *Regulations for the Government of the Slaves at Clifton and Tusculum in New Providence* (1815) demonstrated, he provided good housing, encouraged stable marital unions, family life and church attendance, and was prepared to give faithful and hard-working slaves a long weekend from estate tasks in order to work their own provision grounds and carry goods to market in Nassau. Cynics, however, pointed out that he may have been lenient because cotton planting was no longer profitable, and that he was actually saving money by having his slaves support themselves. That conditions for the Wylly slaves were relatively benign, however, is attested to by the fact that (unlike the majority of sugar plantation slaves in the West Indies) their numbers grew by natural increase – from 46 to 67 within ten years.

Yet, despite his upholding of the amelioration laws and relatively enlightened treatment of his own slaves, William Wylly was not a dedicated abolitionist. He punished recalcitrant or runaway slaves, and manumitted none. When he was appointed Chief Justice of St Vincent in 1823, those slaves he could not carry with him he sold – some of them, indeed, to James Moss, the owner of the largest number of Bahamian slaves and nephew of a planter whom he had earlier prosecuted for cruelty. The slaves sold by Wylly to Moss were shipped from their familiar houses, grounds and market in New Providence to toil at the SALT-pans in the southern Bahamas until slavery ended a decade later.

Further reading: S. Riley, *Homeward Bound: A History of the Bahama Islands to 1850, with a Definitive Study of Abaco in the American Loyalist Plantation Period*, Island Research, 1983, 170–88, 203–6; Craton and Saunders, *Islanders*, i. 187–204, 221–4, 297–303.

YELLOW FEVER A dangerous mosquito-borne viral disease formerly widely spread throughout the Americas, including The Bahamas. More or less eradicated from the Caribbean and North America since the beginning of the twentieth century, it is still prevalent and may be on the increase in parts of tropical South America, Africa and Asia

Thought to have originated in Africa, yellow fever was a dreaded scourge in the New World from the coming of the Spaniards and their African slaves. With its causes unknown (or wrongly attributed) and with no known cure, it was particularly lethal to 'unseasoned' newcomers. 'Yellow Jack' killed far more European troops campaigning in the West Indies than did enemy bullets, and its effects were equally devastating in townships and crowded plantations, in jungle work-gangs, and among sailors and other visitors. With epidemics reaching as far north as Boston, Nassau and other Bahamian settlements were also vulnerable. There were periodic outbreaks, notably during the blockade-running era of the AMERICAN CIVIL WAR (1861–5), and fears of yellow fever (not to mention malaria, CHOLERA or TYPHOID) retarded Bahamian tourism throughout the nineteenth century.

After yellow fever seriously threatened the completion of the Panama Canal, the *Aedes* aegyptiae mosquito was identified as the carrier of the disease, enabling eradication programmes to be carried out. A vaccine was developed and was available worldwide by the 1940s. The last case of yellow fever occurred in the United States in 1905, and in The Bahamas and the rest of the Caribbean soon thereafter.

Further information: www.who.int/inf-fs/en/fact100

YOUNG, Leon Walton (1876–1962) A black businessman and politician who represented the Eastern District of New Providence for 30 years (1912–42). He probably did the best he could for his people during the era of white paternalism. But he achieved even more for himself by means which make him seem in retrospect something of an 'Uncle Tom'. Born in Congo Town in the FOX HILL district in 1876 of proud YORUBA and LIBERATED AFRICAN descent, Walton Young trained as a ship and house carpenter and spent some of his formative years in Key West, Florida. On his return he became a trusted building superintendant of the BAY STREET liquor merchant and property developer Charles Bethel.

Though with minimal formal education, Young had the gift of wit and was an inspiring and outspoken orator. With Bay Street patronage and strong popular support in Fox Hill (and now sufficiently prosperous to afford involvement in active politics) he stood successfully for the House of Assembly at the age of 36.

As a parliamentarian, Walton Young spoke up for the poor, the overtaxed and the underpaid. He was influential in the suspension of property taxes for the poor, and in the passage of the first Minimum Wage Act in 1936. At the same time, he was an enterprising property developer and employer on his own account. Having been a favoured subcontractor in 'Bay Street' projects, notably the construction of the Montagu Beach Hotel (1926), he bought up large acreages in Fox Hill and the southern parts of Over-the-Hill Nassau, which he developed as Village Estates and Youngville. In his own district he built a small hotel and night-club called (after himself) the Walliyou.

Walton Young was already ageing and ailing when the PROGRESSIVE LIBERAL PARTY was formed in 1953 and he played no significant part in the movement that eventually brought it to power. Suffering a severe stroke in 1960, he died after a second attack in 1962.

ZEMIS The name somewhat indiscriminately given to both the sacred icons found in Lucayan and other Taino archaeological sites and to the deities and spirits they are thought to represent. Either anthropomorphic or zoomorphic (particularly bird or turtle-shaped) zemi items are found in a wide variety of forms: as carved and polished stones, the broken-off decorations of pottery vessels, carved items in rough stone, wood and human bone, and as incised or painted petroglyphs in caves or on exposed stone outcrops. The Tainos were also reported to have painted or tattooed similar forms and patterns on their bodies.

Though clearly of spiritual and probably ceremonial significance, the exact role of such zemis has provoked speculations almost as varied as the objects themselves. The more elaborate carvings are said to be status symbols held by caciques (local chiefs), representing the spirits of distinguished ancestors – probably through the maternal line of descent. The most common shape is triangular – thought by some ethnographers to represent the sacred volcanoes of the islands in the Lesser Antilles from which the Lucayans' ancestors came.

These and many other objects, especially those found in seaside or riverside caves or other numinous places, are held to have been used (much like African or Afro-American OBEAH objects) as charms to gain the help of friendly spirits or to placate the inimical. The most ingenious theory is that the detached pottery 'adorno' images may have been broken off intentionally during religious ceremonies in which food offerings were made to the spirits. However, other zemis or their representations may simply have been personal talismans, or even little more than stylistic decorations like modern tattoos.

Further reading: I. Rouse, *The Taino: Rise and Fall of the People who Greeted Columbus*, Yale University Press, 1992.

Zemis

405

Index

A

Aarons, Tony, 17
Abaco, 1–2, 256
    architecture, 19
        Cherokee Sound, 80–81
        Green Turtle Cay, 181–2
        Hole-In-The-Wall, 192
        Hope Town, 194
        logging, 282–3
        Marsh Harbour, 249
Abaco Home Rule Movement (AHRM), 2
Abaco Independence Movement (AIM), 2
Acklins Island, 2–3
Adderley Family (Black), 3–4
Adderley Family (White), 4–5
Adderley, Paul, 268
Adelaide Village, 5
African heritage, 5–6, 152, 171, 172, 186, 224, 265
    See also Friendly Societies; Junkanoos; Obeah; Proverbs; Riddles; Vodun
Africans *See* Congoes; Liberated Africans; Yorubas
Agoutis, 6, 22
Agriculture, 7–8, 101
    See also Bahamas Agricultural Industries Limited (BAIL)
AIDS, 8–9
Airlines *See* Bahamasair; Chalk's Airline
Airports, 9 *See also* Aviation
Albert Town, Long Cay, 231
Albury, Ben, 244
Albury, Dr Paul, 1, 9, 259
Ambergris, 9
American Civil War, 9–10
American Invasion (1776), 10–11
Amerindians, 1, 11–12, 17 *See also* Seminoles
Andros, 12–14, 20, 391
Androsia, 14
Angel's Trumpets *See* White Bells
Anglicanism, 14–16, 321

Animal welfare *See* Bahamas Humane Society
Anti-semitism, 207
Apartheid *See* Collins' Wall
Aragonite, 260
Arawak Cay, 16–17
Archaeology, 17–18, 57, 231 *See also* Museums
Archer, Rev. Colin, 255
Archer, Eleanor (Nellie), 244
Architecture, 18–21
Archives, 21, 263 *See also* Blue books
Ardastra Gardens, 21–2
Armoury, J.K. *See* J.K.Armoury (firm)
Army *See* Militia; West India Regiments
Art, 22–3
Asue (su-su), 23–4
Athletics, 24–5
Atlantis Resort, 25–6, 285
AUTEC (Atlantic Undersea Testing and Evaluation Centre), 14, 26–7
Aviation, 27–8 *See also* Airports
Awards *See* Honours system and national awards

B

Bacardi, 29–30
Bahama Platform, 167
Bahamas (name), 30
Bahamas Agricultural Industries Limited (BAIL), 7, 283
Bahamas Agricultural Research, Training and Development programme (BARTAD), 8
Bahamas Air Sea Rescue Association (BASRA), 47–8
Bahamas Airways (BAL), 28
Bahamas Bar Association, 210–11
Bahamas Chamber of Commerce, 30–31
Bahamas Christian Council, 31, 44
Bahamas Electricity Corporation (BEC), 31–2
Bahamas General Hospital, 252–3
Bahamas Historical Society (BHS), 32–3
Bahamas Humane Society, 33, 303
Bahamas National Trust (BNT), 18, 33–4, 137, 146, 157–8
Bahamas Red Cross, 35–6
Bahamas Telecommunications Corporation (Batelco), 36–7
Bahamasair, 3, 28
Bahamian Belongers, 88
Bahamian Nationality Act (1973), 89
Bahamianisation, 37–9, 157, 219, 258
    See also Citizenship; Independence
Bailey, Robert Melville, 39
Baillou, Isaac, 56
Bain, Charles H., 40
Bain, Hon. Clarence A., 39, 45
Bain Town, 39–40
Balcony House, Nassau, 19, 40, 263
Baltimore Geographical Society Report (1905), 41
'Banana holes', 7
Bank of Nassau, 41–2
Banking, 41–2
    See also Asue; Offshore banking and finance; People's Penny Savings Bank
Baptists, 42–4, 261, 322
Barrier reef, 1
Bars, 44–5
Baseball, 45–6
Basketball, 46–7
BASRA *See* Bahamas Air Sea Rescue Association
Batelco *See* Bahamas Telecommunications Corporation (Batelco)
Batik See Androsia
Bats, 48
Bay Geraniums (*Ambrosia hispida*), 68

406

INDEX

Bay Street, 5, 7, 49, 142
Bay Street group, 37, 49, 125, 126, 155, 166, 338–9, 363, 383
Beadle, John, 22
Bell, Hugh MacLachlan, 276
Belonger status *See* Citizenship
Bermuda Triangle, 49–50
Berry Islands, 50–51
Bethel, Cecil Valentine, 51
Bethel, Clement, 51, 319
Bethel, Nicolette, 115–16, 228
Bethel, Patrick, 81
Bethel, Spurgeon, 268
'Big Yard' *See* Andros
Bimini Museum, 264
Biminis, 51–2, 123, 401, 402
Binyon, Lawrence, 327
Birch family, 14
Birds, 52–3
Birth rate, 299
Black Crab mentality, 37, 54
'Black Hole', 57
'Black Loyalists' *See* Loyalists
'Black Tuesday' (27 April 1965), 54–5
'Blackbeard', 53–54 *See also* Pirates
Blacklands, 376
Blackwell, Chris *See* Compass Point
'Blind Blake' (Alphonso Higgs), 55
Blue books, 56, 113
Blue Flowers (*Valerianoides jamaicensis*), 68
Blue Hills, 56
Blue holes, 13, 56–7
Board of Health, 121
Boatbuilding, 57–60
Bodybuilding, 60–61
Bond, James, 61–2, 137
Bonefish *See* Fishing
Bonny, Anne *See* Pirates
Booth Family *See* Salvation Army
Bostwick, Hon. Janet G., 62, 397
Botanical gardens, 157–8
Bowlegs, Billy, 12
Boxing, 62–4
Braynen, Sir Alvin O., 64
Brazilettos (*Caesalpina vesicaria*), 64
Breadfruit (*Artocarpus altilis*), 68
British Colonial Hotel, 21, 65
British Empire *See* Honours system and national awards; Imperial Order of Daughters of the Empire (IODE); Independence
Brown, Rev. Harcourt, 44
Browne, Governor Montfort, 10
Bruce, Peter Henry, 65–6, 202
Buildings *See* Architecture
'Burma Road' riots, 1942, 66–7
Burton, Bishop Spence, 16
Bush medicine, 12, 67–9, 378
Businesses, 38
  See also Bahamas Chamber of Commerce; Banking; 'Suitcase companies'
Butler, Frances Manester, 69, 70
Butler, Hon. Sir Milo Boughton, 45, 54–5, 69–70, 233
Butlin, Sir 'Billy', 70–71, 177

C

Cable Beach, 72
Campbell, David, 203, 229, 317, 364, 382
Campbell, Hugh *See* Education
Captive insurance *See* Insurance industry
Carleton, 1
Carman, Bliss, 72–3
Carmichael Village, 73–4
Carroll, Anthony (Tony), 60, 61
Carstairs, Marion 'Joe', 74
Cascarilla (*Croton eluteria*), 3, 74
Cash His Excellency Sir Gerald, 74–5
Casinos, 75–6, 162, 372
Cassava (*Manihot esculenta*), 76–7
Casuarina (*Casuarina equestifolia*), 77
Cat Cay, 77
Cat Island, 7, 19, 20, 78–9, 206, 264, 402
Catesby, Mark, 77–8, 108, 197
Catnip (*Salvia serotina*), 68
Caves *See* Blue holes
Cay Sal Bank, 79
Celestials *See* Chinese Bahamians
Central Bank, 42
Cerasee (*Mormodica charantia*), 68
Chalk's Airline, 79–80
Chamberlain, Neville, 348
Charities *See* Bahamas Humane Society
Cherokee, 1
Cherokee Sound, 80–81
Chickcharnies, 13
Children *See* Families
Chinese Bahamians, 81–2, 110, 362
Chippingham, 21, 82
Cholera, 82
Chowder, 98–9
Christ Church Cathedral, 15, 19, 82–4
Christianity *See* Anglicanism; Bahamas Christian Council; Baptists; Churches; Greek Orthodox Church; Methodism; Missionaries; Presbyterians; Roman Catholicism; Salvation Army; Seventh Day Adventists
Christie, Sir Harold George, 22, 84, 238, 275
Christie, Rt. Hon. Perry Gladstone, 84–5
Christmas customs, 85–6
Church of England *See* Anglicanism
Churches, 232 *See also* Anglicanism; Baptists; Methodism; Roman Catholicism
  architecture, 20
  Christ Church Cathedral, 15, 19, 82–4
  Roman Catholic, 206
  Saint Andrew's Kirk, 305
  Saint Francis Xavier Cathedral, 334–5
  Saint Mary's Church, 335–6
  Saint Matthew's Church, 336
  Seventh Day Adventist Church, 344
Churches of God, 86–8, 262
Churchill, Sir Winston, 179, 200, 400
Citizenship, 37, 38, 88–9
Clarence Town, Long Island, 232

INDEX

Clarke, Eldece, 25
Clifford, Governor Hon. Sir Bede, 89–90
Clifton Cay controversy, 90–91
Clifton Estate, 18
Climate, 91–2
Club Mediterranée, 92–4
Coastal rocklands, 376–7
Coat of arms *See* National symbols
Coke, Dr. Thomas, 254
College of the Bahamas (COB), 94–5, 225, 253
Collins' Wall, 95–6
Colonial Hotel, 142
Colonialism *See* English heritage
Columbus, Christopher, 6, 96–7, 231, 264, 330, 338
Commonages *See* Land tenure
Commonwealth *See* West Indies Federation
Commonwealth Games, 24, 25
Compass Point, 97–8
Conception Island, 98
Conchs, 98–9, 112, 343
'Conchy Joes', 41, 42, 99, 214
   See also Man-O'-War Cay
Congoes, 224
Conquistadors *See* Ponce de Leon, Juan
Constitution, 311
Contract, The (1943-1963), 99–101, 257
Coonley, Jacob F., 302
Corals and coral reefs, 13, 101–2
Corn *See* Maize
Cost of living, 102–3
Cottman, Evans W., 103–4
Cotton, 1, 104, 138
Council for a Free Abaco (CFA), 2
Courts *See* Judicial system
Crabs, 105
Crawfish, 230
Creole, 219
Creole incident (1841), 106
Creole language *See* Kweyole
Cricket, 106–8
Crocodiles, 108
Crooked Island, 2–3, 108–10
Cruise ships, 373–4
Cuba, *See also Flamingo* incident (1980), 110–11

Cuisine, 111–12
Currency, 112–14
Curry, William, 214
Customs *See* Marriage customs
Customs duties, 114

D

Dahl, Anthony, 228
Dance, 115–16
D'Arcy Ryan case *See* Bahamianisation
Darling, Governor General Sir Clifford, 3, 116–17, 375
Davis, Pauline, 25
Deadman's Cay *See* Long Island
Dean-Dumont, Dame Ivy, 397
Dean, 'Sweet Richard', 117
Death *See* Funerals
Defries, Amelia, 35, 117–18
Delancey Town, 3, 118–19
Demeritte, Johnny, 400
Deveaux, Andrew Jr., 119–20
Devil's Triangle *See* Bermuda Triangle
Dillet, Joseph Eugene, 120
Dillet, Stephen, 120–21
Dillet, Thomas William, 120
Diseases, 120–21
Disney Company, 172
Dodge, Steve, 243, 244, 249
Dogs *See* Potcakes
Dominoes, 121–2
Douglass, Frederick, 106
Drug trafficking, 122–3, 273, 278, 296, 309
Duhos, 12, 17, 21
Dundas Centre of the Performing Arts, 369
Dundas, Governor Hon. Sir Charles, 123–4
Dunmore, Governor Lord John Murray, 124–5, 151, 188
Dupuch, Sir Etienne, 125–6, 271
Dupuch, Hon. Eugene Aubrey Pyfrom, 126, 400
Dupuch, Leon, 271

E

East Plana Cay, 6

Economy *See* Cost of living
Education, 14, 15, 16, 127–31, 136
Edwards, Hedley, 21
Elbow Cay *See* Hope Town
Eldon, Rt. Rev. Michael Hartley, 16, 131
Elections *See* General Elections
Electoral reform *See* 'Black Tuesday'
Electricity *See* Bahamas Electricity Corporation
Eleuthera, 7, 15, 19, 131–2
Eleutherian Adventurers, 4, 132–3, 217
Emancipation, 134–5, 154, 349
   See also Liberated Africans
Emigration, 140
Eneas, Dr Cleveland Wilmore, 135
Eneas, Wilmore Venable, 87
English heritage, 135–6
Equal opportunities, 42
Eve, Joseph, 30, 136–7, 271
'Exuma' *See* McKay, Tony
Exumas, 137–8, 168, 264

F

Families, 139–40, 189 *See also* Marriage customs
Family Island Regatta *See* Out Island Regatta
Farming *See* Agriculture
Farquharson, Charles, 340
Fauna *See* Wildlife
Fawkes, Hon. Sir Randol F., 140–41, 374
Female emancipation *See* Women's Suffrage Movement
Ferguson, Amos, 141–2
Ferguson, Debbie, 24, 25
Ferguson, Stanley, 87
Financial Action Task Force (FATF) *See* Banking
Financial services *See* Offshore banking and finance
FINCO, 23
Fires, 142–3
Fish markets, 246
Fishing, 81, 143–5
Flags *See* National symbols
Flamingo incident (1980), 146

INDEX

Flamingos, 145–6, 199
Fleming, Ian, 61, 62
Flora, 146–7
Flying boats *See* Chalk's Airline
Folklore, 148, 182 *See also* Chickcharnies; Obeah
Football (soccer), 148–9 *See also* Rugby football
Forbes, (Joan) Rosita, 149, 218
Ford, Jack, 165–6
Forests, 13
Forsyth, Dr Albert E., 27–8
Forsyth, Elgin, 332
Fort Charlotte, 125
'Fort Hill', 150
Fort Nassau, 65
Forts, 150–53
Fortune Island *See* Long Cay
Fountain of Youth *See* Biminis; Ponce de Leon, Juan
Fountain, Patricia (Isaacs) *See* Isaacs, Sir Kendal George Lamon
Fowles, L.D., 165
Fox Hill, 152–3
Fox, Ulrick Alexander (Rick), 47
Free Coloureds, 6, 153–4
Free National Movement (FNM), 2, 155–6, 185, 201, 202, 205, 219
Freeport, 20, 225, 254, 391
Freeport International Airport, 9
Freeport-Lucaya, 156–8, 170
French language *See* Kweyole
French surnames, 184, 199, 362
Friendly Societies, 6, 158–9
Funerals, 159–61
Fynes, Sevatheda, 25

G

'Gallant Thirty' *See* World War I
Gambier Village, 162
Gambling, 31, 162–3 *See also* Casinos
Gardens 147 *See also* Ardastra Gardens; Loyalist Memorial Sculpture Garden, New Plymouth; Sea Gardens
Gardiner, Cordney, 143
Garfunkel family, 207
Garvey, Marcus Massiah, 163, 165, 233, 257
Garveyism, 163–5
Geckos, 229
General Elections, 165–6
General Strike (1958), 166–7
Generation land *See* Land tenure
Geology, 167–8
George Town, Exuma, 168–9
Georgeside, 19
Gibson, Timothy, 169–70
Glinton-Meicholas, Patricia, 148, 248, 277, 312
'Golden Girls' *See* Athletics
Golf 170
Gomez, Archbishop Drexel Wellington, 16, 170–71
Good Samaritans *See* Masonic lodges
Goombay music, 171–2 *See also* 'Blind Blake'
Gorda Cay, 172
Gould, Steven Jay, 172–3
Government High School, 173–5
Government House, 175
Governors, 175–6, 286 *See also* Windsor, Governor Edward, Duke of Governors-General, 287
Grand Bahama, 176–7, 225, 264 *See also* Freeport-Lucaya
Grant's Town, 66, 177–8, 225
Gray, Captain Rolly, 178–9
Graycliff, 179–80
Great Guana Cay, 1, 180
Greek Bahamians, 180, 362
Greek Orthodox Church, 322
Green Turtle Cay, 1, 181–2
Griffin, Merv, 285
Groupers *See* Nassau groupers
Groves, Wallace, 156, 177
Guanahani *See* San Salvador
Guanahatabey people *See* Siboney people
Guava duff, 182
Guidebooks, 371
Gulf Stream, 49, 182–3
Gum Elemi (*Bursera simarouba*), 68
Guy Fawkes Day, 183

H

Haiti, 184
Haitians, 6, 38, 184–6, 352 *See also* Kweyole
Hall, Chuck, 2
Hanna, Hon. Arthur Dion, 3, 37, 186–7
Harbour Island, 19, 20, 187–8
Hard Bargain, 188–9
Hartford, Huntingdon II, 284–5
Hawes, John *See* Jerome, Father
Hawksbill Creek Agreement, 156–7
Hayward, Sir Jack, 189–190
Health *See* Board of Health; Diseases; Medicines
Heath, Sir Robert, 190
Hemingway, Ernest, 52, 63
Higglers *See* Retail trade
Higgs, Alphonso *See* 'Blind Blake'
Historic buildings, 34
HIV *See* AIDS
Hobby Horse Hall, 191
Hoffman, Charles, 17
Hog Island *See* Paradise Island
Hogsty Reef, 191–2
Hole-In-The-Wall, Abaco, 192
Holidays *See* Public Holidays
Homer, Winslow, 192–3
Homosexuality, 31
Honours system and national awards, 193–4
Hope Town, 1, 41, 194
Hopkins, Commodore Ezekiel, 10
Horse racing, 191
Hospitals *See* Medical services
Hotels, 372
    British Colonial Hotel, 65
    Cable Beach, 72
    Jack Tar chain, 71
    Pink Sands, 188
    Royal Victoria Hotel, 328–329
    See also Atlantis Resort
House of Assembly *See* Parliament
Hurricanes, 195–6
Hutias, *See* agoutis

I

Iguanas, 22, 197

INDEX

Immigration, 37–8, 88–9
Imperial Order of Daughters of the Empire (IODE), 197–8
Inagua, 53, 198–200
Independence, 2, 200–202
Indians *See* Amerindians
Ingraham, Rt. Hon. Hubert Alexander, 1, 44, 85, 155, 156, 201–202
Insects, 120, 202–203
   See also spiders
Insurance industry, 204
   See also National insurance
IODE Hall, 198
Isaacs, Sir Kendal George Lamon, 201, 204–5, 238, 368
Islanders in the Stream, 22, 234, 246, 247–8, 302–3, 379

J

J.K. Armoury (firm), 222
Jack Tar hotels, 71
Jails *See* Prisons
Jehovah's Witnesses *See* Minnis, Edward A. ('Eddie')
Jerome, Father (Monsignor John Hawes), 20, 79, 206, 232, 326
Jewish Bahamians, 207
Jitneys, 207–8
Johnson, Dame Doris L., 397
Johnson, J.S. Company *See* Pineapples
Johnston, Randolph W., 209
Judicial system, 210–11
Jumbey (*Leucaena glauca*), 68
Jumbey Village, 211
'Jumper churches' *See* Baptists; Churches of God
Junkanoos, 6, 86, 115, 118, 182, 212–13
Justices of the Peace, 210

K

Kerzner, Sol, 25, 26, 285
Key West, 214, 257
King Charles II, 311
King, Dr Martin Luther, 52
Kinship *See* Families
Kirk *See* Saint Andrew's Kirk

Klingel, Gilbert, 199
Knowles, Mark, 368
Knowles, Sir Durward, 214–15, 332
Kweyole (Haitian Creole language), 215

L

Lake Cunningham, 216
Lake Killarney, 216
Land tenure, 217–19
Language, 219–21
Law of the Sea negotiations, 221
Lebanese Bahamians, 221–2, 362
Leprosy, 222, 253
Levy, Austin, 207
Lewis, Eloise, 222–3
Liberated Africans, 5, 6, 218, 223–4
   See also Adderley Family (Black)
Libraries, 224–6
Life Leaf (*Kalanchoe pinnata*), 68
Lighthouses, 226–7
Lignum vitae (*guaiacum officinale*), 67, 68, 227
Limestone, 18, 167–8, 259, 260
Lipscomb, Bishop, 15
Literature, 227–8 *See also* Poetry
Lizards, 228–9 *See also* Iguanas
Lobsters, 230
Logging *See* Owens-Illinois Company
Long Bay (San Salvador), 17
Long Cay, 2–3, 230–31
Long Island, 20, 231–3, 235
Lords Proprietors *See* Proprietors, Lord
Lotteries, 31
Love, Rev. Dr Joseph Robert, 233
Love Vines (*Cascuta*), 68
Lowe, Alton Roland, 22, 182, 234
Loyalist era architecture, 19
Loyalist Memorial Sculpture Garden, New Plymouth, 2
Loyalists, 1, 15, 168, 181, 217, 231, 234–6, 256, 298, 321, 331, 336
   See also Rolle, Lord John
Lucayans, 3, 11–12, 17, 77, 120, 194, 217, 231, 256, 298, 336, 357
Ludwig, Daniel K., 236
Lumber, 177

Lunatic asylum, 252
Lusca *See* Andros
Lyford, William, 237
Lyford Cay, 18, 237–8

M

McKay, Tony, 239
McKinnen, Daniel, 108, 239
McKinney, A. Leon, 42
Magistrates *See* Judicial system
Mailboats, 59, 80, 137, 239–41, 304
Maize, 241–2
Major, Charles William, 24
Malcolm, Michael, 304, 305
Malone, Brent, 22, 242–3
Malone, Wyannie, 41, 194, 243
Man-O'-War Cay, 1, 244–5
Manatees, 243
Mangroves, 13, 243–4, 377
Maravilla (wreck), 18
Mardon, Michael, 240
Marigny, Count Alfred de, 274
Marketing, 245–7
Marriage customs, 247–8
Marsh Harbour, Abaco, 249
Masonic Lodges, 250–51
Match-Me-If-You-Can (*Acalypha wilkesina*), 68
Matthew Town, Inagua, 199
Maxwell, Governor John, 351
Mayaguana, 251
Maynard, Hon. Sir Clement, 251–2
Medical services, 252–3
Meeres, Paul Sr., 253–4
Meicholas, Patricia Glinton *See* Glinton-Meicholas, Patricia
Methodism, 254–6, 322
Metropolitan effect *See* Population
Migration, 184, 185, 256–8, 299
   See also Contract, The
Militia, 258–9
Mineral resources, 259–60
Minnis, Edward A. ('Eddie'), 260–61
Miscegenation, 4, 153, 233
Missionaries, *See also* Jerome, Father 15, 16, 261–2, 326
Monarchy, 136 *See also* Honours system and national awards; King Charles II; Prince Charles;

INDEX

Queen Elizabeth II; Queen Victoria
Moncur, Avard, 25
Morris, Elisha, 106
Moseley, Edwin Charles, 271
Moseley, Miss Mary, 262, 271
Mosquitoes, 202–3, 404
Moxey, Edmund, 211
Munnings, Freddie Alfred, 262–3
Museums, 2, 263–4
    See also Bahamas Historical Society
Music See Rake n' scrape

N

Names, 30, 199, 265
    See also Place names; Surnames
Nassau, 9, 65, 66, 150–51, 235, 257, 265–7, 269–70, 347
    architecture, 18–19, 20–21
    Balcony House, 263
    Bay Street, 49
    Chippingham, 82
    Christ Church Cathedral, 82–4
    Delancey Town, 118–19
    electricity, 32
    fires, 142–3
    Fort Charlotte, 125
    'Fort Hill', 150
    Government High School, 173–5
    Government House, 175
    Grant's Town, 177–8
    Graycliff, 179–80
    harbour, 10
    hospitals, 252–3
    IODE Hall, 198
    market, 246
    Masonic Lodge, 250
    museums, 263
    nightclubs, 272–3
    public library, 18, 224
    Queen's College, 313–14
    Queen's Staircase, 315
    Royal Victoria Hotel, 328–9
    Saint Anne's School, 333
    Saint Augustine's College, 333–4
    Saint Mary's Church, 335–6
    Saint Matthew's Church, 336
    Sea Gardens, 342
    standpipes, 356
    surnames, 361
    Vendue House, 386–7
Nassau groupers (*Epinephilus striatus*), 267–8
National Art Gallery, 23
National Democratic Party (NDP), 4, 268
National Gallery, 18–19
National insurance, 265
National parks, 34, 146
National symbols, 269
New Providence, 90–91, 246–7, 269–70, 327, 400
    electricity, 32
    Lake Cunningham, 216
    Lake Killarney, 216
    Saint Andrew's School, 332–3
    Saint John's College, 335
    Spanish invasion, 351–2
    water supplies, 390–91
Newspapers, 228, 271–2, 386
Nicholl's Town, Andros, 14, 20
Nightclubs, 272–3
Nonconformists, 31
Norman's Cay, 273
North Bimini, 52
North, Gail See Saunders, Dr Gail
Noyes, P. Belcher, 127
'Numbers Game', 162–3

O

Oakes, Sir Harry, 3, 28, 65, 72, 166, 274–5
Obeah, 6, 275–7 See also Vodun
'Obeah man' See McKay, Tony
Obed, Elisha, 63–4
Offshore banking and finance, 277–8
Old Bahama Channel, 279
Old Bight (Cat Island), 19, 20
Old Fort, New Providence, 279
Old Providence, Providencia, 280
Oldmixon, John, 280
Oral tradition See Literature; Proverbs; Riddles
Orchids, 147
Organization of American States (OAS), 280
Out Island Regatta, 280–82
Ouwade family, 222
Owens-Illinois Company, 282–3

P

'Pa Beah' See Obeah
Paine, Art, 281
Paradise Island, 217, 284–5
Parker, Keith, 24, 25
Parks See Gardens, public; National parks
Parliament, 285–7 See General Elections
Parliament Square, 18
Parrots, 22, 53
Patton, David Willard, 287–8
Paul, Joseph, 254, 335
Peas n' rice, 288
Peggs, Dr Alfred Deans, 174
Penrose, Clement, 41
Pentecostalism See Churches of God
People-to-People programme, 175, 288
People's Penny Savings Bank, 42
Phenney, George, 279, 323
Pidgin language, 219–20
Pigeon Plums (*Cocoloba*), 68
Pindling, Lady Marguerite, 288–289
Pindling, Michelle, 291
Pindling, Rt. Hon. Sir Lynden Oscar, 2, 3, 14, 37, 39, 44, 54, 55, 122, 123, 161, 187, 200–201, 289–92, 374, 375
Pineapples (*Ananas comosus*), 291–2
Pinelands, 377
Pirates, 292–3
Place names, 12, 199
Poetry, 228
Poitier, Sir Sidney, 139, 140, 294–5
Police, 163, 178, 295–6
Pollution, 57, 102
Pompey Museum of Slavery and Emancipation, 263, 387
Pompey's Rebellion (1830), 296–7, 349
Ponce de Leon, Juan, 297–8
Population, 1, 267, 270, 298–300, 341
Postage stamps, 300–301

INDEX

Postal services, 301–2
Postcards, 302–3
Potcakes, 303
Potter's Cay, 34, 241, 303–4
Poultry farms, 8
Pound Cake Bushes (*Parthenium*), 68
Powles, Louis Diston, 112, 265, 272, 304, 311–12, 328–9, 379
Presbyterians, 15, 304–5
Prince Charles, 201
Prince Hall Lodges, 250–51
Princess Margaret Hospital, 252, 253
Prisons, 305–6
Pritchard, Sir Asa H., 307
Privateers, 307 *See also* Pirates
Progressive Liberal Party (PLP), 2, 4, 7, 8, 37, 54, 166, 175, 185, 200, 201, 219, 258, 286–7, 308–9, 365, 374, 375, 384
    See also Pindling, Rt. Hon. Sir Lynden Oscar
Prohibition era, 309–10
Proprietors, Lord, 310–11
Proverbs, 311–12
Providencia *See* Old Providence
Public Bank of the Bahamas, 41
Public Holidays, 312
Public libraries *See* Libraries
Public records *See* Archives
Pyfrom, Florence, 357

Q

Queen Elizabeth II, 313
Queen Victoria, 315–16
Queen's College, 313–14
Queen's Staircase, 315
Quit rents *See* Land tenure

R

Raccoons, 317
Racism, 100
Radio, 36, 317–18
Ragged Islands, 146, 318
Rainfall, 13
Rake n' scrape, 318–19
Ranfurly, Countess Hermione, 319
Ranfurly, Governor Lord, 319
Ranfurly Out Island Library Service, 225, 319
Rastafarianism, 320
Rawnsley, David, 22
Read, Mary *See* Pirates
Records *See* World records, Bahamian
Reefs, 13, 167
Regattas, 280–82, 320–21
Religions, 321–2
Renouard, Gustave, 354
Residency, rights of, 38
Retail trade, 246
Riddles, 322–3
Rigg, J. Linton, 280–81
Roberts, Antonius, 22
Robinson, Jackie, 45
Robinson, Thomas Augustus, 24
Rodgers, Andre, 45–6
Rogers, Governor Captain Woodes, 258–9, 293, 323–4
Rolle, 'Baby Boy', 63
Rolle, Lord John, 138, 324–5
    See also Pompey's Rebellion
Roman Catholicism, 16, 322, 325–7
Rose, Rev. D.W., 43
Royal Air Force, 327
Royal Bahamas Defence Force, 327–8
Royal Bank of Canada, 41, 42
Royal Victoria Hotel, 10, 328–9
Rugby football, 329–30
Rum *See* Bacardi
Rum Cay, 17, 330–31
Russell, Don, 22
Russell, Oris Stanley, 331
Russell Report, 67

S

Sailing, 332 *See also* Gray, Captain Rolly
Saint Andrew's Kirk, 305, 322
Saint Andrew's School, 332–3
Saint Anne's School, 333
Saint Augustine's College, 333–4
Saint Augustine's monastery, New Providence, 206
Saint Francis Xavier Cathedral, 334–5
Saint John's College, 3, 335
Saint Mary's Church, 335–6
Saint Matthew's Church, 18, 336
Salt industry, 336–7
Salvation Army, 337–8
Samana Cay, 338
Samaritan Ministry, 8
San Salvador (Watling's Island), 339–41
Sandflies, 203
Sandilands, Chief Justice Robert, 152
Sandilands Hospital, 253
Sandilands Village *See* Fox Hill
Sands, Hon. Sir Stafford Lofthouse, 338–9
Sands Report, 67
Saunders, Dr Gail, 21, 341
Sayings *See* Proverbs
Sayle, Captain William, 132, 133, 341–2
Schools, 16 *See also* Education
Schooners, 58, 59
Schreiner, Father Chrysostom, 325–6, 334, 335
Scottish settlers, 304
Scriven, Sam, 43
Scuba diving *See* Blue holes; Stella Maris
Sea *See* Law of the Sea negotiations
Sea Gardens, 342
Seashells, 342–3
Segatoo *See* Eleuthera
Seminoles, 12, 13, 343–4
Senate, 287
Serasee *See* Cerasee
Settlers, 1
Seventh Day Adventists, 344–5
Share cropping *See* Emancipation; Land tenure; Truck system
Sharks, 345
Shea, Sir Ambrose, 347
Shepherd's Needles (*Bidens pilosa*), 68
Ship registration, 345–6
Shirley, Governor William, 346–7
Shops *See* Retail trade
Shouter Chapel, 43
Shriners *See* Masonic Lodges
Siboney people, 11

INDEX

Simms family, 231
Sinkholes *See* Blue holes
Sisal, 347–8
Slavery, 348–350
    See also Truck system; Wylly, William
Slaves, 5–6, 17–18, 73–4, 106, 110, 120, 138, 139, 154, 184, 188–9, 210, 217, 218, 247, 255, 259, 298, 324–5, 340, 391
    See also Emancipation; Liberated Africans; Pompey's Rebellion
Sloops, 58, 59
Smallpox, 120
Smith, Roger, 368
Smuggling *See* Ragged Islands
Smyth, Governor Sir James Carmichael, 73, 134, 350
Snakes, 350–51
Soccer *See* Football
Socialism *See* Vanguard Party
Society for the Propagation of the Gospel (SPG), 15
Soils *See* Trees
Souse, 112
South Bimini, 52
Spaniards, 12
Spanish invasion (1782-1783), 351–2
Spanish Wells, 20, 264, 352–3
Spence, Frank, 43
Spiders, 353–4
Sponging, 13–14, 59, 180, 354–5
Sports, 136
    baseball, 45–6
    basketball, 46–7
    boxing, 62–4
    cricket, 106–8
    football (soccer), 148–9
    golf, 170
    horse racing, 191
    Rugby football, 329–30
    sailing, 332
    tennis, 367–8
    See also Athletics
Spotted basil (Basily), 69
Squatters' rights *See* Land tenure
Stamps *See* Postage stamps
Standpipes, 356
Stella Maris, 357

Stirrup Cays, 50
Storytelling, 227–8
Strachan, Miss Telator, 358
Straw markets, 246, 247
Straw work, 357–8
Strikes *See* General Strike (1958)
Stromatolites, 358–9
Sturrup, Chandra, 25
Sugar, 7, 359
Sugar cane, 283
'Suitcase companies', 360–61
Surnames, 1, 3, 4, 184, 199, 214, 265, 352, 361–2
Surreys, 362–3
Symbols *See* National symbols
Symonette, George, 363
Symonette, Rt. Hon. Sir Roland Theodore, 363–4
Syphilis, 120
Syrians *See* Lebanese Bahamians

T

Tainos *See* Amerindians
Taxes *See* Customs duties
Taylor, Berkeley 'Peanuts', 365
Taylor, E.P., 238
Taylor, Sir Henry Morton, 365–6
Taylor, Malone, 22
Taylor, Maxwell, 365
Teach, Edward *See* 'Blackbeard'
Teachers, 128, 130
Telecommunications *See* Bahamas Telecommunications Corporation (Batelco)
Television, 366–7
Tennis, 367–8
Termites, 203
Theatre, 369
Thompson, Leonard, 2
Thompson, Mychal, 46–7
Timber, 58–9 *See also* Owens-Illinois Company
Tinker, Governor John, 56, 250
Tongue of the Ocean, 369–70
Tourism, 1, 14, 90, 172, 328–9, 370–74
    See also Atlantis Resort; Butlin, Sir 'Billy'; Club Mediterranée; Hotels; People-To-People programme; Postcards

Trade unions, 374–6
Treasure hunting, 18
Tree of life *See* Lignum vitae
Trees, 376–8
    See also Forests; Lumber
Trinity chapel, Nassau, 254, 255
Trott, Governor Nicholas, 378
Truck system, 378–9
Turks and Caicos Islands, 11, 379–80
Turnquest, Hon. Sir Orville Alton, 268, 380–81
Turnquest, Tommy, 156
Turtles, 112, 381–2
Turton, William, 254–5
Typhoid, 382

U

UMA (United Union Mercantile Association), 164
Undersea Post Office, 395
UNIA (United Negro Improvement Association), 163, 164
United Bahamian Party (UBP), 54, 166, 200, 286, 287, 308, 309, 383–4
University of the West Indies, 384–5

V

Vanguard Party, 386
Venables, Bishop Addington, 15
Vendue House, 386–7
Vesco, Robert, 387
Villa Doyle, 18–19
Vodun, 387–8
Voting *See* General Elections

W

Wages *See* 'Burma Road' riots
Wakes *See* Funerals
Walker, Claudius R., 164
Walker's Cay, 389
Wallace-Whitfield, Hon. Sir Cecil, 155, 389–90
Ward, James E., 371
Warri, 390

INDEX

Washington, George, 370
Water supplies, 13, 14, 356, 390–91
Watkins, Errington, 2
Watling's Island *See* San Salvador
Wells, John, 271
Wenner-Gren, Axel, 284
Wentworth, Hugh, 311
Wentworth, John, 311
West India Regiments, 391–3
West Indies Federation, 393
Whales, 393–4
White Bells (*datura*), 69
White Elder (*Sanbucus intermedia*), 69
White Sage *See* Catnip
Williams, Burton, 188–9, 340
Williams, Egbert Austin 'Bert', 394–5
Williamson, John Ernest, 395
Windsor, Governor Edward, Duke of, 55, 66–7, 99–100, 175, 395–6
Windsor, Wallis, Duchess of, 35, 55, 99, 396
Women's rights *See* Johnson, Dame Doris L.
Women's Suffrage Movement, 397
Wood, Kathleen McNary, 147, 227
World records, Bahamian, 397–8
World War One (1914-1918), 398–400
World War Two (1939-1945), 400–402
See also Contract, The
Wrecking, 18, 194–5, 280, 401–2
Wright, Horace, 22
Writing *See* Literature
Wyannie Malone Museum, Hope Town, 2
Wylly, William, 237, 255, 402–3

Y

Yachtsman's Guide, 332
Yama Bahama, 63
Yellow fever, 404
Yorubas, 40, 224 *See also* Vodun
Young, J.W., 45
Young, Leon Walton, 164, 404

Z

Zemis, 12, 405
ZNS *See* Radio; Television
Zoos *See* Ardastra Gardens

Text Credits

The author and publishers are grateful to the following for their permission to reproduce copyright material:

Extracts from *An Evening in Guanima, More Talking' Bahamian* 1995, *How to be a true-true Bahamian: a hilarious look at life in the Bahamas* by Patricia Glinton-Meicholas, with permission of the author.

Extract from Blackbeard from *A History of the Bahamas* by Michael Craton with permission of the author.

Extract from *Jamaica Talk: three hundred years of the English language in Jamaica* by Frederic Cassidy, with permission of the University of West Indies Press, © 2007.

Extract Mail boats from *Bahamas, Turks & Caicos, 2* © 2001 Lonely Planet Publications reproduced with permission.

Extract from Out Island Regatta by Art Paine from *Wooden Boat Magazine*, Jan-Feb 1992, pp 66-77 with permission of the author.

Goombay song from *Reminiscing – Memories of Old Nassau* by Valeria Moseley Moss, with permission of the author.

Extract from *Island Heritage: architecture of The Bahamas* by Robert Douglas, with permission of the author.

Bahamas National Anthem by Timothy Gibson used with permission of the Office of the Deputy Prime Minister & Ministry of National Security.

Extract from *The Ephemeral Islands: a Natural history of the Bahamas* by David G Campbell, with permission of Macmillan Education.

Extracts Funeral – 1970, Golf – 1966, Geology by Paul Hearty – 1994, Rake and scrape – 1983 from Bahamas Handbook and Business Annual with permission of Etienne Dupuch, Jr Publications.

If any copyright holders have been omitted, please contact the publishers who will make the necessary arrangements at the first opportunity.

Picture Credits

The author and publishers are grateful to the following for their permission to reproduce copyright illustrations:

Anglican Church, Bahamas: page 43 (Mary Moseley collection)

Antiquities and Monuments and Museums Corporation, Bahamas, page 19

APA Publications: page 76

Bahamian Archives: pages 3, 4, 10 (top), 124, 200, 235, 291, 293, 310, 325, 349, 399, 401

Bahamas Information Services: pages 129 (Peter Ramsey photo), 368

Bahamas Ministry of Tourism: page 285 (Ronald Rose photo)

Bahamas News Bureau: pages 1, 35, 64, 84, 111, 169 (bottom), 201, 208, 225, 275, 308, 329, 366, 383, 397

Ping Amranand, with permission of Superstock Ltd, UK: page 76

Anthony Carroll: page 60

College of The Bahamas: page 94

Colonel Charles Waterhouse Historical Museum, Inc.: page 10 from *Marines in the Revolution 1776*

Etienne Dupuch Jr Publications, Georgeside, George Street, Nassau: pages 125, 142, 226, 318 (from Bahamas Handbook and Business Annual 1982)

FINCO and The Counsellors, Nassau: page 141 (bottom)

Bruce Hallett: page 52 (bottom)

Linda M. Huber (from L. Huber, *Nassau's Historical Landmarks*): pages 173, 250, 255

Imperial War Museum, London: page 392

William R. Johnson: page 57

Nicholas Klonaris: title page and page 213

Ronald G. Lightbourne: pages 80, 117, 279

Brent Malone: pages 12, 242

Meeres family: page 254

Metropolitan Museum of Art, Catharine Lorillard Wolfe Collection, Wolfe Fund 1906 (06.1234) Photograph © 1995 The Metropolitan Museum of Art: page 183

Metropolitan Museum of Art, Amelia B. Lazarus Fund 1910 (10.228.9) © 1995 The Metropolitan Museum of Art: page 193

Nassau Guardian: page 47

Nassau Nostalgia: page 395

Nassau Tribune: page 24 (Felipe Major photo)

National Geographic Image Collection: page 365

Art G. Paine: page 281

Nicolas Popov: Pages 2, 4, 45, 61, 98, 105, 121, 160, 163, 179 (top), 239, 276, 322, 323, 328, 340, 345, 359 (bottom), 394

Ruth Rhodriguez: pages 129, 240, 245

Gail Saunders collection: page 376 ('Doc Sands' photo)

Neil Sealey: pages 5, 7, 13, 14, 15, 16, 22, 26, 29, 31, 33, 34, 40, 42, 48, 50, 51, 56, 63, 65, 71, 77, 78, 79, 81, 91, 93, 97, 101, 103, 109, 132, 133, 137, 144, 145, 147, 168, 169 (top), 174, 177, 181, 185, 189, 195 (bottom), 197, 198, 203, 209, 211, 212, 216, 227, 228, 230, 232, 236, 237, 244, 249, 258, 260, 264, 269, 273, 277, 283, 284, 303, 304, 305, 314, 315, 316, 330, 338, 343, 344, 350, 356, 357, 359 (top), 370, 373, 377, 381, 385, 391, 405

B. Anthony Stewart/National Geographic Image Collection: page 135

Michael Toogood: pages 23, 39, 49, 55, 69, 72, 75, 83, 87, 90, 113, 116, 141 (top), 186, 195 (top), 204, 248, 262, 288, 289, 294, 296, 313, 317, 321, 339, 353, 380, 396

Monica Warner: page 68

Charles Waterhouse: page 10 (bottom)

The following illustrations are from the author's collection: pages 8, 17, 54, 96, 119, 134, 149, 151, 153, 178, 180, 190, 223, 247, 297, 330, 334, 347, 355, 358

If any copyright holders have been omitted, please contact the publishers, who will make the necessary arrangements at the first opportunity